Practical Business Math Procedures

Eleventh Edition

JEFFREY SLATER
North Shore Community College
Danvers, Massachusetts

SHARON M. WITTRY
Pikes Peak Community College
Colorado Springs, Colorado

BUS 103 Business Math
Spokane Community College

2 3 4 5 6 7 8 9 0 BKM BKM 18 17 16 15

ISBN-13: 978-1-259-76210-9
ISBN-10: 1-259-76210-6

Solutions Program Manager: Joyce Berendes
Project Manager: Tina Bower
Cover Photo Credits:
(building) - Andrew Lundquist
(sky) - Hemera Technologies

Dedication

To Mia, Matt, Sam, and Hope.
How lucky I am to have such wonderful grandkids!
—Love, PaPa Jeff

To my loving husband. You make every day shine.
—Love, Sharon

Note to Students

ROADMAP TO SUCCESS

How to use this book and the Total Slater/Wittry Learning System.

Step 1: **Each chapter is broken down into Learning Units. Read and master one Learning Unit at a time.**

How do I know whether I understand it?

- Try the practice quiz. All the worked-out solutions are provided. If you still have questions, watch the authors on your DVD (comes with your text) or on YouTube or Connect and work each problem out.
- For more practice, try the extra practice quiz. Worked-out solutions are in Appendix B.

Once you feel confident with the subject matter, go on to the next Learning Unit in the chapter.

Step 2: **Review the Interactive Chapter Organizer at the end of the chapter.**

How do I know if I understand it?

- The third column, "You try it," gives you the chance to do additional practice.

Step 3: **Do assigned problems at the end of the chapter (or Appendix A). These may include discussion questions, drill, word problems, challenge problems, video cases, as well as projects from Surf to Save and Kiplinger's magazine.**

Can I check my homework?

- Appendix C has check figures for all the odd-numbered problems.

Step 4: **Take the Summary Practice Test.**

Can I check my progress?

- Appendix C has check figures for all problems.

What do I do if I do not match check figures?

- Review the video tutorial on the student DVD—the authors work out each problem. You can also see the videos on YouTube and Connect.

To aid you in studying the book, we have developed the following color code:

 Blue: Movement, cancellations, steps to solve, arrows, blueprints

 Purple and yellow: Formulas and steps

 Green: Tables and forms

 Red: Key items we are solving for

If you have difficulty with any text examples, pay special attention to the red and the blue. These will help remind you of what you are looking for as well as what the procedures are.

FEATURES	The following are the features students have told us have helped them the most.
Blueprint Aid Boxes	For the first eight chapters (not in Chapter 4), blueprint aid boxes are available to help you map out a plan to solve a word problem. We know the harder thing to do in solving word problems is often figuring out where to start. Use the blueprint as a model to get started.
Business Math Handbook	This reference guide contains all the tables found in the text. It makes homework, exams, etc., easier to deal with than flipping back and forth through the text.
Interactive Chapter Organizer	At the end of each chapter is a quick reference guide called the Interactive Chapter Organizer, in which key points, formulas, and examples are provided. A list of vocabulary terms is also included, as well as Check Figures for Extra Practice Quizzes. All have page references. A new column called "You Try It" gives you a chance to do additional practice. And solutions are provided in Appendix B. (A complete glossary is found at the end of the text.) Think of the Interactive Chapter Organizer as your set of notes and use it as a reference when doing homework problems and reviewing before exams.
DVD-ROM	The DVD packaged with the text includes tutorial videos that cover all of the Learning Unit Practice Quizzes and Summary Practice Tests.

*For **extra help** from your authors–Sharon and Jeff–see the student DVD*

The Business Math Website	Visit the site at www.mhhe.com/slater11e and find the Internet Resource Guide with hot links, tutorials, practice quizzes, Excel® workbook and templates, and other study materials useful for the course.
Video Cases	There are six video cases applying business math concepts to real companies such as Six Flags, Subaru of Indiana Automotive, Noodles & Company, Buycostume.com, and DHL. You can watch these videos at **www.mhhe.com/slater11e.** Some background case information and assignment problems incorporating information on the companies are included at the end of Chapters 6, 7, 8, 13, 16, and 19.
Compounding/Present Value Overlays	A set of color overlays are inserted in Chapter 13. These color graphics are intended to demonstrate the concepts of present value and future value and, even more important, the basic relationship between the two.
Surf to Save	At the end of each chapter you will find word problems with links to sites and publications. These problems give you a chance to apply the theory provided in the chapter to the real world. Put your math skills to work.
Group Activity: Personal Finance, a Kiplinger Approach	In each chapter you can debate a business math issue based on a *Kiplinger's Personal Finance* magazine article. This is great for critical thinking, as well as improving your writing skills.
Spreadsheet Templates	Excel® templates are available for selected end-of-chapter problems. You can run these templates as-is or enter your own data. The templates also include an interest table feature that enables you to input any percentage rate and any terms. The program then generates table values for you.
Cumulative Reviews	At the end of Chapters 3, 8, and 13 are word problems that test your retention of business math concepts and procedures. Check figures for *all* cumulative review problems are in Appendix C.
Vocabulary	Each chapter opener includes a Vocabulary Preview covering the key terms in the chapter. The Interactive Chapter Organizer includes page references to the terms. There's also a glossary at the end of the text.

Acknowledgments

Academic Experts, Contributors

Dawn P. Addington

Tom Bilyeu

James P. DeMeuse

Joe Hanson

Deborah Layton

Lynda L. Mattes

Joseph M. Nicassio

Jo Ann Rawley

Karen Ruedinger

Kelly Russell

Marge Sunderland

Mary Frey

Jason Tanner

Patrick Cunningham

Paul Tomko

Peter VanderWeyst

Company/*Applications*

Chapter 1

Subway—*Chapter introduction*

Starbucks—*Problem solving*

Whole Foods—*Reading and writing numbers*

Disney—*Rounding numbers*

Tootsie Roll Industries—*Dissecting word problems and rounding*

Walmart—*Subtraction of whole numbers*

Hershey—*Subtraction of whole numbers*

Facebook—*Multiplying and dividing whole numbers*

Chapter 2

McDonald's—*Fractions*

M&M'S/Mars—*Fractions and multiplication*

Albertsons—*Dissecting word problems with fractions*

Chapter 3

Honda, Toyota, BMW, GM, Chrysler, Mercedes-Benz—*Decimals*

Google—*Adding, subtracting, multiplying, and dividing decimals*

Apple—*International currency*

Chapter 4

Charles Schwab, Fidelity Investments, JPMorgan Chase & Co., T. Rowe Price—*New deposits with use of technology*

TD Bank Financial Group—*ATM fees*

JPMorgan Chase Bank—*Mobile banking*

Chapter 5

Stop & Shop—*Word problems*

Chapter 6

Google, Facebook—*Introduction to percents*

Family Dollar Stores, J.M. Smucker Co.—*Understanding percents*

Walt Disney Co.—*Converting decimals to percents*

Ford, Toyota, Honda, Chrysler, Nissan—*Percent increase and decrease*

M&M'S/Mars—*Rate, portion, and base*

Chapter 7

Groupon, Facebook—*Introduction to decimals*

Procter & Gamble, Samsung Venture Investment Corp.—*Trade discounts*

Amazon.com Inc., Toys "R" Us, Newegg.com—*Shipping terms*

Chapter 8

Macy's Inc., Microsoft, Mozilla Corp.—*Introduction to retailing*

Gap—*Markup on cost and selling price*

Chapter 9

McDonald's—*Health plans*

Google Inc., Apple Inc., Walt Disney Co., Facebook—*Employee satisfaction*

IRS—*Circular E tables*

Chapter 10

Research Services Inc.—*Credit unions versus banks for borrowing*

Chapter 11

Prosper Marketplace Inc., Lending Club Corp., eBay—*Introduction to promissory notes*

U.S. Treasury—*Buying treasuries*

General Motors Co.—*Lines of credit*

Chapter 12

U.S. Department of Labor—*Magic of compounding*

Chapter 13

T. Rowe Price Group—*Retirement payoff*

Dunkin' Donuts—*Power of compounding*

Chapter 14

Edmunds.com—*FICO scores*

U.S. government—*Credit Card Act of 2009*

Citibank Mastercard—*Calculation of finance charge*

Chapter 15

Bank of America, JPMorgan Chase & Co., Freddie Mac—*Lowering mortgage payment*

FICO—*Credit score*

HSH Associates—*Refinancing a mortgage*

Chapter 16

SEC—*Sarbanes-Oxley Act*

Greystone Bakery—*Benefit corporation*

Campbell Soup Co.—*Income statement*

Zyngz Corp.—*Elements of the income statement*

General Mills Inc.—*Gross margin*

Sara Lee, ConAgra, Kraft, Hershey, Kellogg, Heinz—*Cost of goods sold*

Chapter 17

Intellichoice.com—*Depreciation reductions over the years for cars*

Joint Committee on Taxation—*Corporate tax breaks*

Chapter 18

Walmart—*Electronic inventory tags*

American Eagle Outfitters, Abercrombie & Fitch, Aeropostale—*Inventory competition*

Certified Public Accountants—*GAAP and IFRS*

McGraw-Hill Co.—*Textbook pricing*

Gap—*Distribution of overhead*

Chapter 19

Target, Walmart, Amazon—*Collecting taxes online*

Chapter 20

TIAA-CREF, USAA—*Introduction to insurance*

Chapter 21

Morningstar—*Mix of investments*

Putnam Investments Inc., Schwab Funds—*Mutual funds*

Chapter 22

Ford Motor Inc., Facebook, Yahoo!, AOL, Microsoft, Google—*Internet advertising breakdown*

Pike Research—*Bar chart of electric vehicles*

Contents

Practical
Business
Math
Procedures

CHAPTER 1

Whole Numbers: How to Dissect and Solve Word Problems

A Foot Long but a Dollar Short

New numbers released this week prove it: There are more Subway stores on the planet then McDonald's. Has McDonald's lost its grip? Not overseas, where it has nearly twice as many stores as the sandwich chain, and not in terms of world-wide sales. Still, it's a coup for Subway. The chain has been promoting the healthful aspects of its food since 1996, well before Jared went on TV with his Subway diet in 2000, and this without even 'reformulating the meat,' according to Subway spokesman Les Winograd.

—Sarah Slobin

TOTAL STORES IN 2010		U.S.	International
33,749	Subway	23,722	10,027
32,737	McDonald's	14,027	18,710
17,009	Starbucks	11,158	5,851
16,756	KFC	4,986	11,770
13,356	Pizza Hut	7,528	5,828

Are You What You Eat?
Some of the most popular sandwiches world-wide and their vital statistics.

	6" turkey breast sub	Big Mac
Serving size (g)	219	214
Calories	280	540
Calories from fat	30	260
Total fat (g)	3.5	29
Saturated fat	1.0	10
Trans fat	0.0	1.5
Cholesterol (mg)	20	75
Sodium (mg)	920	1,040
Carbohydrates	47	45
Dietary fiber (g)	5	3
Sugars (g)	6	9
Protein (g)	18	25

Sources: Technomic Top 500 Report; the companies

LU 1–1: Reading, Writing, and Rounding Whole Numbers

1. Use place values to read and write numeric and verbal whole numbers *(pp. 4–6)*.

2. Round whole numbers to the indicated position *(pp. 6–7)*.

3. Use blueprint aid for dissecting and solving a word problem *(pp. 7–8)*.

LU 1–2: Adding and Subtracting Whole Numbers

1. Add whole numbers; check and estimate addition computations *(pp. 10–11)*.

2. Subtract whole numbers; check and estimate subtraction computations *(pp. 11–12)*.

LU 1–3: Multiplying and Dividing Whole Numbers

1. Multiply whole numbers; check and estimate multiplication computations *(pp. 14–16)*.

2. Divide whole numbers; check and estimate division computations *(pp. 16–17)*.

VOCABULARY PREVIEW

Here are key terms in this chapter. After completing the chapter, if you know the term, place a checkmark in the parentheses. If you don't know the term, look it up and put the page number where it can be found.

Addends ( ) Decimal point ( ) Decimal system ( ) Difference ( ) Dividend ( ) Divisor ( ) Minuend ( ) Multiplicand ( ) Multiplier ( ) Partial products ( ) Partial quotient ( ) Product ( ) Quotient ( ) Remainder ( ) Rounding all the way ( ) Subtrahend ( ) Sum ( ) Whole number ( )

In the chapter opener we see that Subway has more total stores in the United States (23,722) than does McDonald's (14,027). Keeping track of store count is just one way numbers tell us something about a business.

GLOBAL

People of all ages make personal business decisions based on the answers to number questions. Numbers also determine most of the business decisions of companies. For example, go to the website of a company such as Starbucks and note the importance of numbers in the company's business decision-making process.

The following *Wall Street Journal* clipping "Starbucks Menu Expands in China" announces plans to reach a greater number of people in China:

© Yan daming–Imaginechina via AP Images

Starbucks Menu Expands in China

By Laurie Burkitt

BEIJING—**Starbucks** Corp. is introducing its instant-coffee packets in China, expanding beyond coffee stores to also sell consumer packaged goods.

The Seattle-based coffee company's Via single-serving coffee packets will be available in at least 800 Starbucks stores across China, Hong Kong and Taiwan beginning on April 6, John Culver, president of Starbucks International, said Tuesday at a news conference here.

The packets also will be distributed in grocery and convenience stores and later in hotels and entertainment venues, Mr.

Culver said. He added that a schedule hasn't been set. "We see a big opportunity in packaged goods in China," he said.

The move signals Starbucks's intention to expand not only its coffee business in China but beyond the beverage as well.

Starbucks has been exploring new tactics in the U.S. and internationally to boost its offerings into a broader array of consumer goods. Starbucks dropped the company's name and the word "coffee" from its logo in January.

The company rolled out the new logo Tuesday in China.

Companies often follow a general problem-solving procedure to arrive at a change in company policy. Using Starbucks as an example, the following steps illustrate this procedure:

Step 1. State the problem(s).   Globally increase market share and
                                                 profitability.

Step 2. Decide on the best methods   Expand operations in China beyond
           to solve the problem(s).   coffee sales.

Step 3. Does the solution make   Adapt to Chinese eating habits—more
           sense?   tea products and consumer packaged goods.

Step 4. Evaluate the results.   Starbucks will evaluate new plan.

Your study of numbers begins with a review of basic computation skills that focuses on speed and accuracy. You may think, "But I can use my calculator." Even if your instructor allows you to use a calculator, you still must know the basic computation skills. You need these skills to know what to calculate, how to interpret your calculations, how to make estimates to recognize errors you made in using your calculator, and how to make calculations when you do not have a calculator.

The United States' numbering system is the **decimal system** or *base 10 system.* Your calculator gives the 10 single-digit numbers of the decimal system—0, 1, 2, 3, 4, 5, 6, 7, 8, and 9. The center of the decimal system is the **decimal point.** When you have a number with a decimal point, the numbers to the left of the decimal point are **whole numbers** and the numbers to the right of the decimal point are decimal numbers (discussed in Chapter 3). When you have a number *without* a decimal, the number is a whole number and the decimal is assumed to be after the number.

This chapter discusses reading, writing, and rounding whole numbers; adding and subtracting whole numbers; and multiplying and dividing whole numbers.

Learning Unit 1–1: Reading, Writing, and Rounding Whole Numbers

LO 1

Whole Foods Market has more than 2,100,000 followers on Twitter. Tweets involve recipes, food tips, and answers to customer questions. Are you one of those two million, one hundred thousand followers?

Now let's begin our study of whole numbers.

GLOBAL

Reading and Writing Numeric and Verbal Whole Numbers

The decimal system is a *place-value system* based on the powers of 10. Any whole number can be written with the 10 digits of the decimal system because the position, or placement, of the digits in a number gives the value of the digits.

To determine the value of each digit in a number, we use a place-value chart (Figure 1.1) that divides numbers into named groups of three digits, with each group separated by a comma. To separate a number into groups, you begin with the last digit in the number and insert commas every three digits, moving from right to left. This divides the number into the named groups (units, thousands, millions, billions, trillions) shown in the place-value chart. Within each group, you have a ones, tens, and hundreds place. Keep in mind that the leftmost group may have fewer than three digits.

In Figure 1.1 (p. 5), the numeric number 1,605,743,891,412 illustrates place values. When you study the place-value chart, you can see that the value of each place in the chart is 10 times the value of the place to the right. We can illustrate this by analyzing the last four digits in the number 1,605,743,891,412:

$$1,412 = (1 \times 1,000) + (4 \times 100) + (1 \times 10) + (2 \times 1)$$

So we can also say, for example, that in the number 745, the "7" means seven hundred (700); in the number 75, the "7" means 7 tens (70).

To read and write a numeric number in verbal form, you begin at the left and read each group of three digits as if it were alone, adding the group name at the end (except the last units group and groups of all zeros). Using the place-value chart in Figure 1.1, the number 1,605,743,891,412 is read as one trillion, six hundred five billion, seven hundred forty-three million, eight hundred ninety-one thousand, four hundred twelve. You do not read zeros. They fill vacant spaces as placeholders so that you can correctly state the number values. Also, the numbers twenty-one to ninety-nine must have a hyphen. And most important, when you read or write whole numbers in

FIGURE   1.1

Whole number place-value chart

Whole Number Groups

	Trillions			Billions			Millions			Thousands			Units			
Hundred trillions	Ten trillions	Trillions	Comma	Hundred billions	Ten billions	Billions	Comma	Hundred millions	Ten millions	Millions	Comma	Hundred thousands	Ten thousands	Thousands	Comma	Hundreds	Tens	Ones (units)	Decimal Point
		1	,	6	0	5	,	7	4	3	,	8	9	1	,	4	1	2	.

verbal form, do not use the word *and*. In the decimal system, *and* indicates the decimal, which we discuss in Chapter 3.

By reversing this process of changing a numeric number to a verbal number, you can use the place-value chart to change a verbal number to a numeric number. Remember that you must keep track of the place value of each digit. The place values of the digits in a number determine its total value.

Before we look at how to round whole numbers, we should look at how to convert a number indicating parts of a whole number to a whole number. We will use the following *Wall Street Journal* clip about Whole Foods as an example.

Reprinted with permission of *The Wall Street Journal*, Copyright © 2011 Dow Jones & Company, Inc. All Rights Reserved Worldwide.

Whole Foods' 2,100,000 followers on Twitter could be written as 2.1 million. This amount is two million plus one hundred thousand of an additional million. The following steps explain how to convert these decimal numbers into a regular whole number:

CONVERTING PARTS OF A MILLION, BILLION, TRILLION, ETC., TO A REGULAR WHOLE NUMBER

Step 1. Drop the decimal point and insert a comma.

Step 2. Add zeros so the leftmost digit ends in the word name of the amount you want to convert. Be sure to add commas as needed.

EXAMPLE   Convert 2.1 million to a regular whole number.

Step 1.   2.1 million

2,1   Change the decimal point to a comma.

Step 2.   2,100,000   Add zeros and commas so the whole number indicates million.

LO 2

Rounding Whole Numbers

Many of the whole numbers you read and hear are rounded numbers. Government statistics are usually rounded numbers. The financial reports of companies also use rounded numbers. All rounded numbers are *approximate* numbers. The more rounding you do, the more you approximate the number.

Rounded whole numbers are used for many reasons. With rounded whole numbers you can quickly estimate arithmetic results, check actual computations, report numbers that change quickly such as population numbers, and make numbers easier to read and remember.

Numbers can be rounded to any identified digit place value, including the first digit of a number (rounding all the way). To round whole numbers, use the following three steps:

ROUNDING WHOLE NUMBERS
Step 1. Identify the place value of the digit you want to round.
Step 2. If the digit to the right of the identified digit in Step 1 is 5 or more, increase the identified digit by 1 (round up). If the digit to the right is less than 5, do not change the identified digit.
Step 3. Change all digits to the right of the rounded identified digit to zeros.

EXAMPLE 1   Round 9,362 to the nearest hundred.

Step 1.   9,362   The digit 3 is in the hundreds place value.

Step 2.   The digit to the right of 3 is 5 or more (6). Thus, 3, the identified digit in Step 1, is now rounded to 4. You change the identified digit only if the digit to the right is 5 or more.

9,462

Step 3.   9,400   Change digits 6 and 2 to zeros, since these digits are to the right of 4, the rounded number.

By rounding 9,362 to the nearest hundred, you can see that 9,362 is closer to 9,400 than to 9,300.

Next, we show you how to round to the nearest thousand.

EXAMPLE 2   Round 67,951 to the nearest thousand.

Step 1.   67,951   The digit 7 is in the thousands place value.

Step 2.   The digit to the right of 7 is 5 or more (9). Thus, 7, the identified digit in Step 1, is now rounded to 8.

68,951

Step 3.   68,000   Change digits 9, 5, and 1 to zeros, since these digits are to the right of 8, the rounded number.

By rounding 67,951 to the nearest thousand, you can see that 67,951 is closer to 68,000 than to 67,000.

Now let's look at **rounding all the way.** To round a number all the way, you round to the first digit of the number (the leftmost digit) and have only one nonzero digit remaining in the number.

EXAMPLE 3 Round 7,843 all the way.

Step 1. 7,843   Identified leftmost digit is 7.

Step 2.   Digit to the right of 7 is greater than 5, so 7 becomes 8.

       8,843

Step 3. 8,000   Change all other digits to zeros.

Rounding 7,843 all the way gives 8,000.

Remember that rounding a digit to a specific place value depends on the degree of accuracy you want in your estimate. For example, in the *Wall Street Journal* clip "Phineas and Ferb," 628,000 rounds all the way to 600,000 because the digit to the right of 6 (leftmost digit) is less than 5. The 600,000 is 28,000 less than the original 628,000. You would be more accurate if you rounded 628,000 to the ten thousand place value of 1 identified digit, which is 630,000.

Before concluding this unit, let's look at how to dissect and solve a word problem.

Disney Channel
628,000 boys 6 to 11, on average, watching per episode

© Disney XD/Photofest

Reprinted with permission of *The Wall Street Journal*, Copyright © 2011 Dow Jones & Company, Inc. All Rights Reserved Worldwide.

How to Dissect and Solve a Word Problem

As a student, your author found solving word problems difficult. Not knowing where to begin after reading the word problem caused the difficulty. Today, students still struggle with word problems as they try to decide where to begin.

Solving word problems involves *organization* and *persistence*. Recall how persistent you were when you learned to ride a two-wheel bike. Do you remember the feeling of success you experienced when you rode the bike without help? Apply this persistence to word problems. Do not be discouraged. Each person learns at a different speed. Your goal must be to FINISH THE RACE and experience the success of solving word problems with ease.

To be organized in solving word problems, you need a plan of action that tells you where to begin—a blueprint aid. Like a builder, you will refer to this blueprint aid constantly until you know the procedure. The blueprint aid for dissecting and solving a word problem appears below. Note that the blueprint aid serves an important function—**it decreases your math anxiety.**

Blueprint Aid for Dissecting and Solving a Word Problem

LO 3

	The facts	Solving for?	Steps to take	Key points
BLUEPRINT				

© Roberts Publishing Services

Now let's study this blueprint aid. The first two columns require that you *read* the word problem slowly. Think of the third column as the basic information you must know or calculate before solving the word problem. Often this column contains formulas that provide the foundation for the step-by-step problem solution. The last column reinforces the key points you should remember.

It's time now to try your skill at using the blueprint aid for dissecting and solving a word problem.

The Word Problem On the 100th anniversary of Tootsie Roll Industries, the company reported sharply increased sales and profits. Sales reached one hundred ninety-four million dollars and a record profit of twenty-two million, five hundred fifty-six thousand dollars. The company president requested that you round the sales and profit figures all the way.

Study the following blueprint aid and note how we filled in the columns with the information in the word problem. You will find the organization of the blueprint aid most helpful. Be persistent! You *can* dissect and solve word problems! When you are finished with the word problem, make sure the answer seems reasonable.

	The facts	Solving for?	Steps to take	Key points
BLUEPRINT	*Sales:* One hundred ninety-four million dollars. *Profit:* Twenty-two million, five hundred fifty-six thousand dollars.	Sales and profit rounded all the way.	Express each verbal form in numeric form. Identify leftmost digit in each number.	Rounding all the way means only the left-most digit will remain. All other digits become zeros.

MONEY tips

Do not carry your Social Security card in your wallet. Keep it and other important documents in a safe deposit box or fireproof container. Shred any document that contains personal information, such as anything with your Social Security number on it, old bank statements, applications for loans, and so on.

Steps to solving problem

1. Convert verbal to numeric.
   One hundred ninety-four million dollars ⟶ $194,000,000
   Twenty-two million, five hundred fifty-six thousand dollars ⟶ $ 22,556,000

2. Identify leftmost digit of each number.
   $194,000,000 $22,556,000

3. Round.
   $200,000,000 $20,000,000

Note that in the final answer, $200,000,000 and $20,000,000 have only one nonzero digit.

Remember that you cannot round numbers expressed in verbal form. You must convert these numbers to numeric form.

Now you should see the importance of the information in the third column of the blueprint aid. When you complete your blueprint aids for word problems, do not be concerned if the order of the information in your boxes does not follow the order given in the text boxes. Often you can dissect a word problem in more than one way.

Your first Practice Quiz follows. Be sure to study the paragraph that introduces the Practice Quiz.

LU 1–1 PRACTICE QUIZ

Complete this **Practice Quiz** to see how you are doing.

At the end of each learning unit, you can check your progress with a Practice Quiz. If you had difficulty understanding the unit, the Practice Quiz will help identify your area of weakness. Work the problems on scrap paper. Check your answers with the worked-out solutions that follow the quiz. Ask your instructor about specific assignments and the videos available on your DVD for each unit Practice Quiz.

1. Write in verbal form:
   a. 7,948   b. 48,775   c. 814,410,335,414

2. Round the following numbers as indicated:

Nearest ten	Nearest hundred	Nearest thousand	Rounded all the way
a. 92	**b.** 745	**c.** 8,341	**d.** 4,752

3. Kellogg's reported its sales as five million, one hundred eighty-one thousand dollars. The company earned a profit of five hundred two thousand dollars. What would the sales and profit be if each number were rounded all the way? (*Hint:* You might want to draw the blueprint aid since we show it in the solution.)

For **extra help** from your authors–Sharon and Jeff–see the student DVD

YouTube

✓ **Solutions**

1. **a.** Seven thousand, nine hundred forty-eight

    b. Forty-eight thousand, seven hundred seventy-five

    c. Eight hundred fourteen billion, four hundred ten million, three hundred thirty-five thousand, four hundred fourteen

2. **a.** 90   **b.** 700   **c.** 8,000   **d.** 5,000

3. Kellogg's sales and profit:

BLUEPRINT	The facts	Solving for?	Steps to take	Key points
	Sales: Five million, one hundred eighty-one thousand dollars. *Profit:* Five hundred two thousand dollars.	Sales and profit rounded all the way.	Express each verbal form in numeric form. Identify leftmost digit in each number.	Rounding all the way means only the left-most digit will remain. All other digits become zeros.

Steps to solving problem

1. Convert verbal to numeric.

Five million, one hundred eighty-one thousand ————————————→ $5,181,000

Five hundred two thousand ————————————————————→ $ 502,000

2. Identify leftmost digit of each number.

        $5,181,000 $502,000

3. Round.

        $5,000,000 $500,000

LU 1–1a | **EXTRA PRACTICE QUIZ WITH WORKED-OUT SOLUTIONS**

Need more practice? Try this **Extra Practice Quiz** (check figures in the Interactive Chapter Organizer, p. 21). Worked-out Solutions can be found in Appendix B at end of text.

1. Write in verbal form:

    a. 8,682   **b.** 56,295   **c.** 732,310,444,888

2. Round the following numbers as indicated:

Nearest ten	Nearest hundred	Nearest thousand	Rounded all the way
a. 43	**b.** 654	**c.** 7,328	**d.** 5,980

3. Kellogg's reported its sales as three million, two hundred ninety-one thousand dollars. The company earned a profit of four hundred five thousand dollars. What would the sales and profit be if each number were rounded all the way?

Learning Unit 1–2: Adding and Subtracting Whole Numbers

LO 1

We all know the cost of car rentals and hotel rates vary around the world. The following *Wall Street Journal* clip identifies some of the most and least expensive car rental and hotel rates in the world. For example, note the difference in daily costs between the hotel rates in Brisbane, Australia, and Albuquerque, New Mexico.

Brisbane	$259
Albuquerque	− 65
	$194

Reprinted with permission of *The Wall Street Journal*, Copyright © 2011 Dow Jones & Company, Inc. All Rights Reserved Worldwide.

This unit teaches you how to manually add and subtract whole numbers. When you least expect it, you will catch yourself automatically using this skill.

Addition of Whole Numbers

To add whole numbers, you unite two or more numbers called **addends** to make one number called a **sum,** *total,* or *amount.* The numbers are arranged in a column according to their place values—units above units, tens above tens, and so on. Then, you add the columns of numbers from top to bottom. To check the result, you re-add the columns from bottom to top. This procedure is illustrated in the steps that follow.

"Mistakes were made."

From The Wall Street Journal, copyright © 2010, permission of Cartoon Features Syndicate.

ADDING WHOLE NUMBERS
Step 1. Align the numbers to be added in columns according to their place values, beginning with the units place at the right and moving to the left.
Step 2. Add the units column. Write the sum below the column. If the sum is more than 9, write the units digit and carry the tens digit.
Step 3. Moving to the left, repeat Step 2 until all place values are added.

※ Addends : ~~two or more numbers~~
— The "numbers" that are added together

EXAMPLE

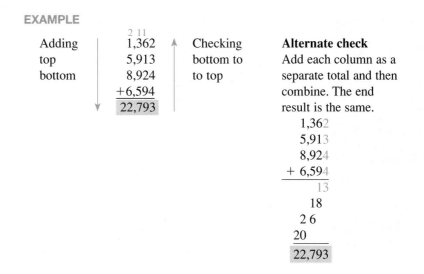

Adding	2 11	Checking	**Alternate check**
top	1,362	bottom to	Add each column as a
bottom	5,913	to top	separate total and then
	8,924		combine. The end
	+6,594		result is the same.
	22,793		

$$
\begin{array}{r}
1,362 \\
5,913 \\
8,924 \\
+\ 6,594 \\
\hline
13 \\
18 \\
2\ 6 \\
20 \\
\hline
22,793
\end{array}
$$

How to Quickly Estimate Addition by Rounding All the Way   In Learning Unit 1–1, you learned that rounding whole numbers all the way gives quick arithmetic estimates. Using the following *Wall Street Journal* clipping "International Ambitions" note how you can round each number all the way and the total will not be rounded all the way. Remember that rounding all the way does not replace actual computations, but it is helpful in making quick commonsense decisions.

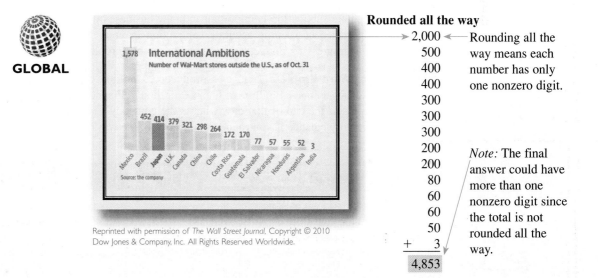

GLOBAL

International Ambitions
Number of Wal-Mart stores outside the U.S., as of Oct. 31

1,578   452   414   379   321   298   264   172   170   77   57   55   52   3

Mexico   Brazil   Japan   U.K.   Canada   China   Chile   Costa Rica   Guatemala   El Salvador   Nicaragua   Honduras   Argentina   India

Source: the company

Reprinted with permission of *The Wall Street Journal*, Copyright © 2010 Dow Jones & Company, Inc. All Rights Reserved Worldwide.

Rounded all the way

$$
\begin{array}{r}
2,000 \\
500 \\
400 \\
400 \\
300 \\
300 \\
300 \\
200 \\
200 \\
80 \\
60 \\
60 \\
50 \\
+\ \ \ 3 \\
\hline
4,853
\end{array}
$$

Rounding all the way means each number has only one nonzero digit.

Note: The final answer could have more than one nonzero digit since the total is not rounded all the way.

LO 2

Subtraction of Whole Numbers

Subtraction is the opposite of addition. Addition unites numbers; subtraction takes one number away from another number. In subtraction, the top (largest) number is the **minuend.** The number you subtract from the minuend is the **subtrahend,** which gives you the **difference** between the minuend and the subtrahend. The steps for subtracting whole numbers follow.

SUBTRACTING WHOLE NUMBERS
Step 1. Align the minuend and subtrahend according to their place values.
Step 2. Begin the subtraction with the units digits. Write the difference below the column. If the units digit in the minuend is smaller than the units digit in the subtrahend, borrow 1 from the tens digit in the minuend. One tens digit is 10 units.
Step 3. Moving to the left, repeat Step 2 until all place values in the subtrahend are subtracted.

✳ minued: The top (largest) number

✳ Subtrahend: The number subtracted from the minuend.   ✳ Difference: The number after you subtract the minuend and subtrahend

© AP Photo/Matt York

EXAMPLE   The *Wall Street Journal* clipping "International Ambitions" illustrates the subtraction of whole numbers:

What is the difference in the number of Walmart stores in Japan and the UK? As shown below you can use subtraction to arrive at the 35 difference.

```
  3 10 14
  4̶ 1̶ 4̶  ← Minuend (larger number)
 −379  ← Subtrahend
   35  ← Difference
```

Check   35
         +379
         ────
          414

In subtraction, borrowing from the column at the left is often necessary. Remember that 1 ten = 10 units, 1 hundred = 10 tens, and 1 thousand = 10 hundreds.

In the units column in the example above, 9 cannot be subtracted from 4 so we borrow from the tens column, resulting in 14 less 9 equals 5. In the tens column, we cannot subtract 7 from 0 so we borrow 10 tens from the hundreds column, leaving 3 hundreds. Ten less 7 equals 3.

Checking subtraction requires adding the difference (35) to the subtrahend (379) to arrive at the minuend (414).

How to Dissect and Solve a Word Problem

Accurate subtraction is important in many business operations. In Chapter 4 we discuss the importance of keeping accurate subtraction in your checkbook balance. Now let's check your progress by dissecting and solving a word problem.

The Word Problem   Hershey's produced 25 million Kisses in one day. The same day, the company shipped 4 million to Japan, 3 million to France, and 6 million throughout the United States. At the end of that day, what is the company's total inventory of Kisses? What is the inventory balance if you round the number all the way?

	The facts	Solving for?	Steps to take	Key points
BLUEPRINT	*Produced:* 25 million. *Shipped:* Japan, 4 million; France, 3 million; United States, 6 million.	Total Kisses left in inventory. Inventory balance rounded all the way.	Total Kisses produced − Total Kisses shipped = Total Kisses left in inventory.	Minuend − Subtrahend = Difference. Rounding all the way means rounding to last digit on the left.

Steps to solving problem

1. Calculate the total Kisses shipped.

2. Calculate the total Kisses left in inventory.

3. Rounding all the way.

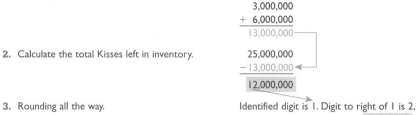

The Practice Quiz that follows will tell you how you are progressing in your study of Chapter 1.

LU 1–2   PRACTICE QUIZ

Complete this **Practice Quiz** to see how you are doing.

1. Add by totaling each separate column:

    8,974
    6,439
    + 6,941

2. Estimate by rounding all the way (do not round the total of estimate) and then do the actual computation:

    4,241
    8,794
    + 3,872

3. Subtract and check your answer:

    9,876
    − 4,967

4. Jackson Manufacturing Company projected its year 2013 furniture sales at $900,000. During 2013, Jackson earned $510,000 in sales from major clients and $369,100 in sales from the remainder of its clients. What is the amount by which Jackson over- or underestimated its sales? Use the blueprint aid, since the answer will show the completed blueprint aid.

For **extra help** from your authors–Sharon and Jeff–see the student DVD

You Tube

✓ Solutions

1.		2. **Estimate**	**Actual**	3.		**Check**
	14				8 18 6 16	
	14	4,000	4,241		9,876 ←	4,909
	2 2	9,000	8,794		− 4,967	+ 4,967
	20	+ 4,000	+ 3,872		4,909	9,876
	22,354	17,000	16,907			

4. Jackson Manufacturing Company over- or underestimated sales:

	The facts	Solving for?	Steps to take	Key points
BLUEPRINT	*Projected 2013 sales:* $900,000. *Major clients:* $510,000. *Other clients:* $369,100.	How much were sales over- or underestimated?	Total projected sales − Total actual sales = Over- or underestimated sales.	Projected sales (minuend) − Actual sales (subtrahend) = Difference.

Steps to solving problem

1. Calculate total actual sales.

    $510,000
    + 369,100
    $879,100

2. Calculate overestimated or underestimated sales.

    $900,000
    − 879,100
    $ 20,900 (overestimated)

LU 1–2a   EXTRA PRACTICE QUIZ WITH WORKED-OUT SOLUTIONS

Need more practice? Try this **Extra Practice Quiz** (check figures in the Interactive Chapter Organizer, p. 21). Worked-out Solutions can be found in Appendix B at end of text.

1. Add by totaling each separate column:

    9,853
    7,394
    +8,843

2. Estimate by rounding all the way (do not round the total of estimate) and then do the actual computation:

    3,482
    6,981
    +5,490

3. Subtract and check your answer:

   9,787
  −5,968

4. Jackson Manufacturing Company projected its year 2013 furniture sales at $878,000. During 2013, Jackson earned $492,900 in sales from major clients and $342,000 in sales from the remainder of its clients. What is the amount by which Jackson over- or underestimated its sales?

Learning Unit 1–3: Multiplying and Dividing Whole Numbers

LO 1

The *Wall Street Journal* clip in the margin shows that Facebook agreed to a 20-year privacy settlement with the government. If Facebook violates the settlement, it can be fined $16,000 per day. What would it cost if Facebook violated the settlement for 4 days?

   4 days × $16,000 = $64,000

If you divide $64,000 by $16,000 per day you get 4 days.

   This unit will sharpen your skills in two important arithmetic operations—multiplication and division. These two operations frequently result in knowledgeable business decisions.

Multiplication of Whole Numbers—Shortcut to Addition

From calculating the cost of Facebook's settlement you know that multiplication is a *shortcut to addition*:

   $16,000 × 4 = $64,000   or $16,000 + $16,000 + $16,000 + $16,000 = $64,000

Before learning the steps used to multiply whole numbers with two or more digits, you must learn some multiplication terminology.

   Note in the following example that the top number (number we want to multiply) is the **multiplicand.** The bottom number (number doing the multiplying) is the **multiplier.** The final number (answer) is the **product.** The numbers between the multiplier and the product are **partial products.** Also note how we positioned the partial product 2090. This number is the result of multiplying 418 by 50 (the 5 is in the tens position). On each line in the partial products, we placed the first digit directly below the digit we used in the multiplication process.

EXAMPLE

	418 ⟵	Top number (multiplicand)
Partial	× 52 ⟵	Bottom number (multiplier)
products	836	2 × 418 = 836
	20 90	50 × 418 = + 20,900
	21,736 ⟵	Product answer ⟶ **21,736**

"I'm not late. Everyone learns at their own speed."

We can now give the following steps for multiplying whole numbers with two or more digits:

MULTIPLYING WHOLE NUMBERS WITH TWO OR MORE DIGITS
Step 1. Align the multiplicand (top number) and multiplier (bottom number) at the right. Usually, you should make the smaller number the multiplier.
Step 2. Begin by multiplying the right digit of the multiplier with the right digit of the multiplicand. Keep multiplying as you move left through the multiplicand. Your first partial product aligns at the right with the multiplicand and multiplier.
Step 3. Move left through the multiplier and continue multiplying the multiplicand. Your partial product right digit or first digit is placed directly below the digit in the multiplier that you used to multiply.
Step 4. Continue Steps 2 and 3 until you have completed your multiplication process. Then add the partial products to get the final product.

Checking and Estimating Multiplication   We can check the multiplication process by reversing the multiplicand and multiplier and then multiplying. Let's first estimate 52×418 by rounding all the way.

EXAMPLE

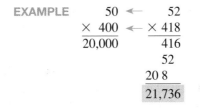

$$
\begin{array}{r}
50 \leftarrow \\
\times\ 400 \leftarrow \\
\hline
20{,}000
\end{array}
\qquad
\begin{array}{r}
52 \\
\times\ 418 \\
\hline
416 \\
52 \\
20\ 8 \\
\hline
21{,}736
\end{array}
$$

By estimating before actually working the problem, we know our answer should be about 20,000. When we multiply 52 by 418, we get the same answer as when we multiply 418×52—and the answer is about 20,000. Remember, if we had not rounded all the way, our estimate would have been closer. If we had used a calculator, the rounded estimate would have helped us check the calculator's answer. Our commonsense estimate tells us our answer is near 20,000—not 200,000.

Before you study the division of whole numbers, you should know (1) the multiplication shortcut with numbers ending in zeros and (2) how to multiply a whole number by a power of 10.

MULTIPLICATION SHORTCUT WITH NUMBERS ENDING IN ZEROS
Step 1. When zeros are at the end of the multiplicand or the multiplier, or both, disregard the zeros and multiply.
Step 2. Count the number of zeros in the multiplicand and multiplier.
Step 3. Attach the number of zeros counted in Step 2 to your answer.

EXAMPLE

$$
\begin{array}{r}
65{,}000 \\
\times\ 420 \\
\hline
\end{array}
\qquad
\begin{array}{r}
65 \\
\times\ 42 \\
\hline
1\ 30 \\
26\ 0 \\
\hline
27{,}300{,}000
\end{array}
\qquad
\begin{array}{r}
3\ \text{zeros} \\
+\ 1\ \text{zero} \\
\hline
4\ \text{zeros}
\end{array}
\qquad
\begin{array}{l}
\text{No need to multiply rows} \\
\text{of zeros} \\
\begin{array}{r}
65{,}000 \\
\times\ \ \ \ 420 \\
\hline
00\ 000 \\
1\ 300\ 00 \\
26\ 000\ 0 \\
\hline
27{,}300{,}000
\end{array}
\end{array}
$$

MULTIPLYING A WHOLE NUMBER BY A POWER OF 10
Step 1. Count the number of zeros in the power of 10 (a whole number that begins with 1 and ends in one or more zeros such as 10, 100, 1,000, and so on).
Step 2. Attach that number of zeros to the right side of the other whole number to obtain the answer. Insert comma(s) as needed every three digits, moving from right to left.

EXAMPLE 99×10 $= 990$ $= 990$ ← Add 1 zero

99×100 $= 9,900$ $= 9,900$ ← Add 2 zeros

$99 \times 1,000 = 99,000 = 99,000$ ← Add 3 zeros

When a zero is in the center of the multiplier, you can do the following:

EXAMPLE

$$
\begin{array}{r}
658 \\
\times \;\; 403 \\
\hline
1\,974 \\
263\,2\square \\
\hline
265,174
\end{array}
$$

$$
\begin{array}{r}
3 \times 658 = \quad 1,974 \\
400 \times 658 = +\,263,200 \\
\hline
265,174
\end{array}
$$

Division of Whole Numbers

LO 2

Division is the reverse of multiplication and a time-saving shortcut related to subtraction. For example, in the introduction of this learning unit you determined that Facebook would pay $64,000 for a 4-day settlement penalty. You multiplied $16,000 × 4 to get $64,000. Since division is the reverse of multiplication you can also say that $64,000 ÷ 4 = $16,000.

Division can be indicated by the common symbols ÷ and $\overline{)}$, or by the bar — in a fraction and the forward slant / between two numbers, which means the first number is divided by the second number. Division asks how many times one number (**divisor**) is contained in another number (**dividend**). The answer, or result, is the **quotient.** When the divisor (number used to divide) doesn't divide evenly into the dividend (number we are dividing), the result is a **partial quotient,** with the leftover amount the **remainder** (expressed as fractions in later chapters). The following example illustrates *even division* (this is also an example of *long division* because the divisor has more than one digit).

EXAMPLE

$$
\begin{array}{r}
18 \quad \leftarrow \text{Quotient} \\
\text{Divisor} \longrightarrow 15\overline{)270} \quad \leftarrow \text{Dividend} \\
\underline{15} \\
120 \\
\underline{120}
\end{array}
$$

This example divides 15 into 27 once with 12 remaining. The 0 in the dividend is brought down to 12. Dividing 120 by 15 equals 8 with no remainder; that is, even division. The following example illustrates *uneven division with a remainder* (this is also an example of *short division* because the divisor has only one digit).

EXAMPLE

$$
\begin{array}{r}
24\,R1 \quad \leftarrow \text{Remainder} \\
7\overline{)169} \\
\underline{14} \\
29 \\
\underline{28} \\
1
\end{array}
$$

Check

$(7 \times 24) + 1 = 169$

Divisor × Quotient + Remainder = Dividend

Note how doing the check gives you assurance that your calculation is correct. When the divisor has one digit (short division) as in this example, you can often calculate the division mentally as illustrated in the following examples:

EXAMPLES

$$
\begin{array}{r}
108 \\
8\overline{)864}
\end{array}
\qquad
\begin{array}{r}
16\,R6 \\
7\overline{)118}
\end{array}
$$

Next, let's look at the value of estimating division.

Estimating Division   Before actually working a division problem, estimate the quotient by rounding. This estimate helps you check the answer. The example that follows is rounded all the way. After you make an estimate, work the problem and check your answer by multiplication.

EXAMPLE

```
              36 R111        Estimate        Check
        138)5,079                 50          138
            4 14          100)5,000         ×  36
            ───                              ───
             939                             828
             828                             4 14
             ───                             ─────
             111                             4,968
                                           + 111  ←── Add remainder
                                             ─────
                                             5,079
```

Now let's turn our attention to division shortcuts with zeros.

Division Shortcuts with Zeros   The steps that follow show a shortcut that you can use when you divide numbers with zeros.

DIVISION SHORTCUT WITH NUMBERS ENDING IN ZEROS

Step 1. When the dividend and divisor have ending zeros, count the number of ending zeros in the divisor.

Step 2. Drop the same number of zeros in the dividend as in the divisor, counting from right to left.

Note the following examples of division shortcuts with numbers ending in zeros. Since two of the symbols used for division are ÷ and $\overline{)}$, our first examples show the zero shortcut method with the ÷ symbol.

EXAMPLES

One ending zero

Dividend   Divisor

Drop 1 zero in dividend

```
95,000 ÷ 10  ────→ 95,000 =  9,500
95,000 ÷ 100 ────→ 95,000 =   950   Drop 2 zeros
95,000 ÷ 1,000 ──→ 95,000 =    95   Drop 3 zeros
```

In a long division problem with the $\overline{)}$ symbol, you again count the number of ending zeros in the divisor. Then drop the same number of ending zeros in the dividend and divide as usual.

EXAMPLE   6,500)88,000 ←── Drop 2 zeros

```
                                       13 R35
                                    65)880
                                       65
                                       ───
                                       230
                                       195
              65)880 ←──                ───
                                        35
```

You are now ready to practice what you learned by dissecting and solving a word problem.

How to Dissect and Solve a Word Problem

The blueprint aid on page 18 will be your guide to dissecting and solving the following word problem.

The Word Problem   Dunkin' Donuts sells to four different companies a total of $3,500 worth of doughnuts per week. What is the total annual sales to these companies? What is the yearly sales per company? (Assume each company buys the same amount.) Check your answer to show how multiplication and division are related.

MONEY tips

College *is* worth it! College graduates earn substantially more money each year than high school graduates *and* that wage premium is increasing steadily—almost twice as much. Stay in school.

	The facts	Solving for?	Steps to take	Key points
BLUEPRINT	Sales per week: $3,500. Companies: 4.	Total annual sales to all four companies. Yearly sales per company.	Sales per week × Weeks in year (52) = Total annual sales. Total annual sales ÷ Total companies = Yearly sales per company.	Division is the reverse of multiplication.

Steps to solving problem

1. Calculate total annual sales. $3,500 × 52 weeks = $182,000

2. Calculate yearly sales per company, $182,000 ÷ 4 = $45,500

Check

$45,500 × 4 = $182,000

It's time again to check your progress with a Practice Quiz.

LU 1–3 PRACTICE QUIZ

Complete this **Practice Quiz** to see how you are doing.

1. Estimate the actual problem by rounding all the way, work the actual problem, and check:

    Actual   **Estimate**   **Check**
    3,894
    × 18

2. Multiply by shortcut method: 3. Multiply by shortcut method:
    77,000   95 × 10,000
    × 1,800

4. Divide by rounding all the way, complete the actual calculation, and check, showing remainder as a whole number.
    26)5,325

5. Divide by shortcut method:
    4,000)96,000

6. Assume General Motors produces 960 Chevrolets each workday (Monday through Friday). If the cost to produce each car is $6,500, what is General Motors' total cost for the year? Check your answer.

*For **extra help** from your authors—Sharon and Jeff—see the student DVD*

✓ **Solutions**

1. **Estimate**   **Actual**   **Check**
    4,000   3,894   8 × 3,894 =   31,152
    ×   20   ×   18   10 × 3,894 = + 38,940
    80,000   31 152   70,092
                                    38 94
                                    70,092

2. 77 × 18 = 1,386 + 5 zeros = 138,600,000   3. 95 + 4 zeros = 950,000

4. **Rounding**   **Actual**   **Check**
        166 R20   204 R21   26 × 204 = 5,304
    30)5,000   26)5,325   +   21
        3 0   5 2   5,325
        2 00   125
        1 80   104
          200   21
          180
            20

5. Drop 3 zeros =
$$\begin{array}{r} 24 \\ 4\overline{)96} \end{array}$$

6. General Motors' total cost per year:

	The facts	Solving for?	Steps to take	Key points
BLUEPRINT	Cars produced each workday: 960. Workweek: 5 days. Cost per car: $6,500.	Total cost per year.	Cars produced per week × 52 = Total cars produced per year. Total cars produced per year × Total cost per car = Total cost per year.	Whenever possible, use multiplication and division shortcuts with zeros. Multiplication can be checked by division.

Steps to solving problem

1. Calculate total cars produced per week.

$5 \times 960 = 4{,}800$ cars produced per week

2. Calculate total cars produced per year.

$4{,}800$ cars $\times 52$ weeks $= 249{,}600$ total cars produced per year

3. Calculate total cost per year.

$249{,}600$ cars $\times \$6{,}500 = \$1{,}622{,}400{,}000$ (multiply $2{,}496 \times 65$ and add zeros)

Check

$\$1{,}622{,}400{,}000 \div 249{,}600 = \$6{,}500$ (drop 2 zeros before dividing)

LU 1–3a EXTRA PRACTICE QUIZ WITH WORKED-OUT SOLUTIONS

Need more practice? Try this **Extra Practice Quiz** (check figures in the Interactive Chapter Organizer, p. 21). Worked-out Solutions can be found in Appendix B at end of text.

1. Estimate the actual problem by rounding all the way, work the actual problem, and check:

Actual   **Estimate**   **Check**

$\begin{array}{r} 4{,}938 \\ \times\ \ \ 19 \end{array}$

2. Multiply by shortcut method:
$\begin{array}{r} 86{,}000 \\ \times\ 1{,}900 \end{array}$

3. Multiply by shortcut method:
$86 \times 10{,}000$

4. Divide by rounding all the way, complete the actual calculation, and check, showing remainder as a whole number.
$26\overline{)6{,}394}$

5. Divide by the shortcut method:
$3{,}000\overline{)99{,}000}$

6. Assume General Motors produces 850 Chevrolets each workday (Monday through Friday). If the cost to produce each car is $7,000, what is General Motors' total cost for the year? Check your answer.

INTERACTIVE CHAPTER ORGANIZER

Topic/procedure/formula	Examples	You try it*
Reading and writing numeric and verbal whole numbers, p. 4 Placement of digits in a number gives the value of the digits (Figure 1.1). Commas separate every three digits, moving from right to left. Begin at left to read and write number in verbal form. Do not read zeros or use *and*. Hyphenate numbers twenty-one to ninety-nine. Reverse procedure to change verbal number to numeric.	462 → Four hundred sixty-two 6,741 → Six thousand, seven hundred forty-one	**Write in verbal form** 571 → 7,943 →
Rounding whole numbers, p. 6 1. Identify place value of the digit to be rounded. 2. If digit to the right is 5 or more, round up; if less than 5, do not change. 3. Change all digits to the right of rounded identified digit to zeros.	643 to nearest ten 4 in tens place value 　　3 is not 5 or more Thus, 643 rounds to 640.	**Round to nearest ten** 691
Rounding all the way, p. 6 Round to first digit of number. One nonzero digit remains. In estimating, you round each number of the problem to one nonzero digit. The final answer is not rounded.	468,451 → 500,000 The 5 is the only nonzero digit remaining.	**Round all the way** 429,685 →
Adding whole numbers, p. 10 1. Align numbers at the right. 2. Add units column. If sum is more than 9, carry tens digit. 3. Moving left, repeat Step 2 until all place values are added. Add from top to bottom. Check by adding bottom to top or adding each column separately and combining.	$\begin{array}{r}1\\65\\+47\\\hline112\end{array}$ $\begin{array}{r}12\\+10\\\hline112\end{array}$ Checking sum of each digit	**Add** 76 +38
Subtracting whole numbers, p. 11 1. Align minuend and subtrahend at the right. 2. Subtract units digits. If necessary, borrow 1 from tens digit in minuend. 3. Moving left, repeat Step 2 until all place values are subtracted. Minuend less subtrahend equals difference.	**Check** $\begin{array}{r}5\ 18\\\cancel{6}\cancel{8}5\\-492\\\hline193\end{array}$ $\begin{array}{r}193\\+492\\\hline685\end{array}$	**Subtract** 629 −134
Multiplying whole numbers, p. 14 1. Align multiplicand and multiplier at the right. 2. Begin at the right and keep multiplying as you move to the left. First partial product aligns at the right with multiplicand and multiplier. 3. Move left through multiplier and continue multiplying multiplicand. Partial product right digit or first digit is placed directly below digit in multiplier. 4. Continue Steps 2 and 3 until multiplication is complete. Add partial products to get final product.	$\begin{array}{r}223\\\times\ 32\\\hline446\\6\ 69\\\hline7,136\end{array}$	**Multiply** 491 × 28
Shortcuts: (a) When multiplicand or multiplier, or both, end in zeros, disregard zeros and multiply; attach same number of zeros to answer. If zero is in center of multiplier, no need to show row of zeros. (b) If multiplying by power of 10, attach same number of zeros to whole number multiplied.	a.　48,000　48　　3 zeros　　　524 　　× 40　 4　　+1 zero　× 206 　　　　1,920,000 ◄4 zeros　3 144 　　　　　　　　　　　　104 8 　　　　　　　　　　　　107,944 b. 14 × 　10 = 140 (attach 1 zero) 　 14 × 1,000 = 14,000 (attach 3 zeros)	**Multiply by shortcut** 13 × 10 = 13 × 1,000 =

(continues)

INTERACTIVE CHAPTER ORGANIZER

Topic/procedure/formula	Examples	You try it*
Dividing whole numbers, p. 16 1. When divisor is divided into the dividend, the remainder is less than divisor. 2. Drop zeros from dividend right to left by number of zeros found in the divisor. Even division has no remainder; uneven division has a remainder; divisor with one digit is short division; and divisor with more than one digit is long division.	1. $\begin{array}{r} 5\ R6 \\ 14\overline{)76} \\ \underline{70} \\ 6 \end{array}$ 2. $5{,}000 \div 100 = 50 \div 1 = \boxed{50}$ $5{,}000 \div 1{,}000 = 5 \div 1 = \boxed{5}$	**Divide** 1. $16\overline{)95}$ **Divide by shortcut** 2. $4{,}000 \div 100$ $4{,}000 \div 1{,}000$
KEY TERMS	Addends, *p. 10* Decimal point, *p. 4* Decimal system, *p. 4* Difference, *p. 11* Dividend, *p. 16* Divisor, *p. 16*	Minuend, *p. 11* Multiplicand, *p. 14* Multiplier, *p. 14* Partial products, *p. 14* Partial quotient, *p. 16* Product, *p. 14*	Quotient, *p. 16* Remainder, *p. 16* Rounding all the way, *p. 6* Subtrahend, *p. 11* Sum, *p. 10* Whole number, *p. 4*
Check Figures for Extra Practice Quizzes with Page References. (Worked-out Solutions in Appendix B.)	LU 1–1a (p. 9) 1. A. Eight thousand, six hundred eighty-two; B. Fifty-six thousand, two hundred ninety-five; C. Seven hundred thirty-two billion, three hundred ten million, four hundred forty-four thousand, eight hundred eighty-eight 2. A. 40; B. 700; C. 7,000; D. 6,000 3. $3,000,000; $400,000	LU 1–2a (p. 13) 1. 26,090 2. 15,000; 15,953 3. 3,819 4. $43,100 (over)	LU 1–3a (p. 19) 1. 100,000; 93,822 2. 163,400,000 3. 860,000 4. 245 R24 5. 33 6. $1,547,000,000

*Worked-out solutions are in Appendix B.

Critical Thinking Discussion Questions with Chapter Concept Check

1. List the four steps of the decision-making process. Do you think all companies should be required to follow these steps? Give an example.

2. Explain the three steps used to round whole numbers. Pick a whole number and explain why it should not be rounded.

3. How do you check subtraction? If you were to attend a movie, explain how you might use the subtraction check method.

4. Explain how you can check multiplication. If you visit a local supermarket, how could you show multiplication as a shortcut to addition?

5. Explain how division is the reverse of multiplication. Using the supermarket example, explain how division is a time-saving shortcut related to subtraction.

6. **Chapter Concept Check.** Using all the math you learned in Chapter 1, go to the chapter opener and plan out a dinner for a family of four. You need to calculate the difference in cost and calories from dining at Subway versus McDonald's. Go online or visit these stores in your area to find current food prices.

Classroom Notes

WORD PROBLEMS

1–47. The *Wall Street Journal* reported that the cost for lightbulbs over a 10-year period at a local Walmart parking lot in Kansas would be $248,134 if standard lightbulbs were used. If LED lightbulbs were used over the same period, the total cost would be $220,396. What would Walmart save by using LED bulbs? *LU 1-2(2)*

1–48. An education can be the key to higher earnings. In a U.S. Census Bureau study, high school graduates earned $30,400 per year. Associate's degree graduates averaged $38,200 per year. Bachelor's degree graduates averaged $52,200 per year. Assuming a 50-year work-life, calculate the lifetime earnings for a high school graduate, associate's degree graduate, and bachelor's degree graduate. What's the lifetime income difference between a high school and associate's degree? What about the lifetime difference between a high school and bachelor's degree? *LU 1-3(1), LU 1-2(2)*

1–49. Assume season-ticket prices in the lower bowl for the Buffalo Bills will rise from $480 for a 10-game package to $600. Fans sitting in the best seats in the upper deck will pay an increase from $440 to $540. Don Manning plans to purchase two season tickets for either lower bowl or upper deck. **(a)** How much more will two tickets cost for lower bowl? **(b)** How much more will two tickets cost for upper deck? **(c)** What will be his total cost for a 10-game package for lower bowl? **(d)** What will be his total cost for a 10-game package for upper deck? *LU 1-2(2), LU 1-3(1)*

1–50. Some ticket prices for *Lion King* on Broadway were $70, $95, $200, and $250. For a family of four, estimate the cost of the $95 tickets by rounding all the way and then do the actual multiplication: *LU 1-1(2), LU 1-3(1)*

1–51. Walt Disney World Resort and United Vacations got together to create a special deal. The air-inclusive package features accommodations for three nights at Disney's All-Star Resort, hotel taxes, and a four-day unlimited Magic Pass. Prices are $609 per person traveling from Washington, DC, and $764 per person traveling from Los Angeles. **(a)** What would be the cost for a family of four leaving from Washington, DC? **(b)** What would be the cost for a family of four leaving from Los Angeles? **(c)** How much more will it cost the family from Los Angeles? *LU 1-3(1)*

1–52. NTB Tires bought 910 tires from its manufacturer for $36 per tire. What is the total cost of NTB's purchase? If the store can sell all the tires at $65 each, what will be the store's gross profit, or the difference between its sales and costs (Sales − Costs = Gross profit)? *LU 1-3(1), LU 1-2(2)*

1–53. What was the total average number of visits for these websites?   *LU 1-2(1), LU 1-3(2)*

Website	Average daily unique visitors
1. Orbitz.com	1,527,000
2. Mypoints.com	1,356,000
3. Americangreetings.com	745,000
4. Bizrate.com	503,000
5. Half.com	397,000

1–54. As the Boston MarketWatch for January 2012 states, "The Approved Card" from Suze Orman provides a pretty fair deal. This prepaid debit card costs $3 to purchase and there is a $3 monthly account maintenance fee (the first month's charge is waived). Withdrawals at ATMs cost $2. If Hanna Lind used this card for 8 months and had nine ATM withdrawals, what would her charge be?   *LU 1-3(1)*

1–55. A report from the Center for Science in the Public Interest—a consumer group based in Washington, DC—released a study listing calories of various ice cream treats sold by six of the largest ice cream companies. The worst treat tested by the group was 1,270 total calories. People need roughly 2,200 to 2,500 calories per day. Using a daily average, how many additional calories should a person consume after eating ice cream?   *LU 1-2(1), LU 1-3(2)*

1–56. At Rose State College, Alison Wells received the following grades in her online accounting class: 90, 65, 85, 80, 75, and 90. Alison's instructor, Professor Clark, said he would drop the lowest grade. What is Alison's average?   *LU 1-2(1)*

1–57. The Bureau of Transportation's list of the 10 most expensive U.S. airports and their average fares is given below. Please use this list to answer the questions that follow.   *LU 1-2(1, 2)*

1. Houston, TX	$477
2. Huntsville, AL	473
3. Newark, NJ	470
4. Cincinnati, OH	466
5. Washington, DC	465
6. Charleston, SC	460
7. Memphis, TN	449
8. Knoxville, TN	449
9. Dallas–Fort Worth, TX	431
10. Madison, WI	429

a. What is the total of all the fares?
b. What would the total be if all the fares were rounded all the way?
c. How much does the actual number differ from the rounded estimate?

1–58. Ron Alf, owner of Alf's Moving Company, bought a new truck. On Ron's first trip, he drove 1,200 miles and used 80 gallons of gas. How many miles per gallon did Ron get from his new truck? On Ron's second trip, he drove 840 miles and used 60 gallons. What is the difference in miles per gallon between Ron's first trip and his second trip? *LU 1-3(2)*

1–59. In Bankrate.com's Smart Spending column for early 2012, Jan Fandrich of Billings, Montana, explains how she saves money, stays healthy, and helps the environment by using baking soda and vinegar instead of toxic commercial cleaners. She puts a little bit of vinegar in the rinse cycle instead of fabric softener, and mops the floors and cleans the showers with a mix of baking soda and vinegar in water. If a box of baking soda costs $1 and a bottle of vinegar is $2, how much will her cleaning supplies cost if she uses five boxes of baking soda and 10 bottles of vinegar in 1 year? *LU 1-3(1)*

1–60. Assume BarnesandNoble.com has 289 business math texts in inventory. During one month, the online bookstore ordered and received 1,855 texts; it also sold 1,222 on the web. What is the bookstore's inventory at the end of the month? If each text costs $59, what is the end-of-month inventory cost? *LU 1-2(1), LU 1-2(2)*

1–61. Assume Cabot Company produced 2,115,000 cans of paint in August. Cabot sold 2,011,000 of these cans. If each can cost $18, what were Cabot's ending inventory of paint cans and its total ending inventory cost? *LU 1-2(2), LU 1-3(1)*

1–62. A local community college has 20 faculty members in the business department, 40 in psychology, 26 in English, and 140 in all other departments. What is the total number of faculty at this college? If each faculty member advises 25 students, how many students attend the local college? *LU 1-2(1), LU 1-3(1)*

1–63. Hometown Buffet had 90 customers on Sunday, 70 on Monday, 65 on Tuesday, and a total of 310 on Wednesday to Saturday. How many customers did Hometown Buffet serve during the week? If each customer spends $9, what were the total sales for the week? *LU 1-2(1), LU 1-3(1)*

If Hometown Buffet had the same sales each week, what were the sales for the year?

1–64. A local travel agency projected its year 2013 sales at $880,000. During 2013, the agency earned $482,900 sales from its major clients and $116,500 sales from the remainder of its clients. How much did the agency overestimate its sales? *LU 1-2(2)*

1–65. Ryan Seary works at US Airways and earned $71,000 last year before tax deductions. From Ryan's total earnings, his company subtracted $1,388 for federal income taxes, $4,402 for Social Security, and $1,030 for Medicare taxes. What was Ryan's actual, or net, pay for the year? *LU 1-2(1, 2)*

1–66. An article in *The New York Times* on January 5, 2012, discussed how individuals with little or no prior credit sources may benefit from a new tracking procedure. Experian, one of the three leading credit reporting companies, is now tracking on-time rent payments, thereby raising the credit scores of many people. Experian uses FICO scores, a three-digit rating system ranging generally from 300–850, to rate how risky a borrower is. If you currently have a FICO score of 550 and on-time rent payments increase your FICO score by 80, what is your new FICO score? *LU 1-2(1)*

1–67. Roger Company produces beach balls and operates three shifts. Roger produces 5,000 balls per shift on shifts 1 and 2. On shift 3, the company can produce 6 times as many balls as on shift 1. Assume a 5-day workweek. How many beach balls does Roger produce per week and per year? *LU 1-2(1), LU 1-3(1)*

1–68. Assume 6,000 children go to Disneyland today. How much additional revenue will Disneyland receive if it raises the cost of admission from $31 to $41 and lowers the age limit for adults from 12 years old to 10 years old? *LU 1-2(1), LU 1-3(1)*

1–69. Moe Brink has a $900 balance in his checkbook. During the week, Moe wrote the following checks: rent, $350; telephone, $44; food, $160; and entertaining, $60. Moe also made a $1,200 deposit. What is Moe's new checkbook balance? *LU 1-2(1, 2)*

1–70. A local Sports Authority store, an athletic sports shop, bought and sold the following merchandise: *LU 1-2(1, 2)*

	Cost	Selling price
Tennis rackets	$ 2,900	$ 3,999
Tennis balls	70	210
Bowling balls	1,050	2,950
Sneakers	+ 8,105	+ 14,888

What was the total cost of the merchandise bought by Sports Authority? If the shop sold all its merchandise, what were the sales and the resulting gross profit (Sales − Costs = Gross profit)?

1–71. Rich Engel, the bookkeeper for Engel's Real Estate, and his manager are concerned about the company's telephone bills. *eXcel* Last year the company's average monthly phone bill was $32. Rich's manager asked him for an average of this year's phone bills. Rich's records show the following: *LU 1-2(1), LU 1-3(2)*

January	$ 34	July	$ 28
February	60	August	23
March	20	September	29
April	25	October	25
May	30	November	22
June	59	December	41

What is the average of this year's phone bills? Did Rich and his manager have a justifiable concern?

1–72. On Monday, a local True Value Hardware sold 15 paint brushes at $3 each, six wrenches at $5 each, seven bags of grass
*e**X**cel* seed at $3 each, four lawn mowers at $119 each, and 28 cans of paint at $8 each. What were True Value's total dollar sales on Monday?   *LU 1-2(1), LU 1-3(1)*

1–73. While redecorating, Lee Owens went to Carpet World and bought 150 square yards of commercial carpet. The total cost of the carpet was $6,000. How much did Lee pay per square yard?   *LU 1-3(2)*

1–74. Washington Construction built 12 ranch houses for $115,000 each. From the sale of these houses, Washington received
*e**X**cel* $1,980,000. How much gross profit (Sales − Costs = Gross profit) did Washington make on the houses?   *LU 1-2(2), LU 1-3(1, 2)*

The four partners of Washington Construction split all profits equally. How much will each partner receive?

CHALLENGE PROBLEMS

1–75. A mall in Lexington has 18 stores. The following is a breakdown of what each store pays for rent per month. The rent is based on square footage.

5 department/computer stores	$1,250	2 bakeries	$ 500
5 restaurants	860	2 drugstores	820
3 bookstores	750	1 supermarket	1,450

Calculate the total rent that these stores pay annually. What would the answer be if it were rounded all the way? How much more each year do the drugstores pay in rent compared to the bakeries?   *LU 1-2(2), LU 1-3(1)*

1–76. Paula Sanchez is trying to determine her 2014 finances. Paula's actual 2013 finances were as follows: *LU 1-1, LU 1-2, LU 1-3*

Income:		Assets:	
Gross income	$69,000	Checking account	$ 1,950
Interest income	450	Savings account	8,950
Total	$69,450	Automobile	1,800
Expenses:		Personal property	14,000
Living	$24,500	Total	$26,700
Insurance premium	350	Liabilities:	
Taxes	14,800	Note to bank	4,500
Medical	585	Net worth	$22,200 ($26,700 − $4,500)
Investment	4,000		
Total	$44,235		

Net worth = Assets − Liabilities
(own)   (owe)

Paula believes her gross income will double in 2014 but her interest income will decrease $150. She plans to reduce her 2014 living expenses by one-half. Paula's insurance company wrote a letter announcing that her insurance premiums would triple in 2014. Her accountant estimates her taxes will decrease $250 and her medical costs will increase $410. Paula also hopes to cut her investments expenses by one-fourth. Paula's accountant projects that her savings and checking accounts will each double in value. On January 2, 2014, Paula sold her automobile and began to use public transportation. Paula forecasts that her personal property will decrease by one-seventh. She has sent her bank a $375 check to reduce her bank note. Could you give Paula an updated list of her 2014 finances? If you round all the way each 2013 and 2014 asset and liability, what will be the difference in Paula's net worth?

 SUMMARY PRACTICE TEST You Tube™

Do you need help? The DVD has step-by-step worked-out solutions.

1. Translate the following verbal forms to numbers and add. *(p. 4)   LU 1-1(1), LU 1-2(1)*

    a. Four thousand, eight hundred thirty-nine

    b. Seven million, twelve

    c. Twelve thousand, three hundred ninety-two

2. Express the following number in verbal form. *(p. 4)   LU 1-1(1)*

    9,622,364

3. Round the following numbers. *(p. 6)   LU 1-1(2)*

Nearest ten	Nearest hundred	Nearest thousand	Round all the way
a. 68	**b.** 888	**c.** 8,325	**d.** 14,821

4. Estimate the following actual problem by rounding all the way, work the actual problem, and check by adding each column of digits separately. *(pp. 6, 10)   LU 1-1(2), LU 1-2(1)*

Actual	Estimate	Check
1,886		
9,411		
+ 6,395		

5. Estimate the following actual problem by rounding all the way and then do the actual multiplication. *(pp. 6, 14)   LU 1-1(2), LU 1-3(1)*

Actual	Estimate
8,843	
× 906	

6. Multiply the following by the shortcut method. *(p. 14)   LU 1-3(1)*

829,412 × 1,000

7. Divide the following and check the answer by multiplication. *(pp. 14, 16)   LU 1-3(1, 2)*

Check

39)‾14,800‾

8. Divide the following by the shortcut method. *(p. 16)   LU 1-3(2)*

6,000 ÷ 60

9. Ling Wong bought a $299 iPod that was reduced to $205. Ling gave the clerk three $100 bills. What change will Ling receive? *(p. 11)   LU 1-2(2)*

10. Sam Song plans to buy a $16,000 Ford Focus with an interest charge of $4,000. Sam figures he can afford a monthly payment of $400. If Sam must pay 40 equal monthly payments, can he afford the Ford Focus? *(pp. 10, 16)   LU 1-2(1), LU 1-3(2)*

11. Lester Hal has the oil tank at his business filled 20 times per year. The tank has a capacity of 200 gallons. Assume **(a)** the price of oil fuel is $3 per gallon and **(b)** the tank is completely empty each time Lester has it filled. What is Lester's average monthly oil bill? Complete the following blueprint aid for dissecting and solving the word problem. *(pp. 14, 16) LU 1-3(1, 2)*

	The facts	Solving for?	Steps to take	Key points
BLUEPRINT				

Steps to solving problem

SURF TO SAVE

PROBLEM 1
Budget your laptop purchase

Imagine you have a budget of $2,500 to purchase 5 identical laptops for your family. Go to http://www.officemax.com, select a laptop to meet your needs, and then calculate how much 5 of those laptops would cost. Round prices to the nearest dollar and ignore sales tax and delivery charges. Is $2,500 enough? If so, how much money do you have left? If not, how much more money do you need?

Discussion Questions

1. What is the importance of having a budget?
2. Should college students, who are traditionally low wage earners, still utilize a budget? Why?

PROBLEM 2
Budget expenses for a trip

Imagine you are planning a 4-night stay, Monday through Thursday, in New York City. Go to http://www.hertz.com to find the daily rate for the car you'd like. Then, go to http://www2.choicehotels.com to choose a hotel and determine the nightly room rate. Calculate your total cost for the car and lodging, ignoring taxes and rounding rates to the nearest dollar.

Discussion Questions

1. Using your existing salary, how would you budget for this trip to ensure you have the appropriate funds? Be specific.
2. What types of expenses might you incur once you are on this trip?

PROBLEM 3
Determine wage breakdowns

Go to http://www.nascar.com. Choose the Standings, Spring Cup Series link. Look at the Top 5 money earners for any 3-year period. Based on total winnings, how much money did each earn per month, per week, per day, and per hour, assuming a 40-hour workweek? What is the difference in each of these earning amounts across the 3 years you selected?

Discussion Questions

1. How much do you expect to earn after graduating from college?
2. What is your expected salary breakdown by month, week, day, and hour?

PROBLEM 4
How much reading can you afford?

Go to http://www.amazon.com. Search for the list of "Top 100 books." If you have $100 to spend, how many of the Top 100 books could you buy if you started with the number one book and worked your way down the list? Ignore shipping and handling and taxes.

Discussion Questions

1. If you owned an e-reader, how many more e-books could you purchase with the same $100?
2. Based on your current salary, how many hours must you work to afford spending this $100 on books?

MOBILE APPS ✖

MathPad 4 (Clay Cat Designs) Focuses on solving word problems through addition, subtraction, division, and multiplication.

Basic Math (Explorer Technologies) Uses repetition of problems to build up basic math skills.

INTERNET PROJECTS ✖

See text website
www.mhhe.com/slater11e_sse_ch01

PAID FOR COLLEGE ON HIS OWN

that offer a bachelor's degree in HVAC. The community college had a program with Ferris, so I had a guarantee that I wouldn't have a problem transferring my credits.

YOU HAVE FOUR YOUNGER SIBLINGS. WERE YOUR PARENTS ABLE TO HELP WITH THE COLLEGE COSTS? They said that I could live at home free and eat all I wanted. But I haven't gotten any money from them for college.

WHAT WERE SOME OF THE WAYS IN WHICH YOU PAID FOR COLLEGE? I had a paper route from ages 12 to 18, and I saved all my money from that—about $6,000. I saved most of my money while I worked at Sam's Club. At the community college, I had a Pell grant [a need-based federal grant, up to $5,550 this year] that covered most of my college costs. I still get a Pell grant, and I also have a scholarship—$4,000 a year, which covers over half of my tuition. I pay a couple of thousand dollars a year more for tuition and fees, plus $3,000 a year for room and board. I have enough money to cover this year's costs, and I should have enough to cover my last year.

David Leestma, 21, is a junior at Ferris State University, in Big Rapids, Mich. He will graduate in 2012 with a bachelor's degree in heating, ventilating and air conditioning, and with zero debt.

YOU TOOK A YEAR OFF BETWEEN HIGH SCHOOL AND COLLEGE. HOW COME? I wasn't sure what I wanted to do for a career, and I didn't want to go to school unless I knew. So I got a job at Sam's Club working at the café for $9 an hour. Over the year, it became clear what I *didn't* want to do— I didn't want to work in retail the rest of my life. I went on a couple of job shadows with friends of my family. On one, I spent time with a mechanical engineer. He designed HVAC systems and got me interested in that.

WHY DID YOU START AT A COMMUNITY COLLEGE RATHER THAN A FOUR-YEAR COLLEGE? Grand Rapids Community College was cheaper, and it gave me the option to live at home. The plan when I started was to transfer to Ferris. As far as I know, it is one of only a few colleges in the country

WHAT HAS BEEN YOUR BIGGEST CHALLENGE SO FAR? At Grand Rapids, I did two summer, two fall and two winter semesters in one year, and I worked part-time at Sam's Club. I went to school and worked pretty much round the clock, except for Sundays. I did homework on lunch breaks. It was crazy.

DO YOU HAVE ADVICE FOR OTHER STUDENTS? From the start, I've always looked at what job I'm going to get when I finish. That's the whole goal of going to college for me. So take your time to choose what you want to do. You can change your mind after you start college, but taking more classes costs money and extra time.

ANY REGRETS ABOUT THE WAY YOU'VE DONE IT? No. A lot of the other students I talk to are $10,000 or more in debt. I like where I'm sitting financially right now. It's a blessing. ∎

Interview by
JANE BENNETT CLARK

BUSINESS MATH ISSUE

Going into debt in order to attend college will always pay off.

1. List the key points of the article and information to support your position.
2. Write a group defense of your position using math calculations to support your view.

CHAPTER 2

Fractions

Rhymes with Orange © 2012 Hilary B. Price. King Features Syndicate.

About half of the vehicles sold in the U.S. are now made foreign-owned firm

LU 2–1: Types of Fractions and Conversion Procedures

1. Recognize the three types of fractions (pp. 36–37).

2. Convert improper fractions to whole or mixed numbers and mixed numbers to improper fractions (pp. 37–38).

3. Convert fractions to lowest and highest terms (pp. 38–39).

LU 2–2: Adding and Subtracting Fractions

1. Add like and unlike fractions (pp. 41–42).

2. Find the least common denominator by inspection and prime numbers (pp. 42–43).

3. Subtract like and unlike fractions (p. 44).

4. Add and subtract mixed numbers with the same or different denominators (pp. 44–46).

LU 2–3: Multiplying and Dividing Fractions

1. Multiply and divide proper fractions and mixed numbers (pp. 47–48).

2. Use the cancellation method in the multiplication and division of fractions (pp. 48–49).

VOCABULARY PREVIEW

Here are key terms in this chapter. After completing the chapter, if you know the term, place a checkmark in the parentheses. If you don't know the term, look it up and put the page number where it can be found.

Cancellation ( ) **Common denominator** ( ) **Denominator** ( ) **Equivalent** ( ) **Fraction** ( ) **Greatest common divisor** ( ) **Higher terms** ( ) **Improper fraction** ( ) **Least common denominator (LCD)** ( ) **Like fractions** ( ) **Lowest terms** ( ) **Mixed numbers** ( ) **Numerator** ( ) **Prime numbers** ( ) **Proper fraction** ( ) **Reciprocal** ( ) **Unlike fractions** ( )

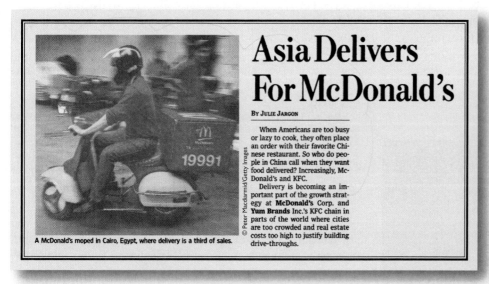

Asia Delivers For McDonald's

BY JULIE JARGON

When Americans are too busy or lazy to cook, they often place an order with their favorite Chinese restaurant. So who do people in China call when they want food delivered? Increasingly, McDonald's and KFC.

Delivery is becoming an important part of the growth strategy at **McDonald's** Corp. and **Yum Brands** Inc.'s KFC chain in parts of the world where cities are too crowded and real estate costs too high to justify building drive-throughs.

A McDonald's moped in Cairo, Egypt, where delivery is a third of sales.

© Peter Macdiarmid/Getty Images

The *Wall Street Journal* clipping "Asia Delivers for McDonald's" illustrates the use of a fraction. From the clipping you learn that one-third ($\frac{1}{3}$) of sales at a McDonald's in Cairo, Egypt, is from delivery.

Now let's look at Milk Chocolate M&M'S® candies as another example of using fractions.

As you know, M&M'S® candies come in different colors. Do you know how many of each color are in a bag of M&M'S®? If you go to the M&M'S website, you learn that a typical bag of M&M'S® contains approximately 17 brown, 11 yellow, 11 red, and 5 each of orange, blue, and green M&M'S®.[1]

GLOBAL

The 1.69-ounce bag of M&M'S® shown on page 36 contains 55 M&M'S®. In this bag, you will find the following colors:

18 yellow	9 blue	6 brown
10 red	7 orange	5 green

[1] Off 1 due to rounding.

55 pieces in the bag

The number of yellow candies in a bag might suggest that yellow is the favorite color of many people. Since this is a business math text, however, let's look at the 55 M&M'S® in terms of fractional arithmetic.

Of the 55 M&M'S® in the 1.69-ounce bag, 5 of these M&M'S® are green, so we can say that 5 parts of 55 represent green candies. We could also say that 1 out of 11 M&M'S® is green. Are you confused?

For many people, fractions are difficult. If you are one of these people, this chapter is for you. First you will review the types of fractions and the fraction conversion procedures. Then you will gain a clear understanding of the addition, subtraction, multiplication, and division of fractions.

Learning Unit 2–1: Types of Fractions and Conversion Procedures

LO 1

This chapter explains the parts of whole numbers called **fractions.** With fractions you can divide any object or unit—a whole—into a definite number of equal parts. For example, the bag of 55 M&M'S® described above contains 6 brown candies. If you eat only the brown M&M'S®, you have eaten 6 parts of 55, or 6 parts of the whole bag of M&M'S®. We can express this in the following fraction:

$$\frac{6}{55}$$

6 is the **numerator,** or top of the fraction. The numerator describes the number of equal parts of the whole bag that you ate.

55 is the **denominator,** or bottom of the fraction. The denominator gives the total number of equal parts in the bag of M&M'S®.

Before reviewing the arithmetic operations of fractions, you must recognize the three types of fractions described in this unit. You must also know how to convert fractions to a workable form.

Types of Fractions

In *The Wall Street Journal* it was reported that in the United States two-thirds ($\frac{2}{3}$) of all sales in fast-food restaurants is from drive-through orders. The fraction $\frac{2}{3}$ is a proper fraction.

© Photodisc/Getty Images

PROPER FRACTIONS

A **proper fraction** has a value less than 1; its numerator is smaller than its denominator.

EXAMPLES $\dfrac{1}{4}, \dfrac{1}{2}, \dfrac{1}{10}, \dfrac{1}{12}, \dfrac{1}{3}, \dfrac{4}{7}, \dfrac{2}{3}, \dfrac{9}{10}, \dfrac{12}{13}, \dfrac{18}{55}$

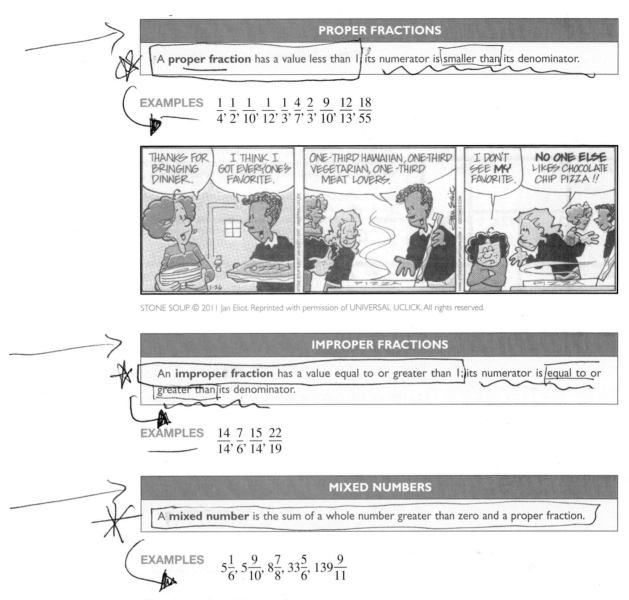

STONE SOUP © 2011 Jan Eliot. Reprinted with permission of UNIVERSAL UCLICK. All rights reserved.

IMPROPER FRACTIONS

An **improper fraction** has a value equal to or greater than 1; its numerator is equal to or greater than its denominator.

EXAMPLES $\dfrac{14}{14}, \dfrac{7}{6}, \dfrac{15}{14}, \dfrac{22}{19}$

MIXED NUMBERS

A **mixed number** is the sum of a whole number greater than zero and a proper fraction.

EXAMPLES $5\dfrac{1}{6}, 5\dfrac{9}{10}, 8\dfrac{7}{8}, 33\dfrac{5}{6}, 139\dfrac{9}{11}$

Conversion Procedures

In Chapter 1 we worked with two of the division symbols (÷ and $\overline{)}$). The horizontal line (or the diagonal) that separates the numerator and the denominator of a fraction also indicates division. The numerator, like the dividend, is the number we are dividing into. The denominator, like the divisor, is the number we use to divide. Then, referring to the 6 brown M&M'S® in the bag of 55 M&M'S® ($\frac{6}{55}$) shown at the beginning of this unit, we can say that we are dividing 55 into 6, or 6 is divided by 55. Also, in the fraction $\frac{3}{4}$, we can say that we are dividing 4 into 3, or 3 is divided by 4.

Working with the smaller numbers of simple fractions such as $\frac{3}{4}$ is easier, so we often convert fractions to their simplest terms. In this unit we show how to convert improper fractions to whole or mixed numbers, mixed numbers to improper fractions, and fractions to lowest and highest terms.

Converting Improper Fractions to Whole or Mixed Numbers   Business situations often make it necessary to change an improper fraction to a whole number or mixed number. You can use the following steps to make this conversion:

CONVERTING IMPROPER FRACTIONS TO WHOLE OR MIXED NUMBERS

LO 2

Step 1. Divide the numerator of the improper fraction by the denominator.

Step 2. **a.** If you have no remainder, the quotient is a whole number.

  b. If you have a remainder, the whole number part of the mixed number is the quotient. The remainder is placed over the old denominator as the proper fraction of the mixed number.

EXAMPLES

$$\frac{15}{15} = 1 \qquad \frac{16}{5} = 3\frac{1}{5}$$

$$\begin{array}{r} 3\,\text{R}1 \\ 5\overline{)16} \\ \underline{15} \\ 1 \end{array}$$

Converting Mixed Numbers to Improper Fractions   By reversing the procedure of converting improper fractions to mixed numbers, we can change mixed numbers to improper fractions.

CONVERTING MIXED NUMBERS TO IMPROPER FRACTIONS
Step 1. Multiply the denominator of the fraction by the whole number.
Step 2. Add the product from Step 1 to the numerator of the old fraction.
Step 3. Place the total from Step 2 over the denominator of the old fraction to get the improper fraction.

EXAMPLE $6\frac{1}{8} = \frac{(8 \times 6) + 1}{8} = \frac{49}{8}$ Note that the denominator stays the same.

Converting (Reducing) Fractions to Lowest Terms   When solving fraction problems, you always reduce the fractions to their lowest terms. This reduction does not change the value of the fraction. For example, in the bag of M&M'S®, 5 out of 55 were green. The fraction for this is $\frac{5}{55}$. If you divide the top and bottom of the fraction by 5, you have reduced the fraction to $\frac{1}{11}$ without changing its value. Remember, we said in the chapter introduction that 1 out of 11 M&M'S® in the bag of 55 M&M'S® represents green candies. Now you know why this is true.

To reduce a fraction to its lowest terms, begin by inspecting the fraction, looking for the largest whole number that will divide into both the numerator and the denominator without leaving a remainder. This whole number is the **greatest common divisor,** which cannot be zero. When you find this largest whole number, you have reached the point where the fraction is reduced to its **lowest terms.** At this point, no number (except 1) can divide evenly into both parts of the fraction.

LO 3

REDUCING FRACTIONS TO LOWEST TERMS BY INSPECTION
Step 1. By inspection, find the largest whole number (greatest common divisor) that will divide evenly into the numerator and denominator (does not change the fraction value).
Step 2. Divide the numerator and denominator by the greatest common divisor. Now you have reduced the fraction to its lowest terms, since no number (except 1) can divide evenly into the numerator and denominator.

EXAMPLE $\frac{24}{30} = \frac{24 \div 6}{30 \div 6} = \frac{4}{5}$

Using inspection, you can see that the number 6 in the above example is the greatest common divisor. When you have large numbers, the greatest common divisor is not so obvious. For large numbers, you can use the following step approach to find the greatest common divisor:

STEP APPROACH FOR FINDING GREATEST COMMON DIVISOR
Step 1. Divide the smaller number (numerator) of the fraction into the larger number (denominator).
Step 2. Divide the remainder of Step 1 into the divisor of Step 1.
Step 3. Divide the remainder of Step 2 into the divisor of Step 2. Continue this division process until the remainder is a 0, which means the last divisor is the greatest common divisor.

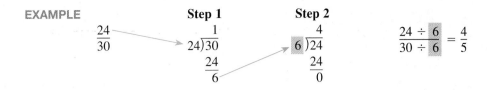

EXAMPLE

$$\frac{24}{30}$$

Step 1

$$\begin{array}{r} 1 \\ 24\overline{)30} \\ \underline{24} \\ 6 \end{array}$$

Step 2

$$\begin{array}{r} 4 \\ 6\overline{)24} \\ \underline{24} \\ 0 \end{array}$$

$$\frac{24 \div 6}{30 \div 6} = \frac{4}{5}$$

Reducing a fraction by inspection is to some extent a trial-and-error method. Sometimes you are not sure what number you should divide into the top (numerator) and bottom (denominator) of the fraction. The following reference table on divisibility tests will be helpful. Note that to reduce a fraction to lowest terms might result in more than one division.

	2	3	4	5	6	10
Will divide evenly into number if	Last digit is 0, 2, 4, 6, 8.	Sum of the digits is divisible by 3.	Last two digits can be divided by 4.	Last digit is 0 or 5.	The number is even and 3 will divide into the sum of the digits.	The last digit is 0.
Examples	$\frac{12}{14} = \frac{6}{7}$	$\frac{36}{69} = \frac{12}{23}$ $3 + 6 = 9 \div 3 = 3$ $6 + 9 = 15 \div 3 = 5$	$\frac{140}{160} = \frac{1(40)}{1(60)}$ $= \frac{35}{40} = \frac{7}{8}$	$\frac{15}{20} = \frac{3}{4}$	$\frac{12}{18} = \frac{2}{3}$	$\frac{90}{100} = \frac{9}{10}$

Converting (Raising) Fractions to Higher Terms   Later, when you add and subtract fractions, you will see that sometimes fractions must be raised to **higher terms.** Recall that when you reduced fractions to their lowest terms, you looked for the largest whole number (greatest common divisor) that would divide evenly into both the numerator and the denominator. When you raise fractions to higher terms, you do the opposite and multiply the numerator and the denominator by the same whole number. For example, if you want to raise the fraction $\frac{1}{4}$, you can multiply the numerator and denominator by 2.

EXAMPLE $\frac{1}{4} \times \frac{2}{2} = \frac{2}{8}$

The fractions $\frac{1}{4}$ and $\frac{2}{8}$ are **equivalent** in value. By converting $\frac{1}{4}$ to $\frac{2}{8}$, you only divided it into more parts.

Let's suppose that you have eaten $\frac{4}{7}$ of a pizza. You decide that instead of expressing the amount you have eaten in 7ths, you want to express it in 28ths. How would you do this?

To find the new numerator when you know the new denominator (28), use the steps that follow.

MONEY tips

Visit ethnic grocery stores for great buys on avocados, mangoes, limes, red onions, and other fruits and vegetables. Prices tend to be much cheaper.

> **RAISING FRACTIONS TO HIGHER TERMS WHEN DENOMINATOR IS KNOWN**
>
> **Step 1.** Divide the *new* denominator by the *old* denominator to get the common number that raises the fraction to higher terms.
>
> **Step 2.** Multiply the common number from Step 1 by the old numerator and place it as the new numerator over the new denominator.

EXAMPLE $\frac{4}{7} = \frac{?}{28}$

Step 1. Divide 28 by 7 = 4.

Step 2. Multiply 4 by the numerator 4 = 16.

Result:

$$\frac{4}{7} = \frac{16}{28} \qquad \left(\textit{Note}: \text{This is the same as multiplying } \frac{4}{7} \times \frac{4}{4}.\right)$$

Note that the $\frac{4}{7}$ and $\frac{16}{28}$ are equivalent in value, yet they are different fractions.

Now try the following Practice Quiz to check your understanding of this unit.

LU 2–1   PRACTICE QUIZ

Complete this **Practice Quiz** to see how you are doing.

1. Identify the type of fraction—proper, improper, or mixed:

    a. $\dfrac{4}{5}$ b. $\dfrac{6}{5}$ c. $19\dfrac{1}{5}$ d. $\dfrac{20}{20}$

2. Convert to a mixed number:

    $\dfrac{160}{9}$

3. Convert the mixed number to an improper fraction:

    $9\dfrac{5}{8}$

4. Find the greatest common divisor by the step approach and reduce to lowest terms:

    a. $\dfrac{24}{40}$ b. $\dfrac{91}{156}$

5. Convert to higher terms:

    a. $\dfrac{14}{20} = \dfrac{}{200}$ b. $\dfrac{8}{10} = \dfrac{}{60}$

*For **extra help** from your authors–Sharon and Jeff–see the student DVD*

YouTube

✓ Solutions

1. a. Proper
    b. Improper
    c. Mixed
    d. Improper

2. $17\dfrac{7}{9}$

$$9)\overline{160}$$
$$\underline{9}$$
$$70$$
$$\underline{63}$$
$$7$$

3. $\dfrac{(9 \times 8) + 5}{8} = \dfrac{77}{8}$

4. a.

    $$24)\overline{40} \quad 16)\overline{24} \quad 8\,)\overline{16}$$
    $$\underline{24} \qquad \underline{16} \qquad \underline{16}$$
    $$16 \qquad\quad 8 \qquad\quad 0$$

    8 is greatest common divisor.

    $\dfrac{24 \div 8}{40 \div 8} = \dfrac{3}{5}$

    b.

    $$91)\overline{156} \quad 65)\overline{91} \quad 26)\overline{65} \quad 13\,)\overline{26}$$
    $$\underline{91} \qquad\quad \underline{65} \qquad \underline{52} \qquad \underline{26}$$
    $$65 \qquad\quad 26 \qquad\quad 13 \qquad\quad 0$$

    13 is greatest common divisor.

    $\dfrac{91 \div 13}{156 \div 13} = \dfrac{7}{12}$

5. a.

    $$20)\overline{200}^{\,10}$$

    $10 \times 14 = 140$

    $\dfrac{14}{20} = \dfrac{140}{200}$

    b.

    $$10)\overline{60}^{\,6}$$

    $6 \times 8 = 48$

    $\dfrac{8}{10} = \dfrac{48}{60}$

LU 2–1a   EXTRA PRACTICE QUIZ WITH WORKED-OUT SOLUTIONS

Need more practice? Try this **Extra Practice Quiz** (check figures in the Interactive Chapter Organizer, p. 53). Worked-out Solutions can be found in Appendix B at end of text.

1. Identify the type of fraction—proper, improper, or mixed:

    a. $\dfrac{2}{5}$ b. $\dfrac{7}{6}$ c. $18\dfrac{1}{3}$ d. $\dfrac{40}{40}$

2. Convert to a mixed number (do not reduce):

    $\dfrac{155}{7}$

3. Convert the mixed number to an improper fraction:

    $8\dfrac{7}{9}$

4. Find the greatest common divisor by the step approach and reduce to lowest terms:

    a. $\dfrac{42}{70}$ **b.** $\dfrac{96}{182}$

5. Convert to higher terms:

    a. $\dfrac{16}{30} = \dfrac{}{300}$ **b.** $\dfrac{9}{20} = \dfrac{}{60}$

Learning Unit 2–2: Adding and Subtracting Fractions

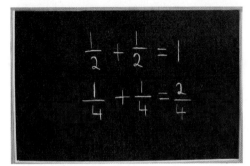

© Roberts Publishing Services

LO 1

More teachers are using online video-sharing sites that are modeled after Google Inc.'s YouTube. As you can see in the video screenshot provided, these fractions can be added because the fractions have the same denominator. These are called *like fractions.*

In this unit you learn how to add and subtract fractions with the same denominators (**like fractions**) and fractions with different denominators (**unlike fractions**). We have also included how to add and subtract mixed numbers.

Addition of Fractions

When you add two or more quantities, they must have the same name or be of the same denomination. You cannot add 6 quarts and 3 pints unless you change the denomination of one or both quantities. You must either make the quarts into pints or the pints into quarts. The same principle also applies to fractions. That is, to add two or more fractions, they must have a **common denominator.**

Adding Like Fractions   In our video-sharing clipping at the beginning of this unit we stated that because the fractions had the same denominator, or a common denominator, they were *like fractions.* Adding like fractions is similar to adding whole numbers.

ADDING LIKE FRACTIONS
Step 1. Add the numerators and place the total over the original denominator.
Step 2. If the total of your numerators is the same as your original denominator, convert your answer to a whole number; if the total is larger than your original denominator, convert your answer to a mixed number.

EXAMPLE $\dfrac{1}{7} + \dfrac{4}{7} = \dfrac{5}{7}$

The denominator, 7, shows the number of pieces into which some whole was divided. The two numerators, 1 and 4, tell how many of the pieces you have. So if you add 1 and 4, you get 5, or $\frac{5}{7}$.

Adding Unlike Fractions   Since you cannot add *unlike fractions* because their denominators are not the same, you must change the unlike fractions to *like fractions*—fractions with the same denominators. To do this, find a denominator that is common to all the fractions you want to add. Then look for the **least common denominator (LCD)**.[2] The LCD is the smallest nonzero whole number into which all denominators will divide evenly. You can find the LCD by inspection or with prime numbers.

Finding the Least Common Denominator (LCD) by Inspection The example that follows shows you how to use inspection to find an LCD (this will make all the denominators the same).

EXAMPLE $\dfrac{3}{7} + \dfrac{5}{21}$

Inspection of these two fractions shows that the smallest number into which denominators 7 and 21 divide evenly is 21. Thus, 21 is the LCD.

[2]Often referred to as the *lowest common denominator.*

You may know that 21 is the LCD of $\frac{3}{7} + \frac{5}{21}$, but you cannot add these two fractions until you change the denominator of $\frac{3}{7}$ to 21. You do this by building (raising) the equivalent of $\frac{3}{7}$, as explained in Learning Unit 2–1. You can use the following steps to find the LCD by inspection:

Step 1. Divide the new denominator (21) by the old denominator (7): $21 \div 7 = 3$.

Step 2. Multiply the 3 in Step 1 by the old numerator (3): $3 \times 3 = 9$. The new numerator is 9.

Result:

$$\frac{3}{7} = \frac{9}{21}$$

Now that the denominators are the same, you add the numerators.

$$\frac{9}{21} + \frac{5}{21} = \frac{14}{21} = \frac{2}{3}$$

Note that $\frac{14}{21}$ is reduced to its lowest terms $\frac{2}{3}$. Always reduce your answer to its lowest terms.

You are now ready for the following general steps for adding proper fractions with different denominators. These steps also apply to the following discussion on finding LCD by prime numbers.

ADDING UNLIKE FRACTIONS
Step 1. Find the LCD.
Step 2. Change each fraction to a like fraction with the LCD.
Step 3. Add the numerators and place the total over the LCD.
Step 4. If necessary, reduce the answer to lowest terms.

LO 2

Finding the Least Common Denominator (LCD) by Prime Numbers   When you cannot determine the LCD by inspection, you can use the prime number method. First you must understand prime numbers.

PRIME NUMBERS
A **prime number** is a whole number greater than 1 that is only divisible by itself and 1. The number 1 is not a prime number.

EXAMPLES   2, 3, 5, 7, 11, 13, 17, 19, 23, 29, 31, 37, 41, 43

Note that the number 4 is not a prime number. Not only can you divide 4 by 1 and by 4, but you can also divide 4 by 2. A whole number that is greater than 1 and is only divisible by itself and 1 has become a source of interest to some people.

EXAMPLE $\dfrac{1}{3} + \dfrac{1}{8} + \dfrac{1}{9} + \dfrac{1}{12}$

Step 1. Copy the denominators and arrange them in a separate row.

3   8   9   12

Step 2. Divide the denominators in Step 1 by prime numbers. Start with the smallest number that will divide into at least two of the denominators. Bring down any number that is not divisible. Keep in mind that the lowest prime number is 2.

$$2 \,/\!\!\underline{\begin{array}{cccc} 3 & 8 & 9 & 12 \end{array}}$$
$$\begin{array}{cccc} 3 & 4 & 9 & 6 \end{array}$$

Note: The 3 and 9 were brought down, since they were not divisible by 2.

Step 3. Continue Step 2 until no prime number will divide evenly into at least two numbers.

Note: The 3 is used, since 2 can no longer divide evenly into at least two numbers.

$$2 \,/\!\!\underline{\begin{array}{cccc} 3 & 8 & 9 & 12 \end{array}}$$
$$2 \,/\!\!\underline{\begin{array}{cccc} 3 & 4 & 9 & 6 \end{array}}$$
$$3 \,/\!\!\underline{\begin{array}{cccc} 3 & 2 & 9 & 3 \end{array}}$$
$$\begin{array}{cccc} 1 & 2 & 3 & 1 \end{array}$$

Step 4. To find the LCD, multiply all the numbers in the divisors (2, 2, 3) and in the last row (1, 2, 3, 1).

$$\boxed{2 \times 2 \times 3} \times \boxed{1 \times 2 \times 3 \times 1} = \boxed{72} \text{ (LCD)}$$

Divisors $\times$ Last row

Step 5. Raise each fraction so that each denominator will be 72 and then add fractions.

$$\dfrac{1}{3} = \dfrac{?}{72} \qquad \begin{array}{l} 72 \div 3 = 24 \\ 24 \times 1 = 24 \end{array}$$

$$\dfrac{24}{72} + \dfrac{9}{72} + \dfrac{8}{72} + \dfrac{6}{72} = \dfrac{47}{72}$$

$$\dfrac{1}{8} = \dfrac{?}{72} \qquad \begin{array}{l} 72 \div 8 = 9 \\ 9 \times 1 = 9 \end{array}$$

The above five steps used for finding LCD with prime numbers are summarized as follows:

FINDING LCD FOR TWO OR MORE FRACTIONS
Step 1. Copy the denominators and arrange them in a separate row.
Step 2. Divide the denominators by the smallest prime number that will divide evenly into at least two numbers.
Step 3. Continue until no prime number divides evenly into at least two numbers.
Step 4. Multiply all the numbers in divisors and last row to find the LCD.
Step 5. Raise all fractions so each has a common denominator and then complete the computation.

Adding Mixed Numbers   The following steps will show you how to add mixed numbers:

ADDING MIXED NUMBERS
Step 1. Add the fractions (remember that fractions need common denominators, as in the previous section).
Step 2. Add the whole numbers.
Step 3. Combine the totals of Steps 1 and 2. Be sure you do not have an improper fraction in your final answer. Convert the improper fraction to a whole or mixed number. Add the whole numbers resulting from the improper fraction conversion to the total whole numbers of Step 2. If necessary, reduce the answer to lowest terms.

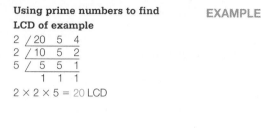

EXAMPLE
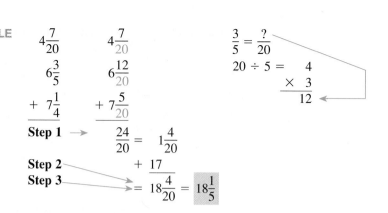

$$4\frac{7}{20} \qquad 4\frac{7}{20}$$

$$6\frac{3}{5} \qquad 6\frac{12}{20}$$

$$+\ 7\frac{1}{4} \qquad +\ 7\frac{5}{20}$$

Step 1 $\rightarrow \qquad \dfrac{24}{20} = 1\dfrac{4}{20}$

Step 2 $\qquad\qquad +\ 17$

Step 3 $\qquad\qquad = 18\dfrac{4}{20} = \boxed{18\dfrac{1}{5}}$

Subtraction of Fractions

The subtraction of fractions is similar to the addition of fractions. This section explains how to subtract like and unlike fractions and how to subtract mixed numbers.

Subtracting Like Fractions   To subtract like fractions, use the steps that follow.

LO 3

SUBTRACTING LIKE FRACTIONS
Step 1. Subtract the numerators and place the answer over the common denominator.
Step 2. If necessary, reduce the answer to lowest terms.

EXAMPLE $\dfrac{9}{10} - \dfrac{1}{10} = \dfrac{8 \div 2}{10 \div 2} = \boxed{\dfrac{4}{5}}$

$\qquad\qquad\qquad\qquad \uparrow \qquad \uparrow$

$\qquad\qquad\quad$ **Step 1   Step 2**

Subtracting Unlike Fractions   Now let's learn the steps for subtracting unlike fractions.

SUBTRACTING UNLIKE FRACTIONS
Step 1. Find the LCD.
Step 2. Raise the fraction to its equivalent value.
Step 3. Subtract the numerators and place the answer over the LCD.
Step 4. If necessary, reduce the answer to lowest terms.

EXAMPLE

$$\frac{5}{8} \qquad \frac{40}{64}$$

$$-\ \frac{2}{64} \qquad -\ \frac{2}{64}$$

$$\qquad\qquad \frac{38}{64} = \boxed{\frac{19}{32}}$$

By inspection, we see that LCD is 64.
Thus $64 \div 8 = 8 \times 5 = 40$.

Subtracting Mixed Numbers   When you subtract whole numbers, sometimes borrowing is not necessary. At other times, you must borrow. The same is true of subtracting mixed numbers.

LO 4

SUBTRACTING MIXED NUMBERS	
When Borrowing Is Not Necessary	*When Borrowing Is Necessary*
Step 1. Subtract fractions, making sure to find the LCD.	**Step 1.** Make sure the fractions have the LCD.
Step 2. Subtract whole numbers.	**Step 2.** Borrow from the whole number of the minuend (top number).
Step 3. Reduce the fraction(s) to lowest terms.	**Step 3.** Subtract the whole numbers and fractions.
	Step 4. Reduce the fraction(s) to lowest terms.

EXAMPLE   Where borrowing is not necessary: Find LCD of 2 and 8. LCD is 8.

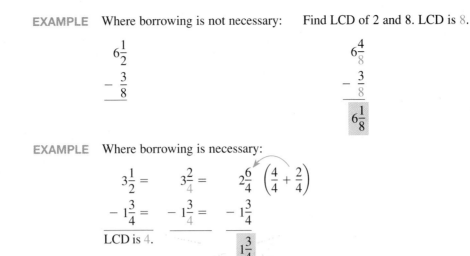

$$6\frac{1}{2}$$

$$-\frac{3}{8}$$

$$6\frac{4}{8}$$

$$-\frac{3}{8}$$

$$6\frac{1}{8}$$

EXAMPLE   Where borrowing is necessary:

$$3\frac{1}{2} = \qquad 3\frac{2}{4} = \qquad 2\frac{6}{4} \left(\frac{4}{4} + \frac{2}{4}\right)$$

$$-1\frac{3}{4} = \qquad -1\frac{3}{4} = \qquad -1\frac{3}{4}$$

LCD is 4.

$$1\frac{3}{4}$$

© Stockbroker/Purestock/Superstock

Since $\frac{3}{4}$ is larger than $\frac{2}{4}$, we must borrow 1 from the 3. This is the same as borrowing $\frac{4}{4}$. A fraction with the same numerator and denominator represents a whole. When we add $\frac{4}{4} + \frac{2}{4}$, we get $\frac{6}{4}$. Note how we subtracted the whole number and fractions, being sure to reduce the final answer if necessary.

How to Dissect and Solve a Word Problem

Let's now look at how to dissect and solve a word problem involving fractions.

The Word Problem The Albertsons grocery store has $550\frac{1}{4}$ total square feet of floor space. Albertsons' meat department occupies $115\frac{1}{2}$ square feet, and its deli department occupies $145\frac{7}{8}$ square feet. If the remainder of the floor space is for groceries, what square footage remains for groceries?

MONEY tips

Create an emergency fund for the unexpected. Having three to six months of monthly expenses in a liquid account will provide you with a great cushion in the event of an unforeseen expense.

	The facts	Solving for?	Steps to take	Key points
BLUEPRINT	*Total square footage:* $550\frac{1}{4}$ sq. ft. *Meat department:* $115\frac{1}{2}$ sq. ft. *Deli department:* $145\frac{7}{8}$ sq. ft.	Total square footage for groceries.	Total floor space − Total meat and deli floor space = Total grocery floor space.	Denominators must be the same before adding or subtracting fractions. $\frac{8}{8} = 1$ Never leave improper fraction as final answer.

Steps to solving problem

1. Calculate total square footage of the meat and deli departments.

Meat: $115\frac{1}{2} = \qquad 115\frac{4}{8}$

Deli: $+145\frac{7}{8} = +145\frac{7}{8}$

$\qquad\qquad\qquad 260\frac{11}{8} = 261\frac{3}{8}$ sq. ft.

2. Calculate total grocery square footage.

Check

$550\frac{1}{4} = \qquad 550\frac{2}{8} = \qquad 549\frac{10}{8}$ $\qquad\qquad 261\frac{3}{8}$

$-261\frac{3}{8} = -261\frac{3}{8} = -261\frac{3}{8}$ $\left(\frac{2}{8} + \frac{8}{8}\right)$ $+288\frac{7}{8}$

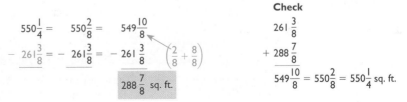

$\qquad\qquad\qquad\qquad\qquad 288\frac{7}{8}$ sq. ft. $549\frac{10}{8} = 550\frac{2}{8} = 550\frac{1}{4}$ sq. ft.

Note how the above blueprint aid helped to gather the facts and identify what we were looking for. To find the total square footage for groceries, we first had to sum the areas for meat and deli. Then we could subtract these areas from the total square footage. Also note that in Step 1 above, we didn't leave the answer as an improper fraction. In Step 2, we borrowed from the 550 so that we could complete the subtraction.

It's your turn to check your progress with a Practice Quiz.

LU 2–2   PRACTICE QUIZ

Complete this **Practice Quiz** to see how you are doing.

1. Find LCD by the division of prime numbers:

   12, 9, 6, 4

2. Add and reduce to lowest terms if needed:

   a. $\dfrac{3}{40} + \dfrac{2}{5}$ b. $2\dfrac{3}{4} + 6\dfrac{1}{20}$

3. Subtract and reduce to lowest terms if needed:

   a. $\dfrac{6}{7} - \dfrac{1}{4}$ b. $8\dfrac{1}{4} - 3\dfrac{9}{28}$ c. $4 - 1\dfrac{3}{4}$

4. Computerland has $660\frac{1}{4}$ total square feet of floor space. Three departments occupy this floor space: hardware, $201\frac{1}{8}$ square feet; software, $242\frac{1}{4}$ square feet; and customer service, _____ square feet. What is the total square footage of the customer service area? You might want to try a blueprint aid, since the solution will show a completed blueprint aid.

*For **extra help** from your authors–Sharon and Jeff–see the student DVD*

✓ **Solutions**

1. 2 / 12 9 6 4   LCD = $2 \times 2 \times 3 \times 1 \times 3 \times 1 \times 1 = \boxed{36}$
    2 / 6 9 3 2
    3 / 3 9 3 1
        1 3 1 1

2. a. $\dfrac{3}{40} + \dfrac{2}{5} = \dfrac{3}{40} + \dfrac{16}{40} = \boxed{\dfrac{19}{40}}$ $\left(\dfrac{2}{5} = \dfrac{?}{40}\quad 40 \div 5 = 8 \times 2 = 16\right)$

   b. $2\dfrac{3}{4}\quad 2\dfrac{15}{20}$
      $+6\dfrac{1}{20}\quad +6\dfrac{1}{20}$
      $8\dfrac{16}{20} = 8\dfrac{4}{5}$ $\dfrac{3}{4} = \dfrac{?}{20}\quad 20 \div 4 = 5 \times 3 = 15$

3. a. $\dfrac{6}{7} = \dfrac{24}{28}$
      $-\dfrac{1}{4} = -\dfrac{7}{28}$
      $\boxed{\dfrac{17}{28}}$

   b. $8\dfrac{1}{4} = 8\dfrac{7}{28} = 7\dfrac{35}{28}$ $\left(\dfrac{28}{28} + \dfrac{7}{28}\right)$
      $-3\dfrac{9}{28} = -3\dfrac{9}{28} = -3\dfrac{9}{28}$
      $4\dfrac{26}{28} = \boxed{4\dfrac{13}{14}}$

   c. $3\dfrac{4}{4}$ Note how we showed the 4 as $3\dfrac{4}{4}$.
      $-1\dfrac{3}{4}$
      $\boxed{2\dfrac{1}{4}}$

4. Computerland's total square footage for customer service:

	The facts	Solving for?	Steps to take	Key points
BLUEPRINT	Total square footage: $660\frac{1}{4}$ sq. ft. Hardware: $201\frac{1}{8}$ sq. ft. Software: $242\frac{1}{4}$ sq. ft.	Total square footage for customer service.	Total floor space − Total hardware and software floor space = Total customer service floor space.	Denominators must be the same before adding or subtracting fractions.

Steps to solving problem

1. Calculate the total square footage of hardware and software.

$$201\tfrac{1}{8} = \quad 201\tfrac{1}{8} \text{ (hardware)}$$
$$+ \ 242\tfrac{1}{4} = \ + \ 242\tfrac{2}{8} \text{ (software)}$$
$$\overline{\qquad\qquad\qquad 443\tfrac{3}{8}}$$

2. Calculate the total square footage for customer service.

$$660\tfrac{1}{4} = \quad 660\tfrac{2}{8} = \ 659\tfrac{10}{8} \text{ (total square footage)}$$
$$-443\tfrac{3}{8} = \ - \ 443\tfrac{3}{8} = \ - \ 443\tfrac{3}{8} \text{ (hardware plus software)}$$
$$\overline{\qquad\qquad\qquad\qquad 216\tfrac{7}{8} \text{ sq. ft. (customer service)}}$$

LU 2–2a   EXTRA PRACTICE QUIZ WITH WORKED-OUT SOLUTIONS

Need more practice? Try this **Extra Practice Quiz** (check figures in the Interactive Chapter Organizer, p. 53). Worked-out Solutions can be found in Appendix B at end of text.

1. Find the LCD by the division of prime numbers:
   10, 15, 9, 4

2. Add and reduce to lowest terms if needed:

   a. $\dfrac{2}{25} + \dfrac{3}{5}$ **b.** $3\tfrac{3}{8} + 6\tfrac{1}{32}$

3. Subtract and reduce to lowest terms if needed:

   a. $\dfrac{5}{6} - \dfrac{1}{3}$ **b.** $9\tfrac{1}{8} - 3\tfrac{7}{32}$ **c.** $6 - 1\tfrac{2}{5}$

4. Computerland has $985\tfrac{1}{4}$ total square feet of floor space. Three departments occupy this floor space: hardware, $209\tfrac{1}{8}$ square feet; software, $382\tfrac{1}{4}$ square feet; and customer service, _____ square feet. What is the total square footage of the customer service area?

Learning Unit 2–3: Multiplying and Dividing Fractions

LO 1

The following recipe for Coconutty "M&M'S"® Brand Brownies makes 16 brownies. What would you need if you wanted to triple the recipe and make 48 brownies?

Coconutty "M&M'S"® Brand Brownies

6 squares (1 ounce each) semi-sweet chocolate
½ cup (1 stick) butter
¾ cup granulated sugar
2 large eggs
1 tablespoon vegetable oil
1 teaspoon vanilla extract
1¼ cups all-purpose flour
3 tablespoons unsweetened cocoa powder
1 teaspoon baking powder
½ teaspoon salt
1½ cups "M&M'S"® Brand MINIS Chocolate
   Candies, divided

M&M'S® are registered trademarks of Mars, Incorporated and its affiliates. These trademarks are used with permission. Mars, Incorporated and its affiliates are not associated with McGraw-Hill Higher Education. The M&M'S® Brand brownie image and recipe are printed with permission of Mars, Incorporated.

Preheat oven to 350°F. Grease 8 × 8 × 2-inch pan; set aside. In small saucepan combine chocolate, butter, and sugar over low heat; stir constantly until smooth. Remove from heat; let cool. In bowl beat eggs, oil, and vanilla; stir in chocolate mixture until blended. Stir in flour, cocoa powder, baking powder, and salt. Stir in 1 cup "M&M'S"® Brand MINIS

Chocolate Candies. Spread batter in prepared pan. Bake 35 to 40 minutes or until toothpick inserted in center comes out clean. Cool. Prepare a coconut topping. Spread over brownies; sprinkle with $\frac{1}{2}$ cup "M&M'S"® Brand MINIS Chocolate Candies.

In this unit you learn how to multiply and divide fractions.

Multiplication of Fractions

Multiplying fractions is easier than adding and subtracting fractions because you do not have to find a common denominator. This section explains the multiplication of proper fractions and the multiplication of mixed numbers.

MULTIPLYING PROPER FRACTIONS[3]

Step 1. Multiply the numerators and the denominators.

Step 2. Reduce the answer to lowest terms or use the cancellation method.

First let's look at an example that results in an answer that we do not have to reduce.

EXAMPLE $\dfrac{1}{7} \times \dfrac{5}{8} = \boxed{\dfrac{5}{56}}$

In the next example, note how we reduce the answer to lowest terms.

EXAMPLE $\dfrac{5}{1} \times \dfrac{1}{6} \times \dfrac{4}{7} = \dfrac{20}{42} = \boxed{\dfrac{10}{21}}$ Keep in mind $\dfrac{5}{1}$ is equal to 5.

We can reduce $\frac{20}{42}$ by the step approach as follows:

$$
\begin{array}{r} 2 \\ 20\overline{)42} \\ 40 \\ \hline 2 \end{array}
\qquad
\begin{array}{r} 10 \\ 2\overline{)20} \\ 20 \\ \hline 0 \end{array}
$$

We could also have found the greatest common divisor by inspection.

$$\dfrac{20 \div 2}{42 \div 2} = \boxed{\dfrac{10}{21}}$$

As an alternative to reducing fractions to lowest terms, we can use the **cancellation** technique. Let's work the previous example using this technique.

EXAMPLE $\dfrac{5}{1} \times \dfrac{1}{\cancel{6}_{3}} \times \dfrac{\cancel{4}^{2}}{7} = \boxed{\dfrac{10}{21}}$ 2 divides evenly into 4 twice and into 6 three times.

Note that when we cancel numbers, we are reducing the answer before multiplying. We know that multiplying or dividing both numerator and denominator by the same number gives an equivalent fraction. So we can divide both numerator and denominator by any number that divides them both evenly. It doesn't matter which we divide first. Note that this division reduces $\frac{10}{21}$ to its lowest terms.

Multiplying Mixed Numbers   The following steps explain how to multiply mixed numbers:

MULTIPLYING MIXED NUMBERS

Step 1. Convert the mixed numbers to improper fractions.

Step 2. Multiply the numerators and denominators.

Step 3. Reduce the answer to lowest terms or use the cancellation method.

EXAMPLE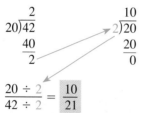

Step 1   Step 2   Step 3

[3]You would follow the same procedure to multiply improper fractions.

Division of Fractions

When you studied whole numbers in Chapter 1, you saw how multiplication can be checked by division. The multiplication of fractions can also be checked by division, as you will see in this section on dividing proper fractions and mixed numbers.

Dividing Proper Fractions   The division of proper fractions introduces a new term—the **reciprocal.** To use reciprocals, we must first recognize which fraction in the problem is the divisor—the fraction that we divide by. Let's assume the problem we are to solve is $\frac{1}{8} \div \frac{2}{3}$. We read this problem as "$\frac{1}{8}$ divided by $\frac{2}{3}$." The divisor is the fraction after the division sign (or the second fraction). The steps that follow show how the divisor becomes a reciprocal.

DIVIDING PROPER FRACTIONS
Step 1. Invert (turn upside down) the divisor (the second fraction). The inverted number is the *reciprocal.*
Step 2. Multiply the fractions.
Step 3. Reduce the answer to lowest terms or use the cancellation method.

Do you know why the inverted fraction number is a reciprocal? Reciprocals are two numbers that when multiplied give a product of 1. For example, 2 (which is the same as $\frac{2}{1}$) and $\frac{1}{2}$ are reciprocals because multiplying them gives 1.

EXAMPLE $\dfrac{1}{8} \div \dfrac{2}{3}$ $\dfrac{1}{8} \times \dfrac{3}{2} = \boxed{\dfrac{3}{16}}$

Dividing Mixed Numbers   Now you are ready to divide mixed numbers by using improper fractions.

DIVIDING MIXED NUMBERS
Step 1. Convert all mixed numbers to improper fractions.
Step 2. Invert the divisor (take its reciprocal) and multiply. If your final answer is an improper fraction, reduce it to lowest terms. You can do this by finding the greatest common divisor or by using the cancellation technique.

EXAMPLE $8\dfrac{3}{4} \div 2\dfrac{5}{6}$

Step 1. $\dfrac{35}{4} \div \dfrac{17}{6}$

Step 2. $\dfrac{35}{\cancel{4}_2} \times \dfrac{\cancel{6}^3}{17} = \dfrac{105}{34} = \boxed{3\dfrac{3}{34}}$ Here we used the cancellation technique.

How to Dissect and Solve a Word Problem

The Word Problem   Jamie Slater ordered $5\frac{1}{2}$ cords of oak. The cost of each cord is $150. He also ordered $2\frac{1}{4}$ cords of maple at $120 per cord. Jamie's neighbor, Al, said that he would share the wood and pay him $\frac{1}{5}$ of the total cost. How much did Jamie receive from Al?

Note how we filled in the blueprint aid columns. We first had to find the total cost of all the wood before we could find Al's share—$\frac{1}{5}$ of the total cost.

MONEY tips

Make good buying decisions. Do not spend more money than you make. In fact, remember to pay yourself first by putting away money each paycheck for your retirement—even $10 each paycheck adds up.

	The facts	Solving for?	Steps to take	Key points
BLUEPRINT	Cords ordered: $5\frac{1}{2}$ at $150 per cord; $2\frac{1}{4}$ at $120 per cord. Al's cost share: $\frac{1}{5}$ the total cost.	What will Al pay Jamie?	Total cost of wood $\times$ $\frac{1}{5}$ = Al's cost.	Convert mixed numbers to improper fractions when multiplying. Cancellation is an alternative to reducing fractions.

Steps to solving problem

1. Calculate the cost of oak.

$$5\frac{1}{2} \times \$150 = \frac{11}{2} \times \overset{\$75}{\cancel{\$150}} = \$825$$

2. Calculate the cost of maple.

$$2\frac{1}{4} \times \$120 = \frac{9}{4} \times \overset{\$30}{\cancel{\$120}} = +270$$

$$\overline{\$1,095} \text{ (total cost of wood)}$$

3. What Al pays.

$$\frac{1}{5} \times \overset{\$219}{\cancel{\$1,095}} = \boxed{\$219}$$

You should now be ready to test your knowledge of the final unit in the chapter.

LU 2–3 **PRACTICE QUIZ**

Complete this **Practice Quiz** to see how you are doing.

1. Multiply (use cancellation technique):

 a. $\dfrac{4}{8} \times \dfrac{4}{6}$ b. $35 \times \dfrac{4}{7}$

2. Multiply (do not use canceling; reduce by finding the greatest common divisor):

 $$\dfrac{14}{15} \times \dfrac{7}{10}$$

3. Complete the following. Reduce to lowest terms as needed.

 a. $\dfrac{1}{9} \div \dfrac{5}{6}$ b. $\dfrac{51}{5} \div \dfrac{5}{9}$

4. Jill Estes bought a mobile home that was $8\frac{1}{8}$ times as expensive as the home her brother bought. Jill's brother paid $16,000 for his mobile home. What is the cost of Jill's new home?

For **extra help** from your authors—Sharon and Jeff—see the student DVD

YouTube

✓ Solutions

1. a. $\dfrac{\overset{\overset{1}{\cancel{2}}}{\cancel{4}}}{\underset{\underset{1}{\cancel{2}}}{\cancel{8}}} \times \dfrac{\overset{1}{\cancel{4}}}{\underset{3}{\cancel{6}}} = \boxed{\dfrac{1}{3}}$ b. $\overset{5}{\cancel{35}} \times \dfrac{4}{\underset{1}{\cancel{7}}} = \boxed{20}$

2. $\dfrac{14}{15} \times \dfrac{7}{10} = \dfrac{98 \div 2}{150 \div 2} = \boxed{\dfrac{49}{75}}$

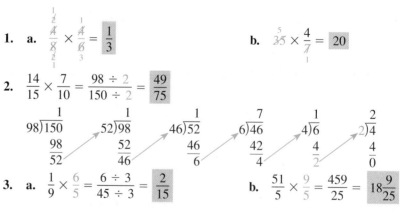

3. a. $\dfrac{1}{9} \times \dfrac{6}{5} = \dfrac{6 \div 3}{45 \div 3} = \boxed{\dfrac{2}{15}}$ b. $\dfrac{51}{5} \times \dfrac{9}{5} = \dfrac{459}{25} = \boxed{18\dfrac{9}{25}}$

4. Total cost of Jill's new home:

	The facts	Solving for?	Steps to take	Key points
BLUEPRINT	Jill's mobile home: $8\frac{1}{8}$ as expensive as her brother's. Brother paid: $16,000.	Total cost of Jill's new home.	$8\frac{1}{8} \times$ Total cost of Jill's brother's mobile home = Total cost of Jill's new home.	Canceling is an alternative to reducing.

Steps to solving problem

1. Convert $8\frac{1}{8}$ to a mixed number. $\frac{65}{8}$

2. Calculate the total cost of Jill's home. $\frac{65}{8} \times \overset{\$2,000}{\cancel{\$16,000}} = \boxed{\$130,000}$

LU 2–3a | EXTRA PRACTICE QUIZ WITH WORKED-OUT SOLUTIONS

Need more practice? Try this **Extra Practice Quiz** (check figures in the Interactive Chapter Organizer, p. 53). Worked-out Solutions can be found in Appendix B at end of text.

1. Multiply (use cancellation technique):

    a. $\frac{6}{8} \times \frac{3}{6}$ **b.** $42 \times \frac{1}{7}$

2. Multiply (do not use canceling; reduce by finding the greatest common divisor):

    $\frac{13}{117} \times \frac{9}{5}$

3. Complete the following. Reduce to lowest terms as needed.

    a. $\frac{1}{8} \div \frac{4}{5}$ **b.** $\frac{61}{6} \div \frac{6}{7}$

4. Jill Estes bought a mobile home that was $10\frac{1}{8}$ times as expensive as the home her brother bought. Jill's brother paid $10,000 for his mobile home. What is the cost of Jill's new home?

INTERACTIVE CHAPTER ORGANIZER

Topic/procedure/formula	Examples	You try it*
Types of fractions, p. 36 *Proper:* Value less than 1; numerator smaller than denominator. *Improper:* Value equal to or greater than 1; numerator equal to or greater than denominator. *Mixed:* Sum of whole number greater than zero and a proper fraction.	$\frac{3}{5}, \frac{7}{9}, \frac{8}{15}$ $\frac{14}{14}, \frac{19}{18}$ $6\frac{3}{8}, 9\frac{8}{9}$	**Identify type of fraction** $\frac{3}{10}, \frac{9}{8}, 1\frac{4}{5}$
Fraction conversions, p. 37 *Improper to whole or mixed:* Divide numerator by denominator; place remainder over *old* denominator. *Mixed to improper:* $\frac{\text{Whole number} \times \text{Denominator} + \text{Numerator}}{\text{Old denominator}}$	$\frac{17}{4} = 4\frac{1}{4}$ $4\frac{1}{8} = \frac{32+1}{8} = \frac{33}{8}$	**Convert to mixed number** $\frac{18}{7}$ **Convert to improper fraction** $5\frac{1}{7}$
Reducing fractions to lowest terms, p. 38 1. Divide numerator and denominator by largest possible divisor (does not change fraction value). 2. When reduced to lowest terms, no number (except 1) will divide evenly into both numerator and denominator.	$\frac{18 \div 2}{46 \div 2} = \boxed{\frac{9}{23}}$	**Reduce to lowest terms** $\frac{16}{24}$
Step approach for finding greatest common denominator, p. 38 1. Divide smaller number of fraction into larger number. 2. Divide remainder into divisor of Step 1. Continue this process until no remainder results. 3. The last divisor used is the greatest common divisor.	$\begin{array}{r}\;\;\;\;4\\15\overline{)65}\\60\\\hline 5\end{array}$ $\begin{array}{r}3\\5\overline{)15}\\15\\\hline 0\end{array}$ $15 \longrightarrow$ 65 $\boxed{5}$ is greatest common divisor.	**Find greatest common denominator** $\frac{20}{50}$
Raising fractions to higher terms, p. 39 Multiply numerator and denominator by same number. Does not change fraction value.	$\frac{15}{41} = \frac{?}{410}$ $410 \div 41 = 10 \times 15 = \boxed{150}$	**Raise to higher terms** $\frac{16}{31} = \frac{?}{310}$

(continues)

INTERACTIVE CHAPTER ORGANIZER

Topic/procedure/formula	Examples	You try it*
Adding and subtracting like and unlike fractions, p. 41 When denominators are the same (like fractions), add (or subtract) numerators, place total over original denominator, and reduce to lowest terms. When denominators are different (unlike fractions), change them to like fractions by finding LCD using inspection or prime numbers. Then add (or subtract) the numerators, place total over LCD, and reduce to lowest terms.	$\frac{4}{9} + \frac{1}{9} = \boxed{\frac{5}{9}}$ $\frac{4}{9} - \frac{1}{9} = \frac{3}{9} = \boxed{\frac{1}{3}}$ $\frac{4}{5} + \frac{2}{7} = \frac{28}{35} + \frac{10}{35} = \frac{38}{35} = \boxed{1\frac{3}{35}}$	**Add** $\frac{3}{7} + \frac{2}{7}$ **Subtract** $\frac{5}{7} - \frac{2}{7}$ **Add** $\frac{5}{8} + \frac{3}{40}$
Prime numbers, p. 42 Whole numbers larger than 1 that are only divisible by itself and 1.	$2, 3, 5, 7, 11$	**List the next two prime numbers after 11**
LCD by prime numbers, p. 42 1. Copy denominators and arrange them in a separate row. 2. Divide denominators by smallest prime number that will divide evenly into at least two numbers. 3. Continue until no prime number divides evenly into at least two numbers. 4. Multiply all the numbers in the divisors and last row to find LCD. 5. Raise fractions so each has a common denominator and complete computation.	$\frac{1}{3} + \frac{1}{6} + \frac{1}{8} + \frac{1}{12} + \frac{1}{9}$ $2\ /\ \underline{3\quad 6\quad 8\quad 12\quad 9}$ $2\ /\ \underline{3\quad 3\quad 4\quad 6\quad 9}$ $3\ /\ \underline{3\quad 3\quad 2\quad 3\quad 9}$ $\quad\ \ 1\quad 1\quad 2\quad 1\quad 3$ $2 \times 2 \times 3 \times 1 \times 1 \times 2 \times 1 \times 3 = \boxed{72}$	**Find LCD** $\frac{1}{2} + \frac{1}{4} + \frac{1}{5}$
Adding mixed numbers, p. 43 1. Add fractions. 2. Add whole numbers. 3. Combine totals of Steps 1 and 2. If denominators are different, a common denominator must be found. Answer cannot be left as improper fraction.	$1\frac{4}{7} + 1\frac{3}{7}$ Step 1: $\frac{4}{7} + \frac{3}{7} = \frac{7}{7}$ Step 2: $1 + 1 = 2$ Step 3: $2\frac{7}{7} = \boxed{3}$	**Add mixed numbers** $2\frac{1}{4} + 3\frac{3}{4}$
Subtracting mixed numbers, p. 44 1. Subtract fractions. 2. If necessary, borrow from whole numbers. 3. Subtract whole numbers and fractions if borrowing was necessary. 4. Reduce fractions to lowest terms. If denominators are different, a common denominator must be found.	$12\frac{2}{5} - 7\frac{3}{5}$ $11\frac{7}{5} - 7\frac{3}{5}$ $= \boxed{4\frac{4}{5}}$ Due to borrowing $\frac{5}{5}$ from number 12 $\frac{5}{5} + \frac{2}{5} = \frac{7}{5}$ The whole number is now 11.	**Subtract mixed numbers** $11\frac{1}{3}$ $-2\frac{2}{3}$
Multiplying proper fractions, p. 48 1. Multiply numerators and denominators. 2. Reduce answer to lowest terms or use cancellation method.	$\frac{4}{7} \times \frac{7}{9} = \boxed{\frac{4}{9}}$	**Multiply and reduce** $\frac{4}{5} \times \frac{25}{26}$
Multiplying mixed numbers, p. 48 1. Convert mixed numbers to improper fractions. 2. Multiply numerators and denominators. 3. Reduce answer to lowest terms or use cancellation method.	$1\frac{1}{8} \times 2\frac{5}{8}$ $\frac{9}{8} \times \frac{21}{8} = \frac{189}{64} = \boxed{2\frac{61}{64}}$	**Multiply and reduce** $2\frac{1}{4} \times 3\frac{1}{4}$

(continues)

INTERACTIVE CHAPTER ORGANIZER

Topic/procedure/formula	Examples	You try it*
Dividing proper fractions, p. 49 1. Invert divisor. 2. Multiply. 3. Reduce answer to lowest terms or use cancellation method.	$\frac{1}{4} \div \frac{1}{8} = \frac{1}{4} \times \frac{\overset{2}{\cancel{8}}}{\underset{1}{\cancel{1}}} = 2$	**Divide** $\frac{1}{8} \div \frac{1}{4}$
Dividing mixed numbers, p. 49 1. Convert mixed numbers to improper fractions. 2. Invert divisor and multiply. If final answer is an improper fraction, reduce to lowest terms by finding greatest common divisor or using the cancellation method.	$1\frac{1}{2} \div 1\frac{5}{8} = \frac{3}{2} \div \frac{13}{8}$ $= \frac{3}{\underset{1}{\cancel{2}}} \times \frac{\overset{4}{\cancel{8}}}{13}$ $= \frac{12}{13}$	**Divide mixed numbers** $3\frac{1}{4} \div 1\frac{4}{5}$

KEY TERMS	Cancellation, *p. 48* Common denominator, *p. 41* Denominator, *p. 36* Equivalent, *p. 39* Fraction, *p. 36* Greatest common divisor, *p. 38*	Higher terms, *p. 39* Improper fraction, *p. 37* Least common denominator (LCD), *p. 41* Like fractions, *p. 41* Lowest terms, *p. 38*	Mixed numbers, *p. 37* Numerator, *p. 36* Prime numbers, *p. 42* Proper fraction, *p. 37* Reciprocal, *p. 49* Unlike fractions, *p. 41*

Check Figures for Extra Practice Quizzes with Page References. (Worked-out Solutions in Appendix B.)	**LU 2–1a (p. 40)** 1. a. P b. I c. M d. I 2. $22\frac{1}{7}$ 3. $\frac{79}{9}$ 4. a. 14; $\frac{3}{5}$ b. 2; $\frac{48}{91}$ 5. a. 160; b. 27	**LU 2–2a (p. 47)** 1. 180 2. a. $\frac{17}{25}$ b. $9\frac{13}{32}$ 3. a. $\frac{1}{2}$ b. $5\frac{29}{32}$ c. $4\frac{3}{5}$ 4. $393\frac{7}{8}$ sq. ft.	**LU 2–3a (p. 51)** 1. a. $\frac{3}{8}$ b. 6 2. $117; \frac{1}{5}$ 3. a. $\frac{5}{32}$ b. $11\frac{31}{36}$ 4. $101,250

*Worked-out solutions are in Appendix B.

Critical Thinking Discussion Questions with Chapter Concept Check

1. What are the steps to convert improper fractions to whole or mixed numbers? Give an example of how you could use this conversion procedure when you eat at Pizza Hut.

2. What are the steps to convert mixed numbers to improper fractions? Show how you could use this conversion procedure when you order doughnuts at Dunkin' Donuts.

3. What is the greatest common divisor? How could you use the greatest common divisor to write an advertisement showing that 35 out of 60 people prefer MCI to AT&T?

4. Explain the step approach for finding the greatest common divisor. How could you use the MCI–AT&T example in question 3 to illustrate the step approach?

5. Explain the steps of adding or subtracting unlike fractions. Using a ruler, measure the heights of two different-size cans of food and show how to calculate the difference in height.

6. What is a prime number? Using the two cans in question 5, show how you could use prime numbers to calculate the LCD.

7. Explain the steps for multiplying proper fractions and mixed numbers. Assume you went to Staples (a stationery superstore). Give an example showing the multiplying of proper fractions and mixed numbers.

8. **Chapter Concept Check.** In the chapter opener it was stated that half of the vehicles sold in the United States are made by foreign firms. Using all the information you have learned about fractions, search the web to find out how many cars are produced in the United States in a year and what fractional part represents cars produced by foreign-owned firms. Finally, present calculations using fractions to agree or disagree with the chapter opener statement.

Classroom Notes

END-OF-CHAPTER PROBLEMS   Mc Graw Hill **connect** (plus+)   www.mhhe.com/slater11e

Check figures for odd-numbered problems in Appendix C.   Name _____   Date _____

DRILL PROBLEMS

Identify the following types of fractions: *LU 2-1(1)*

2–1. $\dfrac{6}{7}$ **2–2.** $\dfrac{12}{11}$ **2–3.** $\dfrac{14}{11}$

Convert the following to mixed numbers: *LU 2-1(2)*

2–4. $\dfrac{91}{10} =$ **2–5.** $\dfrac{921}{15} =$

Convert the following to improper fractions: *LU 2-1(2)*

2–6. $8\dfrac{7}{8}$ **2–7.** $19\dfrac{2}{3}$

Reduce the following to the lowest terms. Show how to calculate the greatest common divisor by the step approach.   *LU 2-1(3)*

2–8. $\dfrac{16}{38}$ **2–9.** $\dfrac{44}{52}$

Convert the following to higher terms: *LU 2-1(3)*

2–10. $\dfrac{9}{10} = \dfrac{}{70}$

Determine the LCD of the following (a) by inspection and (b) by division of prime numbers: *LU 2-2(2)*

2–11. $\dfrac{3}{4}, \dfrac{7}{12}, \dfrac{5}{6}, \dfrac{1}{5}$ **Check**

      Inspection

2–12. $\dfrac{5}{6}, \dfrac{7}{18}, \dfrac{5}{9}, \dfrac{2}{72}$ **Check**

      Inspection

2–13. $\dfrac{1}{4}, \dfrac{3}{32}, \dfrac{5}{48}, \dfrac{1}{8}$ **Check**

      Inspection

Add the following and reduce to lowest terms: *LU 2-2(1), LU 2-1(3)*

2–14. $\dfrac{3}{9} + \dfrac{3}{9}$ **2–15.** $\dfrac{3}{7} + \dfrac{4}{21}$

2–16. $6\dfrac{1}{8} + 4\dfrac{3}{8}$ **2–17.** $6\dfrac{3}{8} + 9\dfrac{1}{24}$

2–18. $9\dfrac{9}{10} + 6\dfrac{7}{10}$

Subtract the following and reduce to lowest terms: *LU 2-2(3), LU 2-1(3)*

2–19. $\dfrac{11}{12} - \dfrac{1}{12}$

2–20. $14\dfrac{3}{8} - 10\dfrac{5}{8}$

2–21. $12\dfrac{1}{9} - 4\dfrac{2}{3}$

Multiply the following and reduce to lowest terms. Do not use the cancellation technique for these problems. *LU 2-3(1), LU 2-1(3)*

2–22. $17 \times \dfrac{4}{2}$

2–23. $\dfrac{5}{6} \times \dfrac{3}{8}$

2–24. $8\dfrac{7}{8} \times 64$

Multiply the following. Use the cancellation technique. *LU 2-3(1), LU 2-1(2)*

2–25. $\dfrac{4}{10} \times \dfrac{30}{60} \times \dfrac{6}{10}$

2–26. $3\dfrac{3}{4} \times \dfrac{8}{9} \times 4\dfrac{9}{12}$

Divide the following and reduce to lowest terms. Use the cancellation technique as needed. *LU 2-3(2), LU 2-1(2)*

2–27. $\dfrac{12}{9} \div 4$

2–28. $18 \div \dfrac{1}{5}$

2–29. $4\dfrac{2}{3} \div 12$

2–30. $3\dfrac{5}{6} \div 3\dfrac{1}{2}$

WORD PROBLEMS

2–31. Michael Wittry has been investing in his Roth IRA retirement account for 20 years. Two years ago, his account was worth $215,658. After losing $\frac{1}{3}$ of its original value, it then gained $\frac{1}{2}$ of its new value back. What is the current value of his Roth IRA? *LU 2-3(1)*

2–32. Delta pays Pete Rose $180 per day to work in the maintenance department at the airport. Pete became ill on Monday and went home after $\frac{1}{6}$ of a day. What did he earn on Monday? Assume no work, no pay. *LU 2-3(1)*

2–33 As reported by *The New York Times* in January 2012, about $\frac{3}{4}$ of the top 1% of North America's wealthiest people reported they spent less than they earned in 2011—compared to almost $\frac{1}{2}$ for all others. If the top 1% equals 312,935 people, how many spent less than they earned (round to the nearest person)? *LU 2-3(3)*

2–34. Joy Wigens, who works at Putnam Investments, received a check for $1,600. She deposited $\frac{1}{4}$ of the check in her Citibank account. How much money does Joy have left after the deposit? *LU 2-3(1)*

2–35. Lee Jenkins worked the following hours as a manager for a local Pizza Hut: $14\frac{1}{4}$, $5\frac{1}{4}$, $8\frac{1}{2}$, and $7\frac{1}{4}$. How many total hours did Lee work? *LU 2-2(1)*

2–36. Lester bought a piece of property in Vail, Colorado. The sides of the land measure $115\frac{1}{2}$ feet, $66\frac{1}{4}$ feet, $106\frac{1}{8}$ feet, and $110\frac{1}{4}$ feet. Lester wants to know the perimeter (sum of all sides) of his property. Can you calculate the perimeter for Lester? *LU 2-2(1)*

2–37. Tiffani Lind got her new weekly course schedule from Roxbury Community College in Boston. Following are her classes and their length: Business Math, $2\frac{1}{2}$ hours; Introduction to Business, $1\frac{1}{2}$ hours; Microeconomics, $1\frac{1}{2}$ hours; Spanish, $2\frac{1}{4}$ hours; Marketing, $1\frac{1}{4}$ hours; and Business Statistics, $1\frac{3}{4}$ hours. How long will she be in class each week? *LU 2-2(1)*

2–38. Seventy-seven million people were born between 1946 and 1964. The U.S. Census classifies this group of individuals as baby boomers. It is said that today and every day for the next 18 years, 10,000 baby boomers will reach 65. If $\frac{1}{4}$ of the 65 and older age group uses e-mail, $\frac{1}{5}$ obtains the news from the Internet, and $\frac{1}{6}$ searches the Internet, find the LCD and determine total technology usage for this age group as a fraction. *LU 2-2(1, 2)*

2–39. At a local Walmart store, a Coke dispenser held $19\frac{1}{4}$ gallons of soda. During working hours, $12\frac{3}{4}$ gallons were dispensed. How many gallons of Coke remain? *LU 2-2(2, 3)*

2–40. Bernie Falls bought a home from Century 21 in Houston, Texas, that is $9\frac{1}{2}$ times as expensive as the home his parents bought. Bernie's parents paid $30,000 for their home. What is the cost of Bernie's new home? *LU 2-1(2), LU 2-3(1)*

2–41. A local garden center charges $250 per cord of wood. If Logan Grace orders $3\frac{1}{2}$ cords, what will the total cost be? *LU 2-3(1)*

2–42. A local Target store bought 90 pizzas at Pizza Hut for its holiday party. Each guest ate $\frac{1}{6}$ of a pizza and there was no pizza left over. How many guests did Target have for the party? *LU 2-3(1)*

2–43. Marc, Steven, and Daniel entered into a Subway sandwich shop partnership. Marc owns $\frac{1}{9}$ of the shop and Steven owns $\frac{1}{4}$. What part does Daniel own? *LU 2-2(1, 2)*

2–44. Lionel Sullivan works for Burger King. He is paid time and one-half for Sundays. If Lionel works on Sunday for 6 hours at a regular pay of $8 per hour, what does he earn on Sunday? *LU 2-3(1)*

2–45. InternetWorldStats.com shows $\frac{1}{2}$ of North America's population is on Facebook. If there are 312,934,968 people in the United States, how many are on Facebook? *LU 2-2(3)*

2–46. A trip to the White Mountains of New Hampshire from Boston will take you $2\frac{3}{4}$ hours. Assume you have traveled $\frac{1}{11}$ of the
eXcel way. How much longer will the trip take? *LU 2-3(1, 2)*

2–47. Andy, who loves to cook, makes apple cobbler for his family. The recipe (serves 6) calls for $1\frac{1}{2}$ pounds of apples, $3\frac{1}{4}$ cups
eXcel of flour, $\frac{1}{4}$ cup of margarine, $2\frac{3}{8}$ cups of sugar, and 2 teaspoons of cinnamon. Since guests are coming, Andy wants to make
a cobbler that will serve 15 (or increase the recipe $2\frac{1}{2}$ times). How much of each ingredient should Andy use? *LU 2-3(1, 2)*

2–48. Mobil allocates $1,692\frac{3}{4}$ gallons of gas per month to Jerry's Service Station. The first week, Jerry sold $275\frac{1}{2}$ gallons; second
week, $280\frac{1}{4}$ gallons; and third week, $189\frac{1}{8}$ gallons. If Jerry sells $582\frac{1}{2}$ gallons in the fourth week, how close is Jerry to selling
his allocation? *LU 2-2(4)*

2–49. A marketing class at North Shore Community College conducted a viewer preference survey. The survey showed that $\frac{5}{6}$ of
the people surveyed preferred Apple's iPhone over the Blackberry. Assume 2,400 responded to the survey. How many
favored using a Blackberry? *LU 2-3(1, 2)*

2–50. The price of a used Toyota LandCruiser has increased to $1\frac{1}{4}$ times its earlier price. If the original price of the LandCruiser
was $30,000, what is the new price? *LU 2-3(1, 2)*

2–51. Tempco Corporation has a machine that produces $12\frac{1}{2}$ baseball gloves each hour. In the last 2 days, the machine has run for
a total of 22 hours. How many baseball gloves has Tempco produced? *LU 2-3(2)*

2–52. Alicia, an employee of Dunkin' Donuts, receives $23\frac{1}{4}$ days per year of vacation time. So far this year she has taken $3\frac{1}{8}$ days
in January, $5\frac{1}{2}$ days in May, $6\frac{1}{4}$ days in July, and $4\frac{1}{4}$ days in September. How many more days of vacation does Alicia have
left? *LU 2-2(1, 2, 3)*

2–53. A Hamilton multitouch watch was originally priced at $600. At a closing of the Alpha Omega Jewelry Shop, the watch is
eXcel being reduced by $\frac{1}{4}$. What is the new selling price? *LU 2-3(1)*

2–54. Shelly Van Doren hired a contractor to refinish her kitchen. The contractor said the job would take $49\frac{1}{2}$ hours. To date, the contractor has worked the following hours:

Monday	$4\frac{1}{4}$
Tuesday	$9\frac{1}{8}$
Wednesday	$4\frac{1}{4}$
Thursday	$3\frac{1}{2}$
Friday	$10\frac{5}{8}$

How much longer should the job take to be completed?   *LU 2-2(4)*

ADDITIONAL SET OF WORD PROBLEMS

2–55. An issue of *Taunton's Fine Woodworking* included plans for a hall stand. The total height of the stand is $81\frac{1}{2}$ inches. If the base is $36\frac{5}{16}$ inches, how tall is the upper portion of the stand?   *LU 2-2(4)*

2–56. Albertsons grocery planned a big sale on apples and received 750 crates from the wholesale market. Albertsons will bag these apples in plastic. Each plastic bag holds $\frac{1}{9}$ of a crate. If Albertsons has no loss to perishables, how many bags of apples can be prepared?   *LU 2-3(1)*

2–57. Frank Puleo bought 6,625 acres of land in ski country. He plans to subdivide the land into parcels of $13\frac{1}{4}$ acres each. Each parcel will sell for $125,000. How many parcels of land will Frank develop? If Frank sells all the parcels, what will be his total sales?   *LU 2-3(1)*

If Frank sells $\frac{3}{5}$ of the parcels in the first year, what will be his total sales for the year?

2–58. A local Papa Gino's conducted a food survey. The survey showed that $\frac{1}{9}$ of the people surveyed preferred eating pasta to hamburger. If 5,400 responded to the survey, how many actually favored hamburger?   *LU 2-3(1)*

2–59. Tamara, Jose, and Milton entered into a partnership that sells men's clothing on the web. Tamara owns $\frac{3}{8}$ of the company and Jose owns $\frac{1}{4}$. What part does Milton own?   *LU 2-2(1, 3)*

2–60. *Quilters Newsletter Magazine* gave instructions on making a quilt. The quilt required $4\frac{1}{2}$ yards of white-on-white print, 2 yards blue check, $\frac{1}{2}$ yard blue-and-white stripe, $2\frac{3}{4}$ yards blue scraps, $\frac{3}{4}$ yard yellow scraps, and $4\frac{7}{8}$ yards lining. How many total yards are needed?   *LU 2-2(1, 2)*

2–61. A trailer carrying supplies for a Krispy Kreme from Virginia to New York will take $3\frac{1}{4}$ hours. If the truck traveled $\frac{1}{5}$ of the way, how much longer will the trip take?   *LU 2-3(1, 2)*

2–62. Land Rover has increased the price of a FreeLander by $\frac{1}{5}$ from the original price. The original price of the FreeLander was $30,000. What is the new price?   *LU 2-3(1, 2)*

CHALLENGE PROBLEMS

2–63. *Woodsmith* magazine gave instructions on how to build a pine cupboard. Lumber will be needed for two shelves $10\frac{1}{4}$ inches long, two base sides $12\frac{1}{2}$ inches long, and two door stiles $29\frac{1}{8}$ inches long. Your lumber comes in 6 foot lengths. **(a)** How many feet of lumber will you need? **(b)** If you want $\frac{1}{2}$ a board left over, is this possible with two boards?   *LU 2-2(1, 2, 3, 4)*

2–64. Jack MacLean has entered into a real estate development partnership with Bill Lyons and June Reese. Bill owns $\frac{1}{4}$ of the partnership, while June has a $\frac{1}{5}$ interest. The partners will divide all profits on the basis of their fractional ownership.

   The partnership bought 900 acres of land and plans to subdivide each lot into $2\frac{1}{4}$ acres. Homes in the area have been selling for $240,000. By time of completion, Jack estimates the price of each home will increase by $\frac{1}{3}$ of the current value. The partners sent a survey to 12,000 potential customers to see whether they should heat the homes with oil or gas. One-fourth of the customers responded by indicating a 5-to-1 preference for oil. From the results of the survey, Jack now plans to install a 270-gallon oil tank at each home. He estimates that each home will need five fills per year. The current price of home heating fuel is $1 per gallon. The partnership estimates its profit per home will be $\frac{1}{8}$ the selling price of each home.

   From the above, please calculate the following: *LU 2-1(1, 2, 3), LU 2-2(1, 2, 3, 4), LU 2-3(1, 2)*

a. Number of homes to be built.

b. Selling price of each home.

c. Number of people responding to survey.

d. Number of people desiring oil.

e. Average monthly cost per house to heat using oil.

f. Amount of profit Jack will receive from the sale of homes.

SUMMARY PRACTICE TEST YouTube

Do you need help? The DVD has step-by-step worked-out solutions.

Identify the following types of fractions. *(p. 36)   LU 2-1(1)*

1. $5\frac{1}{8}$ **2.** $\frac{2}{7}$ **3.** $\frac{20}{19}$

4. Convert the following to a mixed number. *(p. 37)   LU 2-1(2)*

$$\frac{163}{9}$$

5. Convert the following to an improper fraction. *(p. 37)   LU 2-1(2)*

$$8\frac{1}{8}$$

6. Calculate the greatest common divisor of the following by the step approach and reduce to lowest terms. *(p. 39)   LU 2-2(1, 2)*

$$\frac{63}{90}$$

7. Convert the following to higher terms. *(p. 39)   LU 2-1(3)*

$$\frac{16}{94} = \frac{?}{376}$$

8. Find the LCD of the following by using prime numbers. Show your work. *(p. 42)   LU 2-2(2)*

$$\frac{1}{8} + \frac{1}{3} + \frac{1}{2} + \frac{1}{12}$$

9. Subtract the following. *(p. 44)   LU 2-2(4)*

$$15\frac{4}{5}$$
$$-8\frac{19}{20}$$

Complete the following using the cancellation technique. *(p. 49)   LU 2-3(1, 2)*

10. $\frac{3}{4} \times \frac{2}{4} \times \frac{6}{9}$ **11.** $7\frac{1}{9} \times \frac{6}{7}$ **12.** $\frac{3}{7} \div 6$

13. A trip to Washington from Boston will take you $5\frac{3}{4}$ hours. If you have traveled $\frac{1}{3}$ of the way, how much longer will the trip take? *(p. 48)   LU 2-3(1)*

14. Quiznos produces 640 rolls per hour. If the oven runs $12\frac{1}{4}$ hours, how many rolls will the machine produce? *(p. 49)   LU 2-3(1, 2)*

15. A taste-testing survey of Zing Farms showed that $\frac{2}{3}$ of the people surveyed preferred the taste of veggie burgers to regular burgers. If 90,000 people were in the survey, how many favored veggie burgers? How many chose regular burgers? *(p. 48)   LU 2-3(1)*

16. Jim Janes, an employee of Enterprise Co., worked $9\frac{1}{4}$ hours on Monday, $4\frac{1}{2}$ hours on Tuesday, $9\frac{1}{4}$ hours on Wednesday, $7\frac{1}{2}$ hours on Thursday, and 9 hours on Friday. How many total hours did Jim work during the week? *(p. 41)   LU 2-2(1, 2)*

17. JCPenney offered a $\frac{1}{3}$ rebate on its $39 hair dryer. Joan bought a JCPenney hair dryer. What did Joan pay after the rebate? *(p. 48)   LU 2-3(1)*

SURF TO SAVE

PROBLEM 1
Avoid fees

Go to http://money.cnn.com/2001/12/12/debt/q_costcutting/index.htm. Read "The hunt for extra cash," by Annelena Lobb, to learn strategies for reducing banking fees and other personal living expenses. Based on the article, determine how many of the 8,300 traditional banks offer free checking. How many of the 10,599 credit unions offer free checking?

Discussion Questions

1. Why do banks charge fees?
2. What types of fees does your bank charge?

PROBLEM 2
Cook up a winner!

Go to http://www.campbellsoup.com. Search for the recipe called "Festive Chicken."

1 tsp. onion powder; 1/2 tsp. paprika; 1/4 tsp. garlic powder; 1/4 tsp. pepper; 2 lb. chicken parts, skin removed; 1 can (10 3/4 oz.) Campbell's Cream of Mushroom soup OR 98% Fat Free Cream of Mushroom soup; 1/3 cup buttermilk; 1 small red pepper, chopped; 4 green onions, sliced; chopped fresh parsley

The recipe makes 4 servings. If you needed 20 servings for a company outing, how much of each ingredient would you need?

Discussion Questions

1. How much would it cost you to make 20 servings?
2. Would it be less expensive for you to purchase five pizzas to share?

PROBLEM 3
What is your grocery budget?

Visit http://www.walmart.com/cp/Grocery/976759 to find the prices for 20 grocery items that you normally buy within a 1-week time frame. What is the total cost for these items? Determine the fraction of your weekly income needed to cover this expenditure. Now expand this expenditure for the entire month and year. Based on the monthly and yearly expense, determine the fraction of your earnings that would be needed to make these purchases.

Discussion Questions

1. Do you prefer to buy name brand or store brand items? Why?
2. Assume your salary will increase by 1/3 of your current earnings. Would it affect which groceries you would purchase?

PROBLEM 4
Saving for a rainy day

Go to http://www.bankrate.com/finance/financial-literacy/family-learns-to-spend-less-live-more-1.aspx. Read "Family learns to spend less, live more." According to the article, what fraction of disposable income are U.S. households now saving? According to Ellie Kay, is this enough? What fraction does she suggest?

Discussion Questions

1. If you saved 1/10 of your current income for 1 year, how much would you have?
2. If you continued, how much would you have after 10 years of saving? What are some ways you would like to spend this money?

MOBILE APPS ✕

Everyday Mathematics Equivalent Fractions (McGraw-Hill School Education Group) Offers a quick and easy approach to understand concepts related to fractions.

Fractions Calculator (PCB Enterprises) Assists in the addition, subtraction, multiplication, and division of fractions.

INTERNET PROJECTS ✕

See text website
www.mhhe.com/slater11e_sse_ch02

A KIPLINGER APPROACH

» **AHEAD**

MONEY & ETHICS
KNIGHT KIPLINGER

IS IT ETHICAL TO OPT OUT OF HEALTH INSURANCE?

Q. I have a 32-year-old friend—single, healthy, earning a good salary—who doesn't have employer health insurance and declines to buy his own. He thinks it's unlikely he'll need expensive care, and he calls the new individual insurance mandate an infringement on his liberty. Is his position ethical?

The Supreme Court will rule on the *constitutionality* of the health care law's mandate, but to me, the key principle of ethical living is taking responsibility for oneself and not putting a burden on others.

The vast majority of people—including your friend—would never be able to pay out-of-pocket for a very expensive medical need. So the cost would fall on someone else—family members, friends, unreimbursed doctors and hospitals, or taxpayers and fellow citizens who have been paying for insurance long before a need arose.

Only the rich—those able to pay personally for an organ transplant, very premature baby or $100,000-a-year miracle drug—can ethically choose to go naked on health insurance.

Hospitals have long been required by law (and motivated by medical ethics) to provide emergency care to everyone who comes through their doors, regardless of insurance. I don't hear *that* mandate being challenged.

Similarly, polls show that some people who oppose an individual mandate also approve of the government's plan to force insurers to accept new customers with a preexisting health problem. That seems ethically inconsistent.

In the absence of an individual mandate, many people would simply wait until they get really sick to start paying into an insurance pool that has to take them. With some restrictions, their near-term medical costs would be covered by the premiums of more-responsible citizens who had been contributing to the system for a long time.

There is ethical symmetry—as well as economic sense—to a health care system into which everyone must be accepted and to which everyone who is financially able to contribute is required to do so.

HAVE A MONEY-AND-ETHICS QUESTION YOU'D LIKE ANSWERED IN THIS COLUMN?
WRITE TO EDITOR IN CHIEF KNIGHT KIPLINGER AT ETHICS@KIPLINGER.COM.

■ SUZANNE BERNIER IS BACK AT MOM AND DAD'S.

■ STARTING OUT

GROUND RULES FOR BOOMERANG KIDS
IT'S OKAY TO HELP, BUT DON'T CODDLE.

SUZANNE BERNIER IS ONE OF the lucky ones. Just before graduating from Brandeis University in 2010, she landed a job at a medical software company. Yet after graduation, the frugal 24-year-old moved back in with her parents. "I wanted to save as much money as possible," she says.

More than one-fifth of people ages 25 to 34 live in multi-generational homes, the highest level since the 1950s, reports Pew Research. The hospitality helps boomerangers stay positive in tough times. More than three-fourths of people ages 25 to 34 who have lived at home are up-beat about their future finances, according to Pew.

Laying ground rules can help prevent a clash of the generations. "Put a game plan together with expectations," says Linda Leitz, a certified financial planner in Colorado. Parents who open their homes should establish a time limit for the stay and get regular progress reports. The child should pay rent, save money or pay off debt. Don't subsidize a lavish lifestyle. If kids can't contribute money, consider requiring household chores instead.

Parents should gradually turn up the heat, Leitz says. Raise the cost of rent by a certain date, for example, even if your plan is to make a gift of the money when your child departs. The comfort of home shouldn't be cushy enough to erode financial independence.
JOHN MILEY

BUSINESS MATH ISSUE

In the long run, living at home after college results in losing one's independence.

1. List the key points of the article and information to support your position.
2. Write a group defense of your position using math calculations to support your view.

CHAPTER 3

Decimals

What retailers and publishers might get from an e-book vs. a traditional print book, using a hypothetical hardcover:

E-Book	Print book
$12.99 retail price per e-book	**$26.00** retail price per hardcover book
−$3.90 to the retailer	**−$13.00** to the retailer
−$2.27 royalty payment to the author	**−$3.90** royalty payment to the author
−$0.90 for digital rights management, digital warehousing, production, and distribution	**−$3.25** for shipping, warehousing and production
$5.92 per unit to the publisher	**$5.85** per unit to the publisher**

... and for total U.S. publishing industry

$27.9 billion

LU 3–1: Rounding Decimals; Fraction and Decimal Conversions

1. Explain the place values of whole numbers and decimals; round decimals *(pp. 66–68)*.

2. Convert decimal fractions to decimals, proper fractions to decimals, mixed numbers to decimals, and pure and mixed decimals to decimal fractions *(pp. 68–70)*.

LU 3–2: Adding, Subtracting, Multiplying, and Dividing Decimals

1. Add, subtract, multiply, and divide decimals *(pp. 71–73)*.

2. Complete decimal applications in foreign currency *(p. 74)*.

3. Multiply and divide decimals by shortcut methods *(pp. 74–75)*.

VOCABULARY PREVIEW

Here are key terms in this chapter. After completing the chapter, if you know the term, place a checkmark in the parentheses. If you don't know the term, look it up and put the page number where it can be found.

Decimal ( )   Decimal fraction ( )   Decimal point ( )   Mixed decimal ( )   Pure decimal ( )   Repeating decimal ( )   Rounding decimals ( )

© AP Photo/David Zalubowski

MPG Goal Post

Average fuel-economy scores for major auto makers.

Goal for 2025: **56.2 mpg**

Honda	32.5
Toyota	31.2
BMW	27.9
GM	25.9
Ford	25.6
Chrysler	23.9
Mercedes-Benz	23.7

Source: EPA

The way gas prices are rising, fuel economy may be a big consideration in your next car purchase. As you can see from the *Wall Street Journal* clip, "MPG Goal Post," automakers' goal for 2025 is to produce vehicles that get 56.2 miles per gallon. To reach this goal, Honda will have to increase its mpg by 23.7.

Honda: 56.2 mpg
  − 32.5
  ───────
  23.7 mpg

TABLE	3.1

Analyzing a bag of M&M'S®

LO 1

© Sharon Hoogstraten

Color*	Fraction	Decimal
Yellow	$\frac{18}{55}$	.33
Red	$\frac{10}{55}$	.18
Blue	$\frac{9}{55}$	.16
Orange	$\frac{7}{55}$	.13
Brown	$\frac{6}{55}$	.11
Green	$\frac{5}{55}$	.09
Total	$\frac{55}{55} = 1$	1.00

*The color ratios currently given are a sample used for educational purposes. They do not represent the manufacturer's color ratios.

Chapter 2 introduced the 1.69-ounce bag of M&M'S® shown in Table 3.1. In Table 3.1, the six colors in the 1.69-ounce bag of M&M'S® are given in fractions and their values expressed in decimal equivalents that are rounded to the nearest hundredths.

This chapter is divided into two learning units. The first unit discusses rounding decimals, converting fractions to decimals, and converting decimals to fractions. The second unit shows you how to add, subtract, multiply, and divide decimals, along with some shortcuts for multiplying and dividing decimals. Added to this unit is a global application of decimals dealing with foreign exchange rates. One of the most common uses of decimals occurs when we spend dollars and cents, which is a *decimal number*.

A **decimal** is a decimal number with digits to the right of a *decimal point*, indicating that decimals, like fractions, are parts of a whole that are less than one. Thus, we can interchange the terms *decimals* and *decimal numbers*. Remembering this will avoid confusion between the terms *decimal, decimal number,* and *decimal point*.

Learning Unit 3–1: Rounding Decimals; Fraction and Decimal Conversions

Remember to read the decimal point as *and*.

In Chapter 1 we stated that the **decimal point** is the center of the decimal numbering system. So far we have studied the whole numbers to the left of the decimal point and the parts of whole numbers called fractions. We also learned that the position of the digits in a whole number gives the place values of the digits (Figure 1.1, p. 5). Now we will study the position (place values) of the digits to the right of the decimal point (Figure 3.1, p. 67). Note that the words to the right of the decimal point end in *ths*.

You should understand why the decimal point is the center of the decimal system. If you move a digit to the left of the decimal point by place (ones, tens, and so on), *you increase its value 10 times for each place (power of 10)*. If you move a digit to the right of the decimal point by place (tenths, hundredths, and so on), *you decrease its value 10 times for each place*.

EXAMPLES $.06 ← — The 6 is in the hundred*ths* place value.

1.527 — → The 5 is in the ten*ths* place value.

2.8394 — → The 4 is in the ten thousand*ths* place value.

.33 — → The thirty-three hundred*ths* represents the yellow M&M'S® in our M&M'S® bag of 55 M&M'S®.

1.69 oz. — → The one ounce and sixty-nine hundred*ths* of another ounce is the weight of our bag of M&M'S®.

Whole Number Groups					Decimal Place Values				
Thousands	Hundreds	Tens	Ones (units)	Decimal point (and)	Tenths	Hundredths	Thousandths	Ten thousandths	Hundred thousandths
1,000	100	10	1	and	$\frac{1}{10}$	$\frac{1}{100}$	$\frac{1}{1,000}$	$\frac{1}{10,000}$	$\frac{1}{100,000}$

Do you recall from Chapter 1 how you used a place-value chart to read or write whole numbers in verbal form? To read or write decimal numbers, you read or write the decimal number as if it were a whole number. Then you use the name of the decimal place of the last digit as given in Figure 3.1. For example, you would read or write the decimal .0796 as seven hundred ninety-six ten thousandths (the last digit, 6, is in the ten thousandths place).

To read a decimal with four or fewer whole numbers, you can also refer to Figure 3.1. For larger whole numbers, refer to the whole-number place-value chart in Chapter 1 (Figure 1.1, p. 5). For example, from Figure 3.1 you would read the number 126.2864 as one hundred twenty-six and two thousand eight hundred sixty-four ten thousandths. Remember that the *and* is the decimal point.

Now let's round decimals. Rounding decimals is similar to the rounding of whole numbers that you learned in Chapter 1.

Rounding Decimals

From Table 3.1, you know that the 1.69-ounce bag of M&M'S® introduced in Chapter 2 contained $\frac{18}{55}$, or .33, yellow M&M'S®. The .33 was rounded to the nearest hundredth. **Rounding decimals** involves the following steps:

ROUNDING DECIMALS TO A SPECIFIED PLACE VALUE

Step 1. Identify the place value of the digit you want to round.

Step 2. If the digit to the right of the identified digit in Step 1 is 5 or more, increase the identified digit by 1. If the digit to the right is less than 5, do not change the identified digit.

Step 3. Drop all digits to the right of the identified digit.

Let's practice rounding by using the $\frac{18}{55}$ yellow M&M'S® that we rounded to .33 in Table 3.1. Before we rounded $\frac{18}{55}$ to .33, the number we rounded was .32727. This is an example of a **repeating decimal** since the 27 repeats itself.

EXAMPLE   Round .3272727 to the nearest hundredth.

Step 1.   .3272727   The identified digit is 2, which is in the hundredths place (two places to the right of the decimal point).

Step 2.   The digit to the right of 2 is more than 5 (7). Thus, 2, the identified digit in Step 1, is changed to 3.

.3372727

Step 3.   .33   Drop all other digits to the right of the identified digit 3.

We could also round the .3272727 M&M'S® to the nearest tenth or thousandth as follows:

	Tenth	**or**	**Thousandth**
.3272727 →	.3		.3272727 → .327

OTHER EXAMPLES

Round to nearest dollar:	$166.39	→	$166
Round to nearest cent:	$1,196.885	→	$1,196.89
Round to nearest hundredth:	$38.563	→	$38.56
Round to nearest thousandth:	$1,432.9981	→	$1,432.998

The rules for rounding can differ with the situation in which rounding is used. For example, have you ever bought one item from a supermarket produce department that was marked "3 for $1" and noticed what the cashier charged you? One item marked "3 for $1" would not cost you $33\frac{1}{3}$ cents rounded to 33 cents. You will pay 34 cents. Many retail stores round to the next cent even if the digit following the identified digit is less than $\frac{1}{2}$ of a penny. In this text we round on the concept of 5 or more.

LO 2

Fraction and Decimal Conversions

In business operations we must frequently convert fractions to decimal numbers and decimal numbers to fractions. This section begins by discussing three types of fraction-to-decimal conversions. Then we discuss converting pure and mixed decimals to decimal fractions.

Converting Decimal Fractions to Decimals   From Figure 3.1 you can see that a **decimal fraction** (expressed in the digits to the right of the decimal point) is a fraction with a denominator that has a power of 10, such as $\frac{1}{10}$, $\frac{17}{100}$, and $\frac{23}{1,000}$. To convert a decimal fraction to a decimal, follow these steps:

CONVERTING DECIMAL FRACTIONS TO DECIMALS

Step 1. Count the number of zeros in the denominator.

Step 2. Place the numerator of the decimal fraction to the right of the decimal point the same number of places as you have zeros in the denominator. (The number of zeros in the denominator gives the number of digits your decimal has to the right of the decimal point.) Do not go over the total number of denominator zeros.

Now let's change $\frac{3}{10}$ and its higher multiples of 10 to decimals.

EXAMPLES

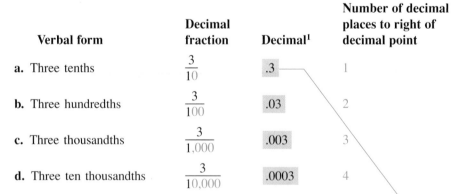

Verbal form	Decimal fraction	Decimal[1]	Number of decimal places to right of decimal point
a. Three tenths	$\frac{3}{10}$	.3	1
b. Three hundredths	$\frac{3}{100}$	.03	2
c. Three thousandths	$\frac{3}{1,000}$	.003	3
d. Three ten thousandths	$\frac{3}{10,000}$	.0003	4

Note how we show the different values of the decimal fractions above in decimals. The zeros after the decimal point and before the number 3 indicate these values. If you add zeros after the number 3, you do not change the value. Thus, the numbers .3 , .30 , and .300 have the same value. So 3 tenths of a pizza, 30 hundredths of a pizza, and 300 thousandths of a pizza are the same total amount of pizza. The first pizza is sliced into 10 pieces. The second pizza is sliced into 100 pieces. The third pizza is sliced into 1,000 pieces. Also, we don't need to place a zero to the left of the decimal point.

[1]From .3 to .0003, the values get smaller and smaller, but if you go from .3 to .3000, the values remain the same.

Converting Proper Fractions to Decimals   Recall from Chapter 2 that proper fractions are fractions with a value less than 1. That is, the numerator of the fraction is smaller than its denominator. How can we convert these proper fractions to decimals? Since proper fractions are a form of division, it is possible to convert proper fractions to decimals by carrying out the division.

CONVERTING PROPER FRACTIONS TO DECIMALS
Step 1. Divide the numerator of the fraction by its denominator. (If necessary, add a decimal point and zeros to the number in the numerator.)
Step 2. Round as necessary.

EXAMPLES

$$\frac{3}{4} = 4\overline{)3.00} \quad \begin{array}{r} .75 \\ \underline{2\,8} \\ 20 \\ \underline{20} \end{array}$$

$$\frac{3}{8} = 8\overline{)3.000} \quad \begin{array}{r} .375 \\ \underline{2\,4} \\ 60 \\ \underline{56} \\ 40 \\ \underline{40} \end{array}$$

$$\frac{1}{3} = 3\overline{)1.000} \quad \begin{array}{r} .33\overline{3} \\ \underline{9} \\ 10 \\ \underline{9} \\ 10 \\ \underline{9} \\ 1 \end{array}$$

Note that in the last example $\frac{1}{3}$, the 3 in the quotient keeps repeating itself (never ends). The short bar over the last 3 means that the number endlessly repeats.

Converting Mixed Numbers to Decimals

A mixed number, you will recall from Chapter 2, is the sum of a whole number greater than zero and a proper fraction. To convert mixed numbers to decimals, use the following steps:

CONVERTING MIXED NUMBERS TO DECIMALS
Step 1. Convert the fractional part of the mixed number to a decimal (as illustrated in the previous section).
Step 2. Add the converted fractional part to the whole number.

EXAMPLE

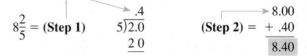

$$8\frac{2}{5} = \textbf{(Step 1)} \quad 5\overline{)2.0} \quad \begin{array}{r} .4 \\ \underline{2\,0} \end{array} \qquad \textbf{(Step 2)} = \begin{array}{r} 8.00 \\ +\ .40 \\ \hline \boxed{8.40} \end{array}$$

Now that we have converted fractions to decimals, let's convert decimals to fractions.

Converting Pure and Mixed Decimals to Decimal Fractions   A **pure decimal** has no whole number(s) to the left of the decimal point (.43, .458, and so on). A **mixed decimal** is a combination of a whole number and a decimal. An example of a mixed decimal follows.

EXAMPLE   737.592 = Seven hundred thirty-seven and five hundred ninety-two
thousandths

Note the following conversion steps for converting pure and mixed decimals to decimal fractions:

CONVERTING PURE AND MIXED DECIMALS TO DECIMAL FRACTIONS

Step 1. Place the digits to the right of the decimal point in the numerator of the fraction. Omit the decimal point. (For a decimal fraction with a fractional part, see examples **c** and **d** below.)

Step 2. Put a 1 in the denominator of the fraction.

Step 3. Count the number of digits to the right of the decimal point. Add the same number of zeros to the denominator of the fraction. For mixed decimals, add the fraction to the whole number.

If desired, you can reduce the fractions in Step 3.

EXAMPLES	Step 1	Step 2	Places	Step 3
a. .3	$\dfrac{3}{}$	$\dfrac{3}{1}$	1	$\dfrac{3}{10}$
b. .24	$\dfrac{24}{}$	$\dfrac{24}{1}$	2	$\dfrac{24}{100}$
c. $.24\frac{1}{2}$	$\dfrac{245}{}$	$\dfrac{245}{1}$	3	$\dfrac{245}{1,000}$

Before completing Step 1 in example **c**, we must remove the fractional part, convert it to a decimal ($\frac{1}{2} = .5$), and multiply it by .01 ($.5 \times .01 = .005$). We use .01 because the 4 of .24 is in the hundredths place. Then we add $.005 + .24 = .245$ (three places to right of the decimal) and complete Steps 1, 2, and 3.

d. $.07\frac{1}{4}$	$\dfrac{725}{}$	$\dfrac{725}{1}$	4	$\dfrac{725}{10,000}$

In example **d**, be sure to convert $\frac{1}{4}$ to .25 and multiply by .01. This gives .0025. Then add .0025 to .07, which is .0725 (four places), and complete Steps 1, 2, and 3.

e. 17.45	$\dfrac{45}{}$	$\dfrac{45}{1}$	2	$\dfrac{45}{100} = 17\dfrac{45}{100}$

Example **e** is a mixed decimal. Since we substitute *and* for the decimal point, we read this mixed decimal as seventeen and forty-five hundredths. Note that after we converted the .45 of the mixed decimal to a fraction, we added it to the whole number 17.

The Practice Quiz that follows will help you check your understanding of this unit.

MONEY tips

Set up automatic payments for the minimum payment due on your debt and eliminate late fees. Create an alert with your smartphone or computer for each bill. Pay more than the minimum whenever possible.

LU 3–1 PRACTICE QUIZ

*Complete this **Practice Quiz** to see how you are doing.*

Write the following as a decimal number.
1. Four hundred eight thousandths

Name the place position of the identified digit:
2. 6.8241   3. 9.3942

Round each decimal to place indicated:

	Tenth	Thousandth
4. .62768	a.	b.
5. .68341	a.	b.

Convert the following to decimals:

6. $\dfrac{9}{10,000}$ 7. $\dfrac{14}{100,000}$

Convert the following to decimal fractions (do not reduce):

8. .819   9. 16.93   10. $.05\frac{1}{4}$

Convert the following fractions to decimals and round answer to nearest hundredth:

11. $\dfrac{1}{6}$ 12. $\dfrac{3}{8}$ 13. $12\frac{1}{8}$

For *extra help* from your authors—Sharon and Jeff—see the student DVD

✓ Solutions

1. .408 (3 places to right of decimal)

2. Hundredths

3. Thousandths

4. a. .6 (identified digit 6—digit to right less than 5)

   b. .628 (identified digit 7—digit to right greater than 5)

5. a. .7 (identified digit 6—digit to right greater than 5)

   b. .683 (identified digit 3—digit to right less than 5)

6. .0009 (4 places)

7. .00014 (5 places)

8. $\dfrac{819}{1,000}$ $\left(\dfrac{819}{1 + 3 \text{ zeros}}\right)$

9. $16\dfrac{93}{100}$

10. $\dfrac{525}{10,000}$ $\left(\dfrac{525}{1 + 4 \text{ zeros}}\ \dfrac{1}{4} \times .01 = .0025 + .05 = .0525\right)$

11. .16666 = .17

12. .375 = .38

13. 12.125 = 12.13

LU 3–1a **EXTRA PRACTICE QUIZ WITH WORKED-OUT SOLUTIONS**

Need more practice? Try this **Extra Practice Quiz** (check figures in the Interactive Chapter Organizer, p. 79). Worked-out Solutions can be found in Appendix B at end of text.

Write the following as a decimal number:

1. Three hundred nine thousandths

Name the place position of the identified digit:

2. 7.9324

3. 8.3682

Round each decimal to place indicated:

	Tenth	**Thousandth**
4. .84361	a.	b.
5. .87938	a.	b.

Convert the following to decimals:

6. $\dfrac{8}{10,000}$

7. $\dfrac{16}{100,000}$

Convert the following to decimal fractions (do not reduce):

8. .938

9. 17.95

10. $.03\frac{1}{4}$

Convert the following fractions to decimals and round answer to nearest hundredth:

11. $\dfrac{1}{8}$

12. $\dfrac{4}{7}$

13. $13\dfrac{1}{9}$

Learning Unit 3–2: Adding, Subtracting, Multiplying, and Dividing Decimals

GLOBAL

The *Wall Street Journal* clip "Google+ Pulls in 20 Million in 3 Weeks" (p. 72) reveals that Google reported 19.93 million visitors since the launch of its social networking service, Google+. The following calculations show how many visitors were from outside the United States.

Total visitors:	19.93 million
U.S. visitors:	−5.31
International visitors:	14.62 million

This learning unit shows you how to add, subtract, multiply, and divide decimals. You also make calculations involving decimals, including decimals used in foreign currency.

LO 1

Addition and Subtraction of Decimals

Since you know how to add and subtract whole numbers, to add and subtract decimal numbers you have only to learn about the placement of the decimals. The following steps on page 72 will help you:

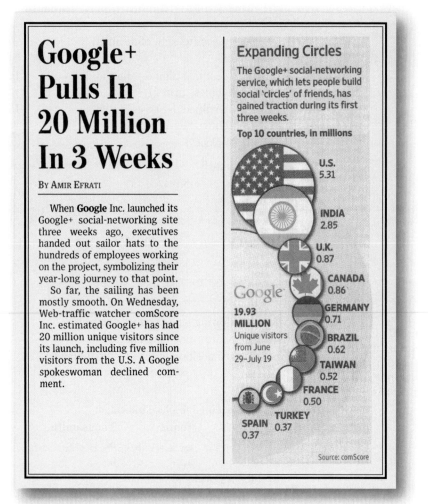

ADDING AND SUBTRACTING DECIMALS

Step 1. Vertically write the numbers so that the decimal points align. You can place additional zeros to the right of the decimal point if needed without changing the value of the number.

Step 2. Add or subtract the digits starting with the right column and moving to the left.

Step 3. Align the decimal point in the answer with the above decimal points.

EXAMPLES   Add $4 + 7.3 + 36.139 + .0007 + 8.22.$

Whole number to → 4.0000   — Extra zeros have
the right of the last   7.3000 ←   been added to make
digit is assumed to   36.1390   calculation easier.
have a decimal.   .0007
                        8.2200
                       55.6597

Subtract $45.3 - 15.273.$ Subtract $7 - 6.9.$

```
      2 9 10                                  6  10
  45.300                                    7.0
- 15.273                                  - 6.9
 30.027                                      .1
```

Multiplication of Decimals

The multiplication of decimal numbers is similar to the multiplication of whole numbers except for the additional step of placing the decimal in the answer (product). The steps that follow simplify this procedure.

MULTIPLYING DECIMALS
Step 1. Multiply the numbers as whole numbers, ignoring the decimal points.
Step 2. Count and total the number of decimal places in the multiplier and multiplicand.
Step 3. Starting at the right in the product, count to the left the number of decimal places totaled in Step 2. Place the decimal point so that the product has the same number of decimal places as totaled in Step 2. If the total number of places is greater than the places in the product, insert zeros in front of the product.

EXAMPLES

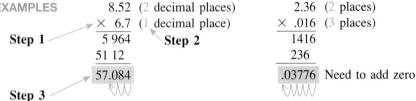

```
          8.52  (2 decimal places)              2.36  (2 places)
Step 1  × 6.7   (1 decimal place)             × .016  (3 places)
          5 964      Step 2                     1416
         51 12                                   236
         57.084                                .03776   Need to add zero
Step 3
```

Division of Decimals

If the divisor in your decimal division problem is a whole number, first place the decimal point in the quotient directly above the decimal point in the dividend. Then divide as usual. If the divisor has a decimal point, complete the steps that follow.

DIVIDING DECIMALS
Step 1. Make the divisor a whole number by moving the decimal point to the right.
Step 2. Move the decimal point in the dividend to the right the same number of places that you moved the decimal point in the divisor (Step 1). If there are not enough places, add zeros to the right of the dividend.
Step 3. Place the decimal point in the quotient above the new decimal point in the dividend. Divide as usual.

EXAMPLE

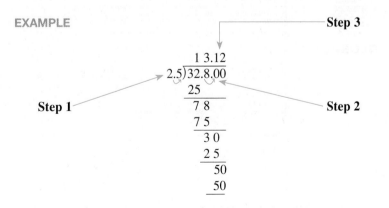

```
                        Step 3
                    1 3.12
          Step 1  2.5)32.8.00
                       25
                        7 8       Step 2
                        7 5
                         3 0
                         2 5
                          50
                          50
```

Stop a moment and study the above example. Note that the quotient does not change when we multiply the divisor and the dividend by the same number. This is why we can move the decimal point in division problems and always divide by a whole number.

GLOBAL

Decimal Applications in Foreign Currency

EXAMPLE

Sharon Wittry, who lives in Canada, wanted to buy a new Apple iPad 2. She went on eBay and found that the cost would be $600 U.S. dollars. Wanting to know how much this would cost in Canadian dollars, Sharon consulted the *Wall Street Journal*'s currency table and found that a Canadian dollar was worth $0.9794 in U.S. dollars. Therefore, for each Canadian dollar it would cost $1.0210 to buy a U.S. good.

Using this information, Sharon completed the following calculation to determine what an iPad would cost her:

$600   × $1.0210   = $612.60
(cost of the iPad in   (cost of the iPad in
U.S. dollars)   Canadian dollars)

To check her findings, Sharon did the following calculation:

$612.60   × $0.9794   = $599.98 (off due to rounding)
(cost of the iPad in   (what the Canadian dollar   (U.S. selling price)
Canadian dollars)   is worth against the
U.S. dollar)

"The dollar held its value today against the yen, the euro, the peso, the comic book and the baseball card."

GLOBAL

Currencies

U.S.-dollar foreign-exchange rates in late New York trading on Friday

Country/currency	Fri in US$	Fri per US$	US$ vs, YTD chg (%)	Country/currency	Fri in US$	Fri per US$	US$ vs, YTD chg (%)
Americas				**Europe**			
Argentina peso*	.2321	4.3089	8.6	Czech Rep. koruna	.05063	19.751	5.8
Brazil real	.5360	1.8657	12.3	Denmark krone	.1743	5.7373	3.1
Canada dollar	.9794	1.0210	2.6	Euro area euro	1.2960	.7716	3.3
Chile peso	.001924	519.86	11.1	Hungary forint	.004113	243.14	17.7
Colombia peso	.0005153	1940.50	1.1	Norway krone	.1673	5.9766	2.6
Ecuador US dollar	1	1	unch	Poland zloty	.2901	3.4470	16.9
Mexico peso*	.0717	13.9461	13.1	Russia ruble‡	.03110	32.150	5.2
Peru new sol	.3709	2.696	-3.9	Sweden krona	.1453	6.8800	2.6
Uruguay peso†	.05047	19.8130	1.9	Switzerland franc	1.0670	.9372	0.2
Venezuela b. fuerte	.229885	4.3500	unch	1-mos forward	1.0675	.9368	0.2
Asia-Pacific				3-mos forward	1.0691	.9354	0.2
				6-mos forward	1.0718	.9330	0.1
Australian dollar	1.0208	.9796	0.3	Turkey lira**	.5217	1.9170	23.5
1-mos forward	1.0170	.9832	0.2	UK pound	1.5542	.6434	0.4
3-mos forward	1.0107	.9894	0.1	1-mos forward	1.5537	.6436	0.4
6-mos forward	1.0024	.9976	-0.2	3-mos forward	1.5528	.6440	0.4
China yuan	.1583	6.3190	-4.3	6-mos forward	1.5513	.6446	0.4
Hong Kong dollar	.1288	7.7669	-0.1				
India rupee	.01886	53.025	18.3	**Middle East/Africa**			
Indonesia rupiah	.0001107	9033	1.6				
Japan yen	.013001	76.92	-5.2	Bahrain dinar	2.6520	.3771	unch
1-mos forward	.013008	76.88	-5.5	Egypt pound*	.1653	6.0498	6.3
3-mos forward	.013025	76.78	-5.6	Israel shekel	.2624	3.8110	7.8
6-mos forward	.013054	76.60	-5.6	Jordan dinar	1.4095	.7095	0.1
Malaysia ringgit	.3147	3.1775	5.1	Kuwait dinar	3.5945	.2782	-1.3
New Zealand dollar	.7776	1.2860	0.3	Lebanon pound	.0006645	1504.95	0.4
Pakistan rupee	.01113	89.845	4.9	Saudi Arabia riyal	.2666	3.7504	unch
Philippines peso	.0228	43.850	0.3	South Africa rand	.1237	8.0873	22.2
Singapore dollar	.7713	1.2965	1.1	UAE dirham	.2722	3.6731	unch
South Korea won	.0008616	1160.60	5.6				
Taiwan dollar	.03304	30.265	4.2	*Floating rate †Financial sGovernment rate			
Thailand baht	.03165	31.600	7.3	‡Russian Central Bank rate **Commercial rate			
Vietnam dong	.00004753	21038	8.2	Source: ICAP plc.			

Multiplication and Division Shortcuts for Decimals

The shortcut steps that follow show how to solve multiplication and division problems quickly involving multiples of 10 (10, 100, 1,000, 10,000, etc.).

SHORTCUTS FOR MULTIPLES OF 10

Multiplication

Step 1. Count the zeros in the multiplier.

Step 2. Move the decimal point in the multiplicand the same number of places to the right as you have zeros in the multiplier.

Division

Step 1. Count the zeros in the divisor.

Step 2. Move the decimal point in the dividend the same number of places to the left as you have zeros in the divisor.

LO 3

© Zumawirewestphotostwo/Newscom

In multiplication, the answers are *larger* than the original number.

EXAMPLE   If Toyota spends $60,000 for magazine advertising, what is the total value if it spends this same amount for 10 years? What would be the total cost?

$$\$60,000 \times 10 = \boxed{\$600,000.} \qquad \text{(1 place to the right)}$$

OTHER EXAMPLES

$6.89 \times 10 = \boxed{68.9}$	(1 place to the right)
$6.89 \times 100 = \boxed{689.}$	(2 places to the right)
$6.89 \times 1,000 = \boxed{6,890.}$	(3 places to the right)

In division, the answers are *smaller* than the original number.

EXAMPLES

$6.89 \div 10 = \boxed{.689}$	(1 place to the left)
$6.89 \div 100 = \boxed{.0689}$	(2 places to the left)
$6.89 \div 1,000 = \boxed{.00689}$	(3 places to the left)
$6.89 \div 10,000 = \boxed{.000689}$	(4 places to the left)

Next, let's dissect and solve a word problem.

How to Dissect and Solve a Word Problem

The Word Problem May O'Mally went to Sears to buy wall-to-wall carpet. She needs 101.3 square yards for downstairs, 16.3 square yards for the upstairs bedrooms, and 6.2 square yards for the halls. The carpet cost $14.55 per square yard. The padding cost $3.25 per square yard. Sears quoted an installation charge of $6.25 per square yard. What was May O'Mally's total cost?

By completing the following blueprint aid, we will slowly dissect this word problem. Note that before solving the problem, we gather the facts, identify what we are solving for, and list the steps that must be completed before finding the final answer, along with any key points we should remember. Let's go to it!

MONEY tips

Formula for Financial Success: Reduce Spending + Decrease Debt + Increase Savings (Investing) = Healthy Net Worth

	The facts	Solving for?	Steps to take	Key points
BLUEPRINT	*Carpet needed:* 101.3 sq. yd.; 16.3 sq. yd.; 6.2 sq. yd. *Costs:* Carpet, $14.55 per sq. yd.; padding, $3.25 per sq. yd.; installation, $6.25 per sq. yd.	Total cost of carpet, padding, and installation.	Total square yards × Cost per square yard = Total cost.	Align decimals. Round answer to nearest cent.

Steps to solving problem

1. Calculate the total number of square yards.

101.3
16.3
6.2
─────
123.8 square yards

2. Calculate the total cost per square yard.

$14.55
3.25
6.25
─────
$24.05

3. Calculate the total cost of carpet, padding, and installation.

123.8 × $24.05 = **$2,977.39**

It's time to check your progress.

LU 3–2 PRACTICE QUIZ

Complete this **Practice Quiz** to see how you are doing.

1. Rearrange vertically and add:
   14, .642, 9.34, 15.87321

2. Rearrange and subtract:
   28.1549 − .885

3. Multiply and round the answer to the nearest tenth:
   28.53 × 17.4

4. Divide and round to the nearest hundredth:
   2,182 ÷ 2.83

Complete by the shortcut method:

5. 14.28 × 100   6. 9,680 ÷ 1,000   7. 9,812 ÷ 10,000

8. Could you help Mel decide which product is the "better buy"?

   Dog food A: $9.01 for 64 ounces   **Dog food B:** $7.95 for 50 ounces

Round to the nearest cent as needed.

9. At Avis Rent-A-Car, the cost per day to rent a medium-size car is $39.99 plus 29 cents per mile. What will it cost to rent this car for 2 days if you drive 602.3 miles? Since the solution shows a completed blueprint, you might use a blueprint also.

10. A trip to Mexico cost 6,000 pesos. What would this be in U.S. dollars? Check your answer.

*For **extra help** from your authors–Sharon and Jeff–see the student DVD*

You Tube

✓ Solutions

1. 14.00000
   .64200
   9.34000
   15.87321
   ─────────
   39.85521

2. 7 101414
   28.1549
   − .8850
   ────────
   27.2699

3. 28.53
   × 17.4
   ──────
   11 412
   199 71
   285 3
   ───────
   496.422   = **496.4**

4. 771.024 = **771.02**
   2.83)218200.000
   1981
   ────
   2010
   1981
   ────
   290
   283
   ───
   7 00
   5 66
   ────
   1 340
   1 132

5. 14.28 = **1,428**   6. 9.680 = **9.680**   7. .9812 = **.9812**

8. A: $9.01 ÷ 64 = **$.14**   B: $7.95 ÷ 50 = **$.16**   **Buy A.**

9. Avis Rent-A-Car total rental charge:

	The facts	Solving for?	Steps to take	Key points
BLUEPRINT	Cost per day, $39.99. 29 cents per mile. Drove 602.3 miles. 2-day rental.	Total rental charge.	Total cost for 2 days' rental + Total cost of driving = Total rental charge.	In multiplication, count the number of decimal places. Starting from right to left in the product, insert decimal in appropriate place. Round to nearest cent.

Steps to solving problem

1.	Calculate total costs for 2 days' rental.	$39.99 × 2 = $79.98
2.	Calculate the total cost of driving.	$.29 × 602.3 = $174.667 = $174.67
3.	Calculate the total rental charge.	$ 79.98 + 174.67 $254.65

10. 6,000 × $.0717 = $430.20

      Check $430.20 × 13.9461 = 5,999.61 pesos due to rounding

---

LU 3–2a EXTRA PRACTICE QUIZ WITH WORKED-OUT SOLUTIONS

Need more practice? Try this **Extra Practice Quiz** (check figures in the Interactive Chapter Organizer, p. 79). Worked-out Solutions can be found in Appendix B at end of text.

1. Rearrange vertically and add: 16, .831, 9.85, 17.8321

2. Rearrange and subtract: 29.5832 − .998

3. Multiply and round the answer to the nearest tenth: 29.64 × 18.2

4. Divide and round to the nearest hundredth: 3,824 ÷ 4.94

Complete by the shortcut method:

5. 17.48 × 100   **6.** 8,432 ÷ 1,000   **7.** 9,643 ÷ 10,000

8. Could you help Mel decide which product is the "better buy"?

    Dog food A: $8.88 for 64 ounces   **Dog food B:** $7.25 for 50 ounces

Round to the nearest cent as needed:

9. At Avis Rent-A-Car, the cost per day to rent a medium-size car is $29.99 plus 22 cents per mile. What will it cost to rent this car for 2 days if you drive 709.8 miles?

10. A trip to Mexico costs 7,000 pesos. What would this be in U.S. dollars? Check your answer.

INTERACTIVE CHAPTER ORGANIZER

Topic/procedure/formula	Examples	You try it*
Identifying place value, p. 67 $$10, 1, \frac{1}{10}, \frac{1}{100}, \frac{1}{1,000}, \text{etc.}$$	.439 in thousandths place value	**Identify place value** .8256
Rounding decimals, p. 67 1. Identify place value of digit you want to round. 2. If digit to right of identified digit in Step 1 is 5 or more, increase identified digit by 1; if less than 5, do not change identified digit. 3. Drop all digits to right of identified digit.	.875 rounded to nearest tenth = .9 Identified digit	**Round to nearest tenth** .841
Converting decimal fractions to decimals, p. 68 1. Decimal fraction has a denominator with multiples of 10. Count number of zeros in denominator. 2. Zeros show how many places are in the decimal.	$\frac{8}{1,000} = .008$ $\frac{6}{10,000} = .0006$	**Convert to decimal** $\frac{9}{1,000}$ $\frac{3}{10,000}$
Converting proper fractions to decimals, p. 69 1. Divide numerator of fraction by its denominator. 2. Round as necessary.	$\frac{1}{3}$ (to nearest tenth) = .3	**Convert to decimal (to nearest tenth)** $\frac{1}{7}$
Converting mixed numbers to decimals, p. 69 1. Convert fractional part of the mixed number to a decimal. 2. Add converted fractional part to whole number.	$6\frac{1}{4}$ $\frac{1}{4} = .25 + 6 = 6.25$	**Convert to decimal** $5\frac{4}{5}$
Converting pure and mixed decimals to decimal fractions, p. 69 1. Place digits to right of decimal point in numerator of fraction. 2. Put 1 in denominator. 3. Add zeros to denominator, depending on decimal places of original number. For mixed decimals, add fraction to whole number.	.984 (3 places) 1. $\frac{984}{\quad}$ 2. $\frac{984}{1}$ 3. $\frac{984}{1,000}$	**Convert to fraction** .865
Adding and subtracting decimals, p. 71 1. Vertically write and align numbers on decimal points. 2. Add or subtract digits, starting with right column and moving to the left. 3. Align decimal point in answer with above decimal points.	Add 1.3 + 2 + .4 1.3 2.0 .4 3.7 Subtract 5 − 3.9 $\overset{4\ 10}{5.0}$ −3.9 1.1	**Add** 1.7 + 3 + .8 **Subtract** 6 − 4.1
Multiplying decimals, p. 73 1. Multiply numbers, ignoring decimal points. 2. Count and total number of decimal places in multiplier and multiplicand. 3. Starting at right in the product, count to the left the number of decimal places totaled in Step 2. Insert decimal point. If number of places greater than space in answer, add zeros.	2.48 (2 places) × .018 (3 places) 1 984 2 48 .04464	**Multiply** 3.49 × .015

(continues)

INTERACTIVE CHAPTER ORGANIZER

Topic/procedure/formula	Examples	You try it*
Dividing a decimal by a whole number, p. 73 **1.** Place decimal point in quotient directly above the decimal point in dividend. **2.** Divide as usual.	 $\begin{array}{r} 1.1 \\ 42\overline{)46.2} \\ \underline{42} \\ 42 \\ \underline{42} \end{array}$	**Divide (to nearest tenth)** $33\overline{)49.5}$
Dividing if the divisor is a decimal, p. 73 **1.** Make divisor a whole number by moving decimal point to the right. **2.** Move decimal point in dividend to the right the same number of places as in Step 1. **3.** Place decimal point in quotient above decimal point in dividend. Divide as usual.	$\begin{array}{r} 14.2 \\ 2.9\overline{)41.39} \\ \underline{29} \\ 123 \\ 116 \\ \underline{}79 \\ 58 \\ \underline{}21 \end{array}$	**Divide (to nearest tenth)** $3.2\overline{)1.48}$
Shortcuts on multiplication and division of decimals, p. 74 When multiplying by 10, 100, 1,000, and so on, move decimal point in multiplicand the same number of places to the right as you have zeros in multiplier. For division, move decimal point to the left.	$4.85 \times 100 = \boxed{485}$ $4.85 \div 100 = \boxed{.0485}$	**Multiply by shortcut** 6.92×100 **Divide by shortcut** $6.92 \div 100$

KEY TERMS	Decimal, *p. 66* Decimal fraction, *p. 68* Decimal point, *p. 66*	Mixed decimal, *p. 69* Pure decimal, *p. 69* Repeating decimal, *p. 67*	Rounding decimals, *p. 67*

Check Figures for Extra Practice Quizzes with Page References. (Worked-out Solutions in Appendix B.)	LU 3–1a (p. 71)		LU 3–2a (p. 77)	

	1. .309
	2. Hundredths
	3. Ten-thousandths
	4. A. .8
	   B. .844
	5. A. .9
	   B. .879
	6. .0008
	7. .00016
		8. $\frac{938}{1,000}$
		9. $17\frac{95}{100}$
		10. $\frac{325}{10,000}$
		11. .13
		12. .57
		13. 13.11
			1. 44.5131
			2. 28.5852
			3. 539.4
			4. 774.09
			5. 1,748
				6. 8.432
				7. .9643
				8. Buy A $.14
				9. $216.14
				10. $501.90

Note: For how to dissect and solve a word problem, see page 75.

*Worked-out solutions are in Appendix B.

Critical Thinking Discussion Questions with Chapter Concept Check

1. What are the steps for rounding decimals? Federal income tax forms allow the taxpayer to round each amount to the nearest dollar. Do you agree with this?

2. Explain how to convert fractions to decimals. If 1 out of 20 people buys a Land Rover, how could you write an advertisement in decimals?

3. Explain why .07, .70, and .700 are not equal. Assume you take a family trip to Disney World that covers 500 miles. Show that $\frac{8}{10}$ of the trip, or .8 of the trip, represents 400 miles.

4. Explain the steps in the addition or subtraction of decimals. Visit a car dealership and find the difference between two sticker prices. Be sure to check each sticker price for accuracy. Should you always pay the sticker price?

5. **Chapter Concept Check.** In the chapter opener, the e-book was compared to a print book through the use of whole numbers and decimals. Visit a publisher's website and calculate the difference between the prices for a printed text and an e-book. Estimate what you think the profit is to the publisher based on what you read in the chapter opener.

Classroom Notes

DRILL PROBLEMS

Identify the place value for the following: *LU 3-1(1)*

3–1. 7.9382

3–2. 462.8391

Round the following as indicated: *LU 3-1(1)*

	Tenth	Hundredth	Thousandth
3–3. .7391			
3–4. 6.8629			
3–5. 5.8312			
3–6. 6.8415			
3–7. 6.5555			
3–8. 75.9913			

Round the following to the nearest cent: *LU 3-1(1)*

3–9. $4,822.775

3–10. $4,892.046

Convert the following types of decimal fractions to decimals (round to nearest hundredth as needed): *LU 3-1(2)*

3–11. $\frac{8}{100}$

3–12. $\frac{3}{10}$

3–13. $\frac{61}{1,000}$

3–14. $\frac{610}{1,000}$

3–15. $\frac{91}{100}$

3–16. $\frac{979}{1,000}$

3–17. $16\frac{61}{100}$

Convert the following decimals to fractions. Do not reduce to lowest terms. *LU 3-1(2)*

3–18. .9

3–19. .71

3–20. .009

3–21. .0125

3–22. .609

3–23. .825

3–24. .9999

3–25. .7065

Convert the following to mixed numbers. Do not reduce to the lowest terms. *LU 3-1(2)*

3–26. 7.1

3–27. 28.48

3–28. 6.025

Write the decimal equivalent of the following: *LU 3-1(2)*

3–29. Five thousandths

3–30. Three hundred three and two hundredths

3–31. Eighty-five ten thousandths

3–32. Seven hundred seventy-five thousandths

Rearrange the following and add: *LU 3-2(1)*

3–33. .115, 10.8318, 4.7, 802.4811

3–34. .005, 2,002.181, 795.41, 14.0, .184

Rearrange the following and subtract: *LU 3-2(1)*

3–35. 9.2 − 5.8

3–36. 7 − 2.0815

3–37. 3.4 − 1.08

Estimate by rounding all the way and multiply the following (do not round final answer): *LU 3-2(1)*

3–38. 6.24 × 3.9

3–39. .413 × 3.07

Estimate

Estimate

3–40. 675 × 1.92

3–41. 4.9 × .825

Estimate

Estimate

Divide the following and round to the nearest hundredth: *LU 3-2(1)*

3–42. .8931 ÷ 3

3–43. 29.432 ÷ .0012

3–44. .0065 ÷ .07

3–45. 7,742.1 ÷ 48

3–46. 8.95 ÷ 1.18

3–47. 2,600 ÷ .381

Convert the following to decimals and round to the nearest hundredth: *LU 3-1(2)*

3–48. $\frac{1}{8}$

3–49. $\frac{1}{25}$

3–50. $\frac{5}{6}$

3–51. $\frac{5}{8}$

Complete these multiplications and divisions by the shortcut method (do not do any written calculations):   *LU 3-2(3)*

3–52. 96.7 ÷ 10

3–53. 258.5 ÷ 100

3–54. 8.51 × 1,000

3–55. .86 ÷ 100

3–56. 9.015 × 100

3–57. 48.6 × 10

3–58. 750 × 10

3–59. 3,950 ÷ 1,000

3–60. 8.45 ÷ 10

3–61. 7.9132 × 1,000

WORD PROBLEMS

As needed, round answers to the nearest cent.

3–62. A Chevy Volt costs $29,000 in the United States. Using the exchange rate given on page 74, what would it cost in Canada? Check your answer.   *LU 3-2(2)*

3–63. Dustin Pedroia got 7 hits out of 12 at bats. What was his batting average to the nearest thousandths place?   *LU 3-1(2)*

3–64. Pete Ross read in a *Wall Street Journal* article that the cost of parts and labor to make an Apple iPhone 4S were as follows: *LU 3-2(1)*

Display	$37.00	Wireless	$23.54
Memory	$28.30	Camera	$17.60
Labor	$ 8.00	Additional items	$81.56

Assuming Pete pays $649 for an iPhone 4S, how much profit does the iPhone generate?

3–65. At the Party Store, Joan Lee purchased 21.50 yards of ribbon. Each yard costs 91 cents. What was the total cost of the ribbon? Round to the nearest cent.   *LU 3-2(1)*

3–66. Douglas Noel went to Home Depot and bought four doors at $42.99 each and six bags of fertilizer at $8.99 per bag. What was the total cost to Douglas? If Douglas had $300 in his pocket, what does he have left to spend?   *LU 3-2(1)*

3–67. The stock of Intel has a high of $30.25 today. It closed at $28.85. How much did the stock drop from its high?   *LU 3-2(1)*

3–68. Pete is traveling by car to a computer convention in San Diego. His company will reimburse him $.48 per mile. If Pete travels 210.5 miles, how much will Pete receive from his company?   *LU 3-2(1)*

3–69. Mark Ogara rented a truck from Avis Rent-A-Car for the weekend (2 days). The base rental price was $29.95 per day plus $14\frac{1}{2}$ cents per mile. Mark drove 410.85 miles. How much does Mark owe?   *LU 3-2(1)*

3–70. Nursing home costs are on the rise as consumeraffairs.com reports in its quarterly newsletter. The average cost is around $192 a day with an average length of stay of 2.5 years. Calculate the cost of the average nursing home stay. *LU 3-2(1)*

3–71. Bob Ross bought a Blackberry on the web for $89.99. He saw the same Blackberry in the mall for $118.99. How much did Bob save by buying on the web? *LU 3-2(1)*

3–72. Russell is preparing the daily bank deposit for his coffee shop. Before the deposit, the coffee shop had a checking account balance of $3,185.66. The deposit contains the following checks:

No. 1	$ 99.50	No. 3	$8.75
No. 2	110.35	No. 4	6.83

Russell included $820.55 in currency with the deposit. What is the coffee shop's new balance, assuming Russell writes no new checks? *LU 3-2(1)*

3–73. Facebook announced it is going public in 2012. As a result, billionaires and millionaires will be created in a scenario similar to what happened when Microsoft and Google went public. Facebook's founder, Mark Zuckerberg, 27 years old, has *eXcel* 533.8 million shares in Facebook worth $28.4 billion. Peter Thiel, Facebook's first outside investor, has 44.7 million shares. Accel Partners has 201.4 million shares. Marc Andreessen, Netscape's founder, has 3.6 million shares. Sheryl Sandberg, the COO of Facebook, has 1.9 million shares. What is the total number of shares owned by these individuals? *LU 3-2(1)*

3–74. Randi went to Lowe's to buy wall-to-wall carpeting. She needs 110.8 square yards for downstairs, 31.8 square yards for the halls, and 161.9 square yards for the bedrooms upstairs. Randi chose a shag carpet that costs $14.99 per square yard. She ordered foam padding at $3.10 per square yard. The carpet installers quoted Randi a labor charge of $3.75 per square yard. What will the total job cost Randi? *LU 3-2(1)*

3–75. Paul Rey bought four new Dunlop tires at Goodyear for $95.99 per tire. Goodyear charged $3.05 per tire for mounting, $2.95 per tire for valve stems, and $3.80 per tire for balancing. If Paul paid no sales tax, what was his total cost for the four tires? *LU 3-2(1)*

3–76. Shelly is shopping for laundry detergent, mustard, and canned tuna. She is trying to decide which of two products is the *eXcel* better buy. Using the following information, can you help Shelly? *LU 3-2(1)*

Laundry detergent A	**Mustard A**	**Canned tuna A**
$2.00 for 37 ounces	$.88 for 6 ounces	$1.09 for 6 ounces

Laundry detergent B	**Mustard B**	**Canned tuna B**
$2.37 for 38 ounces	$1.61 for $12\frac{1}{2}$ ounces	$1.29 for $8\frac{3}{4}$ ounces

3–77. Roger bought season tickets for weekend games to professional basketball games. The cost was $945.60. The season pack-
eXcel age included 36 home games. What is the average price of the tickets per game? Round to the nearest cent. Marcelo, Roger's friend, offered to buy four of the tickets from Roger. What is the total amount Roger should receive? *LU 3-2(1)*

3–78. A nurse was to give each of her patients a 1.32-unit dosage of a prescribed drug. The total remaining units of the drug at the hospital pharmacy were 53.12. The nurse has 38 patients. Will there be enough dosages for all her patients? *LU 3-2(1)*

3–79. Jill Horn went to Japan and bought an animation cel of Spongebob. The price was 25,000 yen. Using the *Wall Street Journal* currency table on page 74, what is the price in U.S. dollars? Check your answer. *LU 3-2(2)*

ADDITIONAL SET OF WORD PROBLEMS

3–80. As *USA TODAY* reported early in 2012, the U.S. debt is now larger than the U.S. economy. The debt is $15.23 trillion while the value of all goods and services the U.S. economy produces in 1 year is $15.17 trillion. How much more debt in trillions does the United States have than it produces each year? *LU 3-2(1)*

3–81. Eastman Kodak announced in a January 19, 2012, press release that it has filed for bankruptcy protection. The 131-year-old company has struggled to adapt to the digital world and has incurred far more debt than assets. The company reported it has $5.1 billion in assets and nearly $6.8 billion in debt. How much more does it have in debt than assets? *LU 3-2(1)*

3–82. Morris Katz bought four new tires at Goodyear for $95.49 per tire. Goodyear also charged Morris $2.50 per tire for mounting, $2.40 per tire for valve stems, and $3.95 per tire for balancing. Assume no tax. What was Morris's total cost for the four tires? *LU 3-2(1)*

3–83. The *Denver Post* reported that Xcel Energy is revising customer charges for monthly residential electric bills and gas bills. Electric bills will increase $3.32. Gas bills will decrease $1.74 a month. **(a)** What is the resulting new monthly increase for the entire bill? **(b)** If Xcel serves 2,350 homes, how much additional revenue would Xcel receive each month? *LU 3-2(1)*

3–84. Steven is traveling to an auto show by car. His company will reimburse him $.29 per mile. If Steven travels 890.5 miles, how much will he receive from his company? *LU 3-2(1)*

3–85. Gracie went to Home Depot to buy wall-to-wall carpeting for her house. She needs 104.8 square yards for downstairs, 17.4 square yards for halls, and 165.8 square yards for the upstairs bedrooms. Gracie chose a shag carpet that costs $13.95 per square yard. She ordered foam padding at $2.75 per square yard. The installers quoted Gracie a labor cost of $5.75 per square yard in installation. What will the total job cost Gracie? *LU 3-2(1)*

CHALLENGE PROBLEMS

3–86. Fred and Winnie O'Callahan have put themselves on a very strict budget. Their goal at the end of the year is to buy a car
eXcel for $14,000 in cash. Their budget includes the following per dollar:

$.40 food and lodging
.20 entertainment
.10 educational

Fred earns $2,000 per month and Winnie earns $2,500 per month. After 1 year will Fred and Winnie have enough cash to buy the car? *LU 3-2(1)*

3–87. Jill and Frank decided to take a long weekend in New York. City Hotel has a special getaway weekend for $79.95. The price is per person per night, based on double occupancy. The hotel has a minimum two-night stay. For this price, Jill and Frank will receive $50 credit toward their dinners at City's Skylight Restaurant. Also included in the package is a $3.99 credit per person toward breakfast for two each morning.

Since Jill and Frank do not own a car, they plan to rent a car. The car rental agency charges $19.95 a day with an additional charge of $.22 a mile and $1.19 per gallon of gas used. The gas tank holds 24 gallons.

From the following facts, calculate the total expenses of Jill and Frank (round all answers to nearest hundredth or cent as appropriate). Assume no taxes. *LU 3-2(1)*

Car rental (2 days):		Dinner cost at Skylight	$182.12
Beginning odometer reading	4,820	Breakfast for two:	
Ending odometer reading	4,940	Morning No. 1	24.17
Beginning gas tank: $\frac{3}{4}$ full		Morning No. 2	26.88
Gas tank on return: $\frac{1}{2}$ full		Hotel room	79.95
Tank holds 24 gallons			

SUMMARY PRACTICE TEST

Do you need help? The DVD has step-by-step worked-out solutions. You Tube™

1. Add the following by translating the verbal form to the decimal equivalent. *(pp. 67, 71)* *LU 3-1(1), LU 3-2(1)*

Three hundred thirty-eight and seven hundred five thousandths
Nineteen and fifty-nine hundredths
Five and four thousandths
Seventy-five hundredths
Four hundred three and eight tenths

Convert the following decimal fractions to decimals. *(p. 68)* *LU 3-1(2)*

2. $\dfrac{7}{10}$

3. $\dfrac{7}{100}$

4. $\dfrac{7}{1,000}$

Convert the following to proper fractions or mixed numbers. Do not reduce to the lowest terms. *(p. 69) LU 3-1(2)*

5. .9   **6.** 6.97   **7.** .685

Convert the following fractions to decimals (or mixed decimals) and round to the nearest hundredth as needed. *(p. 69) LU 3-1(2)*

8. $\dfrac{2}{7}$ **9.** $\dfrac{1}{8}$ **10.** $4\dfrac{4}{7}$ **11.** $\dfrac{1}{13}$

12. Rearrange the following decimals and add. *(p. 71) LU 3-2(1)*

  5.93,   11.862,   284.0382,   88.44

13. Subtract the following and round to the nearest tenth. *(p. 72) LU 3-2(1)*

  $13.111 - 3.872$

14. Multiply the following and round to the nearest hundredth. *(p. 73) LU 3-2(1)*

  7.4821×15.861

15. Divide the following and round to the nearest hundredth. *(p. 73) LU 3-2(1)*

  $203,942 \div 5.88$

Complete the following by the shortcut method. *(p. 74) LU 3-2(3)*

16. $62.94 \times 1,000$

17. $8,322,249.821 \times 100$

18. The average pay of employees is $795.88 per week. Lee earns $820.44 per week. How much is Lee's pay over the average? *(p. 72) LU 3-2(1)*

19. Lowes reimburses Ron $.49 per mile. Ron submitted a travel log for a total of 1,910.81 miles. How much will Lowes reimburse Ron? Round to the nearest cent. *(p. 73) LU 3-2(1)*

20. Lee Chin bought two new car tires from Michelin for $182.11 per tire. Michelin also charged Lee $3.99 per tire for mounting, $2.50 per tire for valve stems, and $4.10 per tire for balancing. What is Lee's final bill? *(pp. 71, 73) LU 3-2(1)*

21. Could you help Judy decide which of the following products is cheaper per ounce? *(p. 73) LU 3-2(1)*

Canned fruit A   **Canned fruit B**

$.37 for 3 ounces $.58 for $3\dfrac{3}{4}$ ounces

22. Paula Smith bought a computer tablet for 350 euros. Using the *Wall Street Journal* currency table on page 74, what is this price in U.S. dollars? *(p. 74) LU 3-2(2)*

23. Google stock traded at a high of $438.22 and closed at $410.12. How much did the stock fall from its high? *(p. 72) LU 3-2(1)*

SURF TO SAVE

How far does your money go? 🔍

 ### PROBLEM 1
Get ready for your new job

Go to http://www.officemax.com. Choose an expensive pen, briefcase, and portfolio. If you were to order all three of these items for your new job, how much would they cost before taxes? (Assume shipping on your order is free.) Assuming your sales tax is 6%, how much would you pay in sales tax on this purchase? Note: Expensive pens are found under "Fine & Better" pens in the pen section. Searching for "Briefcase" is the easiest way to find briefcases at the site.

Discussion Questions

1. What other expenses will you most likely incur as you start your new career?
2. How will these expenses impact the starting salary you will need to earn?

 ### PROBLEM 2
Dollars and yen

Go to http://www.oanda.com/converter/classic. Suppose you converted $10,000 to Japanese yen on July 24, 2004. If you convert those yen back to dollars at today's exchange rate, how much money would you have?

Discussion Questions

1. What did you notice in the conversion of these monetary amounts based on the date of the conversion?
2. What does this tell you about the state of the economy in the U.S. versus Japan?

PROBLEM 3
Affordable trades

Go to http://www.kiplinger.com/columns/ask/archive/2004/q0105.htm. Read the "Ask Kim" question and answer by Kimberly Lankford. At the price quoted in the article for BuyandHold's lower-priced ($6.99) service, how much would it cost to make three trades per month for 1 year?

Discussion Questions

1. Assume you made three trades per month for an entire year. How much would you need to earn in profit on each trade to cover your yearly expense for these trades?
2. How comfortable are you in making such stock trades? By how much would the individual investments have to change in value to encourage you to make these trades? Why?

PROBLEM 4
Mind over matter

Airlines charge almost $200 if a suitcase weighs more than 50 pounds. The skycap tells you your suitcase weighs 22 kilograms. You think that each kilogram is equal to 2.2 pounds. Do you owe additional fees for an overweight suitcase? Use the converter at http://www.metric-conversions.org/weight/kilograms-to-pounds.htm to verify your answer.

Discussion Questions

1. Why do you think airlines charge for overweight baggage and additional baggage?
2. Do these fees impact which airline you fly?

MOBILE APPS ✕

Equations with Decimals (YourTeacher.com) Provides a tutorial on decimals.

Fractions to Decimal and vice versa (Essence Computing) Assists in the conversion of fractions to their decimal equivalents and vice versa.

INTERNET PROJECTS ✕

See text website
www.mhhe.com/slater11e_sse_ch03

Cash In Your Old Electronics

You may be surprised at how much some online retailers will pay. BY JEFF BERTOLUCCI

YOU PROBABLY HAVE PLENTY of old electronic gizmos and gadgets tucked away in drawers. It's easy to convert those cell phones, computers, iPods and movie DVDs into quick cash.

A number of big-name shopping sites, including Amazon, Best Buy, eBay and Gazelle, will offer cash or store credit for your gear. The process is quick and painless, and you won't have to pay shipping costs—even if the buyer rejects your stuff and returns it. Although you may earn more by auctioning gear on eBay, it's hard to top the simplicity of the cash-for-electronics marketplaces.

You'll often get top dollar for trading in high-demand items (such as anything from Apple). That's the case with Gazelle. Gazelle chief gadget officer Anthony Scarsella says you can estimate what you'd get for your used item by seeing what it's selling for at the Gazelle stores on Amazon and eBay. Figure you'll get 10% to 20% less because the merchants add a markup.

Easy sell. As you might expect from the world's top e-tailer, Amazon has an extremely user-friendly interface with its Trade-In Store. The site accepts trade-ins for store credit in four categories: Books, Video Games, Movies & TV (on DVD), and Electronics. To submit an item, you enter the product's name in a search window, then answer a few questions about its condition. If Amazon is interested, you'll get an offer on the spot. If Amazon decides, upon receiving your device, that the product is worth less than its original offer, you can accept a reduced price or have it returned at no charge.

I gave the service a try. Amazon offered $63.25 for my Apple iPod nano, which was a few years old but in excellent condition. I accepted the offer and printed Amazon's free UPS mailing label, which popped up in a browser window. Next, I boxed up the iPod and dropped it off at the nearest UPS store. Painless. Within two weeks, Amazon e-mailed that it had accepted my iPod and credited my gift-card balance.

Could I have made more by auctioning the device on eBay? Probably. I checked eBay and discovered that bidders were offering up to $100 for iPod models similar to mine. Lesson learned: If you want top dollar, trade-ins aren't necessarily the way to go—though getting a good price at auction is always a gamble.

The eBay difference. EBay's Instant Sale works pretty much the same way as Amazon's Trade-In Store, albeit with a notable difference. Unlike Amazon, eBay gives you cash, not store credit. The fastest way to get paid is to open an account with eBay's PayPal service (if you haven't already), then transfer the funds to your checking account.

EBay offered $36.35 for my Apple TV video-streaming device, sight unseen. After examining it, however, eBay lowered the offer to $30.90; "visible scratches" were to blame, they said. (What scratches? I wondered. Am I blind?)

Nevertheless, I accepted the lower offer, mostly because it was higher than competing trade-in sites were willing to pay. Gazelle, for instance, offered just $27, and Amazon wasn't interested in my Apple device at all.

In addition to eBay, other sites offer cash, including Gazelle (www.gazelle.com). Gazelle also operates online trade-in services for big-name retailers, such as Costco and Walmart. If you'd rather not pack up your gear, take it to a participating Best Buy or Radio Shack store, where someone will appraise and buy your products on the spot. Many trade-in services offer to recycle your device free if they don't want to buy it.

Always compare prices at several sites before you accept an offer. While you're at it, surf over to eBay to see how much sellers and auctioneers are asking for your product. ∎

HOW MUCH YOU'LL POCKET

Here's a list of in-demand electronics at two major buyers, and an idea of how much they'll pay.

Trade-in service	Most popular electronic trade-ins	Trade-in price*
Amazon	Apple iPod touch 8GB (Black, 4th generation)	$109
	Amazon Kindle 3G	$30 ▸
	Garmin nuvi 2555LMT GPS Navigator	$87
	Garmin nuvi 1450LMT GPS Navigator	$74
Gazelle	Apple iPhone 3GS	$132
	Apple iPhone 3G	$62
	Apple iPhone 4	$187
	Apple iPad 2	$380
	BlackBerry Torch 9800	$79

*Amazon's prices are maximum offered for the product; Gazelle's are average selling prices for February 2012.

BUSINESS MATH ISSUE

It is better to donate your used electronics than trade them in for cash.

1. List the key points of the article and information to support your position.
2. Write a group defense of your position using math calculations to support your view.

A Word Problem Approach—Chapters 1, 2, 3

1. The top rate at the Waldorf Towers Hotel in New York is $390. The top rate at the Ritz Carlton in Boston is $345. If John spends 9 days at the hotel, how much can he save if he stays at the Ritz? *(pp. 10, 14)   LU 1-2(2), LU 1-3(1)*

2. Robert Half Placement Agency was rated best by 4 to 1 in an independent national survey. If 250,000 responded to the survey, how many rated Robert Half the best? *(p. 47)   LU 2-3(1)*

3. Of the 63.2 million people who watch professional football, only $\frac{1}{5}$ watch the commercials. How many viewers do not watch the commercials? *(p. 47)   LU 2-3(1)*

4. AT&T advertised a 10-minute call for $2.27. MCI WorldCom's rate was $2.02. Assuming Bill Splat makes forty 10-minute calls, how much could he save by using MCI WorldCom? *(pp. 72–73)   LU 3-2(1)*

5. A square foot of rental space in New York City, Boston, and Providence costs as follows: New York City, $6.25; Boston, $5.75; and Providence, $3.75. If Compaq Computer wants to rent 112,500 square feet of space, what will Compaq save by renting in Providence rather than Boston? *(pp. 72–73)   LU 3-2(1)*

6. American Airlines has a frequent-flier program. Coupon brokers who buy and sell these awards pay between 1 and $1\frac{1}{2}$ cents for each mile earned. Fred Dietrich earned a 50,000-mile award (worth two free tickets to any city). If Fred decided to sell his award to a coupon broker, approximately how much would he receive? *(p. 71)   LU 3-2(1)*

7. Lillie Wong bought four new Firestone tires at $82.99 each. Firestone also charged $2.80 per tire for mounting, $1.95 per tire for valves, and $3.15 per tire for balancing. Lillie turned her four old tires in to Firestone, which charged $1.50 per tire to dispose of them. What was Lillie's final bill? *(p. 72)   LU 3-2(1)*

8. Tootsie Roll Industries bought Charms Company for $65 million. Some analysts believe that in 4 years the purchase price could rise to three times as much. If the analysts are right, how much did Tootsie Roll save by purchasing Charms immediately? *(p. 14)   LU 1-3(1)*

9. Today the average business traveler will spend $47.73 a day on food. The breakdown is dinner, $22.26; lunch, $10.73; breakfast, $6.53; tips, $6.23; and tax, $1.98. If Clarence Donato, an executive for Honeywell, spends only .33 of the average, what is Clarence's total cost for food for the day? If Clarence wanted to spend $\frac{1}{3}$ more than the average on the next day, what would be his total cost on the second day? Round to the nearest cent. *(pp. 48, 71)   LU 2-3(1), LU 3-2(1)*

Be sure you use the fractional equivalent in calculating .$\overline{33}$.

CHAPTER 4

Banking

Use a Phone for Deposits on the Go

BY EMILY GLAZER

Depositing checks into investment accounts is getting easier—for some.

Both **Charles Schwab** Corp. and **Fidelity Investments** rolled out new software applications at the end of May allowing customers to deposit checks into brokerage accounts with their smartphones. After signing up for the service, customers photograph the front and back of a check with their iPhone or Android, then follow a few steps to send the deposit on its way in minutes.

"We don't have the pervasive locations that traditional banks and [their] ATMs have," says Richard Blunck, Fidelity's executive vice president for Web distribution. A smartphone, he adds, "is a lot better than stamps and mailing."

After registering for mobile deposits, you select which account the deposits will go to. With Schwab, you'll receive an email acknowledging receipt of a check within four hours if it's sent before 4 p.m., or the next

business day if it's sent after 4, says Diane Russell, Schwab's senior vice president of platform services.

Deposits by smartphone may arrive faster than checks sent in the mail, but the money won't become available in your account any faster. As with most check deposits, the funds become available within a few days of the deposit, based on regulations and financial institution policies.

After the check clears, Ms. Russell recommends shredding or tearing up the paper. If a check is deposited twice, "by accident or abuse," an error message will appear, she says.

Though neither Schwab nor Fidelity enables direct mobile deposit into retirement accounts, Fidelity allows you to transfer money into retirement accounts using the mobile app, Mr. Blunck says. Schwab does not allow that because of "the complexity of IRS rules governing contributions," according to a Schwab spokeswoman.

A recent Schwab survey found nearly seven in 10 Americans between the ages of 18

and 44 were interested in using their mobile phones to deposit checks, largely based on convenience.

Schwab and Fidelity join a batch of banks—including **J.P. Morgan Chase** & Co., **PNC Financial Services Group** Inc. and **U.S. Bancorp**—that have launched similar applications allowing mobile deposits.

Other investment companies say they are exploring the option, including **Vanguard Group** and **T. Rowe Price Group** Inc. "We're on a journey toward that end," says Chip Weldon, T. Rowe Price's vice president of interactive strategies. But he adds he doesn't anticipate rolling out the service in the next year.

"If you fill out this little card, sir, we can switch over to direct deposit."

My
Welcome
Last Login:
18 Dec 2006 at 11:41:32
[1] Account Enquiry
[2] Bill Payment
[3] Funds Transfer To Own Account
[4] Funds Transfer To 3rd Party Account
[5] Account Opening
[#] Logout

Cyber-shot

w you can bank anytime anywh...

Visit www.oc.../mol for more det...ay!

LU 4–1: The Checking Account

1. Define and state the purpose of signature cards, checks, deposit slips, check stubs, check registers, and endorsements *(pp. 92–94)*.
2. Correctly prepare deposit slips and write checks *(pp. 92–94)*.

LU 4–2: Bank Statement and Reconciliation Process; Latest Trends in Mobile Banking

1. Explain trends in the banking industry *(p. 96)*.
2. Define and state the purpose of the bank statement *(pp. 96–98)*.
3. Complete a check register and a bank reconciliation *(pp. 98–101)*.
4. Explain the trends in mobile banking *(p. 101)*.

VOCABULARY PREVIEW

Here are key terms in this chapter. After completing the chapter, if you know the term, place a checkmark in the parentheses. If you don't know the term, look it up and put the page number where it can be found.

Automatic teller machine (ATM) ( ) Bank reconciliation ( ) Bank statement ( ) Banking apps ( ) Blank endorsement ( ) Check ( ) Check register ( ) Check stub ( ) Credit memo (CM) ( ) Debit card ( ) Debit memo (DM) ( ) Deposit slip ( ) Deposits in transit ( ) Draft ( ) Drawee ( ) Drawer ( ) Electronic funds transfer (EFT) ( ) Endorse ( ) Full endorsement ( ) Mobile banking ( ) Nonsufficient funds (NSF) ( ) Outstanding checks ( ) Overdrafts ( ) Payee ( ) Restrictive endorsement ( ) Signature card ( )

The *Wall Street Journal* clip "Use a Phone for Deposits on the Go" in the chapter opener shows how technology is affecting your bank transactions. In this chapter we will look at how to do banking transactions manually, followed by a look at the latest trends in banking.

An important fixture in today's banking is the **automatic teller machine (ATM).** The ability to get instant cash is a convenience many bank customers enjoy.

The effect of using an ATM card is the same as using a **debit card**—both transactions result in money being immediately deducted from your checking account balance. As a re-

sult, debit cards have been called enhanced ATM cards or *check cards.* Often banks charge fees for these card transactions. The frequent complaints of bank customers have made many banks offer their ATMs as a free service, especially if customers use an ATM in the same network as their bank. Some banks charge fees for using another bank's ATM. The following *Wall Street Journal* clip "ATM Fees Heading Higher" (p. 92) shows how ATM fees are on the rise again.

Remember that the use of debit cards involves planning. As *check cards,* you must be aware of your bank balance every time you use a debit card. Also, if you use a credit card instead of a debit card, you can only be held responsible for $50 of illegal charges; and during the time the credit card company

ATM Fees Heading Higher

By ROBIN SIDEL

Some of the nation's biggest banks are imposing a variety of new fees on people who withdraw money from automated-teller machines.

The move is the latest example of the burgeoning new fees that banks are imposing on customers accustomed to years of free services. Banks are scrambling to replace billions of dollars in revenue expected to be lost from new federal regulations on overdraft charges and debit cards.

J.P. Morgan Chase & Co., **TD Bank Financial Group**, and **PNC Financial Services Group** already are changing their ATM policies to collect more fees.

J.P. Morgan's Chase retail division, for example, is going after noncustomers who withdraw money from the bank's ATMs, according to people familiar with the matter. Chase executives have grumbled about customers of rival banks using the company's machines even though it charges them $3, which is standard in the banking industry. Chase is now testing fees of $5

and $4 in Illinois and Texas, respectively, for noncustomer withdrawals.

More ATM fee rises are expected in the coming months. As regulations limit certain profitable practices in the industry, the banks are replacing lost funds with new fees. Some financial institutions recently introduced new charges on checking accounts as a way to make up some of the revenue that will be choked from rules imposed by the Dodd-Frank financial-overhaul law.

investigates the illegal charges, they are removed from your account. However, with a debit card, this legal limit only applies if you report your card lost or stolen within two business days.

This chapter begins with a discussion of the checking account. You will follow Molly Kate as she opens a checking account for Gracie's Natural Superstore and performs her banking transactions. Pay special attention to the procedure used by Gracie's to reconcile its checking account and bank statement. This information will help you reconcile your checkbook records with the bank's record of your account. The chapter concludes by discussing the latest technology trends in banking.

Learning Unit 4–1: The Checking Account

LO 1

A **check** or **draft** is a written order instructing a bank, credit union, or savings and loan institution to pay a designated amount of your money on deposit to a person or an organization. Checking accounts are offered to individuals and businesses. Note that the business checking account usually receives more services than the personal checking account but may come with additional fees.

Most small businesses depend on a checking account for efficient record keeping. In this learning unit you will follow the checking account procedures of a newly organized small business. You can use many of these procedures in your personal check writing. You will also learn about e-checks—a new trend.

Opening the Checking Account

Molly Kate, treasurer of Gracie's Natural Superstore, went to Ipswich Bank to open a business checking account. The bank manager gave Molly a **signature card.** The signature card contained space for the company's name and address, references, type of account, and the signature(s) of the person(s) authorized to sign checks. If necessary, the bank will use the signature card to verify that Molly signed the checks. Some companies authorize more than one person to sign checks or require more than one signature on a check.

Molly then lists on a **deposit slip** (or deposit ticket) the checks and/or cash she is depositing in her company's business account. The bank gave Molly a temporary checkbook to use until the company's printed checks arrived. Molly also will receive *preprinted* checking account deposit slips like the one shown in Figure 4.1 (p. 93). Since the deposit slips are in duplicate, Molly can keep a record of her deposit. Note that the increased use of making deposits at ATM machines has made it more convenient for people to make their deposits.

LO 2

Writing business checks is similar to writing personal checks. Before writing any checks, however, you must understand the structure of a check and know how to write a check. Carefully study Figure 4.2 (p. 93). Note that the verbal amount written in the check should match the figure amount. If these two amounts are different, by law the bank uses

FIGURE   4.1   Deposit slip

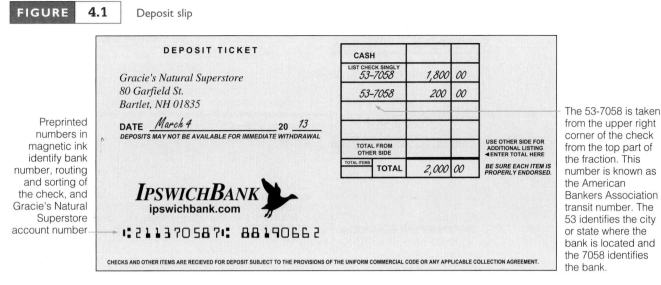

Preprinted numbers in magnetic ink identify bank number, routing and sorting of the check, and Gracie's Natural Superstore account number

The 53-7058 is taken from the upper right corner of the check from the top part of the fraction. This number is known as the American Bankers Association transit number. The 53 identifies the city or state where the bank is located and the 7058 identifies the bank.

Check Stub

It should be completed before the check is written.

the verbal amount. Also, note the bank imprint on the bottom right section of the check. When processing the check, the bank imprints the check's amount. This makes it easy to detect bank errors.

Using the Checking Account

Once the check is written, the writer must keep a record of the check. Knowing the amount of your written checks and the amount in the bank should help you avoid writing a bad check. Business checkbooks usually include attached **check stubs** to keep track of written checks. The sample check stub in the margin shows the information that the check writer will want to record. Some companies use a **check register** to keep their check records instead of check stubs. Figure 4.6 (p. 99) shows a check register with a ✓ column that is often used in balancing the checkbook with the bank statement (Learning Unit 4–2).

FIGURE   4.2   The structure of a check

Date check is written

Bank number and customer's number

To whom check is payable or **payee**

Preprinted check number

Verbal form of amount of check. Note spacing and use of "and" to represent the decimal

Amount of check

Bank ordered to pay is **drawee**

Signature–this is the same as on the signature card

One who writes check is called the **drawer**

(Payer)

Bank number printed with magnetic ink for computer processing matches printed number at upper right-hand corner of check above the date of the check. Customer account number below bank number.

Gracie's Natural Superstore's account number

Preprinted check number

When bank processes check, the 6000 is imprinted here. Note that this should match what is written for amount of check.

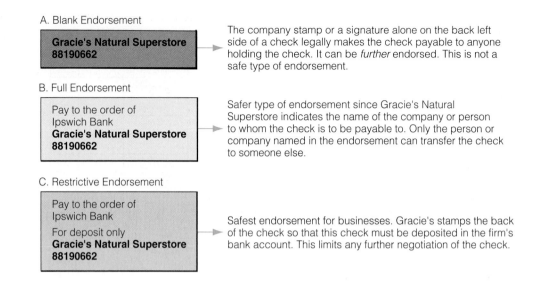

FIGURE   4.3

Types of common endorsements

A. Blank Endorsement

> Gracie's Natural Superstore
> 88190662

The company stamp or a signature alone on the back left side of a check legally makes the check payable to anyone holding the check. It can be *further* endorsed. This is not a safe type of endorsement.

B. Full Endorsement

> Pay to the order of
> Ipswich Bank
> **Gracie's Natural Superstore**
> **88190662**

Safer type of endorsement since Gracie's Natural Superstore indicates the name of the company or person to whom the check is to be payable to. Only the person or company named in the endorsement can transfer the check to someone else.

C. Restrictive Endorsement

> Pay to the order of
> Ipswich Bank
> For deposit only
> **Gracie's Natural Superstore**
> **88190662**

Safest endorsement for businesses. Gracie's stamps the back of the check so that this check must be deposited in the firm's bank account. This limits any further negotiation of the check.

Gracie's Natural Superstore has had a busy week, and Molly must deposit its checks in the company's checking account. However, before she can do this, Molly must **endorse,** or sign, the back left side of the checks. Figure 4.3 above explains the three types of check endorsements: **blank endorsement, full endorsement,** and **restrictive endorsement.** These endorsements transfer Gracie's ownership to the bank, which collects the money from the person or company issuing the check. Federal Reserve regulation limits all endorsements to the top $1\frac{1}{2}$ inches of the trailing edge on the back left side of the check.

After the bank receives Molly's deposit slip, shown in Figure 4.1 (p. 93), it increases (or credits) Gracie's account by $2,000. Often Molly leaves the deposit in a locked bag in a night depository. Then the bank credits (increases) Gracie's account when it processes the deposit on the next working day.

In the following *Wall Street Journal* clip "Fee, Not Free," see how the cost of regular checking has increased. Banks are looking for new ways to increase their profit. Later in the chapter we will look at online banking and the decrease in check writing.

MONEY tips

Conduct an annual check of your bank's interest rates and fees. You may find higher rates and lower fees at a credit union.

Fee, Not Free

The price of many basic banking services has been rising and more increases are expected this year. Industry averages:

	2011	2000	
Using another bank's ATM[1]	$1.63	$1.47	⬆ 16 cents
Overdraft fees[1]	$29.26	$24.87	⬆ $4.39
Interest-bearing checking account[2]	$10.06	$10.81	⬇ 75 cents
Regular checking[2]	$9.04	$6.81	⬆ $2.23

[1]Per transaction fee   [2]Monthly fee   Source: Informa Research Services

LU 4–1   PRACTICE QUIZ

Complete this **Practice Quiz** to see how you are doing.

Complete the following check and check stub for Long Company. Note the $9,500.60 balance brought forward on check stub No. 113. You must make a $690.60 deposit on May 3. Sign the check for Roland Small.

Date	Check no.	Amount	Payable to	For
June 5, 2013	113	$83.76	Angel Corporation	Rent

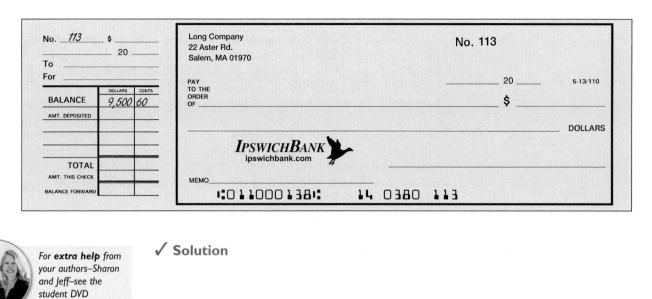

✓ **Solution**

*For **extra help** from your authors–Sharon and Jeff–see the student DVD*

LU 4–1a EXTRA PRACTICE QUIZ WITH WORKED-OUT SOLUTIONS

Need more practice? Try this **Extra Practice Quiz** (check figures in the Interactive Chapter Organizer, p. 103). Worked-out Solutions can be found in Appendix B at end of text.

Complete the following check and stub for Long Company. Note the $10,800.80 balance brought forward on check stub No. 113. You must make an $812.88 deposit on May 3. Sign the check for Roland Small.

Date	Check no.	Amount	Payable to	For
July 8, 2013	113	$79.88	Lowe Corp.	Advertising

Learning Unit 4–2: Bank Statement and Reconciliation Process; Latest Trends in Mobile Banking

LO 1

Trends in Banking Industry

As shown in the chapter opener, more and more people and businesses are using smartphone apps from lenders to do their banking transactions. In the *Wall Street Journal* clip "Need to Bank? Try Phoning It In," we see the latest trend in **mobile banking.** Also, note the other *Wall Street Journal* clip, which shows the recent amount of online banking accounts, the number of bank website visitors, and the penalty for using a teller if a person is signed up as an e-banker.

The rest of this learning unit is divided into two sections: (1) bank statement and reconciliation process, and (2) latest trends in mobile banking. The bank statement discussion will teach you why it was important for Gracie's Natural Superstore to reconcile its checkbook balance with the balance reported on its bank balance. Note that you can also use this reconciliation process in reconciling your personal checking account to avoid the expensive error of an overdrawn account.

Need to Bank? Try Phoning It In.

By Javier Espinoza

Small-business owners are starting to do their banking on the go.

A growing number of entrepreneurs are tapping into smartphone apps from lenders that let them do a range of jobs, from checking their balances and paying bills to depositing checks.

29.7 Million	**24.3 Million**	**$8.95**
Active online banking accounts, more than half of which use bill-paying services.	Unique visitors to the bank's site during August, most among U.S. banks.	Monthly charge to users of Bank of America's eBanking service who visit a teller.

LO 2

Bank Statement and Reconciliation Process

Each month, Ipswich Bank sends Gracie's Natural Superstore a **bank statement** (Figure 4.4, p. 97). We are interested in the following:

1. Beginning bank balance.
2. Total of all the account increases. Each time the bank increases the account amount, it *credits* the account.
3. Total of all account decreases. Each time the bank decreases the account amount, it *debits* the account.
4. Final ending balance.

Due to differences in timing, the bank balance on the bank statement frequently does not match the customer's checkbook balance. Also, the bank statement can show transactions that have not been entered in the customer's checkbook. Figure 4.5, page 97, tells you what to look for when comparing a checkbook balance with a bank balance.

FIGURE   4.4

Bank statement

FIGURE   4.4

Bank statement

Ipswich Online Banking

Online Banking-Windows Internet Explorer			

https//www.onlinebanking.com

File Edit View Favorites Tools Help

Ipswich Online Banking

Privacy   Security   Sign off

Ipswich Online Banking

Last Sign On: Thursday, March 8, 2013 at 11: 32 a.m

My Accounts   Transfer Funds

Ipswich Bank
1 Pleasant St.
Bartlett, NH 01835

Account Statement

Gracie's Natural Superstore
80 Garfield St.
Bartlett, NH 01835

Checking Account: 881900662

Checking Account Summary as of 3/31/13

Beginning Balance	Total Deposits	Total Withdrawals	Service Charge	Ending Balance
$13,112.24	$8,705.28	$9,926.00	$28.50	$11,863.02

Checking Account Transactions

Deposits	Date	Amount
Deposit	3/05	2,000.00
Deposit	3/05	224.00
Deposit	3/09	389.20
EFT leasing: Bakery dept.	3/18	1,808.06
EFT leasing: Meat dept.	3/27	4,228.00
Interest	3/31	56.02

Charges	Date	Amount
Service charge: Check printing	3/31	28.50
EFT: Health insurance	3/21	722.00
NSF	3/21	104.00

Checks			Daily Balance			
Number	Date	Amount	Date	Balance	Date	Balance
301	3/07	200.00	2/28	13,112.24	3/18	10,529.50
633	3/13	6,000.00	3/05	15,232.24	3/21	9,807.50
634	3/13	300.00	3/07	14,832.24	3/28	14,035.50
635	3/11	200.00	3/09	15,221.44	3/31	11,863.02
636	3/18	200.00	3/11	15,021.44		
637	3/31	2,200.00	3/13	8,721.44		

FIGURE   4.5

Reconciling checkbook with
bank statement

Checkbook balance		Bank balance
+ EFT (electronic funds transfer)	− NSF check	+ Deposits in transit
+ Interest earned	− Online fees	− Outstanding checks
+ Notes collected	− Automatic payments*	± Bank errors
+ Direct deposits	− Overdrafts†	
− ATM withdrawals	− Service charges	
− Automatic withdrawals	− Stop payments‡	
	± Book errors§	

*Preauthorized payments for utility bills, mortgage payments, insurance, etc.

†**Overdrafts** occur when the customer has no overdraft protection and a check bounces back to the company or person who received the check because the customer has written a check without enough money in the bank to pay for it.

‡A stop payment is issued when the writer of the check does not want the receiver to cash the check.

§If a $60 check is recorded at $50, the checkbook balance must be decreased by $10.

Gracie's Natural Superstore is planning to offer to its employees the option of depositing their checks directly into each employee's checking account. This is accomplished through the **electronic funds transfer (EFT)**—a computerized operation that electronically transfers funds among parties without the use of paper checks. Gracie's, who sublets space in the store, receives rental payments by EFT. Gracie's also has the bank pay the store's health insurance premiums by EFT.

LO 3

To reconcile the difference between the amount on the bank statement and in the checkbook, the customer should complete a **bank reconciliation.** Today, many companies and home computer owners are using software such as Quicken and QuickBooks to complete their bank reconciliation. Also, we have mentioned the increased use of **banking apps** available to customers. However, you should understand the following steps for manually reconciling a bank statement.

FOR BETTER OR WORSE © 2010 Lynn Johnston Productions. Dist. by Universal Uclick. Reprinted with permission. All rights reserved.

RECONCILING A BANK STATEMENT

Step 1. Identify the outstanding checks (checks written but not yet processed by the bank). You can use the ✓ column in the check register (Figure 4.6) to check the canceled checks listed in the bank statement against the checks you wrote in the check register. The unchecked checks are the outstanding checks.

Step 2. Identify the deposits in transit (deposits made but not yet processed by the bank), using the same method in Step 1.

Step 3. Analyze the bank statement for transactions not recorded in the check stubs or check registers (like EFT).

Step 4. Check for recording errors in checks written, in deposits made, or in subtraction and addition.

Step 5. Compare the adjusted balances of the checkbook and the bank statement. If the balances are not the same, repeat Steps 1–4.

Molly uses a check register (Figure 4.6, p. 99) to keep a record of Gracie's checks and deposits. By looking at Gracie's check register, you can see how to complete Steps 1 and 2 above. The explanation that follows for the first four bank statement reconciliation steps will help you understand the procedure.

Step 1. Identify Outstanding Checks   **Outstanding checks** are checks that Gracie's Natural Superstore has written but Ipswich Bank has not yet recorded for payment when it sends out the bank statement. Gracie's treasurer identifies the following checks written on 3/31 as outstanding:

No. 638	$572.00
No. 639	638.94
No. 640	166.00
No. 641	406.28
No. 642	917.06

FIGURE	4.6

Gracie's Natural Superstore check register

		RECORD ALL CHARGES OR CREDITS THAT AFFECT YOUR ACCOUNT						
NUMBER	DATE 2013	DESCRIPTION OF TRANSACTION	PAYMENT/DEBIT (−)	√	FEE (IF ANY) (−)	DEPOSIT/CREDIT (+)	\$ BALANCE 12,912	24
	3/04	Deposit				2,000 00	+ 2,000	00
							14,912	24
	3/04	Deposit				224 00	+ 224	00
							15,136	24
633	3/08	Staples Company	6,000 00	√			− 6,000	00
							9,136	24
634	3/09	Health Foods Inc.	1,020 00	√			− 1,020	00
							8,116	24
	3/09	Deposit				389 20	+ 389	20
							8,505	44
635	3/10	Liberty Insurance	200 00	√			− 200	00
							8,305	44
636	3/18	Ryan Press	200 00	√			− 200	00
							8,105	44
637	3/29	Logan Advertising	2,200 00	√			− 2,200	00
							5,905	44
	3/30	Deposit				3,383 26	+ 3,383	26
							9,288	70
638	3/31	Sears Roebuck	572 00				− 572	00
							8,716	70
639	3/31	Flynn Company	638 94				− 638	94
							8,077	76
640	3/31	Lynn's Farm	166 00				− 166	00
							7,911	76
641	3/31	Ron's Wholesale	406 28				− 406	28
							7,505	48
642	3/31	Grocery Natural, Inc.	917 06				− 917	06
							\$6,588	42

REMEMBER TO RECORD AUTOMATIC PAYMENTS/DEPOSITS ON DATE AUTHORIZED.

Step 2. Identify Deposits in Transit   **Deposits in transit** are deposits that did not reach Ipswich Bank by the time the bank prepared the bank statement. The March 30 deposit of $3,383.26 did not reach Ipswich Bank by the bank statement date. You can see this by comparing the company's bank statement with its check register.

Step 3. Analyze Bank Statement for Transactions Not Recorded in Check Stubs or Check Register   The bank statement of Gracie's Natural Superstore (Figure 4.4, p. 97) begins with the deposits, or increases, made to Gracie's bank account. Increases to accounts are known as credits. These are the result of a **credit memo (CM).** Gracie's received the following increases or credits in March:

1. *EFT leasing:* $1,808.06 and $4,228.00.   Each month the bakery and meat departments pay for space they lease in the store.
2. *Interest credited:* $56.02.   Gracie's has a checking account that pays interest; the account has earned $56.02.

When Gracie's has charges against its bank account, the bank decreases, or debits, Gracie's account for these charges. Banks usually inform customers of a debit transaction by a **debit memo (DM).** The following items will result in debits to Gracie's account:

1. *Service charge:* $28.50.   The bank charged $28.50 for printing Gracie's checks.
2. *EFT payment:* $722.   The bank made a health insurance payment for Gracie's.
3. *NSF check:* $104.   One of Gracie's customers wrote Gracie's a check for $104. Gracie's deposited the check, but the check bounced for **nonsufficient funds (NSF).** Thus, Gracie's has $104 less than it figured.

Step 4. Check for Recording Errors   The treasurer of Gracie's Natural Superstore, Molly Kate, recorded check No. 634 for the wrong amount—$1,020 (see the check register). The bank statement showed that check No. 634 cleared for $300. To reconcile Gracie's checkbook balance with the bank balance, Gracie's must add $720 to its checkbook balance. Neglecting to record a deposit also results in an error in the company's checkbook balance. As you can see, reconciling the bank's balance with a checkbook balance is a necessary part of business and personal finance.

Step 5. Completing the Bank Reconciliation   Now we can complete the bank reconciliation on the back side of the bank statement as shown in Figure 4.7. This form is usually on the back of a bank statement. If necessary, however, the person reconciling the bank statement can construct a bank reconciliation form similar to Figure 4.8 (p. 101).

FIGURE   4.7

Reconciliation process

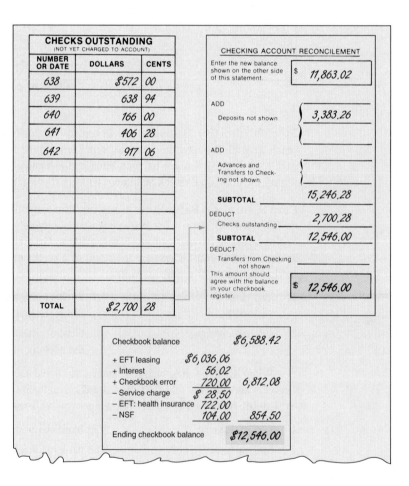

FIGURE **4.8**

Bank reconciliation

GRACIE'S NATURAL SUPERSTORE			
Bank Reconciliation as of March 31, 2013			
Checkbook balance		**Bank balance**	
Gracie's checkbook balance	$6,588.42	Bank balance	$11,863.02
Add:		Add:	
EFT leasing: Bakery dept.	$1,808.06	Deposit in transit, 3/30	3,383.26
EFT leasing: Meat dept.	4,228.00		$15,246.28
Interest	56.02		
Error: Overstated check No. 634	720.00 $ 6,812.08		
	$13,400.50		
Deduct:		Deduct:	
Service charge	$ 28.50	Outstanding checks:	
NSF check	104.00	No. 638	$572.00
EFT health insurance payment	722.00 854.50	No. 639	638.94
		No. 640	166.00
		No. 641	406.28
		No. 642	917.06 2,700.28
Reconciled balance	$12,546.00	Reconciled balance	$12,546.00

LO 4

Trends in Mobile Banking

The hottest trend in banking is the use of bank apps. For example, JPMorgan Chase & Co. offers customers a free app to use with an iPad, iPhone, Android, Blackberry, or Kindle.

MONEY tips

Always review your monthly bank statement to ensure there are no errors. The earlier you catch an error, the easier it is to remedy.

www.chase.com

LU 4–2 PRACTICE QUIZ

Complete this **Practice Quiz** to see how you are doing.

Rosa Garcia received her February 3, 2013, bank statement showing a balance of $212.80. Rosa's checkbook has a balance of $929.15. The bank statement showed that Rosa had an ATM fee of $12.00 and a deposited check returned fee of $20.00. Rosa earned interest of $1.05. She had three outstanding checks: No. 300, $18.20; No. 302, $38.40; and No. 303, $68.12. A deposit for $810.12 was not on her bank statement. Prepare Rosa Garcia's bank reconciliation.

*For **extra help** from your authors–Sharon and Jeff–see the student DVD*

You Tube™

✓ Solution

ROSA GARCIA					
Bank Reconciliation as of February 3, 2013					
Checkbook balance			**Bank balance**		
Rosa's checkbook balance		$929.15	Bank balance		$ 212.80
Add:			Add:		
Interest		1.05	Deposit in transit		810.12
		$930.20			$1,022.92
Deduct:			Deduct:		
Deposited check returned fee	$20.00		Outstanding checks:		
			No. 300	$18.20	
ATM	12.00	32.00	No. 302	38.40	
			No. 303	68.12	124.72
Reconciled balance		$898.20	Reconciled balance		$ 898.20

LU 4–2a EXTRA PRACTICE QUIZ WITH WORKED-OUT SOLUTIONS

Need more practice? Try this **Extra Practice Quiz** (check figures in the Interactive Chapter Organizer, p. 103). Worked-out Solutions can be found in Appendix B at end of text.

Earl Miller received his March 8, 2013, bank statement, which had a $300.10 balance. Earl's checkbook has a $1,200.10 balance. The bank statement showed a $15.00 ATM fee and a $30.00 deposited check returned fee. Earl earned $24.06 interest. He had three outstanding checks: No. 300, $22.88; No. 302, $15.90; and No. 303, $282.66. A deposit for $1,200.50 was not on his bank statement. Prepare Earl's bank reconciliation.

INTERACTIVE CHAPTER ORGANIZER

Topic/procedure/formula	Examples	You try it*
Types of endorsements, p. 94 *Blank:* Not safe; can be further endorsed.	Jones Co. 21-333-9	**Write a sample of a blank, full, and restrictive endorsement.** Use Pete Co. Acct. # 24-111-9
Full: Only person or company named in endorsement can transfer check to someone else.	Pay to the order of Regan Bank Jones Co. 21-333-9	
Restrictive: Check must be deposited. Limits any further negotiation of the check.	Pay to the order of Regan Bank. For deposit only. Jones Co. 21-333-9	

(continues)

INTERACTIVE CHAPTER ORGANIZER

Topic/procedure/formula	Examples	You try it*

Bank reconciliation, p. 98
 	
Checkbook balance
+ EFT (electronic funds transfer)
+ Interest earned
+ Notes collected
+ Direct deposits
− ATM withdrawals
− NSF check
− Online fees
− Automatic withdrawals
− Overdrafts
− Service charges
− Stop payments
± Book errors (see note, below)
CM—adds to balance
DM—deducts from balance
 	
Bank balance
+ Deposits in transit
− Outstanding checks
± Bank errors
	Checkbook balance
	Balance $800
	  − NSF 40
	  $760
	  − Service charge 4
	  $756
	
	Bank balance
	Balance $ 632
	  + Deposits in transit 416
	  $1,048
	  − Outstanding checks 292
	  $ 756
		Calculate ending checkbook balance
		1. Beg. checkbook bal.: $300
		2. NSF: $50
		3. Deposit in transit: $100
		4. Outstanding check: $60
		5. ATM service charge: $20

KEY TERMS	Automatic teller machine (ATM), p. 91 Bank reconciliation, p. 98 Bank statement, p. 96 Banking apps, p. 98 Blank endorsement, p. 94 Check, p. 92 Check register, p. 93 Check stub, p. 93 Credit memo (CM), p. 99	Debit card, p. 91 Debit memo (DM), p. 99 Deposit slip, p. 92 Deposits in transit, p. 99 Draft, p. 92 Drawee, p. 93 Drawer, p. 93 Electronic funds transfer (EFT), p. 98 Endorse, p. 94 Full endorsement, p. 94 Mobile banking, p. 96 Nonsufficient funds (NSF), p. 99 Outstanding checks, p. 98 Overdrafts, p. 97 Payee, p. 93 Restrictive endorsement, p. 94 Signature card, p. 92
Check Figures for Extra Practice Quizzes with Page References. (Worked-out Solutions in Appendix B.)	LU 4–1a (p. 95) Ending Balance Forward $11,533.80	LU 4–2a (p. 102) Reconciled Balance $1,179.16

Note: If a $60 check is recorded as $50, we must decrease checkbook balance by $10.

*Worked-out solutions are in Appendix B.

Critical Thinking Discussion Questions with Chapter Concept Check

1. Explain the structure of a check. The trend in bank statements is not to return the canceled checks. Do you think this is fair?

2. List the three types of endorsements. Endorsements are limited to the top $1\frac{1}{2}$ inches of the trailing edge on the back left side of your check. Why do you think the Federal Reserve made this regulation?

3. List the steps in reconciling a bank statement. Today, many banks charge a monthly fee for certain types of checking accounts. Do you think all checking accounts should be free? Please explain.

4. What are some of the trends in mobile banking? Will we become a cashless society in which all transactions are made with some type of credit card?

5. What do you think of the government's intervention in trying to bail out banks? Should banks be allowed to fail?

6. **Chapter Concept Check.** Create your own company and provide needed data to prepare a bank reconciliation. Then go to a bank website and explain how you would use the bank's app versus the manual system of banking.

Classroom Notes

END-OF-CHAPTER PROBLEMS McGraw Hill connect plus+ www.mhhe.com/slater11e

Check figures for odd-numbered problems in Appendix C. Name _____ Date _____

DRILL PROBLEMS

4–1. Fill out the check register that follows with this information: *LU 4-1(1)*

2013

July 7	Check No. 482 ✓	AOL	$143.50
15	Check No. 483 ✓	Staples	66.10
19	Deposit ✓		800.00
20	Check No. 484 ✓	Sprint	451.88
24	Check No. 485 ✓	Krispy Kreme	319.24
29	Deposit ✓		400.30

		RECORD ALL CHARGES OR CREDITS THAT AFFECT YOUR ACCOUNT					
NUMBER	DATE 2013	DESCRIPTION OF TRANSACTION	PAYMENT/DEBIT (−)	√ FEE (IF ANY) (−)	DEPOSIT/CREDIT (+)	$ BALANCE 4,500 75	
482	7-7	AOL	$143 50 ✓	$	$	4357 25	
483	7-15	Staples	66 10			4291 15	
	7-19	Deposit			800 00	5091 15	
484	7-20	Sprint	451 88			4639 27	
485	7-24	Krispy Kreme	319 24 ✓			4320 03	
	7-29	Deposit			400 30	4720 33	

(handwritten notes to right of table:) 4357 (−14350) (4357.25) need to Show the Adjustment

4–2. November 1, 2013, Payroll.com, an Internet company, has a $10,481.88 checkbook balance. Record the following transactions for Payroll.com by completing the two checks and check stubs provided. Sign the checks Garth Scholten, controller. *LU 4-1(2)*

a. November 8, 2013, deposited $688.10

b. November 8, check No. 190 payable to Staples for office supplies—$766.88 ✓

c. November 15, check No. 191 payable to Best Buy for computer equipment—$3,815.99.

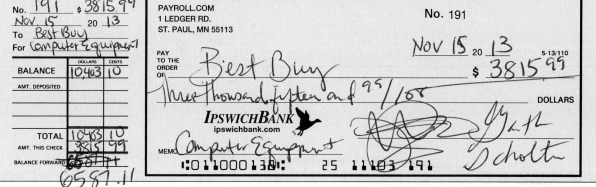

4–3. Using the check register in Problem 4–1 and the following bank statement, prepare a bank reconciliation for Lee.com. *LU 4-2(3)*

BANK STATEMENT			
Date	Checks	Deposits	Balance
7/1 balance			$4,500.75
7/18	$143.50		4,357.25
7/19		$ 800.00	5,157.25
7/26	319.24		4,838.01
7/30	15.00 SC		4,823.01

WORD PROBLEMS

4–4. The World Bank forecasts growth of world trade to be 4.7% in 2012, down from 12.4% in 2010. This change has caused
eXcel Peru's Apple Blossom Florist to analyze its current financial situation, beginning with reconciling its accounts. Apple Blossom received its bank statement showing a balance of $8,788. Its checkbook balance is $15,252. Deposits in transit are $3,450 and $6,521. There is a service charge of $45 and interest earned of $3. Notes collected total $1,575. Outstanding checks are No. 1021 for $1,260 and No. 1022 for $714. All numbers are in U.S. dollars. Help Apple Blossom Florist reconcile its balances. *LU 4-2(3)*

4–5. The U.S. Chamber of Commerce provides a free monthly bank reconciliation template at business.uschamber.com/tools/bankre_m.asp. Annie Moats just received her bank statement notice online. She wants to reconcile her checking account with her bank statement and has chosen to reconcile her accounts manually. Her checkbook shows a balance of $698. Her bank statement reflects a balance of $1,348. Checks outstanding are No. 2146, $25; No. 2148, $58; No. 2152, $198; and No. 2153, $464. Deposits in transit are $100 and $50. There is a $15 service charge and $5 ATM charge in addition to notes collected of $50 and $25. Reconcile Annie's balances. *LU 4-2(3)*

4–6. A local bank began charging $2.50 each month for returning canceled checks. The bank also has an $8.00 "maintenance" fee if a checking account slips below $750. Donna Sands likes to have copies of her canceled checks for preparing her income tax returns. She has received her bank statement with a balance of $535.85. Donna received $2.68 in interest and has been charged for the canceled checks and the maintenance fee. The following checks were outstanding: No. 94, $121.16; No. 96, $106.30; No. 98, $210.12; and No. 99, $64.84. A deposit of $765.69 was not recorded on Donna's bank statement. Her checkbook shows a balance of $806.94. Prepare Donna's bank reconciliation. *LU 4-2(3)*

4–7. Ben Luna received his bank statement with a $27.04 fee for a bounced check (NSF). He has an $815.75 monthly mortgage payment paid through his bank. There was also a $3.00 teller fee and a check printing fee of $3.50. His ATM card fee was $6.40. There was also a $530.50 deposit in transit. The bank shows a balance of $119.17. The bank paid Ben $1.23 in interest. Ben's checkbook shows a balance of $1,395.28. Check No. 234 for $80.30 and check No. 235 for $28.55 were outstanding. Prepare Ben's bank reconciliation. *LU 4-2(3)*

4–8. Kameron Gibson's bank statement showed a balance of $717.72. Kameron's checkbook had a balance of $209.50. Check No. 104 for $110.07 and check No. 105 for $15.55 were outstanding. A $620.50 deposit was not on the statement. He has his payroll check electronically deposited to his checking account—the payroll check was for $1,025.10. There was also a $4 teller fee and an $18 service charge. Prepare Kameron Gibson's bank reconciliation. *LU 4-2(3)*

4–9. Banks are finding more ways to charge fees, such as a $25 overdraft fee. Sue McVickers has an account in Fayetteville; she has received her bank statement with this $25 charge. Also, she was charged a $6.50 service fee; however, the good news is she earned $5.15 interest. Her bank statement's balance was $315.65, but it did not show the $1,215.15 deposit she had made. Sue's checkbook balance shows $604.30. The following checks have not cleared: No. 250, $603.15; No. 253, $218.90; and No. 254, $130.80. Prepare Sue's bank reconciliation. *LU 4-2(3)*

4–10. Carol Stokke receives her April 6 bank statement showing a balance of $859.75; her checkbook balance is $954.25. The bank statement shows an ATM charge of $25.00, NSF fee of $27.00, earned interest of $2.75, and Carol's $630.15 refund check, which was processed by the IRS and deposited to her account. Carol has two checks that have not cleared—No. 115 for $521.15 and No. 116 for $205.50. There is also a deposit in transit for $1,402.05. Prepare Carol's bank reconciliation. *LU 4-2(3)*

4–11. Lowell Bank reported the following checking account fees: $2 to see a real-live teller, $20 to process a bounced check, and $1 to $3 if you need an original check to prove you paid a bill or made a charitable contribution. This past month you had to transact business through a teller six times—a total $12 cost to you. Your bank statement shows a $305.33 balance; your checkbook shows a $1,009.76 balance. You received $1.10 in interest. An $801.15 deposit was not recorded on your statement. The following checks were outstanding: No. 413, $28.30; No. 414, $18.60; and No. 418, $60.72. Prepare your bank reconciliation. *LU 4-2(3)*

4–12. According to New York City's public records, a single-family town house at 247 Central Park West with a 60-foot lap pool,
eXcel fitness/massage area, and media room sold for $22.375 million on January 13, 2012. If you were the owner, reconcile your checkbook and bank balance according to the following: bank statement balance, $18,769; checkbook balance, $22,385,015; interest earned, $3,948; deposits in transit, $100,656 and $22,375,000; ATM card fees, $150; outstanding checks— No. 10189, $55,678; No. 10192, $15,287; No. 10193, $22,350; and No. 10194, $12,297. *LU 4-2(3)*

4–13. Labeled as one of the top 20 best countries to open a small business in, Thailand offers many business strengths as noted by "Doing Business in Thailand: 2011 Country Commercial Guide for U.S. Companies." A restaurant on Koh Phi Phi, Ton Sai Seafood, wants to conduct a bank reconciliation with the following information in U.S. dollars: bank statement balance, $12,568; checkbook balance, $6,485; earned interest, $4; deposits in transit, $2,000; outstanding checks—No. 255, $5,500; No. 261, $2,500; No. 262, $79. Prepare the bank reconciliation.   *LU 4-2(3)*

CHALLENGE PROBLEMS

4–14. Carolyn Crosswell, who banks in New Jersey, wants to balance her checkbook, which shows a balance of $985.20. The bank shows a balance of $1,430.33. The following transactions occurred: $135.20 automatic withdrawal to the gas company, $6.50 ATM fee, $8.00 service fee, and $1,030.05 direct deposit from the IRS. Carolyn used her debit card five times and was charged 45 cents for each transaction; she was also charged $3.50 for check printing. A $931.08 deposit was not shown on her bank statement. The following checks were outstanding: No. 235, $158.20; No. 237, $184.13; No. 238, $118.12; and No. 239, $38.83. Carolyn received $2.33 interest. Prepare Carolyn's bank reconciliation.   *LU 4-2(3)*

4–15. Melissa Jackson, bookkeeper for Kinko Company, cannot prepare a bank reconciliation. From the following facts, can you eXcel help her complete the June 30, 2013, reconciliation? The bank statement showed a $2,955.82 balance. Melissa's checkbook showed a $3,301.82 balance.

Melissa placed a $510.19 deposit in the bank's night depository on June 30. The deposit did not appear on the bank statement. The bank included two DMs and one CM with the returned checks: $690.65 DM for NSF check, $8.50 DM for service charges, and $400.00 CM (less $10 collection fee) for collecting a $400.00 non-interest-bearing note. Check No. 811 for $110.94 and check No. 912 for $82.50, both written and recorded on June 28, were not with the returned checks. The bookkeeper had correctly written check No. 884, $1,000, for a new cash register, but she recorded the check as $1,069. The May bank reconciliation showed check No. 748 for $210.90 and check No. 710 for $195.80 outstanding on April 30. The June bank statement included check No. 710 but not check No. 748. *LU 4-2(3)*

 SUMMARY PRACTICE TEST You Tube™

Do you need help? The DVD has step-by-step worked-out solutions.

1. Walgreens has a $12,925.55 beginning checkbook balance. Record the following transactions in the check stubs provided. *(p. 92) LU 4-1(2)*
   a. November 4, 2013, check No. 180 payable to Ace Medical Corporation, $1,700.88 for drugs.
   b. $5,250 deposit—November 24.
   c. November 24, 2013, check No. 181 payable to John's Wholesale, $825.55 merchandise.

| No. _____ $ _____ |
| _____ 20 ____ |
| To _____ |
| For _____ |

	DOLLARS	CENTS
BALANCE		
AMT. DEPOSITED		
TOTAL		
AMT. THIS CHECK		
BALANCE FORWARD		

| No. _____ $ _____ |
| _____ 20 ____ |
| To _____ |
| For _____ |

	DOLLARS	CENTS
BALANCE		
AMT. DEPOSITED		
TOTAL		
AMT. THIS CHECK		
BALANCE FORWARD		

2. On April 1, 2013, Lester Company received a bank statement that showed a $8,950 balance. Lester showed an $8,000 checking account balance. The bank did not return check No. 115 for $750 or check No. 118 for $370. A $900 deposit made on March 31 was in transit. The bank charged Lester $20 for check printing and $250 for NSF checks. The bank also collected a $1,400 note for Lester. Lester forgot to record a $400 withdrawal at the ATM. Prepare a bank reconciliation. *(p. 98)   LU 4-2(3)*

3. Felix Babic banks at Role Federal Bank. Today he received his March 31, 2013, bank statement showing a $762.80 balance. Felix's checkbook shows a balance of $799.80. The following checks have not cleared the bank: No. 140, $130.55; No. 149, $66.80; and No. 161, $102.90. Felix made a $820.15 deposit that is not shown on the bank statement. He has his $617.30 monthly mortgage payment paid through the bank. His $1,100.20 IRS refund check was mailed to his bank. Prepare Felix Babic's bank reconciliation. *(p. 98)   LU 4-2(3)*

4. On June 30, 2013, Wally Company's bank statement showed a $7,500.10 bank balance. Wally has a beginning check-book balance of $9,800.00. The bank statement also showed that it collected a $1,200.50 note for the company. A $4,500.10 June 30 deposit was in transit. Check No. 119 for $650.20 and check No. 130 for $381.50 are outstanding. Wally's bank charges $.40 cents per check. This month, 80 checks were processed. Prepare a reconciled statement. *(p. 98)* *LU 4-2(3)*

SURF TO SAVE

PROBLEM 1
Bank costs

Go to http://www.bankrate.com/brm/rate/bank_home.asp. Select the Checking/Savings tab. Search for a "Local, Interest Checking Account in a State and City near where you live." Select an interest-bearing account. Which account requires the highest average minimum balance to avoid monthly service fees? Which account requires the lowest average minimum balance to avoid monthly service fees? Which account would you select for your personal checking account from this list?

Discussion Questions

1. What are the most important criteria for you in selecting a checking account? Why?

2. Discuss the pros and cons of using a local versus an Internet-based checking account.

PROBLEM 2
Checkbook vs. bank statement balance

Go to http://googolplex.cuna.org/12433/cnote/article.php?doc_id=2502. Use the Checking/Debit Account Calculator and "Go Figure" based on the following: your register balance, $525.89; interest earnings, $1.23; bank fees, $8.99; statement balance, $698.00; deposits in transit, $150.00; withdrawals in transit, $250.00.

Discussion Questions

1. Based on the difference you found in the adjusted balances, where would you begin to look to determine what is causing this discrepancy?

2. How could this tool be useful for your own checking account?

PROBLEM 3
Online vs. on-site

Go to http://www.bankrate.com/finance/checking/online-banking-still-favorable.aspx. Read the article about online banking. List the pros and cons of online banking compared to a traditional checking account. Which account type do you feel would be the best fit for a typical banking customer? Which type of account would be the best for you, and why?

Discussion Questions

1. In the future, will we see more or less online banking? Why?

2. Why do you feel these differences exist between online and traditional checking accounts?

PROBLEM 4
What's in your checkbook?

Go to http://www.cpasitesolutions.com/content/calcs/CheckBook.html. Calculate your checkbook balance for the month if you started out with $561.00 and wrote four checks for $112.45, $100.00, $45.00, and $245.00, and made three deposits of $100.00, $55.00, and $200.00.

Discussion Questions

1. How often do you update your checkbook balance? Why?

2. Discuss some potential problems that could arise if your checkbook balance is not kept up to date.

MOBILE APPS

Easy Checkbook (Poetry Outdoors) Helps track purchases and balance a check register.

PocketMoney (Catamount Software) Tracks finances on multiple devices and analyzes spending with a variety of reporting functions.

INTERNET PROJECTS

See text website
www.mhhe.com/slater11e_sse_ch04

Credit Unions Anyone Can Join

Become a member and get a better deal on checking accounts, mortgages and car loans.

BY JOAN GOLDWASSER

CREDIT UNIONS OFFER THE same services that banks provide. But they tend to charge lower loan rates, pay higher yields on savings and "treat borrowers who are struggling more sympathetically," says Stephen Brobeck, executive director of the Consumer Federation of America. The rate on new-car loans at credit unions recently averaged 3.4%, or 1.5 percentage points less than at banks; the rate on gold and platinum credit cards was 9.8%, or about 1.4 percentage points lower.

A big reason for the friendlier terms is that credit unions are member-owned, not-for-profit institutions, so they are exempt from federal income taxes. You qualify for membership if you have a "common bond"—because of where you work, live, attend school or worship; because you belong to an affiliated association; or because a family member belongs.

To find a credit union near you, go to www .culookup.com or www .asmarterchoice.org. Or you can bank online at the credit unions below, which are open to anyone if you join the affiliated association (for more choices, go to kiplinger.com/links/ creditunions). Deposits are federally insured by the National Credit Union Administration up to $250,000 per account.

ALLIANT CREDIT UNION
www.alliantcreditunion.org
HOW TO JOIN: Contribute $10 to nonprofit Foster Care to Success and open a $5 savings account.

CHECKING: No monthly service fee or minimum balance. High Rate Checking option pays 0.90%. You have free access to more than 80,000 ATMs.

LOAN RATES: Fixed-rate 30-year mortgages at 4.25%. Loans for new and used cars are 1.99% for up to 72 months.

CONNEXUS CREDIT UNION
www.connexuscu.org
HOW TO JOIN: Make a one-time, $5 donation to the nonprofit Connexus Association and open a $5 savings account.

CHECKING: All three individual accounts have no minimum balance or monthly fees and entitle you to a 1% reduction on consumer loans. With Xtraordinary Checking, you earn 2% on balances up to $25,000 and are eligible for up to $25 a month in ATM rebates.

LOAN RATES: Fixed-rate 30-year mortgages at 4.25%. Auto loans range from 2.49% (36 months) to 5.99% (84 months).

LAKE MICHIGAN CREDIT UNION
www.lmcu.org
HOW TO JOIN: Donate $5 to the West Michigan Chapter of the ALS Association and open a $5 savings account.

CHECKING: Free Checking has no monthly fees but pays no interest. Max Checking pays 3% on balances up to $15,000 and refunds of up to $15 per month in ATM surcharges. Members have free access to 92 proprietary ATMs in Michigan.

LOAN RATES: Fixed-rate 30-year mortgages are as low as 3.9%. Auto loans for new and used cars run 2.99% for up to 63 months. ∎

BUSINESS MATH ISSUE

A credit union is always a better choice than a large bank.

1. List the key points of the article and information to support your position.
2. Write a group defense of your position using math calculations to support your view.

CHAPTER 5

Solving for the Unknown: A How-to Approach for Solving Equations

Study Challenges Old Weight-Loss Equation

BY KATHERINE HOBSON

There's new math out on how to calculate weight loss that may be disappointing to those relying on the old math.

Many people may remember an old—and apparently in-correct—piece of dietary advice: eat 500 fewer calories per day, and in a week you'll have a deficit of 3,500 calories and will thus lose a pound.

BEST OF THE HEALTH BLOG

That calculation, however, assumes that if "I cut 500 calories from my diet … the number of calories I'm burning will stay the same," says Kevin Hall, a physiologist at the National Institute of Diabetes and Digestive and Kidney Diseases. That's not so, however, because metabolism "slows down right away, and continues to slow as body weight is lost," Dr. Hall says.

So if people use that math, they are not going to lose as much weight as they think they should.

Dr. Hall and colleagues just published a paper in the Lancet—part of the journal's obesity series—that provides an alternative model. It is based on data from controlled feeding studies and captures that metabolic slowdown as well as other effects, such as the fact that the same amount and intensity of exercise will burn off fewer calories as a person loses weight.

It predicts that for a typical overweight adult, every reduction of 10 calories per day will lead to a weight loss not of about a pound a year, but only about half a pound. The next half-pound will take about two more years to lose.

The authors note this casts doubt on public-health messages about making small changes (like scrapping a soda a day) in order to reap big weight-loss gains over time. Using their model to predict, say, the effects of a soda tax produces a much more modest impact on obesity.

Eric Ravussin, a professor at Pennington Biomedical Research Center and director of the institution's Nutrition and Obesity Research Center, says this paper is important because many physicians are still advising their patients to rely on the cut-500-calories-per-day-lose-a-pound-a-week model. (He was a reviewer on this paper and has collaborated with Dr. Hall.)

The website for the NIDDK features a Web-based tool that allows you to tailor the rate at which you want to lose weight based on how much you're willing to change your physical activity in the short and long term.

LU 5–1: Solving Equations for the Unknown

1. Explain the basic procedures used to solve equations for the unknown *(pp. 118–119)*.

2. List the five rules and the mechanical steps used to solve for the unknown in seven situations; know how to check the answers *(pp. 119–122)*.

LU 5–2: Solving Word Problems for the Unknown

1. List the steps for solving word problems *(p. 123)*.

2. Complete blueprint aids to solve word problems; check the solutions *(pp. 124–126)*.

VOCABULARY PREVIEW

Here are key terms in this chapter. After completing the chapter, if you know the term, place a checkmark in the parentheses. If you don't know the term, look it up and put the page number where it can be found.

Constants ( ) Equation ( ) Expression ( ) Formula ( ) Knowns ( ) Unknown ( ) Variables ( )

Did you know that Google handles nearly two-thirds of the world's web searches? The following *Wall Street Journal* clip, "Google Revamps To Fight Cheaters," shows how Google uses math formulas to weed out "low-quality" sites.

Learning Unit 5–1 explains how you can solve for unknowns in equations. In Learning Unit 5–2 you learn how to solve for unknowns in word problems. When you complete these learning units, you will not have to memorize as many formulas to solve business and personal math applications. With the increasing use of computer software, a basic working knowledge of solving for the unknown has become necessary.

GLOBAL

© AP Photo/Paul Sakuma

Google Revamps To Fight Cheaters

By Amir Efrati

Google Inc., long considered the gold standard of Internet search, is changing the secret formula it uses to rank Web pages as it struggles to combat websites that have been able to game its system.

The Internet giant, which handles nearly two-thirds of the world's Web searches, has been under fire recently over the quality of its results. Google said it changed its mathematical formula late Thursday in order to better weed out "low-quality" sites that offer users little value. Some such sites offer just enough content to appear in search results and lure users to pages loaded with advertisements.

Google generates billions of dollars from advertising linked to its search engine, whose influence as a front door to the world's online content and commerce continues to grow by the year. Google's power over the fortunes of so many other companies has made it a target of competitor complaints. It has also faced government investigations, including scrutiny by regulators in the U.S. and Europe.

The Silicon Valley company built its business on the strength of algorithms that yield speedy results. The company constantly refines those formulas, and sometimes takes manual action to penalize companies that it believes use tricks to artificially rise in search rankings. In recent weeks, it has cracked down on retailers **J.C. Penney** Co. and **Overstock.com** Inc.

Learning Unit 5–1: Solving Equations for the Unknown

LO 1

The Rose Smith letter below is based on a true story. Note how Rose states that the blueprint aids, the lesson on repetition, and the chapter organizers were important factors in the successful completion of her business math course.

Rose Smith
15 Locust Street
Lynn, MA 01915

Flowers.net
Decorating Service

Dear Professor Slater,

Thank you for helping me get through your Business Math class. When I first started, my math anxiety level was real high. I felt I had no head for numbers. When you told us we would be covering the chapter on solving equations, I'll never forget how I started to shake. I started to panic. I felt I could never solve a word problem. I thought I was having an algebra attack.

Now that it's over (90 on the chapter on unknowns), I'd like to tell you what worked for me so you might pass this on to other students. It was your blueprint aids. Drawing boxes helped me to think things out. They were a tool that helped me more clearly understand how to dissect each word problem. They didn't solve the problem for me, but gave me the direction I needed. Repetition was the key to my success. At first I got them all wrong but after the third time, things started to click. I felt more confident. Your chapter organizers at the end of the chapter were great. Thanks for your patience – your repetition breeds success – now students are asking me to help them solve a word problem. Can you believe it!

Best,

Rose

Rose Smith

Many of you are familiar with the terms *variables* and *constants*. If you are planning to prepare for your retirement by saving only what you can afford each year, your saving is a *variable;* if you plan to save the same amount each year, your saving is a *constant*. Now you can also say that you cannot buy clothes by size because of the many variables involved. This unit explains the importance of mathematical variables and constants when solving equations.

Basic Equation-Solving Procedures

In the chapter opener, the old weight-loss equation was challenged with a new equation based on metabolism. The definition of "equation" that follows may suggest to you what the new equation means.

Do you know the difference between a mathematical expression, equation, and formula? A mathematical **expression** is a meaningful combination of numbers and letters called *terms*. Operational signs (such as + or −) within the expression connect the terms to show a relationship between them. For example, $6 + 2$ and $6A − 4A$ are mathematical expressions. An **equation** is a mathematical statement with an equals sign showing that a mathematical expression on the left equals the mathematical expression on the right. An equation has an equals sign; an expression does not have an equals sign. A **formula** is an equation that expresses in symbols a general fact, rule, or principle. Formulas are shortcuts for expressing a word concept. For example, in Chapter 10 you will learn that the formula for simple interest is Interest (I) = Principal (P) × Rate (R) × Time (T). This means that when you see $I = P \times R \times T$, you recognize the simple interest formula. Now let's study basic equations.

As a mathematical statement of equality, equations show that two numbers or groups of numbers are equal. For example, $6 + 4 = 10$ shows the equality of an equation. Equations also use letters as symbols that represent one or more numbers. These symbols, usually a letter of the alphabet, are **variables** that stand for a number. We can use a variable even though we may not know what it represents. For example, $A + 2 = 6$. The variable A

represents the number or **unknown** (4 in this example) for which we are solving. We distinguish variables from numbers, which have a fixed value. Numbers such as 3 or −7 are **constants** or **knowns,** whereas *A* and 3*A* (this means 3 times the variable *A*) are variables. So we can now say that variables and constants are *terms of mathematical expressions*.

Usually in solving for the unknown, we place variable(s) on the left side of the equation and constants on the right. The following rules for variables and constants are important.

VARIABLES AND CONSTANTS RULES

1. If no number is in front of a letter, it is a 1: *B* = 1*B*; *C* = 1*C*.

2. If no sign is in front of a letter or number, it is a +: *C* = +*C*; 4 = +4.

You should be aware that in solving equations, the meaning of the symbols +, −, ×, and ÷ has not changed. However, some variations occur. For example, you can also write $A \times B$ (*A* times *B*) as $A \cdot B$, $A(B)$, or AB. Also, *A* divided by *B* is the same as A/B. Remember that to solve an equation, you must find a number that can replace the unknown in the equation and make it a true statement. Now let's take a moment to look at how we can change verbal statements into variables.

Assume Dick Hersh, an employee of Nike, is 50 years old. Let's assign Dick Hersh's changing age to the symbol *A*. The symbol *A* is a variable.

Verbal statement	Variable A (age)
Dick's age 8 years ago	$A - 8$
Dick's age 8 years from today	$A + 8$
Four times Dick's age	$4A$
One-fifth Dick's age	$A/5$

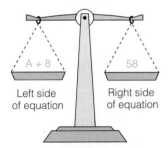

FIGURE 5.1

Equality in equations

A + 8 — Left side of equation

58 — Right side of equation

Dick's age in 8 years will equal 58.

To visualize how equations work, think of the old-fashioned balancing scale shown in Figure 5.1. The pole of the scale is the equals sign. The two sides of the equation are the two pans of the scale. In the left pan or left side of the equation, we have $A + 8$; in the right pan or right side of the equation, we have 58. To solve for the unknown (Dick's present age), we isolate or place the unknown (variable) on the left side and the numbers on the right. We will do this soon. For now, remember that to keep an equation (or scale) in balance, we must perform mathematical operations (addition, subtraction, multiplication, and division) to *both* sides of the equation.

SOLVING FOR THE UNKNOWN RULE

Whatever you do to one side of an equation, you must do to the other side.

How to Solve for Unknowns in Equations

This section presents seven drill situations and the rules that will guide you in solving for unknowns in these situations. We begin with two basic rules—the opposite process rule and the equation equality rule.

OPPOSITE PROCESS RULE

If an equation indicates a process such as addition, subtraction, multiplication, or division, solve for the unknown or variable by using the opposite process. For example, if the equation process is addition, solve for the unknown by using subtraction.

EQUATION EQUALITY RULE

You can add the same quantity or number to both sides of the equation and subtract the same quantity or number from both sides of the equation without affecting the equality of the equation. You can also divide or multiply both sides of the equation by the same quantity or number *(except zero)* without affecting the equality of the equation.

> To check your answer(s), substitute your answer(s) for the letter(s) in the equation. The sum of the left side should equal the sum of the right side.

Drill Situation 1: Subtracting Same Number from Both Sides of Equation

Example	Mechanical steps	Explanation
$A + 8 = 58$	$A + 8 = 58$	8 is subtracted from *both*
Dick's age A plus 8	$\quad\quad -8 \quad -8$	sides of equation to isolate
equals 58.	$A \quad\quad = \boxed{50}$	variable A on the left.
		Check
		$50 + 8 = 58$
		$58 = 58$

Note: Since the equation process used *addition*, we use the opposite process rule and solve for variable A with *subtraction*. We also use the equation equality rule when we subtract the same quantity from both sides of the equation.

Drill Situation 2: Adding Same Number to Both Sides of Equation

Example	Mechanical steps	Explanation
$B - 50 = 80$	$B - 50 = 80$	50 is added to *both* sides to
Some number B less 50	$\quad\quad +50 \quad +50$	isolate variable B on the left.
equals 80.	$B \quad\quad = \boxed{130}$	**Check**
		$130 - 50 = 80$
		$80 = 80$

Note: Since the equation process used *subtraction*, we use the opposite process rule and solve for variable B with *addition*. We also use the equation equality rule when we add the same quantity to both sides of the equation.

Drill Situation 3: Dividing Both Sides of Equation by Same Number

Example	Mechanical steps	Explanation
$7G = 35$	$7G = 35$	By dividing both sides by
Some number G times	$\dfrac{7G}{7} = \dfrac{35}{7}$	7, G equals 5.
7 equals 35.	$G = \boxed{5}$	**Check**
		$7(5) = 35$
		$35 = 35$

Note: Since the equation process used *multiplication*, we use the opposite process rule and solve for variable G with *division*. We also use the equation equality rule when we divide both sides of the equation by the same quantity.

Drill Situation 4: Multiplying Both Sides of Equation by Same Number

Example	Mechanical steps	Explanation
$\dfrac{V}{5} = 70$	$\dfrac{V}{5} = 70$	By multiplying both sides by
		5, V is equal to 350.
Some number V	$5\left(\dfrac{V}{5}\right) = 70(5)$	**Check**
divided by 5		$\dfrac{350}{5} = 70$
equals 70.	$V = \boxed{350}$	$70 = 70$

Note: Since the equation process used *division*, we use the opposite process rule and solve for variable V with *multiplication*. We also use the equation equality rule when we multiply both sides of the equation by the same quantity.

Drill Situation 5: Equation That Uses Subtraction and Multiplication to Solve for Unknown

MULTIPLE PROCESSES RULE
When solving for an unknown that involves more than one process, do the addition and subtraction before the multiplication and division.

Example	**Mechanical steps**	**Explanation**
$\dfrac{H}{4} + 2 = 5$		

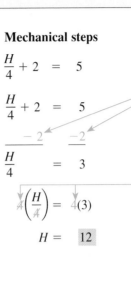

$$\dfrac{H}{4} + 2 = 5$$

$$\dfrac{H}{4} + 2 = 5$$

$$\underline{\quad -2 \qquad -2\quad}$$

$$\dfrac{H}{4} = 3$$

$$4\left(\dfrac{H}{4}\right) = 4(3)$$

$$H = \boxed{12}$$

When we divide unknown H by 4 and add the result to 2, the answer is 5.

1. Move constant to right side by subtracting 2 from both sides.
2. To isolate H, which is divided by 4, we do the opposite process and multiply 4 times *both* sides of the equation.

Check

$$\dfrac{12}{4} + 2 = 5$$
$$3 + 2 = 5$$
$$5 = 5$$

Drill Situation 6: Using Parentheses in Solving for Unknown

PARENTHESES RULE
When equations contain parentheses (which indicate grouping together), you solve for the unknown by first multiplying each item inside the parentheses by the number or letter just outside the parentheses. Then you continue to solve for the unknown with the opposite process used in the equation. Do the additions and subtractions first; then the multiplications and divisions.

Example

$5(P - 4) = 20$

The unknown P less 4, multiplied by 5 equals 20.

Mechanical steps

$$5(P - 4) = 20$$
$$5P - 20 = 20$$
$$\underline{\quad +20 \qquad +20\quad}$$
$$\dfrac{5P}{5} = \dfrac{40}{5}$$
$$P = \boxed{8}$$

Explanation

1. Parentheses tell us that everything inside parentheses is multiplied by 5. Multiply 5 by P and 5 by -4.
2. Add 20 to both sides to isolate $5P$ on left.
3. To remove 5 in front of P, divide both sides by 5 to result in P equals 8.

Check

$$5(8 - 4) = 20$$
$$5(4) = 20$$
$$20 = 20$$

MONEY tips

Negotiate. Over 90% of customers who ask for a discount on items such as electronics, appliances, furniture, and medical bills receive one. Just ask. You could be saving money.

Drill Situation 7: Combining Like Unknowns

LIKE UNKNOWNS RULE
To solve equations with like unkowns, you first combine the unknowns and then solve with the opposite process used in the equation.

Example

$4A + A = 20$

Mechanical steps

$4A + A = 20$

$$\frac{\cancel{5}A}{\cancel{5}} = \frac{20}{5}$$

$\boxed{A} = 4$

Explanation

To solve this equation: $4A + 1A = 5A$. Thus, $5A = 20$. To solve for A, divide both sides by 5, leaving A equals 4.

Check

$4(4) + 4 = 20$

$20 = 20$

Before you go to Learning Unit 5–2, let's check your understanding of this unit.

LU 5–1	PRACTICE QUIZ

Complete this **Practice Quiz** to see how you are doing.

1. Write equations for the following (use the letter Q as the variable). Do not solve for the unknown.
   a. Nine less than one-half a number is fourteen.
   b. Eight times the sum of a number and thirty-one is fifty.
   c. Ten decreased by twice a number is two.
   d. Eight times a number less two equals twenty-one.
   e. The sum of four times a number and two is fifteen.
   f. If twice a number is decreased by eight, the difference is four.

2. Solve the following:
   a. $B + 24 = 60$
   b. $D + 3D = 240$
   c. $12B = 144$
   d. $\dfrac{B}{6} = 50$
   e. $\dfrac{B}{4} + 4 = 16$
   f. $3(B - 8) = 18$

*For **extra help** from your authors–Sharon and Jeff–see the student DVD*

You Tube

✓ Solutions

1. a. $\dfrac{1}{2}Q - 9 = 14$
   b. $8(Q + 31) = 50$
   c. $10 - 2Q = 2$

   d. $8Q - 2 = 21$
   e. $4Q + 2 = 15$
   f. $2Q - 8 = 4$

2. a. $B + 24 = 60$
   $ -24 -24$
   $B = \boxed{36}$

   b. $\dfrac{\cancel{4}D}{\cancel{4}} = \dfrac{240}{4}$
   $D = \boxed{60}$

   c. $\dfrac{\cancel{12}B}{\cancel{12}} = \dfrac{144}{12}$
   $B = \boxed{12}$

   d. $\cancel{6}\left(\dfrac{B}{\cancel{6}}\right) = 50(6)$
   $B = \boxed{300}$

   e. $\dfrac{B}{4} + 4 = 16$
   $\phantom{\dfrac{B}{4}} -4 -4$
   $\dfrac{B}{4} = 12$
   $\cancel{4}\left(\dfrac{B}{\cancel{4}}\right) = 12(4)$
   $B = \boxed{48}$

   f. $3(B - 8) = 18$
   $3B - 24 = 18$
   $ +24 +24$
   $\dfrac{\cancel{3}B}{\cancel{3}} = \dfrac{42}{3}$
   $B = \boxed{14}$

LU 5–1a **EXTRA PRACTICE QUIZ WITH WORKED-OUT SOLUTIONS**

Need more practice? Try this **Extra Practice Quiz** (check figures in the Interactive Chapter Organizer, p. 130). Worked-out Solutions can be found in Appendix B at end of text.

1. Write equations for the following (use the letter Q as the variable). Do not solve for the unknown.
   a. Eight less than one-half a number is sixteen.
   b. Twelve times the sum of a number and forty-one is 1,200.
   c. Seven decreased by twice a number is one.
   d. Four times a number less two equals twenty-four.
   e. The sum of three times a number and three is nineteen.
   f. If twice a number is decreased by six, the difference is five.

2. Solve the following:

   a. $B + 14 = 70$ b. $D + 4D = 250$ c. $11B = 121$

   d. $\dfrac{B}{8} = 90$ e. $\dfrac{B}{2} + 2 = 250$ f. $3(B - 6) = 18$

Learning Unit 5–2: Solving Word Problems for the Unknown

LO 1

When you buy a candy bar such as a Snickers, you should turn the candy bar over and carefully read the ingredients and calories contained on the back of the candy bar wrapper.

For example, on the back of the Snickers wrapper you will read that there are "170 calories per piece." You could misread this to mean that the entire Snickers bar has 170 calories. However, look closer and you will see that the Snickers bar is divided into three pieces, so if you eat the entire bar, instead of consuming 170 calories, you will consume 510 calories. Making errors like this could result in a weight gain that you cannot explain.

$$\frac{1}{3}S = 170 \text{ calories}$$

$$3\left(\frac{1}{3}S\right) = 170 \times 3$$

$$S = \boxed{510} \text{ calories per bar}$$

In this unit, we use blueprint aids in six different situations to help you solve for unknowns. Be patient and *persistent*. Remember that the more problems you work, the easier the process becomes. Do not panic! Repetition is the key. Study the five steps that follow. They will help you solve for unknowns in word problems.

SOLVING WORD PROBLEMS FOR UNKNOWNS
Step 1. Carefully read the entire problem. You may have to read it several times.
Step 2. Ask yourself: What is the problem looking for?
Step 3. When you are sure what the problem is asking, let a variable represent the unknown. If the problem has more than one unknown, represent the second unknown in terms of the same variable. For example, if the problem has two unknowns, Y is one unknown. The second unknown is 4Y—4 times the first unknown.
Step 4. Visualize the relationship between unknowns and variables. Then set up an equation to solve for unknown(s).
Step 5. Check your result to see if it is accurate.

This clip from the *Wall Street Journal,* "How to Ace That Test," may also help you in the process of solving word problems.

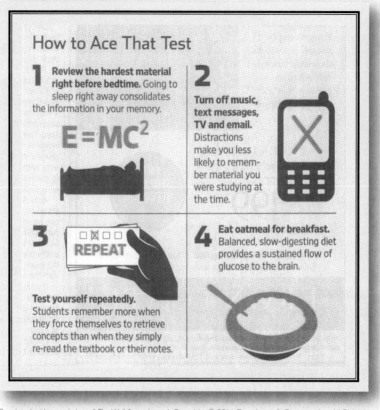

Word Problem Situation 1: Number Problems Today on sale at a local Stop and Shop supermarket, the price of a 1-pound can of Chock full o'Nuts coffee is $9.99. This is a $2 savings. What was the original price of the can of coffee?

© Roberts Publishing Services

LO 2

	Unknown(s)	Variable(s)	Relationship*
B L U E P R I N T	Original price of Chock full o'Nuts	P	$P - \$2 =$ New price

Mechanical steps

$$P - 2 = \$ \, 9.99$$
$$\underline{+ 2 \quad + 2}$$
$$P \quad = \$11.99$$

*This column will help you visualize the equation before setting up the actual equation.

Explanation	**Check**
The original price less $2 = $9.99. Note that we added $2 to both sides to isolate P on the left. Remember, $1P = P$.	$11.99 − 2 = 9.99 $9.99 = $9.99

Word Problem Situation 2: Finding the Whole When Part Is Known A local Burger King budgets $\frac{1}{8}$ of its monthly profits on salaries. Salaries for the month were $12,000. What were Burger King's monthly profits?

	Unknown(s)	Variable(s)	Relationship	Mechanical steps
BLUEPRINT	Monthly profits	P	$\frac{1}{8}P$ Salaries = $12,000	$\frac{1}{8}P = $12,000$ $8\left(\frac{P}{8}\right) = $12,000(8)$ $P = $96,000$

Explanation	**Check**
$\frac{1}{8}P$ represents Burger King's monthly salaries. Since the equation used division, we solve for P by multiplying both sides by 8.	$\frac{1}{8}($96,000) = $12,000$ $12,000 = $12,000

Word Problem Situation 3: Difference Problems ICM Company sold 4 times as many computers as Ring Company. The difference in their sales is 27. How many computers of each company were sold?

	Unknown(s)	Variable(s)	Relationship	Mechanical steps
BLUEPRINT	ICM Ring	$4C$ C	$4C$ $-C$ 27	$4C − C = 27$ $\frac{3C}{3} = \frac{27}{3}$ $C = 9$ Ring = 9 computers ICM = 4(9) = 36 computers

Note: If problem has two unknowns, assign the variable to smaller item or one who sells less. Then assign the other unknown using the same variable. *Use the same letter.*

Explanation	**Check**
The variables replace the names ICM and Ring. We assigned Ring the variable C, since it sold fewer computers. We assigned ICM $4C$, since it sold 4 times as many computers.	36 computers −9 27 computers

Word Problem Situation 4: Calculating Unit Sales Together Barry Sullivan and Mitch Ryan sold a total of 300 homes for Regis Realty. Barry sold 9 times as many homes as Mitch. How many did each sell?

	Unknown(s)	Variable(s)	Relationship	Mechanical steps
BLUEPRINT	Homes sold: B. Sullivan M. Ryan	$9H$ H*	$9H$ $+H$ 300 homes	$9H + H = 300$ $\frac{10H}{10} = \frac{300}{10}$ $H = 30$ Ryan: 30 homes Sullivan: 9(30) = 270 homes

*Assign H to Ryan since he sold less.

Explanation	**Check**
We assigned Mitch H, since he sold fewer homes. We assigned Barry $9H$, since he sold 9 times as many homes. Together Barry and Mitch sold 300 homes.	30 + 270 = 300

Word Problem Situation 5: Calculating Unit and Dollar Sales (Cost per Unit) When Total Units Are Not Given Andy sold watches ($9) and alarm clocks ($5) at a flea market. Total sales were $287. People bought 4 times as many watches as alarm clocks. How many of each did Andy sell? What were the total dollar sales of each?

BLUEPRINT	Unknown(s)	Variable(s)	Price	Relationship
	Unit sales:			
	Watches	4C	$9	36C
	Clocks	C	5	+ 5C
				$287 total sales

Mechanical steps

$$36C + 5C = 287$$
$$\frac{41C}{41} = \frac{287}{41}$$
$$C = \boxed{7}$$

$\boxed{7}$ clocks

$4(7) = \boxed{28}$ watches

Explanation

Number of watches times $9 sales price plus number of alarm clocks times $5 sales price equals $287 total sales.

Check

$$7(\$5) + 28(\$9) = \$287$$
$$\$35 + \$252 = \$287$$
$$\$287 = \$287$$

Word Problem Situation 6: Calculating Unit and Dollar Sales (Cost per Unit) When Total Units Are Given Andy sold watches ($9) and alarm clocks ($5) at a flea market. Total sales for 35 watches and alarm clocks were $287. How many of each did Andy sell? What were the total dollar sales of each?

BLUEPRINT	Unknown(s)	Variable(s)	Price	Relationship
	Unit sales:			
	Watches	W*	$9	9W
	Clocks	35 − W	5	+ 5(35 − W)
				$287 total sales

*The more expensive item is assigned to the variable first only for this situation to make the mechanical steps easier to complete.

Mechanical steps

$$9W + 5(35 - W) = 287$$
$$9W + 175 - 5W = 287$$
$$4W + 175 = 287$$
$$\underline{\quad - 175 \qquad - 175}$$
$$\frac{4W}{4} = \frac{112}{4}$$
$$W = \boxed{28}$$

Watches = $\boxed{28}$

Clocks = $35 - 28 = \boxed{7}$

Explanation

Number of watches (W) times price per watch plus number of alarm clocks times price per alarm clock equals $287. Total units given was 35.

Check

$$28(\$9) + 7(\$5) = \$287$$
$$\$252 + \$35 = \$287$$
$$\$287 = \$287$$

Why did we use $35 - W$? Assume we had 35 pizzas (some cheese, others meatball). If I said that I ate all the meatball pizzas (5), how many cheese pizzas are left? Thirty? Right, you subtract 5 from 35. Think of $35 - W$ as meaning one number.

Note in Word Problem Situations 5 and 6 that the situation is the same. In Word Problem Situation 5, we were not given total units sold (but we were told which sold better). In Word Problem Situation 6, we were given total units sold, but we did not know which sold better.

Now try these six types of word problems in the Practice Quiz. Be sure to complete blueprint aids and the mechanical steps for solving the unknown(s).

LU 5–2   PRACTICE QUIZ

Complete this **Practice Quiz** to see how you are doing.

Situations

1. An L. L. Bean sweater was reduced $30. The sale price was $90. What was the original price?

2. Kelly Doyle budgets $\frac{1}{8}$ of her yearly salary for entertainment. Kelly's total entertainment bill for the year is $6,500. What is Kelly's yearly salary?

3. Micro Knowledge sells 5 times as many computers as Morse Electronics. The difference in sales between the two stores is 20 computers. How many computers did each store sell?

4. Susie and Cara sell stoves at Elliott's Appliances. Together they sold 180 stoves in January. Susie sold 5 times as many stoves as Cara. How many stoves did each sell?

5. Pasquale's Pizza sells meatball pizzas ($6) and cheese pizzas ($5). In March, Pasquale's total sales were $1,600. People bought 2 times as many cheese pizzas as meatball pizzas. How many of each did Pasquale's sell? What were the total dollar sales of each?

6. Pasquale's Pizza sells meatball pizzas ($6) and cheese pizzas ($5). In March, Pasquale's sold 300 pizzas for $1,600. How many of each did Pasquale's sell? What was the dollar sales price of each?

*For **extra help** from your authors–Sharon and Jeff–see the student DVD*

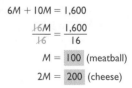

✓ Solutions

1.

	Unknown(s)	Variable(s)	Relationship
BLUEPRINT	Original price	P*	$P - \$30 =$ Sale price Sale price $= \$90$

*P = Original price.

Mechanical steps

$$P - \$30 = \$90$$
$$\underline{+\ 30 \qquad +\ 30}$$
$$P \qquad = \boxed{\$120}$$

2.

	Unknown(s)	Variable(s)	Relationship
BLUEPRINT	Yearly salary	S*	$\frac{1}{8}S$ Entertainment $= \$6,500$

*S = Salary.

Mechanical steps

$$\tfrac{1}{8}S = \$6,500$$
$$8\left(\tfrac{S}{8}\right) = \$6,500(8)$$
$$S = \boxed{\$52,000}$$

3.

	Unknown(s)	Variable(s)	Relationship
BLUEPRINT	Micro	$5C$*	$5C$
	Morse	C	$\underline{-\ C}$ 20 computers

*C = Computers.

Mechanical steps

$$5C - C = 20$$
$$\frac{4C}{4} = \frac{20}{4}$$
$$C = \boxed{5} \text{ (Morse)}$$
$$5C = \boxed{25} \text{ (Micro)}$$

4.

	Unknown(s)	Variable(s)	Relationship
BLUEPRINT	*Stoves sold:*		
	Susie	$5S$*	$5S$
	Cara	S	$\underline{-\ S}$ 180 stoves

*S = Stoves.

Mechanical steps

$$5S + S = 180$$
$$\frac{6S}{6} = \frac{180}{6}$$
$$S = \boxed{30} \text{ (Cara)}$$
$$5S = \boxed{150} \text{ (Susie)}$$

5.

	Unknown(s)	Variable(s)	Price	Relationship
BLUEPRINT	Meatball	M	$\$6$	$6M$
	Cheese	$2M$	5	$\underline{+\ 10M}$ $\$1,600$ total sales

Mechanical steps

$$6M + 10M = 1,600$$
$$\frac{16M}{16} = \frac{1,600}{16}$$
$$M = \boxed{100} \text{ (meatball)}$$
$$2M = \boxed{200} \text{ (cheese)}$$

Check

$$(100 \times \$6) + (200 \times \$5) = \$1,600$$
$$\$600 + \$1,000 = \$1,600$$
$$\$1,600 = \$1,600$$

6.

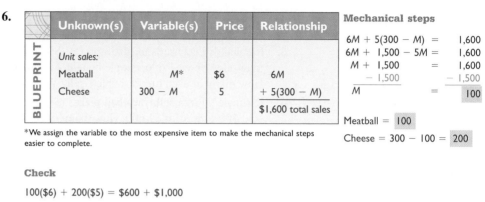

	Unknown(s)	Variable(s)	Price	Relationship
BLUEPRINT	*Unit sales:*			
	Meatball	M^*	$6	$6M$
	Cheese	$300 - M$	5	$+ 5(300 - M)$
				$1,600 total sales

*We assign the variable to the most expensive item to make the mechanical steps easier to complete.

Mechanical steps

$$6M + 5(300 - M) = 1,600$$
$$6M + 1,500 - 5M = 1,600$$
$$M + 1,500 = 1,600$$
$$\underline{-1,500 \qquad -1,500}$$
$$M = 100$$

Meatball = 100

Cheese = 300 − 100 = 200

Check

$$100(\$6) + 200(\$5) = \$600 + \$1,000$$
$$= \$1,600$$

LU 5–2a | EXTRA PRACTICE QUIZ WITH WORKED-OUT SOLUTIONS

Need more practice? Try this **Extra Practice Quiz** (check figures in the Interactive Chapter Organizer, p. 130). Worked-out Solutions can be found in Appendix B at end of text.

Situations

1. An L. L. Bean sweater was reduced $50. The sale price was $140. What was the original price?

2. Kelly Doyle budgets $\frac{1}{7}$ of her yearly salary for entertainment. Kelly's total entertainment bill for the year is $7,000. What is Kelly's yearly salary?

3. Micro Knowledge sells 8 times as many computers as Morse Electronics. The difference in sales between the two stores is 49 computers. How many computers did each store sell?

4. Susie and Cara sell stoves at Elliott's Appliances. Together they sold 360 stoves in January. Susie sold 2 times as many stoves as Cara. How many stoves did each sell?

5. Pasquale's Pizza sells meatball pizzas ($7) and cheese pizzas ($6). In March, Pasquale's total sales were $1,800. People bought 3 times as many cheese pizzas as meatball pizzas. How many of each did Pasquale's sell? What were the total dollar sales of each?

6. Pasquale's Pizza sells meatball pizzas ($7) and cheese pizzas ($6). In March, Pasquale's sold 288 pizzas for $1,800. What was the dollar sales price of each?

INTERACTIVE CHAPTER ORGANIZER

Solving for unknowns from basic equations	Mechanical steps to solve unknowns	Key point(s)	You try it*
Situation 1: Subtracting same number from both sides of equation, p. 120	$D + 10 = 12$ $\underline{-10 \quad -10}$ $D = 2$	Subtract 10 from both sides of equation to isolate variable D on the left. Since equation used addition, we solve by using opposite process—subtraction.	**Solve** $E + 15 = 14$
Situation 2: Adding same number to both sides of equation, p. 120	$L - 24 = 40$ $\underline{+24 \quad +24}$ $L = 64$	Add 24 to both sides to isolate unknown L on left. We solve by using opposite process of subtraction—addition.	**Solve** $B - 40 = 80$
Situation 3: Dividing both sides of equation by same number, p. 120	$6B = 24$ $\dfrac{\cancel{6}B}{\cancel{6}} = \dfrac{24}{6}$ $B = 4$	To isolate B on the left, divide both sides of the equation by 6. Thus, the 6 on the left cancels—leaving B equal to 4. Since equation used multiplication, we solve unknown by using opposite process—division.	**Solve** $5C = 75$

(continues)

INTERACTIVE CHAPTER ORGANIZER

Solving for unknowns from basic equations	Mechanical steps to solve unknowns	Key point(s)	You try it*
Situation 4: Multiplying both sides of equation by same number, p. 120	$\frac{R}{3} = 15$ $3\left(\frac{R}{3}\right) = 15(3)$ $R = \boxed{45}$	To remove denominator, multiply both sides of the equation by 3—the 3 on the left side cancels, leaving R equal to 45. Since equation used division, we solve unknown by using opposite process—multiplication.	**Solve** $\frac{A}{6} = 60$
Situation 5: Equation that uses subtraction and multiplication to solve for unknown, p. 121	$\frac{B}{3} + 6 = 13$ $\underline{\quad -6 \quad -6}$ $\frac{B}{3} = 7$ $3\left(\frac{B}{3}\right) = 7(3)$ $B = 21$	1. Move constant 6 to right side by subtracting 6 from both sides. 2. Isolate B on left by multiplying both sides by 3.	**Solve** $\frac{C}{4} + 10 = 17$
Situation 6: Using parentheses in solving for unknown, p. 121	$6(A - 5) = 12$ $6A - 30 = 12$ $\underline{\quad +30 \quad +30}$ $\frac{6A}{6} = \frac{42}{6}$ $A = \boxed{7}$	Parentheses indicate multiplication. Multiply 6 times A and 6 times −5. Result is 6A − 30 on left side of the equation. Now add 30 to both sides to isolate 6A on left. To remove 6 in front of A, divide both sides by 6, to result in A equal to 7. Note that when deleting parentheses, we did not have to multiply the right side.	**Solve** $7(B - 10) = 35$
Situation 7: Combining like unknowns, p. 122	$6A + 2A = 64$ $\frac{8A}{8} = \frac{64}{8}$ $A = 8$	6A + 2A combine to 8A. To solve for A, we divide both sides by 8.	**Solve** $5B + 3B = 17$

Solving for unknowns from word problems	Blueprint aid	Mechanical steps to solve unknown with check	You try it*
Situation 1: Number problems, p. 124 **U.S. Air reduced its airfare to California by $60. The sale price was $95. What was the original price?**	BLUEPRINT 	Unknown(s)	Variable(s)	Relationship	 |---|---|---| | Original price | P | P − $60 = Sale price Sale price = $95 |	$P - \$60 = \$95$ $\underline{\quad +60 \quad +60}$ $P = \boxed{\$155}$ **Check** $\$155 - \$60 = \$95$ $\$95 = \$95$	**Solve** U.S. Air reduced its airfare to California by $53. The sale price was $110. What was the original price?
Situation 2: Finding the whole when part is known, p. 125 **K. McCarthy spends $1/8$ of her budget for school. What is the total budget if school costs $5,000?**	BLUEPRINT 	Unknown(s)	Variable(s)	Relationship	 |---|---|---| | Total budget | B | $1/8$B School = $5,000 |	$\frac{1}{8}B = \$5,000$ $8\left(\frac{B}{8}\right) = \$5,000(8)$ $B = \boxed{\$40,000}$ **Check** $\frac{1}{8}(\$40,000) = \$5,000$ $\$5,000 = \$5,000$	**Solve** K. McCarthy spends $1/7$ of her budget for school. What is the total budget if school costs $6,000?

(continues)

INTERACTIVE CHAPTER ORGANIZER

Solving for unknowns from word problems	Blueprint aid	Mechanical steps to solve unknown with check	You try it*
Situation 3: Difference problems, p. 125 Moe sold 8 times as many suitcases as Bill. The difference in their sales is 280 suitcases. How many suitcases did each sell?	BLUEPRINT | Unknown(s)	Variable(s)	Relationship
---	---	---
Suitcases sold:		
Moe	8S	8S
Bill	S	− S
		280 suitcases		$8S - S = 280$ $\dfrac{7S}{7} = \dfrac{280}{7}$ $S = \boxed{40}$ (Bill) $8(40) = \boxed{320}$ (Moe) **Check** $320 - 40 = 280$ $280 = 280$	**Solve** Moe sold 9 times as many suitcases as Bill. The difference in their sales is 640 suitcases. How many suitcases did each sell?
Situation 4: Calculating unit sales, p. 125 Moe sold 8 times as many suitcases as Bill. Together they sold a total of 360. How many did each sell?	BLUEPRINT | Unknown(s)	Variable(s)	Relationship
---	---	---
Suitcases sold:		
Moe	8S	8S
Bill	S	+ S
		360 suitcases		$8S + S = 360$ $\dfrac{9S}{9} = \dfrac{360}{9}$ $S = \boxed{40}$ (Bill) $8(40) = \boxed{320}$ (Moe) **Check** $320 + 40 = 360$ $360 = 360$	**Solve** Moe sold 9 times as many suitcases as Bill. Together they sold a total of 640. How many did each sell?
Situation 5: Calculating unit and dollar sales (cost per unit) when *total units not given*, p. 126 Blue Furniture Company ordered sleepers ($300) and nonsleepers ($200) that cost $8,000. Blue expects sleepers to out-sell nonsleepers 2 to 1. How many units of each were ordered? What were dollar costs of each?	BLUEPRINT 	Unknown(s)	Variable(s)	Price	Relationship
Sleepers	2N	$300	600N
Nonsleepers	N	200	+200N
			$8,000 total cost		$600N + 200N = 8,000$ $\dfrac{800N}{800} = \dfrac{8,000}{800}$ $N = \boxed{10}$ (nonsleepers) $2N = \boxed{20}$ (sleepers) **Check** $10 \times \$200 = \$2,000$ $20 \times \$300 = \underline{\ \ 6,000}$ $= \$8,000$	**Solve** Blue Furniture Company ordered sleepers ($400) and nonsleepers ($300) that cost $15,000. Blue expects sleepers to outsell nonsleepers 3 to 1. How many units of each were ordered? What were dollar costs of each?
Situation 6: Calculating unit and dollar sales (cost per unit) when *total units given*, p. 126 Blue Furniture Company ordered 30 sofas (sleepers and nonsleepers) that cost $8,000. The whole-sale unit cost was $300 for the sleepers and $200 for the nonsleepers. How many units of each were ordered? What were dollar costs of each?	BLUEPRINT 	Unknown(s)	Variable(s)	Price	Relationship
Unit costs			
Sleepers	S	$300	300S
Nonsleepers	30 − S	200	+200(30 − S)
			$8,000 total cost	 *Note:* When the total units are given, the higher-priced item (sleepers) is assigned to the variable first. This makes the mechanical steps easier to complete.	$\begin{aligned}300S + 200(30 - S) &= 8,000\\ 300S + 6,000 - 200S &= 8,000\\ 100S + 6,000 &= 8,000\\ -6,000 \qquad\quad &\ -6,000\\ \dfrac{100S}{100} &= \dfrac{2,000}{100}\\ S &= \boxed{20}\\ \text{Nonsleepers} = 30 - 20 &\\ &= \boxed{10}\end{aligned}$ **Check** $20(\$300) + 10(\$200) = \$8,000$ $\$6,000 + \quad \$2,000 = \$8,000$ $\$8,000 = \$8,000$	**Solve** Blue Furniture Company ordered 40 sofas (sleepers and nonsleepers) that cost $15,000. The wholesale unit cost was $400 for the sleepers and $300 for the non-sleepers. How many units of each were ordered? What were dollar costs of each?
KEY TERMS	Constants, *p. 119* Equation, *p. 118* Expression, *p. 118*	Formula, *p. 118* Knowns, *p. 119* Unknown, *p. 119*	Variables, *p. 118*
Check Figures for Extra Practice Quizzes with Page References. (Worked-out Solutions in Appendix B.)	**LU 5–1a (p. 123)** **1.** a. $Q/2 - 8 = 16$ b. $12(Q + 41) = 1,200$ c. $7 - 2Q = 1$ d. $4Q - 2 = 24$ e. $3Q + 3 = 19$ f. $2Q - 6 = 5$ **2.** a. 56 b. 50 c. 11 d. 720 e. 496 f. 12	**LU 5–2a (p. 128)** **1.** $P = \$190$ **2.** $S = \$49,000$ **3.** Morse 7; Micro 56 **4.** Cara 120; Susie 240 **5.** Meatball 72; cheese 216; Meatball = $504; cheese = $1,296 **6.** Meatball $504; cheese $1,296	

*Worked-out solutions are in Appendix B.

Critical Thinking Discussion Questions with Chapter Concept Check

1. Explain the difference between a variable and a constant. What would you consider your monthly car payment—a variable or a constant?

2. How does the opposite process rule help solve for the variable in an equation? If a Mercedes costs 3 times as much as a Saab, how could the opposite process rule be used? The selling price of the Mercedes is $60,000.

3. What is the difference between Word Problem Situations 5 and 6 in Learning Unit 5–2? Show why the more expensive item in Word Problem Situation 6 is assigned to the variable first.

4. **Chapter Concept Check.** Based on the article in the chapter opener and all of the information you have learned about equations in this chapter, go to a weight-loss website and create several equations on how to lose weight. Be sure to create a word problem and specify the steps you need to take to solve this weight-loss problem.

Classroom Notes

END-OF-CHAPTER PROBLEMS connect (plus+) www.mhhe.com/slater11e

Mc Graw Hill

Check figures for odd-numbered problems in Appendix C.   Name _____ Date _____

DRILL PROBLEMS (First of Three Sets)

Solve the unknown from the following equations: *LU 5-1(2)*

5–1. $C - 40 = 315$

5–2. $B + 110 = 400$

5–3. $Q + 100 = 400$

5–4. $Q - 60 = 850$

5–5. $5Y = 75$

5–6. $\dfrac{P}{6} = 92$

5–7. $8Y = 96$

5–8. $\dfrac{N}{16} = 5$

5–9. $4(P - 9) = 64$

5–10. $3(P - 3) = 27$

WORD PROBLEMS (First of Three Sets)

5–11. Lee and Fred are elementary school teachers. Fred works for a charter school in Pacific Palisades, California, where class size reduction is a goal for 2013. Lee works for a noncharter school where funds do not allow for class size reduction policies. Lee's fifth-grade class has 1.4 times as many students as Fred's. If there are a total of 60 students, how many students does Fred's class have? How many students does Lee's class have?   *LU 5-2(2)*

5–12. In 1955 an antique car that originally cost \$3,668 is valued today at \$62,125 if in excellent condition, which is $1\frac{3}{4}$ times as
eXcel much as a car in very nice condition—if you can find an owner willing to part with one for any price. What would be the value of the car in very nice condition?   *LU 5-2(2)*

5–13. Joe Sullivan and Hugh Kee sell cars for a Ford dealer. Over the past year, they sold 300 cars. Joe sells 5 times as many cars as Hugh. How many cars did each sell?   *LU 5-2(2)*

5–14. Nanda Yueh and Lane Zuriff sell homes for ERA Realty. Over the past 6 months they sold 120 homes. Nanda sold 3 times
eXcel as many homes as Lane. How many homes did each sell?   *LU 5-2(2)*

5–15. Dots sells T-shirts ($2) and shorts ($4). In April, total sales were $600. People bought 4 times as many T-shirts as shorts. How many T-shirts and shorts did Dots sell? Check your answer.   *LU 5-2(2)*

5–16. Dots sells a total of 250 T-shirts ($2) and shorts ($4). In April, total sales were $600. How many T-shirts and shorts did Dots sell? Check your answer. *Hint:* Let S = Shorts.   *LU 5-2(2)*

DRILL PROBLEMS (Second of Three Sets)

Solve the unknown from the following equations: *LU 5-1(2)*

5–17. $7B = 490$

5–18. $7(A - 5) = 63$

5–19. $\dfrac{N}{9} = 7$

5–20. $18(C - 3) = 162$

5–21. $9Y - 10 = 53$

5–22. $7B + 5 = 26$

WORD PROBLEMS (Second of Three Sets)

5–23. On a flight from Boston to San Diego, American reduced its Internet price by $190.00. The new sale price was $420.99. What was the original price?   *LU 5-2(2)*

5–24. Jill, an employee at Old Navy, budgets $\frac{1}{5}$ of her yearly salary for clothing. Jill's total clothing bill for the year is $8,000. What is her yearly salary?   *LU 5-2(2)*

5–25. Bill's Roast Beef sells 5 times as many sandwiches as Pete's Deli. The difference between their sales is 360 sandwiches. **eXcel** How many sandwiches did each sell?   *LU 5-2(2)*

5–26. The count of discouraged unemployed workers rose to 503,000, $2\frac{1}{2}$ times as many as in the previous year. How many discouraged unemployed workers were there in the previous year? *LU 5-2(2)*

5–27. A local Computer City sells batteries ($3) and small boxes of pens ($5). In August, total sales were $960. Customers bought 5 times as many batteries as boxes of pens. How many of each did Computer City sell? Check your answer. *LU 5-2(2)*

5–28. Staples sells boxes of pens ($10) and rubber bands ($4). Leona ordered a total of 24 cartons for $210. How many boxes of each did Leona order? Check your answer. *Hint:* Let P = Pens. *LU 5-2(2)*

DRILL PROBLEMS (Third of Three Sets)

Solve the unknown from the following equations: *LU 5-1(2)*

5–29. $A + 90 - 15 = 210$

5–30. $5Y + 15(Y + 1) = 35$

5–31. $3M + 20 = 2M + 80$

5–32. $20(C - 50) = 19{,}000$

WORD PROBLEMS (Third of Three Sets)

5–33. If Colorado Springs, Colorado, has 1.2 times as many days of sunshine than Boston, Massachusetts, how many days of sunshine does each city have if there are a total of 464 days of sunshine between the two in a year? (Round to the nearest day.) *LU 5-2(2)*

5–34. At General Electric, shift 1 produced 4 times as much as shift 2. General Electric's total production for July was 5,500 jet engines. What was the output for each shift?   *LU 5-2(2)*

5–35. Ivy Corporation gave 84 people a bonus. If Ivy had given 2 more people bonuses, Ivy would have rewarded $\frac{2}{3}$ of the work-force. How large is Ivy's workforce?   *LU 5-2(2)*

5–36. Jim Murray and Phyllis Lowe received a total of $50,000 from a deceased relative's estate. They decided to put $10,000 in a trust for their nephew and divide the remainder. Phyllis received $\frac{3}{4}$ of the remainder; Jim received $\frac{1}{4}$. How much did Jim and Phyllis receive?   *LU 5-2(2)*

5–37. The first shift of GME Corporation produced $1\frac{1}{2}$ times as many lanterns as the second shift. GME produced 5,600 lanterns in November. How many lanterns did GME produce on each shift?   *LU 5-2(2)*

5–38. Walmart sells thermometers ($2) and hot-water bottles ($6). In December, Walmart's total sales were $1,200. Customers bought 7 times as many thermometers as hot-water bottles. How many of each did Walmart sell? Check your answer.   *LU 5-2(2)*

5–39. Ace Hardware sells boxes of wrenches ($100) and hammers ($300). Howard ordered 40 boxes of wrenches and hammers for $8,400. How many boxes of each are in the order? Check your answer.   *LU 5-2(2)*

5–40. The Susan Hansen Group in St. George, Utah, sells $16,000,000 of single-family homes and townhomes a year. If single-family homes, with an average selling price of $250,000, sell 3.5 times more often than townhomes, with an average selling price of $190,000, how many of each are sold? (Round to nearest whole.) *LU 5-2(2)*

5–41. Want to donate to a better cause? Consider micro-lending. Micro-lending is a process where you lend directly to entrepreneurs in developing countries. You can lend starting at $25. Kiva.org boasts a 99% repayment rate. The average loan to an entrepreneur is $388.44 and the average loan amount is $261.14. With a total amount loaned of $283,697,150, how many people are lending money if the average number of loans per lender is 8? *LU 5-2(2)*

CHALLENGE PROBLEMS

5–42. Myron Corporation is sponsoring a walking race at its company outing. Leona Jackson and Sam Peterson love to walk. Leona walks at the rate of 5 miles per hour. Sam walks at the rate of 6 miles per hour. Assume they start walking from the same place and walk in a straight line. Sam starts $\frac{1}{2}$ hour after Leona. Answer the questions that follow. *Hint:* Distance = Rate × Time. *LU 5-2(2)*

    a. How long will it take Sam to meet Leona?

    b. How many miles would each have walked?

    c. Assume Leona and Sam meet in Lonetown Station where two buses leave along parallel routes in opposite directions. The bus travelling east has a 60 mph speed. The bus traveling west has a 40 mph speed. In how many hours will the buses be 600 miles apart?

5–43. Bessy has 6 times as much money as Bob, but when each earns $6, Bessy will have 3 times as much money as Bob. How much does each have before and after earning the $6? *LU 5-2(2)*

 SUMMARY PRACTICE TEST You Tube

Do you need help? The DVD has step-by-step worked-out solutions.

1. Delta reduced its round-trip ticket price from Portland to Boston by $140. The sale price was $401.90. What was the original price? *(p. 124)   LU 5-2(2)*

2. David Role is an employee of Google. He budgets $\frac{1}{7}$ of his salary for clothing. If David's total clothing for the year is $12,000, what is his yearly salary? *(p. 125)   LU 5-2(2)*

3. A local Best Buy sells 8 times as many iPods as Sears. The difference between their sales is 490 iPods. How many iPods did each sell? *(p. 125)   LU 5-2(2)*

4. Working at Staples, Jill Reese and Abby Lee sold a total of 1,200 calculators. Jill sold 5 times as many calculators as Abby. How many did each sell? *(p. 125)   LU 5-2(2)*

5. Target sells sets of pots ($30) and dishes ($20) at the local store. On the July 4 weekend, Target's total sales were $2,600. People bought 6 times as many pots as dishes. How many of each did Target sell? Check your answer. *(p. 126)* *LU 5-2(2)*

6. A local Dominos sold a total of 1,600 small pizzas ($9) and pasta dinners ($13) during the Super Bowl. How many of each did Dominos sell if total sales were $15,600? Check your answer. *(p. 126)* *LU 5-2(2)*

SURF TO SAVE

How can you solve the world's problems? 🔍

 PROBLEM 1
Ticket to ride

Your student business club has U.S. $1,000 to spend on a day trip to Toronto. You estimate U.S. $200 for gas and tolls for the bus, and C$10 for parking at the science center. Go to the Ontario Science Center, website (http://www.ontariosciencecentre.ca), to find the cost of admission, including the two OMNIMAX films. Based on these costs, how many students can the business club afford to send on this trip? (*Hint:* Go to http://www.oanda.com/converter/classic for exchange rates.)

Discussion Questions

1. How much money would you budget for meals and other expenses on this trip?

2. What would be some fundraiser ideas to earn more money for your club to take this trip? How much additional revenue could you gain from these fundraisers?

 PROBLEM 2
More People, More Debt

Go to http://www.census.gov/main/www/popclock.html to find the U.S. population. Then, go to http://www.brillig.com/debt_clock to find the U.S. national debt. Use these data to determine the U.S. government's debt per person. Compare this with the number quoted on the debt clock site.

Discussion Questions

1. What do you feel is fueling the growth in the U.S. population?

2. Do you think the national debt will continue to rise? Why?

PROBLEM 3
Fueling Your Travels

Go to http://www.fuelcostcalculator.com. Find the average cost of fuel for your state. If the vehicle you drive averages 25 miles per gallon, what would it cost for you to travel 1,500 miles for your summer vacation?

Discussion Questions

1. Based on rising fuel prices, should you consider an electric or hybrid car for your next purchase? Why?

2. How would the price of driving to your destination compare to other forms of travel (i.e., air, train, bus, etc.)? Which would be your preferred method of travel for your vacation?

PROBLEM 4
Stocking up on Gap

Go to http://finance.yahoo.com/lookup and find the current stock price for Gap, Inc. How many shares of this stock could be purchased at the current price for $1,500.00?

Discussion Questions

1. Is Gap's stock price a value for the money? Why?

2. What are some factors that would cause Gap's stock price to increase? What factors may cause its stock price to decrease?

MOBILE APPS ✕

Equation Genius (Dinh Ba Thanh) Assists in solving for unknown values.

Word Problems, Math (honeHead) Solving for the unknown using over 250 questions and showing the step-by-step approach for solving the problem.

INTERNET PROJECTS ✕

See text website
www.mhhe.com/slater11e_sse_ch05

Tax-Smart Ways to Help Your Kids

Uncle Sam (and some states) give a little back when you help pay college bills or save for their future. BY KIMBERLY LANKFORD

GENEROSITY MAY BE ITS OWN reward, but it's even better when your gift garners a tax break. There are several tax-smart ways to help your kids or grandkids:

Feed a 529 plan. Money in a 529 plan may be used tax-free for college costs, and you may get a state income-tax break for your contributions. To qualify for a state tax break, you usually need to contribute to your own state's 529 plan (although five states—Arizona, Kan-

sas, Maine, Missouri and Pennsylvania—allow a deduction for contributions made to any state's plan). Some states let anyone take a tax deduction for their contributions; others give the tax break only to the owner of the account. But there's no limit to the number of 529 accounts that may be opened for one child, so parents and grandparents, for example, can open separate accounts and deduct contributions (see www .savingforcollege.com for

details about each state's plan and tax rules).

Get a big gift-tax break. In 2011, you may generally give up to $13,000 per person without being subject to gift-tax rules. Or you may make five years' worth of 529 contributions in one year—up to $65,000 per child, or up to $130,000 per child per married couple—without triggering the gift tax. Caveat: If you give money to that person again within the next five years, you'll eat into your lifetime maximum of $5 million in tax-free gifts.

Take credit for tuition payments. The American Opportunity credit can cut your tax bill by up to $2,500 per student if you're paying tuition for the first four years of college. To qualify for the full credit, the student must be considered your dependent and you must spend at least $4,000 in tuition and qualified expenses (including fees, books and other course materials). Plus, your modified adjusted gross income must be below $160,000 if married filing jointly or $80,000 if single or head of household (couples earning up to $180,000 or singles earning up to $90,000 can get a partial credit).

Pay college tuition directly. Direct payments of tuition (but not room and board) to educational institutions are excluded from the $13,000 annual gift-tax limit. This rule applies to anyone making the tuition payment and is particularly popular with grandparents who want to

give some extra money to their grandkids without running up against the gift-tax limits.

Help contribute to a Roth IRA. Kids of any age can open a Roth IRA as long as they have earned income from a job—even if it's just baby-sitting or lawn mowing. They may contribute up to the amount of their earned income for the year—with a $5,000 maximum in 2011—and you can give them the money to make the contributions. You won't get a tax break for your gift, but the kids will reap the benefits in the future—by withdrawing all of the money (including the earnings) tax-free after age 59½. And they can access the contributions at any time without taxes or penalties.

Open a custodial account. Open an account for your children or grandchildren at a brokerage firm or mutual fund company and make it a learning experience by making the investing decisions together. You can use the money for anything that benefits the child until he or she reaches the age of majority (21 in most states; 18 in a few) and takes over control of the account. Custodial accounts for children younger than 19 and full-time students younger than 24 are generally subject to the kiddie-tax rules: The first $950 of the child's investment income is tax-free; the next $950 is taxed at the child's own, low rate. Any investment income that tops $1,900 in 2011 is taxed at the parents' higher rate. ■

BUSINESS MATH ISSUE

Saving for your kids at an early age is not the best use of your cash.

1. List the key points of the article and information to support your position.
2. Write a group defense of your position using math calculations to support your view.

141

Percents and Their Applications

Google to Give Staff 10% Raise

By Amir Efrati
And Scott Morrison

Moving to staunch the defection of staff to competitors, **Google** Inc. is giving a 10% raise to all of its 23,000 employees, according to people familiar with the matter.

The raise, which will be given to executives and staff across the globe, is effective in January.

The pay hike comes as Google ramps up its battle with competitors, especially neighboring **Facebook** Inc., in a fight to secure talented staff. Roughly 10% of Facebook's employees are Google veterans, and other Silicon Valley companies have aggressively poached employees from the Internet giant.

Chief Executive Eric Schmidt disclosed the raise in an email to employees, saying the company wants to lift morale. "We want to make sure that you feel rewarded for your hard work," Mr. Schmidt wrote. "We want to continue to attract the best people to Google."

DILBERT: © Scott Adams/Dist. by United Feature Syndicate, Inc.

LU 6–1: Conversions

1. Convert decimals to percents (including rounding percents), percents to decimals, and fractions to percents (pp. 143–147).

2. Convert percents to fractions (p. 147).

LU 6–2: Application of Percents—Portion Formula

1. List and define the key elements of the portion formula (p. 149).

2. Solve for one unknown of the portion formula when the other two key elements are given (pp. 149–153).

3. Calculate the rate of percent increases and decreases (pp. 153–156).

VOCABULARY PREVIEW

Here are key terms in this chapter. After completing the chapter, if you know the term, place a checkmark in the parentheses. If you don't know the term, look it up and put the page number where it can be found.

Base ( ) Percent decrease ( ) Percent increase ( ) Percents ( ) Portion ( ) Rate ( )

The following *Wall Street Journal* clips illustrate the use of percents to show relationships between numbers. For example, profit at the Family Dollar is up by 23% from an earlier period of time. On the other hand, J.M. Smucker is reporting that it will cut its workforce by 15% and close four plants. Additionally, in the chapter opener, we read that Google is giving a 10% raise to its employees.

To understand percents, you should first understand the conversion relationship between decimals, percents, and fractions as explained in Learning Unit 6–1. Then, in Learning Unit 6–2, you will be ready to apply percents to personal and business events.

Family Dollar's Profit Rises 23%

BY MELISSA KORN

Family Dollar Stores Inc., which posted a 23% rise in fiscal-fourth-quarter profit Wednesday, said low-income shoppers are being joined by middle-class consumers in the discount chain's aisles.

The company said customers are still struggling financially and continue to seek bargains in apparel, pantry staples and other items. Family Dollar also said it plans to accelerate new-store growth and begin a store-renovation program.

Smucker to Cut Workers, Shut Plants

J.M. Smucker Co. said it will cut 15% of its work force, or about 700 jobs, over the next three years, closing four plants and building a new one.

The company said once the measures are fully in place, it expects to save $60 million annually.

The maker of fruit spreads, Folgers coffee and other foods also will close two fruit-spreads plants in 2013 and consolidate all coffee production into facilities in New Orleans, shuttering two other plants over the next two years.

Meanwhile, the company plans to spend $220 million over the next three years in its coffee and namesake businesses, building a new plant and expenditures for new equipment and technology.

Learning Unit 6–1: Conversions

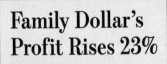

When we described parts of a whole in previous chapters, we used fractions and decimals. Percents also describe parts of a whole. The word *percent* means per 100. The percent symbol (%) indicates hundredths (division by 100). **Percents** are the result of expressing numbers as part of 100.

© Design Pics/Ben Welsh

Percents can provide some revealing information. The *Wall Street Journal* clipping "Animal Instincts" in the margin shows that 30% of pet owners would try another clinic if they had a coupon or special. This 30% represents 30 pet owners out of 100.

Let's return to the M&M'S® example from earlier chapters. In Table 6.1, we use our bag of 55 M&M'S® to show how fractions, decimals, and percents can refer to the same parts of a whole. For example, the bag of 55 M&M'S® contains 18 yellow M&M'S®. As you can see in Table 6.1, the 18 candies in the bag of 55 can be expressed as a fraction ($\frac{18}{55}$), decimal (.33), and percent (32.73%). If you visit the M&M'S® website, you will see that the standard is 11 yellow M&M'S®. The clipping (below) "What Colors Come in Your Bag?" shows an M&M'S® Milk Chocolate Candies Color Chart.

In this unit we discuss converting decimals to percents (including rounding percents), percents to decimals, fractions to percents, and percents to fractions. You will see when you study converting fractions to percents why you should first learn how to convert decimals to percents.

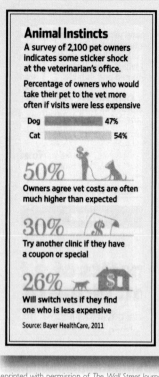

GLOBAL

ⓜ 10% 5.5

ⓜ 10% 5.5

ⓜ 10% 5.5

ⓜⓜⓜ 30% 16.5

ⓜⓜ 20% 11

ⓜⓜ 20% 11

What Colors Come In Your Bag?

Information adapted from http://us.mms.com/us/about/products/milkchocolate/

| TABLE | 6.1 | Analyzing a bag of M&M'S® |

Color	Fraction	Decimal (hundredth)	Percent (hundredth)
Yellow	$\frac{18}{55}$	.33	32.73%
Red	$\frac{10}{55}$	.18	18.18
Blue	$\frac{9}{55}$	.16	16.36
Orange	$\frac{7}{55}$	.13	12.73
Brown	$\frac{6}{55}$	.11	10.91
Green	$\frac{5}{55}$	.09	9.09
Total	$\frac{55}{55} = 1$	1.00	100.00%

Converting Decimals to Percents

The *Wall Street Journal* clip "Disney To Launch Channel In Russia" shows that Disney is starting a new Disney channel in Russia with 49% Disney ownership. If the clipping had stated the 49% as a decimal (.49), could you give its equivalent in percent? The decimal .49 in decimal fraction is $\frac{49}{100}$. As you know, percents are the result of expressing numbers as part of 100, so 49% = $\frac{49}{100}$. You can now conclude that .49 = $\frac{49}{100}$ = 49%.

The steps for converting decimals to percents are as follows:

CONVERTING DECIMALS TO PERCENTS

Step 1. Move the decimal point two places to the right. You are multiplying by 100. If necessary, add zeros. This rule is also used for whole numbers and mixed decimals.

Step 2. Add a percent symbol at the end of the number.

EXAMPLES

$$.49 = .49. = \boxed{49\%} \qquad .8 = .80. = \boxed{80\%} \qquad 8 = 8.00. = \boxed{800\%}$$

Add 1 zero to
make two places.

Add 2 zeros to
make two places.

$$.425 = .42.5 = \boxed{42.5\%} \qquad .007 = .00.7 = \boxed{.7\%} \qquad 2.51 = 2.51. = \boxed{251\%}$$

Caution: One percent means 1 out of every 100. Since .7% is less than 1%, it means $\frac{7}{10}$ of 1%—a very small amount. Less than 1% is less than .01. To show a number less than 1%, you must use more than two decimal places and add 2 zeros. Example: .7% = .007.

Rounding Percents

When necessary, percents should be rounded. Rounding percents is similar to rounding whole numbers. Use the following steps to round percents:

ROUNDING PERCENTS

Step 1. When you convert from a fraction or decimal, be sure your answer is in percent before rounding.

Step 2. Identify the specific digit. If the digit to the right of the identified digit is 5 or greater, round up the identified digit.

Step 3. Delete digits to the right of the identified digit.

For example, Table 6.1 (p. 144) shows that the 18 yellow M&M'S® rounded to the nearest hundredth percent is 32.73% of the bag of 55 M&M'S®. Let's look at how we arrived at this figure.

When using a calculator, you press 18 ÷ 55 % . This allows you to go right to percent, avoiding the decimal step.

Step 1. $\dfrac{18}{55} = .3272727 = 32.72727\%$ Note that the number is in percent! Identify the hundredth percent digit.

Step 2. 32.73727%   Digit to the right of the identified digit is greater than 5, so the identified digit is increased by 1.

Step 3. 32.73%   Delete digits to the right of the identified digit.

Converting Percents to Decimals

Note in the following *Wall Street Journal* clip "The New Ice Age" that ice cream sales are down by .4%.

In the paragraph and steps that follow, you will learn how to convert percents to decimals. The example using .4% comes from the clipping "The New Ice Age."

To convert percents to decimals, you reverse the process used to convert decimals to percents. In our earlier discussion on converting decimals to percents (p. 144), we asked if the 49% in the "Disney" clipping had been in decimals and not percent, could you convert the decimals to the 49%? Once again, the definition of percent states that $49\% = \frac{49}{100}$. The fraction $\frac{49}{100}$ can be written in decimal form as .49. You can conclude that $49\% = \frac{49}{100} = .49$. Now you can see this procedure in the following conversion steps:

CONVERTING PERCENTS TO DECIMALS

Step 1. Drop the percent symbol.

Step 2. Move the decimal point two places to the left. You are dividing by 100. If necessary, add zeros.

EXAMPLES

Note that when a percent is less than 1%, the decimal conversion has at least two leading zeros before the number .004.

.4% = .00.4 = .004   2% = .02. = .02   49% = .49. = .49

Add 2 zeros to make two places.   Add 1 zero to make two places.

54.5% = .54.5 = .545   824.4% = 8.24.4 = 8.244

Now we must explain how to change fractional percents such as $\frac{1}{5}\%$ to a decimal. Remember that fractional percents are values less than 1%. For example, $\frac{1}{5}\%$ is $\frac{1}{5}$ of 1%. Fractional percents can appear singly or in combination with whole numbers. To convert them to decimals, use the following steps:

CONVERTING FRACTIONAL PERCENTS TO DECIMALS

Step 1. Convert a single fractional percent to its decimal equivalent by dividing the numerator by the denominator. If necessary, round the answer.

Step 2. If a fractional percent is combined with a whole number (mixed fractional percent), convert the fractional percent first. Then combine the whole number and the fractional percent.

Step 3. Drop the percent symbol; move the decimal point two places to the left (this divides the number by 100).

EXAMPLES

$\frac{1}{5}\% = .20\% = .00.20 = .0020$

$\frac{1}{4}\% = .25\% = .00.25 = .0025$

$7\frac{3}{4}\% = 7.75\% = .07.75 = .0775$

$6\frac{1}{2}\% = 6.5\% = .06.5 = .065$

Think of $7\frac{3}{4}\%$ as

$7\% = \quad .07$

$+ \frac{3}{4}\% = \quad + .0075$

$7\frac{3}{4}\% = \quad .0775$

Converting Fractions to Percents

When fractions have denominators of 100, the numerator becomes the percent. Other fractions must be first converted to decimals; then the decimals are converted to percents.

CONVERTING FRACTIONS TO PERCENTS
Step 1. Divide the numerator by the denominator to convert the fraction to a decimal.
Step 2. Move the decimal point two places to the right; add the percent symbol.

EXAMPLES

$$\frac{3}{4} = .75 = .75. = \boxed{75\%} \qquad \frac{1}{5} = .20 = .20. = \boxed{20\%} \qquad \frac{1}{20} = .05 = .05. = \boxed{5\%}$$

LO 2

Converting Percents to Fractions

Using the definition of percent, you can write any percent as a fraction whose denominator is 100. Thus, when we convert a percent to a fraction, we drop the percent symbol and write the number over 100, which is the same as multiplying the number by $\frac{1}{100}$. This method of multiplying by $\frac{1}{100}$ is also used for fractional percents.

CONVERTING A WHOLE PERCENT (OR A FRACTIONAL PERCENT) TO A FRACTION
Step 1. Drop the percent symbol.
Step 2. Multiply the number by $\frac{1}{100}$.
Step 3. Reduce to lowest terms.

EXAMPLES

$$76\% = 76 \times \frac{1}{100} = \frac{76}{100} = \boxed{\frac{19}{25}} \qquad \frac{1}{8}\% = \frac{1}{8} \times \frac{1}{100} = \boxed{\frac{1}{800}}$$

$$156\% = 156 \times \frac{1}{100} = \frac{156}{100} = 1\frac{56}{100} = \boxed{1\frac{14}{25}}$$

Sometimes a percent contains a whole number and a fraction such as $12\frac{1}{2}\%$ or 22.5%. Extra steps are needed to write a mixed or decimal percent as a simplified fraction.

MONEY tips

Nearly half, 47%, of adult Americans have no life insurance coverage. Consider the impact on survivors. At a minimum, carry burial insurance and a letter of last instruction stating your burial wishes.

CONVERTING A MIXED OR DECIMAL PERCENT TO A FRACTION
Step 1. Drop the percent symbol.
Step 2. Change the mixed percent to an improper fraction.
Step 3. Multiply the number by $\frac{1}{100}$.
Step 4. Reduce to lowest terms.
Note: If you have a mixed or decimal percent, change the decimal portion to its fractional equivalent and continue with Steps 1 to 4.

EXAMPLES $12\frac{1}{2}\% = \frac{25}{2} \times \frac{1}{100} = \frac{25}{200} = \boxed{\frac{1}{8}}$

$$12.5\% = 12\frac{1}{2}\% = \frac{25}{2} \times \frac{1}{100} = \frac{25}{200} = \boxed{\frac{1}{8}}$$

$$22.5\% = 22\frac{1}{2}\% = \frac{45}{2} \times \frac{1}{100} = \frac{45}{200} = \boxed{\frac{9}{40}}$$

It's time to check your understanding of Learning Unit 6–1.

LU 6–1 PRACTICE QUIZ

Complete this **Practice Quiz** to see how you are doing.

Convert to percents (round to the nearest tenth percent as needed):

1. .6666 _____   **2.** .832 _____

3. .004 _____   **4.** 8.94444 _____

Convert to decimals (remember, decimals representing less than 1% will have at least 2 leading zeros before the number):

5. $\frac{1}{4}\%$ _____   **6.** $6\frac{3}{4}\%$ _____

7. 87% _____   **8.** 810.9% _____

Convert to percents (round to the nearest hundredth percent):

9. $\frac{1}{7}$ _____   **10.** $\frac{2}{9}$ _____

Convert to fractions (remember, if it is a mixed number, first convert to an improper fraction):

11. 19% _____   **12.** $71\frac{1}{2}\%$ _____   **13.** 130% _____

14. $\frac{1}{2}\%$ _____   **15.** 19.9% _____

For **extra help** from your authors—Sharon and Jeff—see the student DVD

You Tube

✓ Solutions

1. .66.66 = 66.7%   **2.** .83.2 = 83.2%

3. .00.4 = .4%   **4.** 8.94.444 = 894.4%

5. $\frac{1}{4}\% = .25\% = .0025$ **6.** $6\frac{3}{4}\% = 6.75\% = .0675$

7. 87% = .87. = .87   **8.** 810.9% = 8.10.9 = 8.109

9. $\frac{1}{7} = .14.285 = 14.29\%$ **10.** $\frac{2}{9} = .22.2\overline{2} = 22.22\%$

11. $19\% = 19 \times \frac{1}{100} = \frac{19}{100}$ **12.** $71\frac{1}{2}\% = \frac{143}{2} \times \frac{1}{100} = \frac{143}{200}$

13. $130\% = 130 \times \frac{1}{100} = \frac{130}{100} = 1\frac{30}{100} = 1\frac{3}{10}$ **14.** $\frac{1}{2}\% = \frac{1}{2} \times \frac{1}{100} = \frac{1}{200}$

15. $19\frac{9}{10}\% = \frac{199}{10} \times \frac{1}{100} = \frac{199}{1,000}$

LU 6–1a EXTRA PRACTICE QUIZ WITH WORKED-OUT SOLUTIONS

Need more practice? Try this **Extra Practice Quiz** (check figures in the Interactive Chapter Organizer, p. 161). Worked-out Solutions can be found in Appendix B at end of text.

Convert to percents (round to the nearest tenth percent as needed):

1. .4444   **2.** .782

3. .006   **4.** 7.93333

Convert to decimals (remember, decimals representing less than 1% will have at least 2 leading zeros before the number):

5. $\frac{1}{5}\%$ **6.** $7\frac{4}{5}\%$

7. 92%   **8.** 765.8%

Convert to percents (round to the nearest hundredth percent):

9. $\frac{1}{3}$ **10.** $\frac{3}{7}$

Convert to fractions (remember, if it is a mixed number, first convert to an improper fraction):

11. 17%   **12.** $82\frac{1}{4}\%$ **13.** 150%

14. $\frac{1}{4}\%$ **15.** 17.8%

Learning Unit 6–2: Application of Percents—Portion Formula

LO 1

The bag of M&M'S® we have been studying contains Milk Chocolate M&M'S®. M&M/Mars also makes Peanut M&M'S® and some other types of M&M'S®. To study the application of percents to problems involving M&M'S®, we make two key assumptions:

1. Total sales of Milk Chocolate M&M'S®, Peanut M&M'S®, and other M&M'S® chocolate candies are $400,000.

2. Eighty percent of M&M'S® sales are Milk Chocolate M&M'S®. This leaves the Peanut and other M&M'S® chocolate candies with 20% of sales (100% − 80%).

80% M&M'S®		20% M&M'S®		100%
Milk Chocolate M&M'S®	+	Peanut and other chocolate candies	=	Total sales ($400,000)

Before we begin, you must understand the meaning of three terms—*base, rate,* and *portion*. These terms are the key elements in solving percent problems.

- **Base (B).** The **base** is the beginning whole quantity or value (100%) with which you will compare some other quantity or value. Often the problems give the base after the word *of*. For example, the whole (total) sales of M&M'S®—Milk Chocolate M&M'S, Peanut, and other M&M'S® chocolate candies—are $400,000.

- **Rate (R).** The **rate** is a percent, decimal, or fraction that indicates the part of the base that you must calculate. The percent symbol often helps you identify the rate. For example, Milk Chocolate M&M'S® currently account for 80% of sales. So the rate is 80%. Remember that 80% is also $\frac{4}{5}$, or .80.

- **Portion (P).** The **portion** is the amount or part that results from the base multiplied by the rate. For example, total sales of M&M'S® are $400,000 (base); $400,000 times .80 (rate) equals $320,000 (portion), or the sales of Milk Chocolate M&M'S®. *A key point to remember is that portion is a number and not a percent. In fact, the portion can be larger than the base if the rate is greater than 100%.*

Solving Percents with the Portion Formula

LO 2

In problems involving portion, base, and rate, we give two of these elements. You must find the third element. Remember the following key formula:

$$\text{Portion } (P) = \text{Base } (B) \times \text{Rate } (R)$$

To help you solve for the portion, base, and rate, this unit shows pie charts. The shaded area in each pie chart indicates the element that you must solve for. For example, since we shaded *portion* in the pie chart at the left, you must solve for portion. To use the pie charts, put your finger on the shaded area (in this case portion). The formula that remains tells you what to do. So in the pie chart at the left, you solve the problem by multiplying base by the rate. Note the circle around the pie chart is broken since we want to emphasize that portion can be larger than base if rate is greater than 100%. The horizontal line in the pie chart is called the dividing line, and we will use it when we solve for base or rate.

The following example summarizes the concept of base, rate, and portion. Assume that you received a small bonus check of $100. This is a gross amount—your company did not withhold any taxes. You will have to pay 20% in taxes.

is

This line is called the dividing line

Portion

Base × Rate

of

%

Base: 100%—whole. Usually given after the word *of*—but not always.	**Rate:** Usually expressed as a percent but could also be a decimal or fraction.	**Portion:** A number—not a percent and not the whole.
$100 bonus check	20% taxes	$20 taxes

First decide what you are looking for. You want to know how much you must pay in taxes—the portion. How do you get the portion? From the portion formula Portion (P) = Base (B) × Rate (R), you know that you must multiply the base ($100) by the rate (20%). When you do this, you get $100 × .20 = $20. So you must pay $20 in taxes.

Let's try our first word problem by taking a closer look at the M&M'S® example to see how we arrived at the $320,000 sales of Milk Chocolate M&M'S® given earlier. We will be using blueprint aids to help dissect and solve each word problem.

Solving for Portion

The Word Problem Sales of Milk Chocolate M&M'S® are 80% of the total M&M'S® sales. Total M&M'S® sales are $400,000. What are the sales of Milk Chocolate M&M'S®?

	The facts	Solving for?	Steps to take	Key points
BLUEPRINT	Milk Chocolate M&M'S® sales: 80%. Total M&M'S® sales: $400,000.	Sales of Milk Chocolate M&M'S®.	Identify key elements. Base: $400,000. Rate: .80. Portion: ? Portion = Base × Rate.	Amount or part of beginning Portion (?) Base × Rate ($400,000) (.80) Beginning whole quantity (often after "of") Percent symbol or word (here we put into decimal) Portion and rate must relate to same piece of base.

Steps to solving problem

1. Set up the formula.   Portion = Base × Rate

2. Calculate portion (sales of Milk   P = $400,000 × .80
   Chocolate M&M'S®).
                                                         P = $320,000

In the first column of the blueprint aid, we gather the facts. In the second column, we state that we are looking for sales of Milk Chocolate M&M'S®. In the third column, we identify each key element and the formula needed to solve the problem. Review the pie chart in the fourth column. Note that the portion and rate must relate to the same piece of the base. In this word problem, we can see from the solution below the blueprint aid that sales of Milk Chocolate M&M'S® are $320,000. The $320,000 does indeed represent 80% of the base. Note here that the portion ($320,000) is less than the base of $400,000 since the rate is less than 100%.

Now let's work another word problem that solves for the portion.

The Word Problem Sales of Milk Chocolate M&M'S® are 80% of the total M&M'S® sales. Total M&M'S® sales are $400,000. What are the sales of Peanut and other M&M'S® chocolate candies?

	The facts	Solving for?	Steps to take	Key points
BLUEPRINT	Milk Chocolate M&M'S® sales: 80%. Total M&M'S® sales: $400,000.	Sales of Peanut and other M&M'S® chocolate candies.	Identify key elements. Base: $400,000. Rate: .20 (100% − 80%). Portion: ? Portion = Base × Rate.	If 80% of sales are Milk Chocolate M&M'S, then 20% are Peanut and other M&M'S® chocolate candies. Portion (?) Base × Rate ($400,000) (.20) Portion and rate must relate to same piece of base.

Steps to solving problem

1. Set up the formula.   Portion = Base $\times$ Rate

2. Calculate portion (sale of Peanut and other $P = \$400,000 \times .20$
   M&M'S® chocolate candies). $P = \$80,000$

In the previous blueprint aid, note that we must use a rate that agrees with the portion so the portion and rate refer to the same piece of the base. Thus, if 80% of sales are Milk Chocolate M&M'S®, 20% must be Peanut and other M&M'S® chocolate candies (100% − 80% = 20%). So we use a rate of .20.

In Step 2, we multiplied $\$400,000 \times .20$ to get a portion of $80,000. This portion represents the part of the sales that were *not* Milk Chocolate M&M'S®. Note that the rate of .20 and the portion of $80,000 relate to the same piece of the base—$80,000 is 20% of $400,000. Also note that the portion ($80,000) is less than the base ($400,000) since the rate is less than 100%.

Take a moment to review the two blueprint aids in this section. Be sure you understand why the rate in the first blueprint aid was 80% and the rate in the second blueprint aid was 20%.

Solving for Rate

The Word Problem Sales of Milk Chocolate M&M'S® are $320,000. Total M&M'S® sales are $400,000. What is the percent of Milk Chocolate M&M'S® sales compared to total M&M'S® sales?

	The facts	Solving for?	Steps to take	Key points
B L U E P R I N T	*Milk Chocolate M&M'S® sales: $320,000.* *Total M&M'S® sales: $400,000.*	Percent of Milk Chocolate M&M'S® sales to total M&M'S® sales.	Identify key elements. *Base:* $400,000. *Rate:* ? *Portion:* $320,000 Rate = $\dfrac{\text{Portion}}{\text{Base}}$	Since portion is less than base, the rate must be less than 100% Portion ($320,000) Base ($400,000) × Rate (?) Portion and rate must relate to the same piece of base.

Steps to solving problem

1. Set up the formula.   Rate = $\dfrac{\text{Portion}}{\text{Base}}$

2. Calculate rate (percent of Milk $R = \dfrac{\$320,000}{\$400,000}$
   Chocolate M&M'S® sales). $R = 80\%$

Note that in this word problem, the rate of 80% and the portion of $320,000 refer to the same piece of the base.

The Word Problem Sales of Milk Chocolate M&M'S® are $320,000. Total sales of Milk Chocolate M&M'S, Peanut, and other M&M'S® chocolate candies are $400,000. What percent of Peanut and other M&M'S® chocolate candies are sold compared to total M&M'S® sales?

(continued on p. 152)

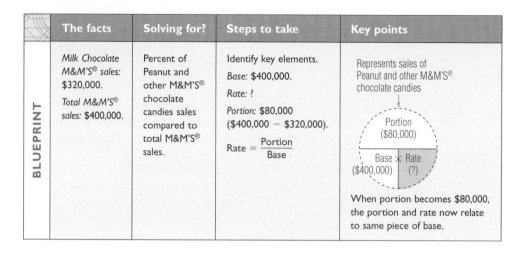

	The facts	Solving for?	Steps to take	Key points
BLUEPRINT	*Milk Chocolate M&M'S® sales: $320,000.* *Total M&M'S® sales: $400,000.*	Percent of Peanut and other M&M'S® chocolate candies sales compared to total M&M'S® sales.	Identify key elements. *Base: $400,000.* *Rate: ?* *Portion: $80,000 ($400,000 − $320,000).* $\text{Rate} = \dfrac{\text{Portion}}{\text{Base}}$	Represents sales of Peanut and other M&M'S® chocolate candies Portion ($80,000) Base × Rate ($400,000) (?) When portion becomes $80,000, the portion and rate now relate to same piece of base.

Steps to solving problem

1. Set up the formula.

$$\text{Rate} = \frac{\text{Portion}}{\text{Base}}$$

2. Calculate rate.

$$R = \frac{\$80,000}{\$400,000} \quad (\$400,000 - \$320,000)$$

$$R = \boxed{20\%}$$

The word problem asks for the rate of candy sales that are *not* Milk Chocolate M&M'S. Thus, $400,000 of total candy sales less sales of Milk Chocolate M&M'S® ($320,000) allows us to arrive at sales of Peanut and other M&M'S® chocolate candies ($80,000). The $80,000 portion represents 20% of total candy sales. The $80,000 portion and 20% rate refer to the same piece of the $400,000 base. Compare this blueprint aid with the blueprint aid for the previous word problem. Ask yourself why in the previous word problem the rate was 80% and in this word problem the rate is 20%. In both word problems, the portion was less than the base since the rate was less than 100%.

Now we go on to calculate the base. Remember to read the word problem carefully so that you match the rate and portion to the same piece of the base.

Solving for Base

The Word Problem   Sales of Peanut and other M&M'S® chocolate candies are 20% of total M&M'S® sales. Sales of Milk Chocolate M&M'S® are $320,000. What are the total sales of all M&M'S®?

	The facts	Solving for?	Steps to take	Key points
BLUEPRINT	*Peanut and other M&M'S® chocolate candies sales: 20%.* *Milk Chocolate M&M'S® sales: $320,000.*	Total M&M'S® sales.	Identify key elements. *Base: ?* *Rate: .80 (100% − 20%)* *Portion: $320,000* $\text{Base} = \dfrac{\text{Portion}}{\text{Rate}}$	Portion ($320,000) Base × Rate (?) (.80) (100% − 20%) Portion ($320,000) and rate (.80) do relate to the same piece of base.

Steps to solving problem

1. Set up the formula.

$$\text{Base} = \frac{\text{Portion}}{\text{Rate}}$$

2. Calculate the base.

$$B = \frac{\$320,000}{.80} \quad \longleftarrow \ \$320,000 \text{ is } 80\% \text{ of base}$$

$$B = \boxed{\$400,000}$$

Note that we could not use 20% for the rate. The $320,000 of Milk Chocolate M&M'S® represents 80% (100% − 20%) of the total sales of M&M'S®. We use 80% so that the portion and rate refer to same piece of the base. Remember that the portion ($320,000) is less than the base ($400,000) since the rate is less than 100%.

Calculating Percent Increases and Decreases

The following *Wall Street Journal* clipping shows that sales for Ford are up 19%, while Toyota showed a 4.4% decrease in sales. Using this clipping, let's look at how to calculate percent increases and decreases.

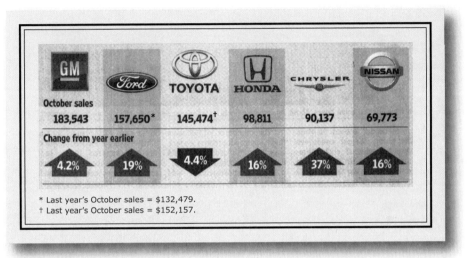

The Ford Example: Rate of Percent Increase
Assume: Sales increase from $132,479 to $157,650.

$$\text{Rate} = \frac{\text{Portion}}{\text{Base}} \quad \begin{matrix} \longleftarrow \text{Difference between old and new sales} \\ \longleftarrow \text{Old sales} \end{matrix}$$

$$R = \frac{\$25,171 \,(\$157,650 - \$132,479)}{\$132,479}$$

$$R = \boxed{18.99\%} \quad \text{(Rounded to 19\% in clip.)}$$

Let's prove the 19% with a pie chart.

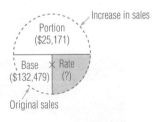

The formula for calculating sales **percent increase** is as follows:

Percent increase

$$\begin{matrix} \text{Percent of} \\ \text{increase } (R) \\ (19\%) \end{matrix} = \frac{\begin{matrix} \text{Amount of sales increase } (P) \\ (\$25,171) \end{matrix}}{\begin{matrix} \text{Original sales } (B) \\ (\$132,479) \end{matrix}}$$

Now let's look at how to calculate the math for a decrease in sales for Toyota.

The Toyota Example: Rate of Percent Decrease
Assume: Sales drop from $152,157 to $145,474.

$$\text{Rate} = \frac{\text{Portion}}{\text{Base}} \leftarrow \text{Difference between old and new sales}$$
$$\leftarrow \text{Old sales}$$

$$R = \frac{\$6,683\,(\$152,157 - \$145,474)}{\$152,157}$$

$$R = \boxed{4.39\%} = 4.4\%$$

Let's prove the 4.4% with a pie chart.

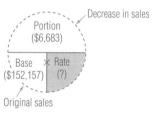

The formula for calculating sales **percent decrease** is as follows:

Percent decrease

Percent of decrease (R) (4.4%)	$=$	Amount of sales decrease (P) ($6,683) / Original sales (B) ($152,157)

In conclusion, the following steps can be used to calculate percent increases and decreases:

CALCULATING PERCENT INCREASES AND DECREASES
Step 1. Find the difference between amounts (such as sales).
Step 2. Divide Step 1 by the original amount (the base): $R = P \div B$. Be sure to express your answer in percent.

Before concluding this chapter, we will show how to calculate a percent increase and decrease using M&M'S® (Figure 6.1).

FIGURE   6.1

Bag of 18.40-ounce M&M'S®

Additional Examples Using M&M'S

The Word Problem Sheila Leary went to her local supermarket and bought the bag of M&M'S® shown in Figure 6.1 (p. 154). The bag gave its weight as 18.40 ounces, which was 15% more than a regular 1-pound bag of M&M'S®. Sheila, who is a careful shopper, wanted to check and see if she was actually getting a 15% increase. Let's help Sheila dissect and solve this problem.

	The facts	Solving for?	Steps to take	Key points
BLUEPRINT	*New bag of M&M'S®:* 18.40 oz. 15% increase in weight. *Original bag of M&M'S®:* 16 oz. (1 lb.)	Checking percent increase of 15%.	Identify key elements. *Base:* 16 oz. *Rate:* ? *Portion:* 2.40 oz. $\left(\begin{array}{r} 18.40 \text{ oz.} \\ -\ 16.00 \\ \hline 2.40 \text{ oz.} \end{array}\right)$ $\text{Rate} = \dfrac{\text{Portion}}{\text{Base}}$	Difference between base and new weight Portion (2.40 oz.) Base × Rate (16 oz.) (?) Original amount sold

Steps to solving problem

1. Set up the formula.
   $$\text{Rate} = \frac{\text{Portion}}{\text{Base}}$$

2. Calculate the rate.
   $$R = \frac{2.40 \text{ oz.}}{16.00 \text{ oz.}} \quad \begin{array}{l} \leftarrow \text{ Difference between base and new weight.} \\ \leftarrow \text{ Old weight equals 100\%.} \end{array}$$

   $R = 15\%$ increase

The new weight of the bag of M&M'S® is really 115% of the old weight:

$$
\begin{array}{rcl}
16.00 \text{ oz.} & = & 100\% \\
+\ 2.40 & = & +\ 15 \\
\hline
18.40 \text{ oz.} & = & 115\% = 1.15
\end{array}
$$

We can check this by looking at the following pie chart:

Portion = Base × Rate

18.40 oz. = 16 oz. × 1.15

Portion (18.40 oz.)
Base × Rate (16 oz.) (1.15)
100%

Why is the portion greater than the base? Remember that the portion can be larger than the base only if the rate is greater than 100%. Note how the portion and rate relate to the same piece of the base—18.40 oz. is 115% of the base (16 oz.).

Let's see what could happen if M&M/Mars has an increase in its price of sugar. This is an additional example to reinforce the concept of percent decrease.

The Word Problem The increase in the price of sugar caused the M&M/Mars company to decrease the weight of each 1-pound bag of M&M'S® to 12 ounces. What is the rate of percent decrease?

	The facts	Solving for?	Steps to take	Key points
BLUEPRINT	*16-oz. bag of M&M'S®:* reduced to 12 oz.	Rate of percent decrease.	Identify key elements. *Base:* 16 oz. *Rate:* ? *Portion:* 4 oz. (16 oz. − 12 oz.) $\text{Rate} = \dfrac{\text{Portion}}{\text{Base}}$	Amount of decrease Portion (4 oz.) Base × Rate (16 oz.) (?) Old base 100%

MONEY tips

When planning for retirement, a rule of thumb is that you will need 70% of your preretirement pay to live comfortably. This number assumes your house is paid off and you are in good health. Automating your savings can be a huge factor in helping you reach your goals. So, begin planning early in life and start saving for a financially sound retirement.

Steps to solving problem

1. Set up the formula.

$$\text{Rate} = \frac{\text{Portion}}{\text{Base}}$$

2. Calculate the rate.

$$R = \frac{4 \text{ oz.}}{16.00 \text{ oz.}}$$

$$R = 25\% \text{ decrease}$$

The new weight of the bag of M&M'S® is 75% of the old weight:

$$
\begin{array}{rcr}
16 \text{ oz.} & = & 100\% \\
- \ 4 & & - \ 25 \\
\hline
12 \text{ oz.} & = & 75\%
\end{array}
$$

We can check this by looking at the following pie chart:

$$\text{Portion} = \text{Base} \times \text{Rate}$$

$$12 \text{ oz.} = 16 \text{ oz.} \times .75$$

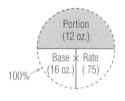

Note that the portion is smaller than the base because the rate is less than 100%. Also note how the portion and rate relate to the same piece of the base—12 ounces is 75% of the base (16 oz.).

After your study of Learning Unit 6–2, you should be ready for the Practice Quiz.

LU 6–2   PRACTICE QUIZ

Complete this **Practice Quiz** to see how you are doing.

Solve for portion:

1. 38% of 900.   **2.** 60% of $9,000.

Solve for rate (round to the nearest tenth percent as needed):

3. 430 is _____% of 5,000.   **4.** 200 is _____% of 700.

Solve for base (round to the nearest tenth as needed):

5. 55 is 40% of _____.   **6.** 900 is $4\frac{1}{2}$% of _____.

Solve the following (blueprint aids are shown in the solution; you might want to try some on scrap paper):

7. Five out of 25 students in Professor Ford's class received an A grade. What percent of the class *did not* receive the A grade?

8. Abby Biernet has yet to receive 60% of her lobster order. Abby received 80 lobsters to date. What was her original order?

9. Assume in 2013, Dunkin' Donuts Company had $300,000 in doughnut sales. In 2014, sales were up 40%. What are Dunkin' Donuts sales for 2014?

10. The price of an Apple computer dropped from $1,600 to $1,200. What was the percent decrease?

11. In 1982, a ticket to the Boston Celtics cost $14. In 2013, a ticket cost $50. What is the percent increase to the nearest hundredth percent?

For **extra help** from your authors–Sharon and Jeff–see the student DVD

✔ **Solutions**

1. $\boxed{342} = 900 \times .38$

     $(P) = (B) \times (R)$

2. $\boxed{\$5,400} = \$9,000 \times .60$

     $(P) \quad = \quad (B) \quad \times (R)$

3. $\dfrac{(P)430}{(B)5,000} = .086 = \boxed{8.6\%}\ (R)$

4. $\dfrac{(P)200}{(B)700} = .2857 = \boxed{28.6\%}\ (R)$

5. $\dfrac{(P)55}{(R).40} = \boxed{137.5}\ (B)$

6. $\dfrac{(P)900}{(R).045} = \boxed{20,000}\ (B)$

7. Percent of Professor Ford's class that did not receive an A grade:

	The facts	Solving for?	Steps to take	Key points
BLUEPRINT	5 As. 25 in class.	Percent that did not receive A.	Identify key elements. *Base:* 25 *Rate:* ? *Portion:* 20 (25 − 5). Rate = $\dfrac{\text{Portion}}{\text{Base}}$	Portion (20) Base × Rate (25) (?) The whole Portion and rate must relate to same piece of base.

Steps to solving problem

1. Set up the formula.   Rate = $\dfrac{\text{Portion}}{\text{Base}}$

2. Calculate the base rate. $R = \dfrac{20}{25}$

        $R = 80\%$

8. Abby Biernet's original order:

	The facts	Solving for?	Steps to take	Key points
BLUEPRINT	60% of the order not in. 80 lobsters received.	Total order of lobsters.	Identify key elements. *Base:* ? *Rate:* .40 (100% − 60%) *Portion:* 80. Base = $\dfrac{\text{Portion}}{\text{Rate}}$	Portion (80) Base × Rate (?) (.40) 80 lobsters represent 40% of the order Portion and rate must relate to same piece of base.

Steps to solving problem

1. Set up the formula.   Base = $\dfrac{\text{Portion}}{\text{Rate}}$

2. Calculate the base rate. $B = \dfrac{80}{.40}$ ← 80 lobsters is 40% of base.

        $B = 200$ lobsters

9. Dunkin' Donuts Company sales for 2014:

	The facts	Solving for?	Steps to take	Key points
BLUEPRINT	*2013:* $300,000 sales. *2014:* Sales up 40% from 2013.	Sales for 2014.	Identify key elements. *Base:* $300,000. *Rate:* 1.40. Old year 100% New year +40 140% *Portion:* ? Portion = Base × Rate.	2014 sales Portion (?) Base × Rate ($300,000) (1.40) 2013 sales When rate is greater than 100%, portion will be larger than base.

Steps to solving problem

1. Set up the formula.   Portion = Base × Rate

2. Calculate the portion. P = \$300,000 × 1.40

$$P = \$420,000$$

10. Percent decrease in Apple computer price:

	The facts	Solving for?	Steps to take	Key points
BLUEPRINT	Apple computer was \$1,600; now, \$1,200.	Percent decrease in price.	Identify key elements. *Base:* \$1,600. *Rate:* ? *Portion:* \$400 (\$1,600 − \$1,200). $Rate = \dfrac{Portion}{Base}$	Difference in price Portion (\$400) Base ($1,600) × Rate (?) Original price

Steps to solving problem

1. Set up the formula. $Rate = \dfrac{Portion}{Base}$

2. Calculate the rate. $R = \dfrac{\$400}{\$1,600}$

$$R = 25\%$$

11. Percent increase in Boston Celtics ticket:

© AP Photo/Charles Krupa

	The facts	Solving for?	Steps to take	Key points
BLUEPRINT	\$14 ticket (old). \$50 ticket (new).	Percent increase in price.	Identify key elements. *Base:* \$14 *Rate:* ? *Portion:* \$36 (\$50 − \$14) $Rate = \dfrac{Portion}{Base}$	Difference in price Portion (\$36) Base ($14) × Rate (?) Original price When portion is greater than base, rate will be greater than 100%.

Steps to solving problem

1. Set up the formula. $Rate = \dfrac{Portion}{Base}$

2. Calculate the rate. $R = \dfrac{\$36}{\$14}$

$$R = 2.5714 = 257.14\%$$

LU 6–2a	EXTRA PRACTICE QUIZ WITH WORKED-OUT SOLUTIONS

Need more practice? Try this **Extra Practice Quiz** (check figures in the Interactive Chapter Organizer, p. 161). Worked-out Solutions can be found in Appendix B at end of text.

Solve for portion:

1. 42% of 1,200

2. 7% of $8,000

Solve for rate (round to nearest tenth percent as needed):

3. 510 is _____% of 6,000.

4. 400 is _____% of 900.

Solve for base (round to the nearest tenth as needed):

5. 30 is 60% of _____.

6. 1,200 is $3\frac{1}{2}$% of _____.

7. Ten out of 25 students in Professor Ford's class received an A grade. What percent of the class did not receive the A grade?

8. Abby Biernet has yet to receive 70% of her lobster order. Abby received 90 lobsters to date. What was her original order?

9. A local Dunkin' Donuts Company had $400,000 in doughnut sales in 2013. In 2014, sales were up 35%. What are Dunkin' Donuts sales for 2014?

10. The price of an Apple computer dropped from $1,800 to $1,000. What was the percent decrease? (Round to the nearest hundredth percent.)

11. In 1982, a ticket to the Boston Celtics cost $14. In 2013, a ticket cost $75. What is the percent increase to the nearest hundredth percent?

INTERACTIVE CHAPTER ORGANIZER

Topic/procedure/formula	Examples	You try it*
Converting decimals to percents, p. 144 1. Move decimal point two places to right. If necessary, add zeros. This rule is also used for whole numbers and mixed decimals. 2. Add a percent symbol at end of number.	.81 = .81. = 81% .008 = .00.8 = .8% 4.15 = 4.15. = 415%	**Convert to percent** .92 .009 5.46
Rounding percents, p. 145 1. Answer must be in percent before rounding. 2. Identify specific digit. If digit to right is 5 or greater, round up. 3. Delete digits to right of identified digit.	Round to the nearest hundredth percent. $\frac{3}{7}$ = .4285714 = 42.85714% = 42.86%	**Round to the nearest hundredth percent** $\frac{2}{9}$
Converting percents to decimals, pp. 145–146 1. Drop percent symbol. 2. Move decimal point two places to left. If necessary, add zeros. For fractional percents: 1. Convert to decimal by dividing numerator by denominator. If necessary, round answer. 2. If a mixed fractional percent, convert fractional percent first. Then combine whole number and fractional percent. 3. Drop percent symbol, move decimal point two places to left.	.89% = .0089 95% = .95 195% = 1.95 $8\frac{3}{4}$% = 8.75% = .0875 $\frac{1}{4}$% = .25% = .0025 $\frac{1}{5}$% = .20% = .0020	**Convert to decimal** .78% 96% 246% $7\frac{3}{4}$% $\frac{3}{4}$% $\frac{1}{2}$%

(continues)

INTERACTIVE CHAPTER ORGANIZER

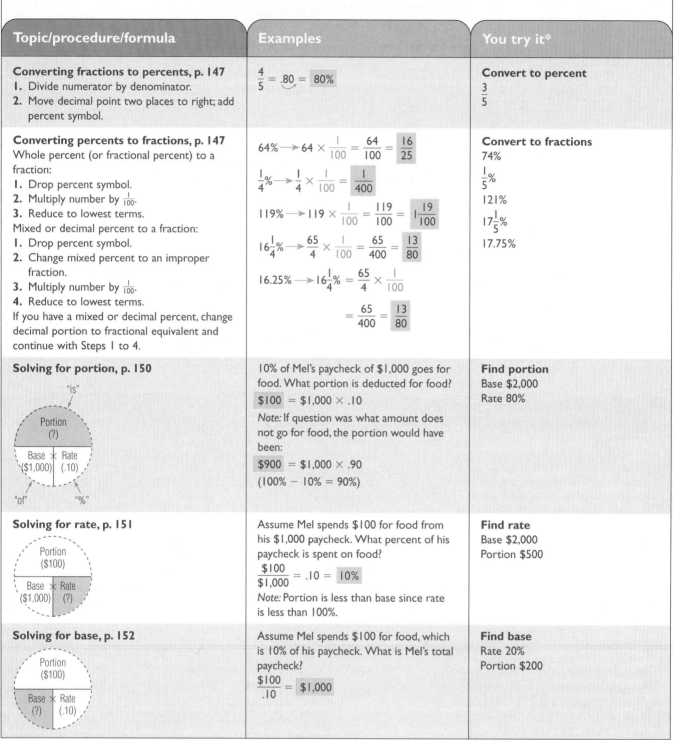

Topic/procedure/formula	Examples	You try it*
Converting fractions to percents, p. 147 1. Divide numerator by denominator. 2. Move decimal point two places to right; add percent symbol.	$\frac{4}{5} = .80 = \boxed{80\%}$	**Convert to percent** $\frac{3}{5}$
Converting percents to fractions, p. 147 Whole percent (or fractional percent) to a fraction: 1. Drop percent symbol. 2. Multiply number by $\frac{1}{100}$. 3. Reduce to lowest terms. Mixed or decimal percent to a fraction: 1. Drop percent symbol. 2. Change mixed percent to an improper fraction. 3. Multiply number by $\frac{1}{100}$. 4. Reduce to lowest terms. If you have a mixed or decimal percent, change decimal portion to fractional equivalent and continue with Steps 1 to 4.	$64\% \longrightarrow 64 \times \frac{1}{100} = \frac{64}{100} = \boxed{\frac{16}{25}}$ $\frac{1}{4}\% \longrightarrow \frac{1}{4} \times \frac{1}{100} = \boxed{\frac{1}{400}}$ $119\% \longrightarrow 119 \times \frac{1}{100} = \frac{119}{100} = \boxed{1\frac{19}{100}}$ $16\frac{1}{4}\% \longrightarrow \frac{65}{4} \times \frac{1}{100} = \frac{65}{400} = \boxed{\frac{13}{80}}$ $16.25\% \longrightarrow 16\frac{1}{4}\% = \frac{65}{4} \times \frac{1}{100}$ $\qquad\qquad = \frac{65}{400} = \boxed{\frac{13}{80}}$	**Convert to fractions** 74% $\frac{1}{5}\%$ 121% $17\frac{1}{5}\%$ 17.75%
Solving for portion, p. 150	10% of Mel's paycheck of $1,000 goes for food. What portion is deducted for food? $\boxed{\$100} = \$1,000 \times .10$ *Note:* If question was what amount does not go for food, the portion would have been: $\boxed{\$900} = \$1,000 \times .90$ $(100\% - 10\% = 90\%)$	**Find portion** Base $2,000 Rate 80%
Solving for rate, p. 151	Assume Mel spends $100 for food from his $1,000 paycheck. What percent of his paycheck is spent on food? $\frac{\$100}{\$1,000} = .10 = \boxed{10\%}$ *Note:* Portion is less than base since rate is less than 100%.	**Find rate** Base $2,000 Portion $500
Solving for base, p. 152	Assume Mel spends $100 for food, which is 10% of his paycheck. What is Mel's total paycheck? $\frac{\$100}{.10} = \boxed{\$1,000}$	**Find base** Rate 20% Portion $200

(continues)

INTERACTIVE CHAPTER ORGANIZER

Topic/procedure/formula	Examples	You try it*
Calculating percent increases and decreases, pp. 153–156 Amount of decrease or increase Portion Base × Rate (?) Original price	Stereo, $2,000 original price. Stereo, $2,500 new price. $$\frac{\$500}{\$2,000} = .25 = \boxed{25\%} \text{ increase}$$ **Check** $2,000 × 1.25 = $2,500 *Note:* Portion is greater than base since rate is greater than 100%. Portion ($2,500) Base ($2,000) × Rate (1.25)	**Find percent increase** Old price $500 New price $600

KEY TERMS	Base, *p. 149* Percent decrease, *p. 154*	Percent increase, *p. 153* Percents, *p. 143*	Portion, *p. 149* Rate, *p. 149*

Check Figures for Extra Practice Quizzes with Page References. (Worked-out Solutions in Appendix B.)	LU 6–1a (p. 148) 1. 44.4% 8. 7.658 2. 78.2% 9. 33.33% 3. .6% 10. 42.86% 4. 793.3% 11. $\frac{17}{100}$ 5. .0020 12. $\frac{329}{400}$ 6. .0780 13. $1\frac{1}{2}$ 7. .92 14. $\frac{1}{400}$ 15. $\frac{89}{500}$	LU 6–2a (p. 159) 1. 504 7. 60% 2. 560 8. 300 3. 8.5% 9. $540,000 4. 44.4% 10. 44.44% 5. 50 11. 435.71% 6. 34,285.7

Note: For how to dissect and solve a word problem, see page 150.

*Worked-out solutions are in Appendix B.

Critical Thinking Discussion Questions with Chapter Concept Check

1. In converting from a percent to a decimal, when will you have at least 2 leading zeros before the whole number? Explain this concept, assuming you have 100 bills of $1.

2. Explain the steps in rounding percents. Count the number of students who are sitting in the back half of the room as a percent of the total class. Round your answer to the nearest hundredth percent. Could you have rounded to the nearest whole percent without changing the accuracy of the answer?

3. Define portion, rate, and base. Create an example using Walt Disney World to show when the portion could be larger than the base. Why must the rate be greater than 100% for this to happen?

4. How do we solve for portion, rate, and base? Create an example using IBM computer sales to show that the portion and rate do relate to the same piece of the base.

5. Explain how to calculate percent decreases or increases. Many years ago, comic books cost 10 cents a copy. Visit a bookshop or newsstand. Select a new comic book and explain the price increase in percent compared to the 10-cent comic. How important is the rounding process in your final answer?

6. **Chapter Concept Check.** Go to the Google or Facebook site and find out how many people the company employs. Assuming a 10% increase in employment this year, calculate the total number of new employees by the end of the year, and identify the base rate and portion. If, in the following year, the 10% increase in employment fell by 5%, what would the total number of current employees be?

Classroom Notes

END-OF-CHAPTER PROBLEMS

connect plus+   www.mhhe.com/slater11e

Check figures for odd-numbered problems in Appendix C.   Name _____   Date _____

DRILL PROBLEMS

Convert the following decimals to percents: *LU 6-1(1)*

6–1. .78   **6–2.** .943   **6–3.** .7

6–4. 8.00   **6–5.** 3.561   **6–6.** 6.006

Convert the following percents to decimals: *LU 6-1(1)*

6–7. 8%   **6–8.** 14%   **6–9.** $64\frac{3}{10}\%$

6–10. 75.9%   **6–11.** 119%   **6–12.** 89%

Convert the following fractions to percents (round to the nearest tenth percent as needed):   *LU 6-1(1)*

6–13. $\frac{1}{12}$ **6–14.** $\frac{1}{400}$

6–15. $\frac{7}{8}$ **6–16.** $\frac{11}{12}$

Convert the following percents to fractions and reduce to the lowest terms: *LU 6-1(2)*

6–17. 4%   **6–18.** $18\frac{1}{2}\%$

6–19. $31\frac{2}{3}\%$ **6–20.** $61\frac{1}{2}\%$

6–21. 6.75%   **6–22.** 182%

Solve for the portion (round to the nearest hundredth as needed):   *LU 6-2(2)*

6–23. 7% of 150   **6–24.** 125% of 4,320   **6–25.** 25% of 410
e**X**cel   e**X**cel   e**X**cel

6–26. 119% of 128.9   **6–27.** 17.4% of 900   **6–28.** 11.2% of 85
e**X**cel   e**X**cel   e**X**cel

6–29. $12\frac{1}{2}\%$ of 919   **6–30.** 45% of 300

6–31. 18% of 90   **6–32.** 30% of 2,000

Solve for the base (round to the nearest hundredth as needed):   *LU 6-2(2)*

6–33. 170 is 120% of _____   **6–34.** 36 is .75% of _____

6–35. 50 is .5% of _____   **6–36.** 10,800 is 90% of _____

6–37. 800 is $4\frac{1}{2}\%$ of _____

Solve for rate (round to the nearest tenth percent as needed):   *LU 6-2(2)*

6–38. _____ of 80 is 50   **6–39.** _____ of 85 is 92

6–40. _____ of 250 is 65   **6–41.** 110 is _____ of 100

6–42. .09 is _____ of 2.25   **6–43.** 16 is _____ of 4

Solve the following problems. Be sure to show your work. Round to the nearest hundredth or hundredth percent as needed: *LU 6-2(2)*

6–44. What is 180% of 310?

6–45. 66% of 90 is what?

6–46. 40% of what number is 20?

6–47. 770 is 70% of what number?

6–48. 4 is what percent of 90?

6–49. What percent of 150 is 60?

Complete the following table: *LU 6-2(3)*

Product	Selling price 2013	Selling price 2014	Amount of decrease or increase	Percent change (to nearest hundredth percent as needed)
6–50. Apple iPad	$650	$500		
6–51. Smartphone	$100	$120		

WORD PROBLEMS (First of Four Sets)

6–52. At a local Dunkin' Donuts, a survey showed that out of 1,200 customers eating lunch, 240 ordered coffee with their meal. e**X**cel What percent of customers ordered coffee? *LU 6-2(2)*

6–53. What percent of customers in Problem 6–52 did not order coffee? *LU 6-2(2)*
e**X**cel

6–54. In January 2012, gas was selling for $3.60 a gallon. The price of a gallon of regular unleaded dropped to $3.50 on February 11, 2012. What was the percent decrease? Round to the nearest hundredth percent. *LU 6-2(3)*

6–55. Wally Chin, the owner of an ExxonMobil station, bought a used Ford pickup truck, paying $2,000 as a down payment. He still owes 80% of the selling price. What was the selling price of the truck? *LU 6-2(2)*

6–56. Maria Fay bought four Dunlop tires at a local Goodyear store. The salesperson told her that her mileage would increase by 8%. Before this purchase, Maria was getting 24 mpg. What should her mileage be with the new tires to the nearest hundredth? *LU 6-2(2)*

6–57. The Social Security Administration announced the following rates to explain what percent of your Social Security benefits *eXcel* you will receive based on how old you are when you start receiving Social Security benefits.

Age	Percent of benefit
62	75
63	80
64	86.7
65	93.3
66	100

Assume Shelley Kate decides to take her Social Security at age 63. What amount of Social Security money will she receive each month, assuming she is entitled to $800 per month? *LU 6-2(2)*

6–58. Assume that in the year 2013, 800,000 people attended the Christmas Eve celebration at Walt Disney World. In 2014, atten- *eXcel* dance for the Christmas Eve celebration is expected to increase by 35%. What is the total number of people expected at Walt Disney World for this event? *LU 6-2(2)*

6–59. Pete Smith found in his attic a Woody Woodpecker watch in its original box. It had a price tag on it for $4.50. The watch was made in 1949. Pete brought the watch to an antiques dealer and sold it for $35. What was the percent of increase in price? Round to the nearest hundredth percent. *LU 6-2(3)*

6–60. Christie's Auction sold a painting for $24,500. It charges all buyers a 15% premium of the final bid price. How much did the bidder pay Christie's? *LU 6-2(2)*

WORD PROBLEMS (Second of Four Sets)

6–61. Out of 9,000 college students surveyed, 540 responded that they do not eat breakfast. What percent of the students do not eat breakfast? *LU 6-2(2)*

6–62. What percent of college students in Problem 6–61 eat breakfast? *LU 6-2(2)*

6–63. The January/February 2012 *Discover* magazine article "Could Random Airplane Boarding Speed Your Trip?" demonstrates that random boarding saved 3.5 minutes off of a typical 22.5-minute boarding process. What percent savings is this to the nearest whole percent? *LU 6-2(2)*

6–64. Rainfall for January in Fiji averages 12″ according to *World Travel Guide*. This year it rained 5% less. How many inches (to the nearest tenth) did it rain this year? *LU 6-2(2)*

6–65. Jim and Alice Lange, employees at Walmart, have put themselves on a strict budget. Their goal at year's end is to buy a boat for $15,000 in cash. Their budget includes the following:

    40% food and lodging   20% entertainment   10% educational

Jim earns $1,900 per month and Alice earns $2,400 per month. After 1 year, will Alice and Jim have enough cash to buy the boat? *LU 6-2(2)*

6–66. Epiq Systems reported bankruptcy filings of 2 million in 2011. Seventy percent of the filings are Chapter 7 bankruptcies allowing individuals to avoid repaying their debts if they meet certain requirements. Thirty percent of the filings are Chapter 13 filings, where a portion of the debt will need to be repaid over 3 to 5 years. How many bankruptcies in 2011 were Chapter 7 and how many bankruptcies were Chapter 13? *LU 6-2(2)*

6–67. The Museum of Science in Boston estimated that 64% of all visitors came from within the state. On Saturday, 2,500 people attended the museum. How many attended the museum from out of state? *LU 6-2(2)*

6–68. Staples pays George Nagovsky an annual salary of $36,000. Today, George's boss informs him that he will receive a $4,600 raise. What percent of George's old salary is the $4,600 raise? Round to the nearest tenth percent. *LU 6-2(2)*

6–69. In 2013, a local Dairy Queen had $550,000 in sales. In 2014, Dairy Queen's sales were up 35%. What were Dairy Queen's sales in 2014? *LU 6-2(2)*

6–70. Blue Valley College has 600 female students. This is 60% of the total student body. How many students attend Blue Valley College? *LU 6-2(2)*

6–71. Dr. Grossman was reviewing his total accounts receivable. This month, credit customers paid $44,000, which represented 20% of all receivables (what customers owe) due. What was Dr. Grossman's total accounts receivable? *LU 6-2(2)*

6–72. Massachusetts has a 5% sales tax. Timothy bought a Toro lawn mower and paid $20 sales tax. What was the cost of the lawn mower before the tax? *LU 6-2(2)*

6–73. The price of an antique doll increased from $600 to $800. What was the percent of increase? Round to the nearest tenth percent. *LU 6-2(3)*

6–74. A local Barnes and Noble bookstore ordered 80 marketing books but received 60 books. What percent of the order was missing? *LU 6-2(2)*

WORD PROBLEMS (Third of Four Sets)

6–75. RealtyTrac reported that the amount of foreclosures filed fell from 2.9 million properties in 2010 to 2 million properties in 2011. This equated to 1 in every 69 U.S. homes. What percent of U.S. homes were foreclosed against (to the nearest tenth percent)? *LU 6-2(2)*

6–76. Due to increased mailing costs, the new rate will cost publishers $50 million; this is 12.5% more than they paid the previous year. How much did it cost publishers last year? Round to the nearest hundreds. *LU 6-2(2)*

6–77. In 2013, Jim Goodman, an employee at Walgreens, earned $45,900, an increase of 17.5% over the previous year. What were Jim's earnings in 2012? Round to the nearest cent. *LU 6-2(2)*

6–78. If the number of mortgage applications declined by 7% to 1,625,415, what had been the previous year's number of applications? *LU 6-2(2)*

6–79. In 2013, the price of a business math text rose to $150. This is 8% more than the 2012 price. What was the old selling price? Round to the nearest cent. *LU 6-2(2)*

6–80. Web Consultants, Inc., pays Alice Rose an annual salary of $48,000. Today, Alice's boss informs her that she will receive a $6,400 raise. What percent of Alice's old salary is the $6,400 raise? Round to the nearest tenth percent. *LU 6-2(2)*

6–81. Earl Miller, a lawyer, charges Lee's Plumbing, his client, 25% of what he can collect for Lee from customers whose accounts are past due. The attorney also charges, in addition to the 25%, a flat fee of $50 per customer. This month, Earl collected $7,000 from three of Lee's past-due customers. What is the total fee due to Earl? *LU 6-2(2)*

6–82. A local Petco ordered 100 dog calendars but received 60. What percent of the order was missing? *LU 6-2(2)*

6–83. Ray's Video uses MasterCard. MasterCard charges $2\frac{1}{2}\%$ on net deposits (credit slips less returns). Ray's made a net deposit of $4,100 for charge sales. How much did MasterCard charge Ray's?   *LU 6-2(2)*

6–84. In 2013, Internet Access had $800,000 in sales. In 2014, Internet Access's sales were up 45%. What are the sales for 2014? *LU 6-2(2)*

WORD PROBLEMS (Fourth of Four Sets)

6–85. Chevrolet raised the base price of its Volt by $1,200 to $33,500. What was the percent increase? Round to the nearest tenth percent.   *LU 6-2(2)*

6–86. The sales tax rate is 8%. If Jim bought a new Buick and paid a sales tax of $1,920, what was the cost of the Buick before the tax?   *LU 6-2(2)*

6–87. Puthina Unge bought a new Compaq computer system on sale for $1,800. It was advertised as 30% off the regular price. What was the original price of the computer? Round to the nearest dollar.   *LU 6-2(2)*

6–88. John O'Sullivan has just completed his first year in business. His records show that he spent the following in advertising:

Internet $600   Radio $650   Yellow Pages $700   Local flyers $400

What percent of John's advertising was spent on the Yellow Pages? Round to the nearest hundredth percent.   *LU 6-2(2)*

6–89. Jay Miller sold his ski house at Attitash Mountain in New Hampshire for $35,000. This sale represented a loss of 15% off the original price. What was the original price Jay paid for the ski house? Round your answer to the nearest dollar. *LU 6-2(2)*

6–90. Out of 4,000 colleges surveyed, 60% reported that SAT scores were not used as a high consideration in viewing their applications. How many schools view the SAT as important in screening applicants? *LU 6-2(2)*

6–91. If refinishing your basement at a cost of $45,404 would add $18,270 to the resale value of your home, what percent of your cost is recouped? Round to the nearest percent. *LU 6-2(2)*

6–92. A major airline laid off 4,000 pilots and flight attendants. If this was a 12.5% reduction in the workforce, what was the size of the workforce after the layoffs? *LU 6-2(2)*

6–93. Assume 450,000 people line up on the streets to see the Macy's Thanksgiving Parade in 2012. If attendance is expected to increase 30%, what will be the number of people lined up on the street to see the 2013 parade? *LU 6-2(2)*

CHALLENGE PROBLEMS

6–94. Each Tuesday, Ryan Airlines reduces its one-way ticket from Fort Wayne to Chicago from $125 to $40. To receive this special $40 price, the customer must buy a round-trip ticket. Ryan has a nonrefundable 25% penalty fare for cancellation; it estimates that about nine-tenths of 1% will cancel their reservations. The airline also estimates this special price will cause a passenger traffic increase from 400 to 900. Ryan expects revenue for the year to be 55.4% higher than the previous year. Last year, Ryan's sales were $482,000. To receive the special rate, Janice Miller bought two round-trip tickets. On other airlines, Janice has paid $100 round trip (with no cancellation penalty). Calculate the following: *LU 6-2(2)*
  a. Percent discount Ryan is offering.

  b. Percent passenger travel will increase.

  c. Sales for new year.
  d. Janice's loss if she cancels one round-trip flight.
  e. Approximately how many more cancellations can Ryan Airlines expect (after Janice's cancellation)?

6–95. A local Dunkin' Donuts shop reported that its sales have increased exactly 22% per year for the last 2 years. This year's sales were $82,500. What were Dunkin' Donuts' sales 2 years ago? Round each year's sales to the nearest dollar. *LU 6-2(2)*

SUMMARY PRACTICE TEST You Tube

Do you need help? The DVD has step-by-step worked-out solutions.

Convert the following decimals to percents. *(p. 144)   LU 6-1(1)*

1.   .921   **2.**   .4   **3.**   15.88   **4.**   8.00

Convert the following percents to decimals. *(p. 145)   LU 6-1(1)*

5.   42%   **6.**   7.98%   **7.**   400%   **8.** $\frac{1}{4}$%

Convert the following fractions to percents. Round to the nearest tenth percent. *(p. 147)   LU 6-1(1)*

9. $\frac{1}{6}$ **10.** $\frac{1}{3}$

Convert the following percents to fractions and reduce to the lowest terms as needed. *(p. 147)   LU 6-1(2)*

11. $19\frac{3}{8}$%   **12.**   6.2%

Solve the following problems for portion, base, or rate:

13.   An Arby's franchise has a net income before taxes of $900,000. The company's treasurer estimates that 40% of the company's net income will go to federal and state taxes. How much will the Arby's franchise have left? *(p. 149)   LU 6-2(2)*

14.   Domino's projects a year-end net income of $699,000. The net income represents 30% of its annual sales. What are Domino's projected annual sales? *(p. 152)   LU 6-2(2)*

15.   Target ordered 400 iPods. When Target received the order, 100 iPods were missing. What percent of the order did Target receive? *(p. 151)   LU 6-2(2)*

16.   Matthew Song, an employee at Putnam Investments, receives an annual salary of $120,000. Today his boss informed him that he would receive a $3,200 raise. What percent of his old salary is the $3,200 raise? Round to the nearest hundredth percent. *(p. 151)   LU 6-2(2)*

17. The price of a Delta airline ticket from Los Angeles to Boston increased to $440. This is a 15% increase. What was the old fare? Round to the nearest cent. *(p. 152)   LU 6-2(2)*

18. Scupper Grace earns a gross pay of $900 per week at Office Depot. Scupper's payroll deductions are 29%. What is Scupper's take-home pay? *(p. 149)   LU 6-2(2)*

19. Mia Wong is reviewing the total accounts receivable of Wong's department store. Credit customers paid $90,000 this month. This represents 60% of all receivables due. What is Mia's total accounts receivable? *(p. 152)   LU 6-2(2)*

www.mhhe.com/
slater11e_vc

In a constantly changing business environment, new product and service development can invigorate a company, improve market share, and ensure desired financial performance. Six Flags, with its "Go Big! Go Six Flags" motto, knows it must regularly add new rides and upgrade existing ones in its theme parks to remain on top.

Located in Grand Prairie, Texas, Six Flags first opened in 1961 and grew to become the largest regional theme park system in the world. Central to this growth was the constant development of new and record-setting theme park rides, following a well-defined process of product development. Consider the Kingda Ka roller coaster that opened in May 2005 at the Six Flags Great Adventure & Wild Safari in Jackson, New Jersey. This is the largest of the Six Flags parks, and Kingda Ka is the tallest and fastest coaster in North America.

Getting to the May 2005 ride opening required significant planning and a coordinated effort. Six Flags' new product development process ensures both. It guides and choreographs the hundreds of tasks involved in building a roller coaster, from preparing the foundation to erecting the steel frame to installing the hydraulic system that allows for speeds of 128 mph to fitting out the cars.

Six Flags relies on several key documents to control and monitor all resources, including raw materials, equipment, and the people involved in the construction of the ride. The Statement of Work (SOW) is a written statement that describes the work to be done and includes a preliminary project schedule and completion dates. The SOW details project milestones, key completion events, and budget parameters. The Work Breakdown Structure (WBS) defines the hierarchy of tasks, subtasks, and work packages and is key to managing the logistics of the project. The project Gantt chart illustrates the project schedule and helps identify the critical path within the project. The critical path represents the longest chain of tasks in terms of time to complete. If there is a delay in any step in the critical path, the whole project can be delayed.

The Kingda Ka ride had a 15-month project schedule of which 9 to 10 months were actual construction time. The coaster took 16 months to complete and came in 10% over budget. Success in new product development requires careful planning, well-defined milestones, teamwork, and flexibility to respond to unforeseen changes. The successful Kingda Ka ride was no exception.

PROBLEM 1

As stated in the case, the original project schedule for the Kingda Ka coaster was 15 months but the project actually took 16 months to complete. What was the percent increase over the original scheduled completion time? Round your answer to the nearest percent.

PROBLEM 2

Review the video case to identify the timing of key steps in the construction of the Kingda Ka, including start of conceptual planning, start of foundation construction, start of steel erection, and completion of the project. What percent of the actual total project time had elapsed by the time foundation construction began? By the time steel erection began? Round answers to the nearest percent.

PROBLEM 3

The project Gantt chart shown in the video indicated that 145 days were planned for site preparation, 119 days for foundations, and 133 for steel erection. What was the percentage of time needed for each of these three steps assuming 397 days were needed in total? Round answers to the nearest percent.

PROBLEM 4

The Kindga Ka is currently the tallest steel roller coaster, at 456 feet high. The second tallest is the Top Thrill Dragster at Cedar Point in Sandusky, Ohio, at 420 feet. How much taller is the Kingda Ka in both feet and percentage (to the nearest tenth percent)?

PROBLEM 5

If Six Flags wanted to build a roller coaster that was 5% taller than the Kingda Ka, how tall would the coaster need to be? Round answer to the nearest foot.

PROBLEM 6

Six Flags rates its rides as mild, moderate, or max. The Six Flags Great Adventure park where the Kingda Ka ride is located has a total of 49 rides. Of these, 12 have a max rating, 8 have a moderate rating, and the remainder are rated mild. Express each of the ride types as a fraction and then determine the percentage each comprises of the total. Reduce fractions to the lowest possible terms and round percentages to the nearest percent.

PROBLEM 7

The Kingda Ka ride covers 3,118 feet of track. The Green Lantern, a new ride at the same park, has ¾ mile of track. Which ride is longer and by what percent? Round answer to the nearest percent.

PROBLEM 8

As the case states, the Kingda Ka ride reaches speeds of 128 mph due to its hydraulic system. The Green Lantern ride is designed to reach speeds of 63 mph. What percent increase would be needed for the Green Lantern ride to match the speed attained on the Kingda Ka? Round answer to the nearest tenth percent.

Class Discussion In any project, project managers must balance three key variables—time, cost, and quality. Typically one variable is most critical in a project and should problems arise, the other two may be sacrificed to achieve the one that is key to the project's success. Discuss how these three variables were managed in the Kingda Ka project.

PROBLEM 1
All-in-one and one for all

Assume you want to buy an all-in-one printer/scanner/copier/fax machine. Go to www.staples.com and choose an all-in-one machine to meet your needs. How much does it cost? If your state charged 7% sales tax; what would be the amount of the tax on this purchase?

Discussion Questions

1. Is the all-in-one machine less expensive than purchasing separate machines for all of these tasks?

2. When might it be a better option to buy individual machines versus an all-in-one? Why?

PROBLEM 2
What do your neighbors earn?

Go to http://www.census.gov/hhes/www/income/data/statemedian/index.html. Find the Median Household Income by State—Single-Year Estimates for a four-person family in your state (use the U.S. average if you are taking this course outside the United States) for the last 3 consecutive years. Find the percent increase (or decrease) in income each year for a family of four.

Discussion Questions

1. How does the median income for your state compare to a neighboring state?

2. What accounts for the differences in median income between your state and neighboring states?

PROBLEM 3
Investment know-how

Go to http://biz.yahoo.com/r. From Research Tools go to the Historical Quotes page. Enter a ticker symbol (search by company name if you do not know the symbol) to find the price of a particular stock last Wednesday and on the same date 1 year ago. (Use the closing price.) What was the percent change in the stock you chose?

Discussion Questions

1. What may have caused this change in stock price?

2. How is the current stock price a reflection of the products the company sells?

PROBLEM 4
On the move, will my money follow?

Assume your employer is relocating to another state. You can keep your current job and salary if you move. Go to http://cgi.money.cnn.com/tools/costofliving/costofliving.html, enter your current state and city, a new destination state and city, and your current yearly salary. Click on Get result. Based on the calculation, what is the percent increase or decrease of your salary? Is this move worth your while financially?

Discussion Questions

1. Other than income, what factors would influence your decision to move to another state?

2. What factors help explain the change in income between the two locations you selected?

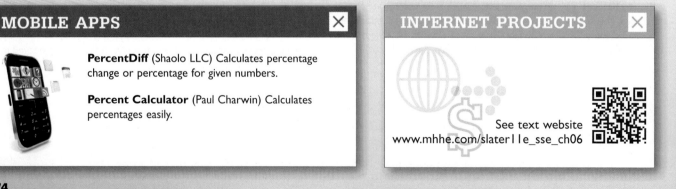

MOBILE APPS ✕

PercentDiff (Shaolo LLC) Calculates percentage change or percentage for given numbers.

Percent Calculator (Paul Charwin) Calculates percentages easily.

INTERNET PROJECTS ✕

See text website
www.mhhe.com/slater11e_sse_ch06

A KIPLINGER APPROACH

New Jobs, New Skills

The best route to a rewarding career
is to pick a growing field and stay flexible.

WHAT IT'S ALL ABOUT.
Jobs will trickle into the labor market over the next several months, but don't expect significant improvement until late next year. We'll recoup the eight million jobs lost in the recession by late 2013 or early 2014. But new workers will be entering the labor force, so achieving a full-employment economy—an unemployment rate of about 5% to 5.5%—could take much longer.

HOW IT'S DIFFERENT THIS TIME. Even profitable companies with plenty of cash aren't hiring until confidence in the economy improves. Nevertheless, job openings have risen 26% since July 2009. Why not a bigger dent in unemployment? Partly it's a mismatch between what employers are looking for and what workers have to offer. Success now depends less on years of experience in a particular industry or finely honed expertise, and more on flexibility and a knack for adapting a set of transferable skills.

HOW YOU CAN PROFIT. New grads will find the highest demand for degrees in accounting, business administration, computer science, engineering and math. An occupational certificate or associate's degree might help snag a lucrative job. But consider the number of job openings in the field. Employment in biomedical engineering is projected to grow 72% from 2008 through 2018—but that works out to just 1,400 openings per year.

The fastest-growing occupations with a lot of openings have a familiar ring, says occupational expert Laurence Shatkin. Over ten years (beginning in 2008), the number of computer network systems and database administrator openings could grow by 46,000 a year on average. Registered nurses could see 104,000 job openings per year. There will be a huge need for accountants and auditors, with about 50,000 openings per year.

Have a job already? Look for a raise of 3% or less, on average, but superstars might see 4.5%. Cover four bases to show you've added value: quantity (more output); quality (reduced errors); cost (on budget or below); and timeliness (deadlines beaten). Ask for a raise immediately after a big success. **ANNE KATES SMITH**

The More You Learn, the More You Earn

What a Degree WILL PAY
You can make a decent wage at the lower end of the educational spectrum. Figures are for median salaries.

BUSINESS

OFFICE MANAGEMENT
CERTIFICATE: $26,952
ASSOCIATE'S DEGREE: $34,296
BUSINESS MANAGEMENT
BACHELOR'S: $57,000
MASTER'S: $75,204

ENGINEERING

DRAFTING
CERTIFICATE: $36,000
ASSOCIATE'S DEGREE: $47,004
CHEMICAL, ELECTRICAL, CIVIL, OTHER
BACHELOR'S: $66,000
MASTER'S: $88,503

HEALTH

HEALTH CARE (LPN)
CERTIFICATE: $23,328
PHYSIOTHERAPIST, X-RAY TECH, OTHER
ASSOCIATE'S DEGREE: $40,524
BACHELOR'S: $45,549
MASTER'S: $60,276

COMPUTERS

INFORMATION MANAGEMENT
CERTIFICATE: $33,504
ASSOCIATE'S DEGREE: $42,000
INFORMATION SCIENCES
BACHELOR'S: $74,406
MASTER'S: $80,004

Where the JOB OPENINGS are
There will be 32.4 million replacement job openings between 2008 and 2018, as baby-boomers exit the workforce.

Financial services	1.9 MILLION
Government and public education services	2.3 MILLION
Manufacturing	2.6 MILLION
Private education services	2.8 MILLION
Health care	3.3 MILLION
Professional and business services	4.5 MILLION

SOURCE: Georgetown University Center on Education and the Workforce

BUSINESS MATH ISSUE

The impact of technology today will result in fewer job openings in the future.

1. List the key points of the article and information to support your position.
2. Write a group defense of your position using math calculations to support your view.

Discounts: Trade and Cash

Facebook Takes Aim at Groupon

BY SCOTT MORRISON

Facebook Inc. will soon start testing a service to provide discounts and other offers to its more than 500 million members, a move that will thrust the social network into direct competition with daily deals provider **Groupon** Inc.

The new service will be tested in Dallas, Austin, Atlanta, San Francisco and San Diego, and will expand upon Facebook's existing service that offers deals to members when they use Facebook Places to check into a specific location, the company said.

Users will be able locate deals on a special page listing all local promotions running at any given time. Users will be able to find a link to the deals page on the left side of their home page.

Facebook said the new service will let people buy deals on Facebook and share them with their friends.

"Local businesses will be able to sign up to use this feature soon and people will be able to find deals in the coming weeks," according to a company statement.

The push into social deals could step up pressure on Groupon and rival LivingSocial, which lead the rapidly growing market but only have a small percentage of Facebook's users.

Facebook declined to say whether it will require members to use the company's virtual currency, Facebook Credits, to purchase deals. The Palo Alto, Calif., company has been pushing the use of Credits for the purchase of digital goods in games, for which Facebook takes a 30% cut of revenue.

Requiring users to buy daily deals with Credits would push the virtual currency beyond the digital realm and could drive adoption among a broader base of users.

Facebook spokeswoman Annie Ta declined to rule out the possibility that deal buyers would be required to use Facebook Credits, saying the company was exploring different ways to purchase deals.

LU 7–1: Trade Discounts—Single and Chain (Includes Discussion of Freight)

1. Calculate single trade discounts with formulas and complements (pp. 178–179).
2. Explain the freight terms FOB shipping point and FOB destination (pp. 179–180).
3. Find list price when net price and trade discount rate are known (pp. 181–182).
4. Calculate chain discounts with the net price equivalent rate and single equivalent discount rate (pp. 182–184).

LU 7–2: Cash Discounts, Credit Terms, and Partial Payments

1. List and explain typical discount periods and credit periods that a business may offer (pp. 185–192).
2. Calculate outstanding balance for partial payments (p. 192).

VOCABULARY PREVIEW

Here are key terms in this chapter. After completing the chapter, if you know the term, place a checkmark in the parentheses. If you don't know the term, look it up and put the page number where it can be found.

Cash discount ( ) Chain discounts ( ) Complement ( ) Credit period ( ) Discount period ( ) Due dates ( ) End of credit period ( ) End of month (EOM) ( ) FOB destination ( ) FOB shipping point ( ) Freight terms ( ) Invoice ( ) List price ( ) Net price ( ) Net price equivalent rate ( ) Ordinary dating ( ) Receipt of goods (ROG) ( ) Series discounts ( ) Single equivalent discount rate ( ) Single trade discount ( ) Terms of the sale ( ) Trade discount ( ) Trade discount amount ( ) Trade discount rate ( )

Have you ever tried to find discounts online when buying fashion products? The *Wall Street Journal* clipping below, "How to Find Discount Fashion Online," shows how searching the web can provide some impressive discounts that you may miss by shopping at your local mall.

This chapter discusses two types of discounts taken by retailers—trade and cash. A **trade discount** is a reduction off the original selling price (list price) of an item and is not related to early payment. A **cash discount** is the result of an early payment based on the terms of the sale.

How to Find Discount Fashion Online

Stephanie Phair, director at discount online retailer **theOut-net.com**, says there are "two different people in the discount world." Some people buy discount but don't tell anyone. Others, like her, tell the world. "There's an element of pride," she says.

But searching site upon site for discounts takes time—just like going from store to store in the mall. A better bet is to try a search engine called an aggregator, which can pull up items from multiple sites. If Ms. Phair has something specific in mind, say, a pair of gold strappy sandals, she starts with ShopStyle or another aggregator. "It's a good way to cover a lot of ground," she says.

Since discount clothes are more likely to be sold out in some sizes, she sorts results by size. Another way to start, if you

have loyalties to specific brands, is to sign up for sales alerts on sites like shopittome.com.

Ms. Phair generally prefers discount sites, which are always open, to flash-sale sites, which offer sales between prescribed hours, because she likes the freedom to shop when her schedule permits. If you try shopping flash sales, also known as "pop-up" sales, being decisive is key: "You can't wait because it will likely be gone," Ms. Phair says. "You have to know what you want and know what your [price] threshold is."

It's helpful to know whether 30% or 60% is a decent discount, though that depends on what's being sold. Shoes and handbags are popular items at full price, so their discounts may hover around the 40% or 50% range. Denim might go for as much as 60% off, while expensive evening

dresses can be found for 70% off.

High-end designer labels, which have limited runs and cult followings, are harder to find at a discount. "Marni is not a brand readily available at discount. If I find [Marni] at 30% or 40% off, that's awesome," Ms. Phair says. Beyond labels, she looks for high-quality pieces that she can expect to last for several seasons and go with items she already owns.

Rather than push bathing suits in September, some discount retailers, including the-Outnet, now highlight season-appropriate clothing. But the collections may include a lot from past seasons—and it often isn't clear what's new and what's from, say, fall 2007. Ms. Phair doesn't scorn older clothes, noting that trends usually run for a few seasons. For example, animal prints, camel and minimalist

dressing, which came into fashion a few years ago, will be in again for fall 2010.

Many online retailers have made the return process as easy as it is at their offline counterparts by including return shipping labels with each purchase. But read the fine print: Very deeply discounted items may be on final sale. Some sites accept returns for store credit only.

There are a few things that Ms. Phair normally won't buy online. Expensive jewelry is one, because she prefers to handle the jewelry in person. Also, Ms. Phair, who plans to get married in February, is debating whether to buy her wedding dress off the web, as new ones are very hard to find at a discount online.

Still, she'll start her search online. "If it's full price, so be it. But if it's discount, even better."
—*Elva Ramirez*

Learning Unit 7–1: Trade Discounts—Single and Chain (Includes Discussion of Freight)

The merchandise sold by retailers is bought from manufacturers and wholesalers who sell only to retailers and not to customers. These manufacturers and wholesalers offer retailer discounts so retailers can resell the merchandise at a profit. The discounts are off the manufacturers' and wholesalers' **list price** (suggested retail price), and the amount of discount that retailers receive off the list price is the **trade discount amount.** The *Wall Street Journal* clip "P&G Clears Plan for Mobile Coupons" shows how consumers use technology, such as smartphones and digital coupons, to obtain discounts. But consumers are not the only ones to benefit; the article also discusses how retailers can track customer preferences based on where and when digital coupons are redeemed.

When you make a purchase, the retailer (seller) gives you a purchase **invoice.** Invoices are important business documents that help sellers keep track of sales transactions and buyers keep track of purchase transactions. North Shore Community College Bookstore is a retail seller of textbooks to students. The bookstore

© Inti St. Clair/Getty Images

P&G Clears Plan for Mobile Coupons

By Hannah Karp

Digital coupons are catching on with consumers, but the market's growth has been hampered by a pesky problem: Many retailers still aren't equipped with laser scanners that can detect bar codes off of the reflective, shiny, backlit screen of a smartphone. **Procter & Gamble** Co. is working on a potential solution. The consumer-goods giant said Monday it is working with start-up **mobeam** Inc. on a pilot program that will allow consumers to redeem coupons for P&G products straight from their

phones. San Francisco-based mobeam has patented a way to beam out a bar code from the screen of a phone that is legible to normal laser scanners.

U.S. consumers saved more than $1.2 billion from redeeming digital coupons in 2010, according to a research report by digital-coupon provider Coupons.com, up 41% from a year earlier.

The challenge for mobeam now will be to get its technology integrated into smartphones so consumers can use it.

The technology must be installed in the guts of a phone,

which requires the cooperation of device makers.

Mobeam says it is working with handset makers so that tens of millions of phones hitting the market in 2012 will include its technology, though it declined to say what device makers it is in discussions with. **Samsung Venture Investment** Corp., the venture-capital arm of **Samsung Group,** a large maker of mobile devices, recently invested money in mobeam.

Scanning technology is improving slowly. Airlines and some retailers like Target and Walgreens have developed tech-

nology to scan bar codes off of the mobile coupons they issue themselves, but consumer companies cannot guarantee exactly where customers will be able to use their coupons since they don't control the checkout lines.

For P&G, another potential payoff could come from the data it could gather from consumers who use the digital coupons. Mobeam says it will provide its partners with a trove of information about their mobile coupon users with consumer permission, allowing companies to track where and when they redeem them and what they buy.

Reprinted with permission of *The Wall Street Journal,* Copyright © 2011 Dow Jones & Company, Inc. All Rights Reserved Worldwide.

usually purchases its textbooks directly from publishers. Figure 7.1 (p. 179) shows a sample of what a textbook invoice from McGraw-Hill/Irwin Publishing Company to the North Shore Community College Bookstore would look like. Note that the trade discount amount is given in percent. This is the **trade discount rate,** which is a percent off the list price that retailers can deduct. The following formula for calculating a trade discount amount gives the numbers from the Figure 7.1 invoice in parentheses:

TRADE DISCOUNT AMOUNT FORMULA
Trade discount amount = List price × Trade discount rate
($1,943.88) ($7,775.50) (25%)

The price that the retailer (bookstore) pays the manufacturer (publisher) or wholesaler is the **net price.** The following formula for calculating the net price gives the numbers from the Figure 7.1 invoice in parentheses:

NET PRICE FORMULA		
Net price = List price − Trade discount amount
($5,831.62) ($7,775.50) ($1,943.88)

Bookstore invoice showing a
trade discount

Invoice No.: 5582

McGraw-Hill/Irwin Publishing Co.
1333 Burr Ridge Parkway
Burr Ridge, Illinois 60527

Date: July 8, 2013
Ship: Two-day UPS
Terms: 2/10, n/30

Sold to: North Shore Community College Bookstore
1 Ferncroft Road
Danvers, MA 01923

Description	Unit list price	Total amount
50 Financial Management—Block/Hirt	$135.10	$6,755.00
10 Introduction to Business—Nichols	102.05	1,020.50
	Total List Price	$7,775.50
	Less: Trade Discount 25%	−1,943.88
	Net Price	$5,831.62
	Plus: Prepaid Shipping Charge	+125.00
	Total Invoice Amount	$5,956.62

© Frances Roberts/Alamy

Frequently, manufacturers and wholesalers issue catalogs to retailers containing list prices of the seller's merchandise and the available trade discounts. To reduce printing costs when prices change, these sellers usually update the catalogs with new *discount sheets.* The discount sheet also gives the seller the flexibility of offering different trade discounts to different classes of retailers. For example, some retailers buy in quantity and service the products. They may receive a larger discount than the retailer who wants the manufacturer to service the products. Sellers may also give discounts to meet a competitor's price, to attract new retailers, and to reward the retailers who buy product-line products. Sometimes the ability of the retailer to negotiate with the seller determines the trade discount amount.

Retailers cannot take trade discounts on freight, returned goods, sales tax, and so on. Trade discounts may be single discounts or a chain of discounts. Before we discuss single trade discounts, let's study freight terms.

LO 2

Freight Terms

The most common **freight terms** are *FOB shipping point* and *FOB destination.* These terms determine how the freight will be paid. The key words in the terms are *shipping point* and *destination.*

FOB shipping point means free on board at shipping point; that is, the buyer pays the freight cost of getting the goods to the place of business.

For example, assume that IBM in San Diego bought goods from Argo Suppliers in Boston. Argo ships the goods FOB Boston by plane. IBM takes title to the goods when the aircraft in Boston receives the goods, so IBM pays the freight from Boston to San Diego. Frequently, the seller (Argo) prepays the freight and adds the amount to the buyer's (IBM) invoice. When paying the invoice, the buyer takes the cash discount off the net price and adds the freight cost. FOB shipping point can be illustrated as follows:

FOB shipping point (Boston)

Boston   San Diego

Argo Suppliers
(IBM takes title here)

IBM
(Buyer pays the freight costs)

Buyer pays the freight

FOB destination means the seller pays the freight cost until it reaches the buyer's place of business. If Argo ships its goods to IBM FOB destination or FOB San Diego, the title to the goods remains with Argo. Then it is Argo's responsibility to pay the freight from Boston to IBM's place of business in San Diego. FOB destination can be illustrated as follows:

FOB destination (San Diego)

Boston

| **Argo Suppliers**
(Has title) | Seller pays the freight → | **IBM**
(Gets title on arrival of goods) |

The following *Wall Street Journal* clipping, "Ship Free or Lose Out," reveals that more and more online and retail stores are offering free shipping.

GLOBAL

Ship Free or Lose Out

More Retailers Absorb Cost of Sending Packages to Vie With Web-Only Rivals

By Ann Zimmerman
And Dana Mattioli

Traditional retailers are taking the expensive step of offering more free-shipping deals this holiday season, as they seek to lure the growing number of Internet shoppers to their websites and away from online-only rivals, particularly Amazon.com Inc.

Amazon offers free shipping on most orders over $25, as well as cheap, low-hassle delivery options such as its Prime membership program, which other retailers have found hard to match. The online retail giant also offers low prices, since it doesn't have to pay for spar-

kly stores or cheery salespeople and— as rivals like to point out—because it doesn't collect sales taxes for the most part.

To fight back, **Toys "R" Us**, which last year had only select items available for free shipping, has made its entire online inventory eligible as long as customers spend $49. Similarly, **Wal-Mart Stores** Inc. has made every consumer-electronics item—rather than just select gadgets—on its website available for free shipping through Dec. 19 with a minimum $45 purchase. And **Best Buy** Co. is offering free shipping for every product it offers online, including giant TV sets.

For consumers, free shipping

can make a big difference in the ultimate price they pay. Amazon and Wal-Mart on Tuesday both were selling a hot holiday toy, Let's Rock Elmo, for $49.66 and offered free standard shipping—about a $6 savings. To keep up, the Toys "R" Us website is waiving its $10 shipping fee for the holidays. (It is charging $10 more for the toy itself, though.)

"Free shipping used to be a way to entice customers to your store over another site, but now it's just the price of entry," said Kevin Mansell, chief executive of **Kohl's** Corp., the discount department store.

Newegg.com, which specializes in electronics and is the

second-biggest online-only retailer, also offers free shipping on many products.

High shipping costs can turn off customers altogether. Amanda Lordy, a 29-year-old from Hoboken, N.J., does about half of her holiday shopping online. She recently canceled an order for $30 of gourmet cheese because the site was charging $14 for shipping.

Now you are ready for the discussion on single trade discounts.

Single Trade Discount

In the introduction to this unit, we showed how to use the trade discount amount formula and the net price formula to calculate the McGraw-Hill/Irwin Publishing Company textbook sale to the North Shore Community College Bookstore. Since McGraw-Hill/Irwin gave the bookstore only one trade discount, it is a **single trade discount.** In the following word problem, we use the formulas to solve another example of a single trade discount. Again, we will use a blueprint aid to help dissect and solve the word problem.

The Word Problem The list price of a Macintosh computer is $2,700. The manufacturer offers dealers a 40% trade discount. What are the trade discount amount and the net price?

	The facts	Solving for?	Steps to take	Key points
BLUEPRINT	List price: $2,700. Trade discount rate: 40%.	Trade discount amount. Net price.	Trade discount amount = List price × Trade discount rate. Net price = List price − Trade discount amount.	

Steps to solving problem

1. Calculate the trade discount amount. $2,700 × .40 = $1,080

2. Calculate the net price. $2,700 − $1,080 = $1,620

Now let's learn how to check the dealers' net price of $1,620 with an alternate procedure using a complement.

How to Calculate the Net Price Using Complement of Trade Discount Rate
The **complement** of a trade discount rate is the difference between the discount rate and 100%. The following steps show you how to use the complement of a trade discount rate:

CALCULATING NET PRICE USING COMPLEMENT OF TRADE DISCOUNT RATE
Step 1. To find the complement, subtract the single discount rate from 100%.
Step 2. Multiply the list price times the complement (from Step 1).

Think of a complement of any given percent (decimal) as the result of subtracting the percent from 100%.

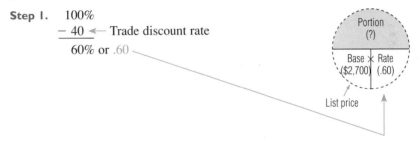

Step 1.   100%
          − 40 ← Trade discount rate
          60% or .60

The complement means that we are spending 60 cents per dollar because we save 40 cents per dollar. Since we planned to spend $2,700, we multiply .60 by $2,700 to get a net price of $1,620.

Step 2. $1,620 = $2,700 × .60

Note how the portion ($1,620) and rate (.60) relate to the same piece of the base ($2,700). The portion ($1,620) is smaller than the base, since the rate is less than 100%.

Be aware that some people prefer to use the trade discount amount formula and the net price formula to find the net price. Other people prefer to use the complement of the trade discount rate to find the net price. The result is always the same.

LO 3

Finding List Price When You Know Net Price and Trade Discount Rate   The following formula has many useful applications:

CALCULATING LIST PRICE WHEN NET PRICE AND TRADE DISCOUNT RATE ARE KNOWN
List price = $\dfrac{\text{Net price}}{\text{Complement of trade discount rate}}$

Next, let's see how to dissect and solve a word problem calculating list price.

The Word Problem A Macintosh computer has a $1,620 net price and a 40% trade discount. What is its list price?

(continued on p. 182)

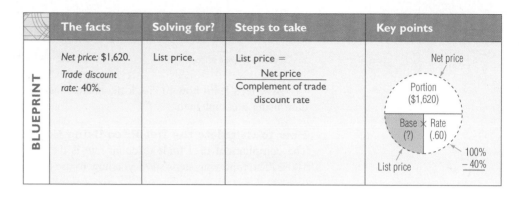

Steps to solving problem

1. Calculate the complement of the trade discount.

$$\begin{array}{r} 100\% \\ -\ 40 \\ \hline 60\% = .60 \end{array}$$

2. Calculate the list price.

$$\frac{\$1,620}{.60} = \boxed{\$2,700}$$

Note that the portion ($1,620) and rate (.60) relate to the same piece of the base.

Let's return to the McGraw-Hill/Irwin invoice in Figure 7.1 (p. 179) and calculate the list price using the formula for finding list price when the net price and trade discount rate are known. The net price of the textbooks is $5,831.62. The complement of the trade discount rate is 100% − 25% = 75% = .75. Dividing the net price $5,831.62 by the complement .75 equals $7,775.50, the list price shown in the McGraw-Hill/Irwin invoice. We can show this as follows:

$$\frac{\$5,831.62}{.75} = \$7,775.50^*, \text{ the list price}$$

*Off one cent due to rounding.

Chain Discounts

LO 4

Frequently, manufacturers want greater flexibility in setting trade discounts for different classes of customers, seasonal trends, promotional activities, and so on. To gain this flexibility, some sellers give **chain** or **series discounts**—trade discounts in a series of two or more successive discounts.

Sellers list chain discounts as a group, for example, 20/15/10. Let's look at how Mick Company arrives at the net price of office equipment with a 20/15/10 chain discount.

EXAMPLE The list price of the office equipment is $15,000. The chain discount is 20/15/10. The long way to calculate the net price is as follows:

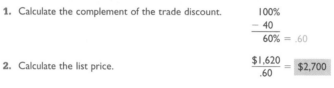

Never add the 20/15/10 together

Note how we multiply the percent (in decimal) times the new balance after we subtract the previous trade discount amount. For example, in Step 3, we change the last discount, 10%, to decimal form and multiply times $10,200. Remember that each percent is multiplied by a successively *smaller* base. You could write the 20/15/10 discount rate in any order and still arrive at the same net price. Thus, you would get the $9,180 net price if the discount were 10/15/20 or 15/20/10. However, sellers usually give the larger discounts first. *Never try to shorten this step process by adding the discounts.* Your net price will be incorrect because, when done properly, each percent is calculated on a different base.

Net Price Equivalent Rate In the example above, you could also find the $9,180 net price with the **net price equivalent rate**—a shortcut method. Let's see how to use this rate to calculate net price.

CALCULATING NET PRICE USING NET PRICE EQUIVALENT RATE
Step 1. Subtract each chain discount rate from 100% (find the complement) and convert each percent to a decimal.
Step 2. Multiply the decimals. Do not round off decimals, since this number is the net price equivalent rate.
Step 3. Multiply the list price times the net price equivalent rate (Step 2).

The following word problem with its blueprint aid illustrates how to use the net price equivalent rate method.

The Word Problem The list price of office equipment is $15,000. The chain discount is 20/15/10. What is the net price?

	The facts	Solving for?	Steps to take	Key points
B L U E P R I N T	*List price:* $15,000. *Chain discount:* 20/15/10	Net price.	Net price equivalent rate. Net price = List price × Net price equivalent rate.	Do not round net price equivalent rate.

Steps to solving problem

1. Calculate the complement of each rate and convert each percent to a decimal.

	100%	100%	100%
	− 20	− 15	− 10
	80%	85%	90%
	↓	↓	↓
	.8	.85	.9

2. Calculate the net price equivalent rate. (Do not round.)

$.8 \times .85 \times .9 = .612$ Net price equivalent rate. For each $1, you are spending about 61 cents.

3. Calculate the net price (actual cost to buyer).

$15,000 \times .612 = \boxed{\$9,180}$

Next we see how to calculate the trade discount amount with a simpler method. In the previous word problem, we could calculate the trade discount amount as follows:

$15,000 ← List price
− 9,180 ← Net price
$ 5,820 ← Trade discount amount

Single Equivalent Discount Rate   You can use another method to find the trade discount by using the **single equivalent discount rate.**

MONEY tips

Double-check invoices. On average 9 out of 10 invoices contain an error.

CALCULATING TRADE DISCOUNT AMOUNT USING SINGLE EQUIVALENT DISCOUNT RATE
Step 1. Subtract the net price equivalent rate from 1. This is the single equivalent discount rate.
Step 2. Multiply the list price times the single equivalent discount rate. This is the trade discount amount.

Let's now do the calculations.

Step 1.   1.000 ← If you are using a calculator, just press 1.
            − .612
             .388 ← This is the single equivalent discount rate.

Step 2. $15,000 × .388 = $5,820 → This is the trade discount amount.

Remember that when we use the net price equivalent rate, the buyer of the office equipment pays $.612 on each $1 of list price. Now with the single equivalent discount rate, we can say that the buyer saves $.388 on each $1 of list price. The .388 is the single equivalent discount rate for the 20/15/10 chain discount. Note how we use the .388 single equivalent discount rate as if it were the only discount.

It's time to try the Practice Quiz.

LU 7–1 PRACTICE QUIZ

Complete this **Practice Quiz** to see how you are doing.[1]

For **extra help** from your authors–Sharon and Jeff–see the student DVD

You Tube™

1. The list price of a dining room set with a 40% trade discount is $12,000. What are the trade discount amount and net price? (Use the complement method for net price.)

2. The net price of a video system with a 30% trade discount is $1,400. What is the list price?

3. Lamps Outlet bought a shipment of lamps from a wholesaler. The total list price was $12,000 with a 5/10/25 chain discount. Calculate the net price and trade discount amount. (Use the net price equivalent rate and single equivalent discount rate in your calculation.)

✓ **Solutions**

1. Dining room set trade discount amount and net price:

	The facts	Solving for?	Steps to take	Key points
BLUEPRINT	List price: $12,000. Trade discount rate: 40%.	Trade discount amount. Net price.	Trade discount amount = List price × Trade discount rate. Net price = List price × Complement of trade discount rate.	Trade discount amount Portion (?) Base × Rate ($12,000) | (.40) List price Trade discount rate

Steps to solving problem

1. Calculate the trade discount. $12,000 × .40 = **$4,800** Trade discount amount

2. Calculate the net price. $12,000 × .60 = **$7,200** (100% − 40% = 60%)

2. Video system list price:

	The facts	Solving for?	Steps to take	Key points
BLUEPRINT	Net price: $1,400. Trade discount rate: 30%.	List price.	List price = $\dfrac{\text{Net price}}{\text{Complement of trade discount}}$	Net price Portion ($1,400) Base × Rate (?) | (.70) List price 100% −30%

Steps to solving problem

1. Calculate the complement of trade discount.

$$\begin{array}{r} 100\% \\ -\ 30 \\ \hline 70\% = .70 \end{array}$$

2. Calculate the list price.

$$\frac{\$1,400}{.70} = \boxed{\$2,000}$$

---

[1]For all three problems we will show blueprint aids. You might want to draw them on scrap paper.

3. Lamps Outlet's net price and trade discount amount:

	The facts	Solving for?	Steps to take	Key points
BLUEPRINT	List price: $12,000. Chain discount: 5/10/25.	Net price. Trade discount amount.	Net price = List price × Net price equivalent rate. Trade discount amount = List price × Single equivalent discount rate.	Do not round off net price equivalent rate or single equivalent discount rate.

Steps to solving problem

1. Calculate the complement of each chain discount.

$$
\begin{array}{ccc}
100\% & 100\% & 100\% \\
-\ \ 5 & -\ 10 & -\ 25 \\
\hline
95\% & 90\% & 75\%
\end{array}
$$

2. Calculate the net price equivalent rate.

$$.95 \times .90 \times .75 = .64125$$

3. Calculate the net price.

$$\$12,000 \times .64125 = \boxed{\$7,695}$$

4. Calculate the single equivalent discount rate.

$$
\begin{array}{r}
1.00000 \\
-\ .64125 \\
\hline
.35875
\end{array}
$$

5. Calculate the trade discount amount.

$$\$12,000 \times .35875 = \boxed{\$4,305}$$

LU 7–1a   EXTRA PRACTICE QUIZ WITH WORKED-OUT SOLUTIONS

Need more practice? Try this **Extra Practice Quiz** (check figures in the Interactive Chapter Organizer, p. 196). Worked-out Solutions can be found in Appendix B at end of text.

1. The list price of a dining room set with a 30% trade discount is $16,000. What are the trade discount amount and net price? (Use the complement method for net price.)
2. The net price of a video system with a 20% trade discount is $400. What is the list price?
3. Lamps Outlet bought a shipment of lamps from a wholesaler. The total list price was $14,000 with a 4/8/20 chain discount. Calculate the net price and trade discount amount. (Use the net price equivalent rate and single equivalent discount rate in your calculation.)

Learning Unit 7–2: Cash Discounts, Credit Terms, and Partial Payments

LO 1

To introduce this learning unit, we will use the New Hampshire Propane Company invoice that follows. The invoice shows that if you pay your bill early, you will receive a 19-cent discount. Every penny counts.

© Alvis Upitis/Getty Images

New Hampshire Propane Company

Date	Description	Qty.	Price	Total
	Previous Balance			**$0.00**
06/24/14	PROPANE	3.60	$3.40	$12.24

Invoice No.		Totals this invoice:	$12.24
004433L		**AMOUNT DUE:**	**$12.24**

Invoice Date	Prompt Pay Discount: $0.19
6/26/14	Net Amount Due if RECEIVED by 07/10/14: $12.05

Due Date	7/26/14

Now let's study cash discounts.

Cash Discounts

In the New Hampshire Propane Company invoice, we receive a cash discount of 19 cents. This amount is determined by the **terms of the sale,** which can include the credit period, cash discount, discount period, and freight terms.

Buyers can often benefit from buying on credit. The time period that sellers give buyers to pay their invoices is the **credit period.** Frequently, buyers can sell the goods bought during this credit period. Then, at the end of the credit period, buyers can pay sellers with the funds from the sales of the goods. When buyers can do this, they can use the consumer's money to pay the invoice instead of their money.

<aside>A cash discount is for prompt payment. A trade discount is not.</aside>

Sellers can also offer a cash discount, or reduction from the invoice price, if buyers pay the invoice within a specified time. This time period is the **discount period,** which is part of the total credit period. Sellers offer this cash discount because they can use the dollars to better advantage sooner than later. Buyers who are not short of cash like cash discounts because the goods will cost them less and, as a result, provide an opportunity for larger profits.

<aside>Trade discounts should be taken before cash discounts.</aside>

Remember that buyers do not take cash discounts on freight, returned goods, sales tax, and trade discounts. Buyers take cash discounts on the *net price* of the invoice. Before we discuss how to calculate cash discounts, let's look at some aids that will help you calculate credit **due dates** and **end of credit periods.**

Aids in Calculating Credit Due Dates   Sellers usually give credit for 30, 60, or 90 days. Not all months of the year have 30 days. So you must count the credit days from the date of the invoice. The trick is to remember the number of days in each month. You can choose one of the following three options to help you do this.

<aside>Years divisible by 4 are leap years. Leap years occur in 2012 and 2016.</aside>

Option 1: Days-in-a-Month Rule   You may already know this rule. Remember that every 4 years is a leap year.

> Thirty days has September, April, June, and November; all the rest have 31 except February has 28, and 29 in leap years.

Option 2: Knuckle Months   Some people like to use the knuckles on their hands to remember which months have 30 or 31 days. Note in the following diagram that each knuckle represents a month with 31 days. The short months are in between the knuckles.

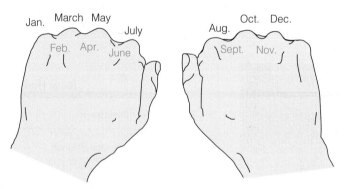

31 days: Jan., March, May, July, Aug., Oct., Dec.

Option 3: Days-in-a-Year Calendar   The days-in-a-year calendar (excluding leap year) is another tool to help you calculate dates for discount and credit periods (Table 7.1, p. 187). For example, let's use Table 7.1 to calculate 90 days from August 12.

EXAMPLE   By Table 7.1: August 12 = $\begin{array}{r} 224 \text{ days} \\ +\ 90 \\ \hline 314 \text{ days} \end{array}$

Search for day 314 in Table 7.1. You will find that day 314 is November 10. In this example, we stayed within the same year. Now let's try an example in which we overlap from year to year.

TABLE   7.1   Exact days-in-a-year calendar (excluding leap year)*

Day of month	31 Jan.	28 Feb.	31 Mar.	30 Apr.	31 May	30 June	31 July	31 Aug.	30 Sept.	31 Oct.	30 Nov.	31 Dec.
1	1	32	60	91	121	152	182	213	244	274	305	335
2	2	33	61	92	122	153	183	214	245	275	306	336
3	3	34	62	93	123	154	184	215	246	276	307	337
4	4	35	63	94	124	155	185	216	247	277	308	338
5	5	36	64	95	125	156	186	217	248	278	309	339
6	6	37	65	96	126	157	187	218	249	279	310	340
7	7	38	66	97	127	158	188	219	250	280	311	341
8	8	39	67	98	128	159	189	220	251	281	312	342
9	9	40	68	99	129	160	190	221	252	282	313	343
10	10	41	69	100	130	161	191	222	253	283	314	344
11	11	42	70	101	131	162	192	223	254	284	315	345
12	12	43	71	102	132	163	193	224	255	285	316	346
13	13	44	72	103	133	164	194	225	256	286	317	347
14	14	45	73	104	134	165	195	226	257	287	318	348
15	15	46	74	105	135	166	196	227	258	288	319	349
16	16	47	75	106	136	167	197	228	259	289	320	350
17	17	48	76	107	137	168	198	229	260	290	321	351
18	18	49	77	108	138	169	199	230	261	291	322	352
19	19	50	78	109	139	170	200	231	262	292	323	353
20	20	51	79	110	140	171	201	232	263	293	324	354
21	21	52	80	111	141	172	202	233	264	294	325	355
22	22	53	81	112	142	173	203	234	265	295	326	356
23	23	54	82	113	143	174	204	235	266	296	327	357
24	24	55	83	114	144	175	205	236	267	297	328	358
25	25	56	84	115	145	176	206	237	268	298	329	359
26	26	57	85	116	146	177	207	238	269	299	330	360
27	27	58	86	117	147	178	208	239	270	300	331	361
28	28	59	87	118	148	179	209	240	271	301	332	362
29	29	—	88	119	149	180	210	241	272	302	333	363
30	30	—	89	120	150	181	211	242	273	303	334	364
31	31	—	90	—	151	—	212	243	—	304	—	365

*Often referred to as a Julian calendar.

EXAMPLE   What date is 80 days after December 5?

Table 7.1 shows that December 5 is 339 days from the beginning of the year. Subtracting 339 from 365 (the end of the year) tells us that we have used up 26 days by the end of the year. This leaves 54 days in the new year. Go back in the table and start with the beginning of the year and search for 54 (80 − 26) days. The 54th day is February 23.

By table

```
  365 days in year
− 339 days until December 5
   26 days used in year

       80 days from December 5
     − 26 days used in year
       54 days in new year or
          February 23
```

Without use of table

```
December  31
− December   5
            26
          + 31 days in January
            57
          + 23 due date (February 23)
            80 total days
```

When you know how to calculate credit due dates, you can understand the common business terms sellers offer buyers involving discounts and credit periods. Remember that discount and credit terms vary from one seller to another.

Common Credit Terms Offered by Sellers

The common credit terms sellers offer buyers include *ordinary dating, receipt of goods (ROG),* and *end of month (EOM).* In this section we examine these credit terms. To determine the due dates, we used the exact days-in-a-year calendar (Table 7.1, p. 187).

Ordinary Dating   Today, businesses frequently use the **ordinary dating** method. It gives the buyer a cash discount period that begins with the invoice date. The credit terms of two common ordinary dating methods are 2/10, n/30 and 2/10, 1/15, n/30.

2/10, n/30 Ordinary Dating Method   The 2/10, n/30 is read as "two ten, net thirty." Buyers can take a 2% cash discount off the gross amount of the invoice if they pay the bill within 10 days from the invoice date. If buyers miss the discount period, the net amount—without a discount—is due between day 11 and day 30. *Freight, returned goods, sales tax, and trade discounts must be subtracted from the gross before calculating a cash discount.*

EXAMPLE $400 invoice dated July 5: terms 2/10, n/30; no freight; paid on July 11.

Step 1. Calculate end of 2% discount period:

>   July   5 date of invoice
>   <u>+ 10</u> days
>   July 15 end of 2% discount period

Step 2. Calculate end of credit period:

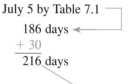

>   July 5 by Table 7.1
>   186 days
>   <u>+ 30</u>
>   216 days

Search in Table 7.1 for 216 → August 4 → end of credit period

Step 3. Calculate payment on July 11:

>   .02 × $400 = $8 cash discount
> $400 − $8 = $392 paid

> *Note:* A 2% cash discount means that you save 2 cents on the dollar and pay 98 cents on the dollar. Thus, $.98 × $400 = $392.

The following time line illustrates the 2/10, n/30 ordinary dating method beginning and ending dates of the above example:

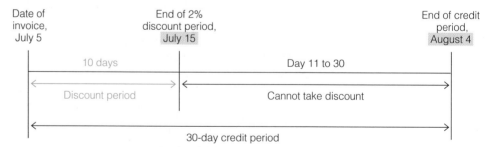

2/10, 1/15, n/30 Ordinary Dating Method   The 2/10, 1/15, n/30 is read "two ten, one fifteen, net thirty." The seller will give buyers a 2% (2 cents on the dollar) cash discount if they pay within 10 days of the invoice date. If buyers pay between day 11 and day 15 from the date of the invoice, they can save 1 cent on the dollar. If buyers do not pay on day 15, the net or full amount is due 30 days from the invoice date.

EXAMPLE $600 invoice dated May 8; $100 of freight included in invoice price; paid on May 22. Terms 2/10, 1/15, n/30.

Step 1. Calculate the end of the 2% discount period:

May   8 date of invoice

+ 10 days

May 18 end of 2% discount period

Step 2. Calculate end of 1% discount period:

May 18 end of 2% discount period

+   5 days

May 23 end of 1% discount period

Step 3. Calculate end of credit period:

May 8 by Table 7.1

128 days

+ 30

158 days

Search in Table 7.1 for 158 → June 7 → end of credit period

Step 4. Calculate payment on May 22 (14 days after date of invoice):

$600 invoice

− 100 freight

$500

× .01

$5.00

$500 − $5.00 + $100 freight = $595

> A 1% discount means we pay $.99 on the dollar or
> $500 × $.99 = $495 + $100 freight = $595.
>
> *Note:* Freight is added back since no cash discount is taken on freight.

The following time line illustrates the 2/10, 1/15, n/30 ordinary dating method beginning and ending dates of the above example:

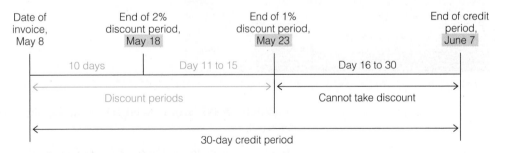

Receipt of Goods (ROG)

3/10, n/30 ROG With the **receipt of goods (ROG),** the cash discount period begins when buyer receives goods, *not* the invoice date. Industry often uses the ROG terms when buyers cannot expect delivery until a long time after they place the order. Buyers can take a 3% discount within 10 days *after* receipt of goods. The full amount is due between day 11 and day 30 if the cash discount period is missed.

EXAMPLE $900 invoice dated May 9; no freight or returned goods; the goods were received on July 8; terms 3/10, n/30 ROG; payment made on July 20.

Step 1. Calculate the end of the 3% discount period:

July   8 date goods arrive

+ 10 days

July 18 end of 3% discount period

(continued on p. 190)

Step 2. Calculate the end of the credit period:

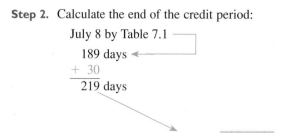

July 8 by Table 7.1

189 days

$+ \;\; 30$

219 days

Search in Table 7.1 for 219 → August 7 → end of credit period

Step 3. Calculate payment on July 20:

Missed discount period and paid net or full amount of $900.

The following time line illustrates 3/10, n/30 ROG beginning and ending dates of the above example:

Date goods arrive, July 8	End of 3% discount period, July 18	End of credit period, August 7
10 days	Day 11 to 30	
Discount period	Cannot take discount	
30-day credit period		

© The McGraw-Hill Companies, Inc./Christopher Kerrigan, photographer

End of Month (EOM)[2]   In this section we look at invoices involving **end of month (EOM)** terms. If an invoice is dated the *25th or earlier* of a month, we follow one set of rules. If an invoice is dated after the 25th of the month, a new set of rules is followed. Let's look at each situation.

Invoice Dated 25th or Earlier in Month, 1/10 EOM If sellers date an invoice on the 25th or earlier in the month, buyers can take the cash discount if they pay the invoice by the first 10 days of the month following the sale (next month). If buyers miss the discount period, the full amount is due within 20 days after the end of the discount period.

EXAMPLE $600 invoice dated July 6; no freight or returns; terms 1/10 EOM; paid on August 8.

Step 1. Calculate the end of the 1% discount period:

August 10 ←   First 10 days of month following sale.

Step 2. Calculate the end of the credit period:

August 10

$+ \;\; 20$ days

August 30 → Credit period is 20 days after discount period.

Step 3. Calculate payment on August 8:

.99 × $600 = $594

The following time line illustrates the beginning and ending dates of the EOM invoice of the previous example:

| Date of invoice, July 6 | Next month following sale, August* | End of 1% discount period, August 10 | End of credit period, August 30 |

*Even though the discount period begins with the next month following the sale, if buyers wish, they can pay before the discount period (date of invoice until the discount period).

Invoice Dated after 25th of Month, 2/10 EOM When sellers sell goods *after* the 25th of the month, buyers gain an additional month. The cash discount period ends on the 10th day of the second month that follows the sale. Why? This occurs because the seller guarantees the 15 days' credit of the buyer. If a buyer bought goods on August 29, September 10 would be only 12 days. So the buyer gets the extra month.

EXAMPLE $800 invoice dated April 29; no freight or returned goods; terms 2/10 EOM; payment made on June 18.

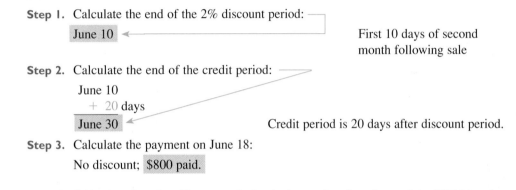

Step 1. Calculate the end of the 2% discount period:

June 10 ◄───────────────────   First 10 days of second month following sale

Step 2. Calculate the end of the credit period:

June 10
+ 20 days
June 30 ◄───────   Credit period is 20 days after discount period.

Step 3. Calculate the payment on June 18:

No discount; $800 paid.

The following time line illustrates the beginning and ending dates of the EOM invoice of the above example:

| Date of invoice, April 29 | 2nd month following sale, June* | End of 2% discount period, June 10 | End of credit period, June 30 |

*Even though the discount period begins with the second month following the sale, if buyers wish, they can pay before the discount date (date of invoice until the discount period)

Solving a Word Problem with Trade and Cash Discount

Now that we have studied trade and cash discounts, let's look at a combination that involves both a trade and a cash discount.

The Word Problem Hardy Company sent Regan Corporation an invoice for office equipment with a $10,000 list price. Hardy dated the invoice July 29 with terms of 2/10 EOM (end of month). Regan receives a 30% trade discount and paid the invoice on September 6. Since terms were FOB destination, Regan paid no freight charge. What was the cost of office equipment for Regan?

	The facts	Solving for?	Steps to take	Key points
BLUEPRINT	List price: $10,000. Trade discount rate: 30%. Terms: 2/10 EOM. Invoice date: 7/29. Date paid: 9/6.	Cost of office equipment.	Net price = List price × Complement of trade discount rate. After 25th of month for EOM. Discount period is 1st 10 days of second month that follows sale.	Trade discounts are deducted before cash discounts are taken. Cash discounts are not taken on freight or returns.

(continued on p. 192)

Steps to solving problem

1. Calculate the net price.

$10,000 × .70 = $7,000

    100%
  − 30% (trade discount)

2. Calculate the discount period.

Sale: 7/29 Month 1: Aug. Month 2: Sept 10 → Paid on Sept. 6—is entitled to 2% off.

3. Calculate the cost of office equipment.

$7,000 × .98 = $6,860

    100%
  − 2%

If you save 2 cents on a dollar, you are spending 98 cents.

Partial Payments

Often buyers cannot pay the entire invoice before the end of the discount period. To calculate partial payments and outstanding balance, use the following steps:

CALCULATING PARTIAL PAYMENTS AND OUTSTANDING BALANCE

Step 1. Calculate the complement of a discount rate.

Step 2. Divide partial payments by the complement of a discount rate (Step 1). This gives the amount credited.

Step 3. Subtract Step 2 from the total owed. This is the outstanding balance.

EXAMPLE   Molly McGrady owed $400. Molly's terms were 2/10, n/30. Within 10 days, Molly sent a check for $80. The actual credit the buyer gave Molly is as follows:

Step 1. $100\% - 2\% = 98\% \rightarrow .98$

Step 2. $\dfrac{\$80}{.98} = \$81.63$ $\dfrac{\$80}{1 - .02}$ ← Discount rate

Step 3. $400.00
            − 81.63 $ partial payment—although sent in $80
            318.37 outstanding balance

Note: We do not multiply .02 × $80 because the seller did not base the original discount on $80. When Molly makes a payment within the 10-day discount period, 98 cents pays each $1 she owes. Before buyers take discounts on partial payments, they must have permission from the seller. Not all states allow partial payments.

   You have completed another unit. Let's check your progress.

LU 7–2   PRACTICE QUIZ

Complete this **Practice Quiz** to see how you are doing.

Complete the following table:

	Date of invoice	Date goods received	Terms	Last day* of discount period	End of credit period
1.	July 6		2/10, n/30		
2.	February 19	June 9	3/10, n/30 ROG		
3.	May 9		4/10, 1/30, n/60		
4.	May 12		2/10 EOM		
5.	May 29		2/10 EOM		

*If more than one discount, assume date of last discount.

6. Metro Corporation sent Vasko Corporation an invoice for equipment with an $8,000 list price. Metro dated the invoice May 26. Terms were 2/10 EOM. Vasko receives a 20% trade discount and paid the invoice on July 3. What was the cost of equipment for Vasko? (A blueprint aid will be in the solution to help dissect this problem.)

7. Complete amount to be credited and balance outstanding:

    Amount of invoice: $600
    Terms: 2/10, 1/15, n/30
    Date of invoice: September 30
    Paid October 3: $400

✓ Solutions

1. End of discount period: July 6 + 10 days = ⎡July 16⎤
   End of credit period: By Table 7.1, July 6 =

   $$\begin{array}{r} 187 \text{ days} \\ + 30 \text{ days} \\ \hline 217 \end{array} \rightarrow \text{search} \longrightarrow \boxed{\text{Aug. 5}}$$

2. End of discount period: June 9 + 10 days = ⎡June 19⎤
   End of credit period: By Table 7.1, June 9 =

   $$\begin{array}{r} 160 \text{ days} \\ + 30 \text{ days} \\ \hline 190 \end{array} \rightarrow \text{search} \longrightarrow \boxed{\text{July 9}}$$

3. End of discount period: By Table 7.1, May 9 =

   $$\begin{array}{r} 129 \text{ days} \\ + 30 \text{ days} \\ \hline 159 \end{array} \rightarrow \text{search} \longrightarrow \boxed{\text{June 8}}$$

   End of credit period: By Table 7.1, May 9 =

   $$\begin{array}{r} 129 \text{ days} \\ + 60 \text{ days} \\ \hline 189 \end{array} \rightarrow \text{search} \longrightarrow \boxed{\text{July 8}}$$

4. End of discount period: ⎡June 10⎤
   End of credit period: June 10 + 20 = ⎡June 30⎤

5. End of discount period: ⎡July 10⎤
   End of credit period: July 10 + 20 = ⎡July 30⎤

6. Vasko Corporation's cost of equipment:

	The facts	Solving for?	Steps to take	Key points
BLUEPRINT	List price: $8,000. Trade discount rate: 20%. Terms: 2/10 EOM. Invoice date: 5/26. Date paid: 7/3.	Cost of equipment.	Net price = List price × Complement of trade discount rate. EOM before 25th: Discount period is 1st 10 days of month that follows sale.	Trade discounts are deducted before cash discounts are taken. Cash discounts are not taken on freight or returns.

Steps to solving problem

1. Calculate the net price.

2. Calculate the discount period.

3. Calculate the cost of office equipment.

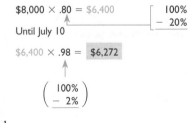

   $8,000 × .80 = $6,400   ⎡ 100%
                            ⎣ − 20%

   Until July 10

   $6,400 × .98 = ⎡$6,272⎤
                  (100%
                    − 2%)

7. $\dfrac{\$400}{.98}$ = $408.16, amount credited.

   $600 − $408.16 = **$191.84,** balance outstanding.

Need more practice? Try this **Extra Practice Quiz** (check figures in the Interactive Chapter Organizer, p. 196). Worked-out Solutions can be found in Appendix B at end of text.

Complete the following table:

	Date of invoice	Date goods received	Terms	Last day of discount period*	End of credit period
1.	July 8		2/10, n/30		
2.	February 24	June 12	3/10, n/30 ROG		
3.	May 12		4/10, 1/30, n/60		
4.	April 14		2/10 EOM		
5.	April 27		2/10 EOM		

*If more than one discount, assume date of last discount.

6. Metro Corporation sent Vasko Corporation an invoice for equipment with a $9,000 list price. Metro dated the invoice June 29. Terms were 2/10 EOM. Vasko receives a 30% trade discount and paid the discount on August 9. What was the cost of equipment for Vasko?

7. Complete amount to be credited and balance outstanding:

Amount of invoice: $700
Terms: 2/10, 1/15, n/30
Date of invoice: September 28
Paid October 3: $600

INTERACTIVE CHAPTER ORGANIZER

Topic/procedure/formula	Examples	You try it*
Trade discount amount, p. 178 Trade discount amount = List price × Trade discount rate	$600 list price 30% trade discount rate Trade discount amount = $600 × .30 = $180	**Calculate trade discount amount** $700 list price 20% trade discount
Calculating net price, p. 178 Net price = List price − Trade discount amount or List price × Complement of trade discount price	$600 list price 30% trade discount rate Net price = $600 × .70 = $420 1.00 − .30 .70	**Calculate net price** $700 list price 20% trade discount
Freight, p. 179 FOB shipping point—buyer pays freight. FOB destination—seller pays freight.	Moose Company of New York sells equipment to Agee Company of Oregon. Terms of shipping are FOB New York. Agee pays cost of freight since terms are FOB shipping point.	**Calculate freight** If a buyer in Boston buys equipment with shipping terms of FOB destination, who will pay cost of freight?
Calculating list price when net price and trade discount rate are known, p. 181 List price = Net price / Complement of trade discount rate	40% trade discount rate Net price, $120 $120/.60 = $200 list price (1.00 − .40)	**Calculate list price** 60% trade discount rate Net price, $240
Chain discounts, p. 182 Successively lower base.	5/10 on a $100 list item $100 $95 × .05 × .10 $5.00 $9.50 (running balance) $95.00 − 9.50 $85.50 net price	**Calculate net price** 6/8 on $200 list item

(continues)

INTERACTIVE CHAPTER ORGANIZER

Topic/procedure/formula	Examples	You try it*
Net price equivalent rate, pp. 182–183 $\dfrac{\text{Actual cost}}{\text{to buyer}} = \dfrac{\text{List}}{\text{price}} \times \dfrac{\text{Net price}}{\text{equivalent rate}}$ Take complement of each chain discount and multiply—do not round. $\dfrac{\text{Trade discount}}{\text{amount}} = \dfrac{\text{List}}{\text{price}} - \dfrac{\text{Actual cost}}{\text{to buyer}}$	Given: 5/10 on $1,000 list price Take complement: .95 × .90 = .855 (net price equivalent) $1,000 × .855 = **$855** (actual cost or net price) $1,000 − 855 **$ 145** trade discount amount	**Calculate net price equivalent rate, net price, and trade discount amount** 6/8 on $2,000 list
Single equivalent discount rate, p. 183 $\dfrac{\text{Trade discount}}{\text{amount}} = \dfrac{\text{List}}{\text{price}} \times \dfrac{1 - \text{Net price}}{\text{equivalent rate}}$	See preceding example for facts: 1 − .855 = .145 .145 × $1,000 = **$145**	**From the above You Try It, calculate single equivalent discount**
Cash discounts, p. 186 Cash discounts, due to prompt payment, are not taken on freight, returns, etc.	Gross $1,000 (includes freight) Freight $25 Terms 2/10, n/30 Returns $25 Purchased: Sept. 9; paid Sept. 15 Cash discount = $950 × .02 = **$19**	**Calculate cash discount** Gross $2,000 (includes freight) Freight $40 Terms 2/10, n/30 Returns $40 Purchased: Sept. 2; paid Sept. 8
Calculating due dates, pp. 186–187 *Option 1:* Thirty days has September, April, June, and November; all the rest have 31 except February has 28, and 29 in leap years. *Option 2:* Knuckles—31-day month; in between knuckles are short months. *Option 3:* Days-in-a-year table.	Invoice $500 on March 5; terms 2/10, n/30 March 5 *End of discount* + 10 *period:* → March 15 *End of credit* March 5 = 64 days *period by* + 30 *Table 7.1:* → 94 days Search in Table 7.1 April 4	**Calculate end of discount and end of credit periods** Invoice $600 on April 2; terms 2/10, n/30
Common terms of sale **a. Ordinary dating, p. 188** Discount period begins from date of invoice. Credit period ends 20 days from the end of the discount period unless otherwise stipulated; example, 2/10, n/60—the credit period ends 50 days from end of discount period.	Invoice $600 (freight of $100 included in price) dated March 8; payment on March 16; 3/10, n/30. March 8 *End of discount* + 10 *period:* → March 18 *End of credit* March 8 = 67 days *period by* + 30 *Table 7.1:* → 97 days Search in Table 7.1 April 7 *If paid on March 16:* .97 × $500 = $485 + 100 freight **$585**	**Calculate amount paid** Invoice $700 (freight of $100 included in price) dated May 7; payment May 15; 2/10, n/30
b. Receipt of goods (ROG), p. 189 Discount period begins when goods are received. Credit period ends 20 days from end of discount period.	4/10, n/30, ROG. $600 invoice; no freight; dated August 5; goods received October 2, payment made October 20. October 2 *End of discount* + 10 *period:* → October 12 *End of* October 2 = 275 *credit period* + 30 *by Table 7.1:* → 305 Search in Table 7.1 November 1 *Payment on October 20:* No discount, pay **$600**	**Calculate amount paid** 3/10, n/30, ROG. $700 invoice; no freight; dated September 6; goods received September 20; payment made October 15.

(continues)

INTERACTIVE CHAPTER ORGANIZER

Topic/procedure/formula	Examples	You try it*
c. End of month (EOM), p. 190 On or before 25th of the month, discount period is 10 days after month following sale. After 25th of the month, an additional month is gained.	$1,000 invoice dated May 12; no freight or returns; terms 2/10 EOM. *End of discount period* → June 10 *End of credit period* → June 30	**Calculate end of discount and end of credit periods** $2,000 invoice dated October 11; terms 2/10 EOM
Partial payments, p. 192 Amount credited $= \dfrac{\text{Partial payment}}{1 - \text{Discount rate}}$	$200 invoice; terms 2/10, n/30; dated March 2; paid $100 on March 5. $\dfrac{\$100}{1-.02} = \dfrac{\$100}{.98} = \$102.04$	**Calculate amount credited** $400 invoice; terms 2/10, n/30; dated May 4; paid $300 on May 7.

KEY TERMS			
	Cash discount, *p. 177* Chain discounts, *p. 182* Complement, *p. 181* Credit period, *p. 186* Discount period, *p. 186* Due dates, *p. 186* End of credit period, *p. 186* End of month (EOM), *p. 190* FOB destination, *p. 180*	FOB shipping point, *p. 179* Freight terms, *p. 179* Invoice, *p. 178* List price, *p. 178* Net price, *p. 178* Net price equivalent rate, *p. 182* Ordinary dating, *p. 188* Receipt of goods (ROG), *p. 189* Series discounts, *p. 182*	Single equivalent discount rate, *p. 183* Single trade discount, *p. 180* Terms of the sale, *p. 186* Trade discount, *p. 177* Trade discount amount, *p. 178* Trade discount rate, *p. 178*

Check Figures for Extra Practice Quizzes with Page References. (Worked-out Solutions in Appendix B.)	LU 7–1a (p. 185) 1. $4,800 TD; $11,200 NP 2. $500 3. $9,891.84 NP; TD $4,108.16	LU 7–2a (p. 194) 1. July 18; Aug. 7 2. June 22; July 12 3. June 11; July 11 4. May 10; May 30 5. June 10; June 30 6. $6,174 7. a) $612.24 b) $87.76

*Worked-out solutions are in Appendix B.

Critical Thinking Discussion Questions with Chapter Concept Check

1. What is the net price? June Long bought a jacket from a catalog company. She took her trade discount off the original price plus freight. What is wrong with June's approach? Who would benefit from June's approach—the buyer or the seller?

2. How do you calculate the list price when the net price and trade discount rate are known? A publisher tells the bookstore its net price of a book along with a suggested trade discount of 20%. The bookstore uses a 25% discount rate. Is this ethical when textbook prices are rising?

3. If Jordan Furniture ships furniture FOB shipping point, what does that mean? Does this mean you get a cash discount?

4. What are the steps to calculate the net price equivalent rate? Why is the net price equivalent rate *not* rounded?

5. What are the steps to calculate the single equivalent discount rate? Is this rate off the list or net price? Explain why this calculation of a single equivalent discount rate may not always be needed.

6. What is the difference between a discount and credit period? Are all cash discounts taken before trade discounts? Do you agree or disagree? Why?

7. Explain the following credit terms of sale:
   a. 2/10, n/30.
   b. 3/10, n/30 ROG.
   c. 1/10 EOM (on or before 25th of month).
   d. 1/10 EOM (after 25th of month).

8. Explain how to calculate a partial payment. Whom does a partial payment favor—the buyer or the seller?

9. **Chapter Concept Check.** Search Facebook to find out what customer discounts companies offer to Facebook users (see chapter opener for specifics). Be sure to talk about shipping charges and trade and cash discounts. What kind of savings can you find?

Check figures for odd-numbered problems in Appendix C.   Name _____   Date _____

DRILL PROBLEMS

For all problems, round your final answer to the nearest cent. Do not round net price equivalent rates or single equivalent discount rates.

Complete the following: *LU 7-1(4)*

Item	List price	Chain discount	Net price equivalent rate (in decimals)	Single equivalent discount rate (in decimals)	Trade discount	Net price
7–1. Apple iPad	$599	3/1				
7–2. Panasonic DVD player	$199	8/4/3				
7–3. IBM scanner	$269	7/3/1				

Complete the following: *LU 7-1(4)*

Item	List price	Chain discount	Net price	Trade discount
7–4. Trotter treadmill	$3,000	9/4		
7–5. Maytag dishwasher	$450	8/5/6		
7–6. Hewlett-Packard scanner	$320	3/5/9		
7–7. Land Rover roofrack	$1,850	12/9/6		

7–8. Which of the following companies, A or B, gives a higher discount? Use the single equivalent discount rate to make your *eXcel* choice (convert your equivalent rate to the nearest hundredth percent).

Company A	Company B
8/10/15/3	10/6/16/5

Complete the following: *LU 7-2(1)*

	Invoice	Date goods are received	Terms	Last day* of discount period	Final day bill is due (end of credit period)
7–9.	June 18		1/10, n/30		
7–10.	Nov. 27		2/10 EOM		
7–11.	May 15	June 5	3/10, n/30, ROG		
7–12.	April 10		2/10, 1/30, n/60		
7–13.	June 12		3/10 EOM		
7–14.	Jan. 10	Feb. 3 (no leap year)	4/10, n/30, ROG		

*If more than one discount, assume date of last discount.

Complete the following by calculating the cash discount and net amount paid: *LU 7-2(1)*

	Gross amount of invoice (freight charge already included)	Freight charge	Date of invoice	Terms of invoice	Date of payment	Cash discount	Net amount paid
7–15.	$7,000	$100	4/8	2/10, n/60	4/15		
7–16.	$600	None	8/1	3/10, 2/15, n/30	8/13		
7–17.	$200	None	11/13	1/10 EOM	12/3		
7–18.	$500	$100	11/29	1/10 EOM	1/4		

Complete the following: *LU 7-2(2)*

	Amount of invoice	Terms	Invoice date	Actual partial payment made	Date of partial payment	Amount of payment to be credited	Balance outstanding
7–19.	$700	2/10, n/60	5/6	$400	5/15		
7–20.	$600	4/10, n/60	7/5	$400	7/14		

WORD PROBLEMS (Round to Nearest Cent as Needed)

7–21. The list price of a smartphone is $299. A local Verizon dealer receives a trade discount of 20%. Find the trade discount amount and the net price. *LU 7-1(1)*

7–22. A model NASCAR race car lists for $79.99 with a trade discount of 40%. What is the net price of the car? *LU 7-1(1)*
eXcel

7–23. Lucky you! You went to couponcabin.com and found a 20% off coupon to your significant other's favorite store. Armed with that coupon, you went to the store only to find a storewide sale offering 10% off everything in the store. In addition, your credit card has a special offer that allows you to save 10% if you use your credit card for all purchases that day. Using your credit card, what will you pay before tax for the $155 gift you found? Use the single equivalent discount to calculate how much you save and then calculate your final price. *LU 7-1(4)*

7–24. Levin Furniture buys a living room set with a $4,000 list price and a 55% trade discount. Freight (FOB shipping point) of $50 is not part of the list price. What is the delivered price (including freight) of the living room set, assuming a cash discount of 2/10, n/30, ROG? The invoice had an April 8 date. Levin received the goods on April 19 and paid the invoice on April 25. *LU 7-1(1, 2)*

7–25. A manufacturer of skateboards offered a 5/2/1 chain discount to many customers. Bob's Sporting Goods ordered 20 skateboards for a total $625 list price. What was the net price of the skateboards? What was the trade discount amount? *LU 7-1(4)*

7–26. Home Depot wants to buy a new line of fertilizers. Manufacturer A offers a 21/13 chain discount. Manufacturer B offers a 26/8
eXcel chain discount. Both manufacturers have the same list price. What manufacturer should Home Depot buy from? *LU 7-1(4)*

7–27. Maplewood Supply received a $5,250 invoice dated 4/15/06. The $5,250 included $250 freight. Terms were 4/10, 3/30, n/60. **(a)** If Maplewood pays the invoice on April 27, what will it pay? **(b)** If Maplewood pays the invoice on May 21, what will it pay? *LU 7-2(1)*

7–28. A local Sports Authority ordered 50 pairs of tennis shoes from Nike Corporation. The shoes were priced at $85 for each
eXcel pair with the following terms: 4/10, 2/30, n/60. The invoice was dated October 15. Sports Authority sent in a payment on October 28. What should have been the amount of the check? *LU 7-2(1)*

7–29. Macy of New York sold LeeCo. of Chicago office equipment with a $6,000 list price. Sale terms were 3/10, n/30 FOB New
eXcel York. Macy agreed to prepay the $30 freight. LeeCo. pays the invoice within the discount period. What does LeeCo. pay Macy? *LU 7-2(2)*

7–30. Royal Furniture bought a sofa for $800. The sofa had a $1,400 list price. What was the trade discount rate Royal received? Round to the nearest hundredth percent. *LU 7-2(1)*

7–31. The Consumer Electronics Show (CES) reports that the HP Spectre laptop computer starts at $999.99 for a base configuration. The model displayed at its recent show costs $1,399, $100 more than the comparable 13-inch Apple MacBook Air. If Computers-R-Us buys the HP Spectre at the show with 3/15, net 30 terms on August 22, how much does it need to pay on September 5? *LU 7-2(1)*

7–32. Bally Manufacturing sent Intel Corporation an invoice for machinery with a $14,000 list price. Bally dated the invoice July 23 with 2/10 EOM terms. Intel receives a 40% trade discount. Intel pays the invoice on August 5. What does Intel pay Bally? *LU 7-2(1)*

7–33. On August 1, Intel Corporation (Problem 7–32) returns $100 of the machinery due to defects. What does Intel pay Bally on August 5? Round to nearest cent.   *LU 7-2(1)*

7–34. Stacy's Dress Shop received a $1,050 invoice dated July 8 with 2/10, 1/15, n/60 terms. On July 22, Stacy's sent a $242 partial payment. What credit should Stacy's receive? What is Stacy's outstanding balance?   *LU 7-2(2)*

7–35. On March 11, Jangles Corporation received a $20,000 invoice dated March 8. Cash discount terms were 4/10, n/30. On March 15, Jangles sent an $8,000 partial payment. What credit should Jangles receive? What is Jangles' outstanding balance?   *LU 7-2(2)*

ADDITIONAL SET OF WORD PROBLEMS

7–36. The 2012 Mini Cooper S retails starting at $23,800. If the dealership can purchase five with a 20/10/5 chain discount, what is its net price?   *LU 7-1(4)*

7–37. A local Barnes and Noble paid a $79.99 net price for each calculus textbook. The publisher offered a 20% trade discount. What was the publisher's list price?   *LU 7-2(3)*

7–38. HomeOffice.com buys a computer from Compaq Corporation. The computer has a $1,200 list price with a 30% trade discount. What is the trade discount amount? What is the net price of the computer? Freight charges are FOB destination. *LU 7-1(1)*

7–39. Vail Ski Shop received a $1,201 invoice dated July 8 with 2/10, 1/15, n/60 terms. On July 22, Vail sent a $485 partial payment. What credit should Vail receive? What is Vail's outstanding balance?   *LU 7-2(2)*

7–40. True Value received an invoice dated 4/15/02. The invoice had a $5,500 balance that included $300 freight. Terms were 4/10, 3/30, n/60. True Value pays the invoice on April 29. What amount does True Value pay?   *LU 7-1(1, 2)*

7–41. Baker's Financial Planners purchased seven new computers for $850 each. It received a 15% discount because it purchased more than five and an additional 6% discount because it took immediate delivery. Terms of payment were 2/10, n/30. Baker's pays the bill within the cash discount period. How much should the check be? Round to the nearest cent.   *LU 7-1(4)*

7–42. On May 14, Talbots of Boston sold Forrest of Los Angeles $7,000 of fine clothes. Terms were 2/10 EOM FOB Boston. Talbots agreed to prepay the $80 freight. If Forrest pays the invoice on June 8, what will Forrest pay? If Forrest pays on June 20, what will Forrest pay? *LU 7-1(2), LU 7-2(1)*

7–43. Sam's Ski Boards.com offers 5/4/1 chain discounts to many of its customers. The Ski Hut ordered 20 ski boards with a total list price of $1,200. What is the net price of the ski boards? What was the trade discount amount? Round to the nearest cent. *LU 7-1(4)*

7–44. Majestic Manufacturing sold Jordans Furniture a living room set for an $8,500 list price with 35% trade discount. The $100 freight (FOB shipping point) was not part of the list price. Terms were 3/10, n/30 ROG. The invoice date was May 30. Jordans received the goods on July 18 and paid the invoice on July 20. What was the final price (include cost of freight) of the living room set? *LU 7-1(1, 2), LU 7-2(1)*

7–45. Boeing Truck Company received an invoice showing 8 tires at $110 each, 12 tires at $160 each, and 15 tires at $180 each. Shipping terms are FOB shipping point. Freight is $400; trade discount is 10/5; and a cash discount of 2/10, n/30 is offered. Assuming Boeing paid within the discount period, what did Boeing pay? *LU 7-1(4)*

7–46. Verizon offers to sell cellular phones listing for $99.99 with a chain discount of 15/10/5. Cellular Company offers to sell its cellular phones that list at $102.99 with a chain discount of 25/5. If Irene is to buy six phones, how much could she save if she buys from the lower-priced company? *LU 7-1(4)*

7–47. The 2012 iPhone 4S launch in China did not go as planned. Because of an overwhelming number of scalpers, Apple halted sales. After implementing a lottery system, Apple resumed selling the device online with shipments promised by March 2. If phones sell for U.S.$199 2/10, n/30 ROG, and 15 were purchased for resale on February 10 and received March 11, how much is owed if the invoice is paid on March 20? *LU 7-2(1)*

7–48. The original price of a 2012 Honda Insight to the dealer is $17,995, but the dealer will pay only $16,495. If the dealer pays Honda within 15 days, there is a 1% cash discount. **(a)** How much is the rebate? **(b)** What percent is the rebate? Round to nearest hundredth percent. **(c)** What is the amount of the cash discount if the dealer pays within 15 days? **(d)** What is the dealer's final price? **(e)** What is the dealer's total savings? Round answer to the nearest hundredth. *LU 7-1(1), LU 7-2(1)*

7–49. On March 30, Century Television received an invoice dated March 28 from ACME Manufacturing for 50 televisions at a cost of $125 each. Century received a 10/4/2 chain discount. Shipping terms were FOB shipping point. ACME prepaid the $70 freight. Terms were 2/10 EOM. When Century received the goods, 3 sets were defective. Century returned these sets to ACME. On April 8, Century sent a $150 partial payment. Century will pay the balance on May 6. What is Century's final payment on May 6? Assume no taxes. *LU 7-1(1, 2, 4), LU 7-2(1)*

 SUMMARY PRACTICE TEST (Round to the Nearest Cent as Needed) You**Tube**

Do you need help? The DVD has step-by-step worked-out solutions.

Complete the following: *(pp. 178–179)   LU 7-1(1)*

	Item	List price	Single trade discount	Net price
1.	Apple iPod	$350	5%	
2.	Palm Pilot		10%	$190

Calculate the net price and trade discount (use net price equivalent rate and single equivalent discount rate) for the following: *(pp. 182–184)   LU 7-1(4)*

	Item	List price	Chain discount	Net price	Trade discount
3.	Sony HD flat-screen TV	$899	5/4		

4. From the following, what is the last date for each discount period and credit period? *(pp. 178–179)   LU 7-1(1)*

	Date of invoice	Terms	End of discount period	End of credit period
a.	Nov. 4	2/10, n/30		
b.	Oct. 3, 2009	3/10, n/30 ROG (Goods received March 10, 2010)		
c.	May 2	2/10 EOM		
d.	Nov. 28	2/10 EOM		

5. Best Buy buys an iPod from a wholesaler with a $300 list price and a 5% trade discount. What is the trade discount amount? *eXcel* What is the net price of the iPod? *(pp. 178–179)   LU 7-1(1)*

6. Jordan's of Boston sold Lee Company of New York computer equipment with a $7,000 list price. Sale terms were 4/10, n/30 FOB Boston. Jordan's agreed to prepay the $400 freight. Lee pays the invoice within the discount period. What does Lee pay Jordan's? *(pp. 179–180; 185–192)   LU 7-1(2), LU 7-2(1)*

7. Julie Ring wants to buy a new line of Tonka trucks for her shop. Manufacturer A offers a 14/8 chain discount. Manufacturer B *eXcel* offers a 15/7 chain discount. Both manufacturers have the same list price. Which manufacturer should Julie buy from? *(pp. 182–184)   LU 7-1(4)*

8. Office.com received a $8,000 invoice dated April 10. Terms were 2/10, 1/15, n/60. On April 14, Office.com sent a $1,900 partial payment. What credit should Office.com receive? What is Office.com's outstanding balance? Round to the nearest cent. *(p. 192)   LU 7-2(2)*

9. Logan Company received from Furniture.com an invoice dated September 29. Terms were 1/10 EOM. List price on the invoice was $8,000 (freight not included). Logan receives a 8/7 chain discount. Freight charges are Logan's responsibility, but Furniture.com agreed to prepay the $300 freight. Logan pays the invoice on November 7. What does Logan Company pay Furniture.com? *(pp. 182–184)   LU 7-1(4)*

www.mhhe.com/
slater11e_vc

In 2002, Fuju Heavy Industries Ltd., parent company of Subaru of Indiana Automotive (SIA), challenged SIA with a goal no domestic manufacturing facility had achieved—zero landfill within 4 years. What seemed like a daunting goal was achieved in half the time by combining a comprehensive approach to identifying and eliminating waste with a powerful motivator.

Located in Lafayette, Indiana, SIA builds the Subaru Outback, Legacy, and Tribeca vehicle lines as well as the Toyota Camry in partnership with Toyota. SIA is currently the only Subaru auto assembly plant in the United States. Getting started on the zero landfill goal, SIA went about systematically identifying, weighing, and inventorying all waste in its 2.3 million-square-foot manufacturing facility, which performs integrated operations from stamping to final assembly.*

Once waste was identified, SIA made section managers responsible for the waste in their section and even went so far as to tie their bonus to waste elimination. Section managers along with their teams eagerly set out to find alternatives to the landfill.

For SIA, a key aspect of the solution included a rigorous approach to sorting waste and finding recyclers who were specifically interested in each type of waste and then only giving them that waste and nothing more. As an example, SIA sorts up to 17 different kinds of plastic. A second key component was SIA's partnership with Allegiant Global Services, which located recyclers, picked up waste line-side, and paid for all shipping charges.

For SIA's part, it invested in equipment that significantly reduced the volume and therefore cost of shipping waste. SIA compacts its cardboard, typically reducing 50–60 cubic yards of material to 2 cubic yards. Smaller bales weigh 350–400 lbs and large ones upwards of 1,000 lbs. SIA also has a bulb crusher on hand to crush fluorescent bulbs, separating the glass from the hazardous chemicals. This saves $2 per bulb to ship them to a recycler.

For its efforts, SIA was the first domestic auto plant to achieve Zero Landfill status in May 2004, the first to receive ISO 14001 certification, and the first to be officially designated a wildlife habitat. Clearly Subaru Indiana Automotive has found responsible environmental stewardship to be the right thing to do for the planet as well as for the bottom line.

Note: The following problems contain data that have been created by the author.

*Subaru of Indiana Automotive Inc. website: http://www.subaru-sia.com/Company/history/index.html.

PROBLEM 1

As the case states, Allegiant Global Services covers the cost of all shipping charges. If the terms included FOB for scraps Allegiant purchased from SIA, what would the terms specify? *Hint:* Research Allegiant's location to detail the terms fully.

PROBLEM 2

Suppose SIA sells each 350–400 lb bale of cardboard to Allegiant for $150. Further assume that SIA has 400 such bales to sell and offers a trade discount of 20% to Allegiant. What would the total trade discount be? What would the net price be? Round answers to the nearest dollar.

PROBLEM 3

If SIA offered a chain discount of 20/15/10 instead of the single discount, what would the net price equivalent rate be? Express your answer as a decimal and do not round.

PROBLEM 4

Suppose an invoice to Allegiant in the amount of $2,500 dated May 11 had the terms 2/10, 1/30, n/60. If the invoice were paid on June 1, how much would Allegiant owe SIA? Round your answer to the nearest dollar.

PROBLEM 5

If Allegiant were to pay $25,000 for recycled steel and SIA offered a 15% trade discount, what would the list price be? Round your answer to the nearest cent.

PROBLEM 6

Imagine an invoice to Allegiant in the amount of $15,250, dated September 8, that had the terms 2/10 EOM. If the invoice were paid on October 11, how much would Allegiant owe SIA? Round your answer to the nearest dollar.

Suppose Allegiant had an invoice from SIA in the amount of $42,000, dated November 16. If the invoice had the terms 2/10, n/30 and Allegiant made a partial payment in the amount of $14,000 on November 23, what would the outstanding balance due be for the invoice? Round your answer to the nearest cent.

Class Discussion The case does not indicate whether Subaru Indiana Automotive has generated a net savings from its recycling efforts. Discuss the economics of the recycling program as you would anticipate them to be and determine whether you feel such a commitment would be warranted even if it cost SIA money to sustain the program.

SURF TO SAVE

Are you taking advantage of discounts? 🔍

PROBLEM 1
Free shipping!

Visit www.staples.com and search for DVD+RW media. Select enough of the DVD+RWs to equal an amount over $45 in order to qualify for free shipping. How much did you save on shipping? What is your discount percent when you receive free shipping on your order?

Discussion Questions

1. Why do online merchants require a certain minimum dollar purchase before giving free shipping?

2. What other incentives could the online merchant use to achieve the same goal?

PROBLEM 2
Pay early, or not?

Go to http://www.fms.treas.gov/prompt/discount.html. If there are 30 days left in the discount period and 60 days left in the payment period, find out what the discount must be for it not to be worthwhile to pay early.

Discussion Questions

1. Would there ever be a situation in which it would still not be advantageous to pay early, even if a discount were available?

2. Why do companies offer a discount for paying early?

PROBLEM 3
Buying software at deep discounts

Go to http://www.academicsuperstore.com. Choose one product listed on the Students tab. What discount off the suggested retail price is the manufacturer offering through Academic Superstore?

Discussion Questions

1. Why do retailers show inflated suggested retail prices?

2. How can consumers be sure they are getting a good deal?

PROBLEM 4
Money in bloom!

Go to http://ww11.1800flowers.com. Click on Deal of the Week. Select any of the flower deals and calculate the discount percentage.

Discussion Questions

1. Why would 1-800-Flowers run promotions such as the Deal of the Week?

2. If there is a deal every week that allows you to save money on flowers, would you ever purchase from its standard flower arrangements? Why?

MOBILE APPS ✕

Calculate Discounts & Sales Tax (Blue Sodium Corp) Helps calculate discounts in percentages or as dollar values.

Discount Calculator (ChuChu Train Productions) Calculates the prices of items after applying discounts to determine item cost and amount saved.

INTERNET PROJECTS ✕

See text website
www.mhhe.com/slater11e_sse_ch07

The App of Haggling

IN THE ARENA OF HAGGLING, knowledge is power. And the right application can put that power at your fingertips. Specifically, free price-matching apps are available for the Apple iPhone and dozens of mobile phones that run Google's Android software.

How do they work? Rather than combing through ads, you check the phone to see which nearby store has the best offer. If you're already at a store and find a better price elsewhere, simply ask the retailer if it will match or beat the competitor's price.

To try phone haggling, I used a T-Mobile G2 ($200 with a two-year contract) and two free apps available in Google's Android Market, an online store with more than 100,000 software programs accessible via the G2's main screen. Because of their power, simplicity and ease of use, my favorite shopping tools are Google Shopper and ShopSavvy, although there are many more.

All price-matching apps work pretty much the same way. The easiest is to use your phone's camera as a bar-code scanner. For instance, using Google Shopper, select "Image Search" on the app's home screen, and then aim the camera at the bar code. Once it recognizes the code, the app beeps. Within seconds, Google Shopper displays all local and online stores that sell the product, the price they're asking, the stores' addresses, and their distance in miles from your current location.

But what if you can't find the bar code? Try a voice-recognition search—say, for example, "Samsung 50-inch 3D plasma HDTV"—or go old school and type in the product's name. A voice search may seem inherently unreliable, but it worked well in my tests of Google Shopper in Best Buy's noisy electronics department. ShopSavvy has a bar-code scanner and text search, but no voice option.

Putting the apps to the test. At Best Buy I spotted a 32-inch Sony LCD TV for $400. Google Shopper found the same model at a Sears 27 miles away for $356. Too far. But at Staples, ShopSavvy discovered that a $210 APC Backup Battery, handy for surge protection and power outages, was $150 at Office Depot and $180 at Best Buy. And both stores were less than a mile away.

Cha-ching. The app showed me that a short drive would save me 60 bucks. But would I have to make the schlep? I asked clerks at both stores whether they'd match the price I'd found with my phone. In both instances, they said they'd need to see a print ad to give me the better deal. (So last century.)

Undaunted, I went to another Best Buy and scanned a Panasonic cordless phone kit with four handsets. Best Buy wanted $100, but a Wal-Mart nine miles away had it for $89. Would Best Buy match Wal-Mart's price? Yes. All I had to do was bring the Panasonic box to customer service, which would call Wal-Mart to verify the lower price.

Next I ventured into Fry's Elec-

TECH WRITER JEFF BERTOLUCCI WORKED APP MAGIC AT STORES NEAR HIS HOME IN THE LOS ANGELES AREA.

tronics, a big-box retailer with stores in nine states, where Shop-Savvy informed me that a $499 Toshiba 32-inch LCD TV was $30 cheaper at a Best Buy a half-mile away. Fry's agreed to match the lower price after making the requisite confirmation call. I couldn't, however, get them to *beat* the competitor's price.

I called retailers to see whether they had a policy on shopping apps, and Best Buy said it does honor prices from them. Given my experiences, it's safe to say some clerks aren't aware of their store's policy, and it's incumbent on shoppers to seek out store managers and push the issue.

Sometimes, shopping apps show that the price you see is the best in town. A Best Buy in my area, for instance, had a Currie Ezip

400 electric scooter on sale for $200; the next best price Google Shopper could find was $300. And Costco's $100 price for the iHome IP45BZ rechargeable stereo speaker (with FM radio and alarm, iPod and iPhone dock) was $3 less than I found elsewhere. No buyer's remorse here.

If you suspect a certain item will go on sale soon—after the holidays, say—use ShopSavvy to create a price alert. Simply enter your target price and e-mail address, and the app will notify you when the price hits your target. Both ShopSavvy and Google Shopper keep a history of the products you've researched—a handy feature for checking prices over time without having to reenter the same information again and again. **JEFF BERTOLUCCI**

BUSINESS MATH ISSUE

Retailers should not allow customers to use the haggling app in their store.

1. List the key points of the article and information to support your position.
2. Write a group defense of your position using math calculations to support your view.

Payroll

McDonald's Says It

Plan With Limits

McDonald's offers hourly workers a set of health-insurance plans that have low weekly premiums and low annual benefit caps. Details of the plans for individual policies for crew members:

	Premiums	Maximum annual benefit
BASIC PLAN	$13.99 (weekly) $727.48 (yearly)	$2,000
MEDIUM BENEFITS	$24.30 $1,263.60	$5,000 (outpatient; $1,500)
HIGHER BENEFITS	$32.30 $1,679.60	$10,000 (outpatient; $2,000)

What all of the plans pay for, up to annual maximum:
- 100% of visit to primary-care or specialist doctor, after $20 co-pay
- 100% of prescription drug costs, after $5 co-pay for generic and $50 co-pay for brand
- 70% of inpatient hospital services

Source: McDonald's benefit handout

"That's $117 for parts, $75 labor and $321 for employee healthcare."

From *The Wall Street Journal*, copyright © 2010, permission of Cartoon Features Syndicate.

© Alex Segre/Alamy

LU 9–1: Calculating Various Types of Employees' Gross Pay

1. Define, compare, and contrast weekly, biweekly, semimonthly, and monthly pay periods *(p. 244)*.

2. Calculate gross pay with overtime on the basis of time *(pp. 244–245)*.

3. Calculate gross pay for piecework, differential pay schedule, straight commission with draw, variable commission scale, and salary plus commission *(pp. 245–247)*.

LU 9–2: Computing Payroll Deductions for Employees' Pay; Employers' Responsibilities

1. Prepare and explain the parts of a payroll register *(pp. 248–251)*.

2. Explain and calculate federal and state unemployment taxes *(pp. 251–252)*.

VOCABULARY PREVIEW

Here are key terms in this chapter. After completing the chapter, if you know the term, place a checkmark in the parentheses. If you don't know the term, look it up and put the page number where it can be found.

Biweekly ( ) Deductions ( ) Differential pay schedule ( ) Draw ( ) Employee's Withholding Allowance Certificate (W-4) ( ) Fair Labor Standards Act ( ) Federal income tax withholding (FIT) ( ) Federal Insurance Contribution Act (FICA) ( ) Federal Unemployment Tax Act (FUTA) ( ) Gross pay ( ) Medicare ( ) Monthly ( ) Net pay ( ) Overrides ( ) Overtime ( ) Payroll register ( ) Percentage method ( ) Semimonthly ( ) Social Security ( ) State income tax (SIT) ( ) State Unemployment Tax Act (SUTA) ( ) Straight commission ( ) Variable commission scale ( ) W-4 ( ) Weekly ( )

Which company would you like to work for? The *Wall Street Journal* clip "Google Is No. 1 on List of Desired Employers" shows the results of a survey of young professionals. Note that the top write-in was Facebook.

This chapter discusses (1) the type of pay people work for, (2) how employers calculate paychecks and deductions, and (3) what employers must report and pay in taxes.

Google Is No. 1 on List Of Desired Employers

BY JOE LIGHT

One in four young professionals wants to work at **Google** Inc., according to a survey by Universum, a consulting firm that helps companies improve their attractiveness to prospective employees.

Nearly 25% of survey respondents picked Google, almost twice as many as chose **Apple** Inc., which ranked second. **Walt Disney** Co., the U.S. State Department and **Amazon.com** Inc. rounded out the top five.

To conduct the survey, Universum asked 10,306 young professionals—defined as college graduates with one to eight years of work experience—to pick as many as five ideal employers out of a list of 150.

Respondents also could write in companies not on the list. The top write-in was **Facebook** Inc., followed by the Department of Homeland Security and the United Nations.

Young professionals generally want to work at companies that the professionals like as consumers, said Kasia Do, a project manager for Universum. Such people also appear to be drawn to companies that seem financially strong and can offer job stability, Ms. Do said.

Google, in particular, has tailored the image it projects to potential employees, said John Sullivan, a management professor at San Francisco State University.

The company regularly hosts open houses and tech-related talks in areas where it wants to recruit, said Yolanda Mangolini, director of outreach programs for Google. "It's incredibly powerful and helps them imagine themselves at Google," she said. The company also runs blogs, Twitter feeds and YouTube channels that try to show what it's like to work there, she said.

Government agencies, such as the National Aeronautics and Space Administration, the Federal Bureau of Investigation and the Central Intelligence Agency, also ranked in the top 10. That might be in part because the federal government hasn't laid off as many employees as the private sector has, Ms. Do said.

Plus, "Those government agencies can articulate a reason for being that gives employees a sense of purpose," said Jon Picoult of brand consultant Watermark Consulting. "For young people looking to make a difference in the world, they have a good story to tell."

Highly Recommended

Percentage of respondents who named the company as an ideal employer

Google	
Apple	
Walt Disney	
U.S. Department of State	
Amazon	
FBI	
Microsoft	
CIA	
NASA	
Teach for America	

0   5   10   15   20   25%

Source: Universum; Note: study of 10,306 professionals with 1 to 8 years of work experience between November 2010 and January 2011; List only includes top 10 companies

Learning Unit 9–1: Calculating Various Types of Employees' Gross Pay

Logan Company manufactures dolls of all shapes and sizes. These dolls are sold worldwide. We study Logan Company in this unit because of the variety of methods Logan uses to pay its employees.

Companies usually pay employees **weekly, biweekly, semimonthly,** or **monthly.** How often employers pay employees can affect how employees manage their money. Some employees prefer a weekly paycheck that spreads the inflow of money. Employees who have monthly bills may find the twice-a-month or monthly paycheck more convenient. All employees would like more money to manage.

Let's assume you earn $50,000 per year. The following table shows what you would earn each pay period. Remember that 13 weeks equals one quarter. Four quarters or 52 weeks equals a year.

Salary paid	Period (based on a year)	Earnings for period (dollars)
Weekly	52 times (once a week)	$ 961.54 ($50,000 ÷ 52)
Biweekly	26 times (every two weeks)	$1,923.08 ($50,000 ÷ 26)
Semimonthly	24 times (twice a month)	$2,083.33 ($50,000 ÷ 24)
Monthly	12 times (once a month)	$4,166.67 ($50,000 ÷ 12)

Now let's look at some pay schedule situations and examples of how Logan Company calculates its payroll for employees of different pay status.

Situation 1: Hourly Rate of Pay; Calculation of Overtime

The **Fair Labor Standards Act** sets minimum wage standards and overtime regulations for employees of companies covered by this federal law. The law provides that employees working for an hourly rate receive time-and-a-half pay for hours worked in excess of their regular 40-hour week. Many managerial people, however, are exempt from the time-and-a-half pay for all hours in excess of a 40-hour week. Other workers may also be exempt.

The current federal hourly minimum wage is $7.25. Various states have passed their own minimum wages. For example, in Illinois it is $8.25; Massachusetts, $8.00; Nevada, $8.25; Ohio, $7.70; Oregon, $8.80; and Washington, $9.04. Note in the *Wall Street Journal* clipping "Stacking Up" how the average hourly wage even varies by different occupations in New York City.

"Don't think of it as overtime. Think of it as an encore."

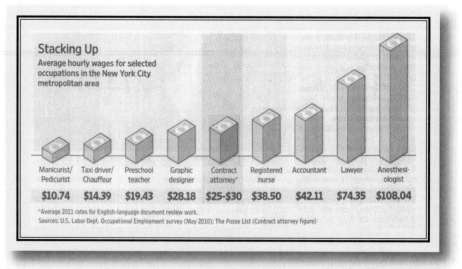

Stacking Up
Average hourly wages for selected occupations in the New York City metropolitan area

Manicurist/ Pedicurist	Taxi driver/ Chauffeur	Preschool teacher	Graphic designer	Contract attorney*	Registered nurse	Accountant	Lawyer	Anesthesiologist
$10.74	$14.39	$19.43	$28.18	$25-$30	$38.50	$42.11	$74.35	$108.04

*Average 2011 rates for English-language document review work.
Sources: U.S. Labor Dept. Occupational Employment survey (May 2010); The Posse List (Contract attorney figure)

Now we return to our Logan Company example. Logan Company is calculating the weekly pay of Ramon Valdez who works in its manufacturing division. For the first 40 hours Ramon works, Logan calculates his **gross pay** (earnings before **deductions**) as follows:

> Gross pay = Hours employee worked × Rate per hour

Ramon works more than 40 hours in a week. For every hour over his 40 hours, Ramon must be paid an **overtime** pay of at least 1.5 times his regular pay rate. The following formula is used to determine Ramon's overtime:

> Hourly overtime pay rate = Regular hourly pay rate × 1.5

Logan Company must include Ramon's overtime pay with his regular pay. To determine Ramon's gross pay, Logan uses the following formula:

> Gross pay = Earnings for 40 hours + Earnings at time-and-a-half rate (1.5)

We are now ready to calculate Ramon's gross pay from the following data:

EXAMPLE

Employee	M	T	W	Th	F	S	Total hours	Rate per hour
Ramon Valdez	13	$8\frac{1}{2}$	10	8	$11\frac{1}{4}$	$10\frac{3}{4}$	$61\frac{1}{2}$	$9

$$\begin{array}{r} 61\frac{1}{2} \text{ total hours} \\ -40 \text{ regular hours} \\ \hline 21\frac{1}{2} \text{ hours overtime}^1 \end{array}$$ Time-and-a-half pay: $9 × 1.5 = $13.50

Gross pay = (40 hours × $9) + ($21\frac{1}{2}$ hours × $13.50)

$\qquad$ = $\qquad$ $360 $\qquad$ + $\qquad$ $290.25

$\qquad$ = $650.25

Note that the $13.50 overtime rate came out even. However, throughout the text, *if an overtime rate is greater than two decimal places, do not round it. Round only the final answer. This gives greater accuracy.*

LO 3

Situation 2: Straight Piece Rate Pay

Some companies, especially manufacturers, pay workers according to how much they produce. Logan Company pays Ryan Foss for the number of dolls he produces in a week. This gives Ryan an incentive to make more money by producing more dolls. Ryan receives $.96 per doll, less any defective units. The following formula determines Ryan's gross pay:

> Gross pay = Number of units produced × Rate per unit

Companies may also pay a guaranteed hourly wage and use a piece rate as a bonus. However, Logan uses straight piece rate as wages for some of its employees.

EXAMPLE   During the last week of April, Ryan Foss produced 900 dolls. Using the above formula, Logan Company paid Ryan $864.

Gross pay = 900 dolls × $.96

$\qquad$ = $864

---

[1]Some companies pay overtime for time over 8 hours in one day; Logan Company pays overtime for time over 40 hours per week.

Situation 3: Differential Pay Schedule

Some of Logan's employees can earn more than the $.96 straight piece rate for every doll they produce. Logan Company has set up a **differential pay schedule** for these employees. The company determines the rate these employees make by the amount of units the employees produce at different levels of production.

EXAMPLE   Logan Company pays Abby Rogers on the basis of the following schedule:

	Units produced	Amount per unit
First 50 →	1–50	$ .50
Next 100 →	51–150	.62
Next 50 →	151–200	.75
	Over 200	1.25

Last week Abby produced 300 dolls. What is Abby's gross pay?
Logan calculated Abby's gross pay as follows:

$$(50 \times \$.50) + (100 \times \$.62) + (50 \times \$.75) + (100 \times \$1.25)$$

$$\$25 \quad + \quad \$62 \quad + \quad \$37.50 \quad + \quad \$125 \quad = \boxed{\$249.50}$$

Now we will study some of the other types of employee commission payment plans.

Situation 4: Straight Commission with Draw

Companies frequently use **straight commission** to determine the pay of salespersons. This commission is usually a certain percentage of the amount the salesperson sells. An example of one group of companies ceasing to pay commissions is the rental-car companies.

Companies such as Logan Company allow some of its salespersons to draw against their commission at the beginning of each month. A **draw** is an advance on the salesperson's commission. Logan subtracts this advance later from the employee's commission earned based on sales. When the commission does not equal the draw, the salesperson owes Logan the difference between the draw and the commission.

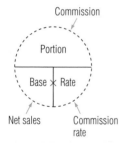

Commission
Portion
Base × Rate
Net sales   Commission rate

EXAMPLE   Logan Company pays Jackie Okamoto a straight commission of 15% on her net sales (net sales are total sales less sales returns). In May, Jackie had net sales of $56,000. Logan gave Jackie a $600 draw in May. What is Jackie's gross pay?
Logan calculated Jackie's commission minus her draw as follows:

$$\$56,000 \times .15 = \$8,400$$
$$- \ 600$$
$$\boxed{\$7,800}$$

Logan Company pays some people in the sales department on a variable commission scale. Let's look at this, assuming the employee had no draw.

Situation 5: Variable Commission Scale

A company with a **variable commission scale** uses different commission rates for different levels of net sales.

EXAMPLE   Last month, Jane Ring's net sales were $160,000. What is Jane's gross pay based on the following schedule?

Up to $35,000	4%
Excess of $35,000 to $45,000	6%
Over $45,000	8%

$$\text{Gross pay} = (\$35,000 \times .04) + (\$10,000 \times .06) + (\$115,000 \times .08)$$

$$= \quad \$1,400 \quad + \quad \$600 \quad + \quad \$9,200$$

$$= \boxed{\$11,200}$$

MONEY tips

Understand the costs of credit. Do not spend money you do not currently have–especially if it is for entertainment. Avoid reaching or coming close to the maximum on your credit cards. Be careful to fully understand the terms of any credit card you use.

Situation 6: Salary Plus Commission

Logan Company pays Joe Roy a $3,000 monthly salary plus a 4% commission for sales over $20,000. Last month Joe's net sales were $50,000. Logan calculated Joe's gross monthly pay as follows:

Gross pay = Salary + (Commission × Sales over $20,000)

= $3,000 + (.04 × $30,000)

= $3,000 + $1,200

= $4,200

Before you take the Practice Quiz, you should know that many managers today receive **overrides.** These managers receive a commission based on the net sales of the people they supervise.

LU 9–1 PRACTICE QUIZ

Complete this **Practice Quiz** to see how you are doing.

1. Jill Foster worked 52 hours in one week for Delta Airlines. Jill earns $10 per hour. What is Jill's gross pay, assuming overtime is at time-and-a-half?

2. Matt Long had $180,000 in sales for the month. Matt's commission rate is 9%, and he had a $3,500 draw. What was Matt's end-of-month commission?

3. Bob Meyers receives a $1,000 monthly salary. He also receives a variable commission on net sales based on the following schedule (commission doesn't begin until Bob earns $8,000 in net sales):

$8,000–$12,000	1%	Excess of $20,000 to $40,000	5%
Excess of $12,000 to $20,000	3%	More than $40,000	8%

Assume Bob earns $40,000 net sales for the month. What is his gross pay?

For **extra help** from your authors–Sharon and Jeff–see the student DVD

✓ **Solutions**

1. 40 hours × $10.00 = $400.00
   12 hours × $15.00 = 180.00 ($10.00 × 1.5 = $15.00)
   $580.00

2. $180,000 × .09 = $16,200
   − 3,500
   $12,700

3. Gross pay = $1,000 + ($4,000 × .01) + ($8,000 × .03) + ($20,000 × .05)
   = $1,000 + $40 + $240 + $1,000
   = $2,280

LU 9–1a EXTRA PRACTICE QUIZ WITH WORKED-OUT SOLUTIONS

Need more practice? Try this **Extra Practice Quiz** (check figures in the Interactive Chapter Organizer, p. 254). Worked-out Solutions can be found in Appendix B at end of text.

1. Jill Foster worked 54 hours in one week for Delta Airlines. Jill earns $12 per hour. What is Jill's gross pay, assuming overtime is at time-and-a-half?

2. Matt Long had $210,000 in sales for the month. Matt's commission rate is 8%, and he had a $4,000 draw. What was Matt's end-of-month commission?

3. Bob Myers receives a $1,200 monthly salary. He also receives a variable commission on net sales based on the following schedule (commission doesn't begin until Bob earns $9,000 in net sales).

$9,000 to $12,000	1%	Excess of $20,000 to $40,000	5%
Excess of $12,000 to $20,000	3%	More than $40,000	8%

Assume Bob earns $60,000 net sales for the month. What is his gross pay?

Learning Unit 9–2: Computing Payroll Deductions for Employees' Pay; Employers' Responsibilities

The following *Wall Street Journal* clip, "Pay Check," shows the average income of the most and least stressful jobs.

This unit begins by dissecting a paycheck. Then we give you an insight into the tax responsibilities of employers.

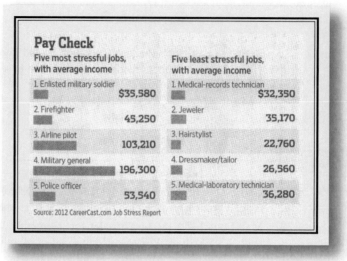

Reprinted with permission of *The Wall Street Journal*, Copyright © 2012 Dow Jones & Company, Inc. All Rights Reserved Worldwide.

LO 1

Computing Payroll Deductions for Employees

Companies often record employee payroll information in a multicolumn form called a **payroll register.** The increased use of computers in business has made computerized registers a time-saver for many companies.

Glo Company uses a multicolumn payroll register. Below is Glo's partial payroll register showing the payroll information for Alice Rey during week 49. Let's check each column to see if Alice's take-home pay of $1,517.81 is correct. Note how the circled letters in the register correspond to the explanations that follow.

GLO COMPANY Payroll Register Week #49															
Employee name	Allow. & marital status	Cum. earn.	Sal. per week	Earnings			Cum. earn.	FICA Taxable Earnings		FICA		Deductions			
				Reg.	Ovt.	Gross		S.S.	Med.	S.S.	Med.	FIT	SIT	Health ins.	Net pay
Rey, Alice	M-2	108,000	2,250	2,250	—	2,250	110,250	2,100	2,250	130.20	32.63	334.36	135	100	1,517.81
	(A)	(B)	(C)		(D)		(E)	(F)	(G)	(H)	(I)	(J)	(K)	(L)	(M)

Payroll Register Explanations

(A)—Allowance and marital status

(B), (C), (D)—Cumulative earnings before payroll, salaries, earnings

(E)—Cumulative earnings after payroll

When Alice was hired, she completed the **W-4 (Employee's Withholding Allowance Certificate)** form shown in Figure 9.1 stating that she is married and claims an allowance (exemption) of 2. Glo Company will need this information to calculate the federal income tax (J).

Before this pay period, Alice has earned $108,000 (48 weeks × $2,250 salary per week). Since Alice receives no overtime, her $2,250 salary per week represents her gross pay (pay before any deductions).

After this pay period, Alice has earned $110,250 ($108,000 + $2,250).

FIGURE 9.1

Employee's W-4 form

Form **W-4**	**Employee's Withholding Allowance Certificate**	OMB No. 1545-0074
Department of the Treasury Internal Revenue Service	▶ Whether you are entitled to claim a certain number of allowances or exemption from withholding is subject to review by the IRS. Your employer may be required to send a copy of this form to the IRS.	**20XX**

1	Your first name and middle initial	Last name		2	Your social security number
	Alice	Rey			021 36 9494

Home address (number and street or rural route)	3 ☐ Single ☒ Married ☐ Married, but withhold at higher Single rate.
2 Roundy Road	**Note.** If married, but legally separated, or spouse is a nonresident alien, check the "Single" box.

City or town, state, and ZIP code	4 If your last name differs from that shown on your social security card,
Marblehead, MA 01945	check here. You must call 1-800-772-1213 for a replacement card. ▶ ☐

5	Total number of allowances you are claiming (from line **H** above **or** from the applicable worksheet on page 2)	5	2
6	Additional amount, if any, you want withheld from each paycheck	6	$
7	I claim exemption from withholding for 2012, and I certify that I meet **both** of the following conditions for exemption.		

• Last year I had a right to a refund of **all** federal income tax withheld because I had **no** tax liability, **and**
• This year I expect a refund of **all** federal income tax withheld because I expect to have **no** tax liability.
If you meet both conditions, write "Exempt" here . . . . ▶ | 7 |

Under penalties of perjury, I declare that I have examined this certificate and, to the best of my knowledge and belief, it is true, correct, and complete.

Employee's signature (This form is not valid unless you sign it.) ▶	*Alice Rey*	Date ▶ 1/1/20XX
8 Employer's name and address (Employer: Complete lines 8 and 10 only if sending to the IRS.)	9 Office code (optional)	10 Employer identification number (EIN)

Cat. No. 10220Q

The **Federal Insurance Contribution Act (FICA)** funds the **Social Security** program. The program includes Old Age and Disability, Medicare, Survivor Benefits, and so on. The FICA tax requires separate reporting for Social Security and **Medicare.** We will use the following rates for Glo Company:

	Rate	Base
Social Security	6.20%	$110,100
Medicare	1.45	No base

These rates mean that Alice Rey will pay Social Security taxes on the first $110,100 she earns this year. After earning $110,100, Alice's wages will be exempt from Social Security. Note that Alice will be paying Medicare taxes on all wages since Medicare has no base cutoff.

F, G—Taxable earnings for Social Security and Medicare

To help keep Glo's record straight, the *taxable earnings column only shows what wages will be taxed. This amount is not the tax.* For example, in week 49, only $2,100 of Alice's salary will be taxable for Social Security.

$110,100 Social Security base
− 108,000 Ⓑ
$ 2,100

H—Social Security

To calculate Alice's Social Security tax, we multiply $2,100 Ⓕ by 6.2%:

$2,100 × .062 = $130.20

I—Medicare

Since Medicare has no base, Alice's entire weekly salary is taxed 1.45%, which is multiplied by $2,250.

$2,250 × .0145 = $32.63

J—FIT

Using the W-4 form Alice completed, Glo deducts **federal income tax withholding (FIT).** The more allowances an employee claims, the less money Glo deducts from the employee's paycheck. Glo uses the percentage method to calculate FIT.[2]

The Percentage Method[3]   Today, since many companies do not want to store the tax tables, they use computers for their payroll. These companies use the **percentage method.** For this method we use Table 9.1 and Table 9.2 on page 250 from Circular E to calculate Alice's FIT.

Step 1. In Table 9.1, locate the weekly withholding for one allowance. Multiply this number by 2.

$73.08 × 2 = $146.16

---

[2]The *Business Math Handbook* has a sample of the wage bracket method.

[3]An alternative method is the wage bracket method shown in the *Business Math Handbook*.

TABLE 9.1

Percentage method income tax withholding allowances

Payroll Period	One Withholding Allowance
Weekly	$ 73.08
Biweekly	146.15
Semimonthly	158.33
Monthly	316.67
Quarterly	950.00
Semiannually	1,900.00
Annually	3,800.00
Daily or miscellaneous (each day of the payroll period)	14.62

TABLE 9.2   Percentage method income tax withholding schedules

TABLE 1—WEEKLY Payroll Period

(a) SINGLE person (including head of household)—

If the amount of wages (after subtracting withholding allowances) is: The amount of income tax to withhold is:

Not over $41 . . . . $0

Over—	But not over—		of excess over—
$41	—$209	. . . . $0.00 plus 10%	—$41
$209	—$721	. . . . $16.80 plus 15%	—$209
$721	—$1,688	. . . . $93.60 plus 25%	—$721
$1,688	—$3,477	. . . . $335.35 plus 28%	—$1,688
$3,477	—$7,510	. . . . $836.27 plus 33%	—$3,477
$7,510	. . . .	$2,167.16 plus 35%	—$7,510

(b) MARRIED person—

If the amount of wages (after subtracting withholding allowances) is: The amount of income tax to withhold is:

Not over $156 . . . . $0

Over—	But not over—		of excess over—
$156	—$490	. . . . $0.00 plus 10%	—$156
$490	—$1,515	. . . . $33.40 plus 15%	—$490
$1,515	—$2,900	. . . . $187.15 plus 25%	—$1,515
$2,900	—$4,338	. . . . $533.40 plus 28%	—$2,900
$4,338	—$7,624	. . . . $936.04 plus 33%	—$4,338
$7,624	. . . .	$2,020.42 plus 35%	—$7,624

TABLE 2—BIWEEKLY Payroll Period

(a) SINGLE person (including head of household)—

If the amount of wages (after subtracting withholding allowances) is: The amount of income tax to withhold is:

Not over $83 . . . . $0

Over—	But not over—		of excess over—
$83	—$417	. . . . $0.00 plus 10%	—$83
$417	—$1,442	. . . . $33.40 plus 15%	—$417
$1,442	—$3,377	. . . . $187.15 plus 25%	—$1,442
$3,377	—$6,954	. . . . $670.90 plus 28%	—$3,377
$6,954	—$15,019	. . . . $1,672.46 plus 33%	—$6,954
$15,019	. . . .	$4,333.91 plus 35%	—$15,019

(b) MARRIED person—

If the amount of wages (after subtracting withholding allowances) is: The amount of income tax to withhold is:

Not over $312 . . . . $0

Over—	But not over—		of excess over—
$312	—$981	. . . . $0.00 plus 10%	—$312
$981	—$3,031	. . . . $66.90 plus 15%	—$981
$3,031	—$5,800	. . . . $374.40 plus 25%	—$3,031
$5,800	—$8,675	. . . . $1,066.65 plus 28%	—$5,800
$8,675	—$15,248	. . . . $1,871.65 plus 33%	—$8,675
$15,248	. . . .	$4,040.74 plus 35%	—$15,248

TABLE 3—SEMIMONTHLY Payroll Period

(a) SINGLE person (including head of household)—

If the amount of wages (after subtracting withholding allowances) is: The amount of income tax to withhold is:

Not over $90 . . . . $0

Over—	But not over—		of excess over—
$90	—$452	. . . . $0.00 plus 10%	—$90
$452	—$1,563	. . . . $36.20 plus 15%	—$452
$1,563	—$3,658	. . . . $202.85 plus 25%	—$1,563
$3,658	—$7,533	. . . . $726.60 plus 28%	—$3,658
$7,533	—$16,271	. . . . $1,811.60 plus 33%	—$7,533
$16,271	. . . .	$4,695.14 plus 35%	—$16,271

(b) MARRIED person—

If the amount of wages (after subtracting withholding allowances) is: The amount of income tax to withhold is:

Not over $338 . . . . $0

Over—	But not over—		of excess over—
$338	—$1,063	. . . . $0.00 plus 10%	—$338
$1,063	—$3,283	. . . . $72.50 plus 15%	—$1,063
$3,283	—$6,283	. . . . $405.50 plus 25%	—$3,283
$6,283	—$9,398	. . . . $1,155.50 plus 28%	—$6,283
$9,398	—$16,519	. . . . $2,027.70 plus 33%	—$9,398
$16,519	. . . .	$4,377.63 plus 35%	—$16,519

TABLE 4—MONTHLY Payroll Period

(a) SINGLE person (including head of household)—

If the amount of wages (after subtracting withholding allowances) is: The amount of income tax to withhold is:

Not over $179 . . . . $0

Over—	But not over—		of excess over—
$179	—$904	. . . . $0.00 plus 10%	—$179
$904	—$3,125	. . . . $72.50 plus 15%	—$904
$3,125	—$7,317	. . . . $405.65 plus 25%	—$3,125
$7,317	—$15,067	. . . . $1,453.65 plus 28%	—$7,317
$15,067	—$32,542	. . . . $3,623.65 plus 33%	—$15,067
$32,542	. . . .	$9,390.40 plus 35%	—$32,542

(b) MARRIED person—

If the amount of wages (after subtracting withholding allowances) is: The amount of income tax to withhold is:

Not over $675 . . . . $0

Over—	But not over—		of excess over—
$675	—$2,125	. . . . $0.00 plus 10%	—$675
$2,125	—$6,567	. . . . $145.00 plus 15%	—$2,125
$6,567	—$12,567	. . . . $811.30 plus 25%	—$6,567
$12,567	—$18,796	. . . . $2,311.30 plus 28%	—$12,567
$18,796	—$33,038	. . . . $4,055.42 plus 33%	—$18,796
$33,038	. . . .	$8,755.28 plus 35%	—$33,038

Step 2. Subtract $146.16 in Step 1 from Alice's total pay.

$$\begin{array}{r} \$2{,}250.00 \\ -\ 146.16 \\ \hline \$2{,}103.84 \end{array}$$

Step 3. In Table 9.2, locate the married person's weekly pay table. The $2,103.84 falls between $1,515 and $2,900. The tax is $187.15 plus 25% of the excess over $1,515.

$$\begin{array}{r} \$2{,}103.84 \\ -\ 1{,}515.00 \\ \hline \$\ \ \ 588.84 \end{array}$$

Tax $187.15 + .25 ($588.84)

$187.15 + $147.21 = $334.36

K—SIT

We assume a 6% **state income tax (SIT).**

$2,250 × .06 = $135.00

L—Health insurance
M—Net pay

Alice contributes $100 per week for health insurance.
Alice's **net pay** is her gross pay less all deductions.

$$\begin{array}{r} \$2{,}250.00 \ \ \text{gross} \\ -\ \ \ \ \ 130.20 \ \ \text{Social Security} \\ -\ \ \ \ \ \ \ 32.63 \ \ \text{Medicare} \\ -\ \ \ \ \ 334.36 \ \ \text{FIT} \\ -\ \ \ \ \ 135.00 \ \ \text{SIT} \\ -\ \ \ \ \ 100.00 \ \ \text{health insurance} \\ \hline =\ \$1{,}517.81 \ \ \text{net pay} \end{array}$$

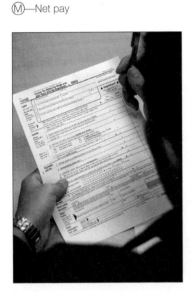

© Corbis/RF

MONEY tips

The IRS has twelve items it looks for on a return that raise the chances of an audit from the average rate of 1.1%: making too much money; failing to report all taxable income; taking large charitable deductions; claiming the home office deduction; claiming rental losses; deducting business meals, travel, and entertainment; claiming 100% business use of a vehicle; writing off a loss for a hobby; running a cash business; failing to report a foreign bank account; engaging in currency transactions; and taking higher-than-average deductions.

Employers' Responsibilities

The chapter opener shows the benefits plan McDonald's is offering its hourly workers. In the first section of this unit, we saw that Alice contributed to Social Security and Medicare. Glo Company has the legal responsibility to match her contributions. Besides matching Social Security and Medicare, Glo must pay two important taxes that employees do not have to pay—federal and state unemployment taxes.

Federal Unemployment Tax Act (FUTA)   The federal government participates in a joint federal-state unemployment program to help unemployed workers. At this writing, employers pay the government a 6.2% **FUTA** tax on the first $7,000 paid to employees as wages during the calendar year. Any wages in excess of $7,000 per worker are exempt wages and are not taxed for FUTA. If the total cumulative amount the employer owes the government is less than $100, the employer can pay the liability yearly (end of January in the following calendar year). If the tax is greater than $100, the employer must pay it within a month after the quarter ends.

Companies involved in a state unemployment tax fund can usually take a 5.4% credit against their FUTA tax. *In reality, then, companies are paying .8% (.008) to the federal unemployment program.* In all our calculations, FUTA is .008.

EXAMPLE   Assume a company had total wages of $19,000 in a calendar year. No employee earned more than $7,000 during the calendar year. The FUTA tax is .8% (6.2% minus the company's 5.4% credit for state unemployment tax). How much does the company pay in FUTA tax?

The company calculates its FUTA tax as follows:

$$\begin{array}{r} 6.2\% \ \ \text{FUTA tax} \\ -\ 5.4\% \ \ \text{credit for SUTA tax} \\ \hline =\ \ .8\% \ \ \text{tax for FUTA} \end{array}$$

.008 × $19,000 = $152 FUTA tax due to federal government

State Unemployment Tax Act (SUTA) The current **SUTA** tax in many states is 5.4% on the first $7,000 the employer pays an employee. Some states offer a merit rating system that results in a lower SUTA rate for companies with a stable employment period. The federal government still allows 5.4% credit on FUTA tax to companies entitled to the lower SUTA rate. Usually states also charge companies with a poor employment record a higher SUTA rate. However, these companies cannot take any more than the 5.4% credit against the 6.2% federal unemployment rate.

EXAMPLE Assume a company has total wages of $20,000 and $4,000 of the wages are exempt from SUTA. What are the company's SUTA and FUTA taxes if the company's SUTA rate is 5.8% due to a poor employment record?

The exempt wages (over $7,000 earnings per worker) are not taxed for SUTA or FUTA. So the company owes the following SUTA and FUTA taxes:

$20,000
$\underline{-\ \ \ 4,000}$ (exempt wages)
$\overline{\$16,000} \times .058 = \boxed{\$928}$ SUTA

Federal FUTA tax would then be:
$\$16,000 \times .008 = \boxed{\$128}$

You can check your progress with the following Practice Quiz.

LU 9–2 | **PRACTICE QUIZ**

Complete this **Practice Quiz** to see how you are doing.

*For **extra help** from your authors—Sharon and Jeff—see the student DVD*

You Tube™

1. Calculate Social Security taxes, Medicare taxes, and FIT for Joy Royce. Joy's company pays her a monthly salary of $9,500. She is single and claims 1 deduction. Before this payroll, Joy's cumulative earnings were $106,600. (Social Security maximum is 6.2% on $110,100, and Medicare is 1.45%.) Calculate FIT by the percentage method.

2. Jim Brewer, owner of Arrow Company, has three employees who earn $300, $700, and $900 a week. Assume a state SUTA rate of 5.1%. What will Jim pay for state and federal unemployment taxes for the first quarter?

✔ **Solutions**

1. **Social Security**

$110,100
$\underline{-\ 106,600}$
$\overline{\$\ \ 3,500} \times .062 = \boxed{\$217.00}$

Medicare

$9,500 \times .0145 = \$137.75$

FIT
Percentage method:
$316.67 \times 1 =$

$9,500.00
$\underline{-\ 316.67}$ (Table 9.1)
$\overline{\$9,183.33}$

$7,317 to $15,067 → $1,453.65 plus 28% of excess over $7,317
(Table 9.2)

$9,183.33
$\underline{-\ 7,317.00}$
$\overline{\$1,866.33} \times .28 = \ \ \ \$\ \ \ 522.57$
$\underline{+\ 1,453.65}$
$\boxed{\$1,976.22}$

2. 13 weeks × $300 = $ 3,900
   13 weeks × $700 = \ \ \ 9,100 ($9,100 − $7,000) → $2,100 ⎱ Exempt wages
   13 weeks × $900 = \ \underline{11,700} ($11,700 − $7,000) → \underline{4,700} ⎰ (not taxed for
   \ \ \ \ \ \ \ \ \ \ \ \ \ \ \ \$24,700 \ $6,800 ⎰ FUTA or SUTA)

$24,700 − $6,800 = $17,900 taxable wages
SUTA = .051 × $17,900 = $\boxed{\$912.90}$
FUTA = .008 × $17,900 = $\boxed{\$143.20}$

Note: FUTA remains at .008 whether SUTA rate is higher or lower than standard.

| LU 9–2a | EXTRA PRACTICE QUIZ WITH WORKED-OUT SOLUTIONS |

Need more practice? Try this **Extra Practice Quiz** (check figures in the Interactive Chapter Organizer, p. 254). Worked-out Solutions can be found in Appendix B at end of text.

1. Calculate Social Security taxes, Medicare taxes, and FIT for Joy Royce. Joy's company pays her a monthly salary of $10,000. She is single and claims 1 deduction. Before this payroll, Joy's cumulative earnings were $109,600. (Social Security maximum is 6.2% on $110,100, and Medicare is 1.45%.) Calculate FIT by the percentage method.

2. Jim Brewer, owner of Arrow Company, has three employees who earn $200, $800, and $950 a week. Assume a state SUTA rate of 5.1%. What will Jim pay for state and federal unemployment taxes for the first quarter?

INTERACTIVE CHAPTER ORGANIZER

Topic/procedure/formula	Examples	You try it*
Gross pay, p. 245 Hours employee worked $\times$ Rate per hour	$6.50 per hour at 36 hours Gross pay = 36 $\times$ $6.50 = $234	**Calculate gross pay** $9.25 per hour; 38 hours
Overtime, p. 245 Gross earnings (pay) = Regular pay + Earnings at overtime rate $(1\frac{1}{2})$	$6 per hour; 42 hours Gross pay = (40 $\times$ $6) + (2 $\times$ $9) = $240 + $18 = $258	**Calculate gross pay** $7 per hour; 43 hours
Straight piece rate, p. 245 Gross pay = Number of units produced $\times$ Rate per unit	1,185 units; rate per unit, $.89 Gross pay = 1,185 $\times$ $.89 = $1,054.65	**Calculate gross pay** 2,250 units; $.79 per unit
Differential pay schedule, p. 246 Rate on each item is related to the number of items produced.	1–500 at $.84; 501–1,000 at $.96; 900 units produced. Gross pay = (500 $\times$ $.84) + (400 $\times$ $.96) = $420 + $384 = $804	**Calculate gross pay** 1–600 at $.79; 601–1,000 at $.88; 900 produced
Straight commission, p. 246 Total sales $\times$ Commission rate Any draw would be subtracted from earnings.	$155,000 sales; 6% commission $155,000 $\times$ .06 = $9,300	**Calculate straight commission** $175,000 sales; 7% commission
Variable commission scale, p. 246 Sales at different levels pay different rates of commission.	Up to $5,000, 5%; $5,001 to $10,000, 8%; over $10,000, 10% Sold: $6,500 Solution: ($5,000 $\times$ .05) + ($1,500 $\times$ .08) = $250 + $120 = $370	**Calculate commission** Up to $6,000, 5%; $6,001 to $8,000, 9%; Over $8,000, 12% Sold: $12,000
Salary plus commission, p. 247 Regular wages (fixed) + Commissions earned	Base $400 per week + 2% on sales over $14,000 Actual sales: $16,000 $400 (base) + (.02 $\times$ $2,000) = $440	**Calculate gross pay** Base $600 per week plus 4% on sales over $16,000. Actual sales $22,000.
Payroll register, p. 248 Multicolumn form to record payroll. Married and paid weekly. (Table 9.2) Claims 1 allowance. FICA rates from chapter.	<table><tr><td rowspan="2">Earnings Gross</td><td colspan="3">Deductions</td><td rowspan="2">Net pay</td></tr><tr><td colspan="3">FICA</td></tr><tr><td></td><td>S.S.</td><td>Med.</td><td>FIT</td><td></td></tr><tr><td>1,515</td><td>93.93</td><td>21.97</td><td>176.19</td><td>1,222.91</td></tr></table>	**Calculate net pay** Gross pay, $490; Married, paid weekly. Claims, one allowance. Use rates in text for Social Security, Medicare, and FIT.
FICA, p. 249 **Social Security Medicare** 6.2% on $110,100 (S.S.) 1.45% (Med.)	If John earns $120,000, what did he contribute for the year to Social Security and Medicare? S.S.: $110,100 $\times$ .062 = $6,826.20 Med.: $120,000 $\times$ .0145 = $1,740.00	**Calculate FICA** If John earns $150,000, what did he contribute to Social Security and Medicare?

(continues)

INTERACTIVE CHAPTER ORGANIZER

Topic/procedure/formula	Examples	You try it*
FIT calculation (percentage method), pp. 249–251 *Facts:* Al Doe: Married Claims: 2 Paid weekly: $1,600	$1,600.00 − 146.16 ($73.08 × 2) Table 9.1 $1,453.84 By Table 9.2 $1,453.84 − 490.00 $ 963.84 $33.40 + .15($963.84) $33.40 + $144.58 = $177.98	**Calculate FIT** Jim Smith, married, claims 3; Paid weekly, $1,400
State and federal unemployment, pp. 251–252 Employer pays these taxes. Rates are 6.2% on $7,000 for federal and 5.4% for state on $7,000. 6.2% − 5.4% = .8% federal rate after credit. If state unemployment rate is higher than 5.4%, no additional credit is taken. If state unemployment rate is less than 5.4%, the full 5.4% credit can be taken for federal unemployment.	Cumulative pay before payroll, $6,400; this week's pay, $800. What are state and federal unemployment taxes for employer, assuming a 5.2% state unemployment rate? State → .052 × $600 = $31.20 Federal → .008 × $600 = $4.80 ($6,400 + $600 = $7,000 maximum)	**Calculate SUTA and FUTA** Cumulative pay before payroll, $6,800. This week's payroll, $9,000. State rate is 5.4%.

KEY TERMS

Biweekly, *p. 244* | Federal Unemployment Tax Act (FUTA), *p. 251* | Social Security, *p. 249*
Deductions, *p. 245* | Gross pay, *p. 245* | State income tax (SIT), *p. 251*
Differential pay schedule, *p. 246* | Medicare, *p. 249* | State Unemployment Tax Act (SUTA), *p. 252*
Draw, *p. 246* | Monthly, *p. 244* | Straight commission, *p. 246*
Employee's Withholding Allowance Certificate (W-4), *p. 248* | Net pay, *p. 251* | Variable commission scale, *p. 246*
Fair Labor Standards Act, *p. 244* | Overrides, *p. 247* | W-4, *p. 248*
Federal income tax withholding (FIT), *p. 249* | Overtime, *p. 245* | Weekly, *p. 244*
Federal Insurance Contribution Act (FICA), *p. 249* | Payroll register, *p. 248* |
 | Percentage method, *p. 249* |
 | Semimonthly, *p. 244* |

Check Figures for Extra Practice Quizzes with Page References. (Worked-out Solutions in Appendix B.)

LU 9–1a (p. 247)
1. $732
2. $12,800
3. $4,070

LU 9–2a (p. 253)
1. $31; 145; $2,116.22
2. $846.60; $132.80

*Worked-out solutions are in Appendix B.

Critical Thinking Discussion Questions with Chapter Concept Check

1. Explain the difference between biweekly and semimonthly. Explain what problems may develop if a retail store hires someone on straight commission to sell cosmetics.

2. Explain what each column of a payroll register records (p. 248) and how each number is calculated. Social Security tax is based on a specific rate and base; Medicare tax is based on a rate but has no base. Do you think this is fair to all taxpayers?

3. What taxes are the responsibility of the employer? How can an employer benefit from a merit-rating system for state unemployment?

4. **Chapter Concept Check.** Visit the Starbucks website to see how its benefits plan compares to McDonald's health insurance plan discussed in the chapter opener. Be sure to discuss the responsibilities of the employee and the employer.

END-OF-CHAPTER PROBLEMS

connect™ (plus+) www.mhhe.com/slater11e

Check figures for odd-numbered problems in Appendix C.   Name _____   Date _____

DRILL PROBLEMS

Complete the following table: *LU 9-1(2)*

Employee	M	T	W	Th	F	Hours	Rate per hour	Gross pay
9–1. Roger Rial	11	6	9	7	6		$7.95	
9–2. Kristina Shaw	5	9	10	8	8		$8.10	

Complete the following table (assume the overtime for each employee is a time-and-a-half rate after 40 hours):   *LU 9-1(2)*

Employee	M	T	W	Th	F	Sa	Total regular hours	Total overtime hours	Regular rate	Overtime rate	Gross earnings
9–3. Blue	12	9	9	9	9	3			$8.00		
9–4. Tagney	14	8	9	9	5	1			$7.60		

Calculate gross earnings: *LU 9-1(3)*

Worker	Number of units produced	Rate per unit	Gross earnings
9–5. Lang	480	$3.50	
9–6. Swan	846	$ .58	

Calculate the gross earnings for each apple picker based on the following differential pay scale: *LU 9-1(3)*

1–1,000: $.03 each	1,001–1,600: $.05 each	Over 1,600: $.07 each

Apple picker	Number of apples picked	Gross earnings
9–7. Ryan	1,600	
9–8. Rice	1,925	

Calculate the end-of-month commission.   *LU 9-1(3)*

Employee	Total sales	Commission rate	Draw	End-of-month commission received
9–9. Reese	$300,000	7%	$8,000	

Ron Company has the following commission schedule:

Commission rate	Sales
2%	Up to $80,000
3.5%	Excess of $80,000 to $100,000
4%	More than $100,000

Calculate the gross earnings of Ron Company's two employees: *LU 9-1(3)*

Employee	Total sales	Gross earnings
9–10. Bill Moore	$ 70,000	
9–11. Ron Ear	$155,000	

Complete the following table, given that A Publishing Company pays its salespeople a weekly salary plus a 2% commission on all net sales over $5,000 (no commission on returned goods):   *LU 9-1(3)*

Employee	Gross sales	Return	Net sales	Given quota	Commission sales	Commission rates	Total commission	Regular wage	Total wage
9–12. Ring *eXcel*	$ 8,000	$ 25		$5,000		2%		$250	
9–13. Porter *eXcel*	$12,000	$100		$5,000		2%		$250	

Calculate the Social Security and Medicare deductions for the following employees (assume a tax rate of 6.2% on $110,100 for Social Security and 1.45% for Medicare):   *LU 9-2(1)*

Employee	Cumulative earnings before this pay period	Pay amount this period	Social Security	Medicare
9–14. Logan	$110,000	$3,000		
9–15. Rouche	$104,000	$7,000		
9–16. Cleaves	$400,000	$6,000		

Complete the following payroll register. Calculate FIT by the percentage method for this weekly period; Social Security and Medicare are the same rates as in the previous problems. No one will reach the maximum for FICA.   *LU 9-2(1)*

Employee	Marital status	Allowances claimed	Gross pay	FIT	FICA S.S.	FICA Med.	Net pay
9–17. Mike Rice	M	2	$1,600				
9–18. Pat Brown	M	4	$2,100				

9–19. Given the following, calculate the state (assume 5.3%) and federal unemployment taxes that the employer must pay for each of the first two quarters. The federal unemployment tax is .8% on the first $7,000.   *LU 9-2(2)*

PAYROLL SUMMARY		
	Quarter 1	Quarter 2
Bill Adams	$4,000	$ 8,000
Rich Haines	8,000	14,000
Alice Smooth	3,200	3,800

WORD PROBLEMS

9–20. Lai Xiaodong, a 22-year-old college-educated man, accepted a job at Foxconn Technology (where the iPad was being produced for Apple) in Chengdu, China, for $22 a day at 12 hours a day, 6 days a week. A company perk included company housing in dorms for the 70,000 employees. It was common for 20 people to be assigned to the same three-bedroom apartment. What were Lai's hourly (rounded to the nearest cent), weekly, and annual gross pay?   *LU 9-1(1)*

9–21. Rhonda Brennan found her first job after graduating from college through the classifieds of the *Miami Herald*. She was delighted when the offer came through at $18.50 per hour. She completed her W-4 stating that she is married with a child and claims an allowance of 3. Her company will pay her biweekly for 80 hours. Calculate her take-home pay for her first check. *LU 9-2(1)*

9–22. The Social Security Administration increased the taxable wage base from $106,800 to $110,100. The 6.2% tax rate is unchanged. Joe Burns earned over $120,000 each of the past two years. **(a)** What is the percent increase in the base? Round to the nearest hundredth percent. **(b)** What is Joe's increase in Social Security tax for the new year?   *LU 9-2(1)*

9–23. In an effort to stimulate economic growth, President Obama proposed "The American Jobs Act," which reduced both employer and employee payroll taxes from 6.2% to 3.1%. If the act passed as originated, how much would Juan Carlos Soto, Jr., have saved in his net pay if he earned $6,548 in March 2012 with earnings to date of $24,356? (Round to the nearest cent.)   *LU 9-2(1)*

9–24. Maggie Vitteta, single, works 38 hours per week at $9.00 an hour. How much is taken out for federal income tax with one withholding exemption? *LU 9-2(1)*

9–25. Robin Hartman earns $600 per week plus 3% of sales over $6,500. Robin's sales are $14,000. How much does Robin earn? *LU 9-1(3)*

9–26. Pat Maninen earns a gross salary of $3,000 each week. What are Pat's first week's deductions for Social Security and Medicare? Will any of Pat's wages be exempt from Social Security and Medicare for the calendar year? Assume a rate of 6.2% on $110,100 for Social Security and 1.45% for Medicare. *LU 9-2(1)*

9–27. Richard Gaziano is a manager for Health Care, Inc. Health Care deducts Social Security, Medicare, and FIT (by percentage method) from his earnings. Assume the same Social Security and Medicare rates as in Problem 9–26. Before this payroll, Richard is $1,000 below the maximum level for Social Security earnings. Richard is married, is paid weekly, and claims 2 exemptions. What is Richard's net pay for the week if he earns $1,300? *LU 9-2(1)*

9–28. Len Mast earned $2,200 for the last 2 weeks. He is married, is paid biweekly, and claims 3 exemptions. What is Len's income tax? Use the percentage method. *LU 9-2(1)*

9–29. Westway Company pays Suzie Chan $2,200 per week. By the end of week 51, how much did Westway deduct for Suzie's eXcel Social Security and Medicare for the year? Assume Social Security is 6.2% on $110,100 and 1.45% for Medicare. What state and federal unemployment taxes does Westway pay on Suzie's yearly salary? The state unemployment rate is 5.1%. FUTA is .8%. *LU 9-2(1, 2)*

9–30. Morris Leste, owner of Carlson Company, has three employees who earn $400, $500, and $700 per week. What are the total state and federal unemployment taxes that Morris owes for the first 11 weeks of the year and for week 30? Assume a state rate of 5.6% and a federal rate of .8%. *LU 9-2(2)*

9–31. Tiffani Lind earned $1,200 during her biweekly pay period. She is married and claims 4 deductions. Her annual earnings *eXcel* to date are $52,521. Calculate her net pay. *LU 9-2(1)*

CHALLENGE PROBLEMS

9–32. The San Bernardino County Fair hires about 150 people during fair time. Their wages range from $6.75 to $8.00. California has a state income tax of 9%. Sandy Denny earns $8.00 per hour; George Barney earns $6.75 per hour. They both worked 35 hours this week. Both are married; however, Sandy claims 2 exemptions and George claims 1 exemption. Assume a rate of 6.2% on $110,100 for Social Security and 1.45% for Medicare. **(a)** What is Sandy's net pay after FIT (use the tables in the text), Social Security tax, state income tax, and Medicare have been taken out? **(b)** What is George's net pay after the same deductions? **(c)** How much more is Sandy's net pay versus George's net pay? Round to the nearest cent. *LU 9-2(1)*

9–33. Bill Rose is a salesperson for Boxes, Inc. He believes his $1,460.47 monthly paycheck is in error. Bill earns a $1,400 salary per month plus a 9.5% commission on sales over $1,500. Last month, Bill had $8,250 in sales. Bill believes his traveling expenses are 16% of his weekly gross earnings before commissions. Monthly deductions include Social Security, $126.56; Medicare, $29.60; FIT, $189.50; union dues, $25.00; and health insurance, $16.99. Calculate the following: **(a)** Bill's monthly take-home pay, and indicate the amount his check was under- or overstated, and **(b)** Bill's weekly traveling expenses. Round your final answer to the nearest dollar. *LU 9-2(1)*

![photo] **SUMMARY PRACTICE TEST** You Tube™

Do you need help? The DVD has step-by-step worked-out solutions.

1. Calculate Sam's gross pay (he is entitled to time-and-a-half). *(p. 245)*   *LU 9-1(2)*

M	T	W	Th	F	Total hours	Rate per hour	Gross pay
$9\frac{1}{4}$	$9\frac{1}{4}$	$10\frac{1}{2}$	$8\frac{1}{2}$	$11\frac{1}{2}$		$8.00	

2. Mia Kaminsky sells shoes for Macy's. Macy's pays Mia $12 per hour plus a 5% commission on all sales. Assume Mia works 37 hours for the week and has $7,000 in sales. What is Mia's gross pay? *(p. 246)*   *LU 9-1(3)*

3. Lee Company pays its employees on a graduated commission scale: 6% on the first $40,000 sales, 7% on sales from $40,001 to $80,000, and 13% on sales of more than $80,000. May West, an employee of Lee, has $230,000 in sales. What commission did May earn? *(p. 246)*   *LU 9-1(3)*

4. Matty Kim, an accountant for Vernitron, earned $102,600 from January to June. In July, Matty earned $20,000. Assume a tax rate of 6.2% for Social Security on $110,100 and 1.45% on Medicare. How much are the July taxes for Social Security and Medicare? *(p. 249)*   *LU 9-2(1)*

5. Grace Kelley earns $2,000 per week. She is married and claims 2 exemptions. What is Grace's income tax? Use the percentage method. *(p. 249)*   *LU 9-2(1)*

6. Jean Michaud pays his two employees $900 and $1,200 per week. Assume a state unemployment tax rate of 5.7% and a federal unemployment tax rate of .8%. What state and federal unemployment taxes will Jean pay at the end of quarter 1 and quarter 2? *(pp. 251–252)*   *LU 9-2(2)*

SURF TO SAVE

Looking for ways to make money? 🔍

PROBLEM 1
Sell it on Amazon.com?

Go to http://www.amazon.com. At the bottom of the page, under Make Money with Us, click on sell on Amazon. Suppose you sold 10 PCs for $500 each and the buyers paid the cost of shipping. After deducting the per-item and referral fees Amazon charges and the $400 you paid for each PC, what was your total profit on these transactions?

Discussion Questions

1. Is it worth the money for you to sell products through this site? Why?

2. Why does Amazon.com charge sellers fees?

PROBLEM 2
Single vs. married taxpayers

Go to http://www.paycheckcity.com/coapa/netpaycalculator.asp. Suppose you are single and earn $2,000 semimonthly. Assume it is July 1 and you have already earned $24,000. How much more federal income tax is withheld from your paycheck compared to a married person, earning the same salary, with four dependents?

Discussion Questions

1. Why do you feel the tax rates differ based on marital status?

2. Will your federal tax withholding likely increase, decrease, or stay the same over the next 10 years? Why?

PROBLEM 3
Can you afford to retire?

Go to http://www.ssa.gov/OACT/quickcalc/index.html. Assume that you plan to retire at the age of 70 and that you will make an average of $55,000 per year. Calculate your benefit using both today's dollars and inflated (future) dollars. How do the two values differ? Click to see the earnings that were used. Which number is more realistic?

Discussion Questions

1. How does this tool help you prepare for your future retirement?

2. Will the amounts you have seen for your eventual retirement cover all of your expected expenses during your retirement? Why or why not?

PROBLEM 4
Worthy commission?

Go to http://www.nytimes.com/2011/01/30/realestate/30cov.html?pagewanted=all and read "You Don't Have to Pay It." According to the article, real estate agents' average commission rate is 6%. If a real estate agent sold five homes with an average price of $250,000 last year, what would be his/her total commission earned for the year?

Discussion Questions

1. Based on the article, what causes drops in agents' commissions?

2. Would you take on more of the tasks involved in selling your house to pay a smaller commission? Why?

MOBILE APPS ✕

Withholding Calc (3 Dogs and a Cat Software) Helps you estimate your paychecks and the impact changes to your withholdings will have on take-home pay.

Payrollguru (Payrollguru, Inc.) Assists in the calculation of paychecks, including the net pay as well as applicable taxes taken out of gross pay amounts.

INTERNET PROJECTS ✕

See text website
www.mhhe.com/slater11e_sse_ch09

Health Coverage on Your Own

New resources and rules help you find an affordable policy. BY KIMBERLY LANKFORD

■ YOU'LL SAVE WITH A HIGH-DEDUCTIBLE POLICY, AND YOU COULD BE ELIGIBLE FOR WELL-CHILD VISITS AT NO COST.

UNLESS A SUPREME COURT decision derails the 2010 health-care-reform law, the marketplace for individual health insurance is scheduled to change drastically in 2014—when policies will be sold on state-run exchanges and insurers will no longer be able to deny you coverage or charge higher rates because of your health. Until then, take advantage of new rules and resources to help you find coverage.

Resources. A new tool at the government's HealthCare .gov site provides extensive information about the poli-

cies available in your area and makes it easy to narrow your search based on the size of the deductible, out-of-pocket expenses and the type of plan (such as HMO or PPO). You'll see details about benefits, co-payment rates, exclusions and base premiums.

For premium information based on your medical condition, go to eHealthInsurance.com, which queries you about your health and lists prices and policy details from many companies. You can also get help from a health insurance agent through www.nahu.org.

If you have the option of continuing coverage through COBRA—the federal law that requires employers to offer coverage for up to 18 months after you leave your job—shop around before you take it. If you're healthy, you may find a better deal on your own.

Adult children can now remain on their parents' policies until age 26 if they don't have coverage through their own jobs. That can be a great deal if you have family coverage for younger siblings and wouldn't need to pay extra to add a grown kid. But if you'd have to switch from coverage for a single or a couple to family coverage, compare the extra cost with the price of buying a separate individual policy—healthy people in their early twenties can generally get a high-deductible policy for $100 per month or less.

High-deductible plans. The money you save in premiums may more than make up for a higher deductible. And new laws now require most insurers to provide preventive-care screenings without charging deductibles or co-payments, even if you have a high-deductible policy. Depending on your age, you could be eligible for blood-pressure, diabetes and cholesterol tests, mammograms and colonoscopies, flu shots, routine vaccines, well-baby and well-child visits, and other preventive services without any out-of-pocket costs (see www.healthcare.gov/prevention for a list of eligible services).

If your health insurance policy has a deductible of at least $1,200 for individual coverage (or $2,400 for family coverage), you can make tax-deductible contributions up to $3,100 ($6,250 for family coverage) to a health savings account for 2012, plus $1,000 if you're 55 or older. That gives you a stash of tax-free money to use for medical expenses in any year.

If you have a preexisting health condition. You'll usually be able to keep coverage from a former employer for up to 18 months under COBRA, no matter how poor your health is. Most states must provide a continuation policy after you've used up your coverage (see www .coverageforall.org for your state's rules).

If you aren't eligible for COBRA, you may be able to find coverage through the new Pre-Existing Condition Insurance Plan, which was introduced as part of the health-care-reform law. The federal government runs the plans in 23 states and the District of Columbia; 27 states run their own plans, which must also follow the federal rules. However, there's a big catch: You can qualify for this coverage only if you've been uninsured for at least six months.

Even if you haven't gone that long without insurance, you may still qualify for a policy through your state's high-risk insurance pool, which may not require a six-month waiting period. For a list of options and rules, see www.healthcare.gov or www.coverageforall.org. ■

Classroom Notes

CHAPTER 10

Simple Interest

From *The Wall Street Journal*, copyright © 2010, permission of Cartoon Features Syndicate.

"*Just why do you think you deserve a better standard of living?*"

Reprinted with permission of *The Wall Street Journal*, Copyright © 2011 Dow Jones & Company, Inc. All Rights Reserved Worldwide.

What's the Difference?
Credit unions typically charge lower fees—and pay out higher rates—than commercial banks. A sampling of current averages:

	Credit Unions	Banks	Difference
DEPOSIT ACCOUNTS			
12-Month CD ($10,000)	0.72%	0.56%	0.16 pts.
Personal Savings ($1,000)	0.29%	0.20%	0.09 pts.
Personal Interest Checking ($2,500)	0.39%	0.23%	0.16 pts.
Insufficient Funds Fee	$26.29	$29.11	$2.82
CONSUMER LOANS			
Unsecured Personal Loan ($5,000; 4 Years)	10.62%	11.05%	0.43 pts
New Auto Loan (5 Years)	3.93%	5.40%	1.47 pt
Used Auto Loan (2-Year-Old Vehicle; 4 Years)	4.06%	5.66%	1.60 pt
CREDIT CARDS			
Platinum	10.22%	12.09%	1.87
Annual Fee	$26.60	$34.63	$8
Maximum Late Fee	$24.98	$34.13	$9
Reward	10.91%	12.91%	2.0
Annual Fee	$27.93	$88.44	$6
Maximum Late Fee	$23.58	$33.56	$

Note: Data as of June

Source: Informa Research Services Inc.

LU 10–1: Calculation of Simple Interest and Maturity Value

1. Calculate simple interest and maturity value for months and years *(pp. 265–266)*.

2. Calculate simple interest and maturity value by **(a)** exact interest and **(b)** ordinary interest *(pp. 266–267)*.

LU 10–2: Finding Unknown in Simple Interest Formula

1. Using the interest formula, calculate the unknown when the other two (principal, rate, or time) are given *(pp. 268–269)*.

LU 10–3: U.S. Rule—Making Partial Note Payments before Due Date

1. List the steps to complete the U.S. Rule as well as calculate proper interest credits *(pp. 270–271)*.

VOCABULARY PREVIEW

Here are key terms in this chapter. After completing the chapter, if you know the term, place a checkmark in the parentheses. If you don't know the term, look it up and put the page number where it can be found.

Adjusted balance ( )   Banker's Rule ( )   Exact interest ( )   Interest ( )   Maturity value ( )   Ordinary interest ( )   Principal ( )   Simple interest ( )   Simple interest formula ( )   Time ( )   U.S. Rule ( )

Do you shop around for the best bank rates? In the chapter opener, the *Wall Street Journal* clip "What's the Difference?" shows that credit unions may be a good choice when it comes to rates for deposits, consumer loans, or credit cards. Note that in the *Wall Street Journal* article "Peer-to-Peer Loans Grow" (in the margin below) borrowers are using the Internet to get loans.

In this chapter, you will study simple interest. The principles discussed apply whether you are paying interest or receiving interest. Let's begin by learning how to calculate simple interest.

Learning Unit 10–1: Calculation of Simple Interest and Maturity Value

Peer-to-Peer Loans Grow
Fed Up With Banks, Entrepreneurs Turn to Internet Sites

BY ANGUS LOTEN

Some small-business owners, rejected by banks or fed up with bad lending terms, are turning to Internet sites that match borrowers with giant pools of lenders when they need funds. That has driven growth and increased the public profile of a sector that was briefly shut down by regulators during the financial crisis.

In the past year, **Prosper Marketplace** Inc. and **Lending Club** Corp., which run the nation's two biggest peer-to-peer lending sites, have reported a sharp upturn in personal loans used to fund small businesses. The sites work like **eBay**-style marketplaces, matching prequalified borrowers to lenders.

Hope Slater, a young attorney, rented an office in a professional building. Since Hope recently graduated from law school, she was short of cash. To purchase office furniture for her new office, Hope went to her bank and borrowed $40,000 for 6 months at a 4% annual interest rate. **Interest** expense is the cost of borrowing money.

The original amount Hope borrowed ($40,000) is the **principal** (face value) of the loan. Hope's price for using the $40,000 is the interest rate (4%) the bank charges on a yearly basis. Since Hope is borrowing the $40,000 for 6 months, Hope's loan will have a **maturity value** of $40,800—the principal plus the interest on the loan. Thus, Hope's price for using the furniture before she can pay for it is $800 interest, which is a percent of the principal for a specific time period. To make this calculation, we use the following formula:

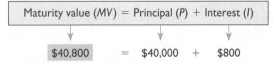

Maturity value (MV) = Principal (P) + Interest (I)

$40,800 = $40,000 + $800

Hope's furniture purchase introduces **simple interest**—the cost of a loan, usually for 1 year or less. Simple interest is only on the original principal or amount borrowed. Let's examine how the bank calculated Hope's $800 interest.

Simple Interest Formula

To calculate simple interest, we use the following **simple interest formula:**

$$\boxed{\text{Simple interest } (I) = \text{Principal } (P) \times \text{Rate } (R) \times \text{Time } (T)}$$

In this formula, rate is expressed as a decimal, fraction, or percent; and time is expressed in years or a fraction of a year.

EXAMPLE   Hope Slater borrowed $40,000 for office furniture. The loan was for 6 months at an annual interest rate of 4%. What are Hope's interest and maturity value?

Using the simple interest formula, the bank determined Hope's interest as follows:

In your calculator, multiply $40,000 times .04 times 6. Divide your answer by 12. You could also use the % key—multiply $40,000 times 4% times 6 and then divide your answer by 12.

Step 1. Calculate the interest.

$$I = \$40,000 \times \underset{(R)}{.04} \times \underset{(T)}{\frac{6}{12}}$$
$$\underset{(P)}{}$$
$$= \$800$$

Step 2. Calculate the maturity value.

$$MV = \underset{(P)}{\$40,000} + \underset{(I)}{\$800}$$
$$= \boxed{\$40,800}$$

Now let's use the same example and assume Hope borrowed $40,000 for 1 year. The bank would calculate Hope's interest and maturity value as follows:

Step 1. Calculate the interest.

$$I = \underset{(P)}{\$40,000} \times \underset{(R)}{.04} \times \underset{(T)}{1 \text{ year}}$$
$$= \$1,600$$

Step 2. Calculate the maturity value.

$$MV = \underset{(P)}{\$40,000} + \underset{(I)}{\$1,600}$$
$$= \boxed{\$41,600}$$

Let's use the same example again and assume Hope borrowed $40,000 for 18 months. Then Hope's interest and maturity value would be calculated as follows:

Step 1. Calculate the interest.

$$I = \$40,000 \times \underset{(R)}{.04} \times \underset{(T)}{\frac{18^{1}}{12}}$$
$$\underset{(P)}{}$$
$$= \$2,400$$

Step 2. Calculate the maturity value.

$$MV = \underset{(P)}{\$40,000} + \underset{(I)}{\$2,400}$$
$$= \boxed{\$42,400}$$

Next we'll turn our attention to two common methods we can use to calculate simple interest when a loan specifies its beginning and ending dates.

LO 2

Two Methods for Calculating Simple Interest and Maturity Value

Method 1: Exact Interest (365 Days)   The Federal Reserve banks and the federal government use the **exact interest** method. The *exact interest* is calculated by using a 365-day year. For **time,** we count the exact number of days in the month that the borrower has the loan. The day the loan is made is not counted, but the day the money is returned is counted

---

[1] This is the same as 1.5 years.

as a full day. This method calculates interest by using the following fraction to represent time in the formula:

$$\text{Time} = \frac{\text{Exact number of days}}{365} \longleftarrow \text{Exact interest}$$

For this calculation, we use the exact days-in-a-year calendar from the *Business Math Handbook*. You learned how to use this calendar in Chapter 7, page 187.

EXAMPLE On March 4, Joe Bench borrowed $50,000 at 5% interest. Interest and principal are due on July 6. What are the interest cost and the maturity value?

Step 1. Calculate the interest.

$$I = P \times R \times T$$
$$= \$50,000 \times .05 \times \frac{124}{365}$$
$$= \$849.32 \text{ (rounded to nearest cent)}$$

Step 2. Calculate the maturity value.

$$MV = P + I$$
$$= \$50,000 + \$849.32$$
$$= \boxed{\$50,849.32}$$

Method 2: Ordinary Interest (360 Days) In the **ordinary interest** method, time in the formula $I = P \times R \times T$ is equal to the following:

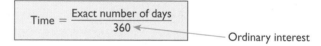

$$\text{Time} = \frac{\text{Exact number of days}}{360} \longleftarrow \text{Ordinary interest}$$

Since banks commonly use the ordinary interest method, it is known as the **Banker's Rule.** Banks charge a slightly higher rate of interest because they use 360 days instead of 365 in the denominator. (Here's a hint: The word *ordinary* starts with an "O" and "360" ends with a "0.") By using 360 instead of 365, the calculation is supposedly simplified. Consumer groups, however, are questioning why banks can use 360 days, since this benefits the bank and not the customer. The use of computers and calculators no longer makes the simplified calculation necessary. For example, after a court case in Oregon, banks began calculating interest on 365 days except in mortgages.

Now let's replay the Joe Bench example we used to illustrate Method 1 to see the difference in bank interest when we use Method 2.

EXAMPLE On March 4, Joe Bench borrowed $50,000 at 5% interest. Interest and principal are due on July 6. What are the interest cost and the maturity value?

Step 1. Calculate the interest.

$$I = \$50,000 \times .05 \times \frac{124}{360}$$
$$= \$861.11$$

Step 2. Calculate the maturity value.

$$MV = P + I$$
$$= \$50,000 + \$861.11$$
$$= \boxed{\$50,861.11}$$

Note: By using Method 2, the bank increases its interest by $11.79.

$$\begin{array}{r} \$861.11 \longleftarrow \text{Method 2} \\ - \ 849.32 \\ \hline \$ \ 11.79 \longleftarrow \text{Method 1} \end{array}$$

Now you should be ready for your first Practice Quiz in this chapter.

MONEY tips

Because debit cards draw money directly from your checking account, it is critical that you protect your account. Be cautious of the ATMs you use. Any outdoor transaction is at risk if the public has access to the machine—even at gas stations. Skimming devices can easily be used to pick up your information and leave your account at risk. Never use an ATM that has been tampered with.

Complete this **Practice Quiz** to see how you are doing.

Calculate simple interest (rounded to the nearest cent):

1. $14,000 at 4% for 9 months
2. $25,000 at 7% for 5 years
3. $40,000 at $10\frac{1}{2}$% for 19 months
4. On May 4, Dawn Kristal borrowed $15,000 at 8%. Dawn must pay the principal and interest on August 10. What are Dawn's simple interest and maturity value if you use the exact interest method?
5. What are Dawn Kristal's (Problem 4) simple interest and maturity value if you use the ordinary interest method?

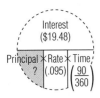

*For **extra help** from your authors–Sharon and Jeff–see the student DVD*

You Tube™

✓ **Solutions**

1. $14,000 \times .04 \times \dfrac{9}{12}$ = $420

2. $25,000 \times .07 \times 5$ = $8,750

3. $40,000 \times .105 \times \dfrac{19}{12}$ = $6,650

4.
   August 10 → 222
   May 4 → − 124
   ───────
   98

   $15,000 \times .08 \times \dfrac{98}{365}$ = $322.19

   MV = $15,000 + $322.19 = $15,322.19

5. $15,000 \times .08 \times \dfrac{98}{360}$ = $326.67   MV = $15,000 + $326.67 = $15,326.67

Need more practice? Try this **Extra Practice Quiz** (check figures in the Interactive Chapter Organizer, p. 273). Worked-out Solutions can be found in Appendix B at end of text.

Calculate simple interest (rounded to the nearest cent):

1. $16,000 at 3% for 8 months
2. $15,000 at 6% for 6 years
3. $50,000 at 7% for 18 months
4. On May 6, Dawn Kristal borrowed $20,000 at 7%. Dawn must pay the principal and interest on August 14. What are Dawn's simple interest and maturity value if you use the exact interest method?
5. What are Dawn Kristal's (Problem 4) simple interest and maturity value if you use the ordinary interest method?

Learning Unit 10–2: Finding Unknown in Simple Interest Formula

LO 1

This unit begins with the formula used to calculate the principal of a loan. Then it explains how to find the *principal, rate,* and *time* of a simple interest loan. In all the calculations, we use 360 days and round only final answers.

Finding the Principal

EXAMPLE Tim Jarvis paid the bank $19.48 interest at 9.5% for 90 days. How much did Tim borrow using the ordinary interest method?

The following formula is used to calculate the principal of a loan:

Interest ($19.48)

Principal × Rate × Time
? (.095) $\left(\dfrac{90}{360}\right)$

$$\text{Principal} = \frac{\text{Interest}}{\text{Rate} \times \text{Time}}$$

Note how we illustrated this in the margin. The shaded area is what we are solving for. When solving for principal, rate, or time, you are dividing. Interest will be in the numerator, and the denominator will be the other two elements multiplied by each other.

Step 2. When using a calculator, press

$\boxed{.095}\ \boxed{\times}\ \boxed{90}\ \boxed{\div}\ \boxed{360}\ \boxed{M+}$.

Step 3. When using a calculator, press

$\boxed{19.48}\ \boxed{\div}\ \boxed{MR}\ \boxed{=}$.

Step 1. Set up the formula.

$$P = \frac{\$19.48}{.095 \times \frac{90}{360}}$$

Step 2. Multiply the denominator.

.095 times 90 divided by 360
(do not round)

$$P = \frac{\$19.48}{.02375}$$

Step 3. Divide the numerator by the result of Step 2. $\boxed{P = \$820.21}$

Step 4. Check your answer.

$$\underset{(I)}{\$19.48} = \underset{(P)}{\$820.21} \times \underset{(R)}{.095} \times \underset{(T)}{\frac{90}{360}}$$

Finding the Rate

EXAMPLE   Tim Jarvis borrowed $820.21 from a bank. Tim's interest is $19.48 for 90 days. What rate of interest did Tim pay using the ordinary interest method?

The following formula is used to calculate the rate of interest:

$$\boxed{\text{Rate} = \frac{\text{Interest}}{\text{Principal} \times \text{Time}}}$$

Step 1. Set up the formula.

$$R = \frac{\$19.48}{\$820.21 \times \frac{90}{360}}$$

Step 2. Multiply the denominator. Do not round the answer.

$$R = \frac{\$19.48}{\$205.0525}$$

Step 3. Divide the numerator by the result of Step 2. $\boxed{R = 9.5\%}$

Step 4. Check your answer.

$$\underset{(I)}{\$19.48} = \underset{(P)}{\$820.21} \times \underset{(R)}{.095} \times \underset{(T)}{\frac{90}{360}}$$

Finding the Time

Step 2. When using a calculator, press

$\boxed{820.21}\ \boxed{\times}\ \boxed{.095}\ \boxed{M+}$.

Step 3. When using a calculator, press

$\boxed{19.48}\ \boxed{\div}\ \boxed{MR}\ \boxed{=}$.

EXAMPLE   Tim Jarvis borrowed $820.21 from a bank. Tim's interest is $19.48 at 9.5%. How much time does Tim have to repay the loan using the ordinary interest method?

The following formula is used to calculate time:

$$\boxed{\text{Time (in years)} = \frac{\text{Interest}}{\text{Principal} \times \text{Rate}}}$$

> **MONEY** tips
>
> For each checking account you have, make certain to apply for overdraft protection to protect your account from human error and unintentional overdrafts.

Step 1. Set up the formula.

$$T = \frac{\$19.48}{\$820.21 \times .095}$$

Step 2. Multiply the denominator. Do not round the answer.

$$T = \frac{\$19.48}{\$77.91995}$$

Step 3. Divide the numerator by the result of Step 2. $T = .25$ years

Step 4. Convert years to days (assume 360 days). $.25 \times 360 = \boxed{90 \text{ days}}$

Step 5. Check your answer.

$$\underset{(I)}{\$19.48} = \underset{(P)}{\$820.21} \times \underset{(R)}{.095} \times \underset{(T)}{\frac{90}{360}}$$

Before we go on to Learning Unit 10–3, let's check your understanding of this unit.

LU 10–2 PRACTICE QUIZ

Complete this **Practice Quiz** to see how you are doing.

Complete the following (assume 360 days):

	Principal	Interest rate	Time (days)	Simple interest
1.	?	5%	90 days	$8,000
2.	$7,000	?	220 days	$350
3.	$1,000	8%	?	$300

For **extra help** from your authors—Sharon and Jeff—see the student DVD

You Tube™

✓ Solutions

1. $\dfrac{\$8,000}{.05 \times \dfrac{90}{360}} = \dfrac{\$8,000}{.0125} =$ $640,000$ $P = \dfrac{I}{R \times T}$

2. $\dfrac{\$350}{\$7,000 \times \dfrac{220}{360}} = \dfrac{\$350}{\$4,277.7777} =$ 8.18% $R = \dfrac{I}{P \times T}$

   (do not round)

3. $\dfrac{\$300}{\$1,000 \times .08} = \dfrac{\$300}{\$80} = 3.75 \times 360 =$ 1,350 days $T = \dfrac{I}{P \times R}$

LU 10–2a EXTRA PRACTICE QUIZ WITH WORKED-OUT SOLUTIONS

Need more practice? Try this **Extra Practice Quiz** (check figures in the Interactive Chapter Organizer, p. 273). Worked-out Solutions can be found in Appendix B at end of text.

Complete the following (assume 360 days):

	Principal	Interest rate	Time (days)	Simple interest
1.	?	4%	90 days	$9,000
2.	$6,000	?	180 days	$280
3.	$900	6%	?	$190

Learning Unit 10–3: U.S. Rule—Making Partial Note Payments before Due Date

Often a person may want to pay off a debt in more than one payment before the maturity date. The **U.S. Rule** allows the borrower to receive proper interest credits. This rule states that any partial loan payment first covers any interest that has built up. The remainder of the partial payment reduces the loan principal. Courts or legal proceedings generally use the U.S. Rule. The Supreme Court originated the U.S. Rule in the case of *Story* v. *Livingston*.

LO 1

EXAMPLE   Jeff Edsell owes $5,000 on a 4%, 90-day note. On day 50, Jeff pays $600 on the note. On day 80, Jeff makes an $800 additional payment. Assume a 360-day year. What is Jeff's adjusted balance after day 50 and after day 80? What is the ending balance due?
   To calculate $600 payment on day 50:

Step 1. Calculate interest on principal from date of loan to date of first principal payment. Round to nearest cent.

$I = P \times R \times T$

$I = \$5,000 \times .04 \times \dfrac{50}{360}$

$I = \$27.78$

Step 2. Apply partial payment to interest due. Subtract remainder of payment from principal. This is the **adjusted balance** (principal).

$600.00 payment
− 27.78 interest
$572.22

$5,000.00 principal
− 572.22
$4,427.78 adjusted balance— principal

(continued on p. 271)

© The McGraw-Hill Companies, Inc./John Flournoy, photographer

MONEY tips

Pay off debt instead of moving it around unless you have been offered 0% interest. Be wary of companies offering to consolidate your debt into a single loan. If you do, be certain to read and understand all the terms.

To calculate $800 payment on day 80:

Step 3. Calculate interest on adjusted balance that starts from previous payment date and goes to new payment date. Then apply Step 2.

Compute interest on $4,427.78 for 30 days (80 − 50)

$$I = \$4,427.78 \times .04 \times \frac{30}{360}$$

$$I = \$14.76$$

$$\begin{array}{r} \$800.00 \text{ payment} \\ -\quad 14.76 \text{ interest} \\ \hline \$785.24 \end{array}$$

$$\begin{array}{r} \$4,427.78 \\ -\quad 785.24 \\ \hline \$3,642.54 \text{ adjusted} \\ \text{balance} \end{array}$$

Step 4. At maturity, calculate interest from last partial payment. *Add* this interest to adjusted balance.

Ten days are left on note since last payment.

$$I = \$3,642.54 \times .04 \times \frac{10}{360}$$

$$I = \$4.05$$

$$\text{Balance owed} = \boxed{\$3,646.59} \left(\begin{array}{r} \$3,642.54 \\ +\quad 4.05 \end{array} \right)$$

Note that when Jeff makes two partial payments, Jeff's total interest is $46.59 ($27.78 + $14.76 + $4.05). If Jeff had repaid the entire loan after 90 days, his interest payment would have been $50—a total savings of $3.41.

Let's check your understanding of the last unit in this chapter.

LU 10–3 | PRACTICE QUIZ

Complete this **Practice Quiz** to see how you are doing.

For **extra help** from your authors—Sharon and Jeff—see the student DVD

You Tube™

Polly Flin borrowed $5,000 for 60 days at 8%. On day 10, Polly made a $600 partial payment. On day 40, Polly made a $1,900 partial payment. What is Polly's ending balance due under the U.S. Rule (assuming a 360-day year)?

✓ **Solutions**

$$\$5,000 \times .08 \times \frac{10}{360} = \$11.11$$

$$\begin{array}{r} \$600.00 \\ -\quad 11.11 \\ \hline \$588.89 \end{array} \qquad \begin{array}{r} \$5,000.00 \\ -\quad 588.89 \\ \hline \$4,411.11 \end{array}$$

$$\$4,411.11 \times .08 \times \frac{30}{360} = \$29.41$$

$$\begin{array}{r} \$1,900.00 \\ -\quad 29.41 \\ \hline \$1,870.59 \end{array} \qquad \begin{array}{r} \$4,411.11 \\ -\quad 1,870.59 \\ \hline \$2,540.52 \end{array}$$

$$\$2,540.52 \times .08 \times \frac{20}{360} = \$11.29$$

$$\begin{array}{r} \$\quad 11.29 \\ +\ 2,540.52 \\ \hline \boxed{\$2,551.81} \end{array}$$

LU 10–3a | EXTRA PRACTICE QUIZ WITH WORKED-OUT SOLUTION

Need more practice? Try this **Extra Practice Quiz** (check figure in the Interactive Chapter Organizer, p. 273). Worked-out Solution can be found in Appendix B at end of text.

Polly Flin borrowed $4,000 for 60 days at 4%. On day 15, Polly made a $700 partial payment. On day 40, Polly made a $2,000 partial payment. What is Polly's ending balance due under the U.S. Rule (assuming a 360-day year)?

INTERACTIVE CHAPTER ORGANIZER

Topic/procedure/formula	Examples	You try it*
Simple interest for months, p. 266 Interest = Principal × Rate × Time (I) (P) (R) (T)	$2,000 at 9% for 17 months $I = \$2,000 \times .09 \times \frac{17}{12}$ $I = \$255$	**Calculate simple interest** $4,000 at 3% for 18 months
Exact interest, pp. 266–267 $T = \dfrac{\text{Exact number of days}}{365}$ $I = P \times R \times T$	$1,000 at 10% from January 5 to February 20 $I = \$1,000 \times .10 \times \frac{46}{365}$ Feb. 20: 51 days Jan. 5: − 5 46 days $I = \$12.60$	**Calculate exact interest** $3,000 at 4% from January 8 to February 22
Ordinary interest (Banker's Rule), p. 267 $T = \dfrac{\text{Exact number of days}}{360}$ $I = P \times R \times T$ [Higher interest costs]	$I = \$1,000 \times .10 \times \frac{46}{360}$ (51 − 5) $I = \$12.78$	**Calculate ordinary interest** $3,000 at 4% from January 8 to February 22
Finding unknown in simple interest formula (use 360 days), p. 268 $I = P \times R \times T$	Use this example for illustrations of simple interest formula parts: $1,000 loan at 9%, 60 days $I = \$1,000 \times .09 \times \frac{60}{360} = \$15$	**Calculate interest (use 360 days)** $2,000 loan at 4%, 90 days
Finding the principal, pp. 268–269 $P = \dfrac{I}{R \times T}$	$P = \dfrac{\$15}{.09 \times \frac{60}{360}} = \dfrac{\$15}{.015} = \$1,000$	**Calculate principal** *Given:* interest, $20; rate, 4%; 90 days
Finding the rate, p. 269 $R = \dfrac{I}{P \times T}$	$R = \dfrac{\$15}{\$1,000 \times \frac{60}{360}} = \dfrac{\$15}{166.66666} = .09$ = 9% *Note:* We did not round the denominator.	**Calculate rate** *Given:* interest, $20; principal, $2,000; 90 days
Finding the time, p. 269 $T = \dfrac{I}{P \times R}$ (in years) Multiply answer by 360 days to convert answer to days for ordinary interest.	$T = \dfrac{\$15}{\$1,000 \times .09} = \dfrac{\$15}{\$90} = .1666666$ $.1666666 \times 360 = 59.99 = 60$ days	**Calculate number of days** *Given:* principal, $2,000; rate, 4%; interest, $20

(continues)

INTERACTIVE CHAPTER ORGANIZER

Topic/procedure/formula	Examples	You try it*

U.S. Rule (use 360 days), pp. 270–271
Calculate interest on principal from date of loan to date of first partial payment.
 	
Calculate adjusted balance by subtracting from principal the partial payment less interest cost. The process continues for future partial payments with the adjusted balance used to calculate cost of interest from last payment to present payment.
	12%, 120 days, $2,000
	Partial payments:
	  On day 40: $250
	  On day 60: $200
	First payment:
	$I = \$2,000 \times .12 \times \dfrac{40}{360}$
	$I = \$26.67$
	  $\$250.00$ payment
	$-\ \ \ 26.67$ interest
	  $\overline{\$223.33}$
	      $\$2,000.00$ principal
	     $-\ \ \ 223.33$
	     $\overline{\$1,776.67}$ adjusted balance
	Second payment:
	$I = \$1,776.67 \times .12 \times \dfrac{20}{360}$
	$I = \$11.84$
	  $\$200.00$ payment
	$-\ \ \ 11.84$ interest
	  $\overline{\$188.16}$
	      $\$1,776.67$
	     $-\ \ \ 188.16$
	     $\overline{\$1,588.51}$ adjusted balance
		Calculate balance due and total interest
		Given: $4,000; 4%; 90 days
		Partial payments:
		  On day 30: $400
		  On day 70: $300

Balance owed equals last adjusted balance plus interest cost from last partial payment to final due date.	*60 days left:*
	$\$1,588.51 \times .12 \times \dfrac{60}{360} = \$31.77$
	$\$1,588.51 + \$31.77 = \boxed{\$1,620.28\ \text{balance due}}$
	Total interest = $\$26.67$
	               11.84
	          $+\ \ 31.77$
	           $\overline{\$70.28}$	

KEY TERMS	Adjusted balance, *p. 270* Banker's Rule, *p. 267* Exact interest, *p. 266* Interest, *p. 265*	Maturity value, *p. 265* Ordinary interest, *p. 267* Principal, *p. 265* Simple interest, *p. 265*	Simple interest formula, *p. 266* Time, *p. 266* U.S. Rule, *p. 270*

Check Figures for Extra Practice Quizzes with Page References. (Worked-out Solutions in Appendix B.)	LU 10–1a (p. 268)
	1. $320
	2. $5,400
	3. $5,250
	4. $20,383.56;
	    Interest = $383.56
	5. $20,388.89;
	    Interest = $388.89
		LU 10–2a (p. 270)
		1. $900,000
		2. 9.33%
		3. 1,267 days
			LU 10–3a (p. 271)
			$1,318.78

*Worked-out solutions are in Appendix B.

Critical Thinking Discussion Questions with Chapter Concept Check

1. What is the difference between exact interest and ordinary interest? With the increase of computers in banking, do you think that the ordinary interest method is a dinosaur in business today?

2. Explain how to use the portion formula to solve the unknowns in the simple interest formula. Why would rounding the answer of the denominator result in an inaccurate final answer?

3. Explain the U.S. Rule. Why in the last step of the U.S. Rule is the interest added, not subtracted?

4. Do you believe the government bailout of banks is in the best interest of the country? Defend your position.

5. **Chapter Concept Check.** Referring to the chapter opener, prepare calculations based on the concepts in this chapter to prove credit unions would save you money in your personal life.

END-OF-CHAPTER PROBLEMS   ■connect™(plus+)   www.mhhe.com/slater11e

Check figures for odd-numbered problems in Appendix C.   Name _____   Date _____

DRILL PROBLEMS

Calculate the simple interest and maturity value for the following problems. Round to the nearest cent as needed.   *LU 10-1(1)*

	Principal	Interest rate	Time	Simple interest	Maturity value
10–1.	$17,000	$2\frac{1}{2}\%$	18 mo.		
10–2.	$21,000	5%	$1\frac{3}{4}$ yr.		
10–3.	$20,000	$6\frac{3}{4}\%$	9 mo.		

Complete the following, using ordinary interest: *LU 10-1(2)*

	Principal	Interest rate	Date borrowed	Date repaid	Exact time	Interest	Maturity value
10–4. eXcel	$1,000	8%	Mar. 8	June 9			
10–5. eXcel	$585	9%	June 5	Dec. 15			
10–6. eXcel	$1,200	12%	July 7	Jan. 10			

Complete the following, using exact interest: *LU 10-1(2)*

	Principal	Interest rate	Date borrowed	Date repaid	Exact time	Interest	Maturity value
10–7.	$1,000	8%	Mar. 8	June 9			
10–8.	$585	9%	June 5	Dec. 15			
10–9.	$1,200	12%	July 7	Jan. 10			

Solve for the missing item in the following (round to the nearest hundredth as needed):   *LU 10-2(1)*

	Principal	Interest rate	Time (months or years)	Simple interest
10–10.	$400	5%	?	$100
10–11.	?	7%	$1\frac{1}{2}$ years	$200
10–12.	$5,000	?	6 months	$300

10–13. Use the U.S. Rule to solve for total interest costs, balances, and final payments (use ordinary interest).   *LU 10-3(1)*

Given   Principal: $10,000, 8%, 240 days
Partial payments: On 100th day, $4,000
On 180th day, $2,000

WORD PROBLEMS

10–14. Diane Van Os decided to buy a new car since her credit union was offering such low interest rates. She borrowed $32,000 at 3.5% on December 26, 2012, and paid it off February 21, 2014. How much did she pay in interest? (Assume ordinary interest.)   *LU 10-1(2)*

10–15. Leslie Hart borrowed $15,000 to pay for her child's education at Riverside Community College. Leslie must repay the loan at the end of 9 months in one payment with $5\frac{1}{2}$% interest. How much interest must Leslie pay? What is the maturity value? *LU 10-1(1)*

10–16. On September 12, Jody Jansen went to Sunshine Bank to borrow $2,300 at 9% interest. Jody plans to repay the loan on
eXcel January 27. Assume the loan is on ordinary interest. What interest will Jody owe on January 27? What is the total
amount Jody must repay at maturity? *LU 10-1(2)*

10–17. Kelly O'Brien met Jody Jansen (Problem 10–16) at Sunshine Bank and suggested she consider the loan on exact interest.
eXcel Recalculate the loan for Jody under this assumption. How much would she save in interest? *LU 10-1(2)*

10–18. On May 3, 2014, Leven Corp. negotiated a short-term loan of $685,000. The loan is due October 1, 2014, and carries a
6.86% interest rate. Use ordinary interest to calculate the interest. What is the total amount Leven would pay on the
maturity date? *LU 10-1(2)*

10–19. Gordon Rosel went to his bank to find out how long it will take for $1,200 to amount to $1,650 at 8% simple interest.
eXcel Please solve Gordon's problem. Round time in years to the nearest tenth. *LU 10-2(1)*

10–20. Bill Moore is buying a used Winnebago. His April monthly interest at 12% was $125. What was Bill's principal balance
at the beginning of April? Use 360 days. *LU 10-2(1)*

10–21. On April 5, 2014, Janeen Camoct took out an $8\frac{1}{2}$% loan for $20,000. The loan is due March 9, 2015. Use ordinary
interest to calculate the interest. What total amount will Janeen pay on March 9, 2015? *LU 10-1(2)*

10–22. Sabrina Bowers took out the same loan as Janeen (Problem 10–21). Sabrina's terms, however, are exact interest. What is
Sabrina's difference in interest? What will she pay on March 9, 2015? *LU 10-1(2)*

10–23. Max Wholesaler borrowed $2,000 on a 10%, 120-day note. After 45 days, Max paid $700 on the note. Thirty days later, Max paid an additional $630. What is the final balance due? Use the U.S. Rule to determine the total interest and ending balance due. Use ordinary interest.   *LU 10-3(1)*

ADDITIONAL SET OF WORD PROBLEMS

10–24. Lane French had a bad credit rating and went to a local cash center. He took out a $100 loan payable in two weeks at $115. What is the percent of interest paid on this loan? Do not round denominator before dividing.   *LU 10-2(1)*

10–25. Joanne and Ed Greenwood built a new barn with an attached arena. To finance the loan, they paid $1,307 interest on $45,000 at 4.0%. What was the time, using exact interest (rounded up to the nearest day)?   *LU 10-2(1)*

10–26. On September 14, Jennifer Rick went to Park Bank to borrow $2,500 at $11\frac{3}{4}$% interest. Jennifer plans to repay the loan on January 27. Assume the loan is on ordinary interest. What interest will Jennifer owe on January 27? What is the total amount Jennifer must repay at maturity?   *LU 10-1(2)*

10–27. Steven Linden met Jennifer Rick (Problem 10–26) at Park Bank and suggested she consider the loan on exact interest. Recalculate the loan for Jennifer under this assumption.   *LU 10-1(2)*

10–28. Lance Lopes went to his bank to find out how long it will take for $1,000 to amount to $1,700 at 12% simple interest. **eXcel** Can you solve Lance's problem? Round time in years to the nearest tenth.   *LU 10-2(1)*

10–29. Andres Michael bought a new boat. He took out a loan for $24,500 at 4.5% interest for 2 years. He made a $4,500 partial payment at 2 months and another partial payment of $3,000 at 6 months. How much is due at maturity?   *LU 10-3(1)*

10–30. Shawn Bixby borrowed $17,000 on a 120-day, 12% note. After 65 days, Shawn paid $2,000 on the note. On day 89, Shawn paid an additional $4,000. What is the final balance due? Determine total interest and ending balance due by the U.S. Rule. Use ordinary interest. *LU 10-3(1)*

10–31. Carol Miller went to Europe and forgot to pay her $740 mortgage payment on her New Hampshire ski house. For her 59 days overdue on her payment, the bank charged her a penalty of $15. What was the rate of interest charged by the bank? Round to the nearest hundredth percent. (Assume 360 days.) *LU 10-2(1)*

10–32. Abe Wolf bought a new kitchen set at Sears. Abe paid off the loan after 60 days with an interest charge of $9. If Sears charges 10% interest, what did Abe pay for the kitchen set? (Assume 360 days.) *LU 10-2(1)*

10–33. Joy Kirby made a $300 loan to Robinson Landscaping at 11%. Robinson paid back the loan with interest of $6.60. How long in days was the loan outstanding? (Assume 360 days.) Check your answer. *LU 10-2(1)*

10–34. Molly Ellen, bookkeeper for Keystone Company, forgot to send in the payroll taxes due on April 15. She sent the payment *eXcel* November 8. The IRS sent her a penalty charge of 8% simple interest on the unpaid taxes of $4,100. Calculate the penalty. (Remember that the government uses exact interest.) *LU 10-1(2)*

10–35. Oakwood Plowing Company purchased two new plows for the upcoming winter. In 200 days, Oakwood must make a single payment of $23,200 to pay for the plows. As of today, Oakwood has $22,500. If Oakwood puts the money in a bank today, what rate of interest will it need to pay off the plows in 200 days? (Assume 360 days.) *LU 10-2(1)*

10–36. Debbie McAdams paid 8% interest on a $12,500 loan balance. Jan Burke paid $5,000 interest on a $62,500 loan. Based on 1 year: **(a)** What was the amount of interest paid by Debbie? **(b)** What was the interest rate paid by Jan? **(c)** Debbie and Jan are both in the 28% tax bracket. Since the interest is deductible, how much would Debbie and Jan each save in taxes? *LU 10-2(1)*

10–37. Janet Foster bought a computer and printer at Computerland. The printer had a $600 list price with a $100 trade discount and 2/10, n/30 terms. The computer had a $1,600 list price with a 25% trade discount but no cash discount. On the computer, Computerland offered Janet the choice of (1) paying $50 per month for 17 months with the 18th payment paying the remainder of the balance or (2) paying 8% interest for 18 months in equal payments. *LU 10-1(2)*

    a. Assume Janet could borrow the money for the printer at 8% to take advantage of the cash discount. How much would Janet save? (Assume 360 days.)

    b. On the computer, what is the difference in the final payment between choices 1 and 2?

 SUMMARY PRACTICE TEST You Tube™

Do you need help? The DVD has step-by-step worked-out solutions.

1. Lorna Hall's real estate tax of $2,010.88 was due on December 14, 2009. Lorna lost her job and could not pay her tax bill until February 27, 2010. The penalty for late payment is $6\frac{1}{2}$% ordinary interest. *(pp. 265–266) LU 10-1(1)*

    a. What is the penalty Lorna must pay?

    b. What is the total amount Lorna must pay on February 27?

2. Ann Hopkins borrowed $60,000 for her child's education. She must repay the loan at the end of 8 years in one payment with $5\frac{1}{2}$% interest. What is the maturity value Ann must repay? *(p. 266) LU 10-1(1)*

3. On May 6, Jim Ryan borrowed $14,000 from Lane Bank at $7\frac{1}{2}$% interest. Jim plans to repay the loan on March 11. Assume the loan is on ordinary interest. How much will Jim repay on March 11? *(p. 267)* *LU 10-1(2)*

4. Gail Ross met Jim Ryan (Problem 3) at Lane Bank. After talking with Jim, Gail decided she would like to consider the same loan on exact interest. Can you recalculate the loan for Gail under this assumption? *(pp. 266–267)* *LU 10-1(2)*

5. Claire Russell is buying a car. Her November monthly interest was $210 at $7\frac{3}{4}$% interest. What is Claire's principal balance (to the nearest dollar) at the beginning of November? Use 360 days. Do not round the denominator in your calculation. *(pp. 268–269)* *LU 10-2(1)*

6. Comet Lee borrowed $16,000 on a 6%, 90-day note. After 20 days, Comet paid $2,000 on the note. On day 50, Comet paid $4,000 on the note. What are the total interest and ending balance due by the U.S. Rule? Use ordinary interest. *(pp. 270–271)* *LU 10-3(1)*

SURF TO SAVE

PROBLEM 1
"Same as cash"?

Go to http://www.consumercity.org/sameascash.html and read the article. Suppose you purchased $5,000 worth of furniture and missed the 90-day deadline to pay it off. If you are charged 18% simple annual interest for the 90 days (1/4 year) on the $5,000, how much will you owe?

Discussion Questions

1 Why do so many companies offer these "same as cash" deals?

2. Do you think most consumers pay off their "same as cash" purchases within the free financing period? Why or why not?

PROBLEM 3
Costs of early out

Go to https://www.afbank.com/rates/cd.cfm. Find the rate for a 60-month certificate of deposit (CD). Now, navigate the site to find the penalty for early withdrawal on 60-month CDs. Calculate the penalty you would pay for early withdrawal if you initially invested $30,000.

Discussion Questions

1. Based on the penalties for early withdrawal, for what reasons would you consider taking money out early?

2. What is the value to the bank to have your money invested for a specific period of time in which you are not allowed to make withdrawals?

PROBLEM 2
Not free forever

Go to http://www.bestbuy.com/site/null/Credit-Cards/ pcmcat102500050032.c?id=pcmcat161200050007 and select a couple of products that would put you over the $149 minimum to receive the 6-month financing offer. Estimate how much interest you would owe if you missed the 6-month deadline.

Discussion Questions

1. What are the pros and cons of "same as cash" offers for the consumer?

2. What are the pros and cons of "same as cash" offers for the seller?

PROBLEM 4
Shopping for a new car

Go to http://www.kbb.com/new-cars and choose a new car you would like to purchase. Note the MSRP and then go to https://www.chase.com and click on Auto Loans. Under new car loans, click on check today's rates. Input your zip code, and click continue. Assume you are taking the loan out for 60 months. What would the simple interest and the maturity value be on your new car purchase?

Discussion Questions

1. What are some options for you to reduce the amount of money you would need to finance your new car purchase?

2. How does the purchase price of the car you desire impact whether you would want to finance your purchase or save money to pay for the car in full?

MOBILE APPS ✕

Simple Loan Calculator (Clean Micro, LLC) Calculates payments based on interest rates and time period based on the amount being borrowed.

Compound Interest Calculator Pro (Pulse2) Helps to figure interest earned as well as future values based on money invested.

INTERNET PROJECTS ✕

See text website
www.mhhe.com/slater11e_sse_ch10

SMART WAYS TO MANAGE STUDENT DEBT

PAYING OFF LOANS EARLY MAY NOT BE THE TOP PRIORITY. **BY MICHAEL STRATFORD**

■ OUR READER

WHO: **CAITLIN KILLAM, 24**
WHERE: **VISALIA, CAL.**
QUESTION: **SHOULD I REPAY MY STUDENT LOANS BEFORE BUILDING SAVINGS?**

SINCE GRADUATING FROM pharmacy school last May, Caitlin has been attempting a balancing act familiar to many recent graduates. She is staring down $120,000 in student debt while also gearing up to buy a house and save for retirement. Fortunately, as a pharmacist for a major retail chain, she's well compensated, with a salary of more than $100,000.

Caitlin knows this income gives her options most of her contemporaries don't enjoy. But that doesn't make managing life a breeze. "I just don't know what to do with my paychecks," Caitlin says. "Should I pay off all my loans right away? Or invest some of the money that I have?" Aside from student loans, Caitlin has no debt and has $20,000 in the bank. She'd like a new car, and hopes to move to Hawaii, where her mother lives, and buy a house there in five to ten years.

Those goals require cash. Caitlin's first step should be to build up her savings and to set aside a rainy-day fund, just in case. Because she has a secure job in a

growing field, a six-month reserve fund should be sufficient. Certificates of deposit are her best bet because CDs aren't easy to spend on a whim. "Having an emergency fund locked up in a CD makes it harder to nibble away at it for items that aren't really emergencies," says Andy Tilp, of Trillium Valley Financial Planning, in Sherwood, Ore.

Caitlin would also do well to buy long-term disability insurance. "Right now, her ability to earn a living is her best asset, and it's important to insure that asset," says William Stewart, of Rehmann Financial, in Troy, Mich. The cost to guarantee 60% of her salary if she were permanently disabled should be in the range of $300 a month—or less, if she can get a discount through her employer.

About those loans. Because Caitlin has other financial goals, her student loans aren't a priority. She's currently paying $1,400

a month on a ten-year repayment plan. If she temporarily extends the term of the debt to 25 years, she'll lower her monthly payment by as much as 50% and be able to put aside the difference for other purposes.

At her salary, Caitlin should aim to save as much as 25% to 30% of her take-home pay, advises Paul Baumbach, of Mallard Advisors, in Newark, Del. He also advises that she rejigger her student-debt repayment schedule while she saves for a down payment on a house in Hawaii, where real estate is expensive. In addition, Baumbach says, she should contribute the full $17,000 permitted in 2012 to her 401(k) once she is eligible for matching contributions. That will save about $6,300 in state and federal taxes.

Still, the longer the payment period on her student loans, the more interest Caitlin will pay overall. So if she can afford at some point to return to the ten-year schedule, she should try.

The principle remains the same even for young people who earn less than Caitlin: Set up a loan-repayment schedule you can live with so that you maximize your cash flow for living expenses and other purposes. Discipline works for everyone. ■

BUSINESS MATH ISSUE

Paying a loan back early is a smart strategy.

1. List the key points of the article and information to support your position.
2. Write a group defense of your position using math calculations to support your view.

Learning Unit 1–1 : Reading, Writing, and Rounding Whole Numbers

DRILL PROBLEMS

1. Express the following numbers in verbal form:

    a. 7,821 _____

    _____

    b. 160,501 _____

    _____

    c. 2,098,767 _____

    _____

    d. 58,003 _____

    _____

    e. 50,025,212,015 _____

    _____

2. Write in numeric form:

    a. Eighty thousand, two hundred eighty-one _____

    b. Fifty-eight thousand, three _____

    c. Two hundred eighty thousand, five _____

    d. Three million, ten _____

    e. Sixty-seven thousand, seven hundred sixty _____

3. Round the following numbers:

    a. To the nearest ten:

    76 _____   379 _____   855 _____   5,981 _____   206 _____

    b. To the nearest hundred:

    9,664 _____   2,074 _____   888 _____   271 _____   75 _____

    c. To the nearest thousand:

    21,486 _____   621 _____   3,504 _____   9,735 _____

4. Round off each number to the nearest ten, nearest hundred, nearest thousand, and round all the way. (Remember that you are rounding the original number each time.)

	Nearest ten	Nearest hundred	Nearest thousand	Round all the way
a. 4,752	_____	_____	_____	_____
b. 70,351	_____	_____	_____	_____
c. 9,386	_____	_____	_____	_____
d. 4,983	_____	_____	_____	_____
e. 408,119	_____	_____	_____	_____
f. 30,051	_____	_____	_____	_____

5. Name the place position (place value) of the underlined digit.

    a. 8,<u>3</u>48 _____   **e.** 2<u>8</u>,200,000,121 _____

    b. <u>9</u>,734 _____   **f.** <u>7</u>06,359,005 _____

    c. 3<u>4</u>7,107 _____   **g.** 27,<u>5</u>63,530 _____

    d. 7<u>2</u>3 _____

WORD PROBLEMS

6. Gim Smith was shopping for an Apple computer. He went to three different websites and found the computer he wanted at three different prices. At website A the price was $2,018, at website B the price was $1,985, and at website C the price was $2,030. What is the approximate price Gim will have to pay for the computer? Round to the nearest thousand. (Just one price.)

7. Amy Parker had to write a check at the bookstore when she purchased her books for the new semester. The total cost of the books was $564. How will she write this amount in verbal form on her check?

8. Matt Schaeffer was listening to the news and heard that steel production last week was one million, five hundred eighty-seven thousand tons. Express this amount in numeric form.

9. Jackie Martin is the city clerk and must go to the aldermen's meetings and take notes on what is discussed. At last night's meeting, they were discussing repairs for the public library, which will cost three hundred seventy-five thousand, nine hundred eighty-five dollars. Write this in numeric form as Jackie would.

10. A government survey revealed that 25,963,400 people are employed as office workers. To show the approximate number of office workers, round the number all the way.

11. Bob Donaldson wished to present his top student with a certificate of achievement at the end of the school year in 2004. To make it appear more official, he wanted to write the year in verbal form. How did he write the year?

12. Nancy Morrissey has a problem reading large numbers and determining place value. She asked her brother to name the place value of the 4 in the number 13,542,966. Can you tell Nancy the place value of the 4? What is the place value of the 3?

    The 4 is in the _____ place.

    The 3 is in the _____ place.

Learning Unit 1–2 : Adding and Subtracting Whole Numbers

DRILL PROBLEMS

1. Add by totaling each separate column:

	a.	b.	c.	d.	e.	f.	g.	h.
	668	43	493	36	716	535	751	75,730
	338	58	826	76	458	107	378	48,531
		96		43	397	778	135	15,797
				24	139	215	747	
					478	391	368	

2. Estimate by rounding all the way, and then add the actual numbers:

a.	b.	c.
580	1,470	475
971	7,631	837
548	4,383	213
430		775
506		432

d.	e.	f.
442	2,571	10,928
609	3,625	9,321
766	4,091	12,654
410	928	15,492
128		

3. Estimate by rounding all the way, and then subtract the actual numbers:

   a. 90
       − 38

   b. 91
       − 33

   c. 68
       − 59

   d. 981
       − 283

   e. 622
       − 328

   f. 1,125
       − 913

4. Subtract and check:

   a. 4,947
       − 4,362

   b. 3,724
       − 2,138

   c. 474,820
       − 85,847

   d. 50,000
       − 21,762

   e. 65,003
       − 24,987

   f. 15,715
       − 3,503

5. In the following sales report, total the rows and the columns, and then check that the grand total is the same both horizontally and vertically.

Salesperson	Region 1	Region 2	Region 3	Total
a. Becker	$ 5,692	$ 7,403	$ 3,591	
b. Edwards	7,652	7,590	3,021	
c. Graff	6,545	6,738	4,545	
d. Jackson	6,937	6,950	4,913	
e. Total				

WORD PROBLEMS

6. June Long owes $8,600 on her car loan for a new chevy volt, plus interest of $620. How much will it cost her to pay off this loan?

7. Sales at Rich's Convenience Store were $3,587 on Monday, $3,944 on Tuesday, $4,007 on Wednesday, $3,890 on Thursday, and $4,545 on Friday. What were the total sales for the week?

8. Poor's Variety Store sold $5,000 worth of lottery tickets in the first week of August; it sold $289 less in the second week. How much were the lottery ticket sales in the second week of August?

9. A truck weighed 9,550 pounds when it was empty. After being filled with rubbish, it was driven to the dump where it weighed in at 22,347 pounds. How much did the rubbish weigh?

10. Joanne Hoster had $610 in her checking account when she went to the bookstore. Joanne purchased an accounting book for $140, the working papers for $30, and a study guide for $35. After Joanne writes a check for the entire purchase, how much money will remain in her checking account?

11. A used Ford truck is advertised with a base price of $6,986 delivered. However, the window sticker on the truck reads as follows: tinted glass, $210; automatic transmission, $650; power steering, $210; power brakes, $215; safety locks, $95; air conditioning, $1,056. Estimate the total price, including the accessories, by rounding all the way and *then* calculating the exact price.

12. Four different stores are offering the same make and model of a Panasonic LCD television:

Store A	Store B	Store C	Store D
$1,285	$1,380	$1,440	$1,355

Find the difference between the highest price and the lowest price. Check your answer.

13. A Xerox XC830 copy machine has a suggested retail price of $1,395. The net price is $649. How much is the discount on the copy machine?

Learning Unit 1–3 : Multiplying and Dividing Whole Numbers

DRILL PROBLEMS

1. In the following problems, first estimate by rounding all the way, and then work the actual problems and check:

	Actual	**Estimate**	**Check**
a.	160 $\times$ 15		
b.	4,216 $\times$ 45		
c.	52,376 $\times$ 309		
d.	3,106 $\times$ 28		

2. Multiply; use the shortcut when applicable:

   a.   4,072
        × 100

   b.   5,100
        × 40

   c.   76,000
        × 1,200

   d. $93 \times 100,000$

3. Divide by rounding all the way; then do the actual calculation and check showing the remainder as a whole number.

      Actual   **Estimate**   **Check**

   a. $8\overline{)7,709}$

   b. $26\overline{)5,910}$

   c. $151\overline{)3,783}$

   d. $46\overline{)19,550}$

4. Divide by the shortcut method:

   a. $200\overline{)5,400}$ **b.** $50\overline{)5,650}$

   c. $1,200\overline{)43,200}$ **d.** $17,000\overline{)510,000}$

WORD PROBLEMS

5. Mia Kaminsky sells state lottery tickets in her variety store. If Mia's Variety Store sells 720 lottery tickets per day, how many tickets will be sold in a 7-day period?

6. Arlex Oil Company employs 100 people who are eligible for profit sharing. The financial manager has announced that the profits to be shared amount to $64,000. How much will each employee receive?

7. John Duncan's employer withheld $4,056 in federal taxes from his pay for the year. If equal deductions are made each week, what is John's weekly deduction?

8. Anne Domingoes drives a Volvo that gets 32 miles per gallon of gasoline. How many miles can she travel on 25 gallons of gas?

9. How many 8-inch pieces of yellow ribbon can be cut from a spool of ribbon that contains 6 yards (1 yard = 36 inches)?

10. The number of commercials aired per day on a local television station is 672. How many commercials are aired in 1 year?

11. The computer department at City College purchased 18 computers at a cost of $2,400 each. What was the total price for the computer purchase?

12. Net income for Goodwin's Partnership was $64,500. The five partners share profits and losses equally. What was each partner's share?

13. Ben Krenshaw's supervisor at the construction site told Ben to divide a load of 1,423 bricks into stacks containing 35 bricks each. How many stacks will there be when Ben has finished the job? How many "extra" bricks will there be?

Learning Unit 2–1 : Types of Fractions and Conversion Procedures

DRILL PROBLEMS

1. Identify the type of fraction—proper, improper, or mixed number:

   a. $\dfrac{7}{8}$

   b. $\dfrac{31}{29}$

   c. $\dfrac{29}{27}$

   d. $9\dfrac{3}{11}$

   e. $\dfrac{18}{5}$

   f. $9\dfrac{1}{8}$

2. Convert to a mixed number:

   a. $\dfrac{29}{4}$

   b. $\dfrac{137}{8}$

   c. $\dfrac{27}{5}$

   d. $\dfrac{29}{9}$

   e. $\dfrac{71}{8}$

   f. $\dfrac{43}{6}$

3. Convert the mixed number to an improper fraction:

   a. $9\dfrac{1}{5}$

   b. $12\dfrac{3}{11}$

   c. $4\dfrac{3}{7}$

   d. $20\dfrac{4}{9}$

   e. $10\dfrac{11}{12}$

   f. $17\dfrac{2}{3}$

4. Tell whether the fractions in each pair are equivalent or not:

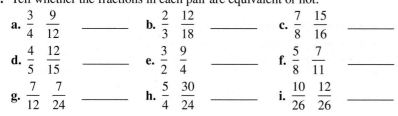

   a. $\dfrac{3}{4}$ $\dfrac{9}{12}$ _____

   b. $\dfrac{2}{3}$ $\dfrac{12}{18}$ _____

   c. $\dfrac{7}{8}$ $\dfrac{15}{16}$ _____

   d. $\dfrac{4}{5}$ $\dfrac{12}{15}$ _____

   e. $\dfrac{3}{2}$ $\dfrac{9}{4}$ _____

   f. $\dfrac{5}{8}$ $\dfrac{7}{11}$ _____

   g. $\dfrac{7}{12}$ $\dfrac{7}{24}$ _____

   h. $\dfrac{5}{4}$ $\dfrac{30}{24}$ _____

   i. $\dfrac{10}{26}$ $\dfrac{12}{26}$ _____

5. Find the greatest common divisor by the step approach and reduce to lowest terms:

a. $\dfrac{36}{42}$

b. $\dfrac{30}{75}$

c. $\dfrac{74}{148}$

d. $\dfrac{15}{600}$

e. $\dfrac{96}{132}$

f. $\dfrac{84}{154}$

6. Convert to higher terms:

a. $\dfrac{9}{10} = \dfrac{}{70}$

b. $\dfrac{2}{15} = \dfrac{}{30}$

c. $\dfrac{6}{11} = \dfrac{}{132}$

d. $\dfrac{4}{9} = \dfrac{}{36}$

e. $\dfrac{7}{20} = \dfrac{}{100}$

f. $\dfrac{7}{8} = \dfrac{}{560}$

WORD PROBLEMS

7. Ken drove to college in $3\frac{1}{4}$ hours. How many quarter-hours is that? Show your answer as an improper fraction.

8. Mary looked in the refrigerator for a dozen eggs. When she found the box, only 5 eggs were left. What fractional part of the box of eggs was left?

9. At a recent meeting of a local Boosters Club, 17 of the 25 members attending were men. What fraction of those in attendance were men?

10. By weight, water is two parts out of three parts of the human body. What fraction of the body is water?

11. Three out of 5 students who begin college will continue until they receive their degree. Show in fractional form how many out of 100 beginning students will graduate.

12. Tina and her friends came in late to a party and found only $\frac{3}{4}$ of a pizza remaining. In order for everyone to get some pizza, she wanted to divide it into smaller pieces. If she divides the pizza into twelfths, how many pieces will she have? Show your answer in fractional form.

13. Sharon and Spunky noted that it took them 35 minutes to do their exercise routine. What fractional part of an hour is that? Show your answer in lowest terms.

14. Norman and his friend ordered several pizzas, which were all cut into eighths. The group ate 43 pieces of pizza. How many pizzas did they eat? Show your answer as a mixed number.

Learning Unit 2–2 : Adding and Subtracting Fractions

DRILL PROBLEMS

1. Find the least common denominator (LCD) for each of the following groups of denominators using the prime numbers:

a. 8, 16, 32

b. 9, 15, 20

c. 12, 15, 32

d. 7, 9, 14, 28

2. Add and reduce to lowest terms or change to a mixed number if needed:

a. $\dfrac{1}{9} + \dfrac{4}{9}$

b. $\dfrac{5}{12} + \dfrac{8}{15}$

c. $\dfrac{7}{8} + \dfrac{5}{12}$

d. $7\dfrac{2}{3} + 5\dfrac{1}{4}$

e. $\dfrac{2}{3} + \dfrac{4}{9} + \dfrac{1}{4}$

3. Subtract and reduce to lowest terms:

a. $\dfrac{5}{9} - \dfrac{2}{9}$

b. $\dfrac{14}{15} - \dfrac{4}{15}$

c. $\dfrac{8}{9} - \dfrac{5}{6}$

d. $\dfrac{7}{12} - \dfrac{9}{16}$

e. $33\dfrac{5}{8} - 27\dfrac{1}{2}$

f. $9 - 2\dfrac{3}{7}$

g. $15\dfrac{1}{3} - 9\dfrac{7}{12}$

h. $92\dfrac{3}{10} - 35\dfrac{7}{15}$

i. $93 - 57\dfrac{5}{12}$

j. $22\dfrac{5}{8} - 17\dfrac{1}{4}$

WORD PROBLEMS

4. Dan Lund took a cross-country trip. He drove $5\dfrac{3}{8}$ hours on Monday, $6\dfrac{1}{2}$ hours on Tuesday, $9\dfrac{3}{4}$ hours on Wednesday, $6\dfrac{3}{8}$ hours on Thursday, and $10\dfrac{1}{4}$ hours on Friday. Find the total number of hours Dan drove in the first 5 days of his trip.

5. Sharon Parker bought 20 yards of material to make curtains. She used $4\dfrac{1}{2}$ yards for one bedroom window, $8\dfrac{3}{5}$ yards for another bedroom window, and $3\dfrac{7}{8}$ yards for a hall window. How much material did she have left?

6. Molly Ring visited a local gym and lost $2\dfrac{1}{4}$ pounds the first weekend and $6\dfrac{1}{8}$ pounds in week 2. What is Molly's total weight loss?

7. Bill Williams had to drive $46\frac{1}{4}$ miles to work. After driving $28\frac{5}{6}$ miles he noticed he was low on gas and had to decide whether he should stop to fill the gas tank. How many more miles does Bill have to drive to get to work?

8. Albert's Lumber Yard purchased $52\frac{1}{2}$ cords of lumber on Monday and $48\frac{3}{4}$ cords on Tuesday. It sold $21\frac{3}{8}$ cords on Friday. How many cords of lumber remain at Albert's Lumber Yard?

9. At Arlen Oil Company, where Dave Bursett is the service manager, it took $42\frac{1}{3}$ hours to clean five boilers. After a new cleaning tool was purchased, the time for cleaning five boilers was reduced to $37\frac{4}{9}$ hours. How much time was saved?

Learning Unit 2-3 : Multiplying and Dividing Fractions

DRILL PROBLEMS

1. Multiply; use the cancellation technique:

a. $\dfrac{6}{13} \times \dfrac{26}{12}$

b. $\dfrac{3}{8} \times \dfrac{2}{3}$

c. $\dfrac{5}{7} \times \dfrac{9}{10}$

d. $\dfrac{3}{4} \times \dfrac{9}{13} \times \dfrac{26}{27}$

e. $6\dfrac{2}{5} \times 3\dfrac{1}{8}$

f. $2\dfrac{2}{3} \times 2\dfrac{7}{10}$

g. $45 \times \dfrac{7}{9}$

h. $3\dfrac{1}{9} \times 1\dfrac{2}{7} \times \dfrac{3}{4}$

i. $\dfrac{3}{4} \times \dfrac{7}{9} \times 3\dfrac{1}{3}$

j. $\dfrac{1}{8} \times 6\dfrac{2}{3} \times \dfrac{1}{10}$

2. Multiply; do not use canceling but reduce by finding the greatest common divisor:

a. $\dfrac{3}{4} \times \dfrac{8}{9}$

b. $\dfrac{7}{16} \times \dfrac{8}{13}$

3. Multiply or divide as indicated:

a. $\dfrac{25}{36} \div \dfrac{5}{9}$

b. $\dfrac{18}{8} \div \dfrac{12}{16}$

c. $2\dfrac{6}{7} \div 2\dfrac{2}{5}$

d. $3\dfrac{1}{4} \div 16$

e. $24 \div 1\dfrac{1}{3}$

f. $6 \times \dfrac{3}{2}$

g. $3\dfrac{1}{5} \times 7\dfrac{1}{2}$

h. $\dfrac{3}{8} \div \dfrac{7}{4}$

i. $9 \div 3\dfrac{3}{4}$

j. $\dfrac{11}{24} \times \dfrac{24}{33}$

k. $\dfrac{12}{14} \div 27$

l. $\dfrac{3}{5} \times \dfrac{2}{7} \div \dfrac{3}{10}$

WORD PROBLEMS

4. Mary Smith plans to make 12 meatloafs to store in her freezer. Each meatloaf requires $2\dfrac{1}{4}$ pounds of ground beef. How much ground beef does Mary need?

5. Judy Carter purchased a real estate lot for $24,000. She sold it 2 years later for $1\dfrac{5}{8}$ times as much as she had paid for it. What was the selling price?

6. Lynn Clarkson saw an ad for a camcorder that cost $980. She knew of a discount store that would sell it to her for a markdown of $\frac{3}{20}$ off the advertised price. How much is the discount she can get?

7. To raise money for their club, the members of the Marketing Club purchased 68 bushels of popcorn to resell. They plan to repackage the popcorn in bags that hold $\frac{2}{21}$ of a bushel each. How many bags of popcorn will they be able to fill?

8. Richard Tracy paid a total of $375 for lumber costing $9\frac{3}{8}$ per foot. How many feet did he purchase?

9. While training for a marathon, Kristin Woods jogged $7\frac{3}{4}$ miles per hour for $2\frac{2}{3}$ hours. How many miles did Kristin jog?

10. On a map, 1 inch represents 240 miles. How many miles are represented by $\frac{3}{8}$ of an inch?

11. In Massachusetts, the governor wants to allot $\frac{1}{6}$ of the total sales tax collections to public education. The total sales tax collected is $2,472,000; how much will go to education?

Learning Unit 3–1 :   Rounding Decimals; Fraction and Decimal Conversions

DRILL PROBLEMS

1. Write in decimal:

   a. Sixty-two hundredths _____

   b. Six tenths _____

   c. Nine hundred fifty-three thousandths _____

   d. Four hundred one thousandths _____

   e. Six hundredths _____

2. Round each decimal to the place indicated:

   a. .8624 to the nearest thousandth _____

   b. .051 to the nearest tenth _____

   c. 8.207 to the nearest hundredth _____

   d. 2.094 to the nearest hundredth _____

   e. .511172 to the nearest ten thousandth _____

3. Name the place position of the underlined digit:

   a. .8$\underline{2}$6 _____

   b. .91$\underline{4}$ _____

   c. 3.$\underline{1}$169 _____

   d. 53.17$\underline{5}$ _____

   e. 1.017$\underline{4}$ _____

4. Convert to fractions (do not reduce):

    a. .91 _____

    b. .426 _____

    c. 2.516 _____

    d. $.62\frac{1}{2}$ _____

    e. 13.007 _____

    f. $5.03\frac{1}{4}$ _____

5. Convert to fractions and reduce to lowest terms:

    a. .4

    b. .44

    c. .53

    d. .336

    e. .096

    f. .125

    g. .3125

    h. .008

    i. 2.625

    j. 5.75

    k. 3.375

    l. 9.04

6. Convert the following fractions to decimals and round your answer to the nearest hundredth:

    a. $\frac{1}{8}$

    b. $\frac{7}{16}$

    c. $\frac{2}{3}$

    d. $\frac{3}{4}$

    e. $\frac{9}{16}$

    f. $\frac{5}{6}$

    g. $\frac{7}{9}$

    h. $\frac{38}{79}$

    i. $2\frac{3}{8}$

    j. $9\frac{1}{3}$

    k. $11\frac{19}{50}$

    l. $6\frac{21}{32}$

    m. $4\frac{83}{97}$

    n. $1\frac{2}{5}$

    o. $2\frac{2}{11}$

    p. $13\frac{30}{42}$

WORD PROBLEMS

7. Alan Angel got 2 hits in his first 7 times at bat. What is his average to the nearest thousandths place?

8. Bill Breen earned $1,555, and his employer calculated that Bill's total FICA deduction should be $118.9575. Round this deduction to the nearest cent.

9. At the local college, .566 of the students are men. Convert to a fraction. Do not reduce.

10. The average television set is watched 2,400 hours a year. If there are 8,760 hours in a year, what fractional part of the year is spent watching television? Reduce to lowest terms.

11. On Saturday, the employees at the Empire Fish Company work only $\frac{1}{3}$ of a day. How could this be expressed as a decimal to the nearest thousandth?

12. The North Shore Cinema has 610 seats. At a recent film screening there were 55 vacant seats. Show as a fraction the number of filled seats. Reduce as needed.

13. Michael Sullivan was planning his marketing strategy for a new product his company had produced. He was fascinated to discover that Rhode Island, the smallest state in the United States, was only twenty thousand, five hundred seven ten millionths the size of the largest state, Alaska. Write this number in decimal.

14. Bull Moose Company purchased a new manufacturing plant, located on an acre of land, for a total price of $2,250,000. The accountant determined that $\frac{3}{7}$ of the total price should be allocated as the price of the building. What decimal portion is the price of the building? Round to the nearest thousandth.

Learning Unit 3–2 : Adding, Subtracting, Multiplying, and Dividing Decimals

DRILL PROBLEMS

1. Rearrange vertically and add:

   a. $7.57 + 6.2 + 13.008 + 4.83$ **b.** $1.0625 + 4.0881 + .0775$

   c. $.903 + .078 + .17 + .1 + .96$ **d.** $3.38 + .175 + .0186 + .2$

2. Rearrange and subtract:

   a. $.96 - .43$ **b.** $.885 - .069$

   c. $11.67 - .935$ **d.** $261.2 - 8.08$

3. Multiply and round to the nearest tenth:

   a. $13.6 \times .02$ **b.** $1.73 \times .069$

c. 400×3.7 **d.** 0.025×5.6

4. Divide and round to the nearest hundredth:

a. $13.869 \div .6$ **b.** $1.0088 \div .14$ **c.** $18.7 \div 2.16$ **d.** $15.64 \div .34$

5. Complete by the shortcut method:

a. $6.87 \times 1,000$ **b.** $927,530 \div 100$ **c.** $27.2 \div 1,000$
d. $.21 \times 1,000$ **e.** 347×100 **f.** $347 \div 100$
g. $.0021 \div 10$ **h.** $85.44 \times 10,000$ **i.** 83.298×100
j. $23.0109 \div 100$

WORD PROBLEMS (Use *Business Math Handbook* Tables as Needed.)

6. Andy Hay noted his Ford Explorer odometer reading of 18,969.4 at the beginning of his vacation. At the end of his vacation the reading was 21,510.4. How many miles did he drive during his vacation?

7. Jeanne Allyn purchased 12.25 yards of ribbon for a craft project. The ribbon cost 37¢ per yard. What was the total cost of the ribbon?

8. Leo Green wanted to find out the gas mileage for his company truck. When he filled the gas tank, he wrote down the odometer reading of 9,650.7. The next time he filled the gas tank the odometer reading was 10,112.2. He looked at the gas pump and saw that he had taken 18.5 gallons of gas. Find the gas mileage per gallon for Leo's truck. Round to the nearest tenth.

9. At Halley's Rent-a-Car, the cost per day to rent a medium-size car is $35.25 plus 37¢ a mile. What would be the charge to rent this car for 1 day if you drove 205.4 miles?

10. A trip to Mexico costs 6,000 pesos. What is this in U.S. dollars? Check your answer.

11. If a commemorative gold coin weighs 7.842 grams, find the number of coins that can be produced from 116 grams of gold. Round to the nearest whole number.

Learning Unit 4–1 : The Checking Account

DRILL PROBLEMS

1. The following is a deposit slip made out by Fred Young of the F. W. Young Company.
    a. How much cash did Young deposit? _____
    b. How many checks did Young deposit? _____
    c. What was the total amount deposited? _____

<table>
<tr><td colspan="3"></td><td>DESCRIPTION</td><td>DOLLARS</td><td>CENTS</td><td colspan="3">ADDITIONAL CHECKS</td></tr>
<tr><td colspan="3" rowspan="2">Fleet Bank
This deposit is subject to: proof and verification, the Uniform Commercial Code, the collection and availability policy of this bank.</td><td></td><td></td><td></td><td>DESCRIPTION</td><td>DOLLARS</td><td>CENTS</td></tr>
<tr><td>BILLS</td><td>415</td><td>XX</td><td>7.</td><td></td><td></td></tr>
<tr><td>Checking Deposit</td><td colspan="2">DATE 3/27/14</td><td>COIN</td><td>15</td><td>64</td><td>8.</td><td></td><td></td></tr>
<tr><td>TO THE ACCOUNT OF</td><td colspan="2"></td><td>LIST CHECKS
1.53-1297</td><td>188</td><td>44</td><td>9.</td><td></td><td></td></tr>
<tr><td>NAME</td><td colspan="2"></td><td>2.51-1509</td><td>98</td><td>37</td><td>10.</td><td></td><td></td></tr>
<tr><td>(PLEASE PRINT)
PLEASE ENDORSE ALL CHECKS</td><td colspan="2">PLEASE ENTER CLEARLY
YOUR ACCOUNT NUMBER</td><td>3.53-1290</td><td>150</td><td>06</td><td>11.</td><td></td><td></td></tr>
<tr><td colspan="3"></td><td>4.</td><td></td><td></td><td>12.</td><td></td><td></td></tr>
<tr><td colspan="3"></td><td>5.</td><td></td><td></td><td>13.</td><td></td><td></td></tr>
<tr><td colspan="3"></td><td>6.</td><td></td><td></td><td>14.</td><td></td><td></td></tr>
<tr><td colspan="3"></td><td>SUB TOTAL
ITEMS 1-6</td><td></td><td></td><td>SUB TOTAL
ITEMS 7-14</td><td></td><td></td></tr>
<tr><td colspan="3"></td><td colspan="3"></td><td>TOTAL</td><td></td><td></td></tr>
</table>

⑆ 5 2 ⑈ 2 0 0 0 ⑈ 7 ⑈

2. Blackstone Company had a balance of $2,173.18 in its checking account. Henry James, Blackstone's accountant, made a deposit that consisted of 2 fifty-dollar bills, 120 ten-dollar bills, 6 five-dollar bills, 14 one-dollar bills, $9.54 in change, plus two checks they had accepted, one for $16.38 and the other for $102.50. Find the amount of the deposit and the new balance in Blackstone's checking account.

3. Answer the following questions using the illustration:

a. Who is the payee? _____

b. Who is the drawer? _____

c. Who is the drawee? _____

d. What is the bank's identification number _____

e. What is Jones Company's account number? _____

f. What was the balance in the account on September 30? _____

g. For how much did Jones write Check No. 113? _____

h. How much was deposited on October 1? _____

i. How much was left after Check No. 113 was written? _____

4. Write each of the following amounts in verbal form as you would on a check:

a. $40 _____

b. $245.75 _____

c. $3.98 _____

d. $1,205.05 _____

e. $3,013 _____

f. $510.10 _____

Learning Unit 4–2 : Bank Statement and Reconciliation Process; Trends in Online Banking

WORD PROBLEMS

1. Find the bank balance on January 31.

Date	Checks and payments			Deposits	Balance
January 1					401.17
January 2	108.64				_____
January 5	116.50			432.16	_____
January 6	14.92	150.00	10.00		_____
January 11	12.29			633.89	_____
January 18	108.64	18.60			_____
January 25	43.91	23.77		657.22	_____
January 26	75.00				_____
January 31	6.75 sc				_____

2. Joe Madruga, of Madruga's Taxi Service, received a bank statement for the month of May showing a balance of $932.36. His records show that the bank had not yet recorded two of his deposits, one for $521.50 and the other for $98.46. There are outstanding checks in the amounts of $41.67, $135.18, and $25.30. The statement also shows a service charge of $3.38. The balance in the check register is $1,353.55. Prepare a bank reconciliation for Madruga's as of May 31.

3. In reconciling the checking account for Nasser Enterprises, Beth Accomando found that the bank had collected a $3,000 promissory note on the company's behalf and had charged a $15 collection fee. There was also a service charge of $7.25. What amount should be added/subtracted from the checkbook balance to bring it up to date?

    Add: _____   Deduct: _____

4. In reconciling the checking account for Colonial Cleaners, Steve Papa found that a check for $34.50 had been recorded in the check register as $43.50. The bank returned an NSF check in the amount of $62.55. Interest income of $8.25 was earned and a service charge of $10.32 was assessed. What amount should be added/subtracted from the checkbook balance to bring it up to date?

    Add: _____   Deduct: _____

5. Matthew Stokes was completing the bank reconciliation for Parker's Tool and Die Company. The check register balance was $1,503.67. Matthew found that a $76.00 check had been recorded in the check register as $67.00; that a note for $1,500 had been collected by the bank for Parker's and the collection fee was $12.00; that $15.60 interest was earned on the account; and that an $8.35 service charge had been assessed. What should the check register balance be after Matthew updates it with the bank reconciliation information?

6. Consumers, community activists, and politicians are decrying the new line of accounts because several include a $3 service charge for some customers who use bank tellers for transactions that can be done through an automated teller machine. Bill Wade banks at a local bank that charges this fee. He was having difficulty balancing his checkbook because he did not notice this fee on his bank statement. His bank statement showed a balance of $822.18. Bill's checkbook had a balance of $206.48. Check No. 406 for $116.08 and Check No. 407 for $12.50 were outstanding. A $521 deposit was not on the statement. Bill has his payroll check electronically deposited to his checking account—the payroll check was for $1,015.12. (Bill's payroll checks vary each month.) There are also a $1 service fee and a teller fee of $6. Complete Bill's bank reconciliation.

7. At First National Bank in San Diego, some customers have to pay $25 each year as an ATM card fee. John Levi banks at First National Bank and just received his bank statement showing a balance of $829.25; his checkbook balance is $467.40. The bank statement shows an ATM card fee of $25.00, teller fee of $9.00, interest of $1.80, and John's $880 IRS refund check, which was processed by the IRS and deposited to his account. John has two checks that have not cleared—No. 112 for $620.10 and No. 113 for $206.05. There is also a deposit in transit for $1,312.10. Prepare John's bank reconciliation.

Learning Unit 5–1 : Solving Equations for the Unknown

DRILL PROBLEMS

1. Write equations for the following situations. Use N for the unknown number. Do not solve the equations.
   a. Three times a number is 180.
   b. A number increased by 13 equals 25.
   c. Seven less than a number is 5.
   d. Fifty-seven decreased by 3 times a number is 21.
   e. Fourteen added to one-third of a number is 18.

   f. Twice the sum of a number and 4 is 32.

   g. Three-fourths of a number is 9.

   h. Two times a number plus 3 times the same number plus 8 is 68.

2. Solve for the unknown number:
   a. $C + 40 = 90$ b. $29 + M = 44$ c. $D - 77 = 98$

   d. $7N = 63$ e. $\dfrac{X}{12} = 11$ f. $3Q + 4Q + 2Q = 108$

   g. $H + 5H + 3 = 57$ h. $2(N - 3) = 62$ i. $\dfrac{3R}{4} = 27$

   j. $E - 32 = 41$ k. $5(2T - 2) = 120$ l. $12W - 5W = 98$

m. $49 - X = 37$ **n.** $12(V + 2) = 84$ **o.** $7D + 4 = 5D + 14$

p. $7(T - 2) = 2T - 9$

Learning Unit 5–2 : Solving Word Problems for the Unknown

WORD PROBLEMS

1. A sweater at the Gap was marked down $30. The sale price was $50. What was the original price?

Unknown(s)	Variables(s)	Relationship

2. Goodwin's Corporation found that $\frac{2}{3}$ of its employees were vested in their retirement plan. If 124 employees are vested, what is the total number of employees at Goodwin's?

Unknown(s)	Variables(s)	Relationship

3. Eileen Haskin's utility and telephone bills for the month totaled $180. The utility bill was 3 times as much as the telephone bill. How much was each bill?

Unknown(s)	Variables(s)	Relationship

4. Ryan and his friends went to the golf course to hunt for golf balls. Ryan found 15 more than $\frac{1}{3}$ of the total number of golf balls that were found. How many golf balls were found if Ryan found 75 golf balls?

Unknown(s)	Variables(s)	Relationship

5. Linda Mills and Sherry Somers sold 459 tickets for the Advertising Club's raffle. If Linda sold 8 times as many tickets as Sherry, how many tickets did each one sell?

Unknown(s)	Variables(s)	Relationship

6. Jason Mazzola wanted to buy a suit at Giblee's. Jason did not have enough money with him, so Mr. Giblee told him he would hold the suit if Jason gave him a deposit of $\frac{1}{5}$ of the cost of the suit. Jason agreed and gave Mr. Giblee $79. What was the price of the suit?

Unknown(s)	Variables(s)	Relationship

7. Peter sold watches ($7) and necklaces ($4) at a flea market. Total sales were $300. People bought 3 times as many watches as necklaces. How many of each did Peter sell? What were the total dollar sales of each?

Unknown(s)	Variables(s)	Price	Relationship

8. Peter sold watches ($7) and necklaces ($4) at a flea market. Total sales for 48 watches and necklaces were $300. How many of each did Peter sell? What were the total dollar sales of each?

Unknown(s)	Variables(s)	Price	Relationship

9. A 3,000 piece of direct mailing cost $1,435. Printing cost is $550, about $3\frac{1}{2}$ times the cost of typesetting. How much did the typesetting cost? Round to the nearest cent.

Unknown(s)	Variables(s)	Relationship

10. In 2014, Tony Rigato, owner of MRM, saw an increase in sales to $13.5 million. Rigato states that since 2011, sales have more than tripled. What were his sales in 2011?

Unknown(s)	Variables(s)	Relationship

Learning Unit 6–1 : Conversions

DRILL PROBLEMS

1. Convert the following to percents; round to the nearest tenth of a percent if needed:

a.	.04	_____ %	**b.**	.729	_____ %	**c.**	.009	_____ %
d.	8.3	_____ %	**e.**	5.26	_____ %	**f.**	6	_____ %
g.	.0105	_____ %	**h.**	.1180	_____ %	**i.**	5.0375	_____ %
j.	.862	_____ %	**k.**	.2615	_____ %	**l.**	.8	_____ %
m.	.025	_____ %	**n.**	.06	_____ %			

2. Convert the following to decimals; do not round:

a. 68% _____   **b.** .09% _____   **c.** 4.7% _____

d. 9.67% _____   **e.** .2% _____   **f.** $\frac{1}{4}$% _____

g. .76% _____   **h.** 110% _____   **i.** $12\frac{1}{2}$% _____

j. 5% _____   **k.** .004% _____   **l.** $7\frac{5}{10}$% _____

m. $\frac{3}{4}$% _____   **n.** 1% _____

3. Convert the following to percents; round to the nearest tenth of a percent if needed:

a. $\frac{7}{10}$ _____ %   **b.** $\frac{1}{5}$ _____ %   **c.** $1\frac{5}{8}$ _____ %

d. $\frac{2}{7}$ _____ %   **e.** 2 _____ %   **f.** $\frac{14}{100}$ _____ %

g. $\frac{1}{6}$ _____ %   **h.** $\frac{1}{2}$ _____ %   **i.** $\frac{3}{5}$ _____ %

j. $\frac{3}{25}$ _____ %   **k.** $\frac{5}{16}$ _____ %   **l.** $\frac{11}{50}$ _____ %

m. $4\frac{3}{4}$ _____ %   **n.** $\frac{3}{200}$ _____ %

4. Convert the following to fractions in simplest form:

a. 40% _____   **b.** 15% _____   **c.** 50% _____

d. 75% _____   **e.** 35% _____   **f.** 85% _____

g. $12\frac{1}{2}$% _____   **h.** $37\frac{1}{2}$% _____   **i.** $33\frac{1}{3}$% _____

j. 3% _____   **k.** 8.5% _____   **l.** $5\frac{3}{4}$% _____

m. 100% _____   **n.** 10% _____

5. Complete the following table by finding the missing fraction, decimal, or percent equivalent:

	Fraction	Decimal	Percent		Fraction	Decimal	Percent
a.	_____	.25	25%	h.	$\frac{1}{6}$	$.16\bar{6}$	_____
b.	$\frac{3}{8}$	_____	$37\frac{1}{2}\%$	i.	_____	$.083\bar{3}$	$8\frac{1}{3}\%$
c.	$\frac{1}{2}$	.5	_____	j.	$\frac{1}{9}$	_____	$11\frac{1}{9}\%$
d.	$\frac{2}{3}$	_____	$66\frac{2}{3}\%$	k.	_____	.3125	$31\frac{1}{4}\%$
e.	_____	.4	40%	l.	$\frac{3}{40}$	.075	_____
f.	$\frac{3}{5}$	.6	_____	m.	$\frac{1}{5}$	_____	20%
g.	$\frac{7}{10}$	_____	70%	n.	_____	1.125	$112\frac{1}{2}\%$

WORD PROBLEMS

6. If in 2013, Mutual of New York reported that 80% of its new sales came from existing clients. What fractional part of its new sales came from existing clients? Reduce to simplest form.

7. Six hundred ninety corporations and design firms competed for the Industrial Design Excellence Award (IDEA). Twenty were selected as the year's best and received gold awards. Show the gold award winners as a fraction; then show what percent of the entrants received gold awards. Round to the nearest tenth of a percent.

8. If in the first half of 2013, stock prices in the Standard & Poor's 500-stock index rose 4.1%. Show the increase as a decimal.

9. In the recent banking crisis, many banks were unable to cover their bad loans. Citicorp, the nation's largest real estate lender, was reported as having only enough reserves to cover 39% of its bad loans. What fractional part of its loan losses was covered?

10. Dave Mattera spent his vacation in Las Vegas. He ordered breakfast in his room, and when he went downstairs to the coffee shop, he discovered that the same breakfast was much less expensive. He had paid 1.884 times as much for the breakfast in his room. What was the percent of increase for the breakfast in his room?

11. Putnam Management Company of Boston recently increased its management fee by .09%. What is the increase as a decimal? What is the same increase as a fraction?

12. Joel Black and Karen Whyte formed a partnership and drew up a partnership agreement, with profits and losses to be divided equally after each partner receives a $7\frac{1}{2}\%$ return on his or her capital contribution. Show their return on investment as a decimal and as a fraction. Reduce.

Learning Unit 6–2 :   Application of Percents—Portion Formula

DRILL PROBLEMS

1. Fill in the amount of the base, rate, and portion in each of the following statements:
   a. The Logans spend $4,000 a month on food, which is 30% of their monthly income of $20,000.
      Base _____   Rate _____   Portion _____

   b. Rocky Norman got a $15 discount when he purchased a new camera. This was 20% off the sticker price of $75.
      Base _____   Rate _____   Portion _____

   c. Mary Burns got a 12% senior citizens discount when she bought a $7.00 movie ticket. She saved $0.84.
      Base _____   Rate _____   Portion _____

   d. Arthur Bogey received a commission of $13,500 when he sold the Brown's house for $225,000. His commission rate is 6%.
      Base _____   Rate _____   Portion _____

   e. Leo Davis deposited $5,000 in a certificate of deposit (CD). A year later he received an interest payment of $450, which was a yield of 9%.
      Base _____   Rate _____   Portion _____

   f. Grace Tremblay is on a diet that allows her to eat 1,600 calories per day. For breakfast she had 600 calories, which is $37\frac{1}{2}$% of her allowance.
      Base _____   Rate _____   Portion _____

2. Find the portion; round to the nearest hundredth if necessary:

a. 7% of 74 _____	b. 12% of 205 _____	c. 16% of 630 _____
d. 7.5% of 920 _____	e. 25% of 1,004 _____	f. 10% of 79 _____
g. 103% of 44 _____	h. 30% of 78 _____	i. .2% of 50 _____
j. 1% of 5,622 _____	k. $6\frac{1}{4}$% of 480 _____	l. 150% of 10 _____
m. 100% of 34 _____	n. $\frac{1}{2}$% of 27 _____	

3. Find the rate; round to the nearest tenth of a percent as needed:

a. 30 is what percent of 90? _____	b. 6 is what percent of 200? _____
c. 275 is what percent of 1,000? _____	d. .8 is what percent of 44? _____
e. 67 is what percent of 2,010? _____	f. 550 is what percent of 250? _____
g. 13 is what percent of 650? _____	h. $15 is what percent of $455? _____
i. .05 is what percent of 100? _____	j. $6.25 is what percent of $10? _____

4. Find the base; round to the nearest tenth as needed:

a. 63 is 30% of _____	b. 60 is 33% of _____	c. 150 is 25% of _____
d. 47 is 1% of _____	e. $21 is 120% of _____	f. 2.26 is 40% of _____
g. 75 is $12\frac{1}{2}$% of _____	h. 18 is 22.2% of _____	i. $37.50 is 50% of _____
j. 250 is 100% of _____		

5. Find the percent of increase or decrease; round to the nearest tenth percent as needed:

Last year	This year	Amount of change	Percent of change
a. 5,962	4,378	_____	_____
b. $10,995	$12,250	_____	_____
c. 120,000	140,000	_____	_____
d. 120,000	100,000	_____	_____

WORD PROBLEMS

6. A machine that originally cost $8,000 was sold for $800 at the end of 5 years. What percent of the original cost is the selling price?

7. Joanne Byrne invested $75,000 in a candy shop and is making 12% per year on her investment. How much money per year is she making on her investment?

8. There was a fire in Bill Porper's store that caused 2,780 inventory items to be destroyed. Before the fire, 9,565 inventory items were in the store. What percent of inventory was destroyed? Round to nearest tenth percent.

9. Elyse's Dress Shoppe makes 25% of its sales for cash. If the cash receipts on January 21 were $799, what were the total sales for the day?

10. The YMCA is holding a fund-raiser to collect money for a new gym floor. So far it has collected $7,875, which is 63% of the goal. What is the amount of the goal? How much more money must the YMCA collect?

11. Leslie Tracey purchased her home for $51,500. She sold it last year for $221,200. What percent profit did she make on the sale? Round to nearest tenth percent.

12. Maplewood Park Tool & Die had an annual production of 375,165 units this year. This is 140% of the annual production last year. What was last year's annual production?

Learning Unit 7–1 :   Trade Discounts—Single and Chain*

DRILL PROBLEMS

1. Calculate the trade discount amount for each of the following items:

Item	List price	Trade discount	Trade discount amount
a. iPhone	$ 200	20%	_____
b. Flat-screen TV	$1,200	30%	_____
c. Suit	$ 500	10%	_____
d. Bicycle	$ 800	$12\frac{1}{2}$	_____
e. David Yurman bracelet	$ 950	40%	_____

2. Calculate the net price for each of the following items:

Item	List price	Trade discount amount	Net price
a. Home Depot table	$600	$250	_____
b. Bookcase	$525	$129	_____
c. Rocking chair	$480	$ 95	_____

3. Fill in the missing amount for each of the following items:

Item	List price	Trade discount amount	Net price
a. Sears electric saw	_____	$19	$56.00
b. Electric drill	$90	_____	$68.50
c. Ladder	$56	$15.25	_____

4. For each of the following, find the percent paid (complement of trade discount) and the net price:

List price	Trade discount	Percent paid	Net price
a. $45	15%	_____	_____
b. $195	12.2%	_____	_____
c. $325	50%	_____	_____
d. $120	18%	_____	_____

5. In each of the following examples, find the net price equivalent rate and the single equivalent discount rate:

Chain discount	Net price equivalent rate	Single equivalent discount rate
a. 25/5	_____	_____
b. 15/15	_____	_____
c. 15/10/5	_____	_____
d. 12/12/6	_____	_____

*Freight problems to be shown in LU 7–2 material.

6. In each of the following examples, find the net price and the trade discount:

List price	Chain discount	Net price	Trade discount
a. $5,000	10/10/5	_____	_____
b. $7,500	9/6/3	_____	_____
c. $898	20/7/2	_____	_____
d. $1,500	25/10	_____	_____

7. The list price of a handheld calculator is $19.50, and the trade discount is 18%. Find the trade discount amount.

8. The list price of a silver picture frame is $29.95, and the trade discount is 15%. Find the trade discount amount and the net price.

9. The net price of a set of pots and pans is $65, and the trade discount is 20%. What is the list price?

10. Jennie's Variety Store has the opportunity to purchase candy from three different wholesalers; each of the wholesalers offers a different chain discount. Company A offers 25/5/5, Company B offers 20/10/5, and Company C offers 15/20. Which company should Jennie deal with? *Hint:* Choose the company with the highest single equivalent discount rate.

11. The list price of a television set is $625. Find the net price after a series discount of 30/20/10.

12. Mandy's Accessories Shop purchased 12 purses with a total list price of $726. What was the net price of each purse if the wholesaler offered a chain discount of 25/20?

13. Kransberg Furniture Store purchased a bedroom set for $1,097.25 from Furniture Wholesalers. The list price of the set was $1,995. What trade discount rate did Kransberg receive?

14. Susan Monk teaches second grade and receives a discount at the local art supply store. Recently she paid $47.25 for art supplies after receiving a chain discount of 30/10. What was the regular price of the art supplies?

Learning Unit 7–2 :   Cash Discounts, Credit Terms, and Partial Payments

DRILL PROBLEMS

1. Complete the following table:

Date of invoice	Date goods received	Terms	Last day of discount period	End of credit period
a. February 8		2/10, n/30		
b. August 26		2/10, n/30		
c. October 17		3/10, n/60		
d. March 11	May 10	3/10, n/30, ROG		
e. September 14		2/10, EOM		
f. May 31		2/10, EOM		

2. Calculate the cash discount and the net amount paid.

Invoice amount	Cash discount rate	Discount amount	Net amount paid
a. $75	3%		
b. $1,559	2%		
c. $546.25	2%		
d. $9,788.75	1%		

3. Use the complement of the cash discount to calculate the net amount paid. Assume all invoices are paid within the discount period.

Terms of invoice	Amount of invoice	Complement	Net amount paid
a. 3/10, n/30	$1,400		
b. 3/10, n/30 ROG	$4,500		
c. 2/10, EOM	$375.50		
d. 1/15, n/45	$3,998		

4. Calculate the amount of cash discount and the net amount paid.

Date of invoice	Terms of invoice	Amount of invoice	Date paid	Cash discount	Amount paid
a. January 12	2/10, n/30	$5,320	January 22		
b. May 28	2/10, n/30	$975	June 7		
c. August 15	2/10, n/30	$7,700	August 26		
d. March 8	2/10, EOM	$480	April 10		
e. January 24	3/10, n/60	$1,225	February 3		

5. Complete the following table:

Total invoice	Freight charges included in invoice total	Date of invoice	Terms of invoice	Date of payment	Cash discount	Amount paid
a. $852	$12.50	3/19	2/10, n/30	3/29		
b. $669.57	$15.63	7/28	3/10, EOM	9/10		
c. $500	$11.50	4/25	2/10, n/60	6/5		
d. $188	$9.70	1/12	2/10, EOM	2/10		

6. In the following table, assume that all the partial payments were made within the discount period.

Amount of invoice	Terms of invoice	Partial payment	Amount to be credited	Balance outstanding
a. $481.90	2/10, n/30	$90.00	_____	_____
b. $1,000	2/10, EOM	$500.00	_____	_____
c. $782.88	3/10, n/30, ROG	$275.00	_____	_____
d. $318.80	2/15, n/60	$200.00	_____	_____

WORD PROBLEMS

7. Ray Chemical Company received an invoice for $16,500, dated March 14, with terms of 2/10, n/30. If the invoice was paid March 22, what was the amount due?

8. On May 27, Trotter Hardware Store received an invoice for trash barrels purchased for $13,650 with terms of 3/10, EOM; the freight charge, which is included in the price, is $412. What are **(a)** the last day of the discount period and **(b)** the amount of the payment due on this date?

9. The Glass Sailboat received an invoice for $930.50 with terms 2/10, n/30 on April 19. On April 29, it sent a payment of $430.50. **(a)** How much credit will be given on the total due? **(b)** What is the new balance due?

10. Dallas Ductworks offers cash discounts of 2/10, 1/15, n/30 on all purchases. If an invoice for $544 dated July 18 is paid on August 2, what is the amount due?

11. The list price of a Luminox watch is $299.90 with trade discounts of 10/20 and terms of 3/10, n/30. If a retailer pays the invoice within the discount period, what amount must the retailer pay?

12. The invoice of a sneakers supplier totaled $2,488.50, was dated February 7, and offered terms 2/10, ROG. The shipment of sneakers was received on March 7. What are **(a)** the last date of the discount period and **(b)** the amount of the discount that will be lost if the invoice is paid after that date?

13. Starburst Toy Company receives an invoice amounting to $1,152.30 with terms of 2/10, EOM and dated November 6. If a partial payment of $750 is made on December 8, what are **(a)** the credit given for the partial payment and **(b)** the balance due on the invoice?

14. Todd's Sporting Goods received an invoice for soccer equipment dated July 26 with terms 3/10, 1/15, n/30 in the amount of $3,225.83, which included shipping charges of $375.50. If this bill is paid on August 5, what amount must be paid?

Learning Unit 8–1 :   Markups Based on Cost (100%)

DRILL PROBLEMS

1. Fill in the missing numbers:

	Cost	Dollar markup	Selling price
a.	$14.80	$4.10	_____
b.	$8.32	_____	$11.04
c.	$25.27	_____	$29.62
d.	_____	$75.00	$165.00
e.	$86.54	$29.77	_____

2. Calculate the markup based on cost; round to the nearest cent.

	Cost	Markup (percent of cost)	Dollar markup
a.	$425.00	30%	_____
b.	$1.52	20%	_____
c.	$9.90	$12\frac{1}{2}$	_____
d.	$298.10	50%	_____
e.	$74.25	38%	_____
f.	$552.25	100%	_____

3. Calculate the dollar markup and rate of the markup as a percent of cost, rounding percents to nearest tenth percent. Verify your result, which may be slightly off due to rounding.

	Cost	Selling price	Dollar markup	Markup (percent of cost)	Verify
a.	$2.50	$4.50	_____	_____	_____
b.	$12.50	$19.00	_____	_____	_____
c.	$0.97	$1.25	_____	_____	_____
d.	$132.25	$175.00	_____	_____	_____
e.	$65.00	$89.99	_____	_____	_____

4. Calculate the dollar markup and the selling price.

	Cost	Markup (percent of cost)	Dollar markup	Selling price
a.	$2.20	40%	_____	_____
b.	$2.80	16%	_____	_____
c.	$840.00	$12\frac{1}{2}\%$	_____	_____
d.	$24.36	30%	_____	_____

5. Calculate the cost, rounding to the nearest cent.

Selling price	Rate of markup based on cost	Cost
a. $1.98	30%	_____
b. $360.00	60%	_____
c. $447.50	20%	_____
d. $1,250.00	100%	_____

6. Find the missing numbers. Round money to the nearest cent and percents to the nearest tenth percent.

Cost	Dollar markup	Percent markup on cost	Selling price
a. $72.00	_____	40%	_____
b. _____	$7.00	_____	$35.00
c. $8.80	$1.10	_____	_____
d. _____	_____	28%	$19.84
e. $175.00	_____	_____	$236.25

WORD PROBLEMS

7. If the cost of a Pottery Barn chair is $499 and the markup rate is 40% of the cost, what are **(a)** the dollar markup and **(b)** the selling price?

8. If Barry's Furniture Store purchased a floor lamp for $120 and plans to add a markup of $90, **(a)** what will the selling price be and **(b)** what is the markup as a percent of cost?

9. If Lesjardin's Jewelry Store is selling a gold bracelet for $349, which includes a markup of 35% on cost, what are **(a)** Lesjardin's cost and **(b)** the amount of the dollar markup?

10. Toll's Variety Store sells an alarm clock for $14.75. The alarm clock cost Toll's $9.90. What is the markup amount as a percent of cost? Round to the nearest whole percent.

11. Swanson's Audio Supply marks up its merchandise by 40% on cost. If the markup on a cassette player is $85, what are **(a)** the cost of the cassette player and **(b)** the selling price?

12. Brown's Department Store is selling a shirt for $55. If the markup is 70% on cost, what is Brown's cost (to the nearest cent)?

13. Ward's Greenhouse purchased tomato flats for $5.75 each. Ward's has decided to use a markup of 42% on cost. Find the selling price.

Learning Unit 8–2 : Markups Based on Selling Price (100%)

DRILL PROBLEMS

1. Calculate the markup based on the selling price.

Selling price	Markup (percent of selling price)	Dollar markup
a. $25.00	40%	_____
b. $230.00	25%	_____
c. $81.00	42.5%	_____
d. $72.88	$37\frac{1}{2}\%$	_____
e. $1.98	$7\frac{1}{2}\%$	_____

2. Calculate the dollar markup and the markup as a percent of selling price (to the nearest tenth percent). Verify your answer, which may be slightly off due to rounding.

	Cost	Selling price	Dollar markup	Markup (percent of selling price)	Verify
a.	$2.50	$4.25	_____	_____	_____
b.	$16.00	$24.00	_____	_____	_____
c.	$45.25	$85.00	_____	_____	_____
d.	$0.19	$0.25	_____	_____	_____
e.	$5.50	$8.98	_____	_____	_____

3. Given the *cost* and the markup as a percent of *selling price,* calculate the selling price.

	Cost	Markup (percent of selling price)	Selling price
a.	$5.90	15%	_____
b.	$600	32%	_____
c.	$15	50%	_____
d.	$120	30%	_____
e.	$0.29	20%	_____

4. Given the selling price and the percent markup on selling price, calculate the cost.

	Cost	Markup (percent of selling price)	Selling price
a.	_____	40%	$6.25
b.	_____	20%	$16.25
c.	_____	19%	$63.89
d.	_____	$62\frac{1}{2}\%$	$44.00

5. Calculate the equivalent rate of markup, rounding to the nearest hundredth percent.

Markup on cost	Markup on selling price		Markup on cost	Markup on selling price
a. 40%	_____		**b.** 50%	_____
c. _____	50%		**d.** _____	35%
e. _____	40%			

WORD PROBLEMS

6. Fisher Equipment is selling a Wet/Dry Shop Vac for $49.97. If Fisher's markup is 40% of the selling price, what is the cost of the Shop Vac?

7. Gove Lumber Company purchased a 10-inch table saw for $225 and will mark up the price 35% on the selling price. What will the selling price be?

8. To realize a sufficient gross margin, City Paint and Supply Company marks up its paint 27% on the selling price. If a gallon of Latex Semi-Gloss Enamel has a markup of $4.02, find **(a)** the selling price and **(b)** the cost.

9. A Magnavox 20-inch color TV cost $180 and sells for $297. What is the markup based on the selling price? Round to the nearest hundredth percent.

10. Bargain Furniture sells a five-piece country maple bedroom set for $1,299. The cost of this set is $700. What are **(a)** the markup on the bedroom set, **(b)** the markup percent on cost, and **(c)** the markup percent on the selling price? Round to the nearest hundredth percent.

11. Robert's Department Store marks up its sundries by 28% on the selling price. If a 6.4-ounce tube of toothpaste costs $1.65, what will the selling price be?

12. To be competitive, Tinker Toys must sell the DS software for $89.99. To meet expenses and make a sufficient profit, Tinker Toys must add a markup on the selling price of 23%. What is the maximum amount that Tinker Toys can afford to pay a wholesaler for the DS software?

13. Nicole's Restaurant charges $7.50 for a linguini dinner that costs $2.75 for the ingredients. What rate of markup is earned on the selling price? Round to the nearest hundredth percent.

Learning Unit 8–3 :   Markdowns and Perishables

DRILL PROBLEMS

1. Find the dollar markdown and the sale price.

Original selling price	Markdown percent	Dollar markdown	Sale price
a. $200	40%	_____	_____
b. $2,099.98	25%	_____	_____
c. $729	30%	_____	_____

2. Find the dollar markdown and the markdown percent on original selling price.

Original selling price	Sale price	Dollar markdown	Markdown percent
a. $19.50	$9.75	_____	_____
b. $250	$175	_____	_____
c. $39.95	$29.96	_____	_____

3. Find the original selling price.

Sale price	Markdown percent	Original selling price
a. $328	20%	_____
b. $15.85	15%	_____

4. Calculate the final selling price.

Original selling price	First markdown	Second markdown	Final markup	Final selling price
a. $4.96	25%	8%	5%	_____
b. $130	30%	10%	20%	_____

5. Find the missing amounts.

Number of units	Unit cost	Total cost	Estimated* spoilage	Desired markup (percent of cost)	Total selling price	Selling price per unit
a. 72	$3	_____	12%	50%	_____	_____
b. 50	$0.90	_____	16%	42%	_____	_____

*Round to the nearest whole unit as needed.

WORD PROBLEMS

6. Speedy King is having a 30%-off sale on their box springs and mattresses. A queen-size, back-supporter mattress is priced at $325. What is the sale price of the mattress?

7. Murray and Sons sells a Dell computer for $602.27. It is having a sale, and the computer is marked down to $499.88. What is the percent of the markdown?

8. Coleman's is having a clearance sale. A lamp with an original selling price of $249 is now selling for $198. Find the percent of the markdown. Round to the nearest hundredth percent.

9. Johnny's Sports Shop has advertised markdowns on certain items of 22%. A soccer ball is marked with a sale price of $16.50. What was the original price of the soccer ball?

10. Sam Grillo sells seasonal furnishings. Near the end of the summer a five-piece patio set that was priced $349.99 had not been sold, so he marked it down by 12%. As Labor Day approached, he still had not sold the patio set, so he marked it down an additional 18%. What was the final selling price of the patio set?

11. Calsey's Department Store sells their down comforters for a regular price of $325. During its white sale the comforters were marked down 22%. Then, at the end of the sale, Calsey's held a special promotion and gave a second markdown of 10%. When the sale was over, the remaining comforters were marked up 20%. What was the final selling price of the remaining comforters?

12. The New Howard Bakery wants to make a 60% profit on the cost of its pies. To calculate the price of the pies, it estimated that the usual amount of spoilage is five pies. Calculate the selling price for each pie if the number of pies baked each day is 24 and the cost of the ingredients for each pie is $1.80.

13. Sunshine Bakery bakes 660 loaves of bread each day and estimates that 10% of the bread will go stale before it is sold and thus will have to be discarded. The owner of the bakery wishes to realize a 55% markup on cost on the bread. If the cost to make a loaf of bread is $0.46, what should the owner sell each loaf for?

Learning Unit 8–4 :   Breakeven Analysis

DRILL PROBLEMS

1.   Calculate the contribution margin.

	Selling Price per unit	Variable cost per unit	Contribution margin
a.	$14.00	$8.00	
b.	$15.99	$4.88	
c.	$18.99	$4.99	
d.	$251.86	$110.00	
e.	$510.99	$310.00	
f.	$1,000.10	$410.00	

2.   Calculate the selling price per unit.

	Selling price per unit	Variable cost per unit	Contribution margin
a.		$12.18	$ 4.10
b.		$19.19	$ 5.18
c.		$21.00	$13.00
d.		$41.00	$14.88
e.		$128.10	$79.50
f.		$99.99	$60.00

3.   Calculate the breakeven point, rounding to the nearest whole unit.

	Break even point	Fixed cost	Selling price per unit	Variable cost per unit
a.		$50,000	$4.00	$1.00
b.		$30,000	$6.00	$2.00
c.		$20,000	$9.00	$3.00
d.		$100,000	$12.00	$4.00
e.		$120,000	$14.00	$5.00
f.		$90,000	$26.00	$8.00

WORD PROBLEMS

4.   Jones Co. produces bars of candy. Each bar sells for $3.99. The variable cost per unit is $2.85. What is the contribution margin for Jones Co.?

5.   Logan Co. produces stuffed animals. They have $40,000 in fixed costs. Logan sells each animal for $19.99 with a $12.10 cost per unit. What is the breakeven point for Logan? Round to the nearest whole number.

6.   Ranyo Company produces lawn mowers. It has a breakeven point of 6,000 lawn mowers. If its contribution margin is $150, what is Ranyo's fixed cost?

7.   Moore company has $100,000 in fixed costs. Its contribution margin is $4.50. Calculate the breakeven point for Moore to the nearest whole number.

Learning Unit 9–1 : Calculating Various Types of Employees' Gross Pay

DRILL PROBLEMS

1. Fill in the missing amounts for each of the following employees. Do not round the overtime rate in your calculations and round your final answers to the nearest cent.

Employee	Total hours	Rate per hour	Regular pay	Overtime pay	Gross pay
a. Mel Jones	38	$11.25	_____	_____	_____
b. Casey Guitare	43	$9.00	_____	_____	_____
c. Norma Harris	37	$7.50	_____	_____	_____
d. Ed Jackson	45	$12.25	_____	_____	_____

2. Calculate each employee's gross from the following data. Do not round the overtime rate in your calculation but round your final answers to the nearest cent.

Employee	S	M	Tu	W	Th	F	S	Total hours	Rate per hour	Regular pay	Overtime pay	Gross pay
a. L. Adams	0	8	8	8	8	8	0	_____	$8.10	_____	_____	_____
b. M. Card	0	9	8	9	8	8	4	_____	$11.35	_____	_____	_____
c. P. Kline	2	$7\frac{1}{2}$	$8\frac{1}{4}$	8	$10\frac{3}{4}$	9	2	_____	$10.60	_____	_____	_____
d. J. Mack	0	$9\frac{1}{2}$	$9\frac{3}{4}$	$9\frac{1}{2}$	10	10	4	_____	$9.95	_____	_____	_____

3. Calculate the gross wages of the following production workers.

Employee	Rate per unit	No. of units produced	Gross pay
a. A. Bossie	$0.67	655	_____
b. J. Carson	$0.87\frac{1}{2}$	703	_____

4. Using the given differential scale, calculate the gross wages of the following production workers.

Units produced	Amount per unit
From 1–50	$.55
From 51–100	.65
From 101–200	.72
More than 200	.95

Employee	Units produced	Gross pay
a. F. Burns	190	_____
b. B. English	210	_____
c. E. Jackson	200	_____

5. Calculate the following salespersons' gross wages.
   a. Straight commission:

Employee	Net sales	Commission	Gross pay
M. Salley	$40,000	13%	_____

b. Straight commission with draw:

Employee	Net sales	Commission	Draw	Commission minus draw
G. Gorsbeck	$38,000	12%	$600	_____

c. Variable commission scale:

Up to $25,000	8%
Excess of $25,000 to $40,000	10%
More than $40,000	12%

Employee	Net sales	Gross pay
H. Lloyd	$42,000	_____

d. Salary plus commission:

Employee	Salary	Commission	Quota	Net sales	Gross pay
P. Floyd	$2,500	3%	$400,000	$475,000	_____

WORD PROBLEMS

For all problems with overtime, be sure to round only the final answer.

6. In the first week of December, Dana Robinson worked 52 hours. His regular rate of pay is $11.25 per hour. What was Dana's gross pay for the week?

7. Davis Fisheries pays its workers for each box of fish they pack. Sunny Melanson receives $.30 per box. During the third week of July, Sunny packed 2,410 boxes of fish. What was Sunny's gross pay?

8. Maye George is a real estate broker who receives a straight commission of 6%. What would her commission be for a house that sold for $197,500?

9. Devon Company pays Eileen Haskins a straight commission of $12\frac{1}{2}\%$ on net sales. In January, Devon gave Eileen a draw of $600. She had net sales that month of $35,570. What was Eileen's commission minus draw?

10. Parker and Company pays Selma Stokes on a variable commission scale. In a month when Selma had net sales of $155,000, what was her gross pay based on the following schedule?

Net sales	Commission rate
Up to $40,000	5%
Excess of $40,000 to $75,000	5.5%
Excess of $75,000 to $100,000	6%
More than $100,000	7%

11. Marsh Furniture Company pays Joshua Charles a monthly salary of $1,900 plus a commission of $2\frac{1}{2}\%$ on sales over $12,500. Last month, Joshua had net sales of $17,799. What was Joshua's gross pay for the month?

12. Amy McWha works at Lamplighter Bookstore where she earns $7.75 per hour plus a commission of 2% on her weekly sales in excess of $1,500. Last week, Amy worked 39 hours and had total sales of $2,250. What was Amy's gross pay for the week?

Learning Unit 9–2 : Computing Payroll Deductions for Employees' Pay; Employers' Responsibilities

DRILL PROBLEMS

Use tables in the *Business Math Handbook* (assume FICA rates in text).

Employee	Allowances and marital status	Cumulative earnings	Salary per week	Taxable earnings S.S.	Medicare
1. Pete Small	M—3	$109,600	$2,300	a. _____	b. _____
2. Alice Hall	M—1	$110,100	$1,100	c. _____	d. _____
3. Jean Rose	M—2	$120,200	$2,000	e. _____	f. _____

4. What is the tax for Social Security and Medicare for Pete in Problem 1?

5. Calculate Pete's FIT by the percentage method.

6. What would employer's contribute for this week's payroll for SUTA and FUTA?

WORD PROBLEMS

7. Cynthia Pratt has earned $108,600 thus far this year. This week she earned $3,500. Find her total FICA tax deduction (Social Security and Medicare).

8. If Cynthia (Problem 7) earns $1,050 the following week, what will be her new total FICA tax deduction?

9. Roger Alley, a service dispatcher, has weekly earnings of $750. He claimed four allowances on his W-4 form and is married. Besides his FIT and FICA deductions, he has deductions of $35.16 for medical insurance and $17.25 for union dues. Calculate his net earnings for the third week in February. Use the percentage method.

10. Nicole Mariotte is unmarried and claimed one withholding allowance on her W-4 form. In the second week of February, she earned $707.35. Deductions from her pay included federal withholding, Social Security, Medicare, health insurance for $47.75, and $30.00 for the company meal plan. What is Nicole's net pay for the week? Use the percentage method.

11. Gerald Knowlton had total gross earnings of $109,800 in the last week of November. His earnings for the first week in December were $804.70. His employer uses the percentage method to calculate federal withholding. If Gerald is married, claims two allowances, and has medical insurance of $52.25 deducted each week from his pay, what is his net pay for the week?

Learning Unit 10–1 : Calculation of Simple Interest and Maturity Value

DRILL PROBLEMS

1. Find the simple interest for each of the following loans:

Principal	Rate	Time	Interest
a. $12,000	2%	1 year	_____
b. $3,000	12%	3 years	_____
c. $18,000	$8\frac{1}{2}\%$	10 months	_____

2. Find the simple interest for each of the following loans; use the exact interest method. Use the days-in-a-year calendar in the text when needed.

Principal	Rate	Time	Interest
a. $900	4%	30 days	_____
b. $4,290	8%	250 days	_____
c. $1,500	8%	Made March 11 Due July 11	_____

3. Find the simple interest for each of the following loans using the ordinary interest method (Banker's Rule).

Principal	Rate	Time	Interest
a. $5,250	$7\frac{1}{2}\%$	120 days	_____
b. $700	3%	70 days	_____
c. $2,600	11%	Made on June 15 Due October 17	_____

WORD PROBLEMS

4. On October 17, Gill Iowa borrowed $6,000 at a rate of 4%. She promised to repay the loan in 7 months. What are (a) the amount of the simple interest and (b) the total amount owed upon maturity?

5. Marjorie Folsom borrowed $5,500 to purchase a computer. The loan was for 9 months at an annual interest rate of $12\frac{1}{2}\%$. What are (a) the amount of interest Marjorie must pay and (b) the maturity value of the loan?

6. Eric has a loan for $1,200 at an ordinary interest rate of 9.5% for 80 days. Julie has a loan for $1,200 at an exact interest rate of 9.5% for 80 days. Calculate (a) the total amount due on Eric's loan and (b) the total amount due on Julie's loan.

7. Roger Lee borrowed $5,280 at $13\frac{1}{2}$% on May 24 and agreed to repay the loan on August 24. The lender calculates interest using the exact interest method. How much will Roger be required to pay on August 24?

8. On March 8, Jack Faltin borrowed $10,225 at $9\frac{3}{4}$%. He signed a note agreeing to repay the loan and interest on November 8. If the lender calculates interest using the ordinary interest method, what will Jack's repayment be?

9. Dianne Smith's real estate taxes of $641.49 were due on November 1, 2013. Due to financial difficulties, Dianne was unable to pay her tax bill until January 15, 2014. The penalty for late payment is $13\frac{3}{8}$% ordinary interest. What is the penalty Dianne will have to pay, and what is Dianne's total payment on January 15?

10. On August 8, Rex Eason had a credit card balance of $550, but he was unable to pay his bill. The credit card company charges interest of $18\frac{1}{2}$% annually on late payments. What amount will Rex have to pay if he pays his bill 1 month late?

11. An issue of *Your Money* discussed average consumers who carry a balance of $2,000 on one credit card. If the yearly rate of interest is 18%, how much are consumers paying in interest per year?

12. AFBA Industrial Bank of Colorado Springs, Colorado, charges a credit card interest rate of 11% per year. If you had a credit card debt of $1,500, what would your interest amount be after 3 months?

Learning Unit 10–2 : Finding Unknown in Simple Interest Formula

DRILL PROBLEMS

1. Find the principal in each of the following. Round to the nearest cent. Assume 360 days. *Calculator hint:* Do denominator calculation first, do not round; when answer is displayed, save it in memory by pressing [M+]. Now key in the numerator (interest amount), [÷], [MR], [=] for the answer. Be sure to clear memory after each problem by pressing [MR] again so that the M is no longer in the display.

Rate	Time	Interest	Principal
a. 8%	70 days	$68	_____
b. 11%	90 days	$125	_____
c. 9%	120 days	$103	_____
d. $8\frac{1}{2}$%	60 days	$150	_____

2. Find the rate in each of the following. Round to the nearest tenth of a percent. Assume 360 days.

	Principal	Time	Interest	Rate
a.	$7,500	120 days	$350	_____
b.	$975	60 days	$25	_____
c.	$20,800	220 days	$910	_____
d.	$150	30 days	$2.10	_____

3. Find the time (to the nearest day) in each of the following. Assuming ordinary interest, use 360 days.

	Principal	Rate	Interest	Time (days)	Time (years) (Round to nearest hundredth)
a.	$400	11%	$7.33	_____	_____
b.	$7,000	12.5%	$292	_____	_____
c.	$1,550	9.2%	$106.95	_____	_____
d.	$157,000	10.75%	$6,797.88	_____	_____

4. Complete the following. Assume 360 days for all examples.

	Principal	Rate (nearest tenth percent)	Time (nearest day)	Simple interest
a.	$345	_____	150 days	$14.38
b.	_____	12.5%	90 days	$46.88
c.	$750	12.2%	_____	$19.06
d.	$20,260	16.7%	110 days	_____

WORD PROBLEMS

Use 360 days.

5. In June, Becky opened a $20,000 bank CD paying 1% interest, but she had to withdraw the money in a few days to cover one child's college tuition. The bank charged her $1,000 in penalties for the withdrawal. What percent of the $20,000 was she charged?

6. Dr. Vaccarro invested his money at $12\frac{1}{2}\%$ for 175 days and earned interest of $760. How much money did Dr. Vaccarro invest?

7. If you invested $10,000 at 5% interest in a 6-month CD compounding interest daily, you would earn $252.43 in interest. How much would the same $10,000 invested in a bank paying simple interest earn?

8. Thomas Kyrouz opened a savings account and deposited $750 in a bank that was paying 2.5% simple interest. How much were his savings worth in 200 days?

9. Mary Millitello paid the bank $53.90 in interest on a 66-day loan at 9.8%. How much money did Mary borrow? Round to the nearest dollar.

10. If Anthony Lucido deposits $2,400 for 66 days and makes $60.72 in interest, what interest rate is he receiving?

11. Find how long in days David Wong must invest $23,500 of his company's cash at 8.4% in order to earn $652.50 in interest.

Learning Unit 10–3 : U.S. Rule—Making Partial Note Payments before Due Date

DRILL PROBLEMS

1. A merchant borrowed $3,000 for 320 days at 11% (assume a 360-day year). Use the U.S. Rule to complete the following table:

Payment number	Payment day	Amount paid	Interest to date	Principal payment	Adjusted balance
					$3,000
1	75	$500	_____	_____	_____
2	160	$750	_____	_____	_____
3	220	$1,000	_____	_____	_____
4	320	_____	_____	_____	_____

2. Use the U.S. Rule to solve for total interest costs, balances, and final payments; use ordinary interest.

    Given
    Principal, $6,000, 5%, 100 days
    Partial payments on 30th day, $2,000
                       on 70th day, $1,000

WORD PROBLEMS

3. John Joseph borrowed $10,800 for 1 year at 14%. After 60 days, he paid $2,500 on the note. On the 200th day, he paid an additional $5,000. Use the U.S. Rule and ordinary interest to find the final balance due.

4. Doris Davis borrowed $8,200 on March 5 for 90 days at $8\frac{3}{4}$%. After 32 days, Doris made a payment on the loan of $2,700. On the 65th day, she made another payment of $2,500. What is her final payment if you use the U.S. Rule with ordinary interest?

5. David Ring borrowed $6,000 on a 13%, 60-day note. After 10 days, David paid $500 on the note. On day 40, David paid $900 on the note. What are the total interest and ending balance due by the U.S. Rule? Use ordinary interest.

Learning Unit 11–1 : Structure of Promissory Notes; the Simple Discount Note

DRILL PROBLEMS

1. Identify each of the following characteristics of promissory notes with an **I** for simple interest note, a **D** for simple discount note, or a **B** if it is true for both.
   ___ Interest is computed on face value, or what is actually borrowed.
   ___ A promissory note for a loan usually less than 1 year.
   ___ Borrower receives proceeds = Face value − Bank discount.
   ___ Maturity value = Face value + Interest.
   ___ Maturity value = Face value.

   ___ Borrower receives the face value.
   ___ Paid back by one payment at maturity.
   ___ Interest computed on maturity value, or what will be repaid, and not on actual amount borrowed.

2. Find the bank discount and the proceeds for the following; assume 360 days:

Maturity value	Discount rate	Time (days)	Bank discount	Proceeds
a. $8,000	3%	120	_____	_____
b. $4,550	8.1%	110	_____	_____
c. $19,350	12.7%	55	_____	_____
d. $63,400	10%	90	_____	_____
e. $13,490	7.9%	200	_____	_____
f. $780	$12\frac{1}{2}\%$	65	_____	_____

3. Find the effective rate of interest for each of the loans in Problem 2. Use the answers you calculated in Problem 2 to solve these problems; round to the nearest tenth percent.

Maturity value	Discount rate	Time (days)	Effective rate
a. $7,000	2%	90	_____
b. $4,550	8.1%	110	_____
c. $19,350	12.7%	55	_____
d. $63,400	10%	90	_____
e. $13,490	7.9%	200	_____
f. $780	$12\frac{1}{2}\%$	65	_____

WORD PROBLEMS

Assume 360 days.

4. Kaylee Putty signed a $8,000 note for 140 days at a discount rate of 5%. Find the discount and the proceeds Kaylee received.

5. The Salem Cooperative Bank charges an $8\frac{3}{4}\%$ discount rate. What are the discount and the proceeds for a $16,200 note for 60 days?

6. Bill Jackson is planning to buy a used car. He went to City Credit Union to take out a loan for $6,400 for 300 days. If the credit union charges a discount rate of $11\frac{1}{2}\%$, what will the proceeds of this loan be?

7. Mike Drislane goes to the bank and signs a note for $9,700. The bank charges a 15% discount rate. Find the discount and the proceeds if the loan is for 210 days.

8. Flora Foley plans to have a deck built on the back of her house. She decides to take out a loan at the bank for $14,300. She signs a note promising to pay back the loan in 280 days. If the note was discounted at 9.2%, how much money will Flora receive from the bank?

9. At the end of 280 days, Flora (Problem 8) must pay back the loan. What is the maturity value of the loan?

10. Dave Cassidy signed a $7,855 note at a bank that charges a 14.2% discount rate. If the loan is for 190 days, find **(a)** the proceeds and **(b)** the effective rate charged by the bank (to the nearest tenth percent).

11. How much money must Dave (Problem 10) pay back to the bank?

Learning Unit 11–2 : Discounting an Interest-Bearing Note before Maturity

DRILL PROBLEMS

1. Calculate the maturity value for each of the following promissory notes; use 360 days:

Date of note	Principal of note	Length of note (days)	Interest rate	Maturity value
a. June 9	$5,000	180	3%	_____
b. August 23	$15,990	85	13%	_____
c. December 10	$985	30	11.5%	_____

2. Find the maturity date and the discount period for the following; assume no leap years. *Hint:* See Exact Days-in-a-Year Calendar, Chapter 7.

Date of note	Length of note (days)	Date of discount	Maturity date	Discount period
a. March 11	200	June 28	_____	_____
b. January 22	60	March 2	_____	_____
c. April 19	85	June 6	_____	_____
d. November 17	120	February 15	_____	_____

3. Find the bank discount for each of the following; use 360 days:

Date of note	Principal of note	Length of note	Interest rate	Bank discount rate	Date of discount	Bank discount
a. October 5	$2,475	88 days	11%	9.5%	December 10	_____
b. June 13	$9,055	112 days	15%	16%	August 11	_____
c. March 20	$1,065	75 days	12%	11.5%	May 24	_____

4. Find the proceeds for each of the discounted notes in Problem 3.

   a. _____

   b. _____

   c. _____

WORD PROBLEMS

5. Connors Company received a $4,000, 90-day, 10% note dated April 6 from one of its customers. Connors Company held the note until May 16, when the company discounted it at a bank at a discount rate of 12%. What were the proceeds that Connors Company received?

6. Souza & Sons accepted a 9%, $22,000, 120-day note from one of its customers on July 22. On October 2, the company discounted the note at Cooperative Bank. The discount rate was 12%. What were (a) the bank discount and (b) the proceeds?

7. The Fargate Store accepted an $8,250, 75-day, 9% note from one of its customers on March 18. Fargate discounted the note at Parkside National Bank at $9\frac{1}{2}$% on March 29. What proceeds did Fargate receive?

8. On November 1, Marjorie's Clothing Store accepted a $5,200, $8\frac{1}{2}$%, 90-day note from Mary Rose in granting her a time extension on her bill. On January 13, Marjorie discounted the note at Seawater Bank, which charged a 10% discount rate. What were the proceeds that Majorie received?

9. On December 3, Duncan's Company accepted a $5,000, 90-day, 12% note from Al Finney in exchange for a $5,000 bill that was past due. On January 29, Duncan discounted the note at The Sidwell Bank at 13.1%. What were the proceeds from the note?

10. On February 26, Sullivan Company accepted a 60-day, 10% note in exchange for a $1,500 past-due bill from Tabot Company. On March 28, Sullivan Company discounted at National Bank the note received from Tabot Company. The bank discount rate was 12%. What are (a) the bank discount and (b) the proceeds?

11. On June 4, Johnson Company received from Marty Russo a 30-day, 11% note for $720 to settle Russo's debt. On June 17, Johnson discounted the note at Eastern Bank at 15%. What proceeds did Johnson receive?

12. On December 15, Lawlers Company went to the bank and discounted a 10%, 90-day, $14,000 note dated October 21. The bank charged a discount rate of 12%. What were the proceeds of the note?

Learning Unit 12–1 : Compound Interest (Future Value)—The Big Picture

DRILL PROBLEMS

1. In the following examples, calculate manually the amount at year-end for each of the deposits, assuming that interest is compounded annually. Round to the nearest cent each year.

Principal	Rate	Number of years	Year 1	Year 2	Year 3	Year 4
a. $530	4%	2	_____	_____		
b. $1,980	12%	4	_____	_____	_____	_____

2. In the following examples, calculate the simple interest, the compound interest, and the difference between the two. Round to the nearest cent; do not use tables.

Principal	Rate	Number of years	Simple interest	Compound interest	Difference
a. $4,600	10%	2	_____	_____	_____
b. $18,400	9%	4	_____	_____	_____
c. $855	$7\frac{1}{5}\%$	3	_____	_____	_____

3. Find the future value and the compound interest using the Future Value of $1 at Compound Interest table or the Compound Daily table. Round to the nearest cent.

Principal	Investment terms	Future value	Compound interest
a. $20,000	6 years at 4% compounded annually	_____	_____
b. $10,000	6 years at 8% compounded quarterly	_____	_____
c. $8,400	7 years at 12% compounded semiannually	_____	_____
d. $2,500	15 years at 10% compounded daily	_____	_____
e. $9,600	5 years at 6% compounded quarterly	_____	_____
f. $20,000	2 years at 6% compounded monthly	_____	_____

4. Calculate the effective rate (APY) of interest using the Future Value of $1 at Compound Interest table.

Investment terms	Effective rate (annual percentage yield)
a. 12% compounded quarterly	_____
b. 12% compounded semiannually	_____
c. 6% compounded quarterly	_____

WORD PROBLEMS

5. John Mackey deposited $7,000 in his savings account at Salem Savings Bank. If the bank pays 2% interest compounded semi annually, what will be the balance of his account at the end of 3 years?

6. Pine Valley Savings Bank offers a certificate of deposit at 12% interest compounded quarterly. What is the effective rate (APY) of interest?

7. Jack Billings loaned $6,000 to his brother-in-law Dan, who was opening a new business. Dan promised to repay the loan at the end of 5 years, with interest of 8% compounded semiannually. How much will Dan pay Jack at the end of 5 years?

8. Eileen Hogarty deposits $5,630 in City Bank, which pays 12% interest compounded quarterly. How much money will Eileen have in her account at the end of 7 years?

9. If Kevin Bassage deposits $3,500 in Scarsdale Savings Bank, which pays 8% interest compounded quarterly, what will be in his account at the end of 6 years? How much interest will he have earned at that time?

10. Arlington Trust pays 6% compounded semiannually. How much interest would be earned on $7,200 for 1 year?

11. Paladium Savings Bank pays 9% compounded quarterly. Find the amount and the interest on $3,000 after three quarters. Do not use a table.

12. David Siderski bought a $8,000 bank certificate paying 4% compounded semiannually. How much money did he obtain upon cashing in the certificate 3 years later?

13. An issue of *Your Money* showed that the more frequently the bank compounds your money, the better. Consider a $10,000 investment earning 6% interest in a 5-year certificate of deposit at the following three banks. What would be the interest earned at each bank?
   a. Bank A (simple interest, no compounding)
   b. Bank B (quarterly compounding)
   c. Bank C (daily compounding)

Learning Unit 12–2 : Present Value—The Big Picture

DRILL PROBLEMS

1. Use the *Business Math Handbook* to find the table factor for each of the following:

	Future value	Rate	Number of years	Compounded	Table value
a.	$1.00	2%	5	Annually	_____
b.	$1.00	12%	8	Semiannually	_____
c.	$1.00	6%	10	Quarterly	_____
d.	$1.00	12%	2	Monthly	_____
e.	$1.00	8%	15	Semiannually	_____

2. Use the *Business Math Handbook* to find the table factor and the present value for each of the following:

	Future value	Rate	Number of years	Compounded	Table value	Present value
a.	$1,000	2%	6	Semiannually	_____	_____
b.	$1,000	16%	7	Quarterly	_____	_____
c.	$1,000	8%	7	Quarterly	_____	_____
d.	$1,000	8%	7	Semiannually	_____	_____
e.	$1,000	8%	7	Annually	_____	_____

3. Find the present value and the interest earned for the following:

	Future value	Number of years	Rate	Compounded	Present value	Interest earned
a.	$2,500	6	8%	Annually	_____	_____
b.	$4,600	10	6%	Semiannually	_____	_____
c.	$12,800	8	10%	Semiannually	_____	_____
d.	$28,400	7	8%	Quarterly	_____	_____
e.	$53,050	1	12%	Monthly	_____	_____

4. Find the missing amount (present value or future value) for each of the following:

	Present value	Investment terms	Future value
a.	$3,500	5 years at 8% compounded annually	_____
b.	_____	6 years at 12% compounded semiannually	$9,000
c.	$4,700	9 years at 14% compounded semiannually	_____

WORD PROBLEMS

Solve for future value or present value.

5. Paul Palumbo assumes that he will need to have a new roof put on his house in 4 years. He estimates that the roof will cost him $17,000 at that time. What amount of money should Paul invest today at 2%, compounded semiannually, to be able to pay for the roof?

6. Tilton, a pharmacist, rents his store and has signed a lease that will expire in 3 years. When the lease expires, Tilton wants to buy his own store. He wants to have a down payment of $35,000 at that time. How much money should Tilton invest today at 6%, compounded quarterly, to yield $35,000?

7. Brad Morrissey loans $8,200 to his brother-in-law. He will be repaid at the end of 5 years, with interest at 10% compounded semiannually. Find out how much he will be repaid.

8. The owner of Waverly Sheet Metal Company plans to buy some new machinery in 6 years. He estimates that the machines he wishes to purchase will cost $39,700 at that time. What must he invest today at 8%, compounded semiannually, to have sufficient money to purchase the new machines?

9. Paul Stevens's grandparents want to buy him a car when he graduates from college in 4 years. They feel that they should have $27,000 in the bank at that time. How much should they invest at 12%, compounded quarterly, to reach their goal?

10. Gilda Nardi deposits $5,325 in a bank that pays 12% interest compounded quarterly. Find the amount she will have at the end of 7 years.

11. Mary Wilson wants to buy a new set of golf clubs in 2 years. They will cost $775. How much money should she invest today at 9%, compounded annually, so that she will have enough money to buy the new clubs?

12. Jack Beggs plans to invest $30,000 at 10%, compounded semiannually, for 5 years. What is the future value of the investment?

13. Ron Thrift expects his Honda Pilot will last 3 more years. Ron does not like to finance his purchases. He went to First National Bank to find out how much money he should put in the bank to purchase a $20,300 car in 3 years. The bank's 3-year CD is compounded quarterly with a 4% rate. How much should Ron invest in the CD?

14. The Downers Grove YMCA had a fund-raising campaign to build a swimming pool in 6 years. Members raised $825,000; the pool is estimated to cost $1,230,000. The money will be placed in Downers Grove Bank, which pays daily interest at 6%. Will the YMCA have enough money to pay for the pool in 6 years?

Learning Unit 13–1 : Annuities: Ordinary Annuity and Annuity Due (Find Future Value)

DRILL PROBLEMS

1. Find the value of the following ordinary annuities; calculate manually:

Amount of each annual deposit	Interest rate	Value at end of year 1	Value at end of year 2	Value at end of year 3
a. $1,000	8%	_____	_____	_____
b. $2,500	12%	_____	_____	_____
c. $7,200	10%	_____	_____	_____

2. Use the Ordinary Annuity Table: Compound Sum of an Annuity of $1 to find the value of the following ordinary annuities:

Annuity payment	Payment period	Term of annuity	Interest rate	Value of annuity
a. $650	Semiannually	5 years	6%	_____
b. $3,790	Annually	13 years	12%	_____
c. $500	Quarterly	1 year	8%	_____

3. Find the annuity due (deposits are made at beginning of period) for each of the following using the Ordinary Annuity Table:

Amount of payment	Payment period	Interest rate	Time (years)	Amount of annuity
a. $900	Annually	7%	6	_____
b. $1,200	Annually	11%	4	_____
c. $550	Semiannually	10%	9	_____

4. Find the amount of each annuity:

Amount of payment	Payment period	Interest rate	Time (years)	Type of annuity	Amount of annuity
a. $600	Semiannually	12%	8	Ordinary	_____
b. $600	Semiannually	12%	8	Due	_____
c. $1,100	Annually	9%	7	Ordinary	_____

WORD PROBLEMS

5. At the end of each year for the next 9 years, D'Aldo Company will deposit $25,000 in an ordinary annuity account paying 9% interest compounded annually. Find the value of the annuity at the end of the 9 years.

6. David McCarthy is a professional baseball player who expects to play in the major leagues for 10 years. To save for the future, he will deposit $50,000 at the beginning of each year into an account that pays 11% interest compounded annually. How much will he have in this account at the end of 10 years?

7. Tom and Sue plan to get married. Because they hope to have a large wedding, they are going to deposit $1,000 at the end of each month into an account that pays 24% compounded monthly. How much will they have in this account at the end of 1 year?

8. Chris Dennen deposits $15,000 at the end of each year for 13 years into an account paying 7% interest compounded annually. What is the value of her annuity at the end of 13 years? How much interest will she have earned?

9. Amanda Blinn is 52 years old today and has just opened an IRA. She plans to deposit $500 at the end of each quarter into her account. If Amanda retires on her 62nd birthday, what amount will she have in her account if the account pays 8% interest compounded quarterly?

10. Jerry Davis won the citywide sweepstakes and will receive a check for $2,000 at the beginning of each 6 months for the next 5 years. If Jerry deposits each check in an account that pays 8% compounded semiannually, how much will he have at the end of 5 years?

11. Mary Hynes purchased an ordinary annuity from an investment broker at 8% interest compounded semiannually. If her semiannual deposit is $600, what will be the value of the annuity at the end of 15 years?

Learning Unit 13–2 : Present Value of an Ordinary Annuity (Find Present Value)

DRILL PROBLEMS

1. Use the Present Value of an Annuity of $1 table to find the amount to be invested today to receive a stream of payments for a given number of years in the future. Show the manual check of your answer. (Check may be a few pennies off due to rounding.)

Amount of expected payments	Payment period	Interest rate	Term of annuity	Present value of annuity
a. $1,500	Yearly	9%	2 years	_____
b. $2,700	Yearly	13%	3 years	_____
c. $2,700	Yearly	6%	3 years	_____

2. Find the present value of the following annuities. Use the Present Value of an Annuity of $1 table.

Amount of each payment	Payment period	Interest rate	Time (years)	Compounded	Present value of annuity
a. $2,000	Year	7%	25	Annually	_____
b. $7,000	Year	11%	12	Annually	_____
c. $850	6 months	12%	5	Semiannually	_____
d. $1,950	6 months	14%	9	Semiannually	_____
e. $500	Quarter	12%	10	Quarterly	_____

WORD PROBLEMS

3. Tom Hanson would like to receive $200 each quarter for the 4 years he is in college. If his bank account pays 8% compounded quarterly, how much must he have in his account when he begins college?

4. Jean Reith has just retired and will receive a $12,500 retirement check every 6 months for the next 20 years. If her employer can invest money at 12% compounded semiannually, what amount must be invested today to make the semiannual payments to Jean?

5. Tom Herrick will pay $4,500 at the end of each year for the next 7 years to pay the balance of his college loans. If Tom can invest his money at 7% compounded annually, how much must he invest today to make the annual payments?

6. Helen Grahan is planning an extended sabbatical for the next 3 years. She would like to invest a lump sum of money at 10% interest so that she can withdraw $6,000 every 6 months while on sabbatical. What is the amount of the lump sum that Helen must invest?

7. Linda Rudd has signed a rental contract for office equipment, agreeing to pay $3,200 at the end of each quarter for the next 5 years. If Linda can invest money at 12% compounded quarterly, find the lump sum she can deposit today to make the payments for the length of the contract.

8. Sam Adams is considering lending his brother John $6,000. John said that he would repay Sam $775 every 6 months for 4 years. If money can be invested at 8%, calculate the equivalent cash value of the offer today. Should Sam go ahead with the loan?

9. The State Lotto Game offers a grand prize of $1,000,000 paid in 20 yearly payments of $50,000. If the state treasurer can invest money at 9% compounded annually, how much must she invest today to make the payments to the grand prize winner?

10. Thomas Martin's uncle has promised him upon graduation a gift of $20,000 in cash or $2,000 every quarter for the next 3 years. If money can be invested at 8%, which offer will Thomas accept? (Thomas is a business major.)

11. Paul Sasso is selling a piece of land. He has received two solid offers. Jason Smith has offered a $60,000 down payment and $50,000 a year for the next 5 years. Kevin Bassage offered $35,000 down and $55,000 a year for the next 5 years. If money can be invested at 7% compounded annually, which offer should Paul accept? (To make the comparison, find the equivalent cash price of each offer.)

12. Abe Hoster decided to retire to Spain in 10 years. What amount should Abe invest today so that he will be able to withdraw $30,000 at the end of each year for 20 years after he retires? Assume he can invest money at 8% interest compounded annually.

Learning Unit 13–3 :   Sinking Funds (Find Periodic Payments)

DRILL PROBLEMS

1. Given the number of years and the interest rate, use the Sinking Fund Table based on $1 to calculate the amount of the periodic payment.

Frequency of payment	Length of time	Interest rate	Future amount	Sinking fund payment
a. Annually	19 years	5%	$125,000	_____
b. Annually	7 years	10%	$205,000	_____
c. Semiannually	10 years	6%	$37,500	_____
d. Quarterly	9 years	12%	$12,750	_____
e. Quarterly	6 years	8%	$25,600	_____

2. Find the amount of each payment into the sinking fund and the amount of interest earned.

	Maturity value	Interest rate	Term (years)	Frequency of payment	Sinking fund payment	Interest earned
a.	$45,500	5%	13	Annually	_____	_____
b.	$8,500	10%	20	Semiannually	_____	_____
c.	$11,000	8%	5	Quarterly	_____	_____
d.	$66,600	12%	$7\frac{1}{2}$	Semiannually	_____	_____

WORD PROBLEMS

3. To finance a new police station, the town of Pine Valley issued bonds totaling $600,000. The town treasurer set up a sinking fund at 8% compounded quarterly in order to redeem the bonds in 7 years. What is the quarterly payment that must be deposited into the fund?

4. Arlex Oil Corporation plans to build a new garage in 6 years. To finance the project, the financial manager established a $250,000 sinking fund at 6% compounded semianually. Find the semiannual payment required for the fund.

5. The City Fisheries Corporation sold $300,000 worth of bonds that must be redeemed in 9 years. The corporation agreed to set up a sinking fund to accumulate the $300,000. Find the amount of the periodic payments made into the fund if payments are made annually and the fund earns 8% compounded annually.

6. Gregory Mines Corporation wishes to purchase a new piece of equipment in 4 years. The estimated price of the equipment is $100,000. If the corporation makes periodic payments into a sinking fund with 12% interest compounded quarterly, find the amount of the periodic payments.

7. The Best Corporation must buy a new piece of machinery in $4\frac{1}{2}$ years that will cost $350,000. If the firm sets up a sinking fund to finance this new machine, what will the quarterly deposits be assuming the fund earns 8% interest compounded quarterly?

8. The Lowest-Price-in-Town Company needs $75,500 in 6 years to pay off a debt. The company makes a decision to set up a sinking fund and make semiannual deposits. What will their payments be if the fund pays 10% interest compounded semiannually?

9. The WIR Company plans to renovate their offices in 5 years. They estimate that the cost will be $235,000. If they set up a sinking fund that pays 12% quarterly, what will their quarterly payments be?

Learning Unit 14–1 : Cost of Installment Buying

DRILL PROBLEMS

1. For the following installment problems, find the amount financed and the finance charge.

	Sale price	Down payment	Number of monthly payments	Monthly payment	Amount financed	Finance charge
a.	$1,500	$300	24	$58	_____	_____
b.	$12,000	$3,000	30	$340	_____	_____
c.	$62,500	$4,700	48	$1,500	_____	_____
d.	$4,975	$620	18	$272	_____	_____
e.	$825	$82.50	12	$67.45	_____	_____

2. For each of the above purchases, find the deferred payment price.

	Sale price	Down payment	Number of monthly payments	Monthly payment	Deferred payment price
a.	$1,500	$300	24	$58	_____
b.	$12,000	$3,000	30	$340	_____
c.	$62,500	$4,700	48	$1,500	_____
d.	$4,975	$620	18	$272	_____
e.	$825	$82.50	12	$67.45	_____

3. Use the Annual Percentage Rate Table per $100 to calculate the estimated APR for each of the previous purchases.

Sale price	Down payment	Number of monthly payments	Monthly payment	Annual percentage rate
a. $1,500	$300	24	$58	_____
b. $12,000	$3,000	30	$340	_____
c. $62,500	$4,700	48	$1,500	_____
d. $4,975	$620	18	$272	_____
e. $825	$82.50	12	$67.45	_____

4. Given the following information, calculate the monthly payment by the loan amortization table.

Amount financed	Interest rate	Number of months of loan	Monthly payment
a. $12,000	10%	18	_____
b. $18,000	11%	36	_____
c. $25,500	13.50%	54	_____

WORD PROBLEMS

5. Jill Walsh purchases a bedroom set for a cash price of $3,920. The down payment is $392, and the monthly installment payment is $176 for 24 months. Find (a) the amount financed, (b) the finance charge, and (c) the deferred payment price.

6. An automaker promotion loan on a $20,000 automobile and a down payment of 20% are being financed for 48 months. The monthly payments will be $367.74. What will be the APR for this auto loan? Use the table in the *Business Math Handbook*.

7. David Nason purchased a recreational vehicle for $25,000. David went to City Bank to finance the purchase. The bank required that David make a 10% down payment and monthly payments of $571.50 for 4 years. Find (a) the amount financed, (b) the finance charge, and (c) the deferred payment that David paid.

8. Calculate the estimated APR that David (Problem 7) was charged per $100 using the Annual Percentage Rate Table.

9. Young's Motors advertised a new car for $16,720. They offered an installment plan of 5% down and 42 monthly payments of $470. What are (a) the deferred payment price and (b) the estimated APR for this car? Use the table.

10. Angie French bought a used car for $9,000. Angie put down $2,000 and financed the balance at 11.50% for 36 months. What is her monthly payment? Use the loan amortization table.

Learning Unit 14–2 : Revolving Charge Credit Cards

DRILL PROBLEMS

1. Use the U.S. Rule to calculate the outstanding balance due for each of the following independent situations:

Monthly payment number	Outstanding balance due	$1\frac{1}{2}$% interest payment	Amount of monthly payment	Reduction in balance due	Outstanding balance due
a. 1	$9,000.00	_____	$600	_____	_____
b. 5	$5,625.00	_____	$1,000	_____	_____
c. 4	$926.50	_____	$250	_____	_____
d. 12	$62,391.28	_____	$1,200	_____	_____
e. 8	$3,255.19	_____	$325	_____	_____

2. Complete the missing data for a $6,500 purchase made on credit. The annual interest charge on this revolving charge account is 18%, or $1\frac{1}{2}\%$ interest on previous month's balance. Use the U.S. Rule.

Monthly payment number	Outstanding balance due	$1\frac{1}{2}\%$ interest payment	Amount of monthly payment	Reduction in balance due	Outstanding balance due
1	$6,500	_____	$700	_____	_____
2	_____	_____	$700	_____	_____
3	_____	_____	$700	_____	_____

3. Calculate the average billing daily balance for each of the monthly statements for the following revolving credit accounts; assume a 30-day billing cycle:

Billing date	Previous balance	Payment date	Payment amount	Charge date(s)	Charge amount(s)	Average daily balance
a. 4/10	$329	4/25	$35	4/29	$56	_____
b. 6/15	$573	6/25	$60	6/26	$25	
				6/30	$72	_____
c. 9/15	$335.50	9/20	$33.55	9/25	$12.50	
				9/26	$108	_____

4. Find the finance charge for each monthly statement (Problem 3) if the annual percentage rate is 15%.

a. _____   b. _____   c. _____

WORD PROBLEMS

5. Niki Marshall is going to buy a new bedroom set at Scottie's Furniture Store, where she has a revolving charge account. The cost of the bedroom set is $5,500. Niki does not plan to charge anything else to her account until she has completely paid for the bedroom set. Scottie's Furniture Store charges an annual percentage rate of 18%, or $1\frac{1}{2}\%$ per month. Niki plans to pay $1,000 per month until she has paid for the bedroom set. Set up a schedule for Niki to show her outstanding balance at the end of each month after her $1,000 payment and also the amount of her final payment. Use the U.S. Rule.

6. Frances Dollof received her monthly statement from Brown's Department Store. The following is part of the information contained on that statement. Finance charge is calculated on the average daily balance.

Date	Reference	Department	Description	Amount
Dec. 15	5921	359	Petite sportswear	84.98
Dec. 15	9612	432	Footwear	55.99
Dec. 15	2600	126	Women's fragrance	35.18
Dec. 23	6247	61	Ralph Lauren towels	20.99
Dec. 24	0129	998	Payment received—thank you	100.00CR

Previous balance		Annual percentage rate		Billing date
719.04	12/13	18%		JAN 13

Brown's Charge Account Terms
Payment is required in monthly installments upon receipt of monthly statement in accordance with Brown's payment terms.

When my new balance is:	My minimum required payment is:	When my new balance is:	My minimum required payment is:
Up to $20.00	New Balance	$350.01 to $400.00	$40.00
$ 20.01 to $200.00	$20.00	$400.01 to $450.00	$45.00
$200.01 to $250.00	$25.00	$450.01 to $500.00	$50.00
$250.01 to $300.00	$30.00	More than $500.00	$50.00 plus
$300.01 to $350.00	$35.00		$10.00 for each $50.00 (or fraction thereof) of New Balance over $500.00

a. Calculate the average daily balance for the month.
b. What is Ms. Dollof's finance charge?
c. What is the new balance for Ms. Dollof's account?
d. What is the minimum payment Frances is required to pay according to Brown's payment terms?

7. What is the finance charge for a Brown's customer who has an average daily balance of $3,422.67?

8. What is the minimum payment for a Brown's customer with a new balance of $522.00?

9. What is the minimum payment for a Brown's customer with a new balance of $325.01?

10. What is the new balance for a Brown's customer with a previous balance of $309.35 whose purchases totaled $213.00, given that the customer made a payment of $75.00 and the finance charge was $4.65?

RECAP OF WORD PROBLEMS IN LU 14–1

11. A home equity loan on a $20,000 automobile with a down payment of 20% is being financed for 48 months. The interest is tax deductible. The monthly payments will be $401.97. What is the APR on this loan? Use the table in the *Business Math Handbook*. If the person is in the 28% income tax bracket, what will be the tax savings with this type of a loan?

12. An automobile with a total transaction price of $20,000 with a down payment of 20% is being financed for 48 months. Banks and credit unions require a monthly payment of $400.36. What is the APR for this auto loan? Use the table in the *Business Math Handbook*.

13. Assume you received a $2,000 rebate that brought the price of a car down to $20,000; the financing rate was for 48 months, and your total interest was $3,279. Using the table in the *Business Math Handbook*, what was your APR?

Learning Unit 15–1 : Types of Mortgages and the Monthly Mortgage Payment

DRILL PROBLEMS

1. Use the table in the *Business Math Handbook* to calculate the monthly payment for principal and interest for the following mortgages:

	Price of home	Down payment	Interest rate	Term in years	Monthly payment
a.	$200,000	15%	6%	25	_____
b.	$200,000	15%	$5\frac{1}{2}\%$	30	_____
c.	$450,000	10%	$11\frac{3}{4}\%$	30	_____
d.	$450,000	10%	11%	30	_____

2. For each of the mortgages, calculate the amount of interest that will be paid over the life of the loan.

	Price of home	Down payment	Interest rate	Term in years	Total interest paid
a.	$200,000	15%	$6\frac{1}{2}\%$	25	_____
b.	$200,000	15%	$10\frac{1}{2}\%$	30	_____
c.	$450,000	10%	$11\frac{3}{4}\%$	30	_____
d.	$450,000	10%	11%	30	_____

3. Calculate the increase in the monthly mortgage payments for each of the rate increases in the following mortgages. Then calculate what percent of change the increase represents, rounded to the nearest tenth percent.

Mortgage amount	Term in years	Interest rate	Increase in interest rate	Increase in monthly payment	Percent change
a. $175,000	22	9%	1%	_____	_____
b. $300,000	30	$11\frac{3}{4}\%$	$\frac{3}{4}\%$	_____	_____

4. Calculate the increase in total interest paid for the increase in interest rates in Problem 3.

Mortgage amount	Term in years	Interest rate	Increase in interest rate	Increase in total interest paid
a. $175,000	22	9%	1%	_____
b. $300,000	30	$11\frac{3}{4}\%$	$\frac{3}{4}\%$	_____

WORD PROBLEMS

5. The Counties are planning to purchase a new home that costs $150,000. The bank is charging them 6% interest and requires a 20% down payment. The Counties are planning to take a 25-year mortgage. How much will their monthly payment be for principal and interest?

6. The MacEacherns wish to buy a new house that costs $299,000. The bank requires a 15% down payment and charges $11\frac{1}{2}\%$ interest. If the MacEacherns take out a 15-year mortgage, what will their monthly payment for principal and interest be?

7. Because the monthly payments are so high, the MacEacherns (Problem 6) want to know what the monthly payments would be for (a) a 25-year mortgage and (b) a 30-year mortgage. Calculate these two payments.

8. If the MacEacherns choose a 30-year mortgage instead of a 15-year mortgage, (a) how much money will they "save" monthly and (b) how much more interest will they pay over the life of the loan?

9. If the MacEacherns choose the 25-year mortgage instead of the 30-year mortgage, (a) how much more will they pay monthly and (b) how much less interest will they pay over the life of the loan?

10. Larry and Doris Davis plan to purchase a new home that costs $415,000. The bank that they are dealing with requires a 20% down payment and charges $12\frac{3}{4}\%$. The Davises are planning to take a 25-year mortgage. What will the monthly payment be?

11. How much interest will the Davises (Problem 10) pay over the life of the loan?

Learning Unit 15–2 : Amortization Schedule—Breaking Down the Monthly Payment

DRILL PROBLEMS

1. In the following, calculate the monthly payment for each mortgage, the portion of the first monthly payment that goes to interest, and the portion of the payment that goes toward the principal.

Amount of mortgage	Interest rate	Term in years	Monthly payment	Portion to interest	Portion to principal
a. $170,000	8%	22	_____	_____	_____
b. $222,000	$11\frac{3}{4}\%$	30	_____	_____	_____
c. $167,000	$10\frac{1}{2}\%$	25	_____	_____	_____
d. $307,000	13%	15	_____	_____	_____
e. $409,500	$12\frac{1}{2}\%$	20	_____	_____	_____

2. Prepare an amortization schedule for the first 3 months of a 25-year, 12% mortgage on $265,000.

Payment number	Monthly payment	Portion to interest	Portion to principal	Balance of loan outstanding
1	_____	_____	_____	_____
2	_____	_____	_____	_____
3	_____	_____	_____	_____

3. Prepare an amortization schedule for the first 4 months of a 30-year, $10\frac{1}{2}$% mortgage on $195,500.

Payment number	Monthly payment	Portion to interest	Portion to principal	Balance of loan outstanding
1	_____	_____	_____	_____
2	_____	_____	_____	_____
3	_____	_____	_____	_____
4	_____	_____	_____	_____

WORD PROBLEMS

4. Jim and Janice Hurst are buying a new home for $235,000. The bank that is financing the home requires a 20% down payment and charges a $13\frac{1}{2}$% interest rate. Janice wants to know **(a)** what the monthly payment for the principal and interest will be if they take out a 30-year mortgage and **(b)** how much of the first payment will be for interest on the loan.

5. The Hursts (Problem 4) thought that a lot of their money was going to interest. They asked the banker just how much they would be paying for interest over the life of the loan. Calculate the total amount of interest that the Hursts will pay.

6. The banker told the Hursts (Problem 4) that they could, of course, save on the interest payments if they took out a loan for a shorter period of time. Jim and Janice decided to see if they could afford a 15-year mortgage. Calculate how much more the Hursts would have to pay each month for principal and interest if they took a 15-year mortgage for their loan.

7. The Hursts (Problem 4) thought that they might be able to afford this, but first wanted to see **(a)** how much of the first payment would go to the principal and **(b)** how much total interest they would be paying with a 15-year mortgage.

8.

	1980	2014
Cost of median-priced new home	$44,200	$136,600
10% down payment	$4,420	
Fixed-rate, 30-year mortgage		
Interest rate	8.9%	$7\frac{1}{2}$%
Total monthly principal and interest	$316	

Complete the 2014 year.

9. You can't count on your home mortgage lender to keep you from getting in debt over your head. The old standards of allowing 28% of your income for mortgage debt (including taxes and insurance) usually still apply. If your total monthly payment is $1,033, what should be your annual income to buy a home?

10. Assume that a 30-year fixed-rate mortgage for $100,000 was 9% at one date as opposed to 7% the previous year. What is the difference in monthly payments for these 2 years?

11. If you had a $100,000 mortgage with $7\frac{1}{2}\%$ interest for 25 years and wanted a $7\frac{1}{2}\%$ loan for 35 years, what would be the change in monthly payments? How much more would you pay in interest?

Learning Unit 16–1 : Balance Sheet—Report as of a Particular Date

DRILL PROBLEMS

1. Complete the balance sheet for David Harrison, Attorney, and show that

Assets = Liabilities + Owner's equity

Account totals are as follows: accounts receivable, $4,800; office supplies, $375; building (net), $130,000; accounts payable, $1,200; notes payable, $137,200; cash, $2,250; prepaid insurance, $1,050; office equipment (net), $11,250; land, $75,000; capital, $85,900; and salaries payable, $425.

DAVID HARRISON, ATTORNEY
Balance Sheet
December 31, 2014

Assets

Current assets:
 Cash _____

 Accounts receivable _____

 Prepaid insurance _____

 Office supplies _____

  Total current assets _____

Plant and equipment:

 Office equipment (net) _____

 Building (net) _____

 Land _____

  Total plant and equipment _____

Total assets ======

Liabilities

Current liabilities:

 Accounts payable _____

 Salaries payable _____

  Total current liabilities _____

Long-term liabilities:

 Notes payable _____

  Total liabilities _____

Owner's Equity

David Harrison, capital, December 31, 2014 _____

Total liabilities and owner's equity ======

---

2. Given the amounts in each of the accounts of Fisher-George Electric Corporation, fill in these amounts on the balance sheet to show that

Assets = Liabilities + Stockholders' equity

Account totals are as follows: cash, $2,500; merchandise inventory, $1,325; automobiles (net), $9,250; common stock, $10,000; accounts payable, $275; office equipment (net), $5,065; accounts receivable, $300; retained earnings, $6,895; prepaid insurance, $1,075; salaries payable, $175; and mortgage payable, $2,170.

FISHER-GEORGE ELECTRIC CORPORATION
Balance Sheet
December 31, 2014

Assets

Current assets:
  Cash   _____

  Accounts receivable   _____

  Merchandise inventory   _____

  Prepaid insurance   _____

    Total current assets   _____

Plant and equipment:

  Office equipment (net)   _____

  Automobiles (net)   _____

    Total plant and equipment   _____

Total assets   ======

Liabilities

Current liabilities:

  Accounts payable   _____

  Salaries payable   _____

    Total current liabilities   _____

Long-term liabilities:

  Mortgage payable   _____

    Total liabilities   _____

Stockholders' Equity

Common stock   _____

Retained earnings   _____

    Total stockholders' equity   _____

Total liabilities and stockholders' equity   ======

3. Complete a vertical analysis of the following partial balance sheet; round all percents to the nearest hundredth percent.

THREEMAX, INC.
Comparative Balance Sheet Vertical Analysis
At December 31, 2013 and 2014

	2013		2014	
	Amount	Percent	Amount	Percent
Assets				
Cash	$ 8,500	_____	$ 10,200	_____
Accounts receivable (net)	11,750	_____	15,300	_____
Merchandise inventory	55,430	_____	54,370	_____
Store supplies	700	_____	532	_____
Office supplies	650	_____	640	_____
Prepaid insurance	2,450	_____	2,675	_____
Office equipment (net)	12,000	_____	14,300	_____
Store equipment (net)	32,000	_____	31,000	_____
Building (net)	75,400	_____	80,500	_____
Land	200,000	_____	150,000	_____
Total assets	$398,880	_____	$359,517	_____

4. Complete a horizontal analysis of the following partial balance sheet; round all percents to the nearest hundredth percent.

THREEMAX, INC. Comparative Balance Sheet Horizontal Analysis At December 31, 2013 and 2014				
	2014	2013	Change	Percent
Assets				
Cash	$ 8,500	$ 10,200	_____	_____
Accounts receivable (net)	11,750	15,300	_____	_____
Merchandise inventory	55,430	54,370	_____	_____
Store supplies	700	532	_____	_____
Office supplies	650	640	_____	_____
Prepaid insurance	2,450	2,675	_____	_____
Office equipment (net)	12,000	14,300	_____	_____
Store equipment (net)	32,000	31,000	_____	_____
Building (net)	75,400	80,500	_____	_____
Land	200,000	150,000	_____	_____
Total assets	$398,880	$359,517		

Learning Unit 16–2 : Income Statement—Report for a Specific Period of Time

DRILL PROBLEMS

1. Complete the income statement for the year ended December 31, 2014, for Foley Realty, doing all the necessary addition. Account totals are as follows: office salaries expense, $15,255; advertising expense, $2,400; rent expense, $18,000; telephone expense, $650; insurance expense, $1,550; office supplies, $980; depreciation expense, office equipment, $990; depreciation expense, automobile, $2,100; sales commissions earned, $98,400; and management fees earned, $1,260.

FOLEY REALTY Income Statement For the Year Ended December 31, 2014	
Revenues:	
Sales commissions earned	_____
Management fees earned	_____
Total revenues	
Operating expenses:	
Office salaries expense	_____
Advertising expense	_____
Rent expense	_____
Telephone expense	_____
Insurance expense	_____
Office supplies expense	_____
Depreciation expense, office equipment	_____
Depreciation expense, automobile	_____
Total operating expenses	_____
Net income	_____

2. Complete the income statement for Toll's, Inc., a merchandising concern, doing all the necessary addition and subtraction. Sales were $250,000; sales returns and allowances were $1,400; sales discounts were $2,100; merchandise inventory, December 31, 2013, was $42,000; purchases were $156,000; purchases returns and allowances were $1,100; purchases discounts were $3,000; merchandise inventory, December 31, 2014, was $47,000; selling expenses were $37,000; and general and administrative expenses were $29,000.

TOLL'S, INC.
Income Statement
For the Year Ended December 31, 2014

Revenues:
  Sales _____
    Less: Sales return and allowances _____
      Sales discounts _____ _____
  Net sales _____
Cost of goods sold:
  Merchandise inventory, December 31, 2013 _____
  Purchases _____
    Less: Purchases returns and allowances _____
      Purchase discounts _____ _____
  Cost of net purchases _____
  Goods available for sale _____
  Merchandise inventory, December 31, 2014 _____
    Total cost of goods sold _____
Gross profit from sales _____
Operating expenses:
  Selling expenses _____
  General and administrative expenses _____
    Total operating expenses _____
Net income _____

3. Complete a vertical analysis of the following partial income statement; round all percents to the nearest hundredth percent. Note net sales are 100%.

THREEMAX, INC.
Comparative Income Statement Vertical Analysis
For Years Ended December 31, 2013 and 2014

	2014 Amount	Percent	2013 Amount	Percent
Sales	$795,450		$665,532	
Sales returns and allowances	−6,250		−5,340	
Sales discounts	−6,470	---------	−5,125	----------
Net sales	$782,730	---------	$655,067	----------
Cost of goods sold:				
Beginning inventory	$ 75,394		$ 81,083	
Purchases	575,980		467,920	
Purchase discounts	−4,976	---------	−2,290	----------
Goods available for sale	$646,398		$546,713	
Less ending inventory	−66,254		−65,712	----------
Total costs of goods sold	$580,144	---------	$481,001	----------
Gross profit	$202,586		$174,066	

4. Complete a horizontal analysis of the following partial income statement. Rround all percents to the nearest hundredth percent.

THREEMAX, INC. Comparative Income Statement Horizontal Analysis For Years Ended December 31, 2014 and 2013				
	2014	2013	Change	Percent
Sales	$795,450	$665,532	___	___
Sales returns and allowances	−6,250	−5,340	___	___
Sales discounts	−6,470	−5,125	___	___
Net sales	$782,730	$655,067	___	___
Cost of goods sold:				
Beginning inventory	$ 75,394	$ 81,083	___	___
Purchases	575,980	467,920	___	___
Purchase discounts	−4,976	−2,290	___	___
Goods available for sale	$646,398	$546,713	___	___
Less ending inventory	−66,254	−65,712	___	___
Total cost of goods sold	$580,144	$481,001	___	___
Gross profit	$202,586	$174,066	___	___

Learning Unit 16–3 : Trend and Ratio Analysis

DRILL PROBLEMS

1. Express each amount as a percent of the base-year (2012) amount. Round to the nearest tenth percent.

	2015	2014	2013	2012
Sales	$562,791	$560,776	$588,096	$601,982
Percent				
Gross profit	$168,837	$196,271	$235,238	$270,891
Percent				
Net income	$67,934	$65,927	$56,737	$62,762
Percent				

2. If current assets = $42,500 and current liabilities = $56,400, what is the current ratio (to the nearest hundredth)?

3. In Problem 2, if inventory = $20,500 and prepaid expenses = $9,750, what is the quick ratio, or acid test (to the nearest hundredth)?

4. If accounts receivable = $36,720 and net sales = $249,700, what is the average day's collection (to the nearest whole day)?

5. If total liabilities = $243,000 and total assets = $409,870, what is the ratio of total debt to total assets (to the nearest hundredth percent)?

6. If net income = $55,970 and total stockholders' equity = $440,780, what is the return on equity (to the nearest hundredth percent)?

7. If net sales = $900,000 and total assets = $1,090,000, what is the asset turnover (to the nearest hundredth)?

8. In Problem 7, if the net income is $36,600, what is the profit margin on net sales (to the nearest hundredth percent)?

WORD PROBLEMS

9. Calculate trend percentages for the following items using 2012 as the base year. Round to the nearest hundredth percent.

	2015	2014	2013	2012
Sales	$298,000	$280,000	$264,000	$249,250
Cost of goods sold	187,085	175,227	164,687	156,785
Accounts receivable	29,820	28,850	27,300	26,250

10. According to the balance sheet for Ralph's Market, current assets = $165,500 and current liabilities = $70,500. Find the current ratio (to the nearest hundredth).

11. On the balance sheet for Ralph's Market (Problem 10), merchandise inventory = $102,000. Find the quick ratio (acid test).

12. The balance sheet of Moses Contractors shows cash of $5,500, accounts receivable of $64,500, an inventory of $42,500, and current liabilities of $57,500. Find Moses' current ratio and acid test ratio (both to the nearest hundredth).

13. Moses' income statement shows gross sales of $413,000, sales returns of $8,600, and net income of $22,300. Find the profit margin on net sales (to the nearest hundredth percent).

14. Given:

Cash	$ 39,000	Retained earnings	$194,000
Accounts receivable	109,000	Net sales	825,000
Inventory	150,000	Cost of goods sold	528,000
Prepaid expenses	48,000	Operating expenses	209,300
Plant and equipment (net)	487,000	Interest expense	13,500
Accounts payable	46,000	Income taxes	32,400
Other current liabilities	43,000	Net income	41,800
Long-term liabilities	225,000		
Common stock	325,000		

Calculate (to nearest hundredth or hundredth percent as needed):

a. Current ratio.   **b.** Quick ratio.   **c.** Average day's collection.

d. Total debt to total assets.   **e.** Return on equity.   **f.** Asset turnover.

g. Profit margin on net sales.

15. The Vale Group lost $18.4 million in profits for the year 2013 as sales dropped to $401 million. Sales in 2012 were $450.6 million. What percent is the decrease in Vale's sales? Round to the nearest hundredth percent.

Learning Unit 17–1 : Concept of Depreciation and the Straight-Line Method

DRILL PROBLEMS

1. Find the annual straight-line rate of depreciation, given the following estimated lives.

Life	Annual rate	Life	Annual rate
a. 25 years	_____	**b.** 4 years	_____
c. 10 years	_____	**d.** 5 years	_____
e. 8 years	_____	**f.** 30 years	_____

2. Find the annual depreciation using the straight-line depreciation method. Round to the nearest whole dollar.

	Cost of asset	Residual value	Useful life	Annual depreciation
a.	$2,460	$400	4 years	_____
b.	$24,300	$2,000	6 years	_____
c.	$350,000	$42,500	12 years	_____
d.	$17,325	$5,000	5 years	_____
e.	$2,550,000	$75,000	30 years	_____

3. Find the annual depreciation and ending book value for the first year using the straight-line depreciation method. Round to the nearest dollar.

	Cost	Residual value	Useful life	Annual depreciation	Ending book value
a.	$6,700	$600	3 years	_____	_____
b.	$11,600	$500	6 years	_____	_____
c.	$9,980	–0–	5 years	_____	_____
d.	$36,950	$2,500	12 years	_____	_____
e.	$101,690	$3,600	27 years	_____	_____

4. Find the first-year depreciation to the nearest dollar for the following assets, which were only owned for part of a year. Round to the nearest whole dollar the annual depreciation for in-between calculations.

	Date of purchase	Cost of asset	Residual value	Useful life	First year depreciation
a.	April 8	$10,500	$1,200	4 years	_____
b.	July 12	$23,900	$3,200	6 years	_____
c.	June 19	$8,880	$800	3 years	_____
d.	November 2	$125,675	$6,000	17 years	_____
e.	May 25	$44,050	–0–	9 years	_____

WORD PROBLEMS

5. North Shore Grinding purchased a lathe for $37,500. This machine has a residual value of $3,000 and an expected useful life of 4 years. Prepare a depreciation schedule for the lathe using the straight-line depreciation method.

6. Colby Wayne paid $7,750 for a photocopy machine with an estimated life of 6 years and a residual value of $900. Prepare a depreciation schedule using the straight-line depreciation method. Round to the nearest whole dollar. (Last year's depreciation may have to be adjusted due to rounding.)

7. The Leo Brothers purchased a machine for $8,400 that has an estimated life of 3 years. At the end of 3 years the machine will have no value. Prepare a depreciation schedule using the straight-line depreciation method for this machine.

8. Fox Realty bought a computer table for $1,700. The estimated useful life of the table is 7 years. The residual value at the end of 7 years is $370. Find (a) the annual rate of depreciation to the nearest hundredth percent, (b) the annual amount of depreciation, and (c) the book value of the table at the end of the *third* year using the straight-line depreciation method.

9. Cashman, Inc., purchased an overhead projector for $560. It has an estimated useful life of 6 years, at which time it will have no remaining value. Find the book value at the end of 5 years using the straight-line depreciation method. Round the annual depreciation to the nearest whole dollar.

10. Shelley Corporation purchased a new machine for $15,000. The estimated life of the machine is 12 years with a residual value of $2,400. Find (a) the annual rate of depreciation by the straight-line method to the nearest hundredth percent, (b) the annual amount of depreciation, (c) the accumulated depreciation at the end of 7 years, and (d) the book value at the end of 9 years.

11. Wolfe Ltd. purchased a supercomputer for $75,000 on July 7, 2013. The computer has an estimated life of 5 years and will have a residual value of $15,000. Find (a) the annual depreciation amount by the straight-line method, (b) the depreciation amount for 2013, (c) the accumulated depreciation at the end of 2014, and (d) the book value at the end of 2015.

Learning Unit 17–2 : Units-of-Production Method

DRILL PROBLEMS

1. Find the depreciation per unit for each of the following assets. Round to three decimal places.

Cost of asset	Residual value	Estimated production	Depreciation per unit
a. $3,500	$800	9,000 units	_____
b. $309,560	$22,000	1,500,000 units	_____
c. $54,890	$6,500	275,000 units	_____

2. Find the annual depreciation expense for each of the assets in Problem 1.

Cost of asset	Residual value	Estimated production	Depreciation per unit	Units produced	Amount of depreciation
a. $3,500	$800	9,000 units	_____	3,000	_____
b. $309,560	$22,000	1,500,000 units	_____	45,500	_____
c. $54,890	$6,500	275,000 units	_____	4,788	_____

3. Find the book value at the end of the first year for each of the assets in Problems 1 and 2.

Cost of asset	Residual value	Estimated production	Depreciation per unit	Units produced	Book value
a. $3,500	$800	9,000 units	_____	3,000	_____
b. $309,560	$22,000	1,500,000 units	_____	45,500	_____
c. $54,890	$6,500	275,000 units	_____	4,788	_____

4. Calculate the accumulated depreciation at the end of year 2 for each of the following machines. Carry out the unit depreciation to three decimal places.

Cost of machine	Residual value	Estimated life	Hours used during year 1	Hours used during year 2	Accumulated depreciation
a. $67,900	$4,300	19,000 hours	5,430	4,856	_____
b. $3,810	$600	33,000 hours	10,500	9,330	_____
c. $25,000	$4,900	80,000 hours	7,000	12,600	_____

WORD PROBLEMS

5. Prepare a depreciation schedule for the following machine: The machine cost $63,400; it has an estimated residual value of $5,300 and expected life of 290,500 units. The units produced were:

Year 1	95,000 units
Year 2	80,000 units
Year 3	50,000 units
Year 4	35,500 units
Year 5	30,000 units

6. Forsmann & Smythe purchased a new machine that cost $46,030. The machine has a residual value of $2,200 and estimated output of 430,000 hours. Prepare a units-of-production depreciation schedule for this machine, rounding the unit depreciation to three decimal places. The hours of use were:

Year 1	90,000 hours
Year 2	150,000 hours
Year 3	105,000 hours
Year 4	90,000 hours

7. Young Electrical Company depreciates its vans using the units-of-production method. The cost of its new van was $24,600, the useful life is 125,000 miles, and the trade-in value is $5,250. What are (a) the depreciation expense per mile (to three decimal places) and (b) the book value at the end of the first year if it is driven 29,667 miles?

8. Tremblay Manufacturing Company purchased a new machine for $52,000. The machine has an estimated useful life of 185,000 hours and a residual value of $10,000. The machine was used for 51,200 hours the first year. Find (a) the depreciation rate per hour, rounded to three decimal places, (b) the depreciation expense for the first year, and (c) the book value of the machine at the end of the first year.

Learning Unit 17–3 : Declining-Balance Method

DRILL PROBLEMS

1. Find the declining-balance rate of depreciation, given the following estimated lives.

Life	Declining rate
a. 25 years	_____
b. 10 years	_____
c. 8 years	_____

2. Find the first year depreciation amount for the following assets using the declining-balance depreciation method. Round to the nearest whole dollar.

Cost of asset	Residual value	Useful life	First year depreciation
a. $2,460	$400	4 years	_____
b. $24,300	$2,000	6 years	_____
c. $350,000	$42,500	12 years	_____
d. $17,325	$5,000	5 years	_____
e. $2,550,000	$75,000	30 years	_____

3. Find the depreciation expense and ending book value for the first year, using the declining-balance depreciation method. Round to the nearest dollar.

Cost	Residual value	Useful life	First year depreciation	Ending book value
a. $6,700	$600	3 years	_____	_____
b. $11,600	$500	6 years	_____	_____
c. $9,980	–0–	5 years	_____	_____
d. $36,950	$2,500	12 years	_____	_____
e. $101,690	$3,600	27 years	_____	_____

WORD PROBLEMS

4. North Shore Grinding purchased a lathe for $37,500. This machine has a residual value of $3,000 and an expected useful life of 4 years. Prepare a depreciation schedule for the lathe using the declining-balance depreciation method. Round to the nearest whole dollar.

5. Colby Wayne paid $7,750 for a photocopy machine with an estimated life of 6 years and a residual value of $900. Prepare a depreciation schedule using the declining-balance depreciation method. Round to the nearest whole dollar.

6. The Leo Brothers purchased a machine for $8,400 that has an estimated life of 3 years. At the end of 3 years, the machine will have no value. Prepare a depreciation schedule for this machine. Round to the nearest whole dollar.

7. Fox Realty bought a computer table for $1,700. The estimated useful life of the table is 7 years. The residual value at the end of 7 years is $370. Find (a) the declining depreciation rate to the nearest hundredth percent, (b) the amount of depreciation at the end of the *third* year, and (c) the book value of the table at the end of the *third* year using the declining-balance depreciation method. Round to the nearest whole dollar.

8. Cashman, Inc., purchased an overhead projector for $560. It has an estimated useful life of 6 years, at which time it will have no remaining value. Find the book value at the end of 5 years using the declining-balance depreciation method. Round to the nearest whole dollar.

9.   Shelley Corporation purchased a new machine for $15,000. The estimated life of the machine is 12 years with a residual value of $2,400. Find (a) the declining-balance depreciation rate as a fraction and as a percent (hundredth percent), (b) the amount of depreciation at the end of the first year, (c) the accumulated depreciation at the end of 7 years, and (d) the book value at the end of 9 years. Round to the nearest dollar.

Learning Unit 17–4 :   Modified Accelerated Cost Recovery System (MACRS) with Introduction to ACRS

DRILL PROBLEMS

1.   Using the MACRS method of depreciation, find the recovery rate, first-year depreciation expense, and book value of the asset at the end of the first year. Round to the nearest whole dollar.

Cost of asset	Recovery period	Recovery rate	Depreciation expense	End-of-year book value
a. $2,500	3 years	____	____	____
b. $52,980	3 years	____	____	____
c. $4,250	5 years	____	____	____
d. $128,950	10 years	____	____	____
e. $13,775	5 years	____	____	____

2.   Find the accumulated depreciation at the end of the second year for each of the following assets. Round to the nearest whole dollar.

Cost of asset	Recovery period	Accumulated depreciation at end of 2nd year using MACRS	Book value at end of 2nd year using MACRS
a. $2,500	3 years	____	____
b. $52,980	3 years	____	____
c. $4,250	5 years	____	____
d. $128,950	10 years	____	____
e. $13,775	5 years	____	____

WORD PROBLEMS

3.   Colby Wayne paid $7,750 for a photocopy machine that is classified as equipment and has a residual value of $900. Prepare a depreciation schedule using the MACRS depreciation method. Round all calculations to the nearest whole dollar.

4.   Fox Realty bought a computer table for $1,700. The table is classified as furniture. The residual value at the end of the table's useful life is $370. Using the MACRS depreciation method, find (a) the amount of depreciation at the end of the *third* year, (b) the total accumulated depreciation at the end of year 3, and (c) the book value of the table at the end of the *third* year. Round all calculations to the nearest dollar.

5.   Cashman, Inc., purchased an overhead projector for $560. It is classified as office equipment and will have no residual value. Find the book value at the end of 5 years using the MACRS depreciation method. Round to the nearest whole dollar.

6.   Shelley Corporation purchased a new machine for $15,000. The machine is comparable to equipment used for two-way exchange of voice and data with a residual value of $2,400. Find (a) the amount of depreciation at the end of the first year, (b) the accumulated depreciation at the end of 7 years, and (c) the book value at the end of 9 years. Round to the nearest dollar.

7.*   Wolfe Ltd. purchased a supercomputer for $75,000 at the beginning of 1996. The computer is classified as a 5-year asset and will have a residual value of $15,000. Using MACRS, find (a) the depreciation amount for 1996, (b) the accumulated depreciation at the end of 1997, (c) the book value at the end of 1998, and (d) the last year that the asset will be depreciated.

*These problems are placed here for a quick review.

8.* Cummins Engine Company uses a straight-line depreciation method to calculate the cost of an asset of $1,200,000 with a $200,000 residual value and a life expectancy of 15 years. How much would Cummins have for depreciation expense for each of the first 2 years? Round to the nearest dollar for each year.

9. An article in an issue of *Management Accounting* stated that Cummins Engine Company changed its depreciation. The cost of its asset was $1,200,000 with a $200,000 residual value (with a life expectancy of 15 years) and an estimated productive capacity of 864,000 products. Cummins produced 59,000 products this year. What would it write off for depreciation using the units-of-production method?

*These problems are placed here for a quick review.

Learning Unit 18-1 : Assigning Costs to Ending Inventory—Specific Identification; Weighted Average; FIFO; LIFO

DRILL PROBLEMS

1. Given the value of the beginning inventory, purchases for the year, and ending inventory, find the cost of goods available for sale and the cost of goods sold.

	Beginning inventory	Purchases	Ending inventory	Cost of goods available for sale	Cost of goods sold
a.	$1,000	$4,120	$2,100	_____	_____
b.	$52,400	$270,846	$49,700	_____	_____
c.	$205	$48,445	$376	_____	_____
d.	$78,470	$2,788,560	$100,600	_____	_____
e.	$965	$53,799	$2,876	_____	_____

2. Find the missing amounts; then calculate the number of units available for sale and the cost of the goods available for sale.

Date	Category	Quantity	Unit cost	Total cost
January 1	Beginning inventory	1,207	$45	_____
February 7	Purchase	850	$46	_____
April 19	Purchase	700	$47	_____
July 5	Purchase	1,050	$49	_____
November 2	Purchase	450	$52	_____
Goods available for sale		_____		_____

3. Using the *specific identification* method, find the ending inventory and cost of goods sold for the merchandising concern in Problem 2.

Remaining inventory	Unit cost	Total cost
20 units from beginning inventory	_____	_____
35 units from February 7	_____	_____
257 units from July 5	_____	_____
400 units from November 2	_____	_____
Cost of ending inventory		_____
Cost of goods sold		_____

4. Using the *weighted-average* method, find the average cost per unit (to the nearest cent) and the cost of ending inventory.

Units available for sale	Cost of goods available for sale	Units in ending inventory	Weighted-average unit cost	Cost of ending inventory
a. 2,350	$120,320	1,265	_____	_____
b. 7,090	$151,017	1,876	_____	_____
c. 855	$12,790	989	_____	_____
d. 12,964	$125,970	9,542	_____	_____
e. 235,780	$507,398	239,013	_____	_____

5. Use the *FIFO* method of inventory valuation to determine the value of ending inventory, which consists of 40 units, and the cost of goods sold.

Date	Category	Quantity	Unit cost	Total cost
January 1	Beginning inventory	37	$219.00	_____
March 5	Purchases	18	230.60	_____
June 17	Purchases	22	255.70	_____
October 18	Purchases	34	264.00	_____
Goods available for sale		___		_____

Ending inventory = _____   Cost of goods sold = _____

6. Use the *LIFO* method of inventory valuation to determine the value of the ending inventory, which consists of 40 units, and the cost of goods sold.

Date	Category	Quantity	Unit cost	Total cost
January 1	Beginning inventory	37	$219.00	_____
March 5	Purchases	18	230.60	_____
June 17	Purchases	22	255.70	_____
October 18	Purchases	34	264.00	_____
Goods available for sale		___		_____

Ending inventory = _____   Cost of goods sold = _____

WORD PROBLEMS

7. At the beginning of September, Green's of Gloucester had 13 yellow raincoats in stock. These raincoats cost $36.80 each. During the month, Green's purchased 14 raincoats for $37.50 each and 16 raincoats for $38.40 each, and they sold 26 raincoats. Calculate **(a)** the average unit cost rounded to the nearest cent and **(b)** the ending inventory value using the weighted-average method.

8. If Green's of Gloucester (Problem 7) used the FIFO method, what would the value of the ending inventory be?

9. If Green's of Gloucester (Problem 7) used the LIFO method, what would the value of the ending inventory be?

10. Hobby Caterers purchased recycled-paper sketch pads during the year as follows:

January	350 pads for $.27 each
March	400 pads for $.31 each
July	200 pads for $.36 each
October	850 pads for $.26 each
November	400 pads for $.31 each

At the end of the year, the company had 775 of these sketch pads in stock. Find the ending inventory value using **(a)** the weighted-average method (round to the nearest cent), **(b)** the FIFO method, and **(c)** the LIFO method.

11. On March 1, Sandler's Shoe Store had the following sports shoes in stock:

   13 pairs running shoes for $33 a pair
   22 pairs walking shoes for $29 a pair
   35 pairs aerobic shoes for $26 a pair
   21 pairs cross-trainers for $52 a pair

   During the month Sandler's sold 10 pairs of running shoes, 15 pairs of walking shoes, 28 pairs of aerobic shoes, and 12 pairs of cross-trainers. Use the specific identification method to find (a) the cost of the goods available for sale, (b) the value of the ending inventory, and (c) the cost of goods sold.

Learning Unit 18–2 : Retail Method; Gross Profit Method; Inventory Turnover; Distribution of Overhead

DRILL PROBLEMS

1. Given the following information, calculate (a) the goods available for sale at cost and retail, (b) the cost ratio (to the nearest thousandth), (c) the ending inventory at retail, and (d) the cost of the March 31 inventory (to the nearest dollar) by the retail inventory method.

	Cost	Retail
Beginning inventory, March 1	$57,300	$95,500
Purchases during March	$28,400	$48,000
Sales during March		$79,000

2. Given the following information, use the gross profit method to calculate (a) the cost of goods available for sale, (b) the cost percentage, (c) the estimated cost of goods sold, and (d) the estimated cost of the inventory as of April 30.

Beginning inventory, April 1	$30,000
Net purchases during April	81,800
Sales during April	98,000
Average gross profit on sales	40%

3. Given the following information, find the average inventory.

Merchandise inventory, January 1, 200A	$82,000
Merchandise inventory, December 31, 200A	$88,000

4. Given the following information, find the inventory turnover for the company in Problem 3 to the nearest hundredth.

Cost of goods sold (12/31/0A)	$625,000

5. Given the following information, calculate the (a) average inventory at retail, (b) average inventory at cost, (c) inventory turnover at retail, and (d) inventory turnover at cost. Round to the nearest hundredth.

	Cost	Retail
Merchandise inventory, January 1	$ 250,000	$ 355,000
Merchandise inventory, December 31	$ 235,000	$ 329,000
Cost of goods sold	$1,525,000	
Sales		$2,001,000

6. Given the floor space for the following departments, find the entire floor space and the percent each department represents.

		Percent of floor space
Department A	15,000 square feet	_____
Department B	25,000 square feet	_____
Department C	10,000 square feet	_____
Total floor space	50,000 square feet	_____

7. If the total overhead for all the departments (Problem 6) is $200,000, how much of the overhead expense should be allocated to each department?

	Overhead/department
Department A	_____
Department B	_____
Department C	_____

WORD PROBLEMS

8. During the accounting period, Ward's Greenery sold $290,000 of merchandise at marked retail prices. At the end of the period, the following information was available from Ward's records:

	Cost	**Retail**
Beginning inventory	$ 53,000	$ 79,000
Net purchases	$204,000	$280,000

Use the retail method to estimate Ward's ending inventory at cost. Round the cost ratio to the nearest thousandth.

9. On January 1, Benny's Retail Mart had a $49,000 inventory at cost. During the first quarter of the year, Benny's made net purchases of $199,900. Benny's records show that during the past several years, the store's gross profit on sales has averaged 35%. If Benny's records show $275,000 in sales for the quarter, estimate the ending inventory for the first quarter, using the gross profit method.

10. On April 4, there was a big fire and the entire inventory of R. W. Wilson Company was destroyed. The company records were salvaged. They showed the following information:

Sales (January 1 through April 4)	$127,000
Merchandise inventory, January 1	16,000
Net purchases	71,250

On January 1, the inventory was priced to sell for $38,000 and additional items bought during the period were priced to sell for $102,000. Using the retail method, calculate the cost of the inventory that was destroyed by the fire. Round the cost ratio to the nearest thousandth.

11. During the past 4 years, the average gross margin on sales for R. W. Wilson Company was 36% of net sales. Using the data in Problem 10 and the gross profit method, calculate the cost of the ending inventory destroyed by fire.

12. Chase Bank has to make a decision on whether to grant a loan to Sally's Furniture store. The lending officer is interested in how often Sally's inventory turns over. Using selected information from Sally's income statement, calculate the inventory turnover for Sally's Furniture Store (to the nearest hundredth).

Merchandise inventory, January 1	$ 43,000
Merchandise inventory, December 31	55,000
Cost of goods sold	128,000

13. Wanting to know more about a business he was considering buying, Jake Paige studied the business's books. He found that beginning inventory for the previous year was $51,000 at cost and $91,800 at retail, ending inventory was $44,000 at cost and $72,600 at retail, sales were $251,000, and cost of goods sold was $154,000. Using this information, calculate for Jake the inventory turnover at cost and the inventory turnover at retail.

14. Ralph's Retail Outlet has calculated its expenses for the year. Total overhead expenses are $147,000. Ralph's accountant must allocate this overhead to four different departments. Given the following information regarding the floor space occupied by each department, calculate how much overhead expense should be allocated to each department.

Department W	12,000 square feet	Department Y	14,000 square feet
Department X	9,000 square feet	Department Z	7,000 square feet

15. How much overhead would be allocated to each department of Ralph's Retail Outlet (Problem 14) if the basis of allocation were the sales of each department? Sales for each of the departments were:

Department W	$110,000	Department Y	$170,000
Department X	$120,000	Department Z	$100,000

Learning Unit 19–1 : Sales and Excise Taxes

DRILL PROBLEMS

1. Calculate the sales tax and the total amount due for each of the following:

	Total sales	Sales tax rate	Sales tax	Total amount due
a.	$536	5%	_____	_____
b.	$11,980	6%	_____	_____
c.	$3,090	$8\frac{1}{4}\%$	_____	_____
d.	$17.65	$5\frac{1}{2}\%$	_____	_____
e.	$294	7.42%	_____	_____

2. Find the amount of actual sales and amount of sales tax on the following total receipts:

	Total receipts	Sales tax rate	Actual sales	Sales tax
a.	$27,932.15	5.5%	_____	_____
b.	$35,911.53	7%	_____	_____
c.	$115,677.06	$6\frac{1}{2}\%$	_____	_____
d.	$142.96	$5\frac{1}{4}\%$	_____	_____
e.	$5,799.24	4.75%	_____	_____

3. Find the sales tax, excise tax, and total cost for each of the following items:

	Retail price	Sales tax, 5.2%	Excise tax, 11%	Total cost
a.	$399	_____	_____	_____
b.	$22,684	_____	_____	_____
c.	$7,703	_____	_____	_____

4. Calculate the amount, subtotal, sales tax, and total amount due of the following:

Quantity	Description	Unit price	Amount
3	Taxable item	$4.30	_____
2	Taxable item	$5.23	_____
4	Taxable item	$1.20	_____
		Subtotal	_____
		5% sales tax	_____
		Total	_____

5. Given the sales tax rate and the amount of the sales tax, calculate the price of the following purchases (before tax was added):

	Tax rate	Tax amount	Price of purchase
a.	7%	$71.61	_____
b.	$5\frac{1}{2}\%$	$3.22	_____

6. Given the sales tax rate and the total price (including tax), calculate the price of the following purchases (before the tax was added):

	Tax rate	Total price	Price of purchase
a.	5%	$340.20	_____
b.	6%	$1,224.30	_____

WORD PROBLEMS

7. In a state with a 4.75% sales tax, what will be the sales tax and the total price of a video game marked $110?

8. Browning's invoice included a sales tax of $38.15. If the sales tax rate is 6%, what was the total cost of the taxable goods on the invoice?

9. David Bowan paid a total of $2,763 for a new computer. If this includes a sales tax of 5.3%, what was the marked price of the computer?

10. After a 5% sales tax and a 12% excise tax, the total cost of a leather jacket was $972. What was the selling price of the jacket?

11. A customer at the RDM Discount Store purchased four tubes of toothpaste priced at $1.88 each, six toothbrushes for $1.69 each, and three bottles of shampoo for $2.39 each. What did the customer have to pay if the sales tax is $5\frac{1}{2}$%?

12. Bill Harrington purchased a mountain bike for $875. Bill had to pay a sales tax of 6% and an excise tax of 11%. What was the total amount Bill had to pay for his mountain bike?

13. Donna DeCoff received a bill for $754 for a new chair she had purchased. The bill included a 6.2% sales tax and a delivery charge of $26. What was the selling price of the chair?

Learning Unit 19–2 : Property Tax

DRILL PROBLEMS

1. Find the assessed value of the following properties, rounding to the nearest whole dollar:

Market value	Assessment rate	Assessed value	Market value	Assessment rate	Assessed value
a. $195,000	35%	_____	d. $2,585,400	65%	_____
b. $1,550,900	50%	_____	e. $349,500	85%	_____
c. $75,000	75%	_____			

2. Find the tax rate for each of the following municipalities, rounding to the nearest tenth of a percent:

Budget needed	Total assessed value	Tax rate	Budget needed	Total assessed value	Tax rate
a. $2,594,000	$44,392,000	_____	d. $13,540,000	$143,555,500	_____
b. $17,989,000	$221,900,000	_____	e. $1,099,000	$12,687,000	_____
c. $6,750,000	$47,635,000	_____			

3. Express each of the following tax rates in all the indicated forms:

By percent	Per $100 of assessed value	Per $1,000 of assessed value	In mills
a. 7.45%	_____	_____	_____
b. _____	$14.24	_____	_____
c. _____	_____	_____	90.8
d. _____	_____	$62.00	_____

4. Calculate the property tax due for each of the following:

Total assessed value	Tax rate	Total property tax due	Total assessed value	Tax rate	Total property tax due
a. $12,900	$6.60 per $100	_____	e. $78,900	59 mills	_____
b. $175,400	43 mills	_____	f. $225,550	$11.39 per $1,000	_____
c. $320,500	2.7%	_____	g. $198,750	$2.63 per $100	_____
d. $2,480,000	$17.85 per $1,000	_____			

WORD PROBLEMS

5. The county of Chelsea approved a budget of $3,450,000, which had to be raised through property taxation. If the total assessed value of properties in the county of Chelsea was $37,923,854, what will the tax rate be? The tax rate is stated per $100 of assessed valuation.

6. Linda Tawse lives in Camden and her home has a market value of $235,000. Property in Camden is assessed at 55% of its market value, and the tax rate for the current year is $64.75 per $1,000. What is the assessed valuation of Linda's home?

7. Using the information in Problem 6, find the amount of property tax that Linda will have to pay.

8. Mary Faye Souza has property with a fair market value of $219,500. Property in Mary Faye's city is assessed at 65% of its market value and the tax rate is $3.64 per $100. How much is Mary Faye's property tax due?

9. Cagney's Greenhouse has a fair market value of $1,880,000. Property is assessed at 35% by the city. The tax rate is 6.4%. What is the property tax due for Cagney's Greenhouse?

10. In Chester County, property is assessed at 40% of its market value, the residential tax rate is $12.30 per $1,000, and the commercial tax rate is $13.85 per $1,000. What is the property tax due on a home that has a market value of $205,000?

11. Using the information in Problem 10, find the property tax due on a grocery store with a market value of $5,875,000.

12. Bob Rose's home is assessed at $195,900. Last year the tax rate was 11.8 mills, and this year the rate was raised to 13.2 mills. How much more will Bob have to pay in taxes this year?

Learning Unit 20–1 : Life Insurance

DRILL PROBLEMS

1. Use the table in the *Business Math Handbook* to find the annual premium per $1,000 of life insurance and calculate the annual premiums for each policy listed. Assume the insureds are males.

	Face value of policy	Type of insurance	Age at issue	Annual premium per $1,000	Number of $1,000s in face value	Annual premium
a.	$25,000	Straight life	31	_____	_____	_____
b.	$40,500	20-year endowment	40	_____	_____	_____
c.	$200,000	Straight life	44	_____	_____	_____
d.	$62,500	20-payment life	25	_____	_____	_____
e.	$12,250	5-year term	35	_____	_____	_____
f.	$42,500	20-year endowment	42	_____	_____	_____

2. Use Table 20.1 to find the annual premium for each of the following life insurance policies. Assume the insured is a 30-year-old male.

	Face value of policy	Five-year term policy	Straight life policy	Twenty-payment life policy	Twenty-year endowment
a.	$50,000	_____	_____	_____	_____
b.	$1,000,000	_____	_____	_____	_____
c.	$250,000	_____	_____	_____	_____
d.	$72,500	_____	_____	_____	_____

3. Use the table in the *Business Math Handbook* to find the annual premium for each of the following life insurance policies. Assume the insured is a 30-year-old female.

	Face value of policy	Five-year term policy	Straight life policy	Twenty-payment life policy	Twenty-year endowment
a.	$50,000	_____	_____	_____	_____
b.	$1,000,000	_____	_____	_____	_____
c.	$250,000	_____	_____	_____	_____
d.	$72,500	_____	_____	_____	_____

4. Use the table in the *Business Math Handbook* to find the nonforfeiture options for the following policies:

Years policy in force	Type of policy	Face value	Cash value	Amount of paid-up insurance	Extended term
a. 10	Straight life	$25,000	_____	_____	_____
b. 20	20-year endowment	$500,000	_____	_____	_____
c. 5	20-payment life	$2,000,000	_____	_____	_____
d. 15	Straight life	$750,000	_____	_____	_____
e. 5	20-year endowment	$93,500	_____	_____	_____

WORD PROBLEMS

5. If Mr. Davis, aged 39, buys a $90,000 straight life policy, what is the amount of his annual premium?

6. If Miss Jennie McDonald, age 27, takes out a $65,000 20-year endowment policy, what premium amount will she pay each year?

7. If Gary Thomas decides to cash in his $45,000 20-payment life insurance policy after 15 years, what cash surrender value will he receive?

8. Mary Allyn purchased a $70,000 20-year endowment policy when she was 26 years old. Ten years later, she decided that she could no longer afford the premiums. If Mary decides to convert her policy to paid-up insurance, what amount of paid-up insurance coverage will she have?

9. Peter and Jane Rizzo are both 28 years old and are both planning to take out $50,000 straight life insurance policies. What is the difference in the annual premiums they will have to pay?

10. Paul Nasser purchased a $125,000 straight life policy when he was 30 years old. He is now 50 years old. Two months ago, he slipped in the bathtub and injured his back; he will not be able to return to his regular job for several months. Due to a lack of income, he feels that he can no longer continue to pay the premiums on his life insurance policy. If Paul decides to surrender his policy for cash, how much cash will he receive?

11. If Paul Nasser (Problem 10) chooses to convert his policy to paid-up insurance, what will the face value of his new policy be?

Learning Unit 20–2 : Fire Insurance

DRILL PROBLEMS

1. Use the tables in the *Business Math Handbook* to find the premium for each of the following:

Rating of area	Building class	Building value	Value of contents	Total annual premium
a. 3	A	$80,000	$32,000	_____
b. 2	B	$340,000	$202,000	_____
c. 2	A	$221,700	$190,000	_____
d. 1	B	$96,400	$23,400	_____
e. 3	B	$65,780	$62,000	_____

2. Use the tables in the *Business Math Handbook* to find the short-term premium and the amount of refund due if the insured cancels.

Annual premium	Months of coverage	Short-term premium	Refund due
a. $1,860	3	_____	_____
b. $650	7	_____	_____
c. $1,200	10	_____	_____
d. $341	12	_____	_____
e. $1,051	4	_____	_____

3. Find the amount to be paid for each of the following losses:

Property value	Coinsurance clause	Insurance required	Insurance carried	Amount of loss	Insurance company pays (indemnity)
a. $85,000	80%	_____	$70,000	$60,000	_____
b. $52,000	80%	_____	$45,000	$50,000	_____
c. $44,000	80%	_____	$33,000	$33,000	_____
d. $182,000	80%	_____	$127,400	$61,000	_____

WORD PROBLEMS

4. Mary Rose wants to purchase fire insurance for her building, which is rated as Class B; the rating of the area is 2. If her building is worth $225,000 and the contents are worth $70,000, what will her annual premium be?

5. Janet Ambrose owns a Class A building valued at $180,000. The contents of the building are valued at $145,000. The territory rating is 3. What is her annual fire insurance premium?

6. Jack Altshuler owns a building worth $355,500. The contents are worth $120,000. The classification of the building is B, and the rating of the area is 1. What annual premium must Jack pay for his fire insurance?

7. Jay Viola owns a store valued at $460,000. His fire insurance policy (which has an 80% coinsurance clause) has a face value of $345,000. A recent fire resulted in a loss of $125,000. How much will the insurance company pay?

8. The building that is owned by Tally's Garage is valued at $275,000 and is insured for $225,000. The policy has an 80% coinsurance clause. If there is a fire in the building and the damages amount to $220,000, how much of the loss will be paid for by the insurance company?

9. Michael Dannon owns a building worth $420,000. He has a fire insurance policy with a face value of $336,000 (there is an 80% coinsurance clause). There was recently a fire that resulted in a $400,000 loss. How much money will he receive from the insurance company?

10. Rice's Rent-A-Center business is worth $375,000. He has purchased a $250,000 fire insurance policy. The policy has an 80% coinsurance clause. What will Rice's reimbursement be **(a)** after a $150,000 fire and **(b)** after a $330,000 fire?

11. If Maria's Pizza Shop is valued at $210,000 and is insured for $147,000 with a policy that contains an 80% coinsurance clause, what settlement is due after a fire that causes **(a)** $150,000 in damages and **(b)** $175,000 in damages?

Learning Unit 20–3 : Auto Insurance

DRILL PROBLEMS

1. Calculate the annual premium for compulsory coverage for each of the following.

Driver classification	Bodily	Property	Total premium
a. 17	_____	_____	_____
b. 20	_____	_____	_____
c. 10	_____	_____	_____

2. Calculate the amount of money the insurance company and the driver should pay for each of the following accidents, assuming the driver carries compulsory insurance only.

Accident and court award	Insurance company pays	Driver pays
a. Driver hit one person and court awarded $15,000.	_____	_____
b. Driver hit one person and court awarded $12,000 for personal injury.	_____	_____
c. Driver hit two people; court awarded first person $9,000 and the second person $12,000.	_____	_____

3. Calculate the additional premium payment for each of the following options.

Optional insurance coverage	Addition to premium
a. Bodily injury 50/100/25, driver class 20	_____
b. Bodily injury 25/60/10, driver class 17	_____
c. Collision insurance, driver class 10, age group 3, symbol 5, deductible $100	_____
d. Comprehensive insurance, driver class 10, age group 3, symbol 5, deductible $200	_____
e. Substitute transportation, towing, and labor; driver class 10, age group 3, symbol 5	_____

4. Compute the annual premium for compulsory insurance with optional liability coverage for bodily injury and damage to someone else's property.

Driver classification	Bodily coverage	Premium
a. 17	50/100/25	_____
b. 20	100/300/10	_____
c. 10	25/60/25	_____
d. 18	250/500/50	_____
e. 20	25/50/10	_____

5. Calculate the annual premium for each of the following drivers with the indicated options. All drivers must carry compulsory insurance.

Driver classification	Car age	Car symbol	Bodily injury	Collision	Comprehensive	Transportation and towing	Annual premium
a. 10	2	4	50/100/10	$100 deductible	$300 deductible	Yes	_____
b. 18	3	2	25/60/25	$200 deductible	$200 deductible	Yes	_____

WORD PROBLEMS

6. Ann Centerino's driver classification is 10. She carries only compulsory insurance coverage. What annual insurance premium must she pay?

7. Gary Hines is a class 18 driver. He wants to add optional bodily injury and property damage of 250/500/50 to his compulsory insurance coverage. What will be Gary's total annual premium?

8. Sara Goldberg wants optional bodily injury coverage of 50/100/25 and collision coverage with a deductible of $300 in addition to the compulsory coverage her state requires. Sara is a class 17 driver and has a symbol 4 car that is 2 years old. What annual premium must Sara pay?

9. Karen Babson has just purchased a new car with a symbol of 8. She wants bodily injury and property liability of 500/1,000/100, comprehensive and collision insurance with a $200 deductible, and transportation and towing coverage. If Karen is a class 10 driver, what will be her annual insurance premium? There is no compulsory insurance requirement in her state. Assume age group 1.

10. Craig Haberland is a class 18 driver. He has a 5-year-old car with a symbol of 4. His state requires compulsory insurance coverage. In addition, he wishes to purchase collision and comprehensive coverage with the maximum deductible. He also wants towing insurance. What will Craig's annual insurance premium be?

11. Nancy Poland has an insurance policy with limits of 10/20. If Nancy injures a pedestrian and the judge awards damages of $18,000, **(a)** how much will the insurance company pay and **(b)** how much will Nancy pay?

12. Peter Bell carries insurance with bodily injury limits of 25/60. Peter is in an accident and is charged with injuring four people. The judge awards damages of $10,000 to each of the injured parties. How much will the insurance company pay? How much will Peter pay?

13. Jerry Greeley carries an insurance policy with bodily injury limits of 25/60. Jerry is in an accident and is charged with injuring four people. If the judge awards damages of $20,000 to each of the injured parties, **(a)** how much will the insurance company pay and **(b)** how much will Jerry pay?

14. An issue of *Your Money* reported that the Illinois Department of Insurance gave a typical premium for a brick house in Chicago built in 1950, assuming no policy discounts and a replacement cost estimated at $100,000. With a $100 deductible, the annual premium will be $653. Using the rate in your textbook, with a rating area 3 and class B, what would be the annual premium? (This problem reviews fire insurance.)

15. An issue of *Money* ran a story on cutting car insurance premiums. Raising the car insurance deductible to $500 will cut the collision premium 15%. Theresa Mendex insures her car; her age group is 5 and symbol is 5. What would be her reduction if she changed her policy to a $500 deductible? What would the collision insurance now cost?

16. Robert Stuono lost his life insurance when he was downsized from an investment banking company early this year. So Stuono, age 44, enlisted the help of an independent agent who works with several insurance companies. His goal is $350,000 in term coverage with a level premium for 5 years. What will Robert's annual premium be for term insurance? (This problem reviews life insurance.)

Learning Unit 21–1 : Stocks

DRILL PROBLEMS

52 weeks		Stocks	SYM	Div	Yld %	PE	Vol 100s	High	Low	Close	Net chg
Hi	Lo										
43.88	25.51	Disney	DIS	.21	.8	49	49633	27.69	26.50	27.69	+0.63

1. From the listed information for Disney, complete the following:
   a. _____ was the highest price at which Disney stock traded during the year.
   b. _____ was the lowest price at which Disney stock traded during the year.
   c. _____ was the amount of the dividend Disney paid to shareholders last year.
   d. _____ is the dividend amount a shareholder with 100 shares would receive.
   e. _____ is the rate of return the stock yielded to its stockholders.
   f. _____ is how many times the earnings per share the stock is selling for.
   g. _____ is the number of shares traded on the day of this stock quote.
   h. _____ is the highest price paid for Disney stock on this day.
   i. _____ is the lowest price paid for Disney stock on this day.
   j. _____ is the change in price from yesterday's closing price.

2. Use the Disney information to show how the yield percent was calculated.

3. What was the price of the last trade of Disney stock yesterday?

WORD PROBLEMS

4. Assume a stockbroker's commission of 2%. What will it cost to purchase 200 shares of Saplent Corporation at $10.75?

5. In Problem 4, the stockbroker's commission for selling stock is the same as that for buying stock. If the customer who purchased 200 shares at $10.75 sells the 200 shares of stock at the end of the year at $18.12, what will be the gain on investment?

6. Holtz Corporation's records show 80,000 shares of preferred stock issued. The preferred dividend is $2 per share, which is cumulative. The records show 750,000 shares of common stock issued. In 2012, no dividends were paid. In 2013, the board of directors declared a dividend of $582,500. What are **(a)** the total amount of dividends paid to preferred stockholders, **(b)** the total amount of dividends paid to common stockholders, and **(c)** the amount of the common dividend per share?

7. Melissa Tucker bought 300 shares of Delta Air Lines stock listed at $61.22 per share. What is the total amount she paid if the stockbroker's commission is 2.5%?

8. A year later, Melissa (Problem 7) sold the stock she had purchased. The market price of the stock at this time was $72.43. Delta Air Lines had paid its shareholders a dividend of $1.20 per share. If the stockbroker's commission to sell stock is 2.5%, what gain did Melissa realize?

9. The board of directors of Parker Electronics, Inc., declared a $539,000 dividend. If the corporation has 70,000 shares of common stock outstanding, what is the dividend per share?

Learning Unit 21–2 : Bonds

DRILL PROBLEMS

Bond	Current yield	Sales	Close	Net change
IBM $10\frac{1}{4}$ 18	10.0	11	102.5	+.125

1. From the bond listing above complete the following:
    a. _____ is the name of the company.
    b. _____ is the percent of interest paid on the bond.
    c. _____ is the year in which the bond matures.
    d. _____ is the total interest for the year.
    e. _____ was the previous day's closing price on the IBM bond.

2. Show how to calculate the current yield of 10.0% for IBM. (Trade commissions have been omitted.)

3. Use the information for the IBM bonds to calculate **(a)** the amount the last bond traded for on this day and **(b)** the amount the last bond traded for yesterday.

4. What will be the annual interest payment **(a)** to the bondholder assuming he paid $101\frac{3}{4}$ and **(b)** to the bondholder who purchased the bond for $102\frac{1}{2}$?

5. If Terry Gambol purchased three IBM bonds at this day's closing price, **(a)** what will be her total cost excluding commission and **(b)** how much interest will she receive for the year?

6. Calculate the bond yield (to the nearest tenth percent) for each of the following:

Bond interest rate	Purchase price	Bond yield
a. 7%	97	_____
b. $9\frac{1}{2}$%	101.625	_____
c. $13\frac{1}{4}$%	104.25	_____

7. For each of the following, state whether the bond sold at a premium or a discount and give the amount of the premium or discount.

Bond interest rate	Purchase price	Premium or discount
a. 7%	97	_____
b. $9\frac{1}{2}\%$	101.625	_____
c. $13\frac{1}{4}\%$	104.25	_____

WORD PROBLEMS

8. Rob Morrisey purchased a $1,000 bond that was quoted at 102.25 and paying $8\frac{7}{8}\%$ interest. **(a)** How much did Rob pay for the bond? **(b)** What was the premium or discount? **(c)** How much annual interest will he receive?

9. Jackie Anderson purchased a bond that was quoted at 62.50 and paying interest of $10\frac{1}{2}\%$. **(a)** How much did Jackie pay for the bond? **(b)** What was the premium or discount? **(c)** What interest will Jackie receive annually? **(d)** What is the bond's current annual yield (to the nearest tenth percent)?

10. Swartz Company issued bonds totaling $2,000,000 in order to purchase updated equipment. If the bonds pay interest of 11%, what is the total amount of interest the Swartz Company must pay semiannually?

11. The RJR and ACyan companies have both issued bonds that are paying $7\frac{3}{8}\%$ interest. The quoted price of the RJR bond is 94.125, and the quoted price of the ACyan bond is $102\frac{7}{8}$. Find the current annual yield on each (to the nearest tenth percent).

12. Mary Rowe purchased 25 of Chrysler Corporation $8\frac{3}{8}\%$ bonds of 2009. The bonds closed at 93.25. Find **(a)** the total purchase price and **(b)** the amount of the first semiannual interest payment Mary will receive.

13. What is the annual yield (to the nearest hundredth percent) of the bonds Mary Rowe purchased?

14. Mary Rowe purchased a $1,000 bond listed as ARch $10\frac{7}{8}$ 19 for 122.75. What is the annual yield of this bond (to the nearest tenth percent)?

Learning Unit 21–3 : Mutual Funds

DRILL PROBLEMS

From the following, calculate the NAV. Round to the nearest cent.

	Current market value of fund investments	Current liabilities	Number of shares outstanding	NAV
1.	$6,800,000	$850,000	500,000	_____
2.	$11,425,000	$690,000	810,000	_____
3.	$22,580,000	$1,300,000	1,400,000	_____

Complete the following using this information:

NAV	Net change	Fund name	Inv. obj.	YTD %Ret	Total return 1 Yr R
$23.48	+.14	EuroA	Eu	+37.3	+7.6 E

4. NAV _____

5. NAV change _____

6. Total return year to date _____

7. Return for the last 12 months _____

8. What does an E rating mean? _____

Calculate the commission (load) charge and the offer to buy.

NAV	% commission (load) charge	Dollar amount of commission (load) charge	Offer price
9. $17.00	$8\frac{1}{2}\%$	_____	_____
10. $21.55	6%	_____	_____
11. $14.10	4%	_____	_____

WORD PROBLEMS

12. Paul wanted to know how his Fidelity mutual fund $14.33 NAV in the newspaper was calculated. He called Fidelity, and he received the following information:

Current market value of fund investment	$7,500,000
Current liabilities	$910,000
Number of shares outstanding	460,000

Please calculate the NAV for Paul. Was the NAV in the newspaper correct?

13. Jeff Jones bought 150 shares of Putnam Vista Fund. The NAV of the fund was $9.88. The offer price was $10.49. What did Jeff pay for these 150 shares?

14. Pam Long purchased 300 shares of the no-load Scudder's European Growth Company Fund. The NAV is $12.61. What did Pam pay for the 300 shares?

15. Assume in Problem 14 that 8 years later Pam sells her 300 shares. The NAV at the time of sale was $12.20. What is the amount of her profit or loss on the sale?

16. Financial planner J. Michael Martin recommended that Jim Kelly choose a long-term bond because it gives high income while Kelly waits for better stock market opportunities down the road. The bond Martin recommended matures in 2012 and was originally issued at $8\frac{1}{2}\%$ interest and the current yield is 7.9%. What would be the current selling price for this bond and how would that price appear in the bond quotations?

17.

Bonds	Vol.	Close	Net chg.
Comp USA $9\frac{1}{2}$ 14	70	102.375	−.125
GMA 7 22	5	101.625	−1.25

From the above information, compare the two bonds for:

a. When the bonds expire.
b. The yield of each bond.
c. The current selling price.
d. Whether the bond is selling at a discount or premium.
e. Yesterday's bond close.

Learning Unit 22–1 : Mean, Median, and Mode

Note: Optional problems for LU 22–3 are found on page 549.

DRILL PROBLEMS

1. Find the mean for the following lists of numbers. Round to the nearest hundredth.
   a. 12, 16, 20, 25, 29   Mean _____
   b. 80, 91, 98, 82, 68, 82, 79, 90   Mean _____
   c. 9.5, 12.3, 10.5, 7.5, 10.1, 18.4, 9.8, 6.2, 11.1, 4.8, 10.6   Mean _____

2. Find the weighted mean for the following. Round to the nearest hundredth.
   a. 4, 4, 6, 8, 8, 13, 4, 6, 8   Weighted mean _____
   b. 82, 85, 87, 82, 82, 90, 87, 63, 100, 85, 87   Weighted mean _____

3. Find the median for the following:
   a. 56, 89, 47, 36, 90, 63, 55, 82, 46, 81   Median _____
   b. 59, 22, 39, 47, 33, 98, 50, 73, 54, 46, 99   Median _____

4. Find the mode for the following:
   24, 35, 49, 35, 52, 35, 52   Mode _____

5. Find the mean, median, and mode for each of the following:
   a. 72, 48, 62, 54, 73, 62, 75, 57, 62, 58, 78
      Mean _____   Median _____   Mode _____
   b. $0.50, $1.19, $0.58, $1.19, $2.83, $1.71, $2.21, $0.58, $1.29, $0.58
      Mean _____   Median _____   Mode _____
   c. $92, $113, $99, $117, $99, $105, $119, $112, $95, $116, $102, $120
      Mean _____   Median _____   Mode _____
   d. 88, 105, 120, 119, 105, 128, 160, 151, 90, 153, 107, 119, 105
      Mean _____   Median _____   Mode _____

WORD PROBLEMS

6. The sales for the year at the 8 Bed and Linen Stores were $1,442,897, $1,556,793, $1,703,767, $1,093,320, $1,443,984, $1,665,308, $1,197,692, and $1,880,443. Find the mean earnings for a Bed and Linen Store for the year.

7. To avoid having an extreme number affect the average, the manager of Bed and Linen Stores (Problem 6) would like you to find the median earnings for the 8 stores.

8. The Bed and Linen Store in Salem sells many different towels. Following are the prices of all the towels that were sold on Wednesday: $7.98, $9.98, $9.98, $11.49, $11.98, $7.98, $12.49, $12.49, $11.49, $9.98, $9.98, $16.00, and $7.98. Find the mean price of a towel.

9. Looking at the towel prices, the Salem manager (Problem 8) decided that he should have calculated a weighted mean. Find the weighted mean price of a towel.

10. The manager of the Salem Bed and Linen Store above would like to find another measure of the central tendency called the *median*. Find the median price for the towels sold.

11. The manager at the Salem Bed and Linen Store would like to know the most popular towel among the group of towels sold on Wednesday. Find the mode for the towel prices for Wednesday.

Learning Unit 22–2 : Frequency Distributions and Graphs

DRILL PROBLEMS

1. A local dairy distributor wants to know how many containers of yogurt health club members consume in a month. The distributor gathered the following data:

17	17	22	14	26	23	23	15	18	16
18	15	23	18	29	20	24	17	12	15
18	19	18	20	28	21	25	21	26	14
16	18	15	19	27	15	22	19	19	13
20	17	13	24	28	18	28	20	17	16

Construct a frequency distribution table to organize these data.

2. Construct a bar graph for the Problem 1 data. The height of each bar should represent the frequency of each amount consumed.

3. To simplify the amount of data concerning yogurt consumption, construct a relative frequency distribution table. The range will be from 1 to 30 with five class intervals: 1–6, 7–12, 13–18, 19–24, and 25–30.

4. Construct a bar graph for the grouped data.

5. Prepare a pie chart to represent the above data.

WORD PROBLEMS

6. The women's department of a local department store lists its total sales for the year: January, $39,800; February, $22,400; March, $32,500; April, $33,000; May, $30,000; June, $29,200; July, $26,400; August, $24,800; September, $34,000; October, $34,200; November, $38,400; December, $41,100. Draw a line graph to represent the monthly sales of the women's department for the year. The vertical axis should represent the dollar amount of the sales.

7. The following list shows the number of television sets sold in a year by the sales associates at Souza's TV and Appliance Store.

115	125	139	127	142	153	169	126	141
130	137	150	169	157	146	173	168	156
140	146	134	123	142	129	141	122	141

Construct a relative frequency distribution table to represent the data. The range will be from 115 to 174 with intervals of 10.

8. Use the data in the distribution table for Problem 7 to construct a bar graph for the grouped data.

9. Expenses for Flora Foley Real Estate Agency for the month of June were as follows: salaries expense, $2,790; utilities expense, $280; rent expense, $2,000; commissions expense, $4,800; and other expenses, $340. Present these data in a circle graph. (First calculate the percent relationship between each item and the total, then determine the number of degrees that represents each item.)

10. Today a new Jeep costs $25,000. In 1970, the Jeep cost $4,500. What is the price relative? (Round to the nearest tenth percent.)

Worked-Out Solutions to Extra Practice Quizzes and You Try It Problems

Chapter 1

LU 1-1a

1. **a.** Eight thousand, six hundred eighty-two
    b. Fifty-six thousand, two hundred ninety-five
    c. Seven hundred thirty-two billion, three hundred ten million, four hundred forty-four thousand, eight hundred eighty-eight

2. **a.** 43 = 40   **b.** 654 = 700   **c.** 7,328 = 7,000   **d.** 5,980 = 6,000

3. Kellogg's sales and profit:

	The facts	Solving for?	Steps to take	Key points
BLUEPRINT	*Sales:* Three million, two hundred ninety-one thousand dollars. *Profit:* Four hundred five thousand dollars.	Sales and profit rounded all the way.	Express each verbal form in numeric form. Identify leftmost digit in each number.	Rounding all the way means only the leftmost digit will remain. All other digits become zeros.

Steps to solving problem

1. Convert verbal to numeric.
   Three million, two hundred ninety-one thousand ⟶ $3,291,000
   Four hundred five thousand ⟶ $ 405,000

2. Identify leftmost digit of each number.
   $3,291,000 $405,000
        ↓   ↓
   $3,000,000 $400,000

LU 1-2a

1.
```
     10
     18
     19
     24
  26,090
```

2.
Estimate	Actual
3,000	3,482
7,000	6,981
+ 5,000	5,490
15,000	15,953

3.
```
  8 17 7 17
  9,787
 −5,968
  3,819
```
Check
```
  3,819
 + 5,968
  9,787
```

4. Jackson Manufacturing Company over- or underestimated sales:

	The facts	Solving for?	Steps to take	Key points
BLUEPRINT	*Projected 2013 sales:* $878,000 *Major clients:* $492,900 *Other clients:* $342,000	How much were sales over- or underestimated?	Total projected sales − Total actual sales = Over- or underestimated sales.	Projected sales (minuend) − Actual sales (subtrahend) = Difference.

Steps to solving problem

1. Calculate total actual sales.
```
  $492,900
 + 342,000
  $834,900
```

2. Calculate over- or underestimated sales.
```
  $878,000
 − 834,900
  $ 43,100  (overestimated)
```

LU 1-3a

1.

Estimate	Actual	Check
5,000	4,938	$9 \times 4,938 = 44,442$
$\times\ \ 20$	$\times\ \ 19$	$10 \times 4,938 = +49,380$
100,000	44442	93,822
	4938	
	93,822	

2. $86 \times 19 = 1,634 + 5$ zeros $= 163,400,000$

3. $86 + 4$ zeros $= 860,000$

4.

Rounding	Actual		Check
200	245	R24	$26 \times 245 = 6,370$
30)6,000	26)6,394		$+\ \ 24$
6 0	52		6,394
	119		
	104		
	154		
	130		
	24		

5.   Drop 3 zeros $= 3)\overline{99}$ (quotient 33)

6.   General Motors' total cost per year:

	The facts	Solving for?	Steps to take	Key points
BLUEPRINT	Cars produced each workday: 850 Workweek: 5 days Cost per car: $7,000	Total cost per year.	Cars produced per week × 52 = Total cars produced per year. Total cars produced per year × Total cost per car = Total cost per year.	Whenever possible, use multiplication and division shortcuts with zeros. Multiplication can be checked by division.

Steps to solving problem

1. Calculate total cars produced per week. $5 \times 850 = 4,250$ cars produced per week

2. Calculate total cars produced per year. $4,250$ cars $\times 52$ weeks $= 221,000$ total cars produced per year

3. Calculate total cost per year. $221,000$ cars $\times \$7,000 = \$1,547,000,000$ (multiply 221×7 and add zeros)

   Check $\$1,547,000,000 \div 221,000 = \$7,000$ (drop 3 zeros before dividing)

You Try It

1. 571 → Five hundred seventy-one
7,943 → Seven thousand, nine hundred forty-three

2. 691 = 691 = 690

Identify digit ↑   Less than 5

3. 429,685 → 429,685 → 400,000

Identify digit ↑   Less than 5

4.
```
  1
  76
+ 38
 114
```

5.
```
 5 12
 629
-134
 495
```

6.
```
    491
 ×   28
   3928
    982
 13,748
```

$13 \times 10 = 130$ (attach 1 zero)
$13 \times 1,000 = 13,000$ (attach 3 zeros)

7.
```
    5 R15
16)95
   80
   15
```

$4,000 \div 100 = 40$ (drop 2 zeros)
$4,000 \div 1,000 = 4$ (drop 3 zeros)

Chapter 2

LU 2-1a

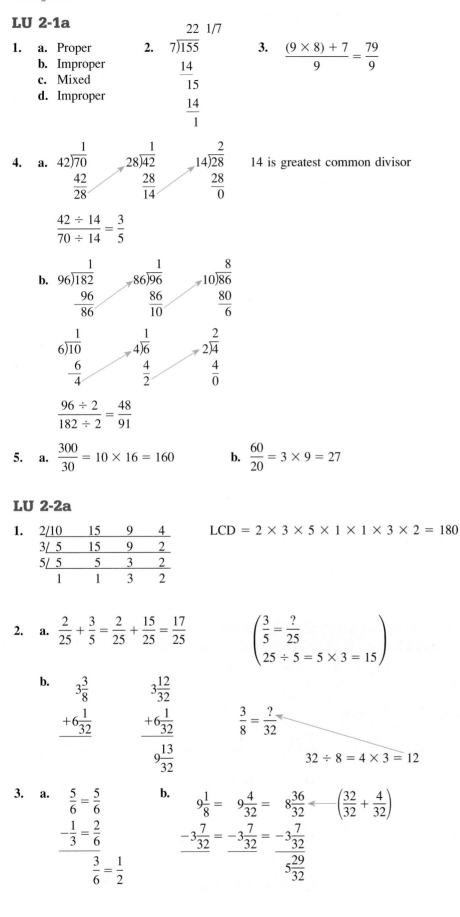

1. a. Proper
    b. Improper
    c. Mixed
    d. Improper

2. $$7\overline{)155} \quad \begin{array}{r} 22 \ 1/7 \\ \hline \end{array}$$
    $$\begin{array}{r} 14 \\ \hline 15 \\ 14 \\ \hline 1 \end{array}$$

3. $\dfrac{(9 \times 8) + 7}{9} = \dfrac{79}{9}$

4. a. $42\overline{)70}^{\,1} \quad 28\overline{)42}^{\,1} \quad 14\overline{)28}^{\,2}$

    $\dfrac{42}{28} \quad \dfrac{28}{14} \quad \dfrac{28}{0}$ 14 is greatest common divisor

    $\dfrac{42 \div 14}{70 \div 14} = \dfrac{3}{5}$

    b. $96\overline{)182}^{\,1} \quad 86\overline{)96}^{\,1} \quad 10\overline{)86}^{\,8}$

    $\dfrac{96}{86} \quad \dfrac{86}{10} \quad \dfrac{80}{6}$

    $6\overline{)10}^{\,1} \quad 4\overline{)6}^{\,1} \quad 2\overline{)4}^{\,2}$

    $\dfrac{6}{4} \quad \dfrac{4}{2} \quad \dfrac{4}{0}$

    $\dfrac{96 \div 2}{182 \div 2} = \dfrac{48}{91}$

5. a. $\dfrac{300}{30} = 10 \times 16 = 160$ b. $\dfrac{60}{20} = 3 \times 9 = 27$

LU 2-2a

1.
    $$\begin{array}{llll} 2/\underline{10} & 15 & 9 & 4 \\ 3/\ \underline{5} & 15 & 9 & 2 \\ 5/\ \underline{5} & \underline{5} & 3 & 2 \\ 1 & 1 & 3 & 2 \end{array}$$
    LCD $= 2 \times 3 \times 5 \times 1 \times 1 \times 3 \times 2 = 180$

2. a. $\dfrac{2}{25} + \dfrac{3}{5} = \dfrac{2}{25} + \dfrac{15}{25} = \dfrac{17}{25}$

    $\left(\begin{array}{l} \dfrac{3}{5} = \dfrac{?}{25} \\ 25 \div 5 = 5 \times 3 = 15 \end{array}\right)$

    b.
    $$\begin{array}{r} 3\frac{3}{8} \\ +6\frac{1}{32} \\ \hline \end{array} \qquad \begin{array}{r} 3\frac{12}{32} \\ +6\frac{1}{32} \\ \hline 9\frac{13}{32} \end{array}$$

    $\dfrac{3}{8} = \dfrac{?}{32}$

    $32 \div 8 = 4 \times 3 = 12$

3. a. $\begin{array}{r} \dfrac{5}{6} = \dfrac{5}{6} \\ -\dfrac{1}{3} = \dfrac{2}{6} \\ \hline \dfrac{3}{6} = \dfrac{1}{2} \end{array}$

    b. $9\dfrac{1}{8} = 9\dfrac{4}{32} = 8\dfrac{36}{32} \longleftarrow \left(\dfrac{32}{32} + \dfrac{4}{32}\right)$

    $ -3\dfrac{7}{32} = -3\dfrac{7}{32} = -3\dfrac{7}{32}$

    $\phantom{b.\ -3\dfrac{7}{32} = -3\dfrac{7}{32} = } \overline{5\dfrac{29}{32}}$

c. Note how we showed the 6 as $5\frac{5}{5}$

$$5\frac{5}{5}$$
$$-1\frac{2}{5}$$
$$\overline{4\frac{3}{5}}$$

4.

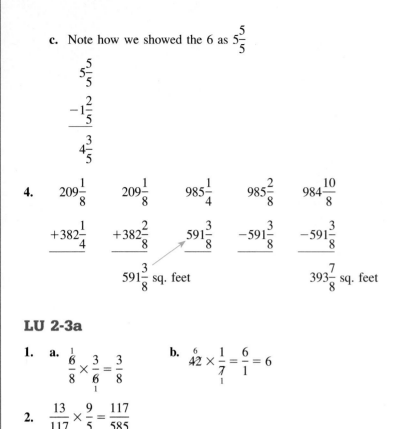

$209\frac{1}{8}$ $209\frac{1}{8}$ $985\frac{1}{4}$ $985\frac{2}{8}$ $984\frac{10}{8}$

$+382\frac{1}{4}$ $+382\frac{2}{8}$ $591\frac{3}{8}$ $-591\frac{3}{8}$ $-591\frac{3}{8}$

$591\frac{3}{8}$ sq. feet $393\frac{7}{8}$ sq. feet

LU 2-3a

1.   **a.** $\dfrac{\overset{1}{\cancel{6}}}{8} \times \dfrac{3}{\underset{1}{\cancel{6}}} = \dfrac{3}{8}$ **b.** $\overset{6}{\cancel{42}} \times \dfrac{1}{\underset{1}{7}} = \dfrac{6}{1} = 6$

2. 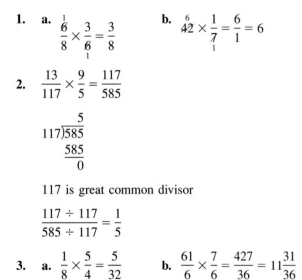 $\dfrac{13}{117} \times \dfrac{9}{5} = \dfrac{117}{585}$

$$117\overline{)585}$$
$$\underline{585}$$
$$0$$

with quotient 5.

117 is great common divisor

$$\frac{117 \div 117}{585 \div 117} = \frac{1}{5}$$

3.   **a.** $\dfrac{1}{8} \times \dfrac{5}{4} = \dfrac{5}{32}$ **b.** $\dfrac{61}{6} \times \dfrac{7}{6} = \dfrac{427}{36} = 11\dfrac{31}{36}$

4.   Total cost of Jill's new home:

	The facts	Solving for?	Steps to take	Key points
BLUEPRINT	Jill's mobile home: $10\frac{1}{8}$ as expensive as her brother's. Brother paid: $10,000	Total cost of Jill's new home.	$10\frac{1}{8}$ × Total cost of Jill's brother's mobile home = Total cost of Jill's new home.	Canceling is an alternative to reducing.

Steps to solving problem

1. Convert $10\frac{1}{8}$ to a mixed number. $\dfrac{81}{8}$

2. Calculate the total cost of Jill's home. $\dfrac{81}{\underset{1}{8}} \times \overset{1,250}{\cancel{\$10,000}} = \$101,250$

You Try It

1. $\frac{3}{10}$ proper, $\frac{9}{8}$ improper, $1\frac{4}{5}$ mixed

2. $\frac{18}{7} = 2\frac{4}{7}$ $5\frac{1}{7} = \frac{35 + 1}{7} = \frac{36}{7}$

3. $\frac{16 \div 8}{24 \div 8} = \frac{2}{3}$ 4. $\frac{20}{50} = 20\overline{)50}$

$$\begin{array}{r} 2 \\ 20\overline{)50} \\ 40 \\ \hline 10 \end{array}$$

$$\begin{array}{r} 2 \\ 10\overline{)20} \\ 20 \\ \hline 0 \end{array}$$

10 is greatest common denominator

5. $\frac{16}{31} = \frac{}{310}$

$310 \div 31 = 10$ $10 \times 16 = 160$

6. $\frac{3}{7} + \frac{2}{7} = \frac{5}{7}$ $\frac{5}{7} - \frac{2}{7} = \frac{3}{7}$

$\frac{5}{8} = \frac{25}{40}$

$+ \frac{3}{40} = \frac{3}{40}$

$\frac{28}{40} = \frac{7}{10}$

7. Prime numbers 2, 3, 5, 7, 11, 13, 17

8. $\frac{1}{2} + \frac{1}{4} + \frac{1}{5} = \dfrac{2\,\underline{/2 \quad 4 \quad 5}}{1 \quad 2 \quad 5}$

$2 \times 1 \times 2 \times 5 = 20$ LCD

9. $2\frac{1}{4}$
$+ 3\frac{3}{4}$
$5\frac{4}{4} = 6$

10. $11\frac{1}{3}$ $10\frac{4}{3}$
$-2\frac{2}{3}$ $-2\frac{2}{3}$
$8\frac{2}{3}$

11. $\frac{4}{5} \times \frac{25}{26} = \frac{\overset{2}{\cancel{4}}}{\underset{1}{\cancel{5}}} \times \frac{\overset{5}{\cancel{25}}}{\underset{13}{\cancel{26}}} = \frac{10}{13}$

12. $2\frac{1}{4} \times 3\frac{1}{4} = \frac{9}{4} \times \frac{13}{4} = \frac{117}{16} = 7\frac{5}{16}$

13. $\frac{1}{8} \div \frac{1}{4} = \frac{1}{8} \times \frac{\cancel{4}}{1} = \frac{1}{2}$

14. $3\frac{1}{4} \div 1\frac{4}{5} = \frac{13}{4} \div \frac{9}{5} = \frac{13}{4} \times \frac{5}{9} = \frac{65}{36}$

Chapter 3

LU 3-1a

1. .309 (3 places to right of decimal)

2. Hundredths

3. Ten thousandths

4. **a.** .8 (identified digit 8 – digit to right less than 5)   **b.** .844 (identified digit 3 – digit to right greater than 5)

5. **a.** .9 (identified digit 6 – digit to right greater than 5)   **b.** .879 (identified digit 9 – digit to right less than 5)

6. .0008 (4 places)

7. .00016 (5 places)

8. $\dfrac{938}{1,000}\left(\dfrac{938}{1 + 3 \text{ zeros}}\right)$

9. $17\dfrac{95}{100}$

10. $\dfrac{325}{10,000}\left(\dfrac{325}{1 + 4 \text{ zeros}} \quad \dfrac{1}{4} \times .01 = .0025 + .03 = .0325\right)$

11. .125 = .13

12. .571 = .57

13. 13.111 = 13.11

LU 3-2a

1. 16.0000
.8310
9.8500
17.8321
44.5131

2. $\overset{14\ 17}{\overset{8\ \ 4\,\cancel{7}\,13}{29.5832}}$
$-\ .9980$
28.5852

3. 29.64
$\times$ 18.2
5928
23712
2964
$\underset{\sim\!\sim}{539.448} = 539.4$

4. $\overset{774.08 = 774.09}{494\overline{)382400.00}}$
$\underset{\sim\!\sim}{3458}$
3660
3458
2020
1976
4400
3952
448

5. 17.48 = 1,748

6. 8.432 = 8.432

7. .9643 = .9643

8. A: $8.88 ÷ 64 = $.14   B: $7.25 ÷ 50 = $.15   Buy A

9. Avis Rent-A-Car total rental charge:

	The facts	Solving for?	Steps to take	Key points
BLUEPRINT	Cost per day: $29.99 22 cents per mile. Drove 709.8 miles. 2-day rental.	Total rental charge.	Total cost for 2 days' rental + Total cost of driving = Total rental charge.	In multiplication, count the number of decimal places. Starting from right to left in the product, insert decimal in appropriate place. Round to nearest cent.

Steps to solving problem

1. Calculate total costs for 2 days' rental. $29.99 × 2 = $59.98

2. Calculate the total cost of driving. $.22 × 709.8 = $156.156 = $156.16

3. Calculate the total rental charge.
$$\begin{array}{r} \$\ 59.98 \\ +\ 156.16 \\ \hline \$216.14 \end{array}$$

10. 7,000 × $.0717 = $501.90

     Check $501.90 × 13.9461 = 6,999.5 pesos due to rounding

You Try It

1. .8256 → Ten thousandths place

2. .841 = .8
     ↑↑
     Less than 5

3. $\frac{9}{1,000}$ = .009

     $\frac{3}{10,000}$ = .0003

4. $\frac{1}{7}$ = .142 = .1

5. $5\frac{4}{5} = \frac{4}{5}$ = .80 + 5 = 5.80

6. .865 $\frac{865}{1}$ $\frac{865}{1,000}$ (attach 3 zeros)

7.
$$\begin{array}{r} 1.7 \\ 3.0 \\ .8 \\ \hline 5.5 \end{array} \qquad \begin{array}{r} {}^{5\ 10} \\ 6.\cancel{0}0 \\ -4.10 \\ \hline 1.90 \end{array}$$

8.
$$\begin{array}{r} 3.49\ (\text{2 places}) \\ .015\ (\text{3 places}) \\ \hline 1745 \\ 349 \\ \hline .05235 \end{array}$$

9.
$$\begin{array}{r} 1.5 \\ 33\overline{)49.5} \\ 33 \\ \hline 165 \\ 165 \\ \hline 0 \end{array}$$

10.
$$\begin{array}{r} .46 = .5 \\ 3.2\overline{)1.480} \\ 128 \\ \hline 200 \\ 192 \end{array}$$

11. 6.92 × 100 = 692 (move 2 places to right)
     6.92 ÷ 100 = .0692 (move 2 places to left)

Chapter 4

LU 4-1a

1.

No. 113	$ 79.88
July 8	20 13

To   Lowe Corp.
For   Advertising

	DOLLARS	CENTS
BALANCE	10,800	80
AMT. DEPOSITED	812	88
TOTAL	11,613	68
AMT. THIS CHECK	79	88
BALANCE FORWARD	11,533	80

Long Company
22 Aster Rd.
Salem, MA 01970

No. 113

PAY
TO THE   July 8   20 13   5-13/110
ORDER
OF   Lowe Corporation $ 79 $\frac{88}{100}$

Seventy-nine and $\frac{88}{100}$ DOLLARS

IPSWICHBANK
ipswichbank.com   Roland Small

MEMO   Advertising

⑈0⑈⑈000⑈38⑈⑉

LU 4-2a

EARL MILLER				
Bank Reconciliation as of March 8, 2013				
Checkbook balance			**Bank balance**	
Earl's checkbook balance	$1,200.10		Bank balance	$ 300.10
Add:			Add:	
Interest	24.06		Deposit in transit	1,200.50
	$1,224.16			$1,500.60
Deduct:			Deduct:	
Deposited check returned fee	$30.00		Outstanding checks:	
			No. 300	$22.88	
ATM	15.00	45.00	No. 302	15.90	
			No. 303	282.66	321.44
Reconciled balance	$1,179.16		Reconciled balance	$1,179.16

You Try It

Sample

1. Pete Co.
   24-111-9

   Pay to the order of
   Reel Bank
   Pete Co. 24-111-9

   Pay to the order
   of Reel Bank for
   deposit only
   Pete Co. 24-111-9

Checkbook

Beg. balance		$300
2. *Less:* NSF	$50	
ATM service charge	20	70
Ending balance		$230

Chapter 5

LU 5-1a

1. **a.** $\frac{1}{2}Q - 8 = 16$ **b.** $12(Q + 41) = 1,200$ **c.** $7 - 2Q = 1$

   d. $4Q - 2 = 24$ **e.** $3Q + 3 = 19$ **f.** $2Q - 6 = 5$

2. **a.** $\begin{array}{r} B + 14 = 70 \\ \underline{-14 \quad -14} \\ B \quad\quad 56 \end{array}$

   b. $\begin{array}{c} \dfrac{\cancel{5}D}{\cancel{5}} = \dfrac{250}{5} \\ D = 50 \end{array}$

   c. $\begin{array}{c} \dfrac{\cancel{11}B}{\cancel{11}} = \dfrac{121}{11} \\ B = 11 \end{array}$

   d. $\begin{array}{c} 8\left(\dfrac{B}{8}\right) = 90(8) \\ B = 720 \end{array}$

   e. $\begin{array}{r} \dfrac{B}{2} + 2 = 250 \\ \underline{-2 \quad -2} \\ \dfrac{B}{2} = 248 \end{array}$

   $\begin{array}{c} 2\left(\dfrac{B}{2}\right) = 248(2) \\ B = 496 \end{array}$

   f. $\begin{array}{r} 3(B - 6) = 18 \\ 3B - 18 = 18 \\ \underline{+ 18 \quad + 18} \\ \dfrac{\cancel{3}B}{\cancel{3}} = \dfrac{36}{3} \\ B = 12 \end{array}$

LU 5-2a

1.

	Unknown(s)	Variable(s)	Relationship
BLUEPRINT	Original price	P*	P − $50 = Sale price Sale price = $140

*P = Original price.

1. **Mechanical steps**

   $\begin{array}{r} P - \$50 = \$140 \\ \underline{+ \quad 50 \quad\quad + \quad 50} \\ P \quad\quad = \$190 \end{array}$

2.

BLUEPRINT	Unknown(s)	Variable(s)	Relationship
	Yearly salary	S^*	$\frac{1}{7}S$ Entertainment = $7,000

*S = Salary.

2.   Mechanical steps

$$\frac{1}{7}S = \$7,000$$

$$7\left(\frac{S}{7}\right) = \$7,000(7)$$

$$S = \$49,000$$

3.

BLUEPRINT	Unknown(s)	Variable(s)	Relationship
	Micro	$8C^*$	$5C$
	Morse	C	$- C$ 49 computers

*C = Computers.

3.   Mechanical steps

$$8C - C = 49$$

$$\frac{7C}{7} = \frac{49}{7}$$

$$C = 7 \ (Morse)$$
$$8C = 56 \ (Micro)$$

4.

BLUEPRINT	Unknown(s)	Variable(s)	Relationship
	Stoves sold:		
	Susie	$2S^*$	$2S$
	Cara	S	$+S$ 360 stoves

*S = Stoves.

4.   Mechanical steps

$$2S + S = 360$$

$$\frac{3S}{3} = \frac{360}{3}$$

$$S = 120 \ (Cara)$$
$$2S = 240 \ (Susie)$$

5.

BLUEPRINT	Unknown(s)	Variable(s)	Price	Relationship
	Meatball	M	$7	$7M$
	Cheese	$3M$	6	$+ 18M$ $1,800 total sales

5.   Mechanical steps

$$7M + 18M = 1,800$$

$$\frac{25M}{25} = \frac{1,800}{25}$$

$$M = 72 \quad (meatball)$$
$$3M = 216 \ (cheese)$$

Check

$$(72 \times \$7) + (216 \times \$6) = \$1,800$$

$$\$504 + \$1,296 = \$1,800$$

$$\$1,800 = \$1,800$$

6.

BLUEPRINT	Unknown(s)	Variable(s)	Price	Relationship
	Unit sales:			
	Meatball	M^*	$7	$6M$
	Cheese	$288 - M$	6	$+ 6(288 - M)$ $1,800 total sales

*We assign the variable to the most expensive item to make the mechanical steps easier to complete.

6.   Mechanical steps

$$7M + 6(288 - M) = \$1,800$$
$$7M + 1,728 - 6M = \$1,800$$
$$M + 1,728 = \$1,800$$
$$-1,728 = -1,728$$
$$M = 72$$
$$Meatball = 72$$
$$Cheese = 288 - 72 = 216$$

Check

$$72(\$7) + 216 \ (\$6) = \$504 + \$1,296$$
$$= \$1,800$$

You Try It

1. $E + 15 = 14$
   $\underline{ -15 \quad -15}$
   $E = -1$

2. $B - 40 = 80$
   $\underline{ +40 \quad +40}$
   $B = 120$

3. $\frac{5C}{5} = 75$
   $C = 15$

4. $\frac{A}{6} = 60 \quad (6)\frac{A}{6} = 6(60)$
   $A = 360$

5. $\frac{C}{4} + 10 = 17$
   $\underline{\phantom{\frac{C}{4} +} -10 \quad -10}$
   $\frac{C}{4} = 7$
   $(4)\frac{C}{4} = 7(4)$
   $C = 28$

6. $7(B - 10) = 35$
   $7B - 70 = 35$
   $\underline{ +70 \quad +70}$
   $\frac{7B}{7} = \frac{105}{7}$
   $B = 15$

7. $5B + 3B = 16$

$\dfrac{8B}{8} = \dfrac{16}{8}$

$B = 2$

Sit. 1. $P - \$53 = \$110$

$\dfrac{+53 \quad +53}{P \qquad = \$163}$

Sit. 2. $\dfrac{1}{7}B = \$6,000$

$7\left(\dfrac{B}{7}\right) = 6,000 \,(7)$

$B = \$42,000$

Sit. 3. $95 - S = 640$

$\dfrac{8S}{8} = \dfrac{640}{8}$

$S = 80 \qquad 9S = 720$

Sit. 4. $9S + S = 640$

$\dfrac{10S}{10} = \dfrac{640}{10}$

$S = 64 \qquad 9S = 576$

Sit. 5. $1,200\,N + 300\,N = 15,000$

$\dfrac{1,500\,N}{1,500} = \dfrac{15,000}{1,500}$

$N = 10$

$3\,N = 30$

Sit. 6. $400\,S + 300\,(40 - S) = 15,000$

$400\,S + 12,000 - 300\,S = 15,000$

$100\,S + 12,000 = 15,000$

$\dfrac{-12,000 \quad -12,000}{\dfrac{100\,S}{100} = \dfrac{3,000}{100}}$

$S = 30$

$40 - S = 10$

Chapter 6

LU 6-1a

1. $.44.44 = 44.4\%$

2. $.78.2 = 78.2\%$

3. $.00.6 = .6\%$

4. $7.93.333 = 793.3\%$

5. $\dfrac{1}{5}\% = .20\% = .0020$

6. $7\dfrac{4}{5}\% = 7.80\% = .0780$

7. $92\% = .92 = .92$

8. $765.8\% = 7.65.8 = 7.658$

9. $\dfrac{1}{3} = .33.333 = 33.33\%$

10. $\dfrac{3}{7} = .42.857 = 42.86\%$

11. $17\% = 17 \times \dfrac{1}{100} = \dfrac{17}{100}$

12. $82\dfrac{1}{4}\% = \dfrac{329}{4} \times \dfrac{1}{100} = \dfrac{329}{400}$

13. $150\% = 150 \times \dfrac{1}{100} = \dfrac{150}{100} = 1\dfrac{50}{100} = 1\dfrac{1}{2}$

14. $\dfrac{1}{4}\% = \dfrac{1}{4} \times \dfrac{1}{100} = \dfrac{1}{400}$

15. $17\dfrac{8}{10}\% = \dfrac{178}{10} \times \dfrac{1}{100} = \dfrac{178}{1,000} = \dfrac{89}{500}$

LU 6-2a

1. $504 = 1,200 \times .42$

$(P) = (B) \times (R)$

2. $\$560 = \$8,000 \times .07$

$(P) = (B) \times (R)$

3. $\dfrac{(P)510}{(B)6,000} = .085 = 8.5\%$

4. $\dfrac{(P)400}{(B)900} = .444 = 44.4\%$

5. $\dfrac{(P)30}{(R).60} = 50(B)$

6. $\dfrac{(P)1,200}{(R).035} = 34,285.7(B)$

7. Percent of Professor Ford's class that did not receive the A grade:

	The facts	Solving for?	Steps to take	Key points
BLUEPRINT	10 As. 25 in class.	Percent that did not receive A.	Identify key elements. *Base:* 25 *Rate:* ? *Portion:* 15(25 − 10). Rate = $\dfrac{\text{Portion}}{\text{Base}}$	Portion (15) Base × Rate (25) (?) The whole Portion and rate must relate to same piece of base.

Steps to solving problem

1. Set up the formula. $\text{Rate} = \dfrac{\text{Portion}}{\text{Base}}$

2. Calculate the rate. $R = \dfrac{15}{25}$

      $R = 60\%$

8. Abby Biernet's original order:

	The facts	Solving for?	Steps to take	Key points
BLUEPRINT	70% of the order not in. 90 lobsters received.	Total order of lobsters.	Identify key elements. *Base:* ? *Rate:* 30 (100% − 70%) *Portion:* 90. $\text{Base} = \dfrac{\text{Portion}}{\text{Rate}}$	Portion (90) Base × Rate (?) (.30) 90 lobsters represent 30% of the order Portion and rate must relate to same piece of base.

Steps to solving problem

1. Set up the formula. $\text{Base} = \dfrac{\text{Portion}}{\text{Rate}}$

2. Calculate the base. $B = \dfrac{90}{.30}$ ← 90 lobsters are 30% of base

      $B = 300$ lobsters

9. Dunkin' Donuts Company sales for 2014:

	The facts	Solving for?	Steps to take	Key points
BLUEPRINT	*2013:* $400,000 sales. *2014:* Sales up 35% from 2013.	Sales for 2014.	Identify key elements. *Base:* $300,000 *Rate:* 1.35. Old year 100% New year + 35 ___ 135% *Portion:* ? Portion = Base × Rate	2014 sales Portion (?) Base × Rate ($400,000) (1.35) 2013 sales When rate is greater than 100%, portion will be larger than base.

Steps to solving problem

1. Set up the formula.   Portion = Base × Rate

2. Calculate the portion. $P = \$400,000 \times 1.35$

      $P = \$540,000$

10. Percent decrease in Apple Computer price:

	The facts	Solving for?	Steps to take	Key points
BLUEPRINT	Apple Computer was $1,800; now $1,000.	Percent decrease in price.	Identify key elements. *Base*: $1,800 *Rate*: ? *Portion*: $800 ($1,800 − $1,000) $\text{Rate} = \dfrac{\text{Portion}}{\text{Base}}$	Difference in price Portion ($800) Base × Rate ($1,800) (?) Original price

Steps to solving problem

1. Set up the formula. $\text{Rate} = \dfrac{\text{Portion}}{\text{Base}}$

2. Calculate the rate. $R = \dfrac{\$800}{\$1,800}$
   $R = 44.44\%$

11. Percent increase in Boston Celtics ticket:

	The facts	Solving for?	Steps to take	Key points
BLUEPRINT	$14 ticket (old). $75 ticket (new).	Percent increase in price.	Identify key elements. *Base*: $14 *Rate*: ? *Portion*: $61 ($75 − $14) $\text{Rate} = \dfrac{\text{Portion}}{\text{Base}}$	Difference in price Portion $61 Base × Rate ($14) (?) Original price When portion is greater than base, rate will be greater than 100%.

Steps to solving problem

1. Set up the formula. $\text{Rate} = \dfrac{\text{Portion}}{\text{Base}}$

2. Calculate the rate. $R = \dfrac{\$61}{\$14}$
   $R = 435,714 = 435.71\%$

You Try It

1. $.92 = 92\%$
   $.009 = .9\%$
   $5.46 = 546\%$

2. $\dfrac{2}{9} = 22.222\% = 22.22\%$

3. $78\% = .0078$ (2 places to left)
   $96\% = .96$ (2 places to left)
   $246\% = 2.46$ (2 places to left)

   $7\dfrac{3}{4}\% = 7.75\% = .0775$

   $\dfrac{3}{4}\% = .75\% = .0075$

   $\dfrac{1}{2}\% = .50\% = .0050$

4. $\dfrac{3}{5} = .60 = 60\%$

5. $74\% \rightarrow 74 \times \dfrac{1}{100} = \dfrac{74}{100} = \dfrac{37}{50}$

   $\dfrac{1}{5}\% \rightarrow \dfrac{1}{5} \times \dfrac{1}{100} = \dfrac{1}{500}$

   $121\% \rightarrow 121 \times \dfrac{1}{100} = \dfrac{121}{100} = 1\dfrac{21}{100}$

   $17\dfrac{1}{5}\% \rightarrow \dfrac{86}{5} \times \dfrac{1}{100} = \dfrac{86}{500} = \dfrac{43}{250}$

   $17.75\% \rightarrow 17\dfrac{3}{4}\% = \dfrac{71}{4} \times \dfrac{1}{100} = \dfrac{71}{400}$

6. Portion ($1,600) = Base ($2,000) × Rate (.80)

7. Rate (25%) = $\dfrac{\text{Portion (\$500)}}{\text{Base (\$2,000)}}$

8. Base ($1,000) = $\dfrac{\text{Portion (\$200)}}{\text{Rate (.20)}}$

9. $\dfrac{\text{Difference in price (\$100)}}{\text{Base (orig. \$500)}} = 20\%$

Chapter 7

LU 7-1a

1. Dining room set trade discount amount and net price:

The facts	Solving for?	Steps to take	Key points
BLUEPRINT	List price: $16,000. Trade discount rate: 30%.	Trade discount amount. Net price.	Trade discount amount = List price × Trade discount rate. Net price = List price × Complement of trade discount rate.	Trade discount amount. Portion (?) Base ($16,000) × Rate (.30). List price. Trade discount rate.

Steps to solving problem

1. Calculate the trade discount. $16,000 × .30 = $4,800 Trade discount amount
2. Calculate the net price. $16,000 × .70 = $11,200 (100% − 30% = 70%)

2. Video system list price:

The facts	Solving for?	Steps to take	Key points
BLUEPRINT	Net price: $400. Trade discount rate: 20%.	List price.	List price = Net price / Complement of trade discount	Net price. Portion $400. Base (?) × Rate (.80). List price. 100% −20%

Steps to solving problem

1. Calculate the complement of trade discount

$$100\% - 20\% = 80\% = .80$$

2. Calculate the list price.

$$\frac{\$400}{.80} = \$500$$

3. Lamps Outlet's net price and trade discount amount:

The facts	Solving for?	Steps to take	Key points
BLUEPRINT	List price: $14,000. Chain discount: 4/8/20.	Net price. Trade discount amount.	Net price = List price × Net price equivalent rate. Trade discount amount = List price × Single equivalent discount rate.	Do not round off net price equivalent rate or single equivalent discount rate.

Steps to solving problem

1. Calculate the complement of each chain discount.

$$100\% - 4 = 96\% \qquad 100\% - 8 = 92\% \qquad 100\% - 20 = 80\%$$

2. Calculate the net price equivalent rate. .96 × .92 × .80 = .70656
3. Calculate the net price. $14,000 × .70656 = $9,891.84
4. Calculate the single equivalent discount rate. 1.00000 − .70656 = .29344
5. Calculate the trade discount amount. $14,000 × .29344 = $4,108.16

LU 7-2a

1. End of discount period: July 8 + 10 days =   July 18
   End of credit period: By Table 7.1, July 8 =   189 days
   $$\underline{+30\ days}$$
   219 → search → Aug. 7

2. End of discount period: June 12 + 10 days = June 22
   End of credit period: By Table 7.1, June 12 =   163 days
   $$\underline{+30\ days}$$
   193 → search → July 12

3. End of discount period: By Table 7.1, May 12 = 132 days
   $$\underline{+30\ days}$$
   162 → search → June 11

   End of credit period: By Table 7.1, May 12 =   132 days
   $$\underline{+60\ days}$$
   192 → search → July 11

4. End of discount period: May 10
   End of credit period: May 10 + 20 = May 30

5. End of discount period: June 10
   End of credit period: June 10 + 20 = June 30

6. Vasko Corporation's cost of equipment:

	The facts	Solving for?	Steps to take	Key points
BLUEPRINT	List price: $9,000. Trade discount rate: 30%. Terms: 2/10 EOM. Invoice date: 6/29 Date paid: 8/9	Cost of equipment.	Net price = List price × Complement of trade discount rate. EOM before 25th: Discount period is 1st 10 days of month that follow sale.	Trade discounts are deducted before cash discounts are taken. Cash discounts are not taken on freight or returns.

Steps to solving problem

1. Calculate the net price. $9,000 × .70 = $6,300   100% − 30%
2. Calculate the discount period. Until Aug. 10
3. Calculate the cost of office equipment. $6,300 × .98 = $6,174   100% − 2%

7. $\frac{\$600}{.98} = \$612.24$ Credited

   $700 − $612.24 = $87.76 Balance outstanding

You Try It

1. $700 × .20 = $140

2. 1.00 $700 × .80 = $560
   $$\underline{-\ .20}$$
   .80

3. Seller will pay the freight

4. $\frac{\$240}{.40} = \$600$
   (100% − 60%)

5. $200 $188
   × .06   × .08
   $12.00 $15.04
   $188.00   .8648 NPER
   − 15.04   .94 × .92 = × $200
   $172.96 $172.96

6. .94 × .92 × $2,000 = $1,729.60

7. 1.0000
   − .8648 (.94 × .92)
   .1352 × $2,000 = $270.40

8. $2,000
   −   80 (Freight and returns)
   $1,920 × .02 = $38.40

9. April 12, May 2

10. $700
    − 100
    $600 × .98 = $588
                + 100
                $688

11. No discount; pay full $700

12. November 10; November 13

13. $300/.98 = $306.12

Chapter 8

LU 8-1a

1. Irene's dollar markup and percent markup on cost:

	The facts	Solving for?	Steps to take	Key points
BLUEPRINT	Desk cost: $800. Desk selling price: $1,200.	% $ C 100% $ 800 + M 50² 400¹ = S 150% $1,200 ¹Dollar markup. ²Percent markup on cost.	Dollar markup = Selling price − Cost. Percent markup on cost = $\frac{\text{Dollar markup}}{\text{Cost}}$	Dollar markup Portion $400 Base × Rate $800 (?) Cost

Steps to solving problem

1. Calculate the dollar markup.

Dollar markup = Selling price − Cost
$400 = $1,200 − $800

2. Calculate the percent markup on cost.

Percent markup on cost = $\frac{\text{Dollar markup}}{\text{Cost}}$

$= \frac{\$400}{\$800} = 50\%$

Check

Selling price = Cost + Markup or Cost (B) = $\frac{\text{Dollar markup }(P)}{\text{Percent markup on cost }(R)}$

$1,200 = $800 + .50($800) $= \frac{\$400}{.50} = \$800$

$1,200 = $800 + $400
$1,200 = $1,200

2. Dollar markup and selling price of doll:

	The facts	Solving for?	Steps to take	Key points
BLUEPRINT	Doll cost: $14 each. Markup on cost: 38%.	% $ C 100% $14.00 +M 38 5.32¹ = S 138% $19.32² ¹Dollar markup. ²Selling price.	Dollar markup: S = C + M S = Cost × (1 + Percent markup on cost)	Selling price Portion (?) Base × Rate ($14) (1.38) Cost 100% +38%

Steps to solving problem

1. Calculate the dollar markup.

S = C + M
S = $14.00 + .38($14.00)
S = $14.00 + $5.32 ← Dollar markup

2. Calculate the selling price.   S = $19.32

Check

Selling price = Cost × (1 + Percent markup on cost) = $14.00 × 1.38 = $19.32
(P) (B) (R)

3. Cost and dollar markup

The facts	Solving for?	Steps to take	Key points
Selling price: $16. Markup on cost: 42%.	$$\begin{array}{ccc} & \% & \$ \\ C & 100\% & \$11.27 \\ +M & 42 & 4.73^1 \\ =S & 142\% & \$16.00^2 \end{array}$$ ¹Cost. ²Dollar markup.	$S = C + M$ or $$Cost = \frac{Selling\ price}{1 + \frac{Percent}{markup\ on\ cost}}$$ $M = S - C$	Selling price; Portion $16; Base × Rate (?) (1.42); Cost; 100% +42%

Steps to solving problem

1. Calculate the cost.

$$S = C + M$$
$$\$16 = C + .42C$$
$$\frac{\$16}{1.42} = \frac{1.42C}{1.42}$$
$$\$11.27 = C$$

2. Calculate the dollar markup.

$$M = S - C$$
$$M = \$16 - \$11.27$$
$$M = \$4.73$$

Check

$$Cost\ (B) = \frac{Selling\ price\ (P)}{1 + Percent\ markup\ on\ cost\ (R)} \qquad \frac{\$16}{1.42} = \$11.27$$

LU 8-2a

1. Irene's dollar markup and percent markup on selling price:

The facts	Solving for?	Steps to take	Key points
Desk cost: $800. Desk selling price: $1,200.	$$\begin{array}{ccc} & \% & \$ \\ C & 66.7\% & \$800 \\ +M & 33.3^2 & 400^1 \\ =S & 100\% & \$1,200 \end{array}$$ ¹Dollar markup. ²Percent markup on selling price.	$$\frac{Dollar}{markup} = \frac{Selling}{price} - Cost$$ $$\frac{Percent}{markup\ on\ selling\ price} = \frac{Dollar\ markup}{Selling\ price}$$	Markup; Portion $400; Base × Rate $1,200 (?); Selling price

Steps to solving problem

1. Calculate the dollar markup.

$$\begin{array}{ccccc} Dollar\ markup & = & Selling\ price & - & Cost \\ \$400 & = & \$1,200 & - & \$800 \end{array}$$

2. Calculate the percent markup on selling price.

$$\frac{Percent\ markup}{on\ selling\ price} = \frac{Dollar\ markup}{Selling\ price}$$
$$= \frac{\$400}{\$1,200} = 33.3\%$$

Check

$$Selling\ price = Cost + Markup \qquad or \qquad Selling\ price\ (B) = \frac{Dollar\ markup\ (P)}{Percent\ markup\ on\ selling\ price\ (R)}$$

$$\$1,200 = \$800 + .333(\$1,200)$$

$$\$1,200 = \$800 + \$399.60$$

$$\$1,200 = \$1,199.60\ (off\ due\ to\ rounding)$$

$$= \frac{\$400}{.333} = \$1,201.20\ (off\ due\ to\ rounding)$$

2. Selling price of doll and dollar markup:

	The facts	Solving for?	Steps to take	Key points
BLUEPRINT	*Doll cost:* $14 each. *Markup on selling price:* 38%.	$\begin{array}{ccc} & \% & \$ \\ C & 62\% & \$14.00 \\ + M & 38 & 8.58^2 \\ \hline = S & 100\% & \$22.58^1 \end{array}$ ^{1}Selling price. ^{2}Dollar markup.	$S = C + M$ or $S = \dfrac{\text{Cost}}{1 - \text{Percent markup on selling price}}$	Cost ↘ Portion $14 Base × Rate (?) (.62) Selling price 100% −38%

Steps to solving problem

1. Calculate the selling price.

$$S = C + M$$
$$S = \$14.00 + .38S$$
$$\underline{-.38S \qquad\qquad -.38S}$$
$$\frac{.62S}{.62} = \frac{\$14.00}{.62}$$
$$S = \$22.58$$

2. Calculate the dollar markup.

$$M = S - C$$
$$\$8.58 = \$22.58 - \$14.00$$

Check

$$\text{Selling price } (B) = \frac{\text{Cost } (P)}{1 - \text{Percent markup on selling price } (R)} = \frac{\$14.00}{.62} = \$22.58$$

3. Dollar markup and cost:

	The facts	Solving for?	Steps to take	Key points
BLUEPRINT	*Selling price:* $16. *Markup on selling price:* 42%.	$\begin{array}{ccc} & \% & \$ \\ C & 58\% & \$\,9.28^2 \\ + M & 42 & 6.72^1 \\ \hline = S & 100\% & \$16.00 \end{array}$ ^{1}Dollar markup. ^{2}Cost.	$S = C + M$ or $\text{Cost} = \text{Selling price} \times$ $\left(1 - \dfrac{\text{Percent markup}}{\text{on selling price}}\right)$	Cost ↘ Portion (?) Base × Rate ($16) (.58) Selling price 100% −42%

Steps to solving problem

1. Calculate the dollar markup.

$$S = C + M$$
$$\$16.00 = C + .42(\$16.00)$$

2. Calculate the cost.

$$\$16.00 = C + \$6.72 \quad\leftarrow\text{ Dollar markup}$$
$$\underline{-6.72 \qquad\qquad -6.72}$$
$$\$9.28 = C$$

Check

$$\underset{(P)}{\text{Cost}} = \underset{(B)}{\text{Selling price}} \times \underset{(R)}{(1 - \text{Percent markup on selling price})} = \$16.00 \times .58 = \$9.28$$

$$(1.00 - .42)$$

4. $\text{Cost} = \dfrac{\$5}{\$7} = 71.4\%$ $\qquad \dfrac{.417}{1 - .417} = \dfrac{.417}{.583} = 71.5\%$

$\text{Selling price} = \dfrac{\$5}{\$12} = 41.7\%$ $\qquad \dfrac{.714}{1 + .714} = \dfrac{.714}{1.714} = 41.7\%$ (due to rounding)

LU 8-3a

1.

$$S = C + M$$

$$S = \$800 + .30S$$

$$-.30S \qquad -.30S$$

$$\frac{.70S}{.70} = \frac{\$800}{.70}$$

$$S = \$1,142.86$$

Check

$$S = \frac{\text{Cost}}{1 - \text{Percent markup on selling price}}$$

$$S = \frac{\$800}{1 - .30} = \frac{\$800}{.70} = \$1,142.86$$

First markdown: $.90 \times \$1,142.86 = \$1,028.57$ selling price
Second markdown: $.95 \times \$1,028.57 = \$977.14$
Markup: $1.02 \times \$977.14 = \$996.68$ final selling price

$$\$1,142.86 - \$996.68 = \frac{\$146.18}{\$1,142.86} = 12.79\%$$

2.

	The facts	Solving for?	Steps to take	Key points
BLUEPRINT	500 lb. tomatoes at $.16 per pound. Spoilage: 10% Markup cost: 55%.	Price of tomatoes per pound.	Total cost. Total dollar markup. Total selling price. Spoilage amount $TS = TC + TM$	Markup is based on cost.

Steps in solving problem

1. Calculate the total cost.

$TC = 500 \text{ lb.} \times \$.16 = \$80.00$

2. Calculate the total dollar markup.

$TS = TC + TM$

$TS = \$80.00 + .55(\$80.00)$

$TS = \$80.00 + \$44.00 \leftarrow$ Total dollar markup

3. Calculate the total selling price.

$TS = \$124.00 \leftarrow$ Total selling price

4. Calculate the tomato loss.

$500 \text{ lb.} \times .10 = 50 \text{ lb. spoilage}$

5. Calculate the selling price per pound of tomatoes.

$\dfrac{\$124.00}{450} = \$.28$ per pound (rounded to nearest hundredth)

$(500 - 50)$

LU 8-4a

$\$240 - \$80 = \$160$ $\dfrac{\$96,000}{\$160} = 600$ units

You Try It

1. $S = C + M$
$S = \$400 + \$200$
$S = \$600$

2. $\dfrac{\$50}{\$200} = 25\%$

$\dfrac{\$50}{.25} = \$200$

3. $S = C + M$
$S = \$8 + .10(\$8)$
$S = \$8 + \$.80$
$S = \$8.80$

4. $S = C + M$
$\$200 = C + .60 C$
$\dfrac{\$200}{1.60} = \dfrac{1.60C}{1.60}$
$\$125 = C$

5. $M = S - C$
$(\$2,500) = (\$4,500) - (\$2,000)$

6. $\dfrac{\$700}{\$2,800} = 25\%$

$\dfrac{\$700}{.50} = \$1,400$

7.
$$S = C + M$$
$$S = \$800 + .40(S)$$
$$\underline{-.40 \qquad -.40}$$
$$\frac{.60\,S}{.60} = \frac{\$800}{.60}$$
$$S = \$1333.33$$

8.
$$S = C + M$$
$$\$2,000 = C + .70(\$2,000)$$
$$2,000 = C + \$1,400$$
$$\underline{-1,400 \qquad -1,400}$$
$$\$600 = C$$

9. $\dfrac{.47}{1 + .47} = \dfrac{.47}{1.47} = 32\%$ rounded

10.
$$\begin{array}{r} \$50 \\ \times\ .20 \\ \hline \$10 \end{array} \qquad \frac{\$10}{\$50} = 20\%$$

11.
$$TS = TC + TM$$
$$TS = \$9 + .30(\$9)$$
$$TS = \$9 + \$2.7$$
$$TS = \$11.70$$
$$\frac{\$11.70}{45} = \$.26$$

12. $\dfrac{\$70,000}{\$20} = 3,500$ units

Chapter 9

LU 9-1a

1. 40 hours × $12.00 = $480.00
14 hours × $18.00 = $252.00 ($12.00 × 1.5 = $18.00)
$732.00

2. $210,000 × .08 = $16,800
$\underline{-\ 4,000}$
$12,800

3. Gross pay = $1,200 + ($3,000 × .01) + ($8,000 × .03) + ($20,000 × .05) + ($20,000 × .08)
= $1,200 + $30 + $240 + $1,000 + $1,600
= $4,070

LU 9-2a

1.
Social Security

$110,100
$\underline{-\ 109,600}$
$\ \ \ \ 500 × .062 = $31

Medicare

$10,000 × .0145 = $145.00

FIT
Percentage method: $10,000.00
$316.67 × 1 = $\underline{-\ \$316.67}$ (Table 9.1)
$\ 9,683.33

$7,317 to $15,067 → $1,453.65 plus 28% of excess over $7,317 (Table 9.2)

$9,683.33 $1,453.65
$\underline{-\ 7,317.00}$ $\underline{+\ \ \ 662.57}$ ($2,366.33 × .28)
$2,366.33 $2,116.22

2. 13 weeks × $200 = $ 2,600
13 weeks × $800 = 10,400 ($10,400 − $7,000) → $3,400
13 weeks × $950 = $\underline{12,350}$ ($12,350 − $7,000) → $\underline{5,350}$ } exempt wages (not taxed for FUTA or SUTA)
$25,350 $8,750

$25,350 − $8,750 = $16,600 taxable wages
SUTA = .051 × $16,600 = $846.60
FUTA = .008 × $16,600 = $132.80

Note: FUTA remains at .008 whether SUTA rate is higher or lower than standard.

You Try It

1. 38 hrs × $9.25 = $351.50

2. **Reg $ Overtime $**
(40 × $7) + (3 × $10.50)
   $280   + $31.50 = $311.50 gross pay

3. 2,250 × $.79 = $1,777.50

4. 600 × $.79 = $474
300 × $.88 = + 264
                $738

5. $175,000 × .07 = $12,286.96

6. $6,000 × .05 = $300
$2,000 × .09 = 180
$4,000 × .12 = 480
                $960

7. $600 + ($6,000 × .04)
$600 + 240 = $840

8. Gross $490.00
   Less: FIT   41.69 $490.00
         SS   30.38   − 73.08
         Med.   7.11 $416.92 × .10 = $41.69
               $410.82

9. Social Security = $110,100 × .062 = $682,62
   Medicare = $150,000 × .0145 = $2,175

10. $1,400.00   ($73.08 × 3)
       219.24 $33.40 + .15($690.76)
     1,180.76 $33.40 + $103.61
     − 490.00 $137.01 FIT
     $ 690.76

11. FUTA $200 × .008 = $1.60
    SUTA $200 × .054 = $10.80

Chapter 10

LU 10-1a

1. $16,000 × .03 × $\dfrac{8}{12}$ = $320

2. $15,000 × .06 × 6 = $5,400

3. $50,000 × .07 × $\dfrac{18}{12}$ = $5,250

4. August 14 → 226 $20,000 × .07 × $\dfrac{100}{365}$ = $383.56
   May 6 → − 126 $MV = $20,000 + $383.56 = $20,383.56
                100

5. $20,000 × .07 × $\dfrac{100}{360}$ = $388.89 $MV = $20,000 + $388.89 = $20,388.89

LU 10-2a

1. $\dfrac{\$9,000}{.04 \times \dfrac{90}{360}} = \dfrac{\$9,000}{.01} = \$900,000$ $P = \dfrac{I}{R \times T}$

2. $\dfrac{\$280}{\$6,000 \times \dfrac{180}{360}} = \dfrac{\$280}{\$3,000} = 9.33\%$ $R = \dfrac{I}{P \times T}$

3. $\dfrac{\$190}{\$900 \times .06} = \dfrac{\$190}{\$54} = 3.52 \times 360 = 1{,}267$ days $T = \dfrac{I}{P \times R}$

LU 10-3a

$4,000 × .04 × $\dfrac{15}{360}$ = $6.67

   $2,000.00 $3,306.67
 −   9.19   −1,990.81
   $1,990.81 $1,315.86

  $ 700.00 $ 4,000.00
 −   6.67   −   693.33
  $ 693.33 $ 3,306.67

$3,306.67 × .04 × $\dfrac{25}{360}$ = $9.19

$1,315.86 × .04 × $\dfrac{20}{360}$ = $2.92

   $ 2.92 ←
 + 1,315.86
   $1,318.78

You Try It

1. $\$4,000 \times .03 \times \dfrac{18}{12} = \$180$

2. $\$3,000 \times .04 \times \dfrac{45}{365} = \$14.79$

Feb 22	53
Jan 8	− 8
	45

3. $\$3,000 \times .04 \times \dfrac{45}{360} = \$15.00$

4. $\$2,000 \times .04 \times \dfrac{90}{360} = \$20$

5. $\dfrac{\$20}{.04 \times \dfrac{90}{360}} = \$2,000$

6. $\dfrac{\$20}{\$2,000 \times \dfrac{90}{360}} = 4\%$

7. $\dfrac{20}{\$2,000 \times .04} = .25 \times 360 = 90 \text{ days}$

8. $\$4,000 \times .04 \times \dfrac{30}{360} = \$13.33$

$$\begin{array}{r} \$400.00 \\ -\ \ 13.33 \\ \hline \$386.67 \end{array}$$

$\$4,000 - 386.67 = \$3,613.33$

$\$3,613.33 \times .04 \times \dfrac{40}{360} = \$16.06$

$\$300 - \$16.06 = \$283.94$
$\$3,613.33 - \$283.94 = \$3,329.39$

$\$3,329.39 \times .04 \times \dfrac{20}{360} = \$7.40$

$\$3,329.39 + \$7.40 = \$3,336.79$
Total interest $= \$13.33 + \$16.06 + \$7.40 = \$36.79$

Chapter 11

LU 11-1a

1. **a.** Maturity value = Face value = $14,000
   b. Bank discount = $MV \times$ Bank discount rate $\times$ Time

$$= \$14,000 \times .045 \times \frac{60}{360}$$

$$= \$105$$

   c. Proceeds = MV − Bank discount
   $$= \$14,000 - \$105$$
   $$= \$13,895$$

   d. Effective rate $= \dfrac{\text{Interest}}{\text{Proceeds} \times \text{Time}}$

$$= \dfrac{\$105}{\$13,895 \times \dfrac{60}{360}}$$

$$= 4.53\%$$

2. $\$10,000 \times .04 \times \dfrac{13}{52} = \$100$ interest $\dfrac{\$100}{\$9,900 \times \dfrac{13}{52}} = 4.04\%$

LU 11-2a

1. **a.** $I = \$40,000 \times .05 \times \dfrac{170}{360} = \$944.44$

   $MV = \$40,000 + \$944.44 = \$40,944.44$

   b. Discount period = 170 − 61 = 109 days.

April	30		**or by table:**	
	− 10		June 8	161
	20		April 8	− 100
May	+ 31			61
	51			
June	+ 10			
	61			

   c. Bank discount $= \$40,944.44 \times .02 \times \dfrac{109}{360} = \$247.94$

   d. Proceeds = $40,944.44 − $247.94 = $40,696.50

You Try It

1. $4,000 \times .02 \times \dfrac{30}{360} = \$6.67$

$$\begin{array}{r} \$\,4000.00 \\ -\quad 6.67 \\ \hline \$3,993.33 \text{ Proceeds} \end{array}$$

2. $15,000 \times .04 \times \dfrac{40}{360} = \$66.67$

$$\begin{array}{r} \$15,000.00 \\ -\quad 66.67 \\ \hline \end{array}$$

$\dfrac{\$66.67}{\$14,933.33 \times \dfrac{40}{360}} = 4.02\%$

3. $\begin{array}{r} \text{Dec 15} \quad 349 \\ \text{Nov 5} \quad -309 \\ \hline 40 \text{ days} \end{array}$ $\$2,000 \times .03 \times \dfrac{60}{360} = \$10$

$MV = \$2,010$ (Left to go)

$\$2,010 \times .05 \times \dfrac{20}{360} = \$5.58$

$\$2,010 - \$5.58 = \$2,004.42$ Proceeds

Chapter 12

LU 12-1a

1. **a.** $4(4 \times 1)$ **b.** $541.21   **c.** $41.27 ($541.27 − $500)

   $500 \times 1.02 = \$510 \times 1.02 = \$520.20 \times 1.02 = \$530.60 \times 1.02 = \$541.21$

2. 500×1.0824 (4 periods at 2%) = $541.20

3. 16 periods, 2%, $7,000 \times 1.3728 = \$9,609.60$

4. 4 periods, $1\frac{1}{2}\%$

   $$\begin{array}{r} \$8,000 \times 1.0614 = \$8,491.20 \\ -\;8,000.00 \\ \hline \$\;\;\;491.20 \end{array}$$ $\dfrac{\$491.20}{\$8,000} = 6.14\%$

5. $1,800 \times 1.3498 = \$2,429.64$

LU 12-2a

1. 14 periods (7 years × 2) $2\frac{1}{2}\%$ (5% ÷ 2)   .7077 $6,369.30 ($9,000 × .7077)

2. 20 periods (20 years × 1)   4% (4% ÷ 1)   .4564 $9,128 ($20,000 × .4564)

3. 6 years × 4 = 24 periods $\dfrac{8\%}{4} = 2\%$ .6217 × $40,000 = $24,868

4. 4 × 4 years = 16 periods $\dfrac{4\%}{4} = 1\%$ .8528 × $28,000 = $23,878.40

You Try It

1. $\begin{array}{r} \$200 \\ \times\,1.04 \\ \hline \$208 \end{array}$ $\begin{array}{r} \$\;\;208 \\ \times\;\;1.04 \\ \hline \$216.32 \end{array}$

2. $4,000 × 1.4258 (3% 12 periods)
   = $5,703.20

3. Table 1.0609 (3% 2 periods)
   ↓
   6.09%

   $$\begin{array}{r} \$4,000 \times 1.0609 = \$4,243.60 \\ -\;4,000.00 \\ \hline \$\;\;\;243.60 \end{array}$$

   $\dfrac{\$243.60}{\$4,000.00} = 6.09\%$

4. Table $.7880 (1.5% 16 periods)
   $\begin{array}{r} \times\;\$6,000 \\ \hline \$4,728 \end{array}$

Chapter 13

LU 13-1a

1. **a. Step 1.** Periods = 4 years × 2 = 8
   4% ÷ 2 = 2%

   b. Periods = 4 years × 2   **Step 1**
   = 8 + 1 = 9
   4% ÷ 2 = 2%

   Step 2. Factor = 8.5829
   Step 3. $5,000 × 8.5829 = $42,914.50

   Factor = 9.7546   **Step 2**
   $5,000 × 9.7546 = $48,773   **Step 3**
   −1 payment   − $ 5,000   **Step 4**
   $43,773

2. **Step 1.** 6 years × 2 = 12 + 1 = 13 Periods $\dfrac{6\%}{2} = 3\%$

    Step 2. Table factor, 15.6178
    Step 3. $2,500 × 15.6178 = $39,044.50
    Step 4. $\qquad\qquad\qquad\dfrac{-\ 2,500.00}{\$36,544.50}$

LU 13-2a

1. **Step 1.** Periods = 5 years × 2 = 10; Rate = 5% ÷ 2 = $2\frac{1}{2}\%$
    Step 2. Factor, 8.7521
    Step 3. $20,000 × 8.7521 = $175,042

2. **Step 1.** Periods = 10; Rate = 4%
    Step 2. Factor, 8.1109
    Step 3. $15,000 × 8.1109 = $121,663.50

3. **Step 1.** Calculate present value of annuity; 30 periods, 3%

              $80,000 × 19.6004 = $1,568,032

    Step 2. Find the present value of $1,568,032 × .8626 = $1,352,584.40

LU 13-3a

20 years × 2 = 40 Per. $\dfrac{6\%}{2} = 3\%$ $120,000 × .0133 = $1,596

Check

$1,596 × 75.4012 = $120,340

You Try It

1.	4.4399 (7% 4 periods)	3.	5.2421 (4% 6 periods)

1. $\dfrac{\times\quad 6{,}000}{\$26{,}639.40}$ 4.4399 (7% 4 periods)

3. $\dfrac{\times\ \$\ 20{,}000}{\$104{,}842}$ 5.2421 (4% 6 periods)

2. $6,000 × 5.7507 = $\dfrac{\$34{,}504.20\ \ (7\%\ 5\ \text{periods})}{\dfrac{-\quad 6000.00}{\$28{,}504.20}}$

4. $\dfrac{\times\ \$400{,}000}{\$\ 12{,}080}$ .0302 (5% 20 periods)

Chapter 14

LU 14-1a

1. **a.** $13,999 − $1,480 = $12,519
    b. $17,700 ($295 × 60) − $12,519 = $5,181
    c. $17,700 ($295 × 60) + $1,480 = $19,180
    d. $\dfrac{\$5{,}181}{\$12{,}519} × \$100 = \$41.39$; between 14.50% and 14.75%
    e. $\dfrac{\$5{,}181 + \$12{,}519}{60} = \$295$

2. $\dfrac{\$8{,}000}{\$1{,}000} = 8 × \$20.28 = \$162.24$ (8%, 60 months)

LU 14-2a

1.

Month	Balance due	Interest	Monthly payment	Reduction in balance	Balance outstanding
1	$300	$3.75 (.0125 × $300)	$20	$16.25 ($20 − $3.75)	$283.75
2	$283.75	$3.55 (.0125 × $283.75)	$20	$16.45	$267.30

2. Average daily balance calculated as follows:

No. of days of current balance	Current balance	Extension
3	$400	$1,200
7	300 ($400 − $100)	2,100
5	360 ($300 + $60)	1,800
5	340 ($360 − $20)	1,700
11	540 ($340 + $200)	5,940

31 − 20 (3 + 7 + 5 + 5)

Average daily balance $= \dfrac{\$12,740}{31} = \$410.97$

Finance charge $= \$410.97 \times 2\% = \$8.22$

You Try It

1. $5,400 amount financed
   − 100
   $5,300

2. $7,799.40
$129.99 × 60 = − 5300.00
              $2,499.40 FC

3. $7,799.40 + $100 = $7,899.40

4. $\dfrac{\$2,499.40}{\$5,300.00} \times \$100 = 47.16$ (between 16.25% and 16.50%)

5. $\dfrac{\$2,499.40 + \$5,300}{60} = \$129.99$

$\dfrac{\$5,300}{1,000} = 5.3 \times 24.32 = \$128.9$
(off due to using 16% instead of using between 16.25% and 16.50%)

6. $5,000 × .035 = $175
   $275 − $175 = $100
   $5,000 − $100 = $4,900

7. 12 days × $200 = $2,400
   4 days × $120 [$200 − $80] = $480
   14 days × $180 [$120 + $60] = $2,520
   Total = $5,400
   $5,400/30 = $180 daily balance
   Finance charge = $180 × 2.5% = $4.50

Chapter 15

LU 15-1a

1. $180,000 − $54,000 = $126,000

$\dfrac{\$126,000}{\$1,000} = 126 \times 6.66 = \$839.16$

$176,097.60 = $302,097.60 − $126,000
($839.16 × 360)   30 years × 12 payments per year

2. 5% = $676.62 monthly payment
        (126 × $5.37)

Total interest cost $117,583.20 = ($676.62 × 360) − $126,000
Savings $58,514.40 = $176,097.60 − $117,583.20

LU 15-2a

$70,000 mortgage; monthly payment of $466.20 (70 × $6.66)

Payment number	Principal (current)	PORTION TO— Interest	Principal reduction	Balance of principal
1	$70,000	$408.33 $70,000 × .07 × $\frac{1}{12}$	$57.87 ($466.20 − $408.33)	$69,942.13 ($70,000 − $57.87)
2	$69,942.13	$69,942.13 × .07 × $\frac{1}{12}$ $408	($466.20 − $408.00) $58.20	($69,942.13 − $58.20) $69,883.93

You Try It

1. $\dfrac{\$70,000}{\$1,000} = 70 \times \$4.50 = \$315$

2. 30 years = $\times$ $\begin{array}{r} 360 \text{ payments} \\ \$\quad 315 \\ \hline \end{array}$
$\$113,400 - \$70,000 = \$43,400$ interest

3.
Payment	Interest	Principal reduction	Balance
1	$204.17	$110.83	$69,889.17

$\left(\$70,000 \times .035 \times \dfrac{1}{12} = \$204.17\right)$ ($315 − $204.17)   ($70,000 − $110.83)

2	203.84	$111.16	$69,778.01

$\left(\$69,889.17 \times .035 \times \dfrac{1}{12}\right)$ ($315 − $203.84)   ($69,889.17 − $111.16)

Chapter 16

LU 16-1a

		2014	2013
1.	a. Cash	$\dfrac{\$38,000}{\$180,000} = 21.11\%$	$\dfrac{\$35,000}{\$140,000} = 25.00\%$
	b. Accounts receivable	$\dfrac{\$19,000}{\$180,000} = 10.56\%$	$\dfrac{\$18,000}{\$140,000} = 12.86\%$
	c. Merchandise inventory	$\dfrac{\$16,000}{\$180,000} = 8.89\%$	$\dfrac{\$11,000}{\$140,000} = 7.86\%$
	d. Prepaid expenses	$\dfrac{\$20,000}{\$180,000} = 11.11\%$	$\dfrac{\$16,000}{\$140,000} = 11.43\%$

2. $\begin{array}{r} \$16,000 \\ -\ 11,000 \\ \hline \$\ 5,000 \end{array}$ Percent $= \dfrac{\$5,000}{\$11,000} = 45.45\%$

LU 16-2a

1. **a.** $36,000 − $2,800 = $33,200
(Gross sales − Sales returns and allowances)
b. $5,900 + $6,800 − $5,200 = $7,500
(Beginning inventory + Net purchases − Ending inventory)
c. $33,200 − $7,500 = $25,700
(Net sales − Cost of merchandise sold)
d. $25,700 − $8,100 = $17,600
(Gross profit from sales − Operating expenses)

LU 16-3a

		2015	2014	2013	2012
1.	Sales	36%	86%	71%	100%
		$\left(\dfrac{\$25,000}{\$70,000}\right)$	$\left(\dfrac{\$60,000}{\$70,000}\right)$	$\left(\dfrac{\$50,000}{\$70,000}\right)$	

2. **a.** $\dfrac{\text{CA}}{\text{CL}} = \dfrac{\$14,000}{\$9,000} = 1.6$ **b.** $\dfrac{\text{CA} - \text{Inv.}}{\text{CL}} = \dfrac{\$14,000 - \$3,900}{\$9,000} = 1.12$

c. $\dfrac{\text{AR}}{\frac{\text{Net sales}}{360}} = \dfrac{\$5,500}{\frac{\$36,500}{360}} = 54.2$ days   **d.** $\dfrac{\text{NI}}{\text{Net sales}} = \dfrac{\$8,000}{\$36,500} = 21.92\%$

You Try It

1.
$$
\begin{array}{rr}
\$\ 400 & 40\% \\
+\ \ 600 & 60\% \\
\hline
\$1,000 & 100\%
\end{array}
$$

2.

	2014	2013	Change	%
Cash	$8,000	2,000	$6,000	300%

$\dfrac{\$6,000}{\$2,000}$

3. $400 − $20 − $5 = $375 net sales

4. $50 + $200 − $20 = $230

5. $400 − $250 = $150 gross profit

6. $210 − $180 = $30 net income

7.
2016	2015	2014
1,200	800	1,000
120%	80%	100%
$\left(\dfrac{1,200}{1,000}\right)$	$\dfrac{200}{1,000}$	

8. $\dfrac{\$40,000}{\$160,000} = .25$

9. $\dfrac{\$40,000 - \$2,000 - \$3,000}{\$160,000} = \dfrac{\$35,000}{\$160,000} = .22$

10. $\dfrac{\$4,000}{\frac{\$60,000}{360}} = 24$ days

11. $\dfrac{\$180,000}{\$70,000} = 257.14$

12. $\dfrac{\$16,000}{-\$90,000} = -17.78\%$

13. $\dfrac{\$60,000}{70,000} = .86$

14. $\dfrac{\$16,000}{\$60,000} = .27$

Chapter 17

LU 17-1a

1.

End of year	Cost of truck	Depreciation expense for year	Accumulated depreciation at end of year	Book value at end of year (Cost − Accumulated depreciation)
1	$20,000	$6,000	$ 6,000	$14,000 ($20,000 − $6,000)
2	20,000	6,000	12,000	8,000
3	20,000	6,000	18,000	2,000

2. $\dfrac{\$20,000 - \$2,000}{3} = \$6,000 \times \dfrac{11}{12} = \$5,500$

LU 17-2a

1. $\dfrac{\$30,000 - \$2,000}{56,000} = \$.50$

End of year	Cost of machine	Units produced	Depreciation expense for year	Accumulated depreciation at end of year	Book value at end of year (Cost − Accumulated depreciation)
2012	$30,000	1,000	$500 ($1,000 × $.50)	$ 500	$ 29,500
2013	30,000	6,000	3,000	3,500	26,500
2014	30,000	4,000	2,000	5,500	24,500
2015	30,000	2,000	1,000	6,500	23,500
2016	30,000	2,500	1,250	7,750	22,250

LU 17-3a

End of year	Cost of machine	Accumulated depreciation at beginning of year	Book value at beginning of year (Cost – Accumulated depreciation)	Depreciation (Book value at beginning of year × Rate)	Accumulated depreciation at end of year	Book value at end of year (Cost – Accumulated depreciation)
1	$31,000	$ -0-	$31,000	$12,400	$12,400	$18,600
2	31,000	12,400	18,600	7,440	19,840	11,160
3	31,000	19,840	11,160	4,464	24,304	*6,696

*An additional $5,696 could have been taken to reach residual value.

LU 17-4a

1. $90,000 \times .1920 = \$17,280$

2. $900,000 \times .05 = \$45,000$

You Try It

1. $\dfrac{\$50,000 - \$10,000}{4} = \dfrac{\$40,000}{4} = \$10,000$ per year

2. $\dfrac{\$4,000 - \$500}{700} = \dfrac{\$3,500}{700} = \$5$ depreciation per unit

   $150 \times \$5 = \$750$

3.

Year	Cost	Depreciation expense	Book value at end of year
1	$40,000	$20,000 ($40,000 × .50)	$20,000
2	$20,000	10,000 ($20,000 × .50) =	$10,000

4. $.20 \times \$7,000 = \$1,400$ depreciation expense

Chapter 18

LU 18-1a

1. **a.** 58 units of ending inventory $\times \$4.76 = \$276.08$ Cost of ending inventory

   b. $\underset{\text{available for sale}}{\text{Cost of goods}} - \underset{\text{inventory}}{\text{Cost of ending}} = \underset{\text{goods sold}}{\text{Cost of}}$

   $\quad\quad \$810 \quad - \quad \$276.08 \quad = \quad \$533.92$

2. **a.** 50 units from November 1 purchased at $7 $350
       _8 units from April 1 purchased at $5   + 40
       58 units $390 Cost of ending inventory

   b. $\underset{\text{available for sale}}{\text{Cost of goods}} - \underset{\text{inventory}}{\text{Cost of ending}} = \underset{\text{goods sold}}{\text{Cost of}}$

   $\quad\quad \$810 \quad - \quad \$390 \quad = \quad \$420$

3. **a.** 20 units from January 1 purchased at $4 $ 80
       38 units from March 1 purchased at $3   + 114
       58 units $194 Cost of ending inventory

   b. $\underset{\text{available for sale}}{\text{Cost of goods}} - \underset{\text{inventory}}{\text{Cost of ending}} = \underset{\text{goods sold}}{\text{Cost of}}$

   $\quad\quad \$810 \quad - \quad \$194 \quad = \quad \$616$

LU 18-2a

	Cost	Retail
1. Beginning inventory	$ 19,000	$ 60,000
Net purchases during the month	265,000	392,000
Cost of goods available for sale	$284,000	$452,000
Less net sales for the month		375,000
Ending inventory at retail		$ 77,000
Cost ratio ($284,000 ÷ $452,000)		62.8%
Ending inventory at cost (.628 × $77,000)		$ 48,356

2. Goods available for sale

Beginning inventory, January 1, 2014		$ 30,000
Net purchases		8,000
Cost of goods available for sale		$ 38,000
Less estimated cost of goods sold:		
Net sales at retail	$ 16,000	
Cost percentage (100% − 30%)	.70	
Estimated cost of goods sold		$ 11,200
Estimated ending inventory, January 31, 2014		$ 26,800

3. Inventory turnover at cost $= \dfrac{\text{Cost of goods sold}}{\text{Average inventory at cost}} = \dfrac{\$76,500}{\$11,200} = 6.83$

Inventory turnover at retail $= \dfrac{\text{Net sales}}{\text{Average inventory at retail}} = \dfrac{\$129,500}{\$21,800} = 5.94$

Ratio

4. Department A   10,000 $\dfrac{10,000}{60,000} = .17 \times \$60,000 = \$10,200$

Department B $\dfrac{50,000}{60,000}$ $\dfrac{50,000}{60,000} = .83 \times \$60,000 = \dfrac{49,800}{\$60,000}$

You Try It

1. $4 \times 9 = 36$
    $3 \times 10 = 30$
    66 total cost
    $1 \times \$9 = \$9$
    $1 \times \$10 = \dfrac{\$10}{\$19}$
    $\$66 - 19 = \$47$ Cost of goods sold

2. $\dfrac{89}{15} = \$5.93$ unit cost
    $4 \times \$5.93 = \$23.72$

3. FIFO $4 \times \$7 = \$28$

4. LIFO $4 \times \$.5 = \$20$

5.

	Cost	Retail
Cost of goods available for sale	$88,000	$117,000
		− 90,000
Net sales		$ 27,000

Cost ratio: $\dfrac{\$88,000}{\$117,000} = 75\%$

$.75 \times \$27,000 = \$20,250$

6. Cost of goods available for sale — $42,000
   Net sales at retail — $20,000
   × .25
   COGS at retail — 5,000
   Ending inventory — $37,000

7. $\dfrac{\$90,000}{\frac{\$40,000 + \$60,000}{2}} = \dfrac{\$90,000}{\$50,000} = 1.8$

8. Total sq. ft. for dept. 10,000
   .40 to Dept A $30,000 × .40 = $12,000
   .60 to Dept B   30,000 × .60 = 18,000

Chapter 19

LU 19-1a

Shampoo	$ 5.90
Laundry detergent	4.10
	$10.00 × .07 = $.70

LU 19-2a

1. $.40 \times \$150,000 = \$60,000$

2. $\dfrac{\$159,000}{\$1,680,000} = .0946$ per dollar

3. a. $.09.46 = 9.46\%$

b. $.09.46 \times 100 = \$9.46$

c. $.094.6 \times 1,000 = \$94.60$

d. $\dfrac{.0946}{.001} = 94.6$ mills (or $.0946 \times 1,000$)

4.
$$
\begin{aligned}
.0946 \times \$60,000 &= \$5,676 \\
\$9.46 \times 600 &= \$5,676 \\
\$94.60 \times 60 &= \$5,676 \\
94.60 \times .001 \times \$60,000 &= \$5,676
\end{aligned}
$$

You Try It

1. $\$62.80 - \$5.02 = \$57.78$
$$
\begin{array}{r}
\times\ .06 \\
\hline
\$3.47 \text{ sales tax}
\end{array}
$$

2. $\$6,000 + \$30 + \$60 = \$6,090$

3. $\$200,000 \times .40 = \$80,000$ assessed value

4. $\dfrac{\$700,000}{\$8,400,000} = .0833$

5. 1. 8.3% 2. \$8.33 3. \$83 4. $\dfrac{.0833}{.001} = 83.3 = 83$ mills

6. 1. $9.5\% \times \$40,000 = \$3,800$

2. $\dfrac{\$40,000}{\$100} = 400 \times \$9.50 = \$3,800$

3. $\dfrac{\$40,000}{\$1,000} = 40 \times \$95 = \$3,800$

4. $\dfrac{\$.0950}{.001} = 95 \times .001 \times \$40,000 = \$3,800$

Chapter 20

LU 20-1a

1. $\dfrac{\$70,000}{\$1,000} = 70 \times \$2.67 = \$186.90$ No cash value in term insurance

2. $\dfrac{\$95,000}{\$1,000} = 95 \times \$7.75^* = \$736.25$

Option 1: Cash value $95 \times \$29 = \$2,755$
Option 2: Paid up $95 \times \$86 = \$8,170$
Option 3: Extended term 9 years 91 days

*For females we subtract 3 years.

LU 20-2a

1. $\dfrac{\$80,000}{100} = 800 \times \$.41 = \$328$ $\dfrac{\$20,000}{100} = 200 \times \$.50 = \dfrac{\$100}{\$428}$ ⟵ total premium

2. $\$428 \times .74 = \$316.72$ $\$428 - \$316.72 = \$111.28$

3. $\dfrac{\$140,000}{\$200,000} = \dfrac{7}{10} \times \$50,000 = \$35,000$

$(.80 \times \$250,000)$ \$170,000 never more than face value

LU 20-3a

Compulsory		
Bodily	$ 98	(Table 20.5)
Property	160	(Table 20.5)
Options		
Bodily	146	(Table 20.6)
Property	164	(Table 20.7)
Collision	174 ($154 + $20)	(Table 20.8)
Comprehensive	71 ($67 + $4)	(Table 20.9)
Towing	4	(Table 20.10)
Towing annual premium	$817	

You Try It

1. 1. $\dfrac{\$90,000}{\$1,000} = 90 \times \$2.44 = \$219.60$

   2. $\dfrac{\$90,000}{\$1,000} = 90 \times \$11.84 = \$1,065.60$

   3. $\dfrac{\$90,000}{\$1,000} = 90 \times \$15.60 = \$1,404.00$

   4. $\dfrac{\$90,000}{\$1,000} = 90 \times \$27.64 = \$2,487.60$

2. Option 1: $\dfrac{\$60,000}{\$1,000} = 60 \times \$265 = \$15,900$

   Option 2: $60 \times \$550 = \$33,000$

   Option 3: 21 yr 300 days

3. $\dfrac{\$80,000}{\$100} = 800 \times \$.61 = \$488$

   $\dfrac{\$20,000}{\$100} = 200 \times \$.65 = \underline{\$130}$

   Total $\underline{\$618}$

4. $600 \times \$.44 = \$264$
   Refund $\$600 - \$264 = \$336$

5. $\$600 \times \dfrac{1}{3} = \$200$

   $\$600 - \$200 = \$400$

6. $\dfrac{\$40,000}{\$60,000} \times \$9,000 = \$6,000$

7.

10/20/5	$184 ($55 + $129)
Bodily	94
Property	132
Collision	196
Comprehensive	178
Comprehensive	$784

Chapter 21

LU 21-1a

1. a. (A) Highest price traded in last 52 weeks.
       (B) Lowest price traded in past 52 weeks.
       (C) Name of corporation is Good Year (symbol GT).
       (D) Dividend per share per year is .07.
       (E) Yield for year is .54%.
       (F) Good Year stock sells at 16 times its earnings.
       (G) Sales volume for the day is 3,080,000.
       (H) The last price (closing price for the day) is $13.08.
       (I) Stock is up $.11 from closing price yesterday.

    b. EPS $= \dfrac{\$13.08}{16} = \$.82$ per share   c. $\dfrac{\$.07}{\$13.08} = .54\%$

2. Preferred: $40,000 \times \$.60 = \$24,000$ Arrears 2014
                                  $+ \ 24,000$ 2015
                                  $\overline{\$48,000}$

    Common: $162,000 ($210,000 − $48,000)

LU 21-2a

1. $100.25\% \times \$1,000 = \$1,002.50 \times 5 = \$5,012.50$

2. $7\frac{1}{2}\% = .075 \times \$1,000 = \$75$ annual interest $\dfrac{\$75.00}{\$1,002.50} = 7.48\%$

LU 21-3a

1. 7.61   2. 0.00   3. 3.8%

You Try It

1. $\dfrac{\$.88}{\$53.88} = 1.63\%$

2. $\dfrac{\$53.88}{\$3.70} = 14.56 = 15$

3. $30,000 \times \$.80 = 24,000$
   $30,000 \times \$.80 = \underline{24,000}$
                     $48,000$ to preferred

$\begin{array}{r} \$300,000 \\ - \ \ 48,000 \\ \hline \$252,000 \end{array}$ $\div \ 60,000 = \$4.20$ to common

4. $\$1,022.25 \times 6 = \$6,133.50$

5. $\dfrac{\$40}{1,011.20} = 3.96\%$

6. $\$12.44 + \$.05 = \$12.49$

Chapter 22

LU 22-1a

$$\text{Mean} = \frac{\$17,000 + \$14,000 + \$11,000 + \$51,000}{4} = \$23,250$$

$$\text{Median} = \frac{\$14,000 + \$17,000}{2} = \$15,500 \qquad \$11,000, \boxed{\$14,000, \$17,000,} \ \$51,000.$$

Note how we arrange numbers from smallest to highest to calculate median.

Median is the better indicator since in calculating the mean, the $51,000 puts the average of $23,250 much too high. There is no mode.

LU 22-2a

1.

Number of sales	Tally	Frequency
0	IIII	4
1	II	2
2	I	1
3	I	1
4	II	2
5		0
6	I	1
7	I	1
8	III	3
9	IIII	4
10	I	1

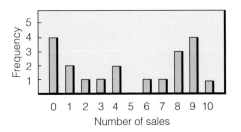

2.

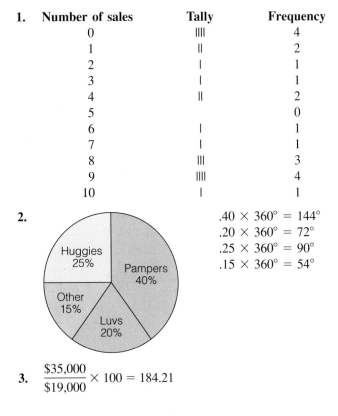

$$.40 \times 360° = 144°$$
$$.20 \times 360° = 72°$$
$$.25 \times 360° = 90°$$
$$.15 \times 360° = 54°$$

3. $\dfrac{\$35,000}{\$19,000} \times 100 = 184.21$

LU 22-3a

1. $60 - 5 = 55$ range

2.

Data	Data − Mean	(Data − Mean)²
120	120 − 103 = 17	289
88	88 − 103 = −15	225
77	77 − 103 = −26	676
125	125 − 103 = 22	484
110	110 − 103 = 7	49
93	93 − 103 = −10	100
111	111 − 103 = 8	64
	Total	1,887

$$1,887 \div (7 - 1) = 314.5$$
$$\sqrt{314.5} = 17.7 \text{ standard deviation}$$

You Try It

1. $\dfrac{41 + 29 + 16 + 15 + 18}{5} = 23.8$

2.
Value	Frequency	Product
80	2	160
90	3	270
100	1	100
	6	690

Mean $= \dfrac{690}{6} = 115$

3. 4 7 ⑨ 14 16

4.
Coffees consumed	Tally	Frequency
0	I	1
1	I	1
2	II	2
3	I	1
4	I	1
5	I	1
6		0
7		0
8	I	1

5.
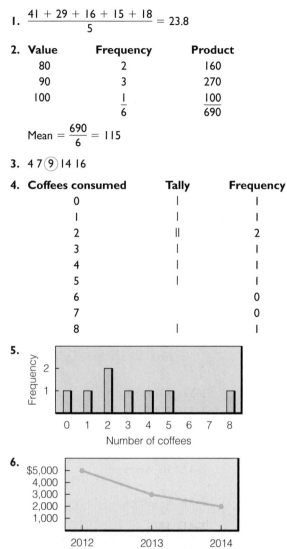

6.

7.
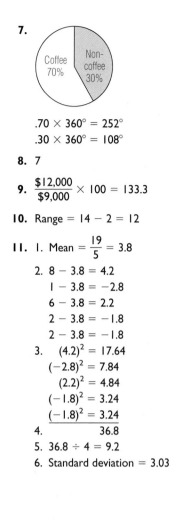

$.70 \times 360° = 252°$
$.30 \times 360° = 108°$

8. 7

9. $\dfrac{\$12,000}{\$9,000} \times 100 = 133.3$

10. Range $= 14 - 2 = 12$

11. 1. Mean $= \dfrac{19}{5} = 3.8$

 2. $8 - 3.8 = 4.2$
  $1 - 3.8 = -2.8$
  $6 - 3.8 = 2.2$
  $2 - 3.8 = -1.8$
  $2 - 3.8 = -1.8$

 3. $(4.2)^2 = 17.64$
  $(-2.8)^2 = 7.84$
  $(2.2)^2 = 4.84$
  $(-1.8)^2 = 3.24$
  $(-1.8)^2 = 3.24$

 4. $\overline{ 36.8}$

 5. $36.8 \div 4 = 9.2$

 6. Standard deviation $= 3.03$

Odd-Numbered Drill and Word Problems for End-of-Chapter Problems.

Challenge Problems (all).

Summary Practice Tests (all).

Cumulative Reviews (all).

Odd-Numbered Additional Assignments by Learning Unit from Appendix A.

Check Figures to Drill and Word Problems (Odds), Challenge Problems, Summary Practice Tests, and Cumulative Reviews

Chapter 1

End-of-Chapter Problems

1–1. 94
1–3. 176
1–5. 13,580
1–7. 113,690
1–9. 38
1–11. 3,600
1–13. 1,074
1–15. 31,110
1–17. 340,531
1–19. 126,000
1–21. 90
1–23. 86 R4
1–25. 405
1–27. 1,616
1–29. 24,876
1–31. 17,989; 18,000
1–33. 80
1–35. 133
1–37. 216
1–39. 19 R21
1–41. 7,690; 6,990
1–43. 70,470; 72,000
1–45. 700
1–47. $27,738
1–49. $240; $200; $1,200; $1,080
1–51. $2,436; $3,056; $620 more
1–53. 905,600
1–55. 1,080
1–57. a. $4,569
      b. $4,600
      c. $31
1–59. $25
1–61. $1,872,000
1–63. $4,815; $250,380
1–65. $64,180
1–67. 200,000; 10,400,000
1–69. $1,486
1–71. Average $33; no concern
1–73. $40 per sq yard

1–75. $7,680 difference between drugstore and bakery
1–76. $12,000 difference

Summary Practice Test

1. 7,017,243
2. Nine million, six hundred twenty-two thousand, three hundred sixty-four
3. a. 70
   b. 900
   c. 8,000
   d. 10,000
4. 17,000; 17,692
5. 8,100,000; 8,011,758
6. 829,412,000
7. 379 R19
8. 100
9. $95
10. $500; no
11. $1,000

Chapter 2

End-of-Chapter Problems

2–1. Proper
2–3. Improper
2–5. $61\frac{2}{5}$
2–7. $\frac{59}{3}$
2–9. $\frac{11}{13}$
2–11. 60 ($2 \times 2 \times 3 \times 5$)
2–13. 96 ($2 \times 2 \times 2 \times 2 \times 2 \times 3$)
2–15. $\frac{13}{21}$
2–17. $15\frac{5}{12}$
2–19. $\frac{5}{6}$
2–21. $7\frac{4}{9}$

2–23. $\frac{5}{16}$
2–25. $\frac{3}{25}$
2–27. $\frac{1}{3}$
2–29. $\frac{7}{18}$
2–31. $215,658
2–33. 234,701
2–35. $35\frac{1}{4}$ hours
2–37. $10\frac{3}{4}$ hours
2–39. $6\frac{1}{2}$ gallons
2–41. $875
2–43. $\frac{23}{36}$
2–45. 156, 467, 484
2–47. $3\frac{3}{4}$ lbs apple; $8\frac{1}{8}$ cups flour; $\frac{5}{8}$ cup marg.; $5\frac{15}{16}$ cups sugar; 5 teaspoons cin.
2–49. 400 people
2–51. 275 gloves
2–53. $450
2–55. $45\frac{3}{16}$
2–57. $62,500,000; $37,500,000
2–59. $\frac{3}{8}$
2–61. $2\frac{3}{5}$ hours
2–63. $8\frac{31}{48}$ feet; Yes
2–64. a. 400 homes b. $320,000
      c. 3,000 people; 2,500 people
      d. $112.50 e. $8,800,000

Summary Practice Test

1. Mixed number
2. Proper
3. Improper
4. $18\frac{1}{9}$
5. $\frac{65}{8}$
6. $9;\frac{7}{10}$
7. 64
8. 24 ($2 \times 2 \times 3 \times 2 \times 1 \times 1 \times 1$)
9. $6\frac{17}{20}$
10. $\frac{1}{4}$
11. $6\frac{2}{21}$
12. $\frac{1}{14}$
13. $3\frac{5}{6}$ hours
14. 7,840 rolls
15. a. 60,000 veggie
    b. 30,000 regular
16. $39\frac{1}{2}$ hours
17. $26

Chapter 3

End-of-Chapter Problems

3–1. Hundredths
3–3. .7; .74; .739
3–5. 5.8; 5.83; 5.831
3–7. 6.6; 6.56; 6.556
3–9. $4,822.78
3–11. .08
3–13. .06
3–15. .91
3–17. 16.61
3–19. $\frac{71}{100}$
3–21. $\frac{125}{10,000}$
3–23. $\frac{825}{1,000}$
3–25. $\frac{7,065}{10,000}$
3–27. $28\frac{48}{100}$
3–29. .005
3–31. .0085
3–33. 818.1279
3–35. 3.4
3–37. 2.32
3–39. 1.2; 1.26791
3–41. 4; 4.0425
3–43. 24,526.67
3–45. 161.29

3–47. 6,824.15
3–49. .04
3–51. .63
3–53. 2.585
3–55. .0086
3–57. 486
3–59. 3.950
3–61. 7,913.2
3–63. .583
3–65. $19.57
3–67. $1.40
3–69. $119.47
3–71. $29.00
3–73. $785.4 million
3–75. $423.16
3–77. $105.08
3–79. $325.03
3–81. $1.7 billion
3–83. $1.58; $3,713
3–85. $6,465.60
3–86. Yes, $16,200
3–87. $560.45

Summary Practice Test

1. 767.849
2. .7
3. .07
4. .007
5. $\frac{9}{10}$
6. $6\frac{97}{100}$
7. $\frac{685}{1,000}$
8. .29
9. .13
10. 4.57
11. .08
12. 390.2702
13. 9.2
14. 118.67
15. 34,684.01
16. 62,940
17. 832,224,982.1
18. $24.56
19. $936.30
20. $385.40
21. A $.12
22. $453.60
23. $28.10

Cumulative Review 1, 2, 3

1. $405
2. $200,000
3. $50,560,000
4. $10.00
5. $225,000
6. $750
7. $369.56
8. $130,000,000
9. $63.64

Chapter 4

End-of-Chapter Problems

4–1. $4,720.33
4–3. $4,705.33
4–5. $753
4–7. $540.82
4–9. $577.95
4–11. $998.86
4–13. $6,489
4–14. $1,862.13
4–15. $3,061.67

Summary Practice Test

1. End Bal. $15,649.12
2. $8,730
3. $1,282.70
4. $10,968.50

Chapter 5

End-of-Chapter Problems

5–1. $C = 355$
5–3. $Q = 300$
5–5. $Y = 15$
5–7. $Y = 12$
5–9. $P = 25$
5–11. Fred 25; Lee 35
5–13. Hugh 50; Joe 250
5–15. 50 shorts; 200 T-shirts
5–17. $B = 70$
5–19. $N = 63$
5–21. $Y = 7$
5–23. $P = \$610.99$
5–25. Pete = 90; Bill = 450
5–27. 48 boxes pens; 240 batteries
5–29. $A = 135$
5–31. $M = 60$
5–33. 211 Boston; 253 Colorado Springs
5–35. $W = 129$
5–37. Shift 1: 3,360; shift 2: 2,240
5–39. 22 boxes of hammers
      18 boxes of wrenches
5–41. 135,797 lenders
5–42. a. 2.5
      b. 15 miles
      c. 6 hours
5–43. $B = 4$

Summary Practice Test

1. $541.90
2. $84,000
3. Sears 70; Buy 560
4. Abby 200; Jill 1,000
5. 13 dishes; 78 pots
6. Pasta 300; 1,300 pizzas

Chapter 6

End-of-Chapter Problems

6–1. 78%
6–3. 70%

6–5. 356.1%
6–7. .08
6–9. .643
6–11. 1.19
6–13. 8.3%
6–15. 87.5%
6–17. $\dfrac{1}{25}$
6–19. $\dfrac{19}{60}$
6–21. $\dfrac{27}{400}$
6–23. 10.5
6–25. 102.5
6–27. 156.6
6–29. 114.88
6–31. 16.2
6–33. 141.67
6–35. 10,000
6–37. 17,777.78
6–39. 108.2%
6–41. 110%
6–43. 400%
6–45. 59.40
6–47. 1,100
6–49. 40%
6–51. +20%
6–53. 80%
6–55. $10,000
6–57. $640 per month
6–59. 677.78%
6–61. 6%
6–63. 16%
6–65. Yes, $15,480
6–67. 900
6–69. $742,500
6–71. $220,000
6–73. 33.3%
6–75. 1.4%
6–77. $39,063.83
6–79. $138.89
6–81. $1,900
6–83. $102.50
6–85. 3.7%
6–87. $2,571
6–89. $41,176
6–91. 40%
6–93. 585,000
6–94. a. 68%
　　　b. 125%
　　　c. $749,028
　　　d. $20
　　　e. 7 people
6–95. $55,429

Summary Practice Test
　1. 92.1%
　2. 40%
　3. 1,588%
　4. 800%
　5. .42

6. .0798
7. 4.0
8. .0025
9. 16.7%
10. 33.3%
11. $\dfrac{31}{160}$
12. $\dfrac{31}{500}$
13. $540,000
14. $2,330,000
15. 75%
16. 2.67%
17. $382.61
18. $639
19. $150,000

Chapter 7

End-of-Chapter Problems
7–1. .9603; .0397; $23.78; $575.22
7–3. .893079; .106921; $28.76; $240.24
7–5. $369.70; $80.30
7–7. $1,392.59; $457.41
7–9. June 28; July 18
7–11. June 15; July 5
7–13. July 10; July 30
7–15. $138; $6,862
7–17. $2; $198
7–19. $408.16; $291.84
7–21. $59.80; $239.20
7–23. .648; .352; $54.56; $100.44
7–25. $576.06; $48.94
7–27. $5,100; $5,250
7–29. $5,850
7–31. $1,357.03
7–33. $8,173.20
7–35. $8,333.33; $11,666.67
7–37. $99.99
7–39. $489.90; $711.10
7–41. $4,658.97
7–43. $1,083.46; $116.54
7–45. $5,008.45
7–47. $2,925.30
7–48. a. $1,500
　　　b. 8.34%
　　　c. $164.95
　　　d. $16,330.05
　　　e. $1,664.95
7–49. $4,794.99

Summary Practice Test
　1. $332.50
　2. $211.11
　3. $819.89; $79.11
　4. a. Nov. 14; Dec. 4
　　　b. March 20; April 9
　　　c. June 10; June 30
　　　d. Jan. 10; Jan. 30
　5. $15; $285

6. $7,120
7. B: 20.95%
8. $1,938.78; $6,061.22
9. $7,076.35

Chapter 8

End-of-Chapter Problems
8–1. $100; $600
8–3. $4,285.71
8–5. $6.90; 45.70%
8–7. $450; $550
8–9. $110.83
8–11. $34.20; 69.8%
8–13. 11%
8–15. $3,830.40; $1,169.60; 23.39%
8–17. 16,250; $4.00
8–19. $166.67
8–21. $14.29
8–23. $600; $262.50
8–25. $84
8–27. 42.86%
8–29. $3.56
8–31. 20,000
8–33. $558.60
8–35. $195
8–37. $129.99
8–39. $2.31
8–41. 12,000
8–42. $266
8–43. $94.98; $20.36; loss

Summary Practice Test
　1. $126
　2. 30.26%
　3. $482.76; $217.24
　4. $79; 37.97%
　5. $133.33
　6. $292.50
　7. 27.27%
　8. $160
　9. 25.9%
　10. $1.15
　11. 11,500

Cumulative Review 6, 7, 8
　1. 650,000
　2. $296.35
　3. $133
　4. $2,562.14
　5. $48.75
　6. $259.26
　7. $1.96; $1.89

Chapter 9

End-of-Chapter Problems
9–1. 39; $310.05
9–3. $12.00; $452
9–5. $1,680
9–7. $60
9–9. $13,000
9–11. $4,500

9–13. $11,900; $6,900; $138; $388
9–15. $378.20; $101.50
9–17. $177.98; $99.20; $23.20; $1,299.62
9–19. $752.60; $113.60
9–21. $1,290.80
9–23. $202.99
9–25. $825
9–27. $1,086.17
9–29. $357; $56
9–31. $1,077.86
9–32. a. $233.38
      b. $196.19
      c. $37.19
9–33. $1,653.60, $193.13 understated; $52

Summary Practice Test
  1. 49; $428
  2. $794
  3. $24,700
  4. $465; $290
  5. $271.86
  6. $798 SUTA; $112 FUTA;
     no tax in quarter 2

Chapter 10

End-of-Chapter Problems
 10–1. $637.50; $17,637.50
 10–3. $1,012.50; $21,012.50
 10–5. $28.23; $613.23
 10–7. $20.38; $1,020.38
 10–9. $73.78; $1,273.78
 10–11. $1,904.76
 10–13. $4,390.61 balance due
 10–15. $618.75; $15,618.75
 10–17. $2,377.70; Save $1.08
 10–19. 4.7 years
 10–21. $21,596.11
 10–23. $714.87; $44.87
 10–25. 266 days
 10–27. $2,608.65
 10–29. $18,666.85
 10–31. 12.37%
 10–33. 72 days
 10–35. 5.6%
 10–36. a. $1,000
      b. 8%
      c. $280; $1,400
 10–37. $7.82; $275.33

Summary Practice Test
  1. $27.23; $2,038.11
  2. $86,400
  3. $14,901.25
  4. $14,888.90
  5. $32,516
  6. $191.09; $10,191.09

Chapter 11

End-of-Chapter Problems
 11–1. $211.11; $15,788.89
 11–3. 25 days

 11–5. $51,451.39; 57; $733.18; $50,718.21
 11–7. 4.04%
 11–9. $7,566.67; 6.9%
 11–11. $8,937
 11–13. ¥20,188
 11–15. $5,133.33; 56; $71.87; $5,061.46
 11–17. $4,836.44
 11–18. a. $90.13
      b. $177.50
      c. 3.64%
      d. 3.61%
 11–19. $2,127.66; 9.57%

Summary Practice Test
  1. $160,000
  2. $302.22; $16,697.98; $17,000; 4.1%
  3. $61,132.87
  4. $71,264.84
  5. $57,462.50; 7.6%
  6. 5.58%

Chapter 12

End-of-Chapter Problems
 12–1. 4; 3%; $1,800.81; $200.81
 12–3. $15,450; $450
 12–5. 12.55%
 12–7. 16; $1\frac{1}{2}$%; .7880; $4,728
 12–9. 28; 3%; .4371; $7,692.96
 12–11. 2.2879 × $7,692.96
 12–13. $64,188
 12–15. Mystic $4,775
 12–17. $25,734.40
 12–19. $3,807
 12–21. 5.06%
 12–23. $37,644
 12–25. Yes, $17,908 (compounding)
     or $8,376 (p. v.)
 12–27. $3,739.20
 12–29. $13,883.30
 12–31. $105,878.50
 12–32. $689,125; $34,125 Bank B

Summary Practice Test
  1. $48,760
  2. $31,160
  3. $133,123.12
  4. No, $26,898 (compounding)
     or $22,308 (p. v.)
  5. 6.14%
  6. $46,137
  7. $187,470
  8. $28,916.10

Chapter 13

End-of-Chapter Problems
 13–1. $203,182
 13–3. $209,278
 13–5. $3,118.59

 13–7. End of first year $2,405.71
 13–9. $1,410
 13–11. $3,397.20
 13–13. $124,937.70; $168,254.70
 13–15. $1,245
 13–17. $900,655
 13–19. $33,444
 13–21. $13,838.25
 13–23. Annuity $12,219.11 or
     $12,219.93
 13–25. $3,625.60
 13–27. $111,013.29
 13–29. $404,313.97
 13–30. $199.29
 13–31. $120,747.09

Summary Practice Test
  1. $100,952.82
  2. $33,914.88 or $33,913.57
  3. $108,722.40
  4. $2,120
  5. $2,054
  6. $264,915.20
  7. $83,304.59
  8. $237,501.36
  9. $473,811.99
  10. $713,776.37

Cumulative Review 10, 11, 12, 13
  1. Annuity $2,058.62 or $2,058.59
  2. $5,118.70
  3. $116,963.02
  4. $3,113.92
  5. $5,797.92
  6. $18,465.20
  7. $29,632.35
  8. $55,251

Chapter 14

End-of-Chapter Problems
 14–1. Finance charge $3,600
 14–3. Finance charge $1,279.76;
     12.75%–13%
 14–5. $119.39; $119.37
 14–7. $2,741; $41.12
 14–9. $1,191.67
 14–11. a. $4,050 b. $1,656 c. $5,756
      d. $40.89, falls between 14.25%
         and 14.50%
      e. $95.10
 14–13. $415.12; $340.66; $74.46
 14–15. $940.36
 14–17. Peg is correct
 14–18. 15.48%

Summary Practice Test
  1. $26,500; $4,100
  2. $52.66
  3. 4.25% to 4.5%
  4. $6,005.30
  5. $400; $8

Chapter 15

End-of-Chapter Problems
- **15–1.** $651.30
- **15–3.** $894.60
- **15–5.** $118,796
- **15–7.** $1,679.04; $1,656.25; $22.79; $158,977.21
- **15–9.** $145,395
- **15–11.** $636.16; $117,017.60
- **15–13.** Payment 3, $119,857.38
- **15–15.** $84,240
- **15–17.** $942.50
- **15–18.** $793.50
- **15–19.** a. $92,495.50
  b. $1,690.15
  c. $415,954

Summary Practice Test
1. $1,020; $850; $169,830
2. $499.84; $91,942.40
3. a. $434.97; $75,589.20
   b. $460.08; $84,628.80
   c. $486; $93,960
   d. $512.73; $103,582.80
4. $5.71; $1,027.80
5. $251,676

Chapter 16

End-of-Chapter Problems
- **16–1.** Total assets $74,000
- **16–3.** Inventory −16.67%; mortgage note +13.79%
- **16–5.** Net sales 13.62%; Net earnings 2013 47.92%
- **16–7.** Depreciation $100; + 16.67%
- **16–9.** 1.43; 1.79
- **16–11.** .20; .23
- **16–13.** .06; .08
- **16–15.** 13.57%
- **16–17.** 87.74%; 34.43%; .13; 55.47%
- **16–19.** 2016 68% sales
- **16–21.** $3,470; $431
- **16–22.** 3.5; 2.3

Summary Practice Test
1. a. $161,000
   b. $21,000
   c. $140,000
   d. $84,000
2. Acc. rec. 15.15%; 24.67%
3. Cash $11,000; 137.50%
4. 2013; 74%
5. Total assets $175,000
6. a. .70 b. .50 c. 45 days
   d. 1.05 e. .25

Chapter 17

End-of-Chapter Problems
- **17–1.** Book value (end of year) $27,000
- **17–3.** Book value (end of year) $21,000
- **17–5.** Book value (end of year) $15,000
- **17–7.** Book value (end of year) $9,000
- **17–9.** Book value (end of year) $15,000
- **17–11.** Book value (end of year) $5,400
- **17–13.** $1,400
- **17–15.** $18,000
- **17–17.** $22,560
- **17–19.** $15,000
- **17–21.** $6,000; $18,000
- **17–23.** $6,760 below
- **17–25.** $83,667
- **17–27.** a. $87,750 b. $11.40
  c. $21,489 d. 4 years
- **17–28.** $13,320; $1.11

Summary Practice Test
1. Book value end of year 2: $10,800
2. $1,713.60
3. Acc. dep., $4,000; $8,000; $12,000; $16,000; $20,000
4. $1,500
5. $12,600

Chapter 18

End-of-Chapter Problems
- **18–1.** $2,409; $6,674
- **18–3.** $543; $932
- **18–5.** $10
- **18–7.** $36
- **18–9.** $72
- **18–11.** $140.80
- **18–13.** $147.75; $345.60
- **18–15.** $188.65; $304.70
- **18–17.** 3.56; 3.25
- **18–19.** .75; $67,500
- **18–21.** $10,550; $24,645
- **18–23.** $45,000
- **18–25.** $55,120
- **18–27.** $38,150
- **18–28.** $13,499.50
- **18–29.** $1,900

Summary Practice Test
1. a. 31 b. $66.87; $93.30; $80.29
2. $40,000
3. 1.10
4. $109,275
5. $97,960

Chapter 19

End-of-Chapter Problems
- **19–1.** $1,044
- **19–3.** $83,018.87
- **19–5.** $39,000
- **19–7.** $.0233
- **19–9.** 6.99%; $6.99; $69.90; 69.90
- **19–11.** $4,462.50
- **19–13.** $16,985.05
- **19–15.** $112.92
- **19–17.** $112,000
- **19–19.** $6,940
- **19–21.** $64,000
- **19–23.** $2,251.50
- **19–25.** $23,065 more in Minn.
- **19–26.** $3,665
- **19–27.** $979

Summary Practice Test
1. $284.76; $14.24
2. $4,710
3. $146,000
4. 5.1 mills
5. $1,237.50
6. $18,141.20

Chapter 20

End-of-Chapter Problems
- **20–1.** $1,657.60
- **20–3.** $277.50
- **20–5.** $53,000
- **20–7.** 21 years, 300 days
- **20–9.** $518; $182
- **20–11.** $16,500
- **20–13.** $1,067
- **20–15.** $1,855 cheaper
- **20–17.** $801
- **20–19.** $118,750
- **20–21.** $1,100
- **20–23.** $373.67
- **20–25.** $22,900; $10,700
- **20–27.** $24,000; $16,300
- **20–28.** $7,512.64; $1,942.00; $787.89
- **20–29.** $176.00

Summary Practice Test
1. $1,993.50; $28,530
2. $2,616.60; $55,650; $115,500; 21 years 300 days
3. $234,375; $450,000
4. $990; $326.70
5. $1,755
6. Insurance company pays $31,600; Roger pays $10,000

Chapter 21

End-of-Chapter Problems
- **21–1.** $151,952
- **21–3.** 1.1%
- **21–5.** 13
- **21–7.** $24,227.04
- **21–9.** 2013 preferred $8,000
  2014 0
  2015 preferred $127,000
  common $33,000
- **21–11.** $2,280
- **21–13.** $260; $2,725; 9.5%
- **21–15.** $12.04; −$.06; 9.6%
- **21–17.** Gain $222.48

21–19. 12; 2.4%
21–21. $5,043.75; $56.25
21–23. 7.3%
21–25. Stock 6.7%; bond 11.9%
21–27. Yes, $16.02
21–29. $443.80
21–30. a. 1,287 shares
　　b. 2,574 shares
　　c. 5,147 shares
　　d. $26,381.76 for (a);
　　　　$52,388.43 for (b);
　　　　$103,756.44 for (c)
21–31. $1,014.33

Summary Practice Test
　1. $18,127.26
　2. 8; 1.3%
　3. $1.23
　4. $10,476
　5. 5.6%
　6. $160,000
　7. $14.52; $11,616

Chapter 22

End-of-Chapter Problems
22–1. 7.50
22–3. $77.23
22–5. 2.7

22–7. 31.5
22–9. 8
22–11. 142.9
22–13. $200–$299.99 ⊪
22–15. Traditional watch 183.6°
22–17.

Golden retriever 11%
Yorkshire terrier 8%
Labrador retriever 39%
Beagle 17%
German shepherd 25%

22–19. Transportation　126°
　　Hotel　100.8°
　　Food　72°
　　Miscellaneous　61.2°

Transportation 35%
Misc. 17%
Hotel 28%
Food and entertainment 20%

22–21. 250
22–23. a. 57,000,000 mean
　　　62,900,000 median
　　b. AAA = 30.42%
　　　Riser = 22.18%
　　　Casto = 22.07%
　　　Balbon = 12.70%
　　　Hunter = 12.63%
22–24. 24.94%; 15.42%; 10.88%; 13.15%;
　　18.59%; 17.01%

Optional Assignment
　1. 98
　3. 4.3
　5. 16%; 2.5%
　7. 68%; 81.5%; 2.5%; 2.5%; 47.5%
　9. 5.02

Summary Practice Test
　1. $143,300; $141,000
　2. 1,100
　3. 2.50
　4. 100; ⊪⊪; 4
　5. Bar 1 on horizontal axis goes up to 800 on vertical axis
　6. Profits　108°
　　Cost of sales　144°
　　Expense　108°
　7. 166.3%
　8. 3.0 standard deviation

Check Figures (Odds) to Additional Assignments by Learning Unit from Appendix A

LU 1–1

1. a. Seven thousand, eight hundred twenty-one
　d. Fifty-eight thousand, three
3. a. 80; 380; 860; 5,980; 210
　c. 21,000; 1,000; 4,000; 10,000
5. a. Hundreds place
　c. Ten thousands place
　e. Billions place
7. Five hundred sixty-five
9. $375,985
11. Two thousand, four

LU 1–2

1. a. 1,006
　c. 1,319
　d. 179
3. a. Estimated 50; 52
　c. Estimated 10; 9
5. $71,577
7. $19,973
9. 12,797 lbs
11. Estimated $9,400; $9,422
13. $746 discount

LU 1–3

1. a. Estimated 4,000; actual 2,400
　c. Estimated 15,000,000; actual 16,184,184

3. a. Estimated 1,000; actual 963 R5
　c. Estimated 20; actual 25 R8
5. 5,040
7. $78
9. 27
11. $43,200
13. 40 stacks and 23 "extra" bricks

LU 2–1

1. a. Proper
　b. Improper
　c. Improper
　d. Mixed number
　e. Improper
　f. Mixed number
3. a. $\frac{46}{5}$　**c.** $\frac{31}{7}$　**f.** $\frac{53}{3}$
5. a. $6; \frac{6}{7}$　**b.** $15; \frac{2}{5}$　**e.** $12; \frac{8}{11}$
7. $\frac{13}{4}$
9. $\frac{17}{25}$
11. $\frac{60}{100}$
13. $\frac{7}{12}$

LU 2–2

1. a. 32　**b.** 180　**c.** 480　**d.** 252
3. a. $\frac{1}{3}$　**b.** $\frac{2}{3}$　**e.** $6\frac{1}{8}$　**h.** $56\frac{5}{6}$
5. $3\frac{1}{40}$ yards
7. $17\frac{5}{12}$ miles
9. $4\frac{8}{9}$ hours

LU 2–3

1. a. $\frac{\overset{1}{\cancel{6}}}{\cancel{13}} \times \frac{\overset{2}{\cancel{26}}}{\cancel{12}} = 1$
3. a. $1\frac{1}{4}$　**b.** 3　**g.** 24　**l.** $\frac{4}{7}$
5. $39,000
7. 714
9. $20\frac{2}{3}$ miles
11. $412,000

LU 3–1

1. a. .62　**b.** .6　**c.** .953
　d. .401　**e.** .06

3. a. Hundredths place
   d. Thousandths place

5. a. $\dfrac{2}{5}$ **b.** $\dfrac{11}{25}$

   g. $\dfrac{5}{16}$ **l.** $9\dfrac{1}{25}$

7. .286

9. $\dfrac{566}{1,000}$

11. .333

13. .0020507

LU 3–2

1. a. 31.608 **b.** 5.2281 **d.** 3.7736
3. a. .3 **b.** .1 **c.** 1,480.0 **d.** .1
5. a. 6,870 **c.** .0272
   e. 34,700 **i.** 8,329.8
7. $4.53
9. $111.25
11. 15

LU 4–1

1. a. $430.64 **b.** 3 **c.** $867.51
3. a. Neuner Realty Co.
   b. Kevin Jones
   h. $2,756.80

LU 4–2

1. $1,435.42
3. Add $3,000; deduct $22.25
5. $2,989.92
7. $1,315.20

LU 5–1

1. a. $3N = 180$ **e.** $14 + \dfrac{N}{3} = 18$

   h. $2N + 3N + 8 = 68$

LU 5–2

1. $80
3. $45 telephone; $135 utility
5. 51 tickets—Sherry;
   408 tickets—Linda
7. 12 necklaces ($48);
   36 watches ($252)
9. $157.14

LU 6–1

1. a. 4% **b.** 72.9% **i.** 503.8% **l.** 80%
3. a. 70% **c.** 162.5%
   h. 50% **n.** 1.5%

5. a. $\dfrac{1}{4}$ **b.** .375 **c.** 50%

   d. $.66\overline{6}$ **n.** $1\dfrac{1}{8}$

7. 2.9%

9. $\dfrac{39}{100}$

11. $\dfrac{9}{10,000}$

LU 6–2

1. a. $20,000; 30%; $4,000
   c. $7.00; 12%; $.84
3. a. 33.3% **b.** 3% **c.** 27.5%
5. a. −1,584; −26.6%
   d. −20,000; −16.7%
7. $9,000
9. $3,196
11. 329.5%

LU 7–1

1. a. $40 **b.** $360 **c.** $50
   d. $100 **e.** $380
3. a. $75 **b.** $21.50; $40.75
5. a. .7125; .2875 **b.** .7225; .2775
7. $3.51
9. $81.25
11. $315
13. 45%

LU 7–2

1. a. February 18; March 10
   d. May 20; June 9
   e. October 10; October 30
3. a. .97; $1,358
   c. .98; $367.99
5. a. $16.79; $835.21
7. $16,170
9. a. $439.29 **b.** $491.21
11. $209.45
13. a. $765.31 **b.** $386.99

LU 8–1

1. a. $18.90 **b.** $2.72
   c. $4.35 **d.** $90 **e.** $116.31
3. a. $2; 80% **b.** $6.50; 52%
   c. $.28; 28.9%
5. a. $1.52 **b.** $225
   c. $372.92 **d.** $625
7. a. $199.60 **b.** $698.60
9. a. $258.52 **b.** $90.48
11. a. $212.50 **b.** $297.50
13. $8.17

LU 8–2

1. a. $5.40 **b.** $57.50
   c. $34.43 **d.** $27.33 **e.** $.15
3. a. $6.94 **b.** $882.35 **c.** $30
   d. $171.43
5. a. 28.57% **b.** 33.33% **d.** 53.85%
7. $346.15
9. 39.39%
11. $2.29
13. 63.33%

LU 8–3

1. a. $80; $120
   b. $525; $1,574.98
3. a. $410 **b.** $18.65

5. a. $216; $324; $5.14
   b. $45; $63.90; $1.52
7. 17%
9. $21.15
11. $273.78
13. $.79

LU 8–4

1. a. $6.00 **b.** $11.11
3. a. 16,667 **b.** 7,500
5. 5,070
7. 22,222

LU 9–1

1. a. $427.50; 0; $427.50
   b. $360; $40.50; $400.50
3. a. $438.85 **b.** $615.13
5. a. $5,200 **b.** $3,960
   c. $3,740 **d.** $4,750
7. $723.00
9. $3,846.25
11. $2,032.48

LU 9–2

1. a. $500; $2,300
3. $0; $2,000
5. $328.59
7. $143.75
9. $594.44
11. $663.50

LU 10–1

1. a. $240 **b.** $1,080 **c.** $1,275
3. a. $131.25 **b.** $4.08 **c.** $98.51
5. a. $515.63 **b.** $6,015.63
7. a. $5,459.66
9. $659.36
11. $360

LU 10–2

1. a. $4,371.44 **b.** $4,545.45
   c. $3,433.33
3. a. 60; .17 **b.** 120; .33
   c. 270; .75 **d.** 145; .40
5. 5%
7. $250
9. $3,000
11. 119 days

LU 10–3

1. a. $2,568.75; $1,885.47; $920.04
3. $4,267.59
5. $4,715.30; $115.30

LU 11–1

1. I; B; D; I; D; I; B; D
3. a. 2%
   c. 13%
5. $15,963.75

7. $848.75; $8,851.25
9. $14,300
11. $7,855

LU 11–2

1. a. $5,075.00
   b. $16,480.80
   c. $994.44
3. a. $14.76
   b. $223.25
   c. $3.49
5. $4,031.67
7. $8,262.74
9. $5,088.16
11. $721.45

LU 12–1

1. a. $573.25 year 2
   b. $3,115.57 year 4
3. a. $25,306; $5,306
   b. $16,084; $6,084
5. $7,430.50
7. $8,881.20
9. $2,129.40
11. $3,207.09; $207.09
13. $3,000; $3,469; $3,498

LU 12–2

1. a. .9804 **b.** .3936 **c.** .5513
3. a. $1,575.50; $924.50
   b. $2,547.02; $2,052.98
5. $14,509.50
7. $13,356.98
9. $16,826.40
11. $652.32
13. $18,014.22

LU 13–1

1. a. $1,000; $2,080; $3,246.40
3. a. $6,888.60 **b.** $6,273.36
5. $325,525
7. $13,412
9. $30,200.85
11. $33,650.94

LU 13–2

1. a. $2,638.65 **b.** $6,375.24; $7,217.10
3. $2,715.54
5. $24,251.85
7. $47,608
9. $456,425
11. Accept Jason $265,010

LU 13–3

1. a. $4,087.50 **b.** $21,607
   c. $1,395 **d.** $201.45
   e. $842.24
3. $16,200
5. $24,030

7. $16,345
9. $8,742

LU 14–1

1. a. $1,200; $192
   b. $9,000; $1,200
3. a. 14.75% **b.** 10%
   c. 11.25%
5. a. $3,528 **b.** $696
   c. $4,616
7. a. $22,500 **b.** $4,932
   c. $29,932
9. a. $20,576 **b.** 12.75%

LU 14–2

1. a. $465; $8,535
   b. $915.62; $4,709.38
3. a. $332.03 **b.** $584.83
   c. $384.28
5. Final payment $784.39
7. $51.34
9. $35
11. $922.48
13. 7.50% to 7.75%

LU 15–1

1. a. $1,096.50 **b.** $965.60;
   $4,090.50; $3,859.65
3. a. $117.25, 7.7%
   b. $174, 5.7%
5. $774
7. $2,584.71; $2,518.63
9. a. $66.08 **b.** $131,293.80
11. $773,560

LU 15–2

1. a. $1,371.90; $1,133.33; $238.57
3. #4 balance outstanding $195,183.05
5. $587,612.80
7. $327.12; $251,581.60
9. $44,271.43
11. $61,800

LU 16–1

1. Total assets $224,725
3. Merch. inventory 13.90%; 15.12%

LU 16–2

1. Net income $57,765
3. Purchases 73.59%; 71.43%

LU 16–3

1. Sales 2015, 93.5%; 2014, 93.2%
3. .22
5. 59.29%
7. .83
9. COGS 119.33%; 111.76%;
   105.04%

11. .90
13. 5.51%
15. 11.01%

LU 17–1

1. a. 4% **b.** 25% **c.** 10%
   d. 20%
3. a. $2,033; $4,667
   b. $1,850; $9,750
5. $8,625 depreciation per year
7. $2,800 depreciation per year
9. $95
11. a. $12,000 **b.** $6,000
   c. $18,000 **d.** $45,000

LU 17–2

1. a. $.300 **b.** $.192 **c.** $.176
3. a. $.300, $2,600
   b. $.192, $300,824
5. $5,300 book value end of year 5
7. a. $.155 **b.** $20,001.61

LU 17–3

1. a. 8% **b.** 20% **c.** 25%
3. a. $4,467; $2,233
   b. $3,867; $7,733
5. $121, year 6
7. a. 28.57% **b.** $248 **c.** $619
9. a. 16.67% **b.** $2,500
   c. $10,814 **d.** $2,907

LU 17–4

1. a. 33%; $825; $1,675
3. Depreciation year 8, $346
5. $125
7. a. $15,000 **b.** $39,000
   c. $21,600 **d.** 2001
9. $68,440

LU 18–1

1. a. $5,120; $3,020
   b. $323,246; $273,546
3. $35,903; $165,262
5. $10,510.20; $16,345
7. $37.62; $639.54
9. $628.40
11. $3,069; $952; $2,117

LU 18–2

1. a. $85,700; $143,500; .597; $64,500;
   $38,507
3. $85,000
5. $342,000; $242,500; 5.85; 6.29
7. $60,000; $100,000; $40,000
9. $70,150
11. $5,970
13. 3.24; 3.05
15. $32,340; $35,280; $49,980;
   $29,400

LU 19–1

1. **a.** $26.80; $562.80
   b. $718.80; $12,698.80
3. **a.** $20.75; $43.89; $463.64
5. Total is **(a)** $1,023; **(b)** $58.55
7. $5.23; $115.23
9. $2,623.93
11. $26.20
13. $685.50

LU 19–2

1. **a.** $68,250   **b.** $775,450
3. **a.** $7.45; $74.50; 74.50
5. $9.10
7. $8,368.94
9. $42,112
11. $32,547.50

LU 20–1

1. **a.** $9.27; 25; $231.75
3. **a.** $93.00; $387.50; $535.00;
   $916.50
5. $1,242.90
7. $14,265
9. $47.50 more
11. $68,750

LU 20–2

1. **a.** $488   **b.** $2,912
3. **a.** $68,000; $60,000
   b. $41,600; $45,000
5. $1,463
7. $117,187.50

9. $336,000
11. **a.** $131,250   **b.** $147,000

LU 20–3

1. **a.** $98; $160; $258
3. **a.** $312   **b.** $233   **c.** $181
   d. $59; $20
5. **a.** $647   **b.** $706
7. $601
9. $781
11. $10,000; $8,000
13. $60,000; $20,000
15. $19.50; $110.50

LU 21–1

1. **a.** $43.88   **f.** 49
3. $27.06
5. $1,358.52 gain
7. $18,825.15
9. $7.70

LU 21–2

1. **a.** IBM   **b.** $10\frac{1}{4}$ **c.** 2018
   d. $102.50   **e.** 102.375
3. **a.** $1,025
   b. $1,023.75
5. **a.** $3,075
   b. $307.50
7. **a.** $30 discount
   b. $16.25 premium
   c. $42.50 premium
9. **a.** $625   **b.** $375 discount
   c. $105   **d.** 16.8%

11. 7.8%; 7.2%
13. 8.98%

LU 21–3

1. $11.90
3. $15.20
5. +$.14
7. 7.6%
9. $1.45; $18.45
11. $.56; $14.66
13. $1,573.50
15. $123.00 loss
17. **a.** 2014; 2022
   b. 9.3% Comp USA; 6.9% GMA
   c. $1,023.75 Comp USA
      $1,016.25 GMA
   d. Both at premium
   e. $1,025 Comp USA; $1,028.75 GMA

LU 22–1

1. **a.** 20.4   **b.** 83.75   **c.** 10.07
3. **a.** 59.5   **b.** 50
5. **a.** 63.7; 62; 62
7. $1,500,388.50
9. $10.75
11. $9.98

LU 22–2

1. 18: ||||| || 7
3. 25–30: ||||| ||| 8
5. 7.2°
7. 145–154: |||| 4
9. 98.4°; 9.9°; 70.5°; 169.2°; 11.9°

Classroom Notes

Classroom Notes

Classroom Notes

Classroom Notes

Metric System

The Boston Globe

John Sullivan: Angie, I drove into the gas station last night to fill the tank up. Did I get upset! The pumps were not in gallons but in liters. This country (U.S.) going to metric is sure making it confusing.

Angie Smith: Don't get upset. Let me first explain the key units of measure in metric, and then I'll show you a convenient table I keep in my purse to convert metric to U.S. (also called customary system), and U.S. to metric. Let's go on.

The metric system is really a decimal system in which each unit of measure is exactly 10 times as large as the previous unit. In a moment, we will see how this aids in conversions. First, look at the middle column (Units) of this to see the basic units of measure:

U.S.	Thousands	Hundreds	Tens	Units	Tenths	Hundredths	Thousandths
Metric	Kilo-	Hecto-	Deka-	Gram	Deci-	Centi-	Milli-
	1,000	100	10	Meter	.1	.01	.001
				Liter			
				1			

- Weight: Gram (think of it as $\frac{1}{30}$ of an ounce).
- Length: Meter (think of it for now as a little more than a yard).
- Volume: Liter (a little more than a quart).

To aid you in looking at this, think of a decimeter, a centimeter, or a millimeter as being "shorter" (smaller) than a meter, whereas a dekameter, hectometer, and kilometer are "larger" than a meter. For example:

1 centimeter $= \frac{1}{100}$ of a meter; or 100 centimeters equals 1 meter.

1 millimeter $= \frac{1}{1,000}$ meter; or 1,000 millimeters equals 1 meter.

1 hectometer $= 100$ meters.

1 kilometer $= 1,000$ meters.

Remember we could have used the same setup for grams or liters. Note the summary here.

Length	Volume	Mass
1 meter:	1 liter:	1 gram:
= 10 decimeters	= 10 deciliters	= 10 decigrams
= 100 centimeters	= 100 centiliters	= 100 centigrams
= 1,000 millimeters	= 1,000 milliliters	= 1,000 milligrams
= .1 dekameter	= .1 dekaliter	= .1 dekagram
= .01 hectometer	= .01 hectoliter	= .01 hectogram
= .001 kilometer	= .001 kiloliter	= .001 kilogram

Practice these conversions and check solutions.

1	PRACTICE QUIZ

Convert the following:

1. 7.2 meters to centimeters
2. .89 meter to millimeters
3. 64 centimeters to meters
4. 350 grams to kilograms
5. 7.4 liters to centiliters
6. 2,500 milligrams to grams

✓ **Solutions**

1. 7.2 meters = 7.2 × 100 = 720 centimeters (remember, 1 meter = 100 centimeters)
2. .89 meter = .89 × 1,000 = 890 millimeters (remember, 1 meter = 1,000 millimeters)
3. 64 centimeters = 64/100 = .64 meters (remember, 1 meter = 100 centimeters)
4. 350 grams = $\dfrac{350}{1,000}$ = .35 kilograms (remember 1 kilogram = 1,000 grams)
5. 7.4 liters = 7.4 × 100 = 740 centiliters (remember, 1 liter = 100 centiliters)
6. 2,500 milligrams = $\dfrac{2,500}{1,000}$ = 2.5 grams (remember, 1 gram = 1,000 milligrams

Angie: Look at the table of conversions and I'll show you how easy it is. Note how we can convert liters to gallons. Using the conversion from meters to U.S. (liters to gallons), we see that you multiply numbers of liters by .26, so for 37.95 liters we get 37.95 × .26 = 9.84 gallons.

Common conversion factors for U.S./metric					
A. To convert from U.S. to	**Metric**	**Multiply by**	**B. To convert from metric to**	**U.S.**	**Multiply by**
Length:			*Length:*		
Inches (in)	Meters (m)	.025	Meters (m)	Inches (in)	39.37
Feet (ft)	Meters (m)	.31	Meters (m)	Feet (ft)	3.28
Yards (yd)	Meters (m)	.91	Meters (m)	Yards (yd)	1.1
Miles	Kilometers (km)	1.6	Kilometers (km)	Miles	.62
Weight:			*Weight:*		
Ounces (oz)	Grams (g)	28	Grams (g)	Ounces (oz)	.035
Pounds (lb)	Grams (g)	454	Grams (g)	Pounds (lb)	.0022
Pounds (lb)	Kilograms (kg)	.45	Kilograms (kg)	Pounds (lb)	2.2
Volume or capacity:			*Volume or capacity:*		
Pints	Liters (L)	.47	Liters (L)	Pints	2.1
Quarts	Liters (L)	.95	Liters (L)	Quarts	1.06
Gallons (gal)	Liters (L)	3.8	Liters (L)	Gallons	.26

John: How would I convert 6 miles to kilometers?

Angie: Take the number of miles times 1.6, thus 6 miles × 1.6 = 9.6 kilometers.

John: If I weigh 120 pounds, what is my weight in kilograms?

Angie: 120 times .45 (use the conversion table) equals 54 kilograms.

John: OK. Last night, when I bought 16.6 liters of gas, I really bought 4.3 gallons (16.6 liters times .26).

2	PRACTICE QUIZ

Convert the following:

1. 10 meters to yards
2. 110 quarts to liters
3. 78 kilometers to miles
4. 52 yards to meters
5. 82 meters to inches
6. 292 miles to kilometers

✓ **Solutions**

1. 10 meters $\times$ 1.1 = 11 yards
2. 110 quarts $\times$ .95 = 104.5 liters
3. 78 kilometers $\times$ .62 = 48.36 miles
4. 52 yards $\times$ .91 = 47.32 meters
5. 82 meters $\times$ 39.37 = 3,228.34 inches
6. 292 miles $\times$ 1.6 = 467.20 kilometers

Appendix D: Problems

DRILL PROBLEMS

Convert:

1. 65 centimeters to meters

2. 7.85 meters to centimeters

3. 44 centiliters to liters

4. 1,500 grams to kilograms

5. 842 millimeters to meters

6. 9.4 kilograms to grams

7. .854 kilograms to grams

8. 5.9 meters to millimeters

9. 8.91 kilograms to grams

10. 2.3 meters to millimeters

Convert, rounding to the nearest tenth:

11. 50.9 kilograms to pounds

12. 8.9 pounds to grams

13. 395 kilometers to miles

14. 33 yards to meters

15. 13.9 pounds to grams

16. 594 miles to kilometers

17. 4.9 feet to meters

18. 9.9 feet to meters

19. 100 yards to meters

20. 40.9 kilograms to pounds

21. 895 miles to kilometers

22. 1,000 grams to pounds

23. 79.1 meters to yards

24. 12 liters to quarts

25. 2.92 meters to feet

26. 5 liters to gallons

27. 8.7 meters to feet

28. 8 gallons to liters

29. 1,600 grams to pounds

30. 310 meters to yards

WORD PROBLEM

31. A metric ton is 39.4 bushels of corn. The Russians bought 450,000 metric tons of U.S. corn, valued at $58 million, for delivery after September 30. Convert the number of bushels purchased from metric tons to bushels of corn.

Glossary/Index

Note: Page numbers followed by n indicate material found in footnotes.

8 DIVIDENDS REPORTED DECEMBER 20

Trading Diary: Volume, Advancers, Decliners

	NYSE	Nasdaq	NYSE Amex	NYSE Arca
Issues traded	3,159	2,633	479	1,225
Advances	2,308	1,945	244	905
Declines	779	601	206	308
Unchanged	72	87	29	12
New highs	128	115	8	66
New lows	4	14	2	34
Adv. volume*	674,259,541	1,600,585,812	7,460,624	178,094,257
Decl. volume*	112,363,056	299,696,122	3,503,877	43,705,118
Total volume*	805,793,430	1,924,543,708	11,391,215	222,077,440
Closing tick	+463	+235	+36	+51
Closing Arms (TRIN)†	0.48	0.61	0.61	0.98
Block trades*	4,537	7,363	97	1,517

©2011 Dow Jones & Company, Inc.

Explanation

Today on the New York Stock Exchange there were more stocks declining than advancing. More trades were made selling than buying, as shown by the decline volume being larger than advance volume.

Applying Your Business Math

What percent of stocks on NASDAQ rose today? Round to nearest hundredth percent.

$$\frac{1,945}{2,633} = 73.87\%$$

(circle diagram: P 1,945 / B 2,633 × R)

9 PERCENTAGE GAINERS... AND LOSERS

Percentage Gainers...

Company	Symbol	Volume (in000s)	Close	NetChg	%Chg	High	Low	%Chg
OakRidgeFnlSvc	BRGR	6	3.73	0.98	35.64	5.00	2.00	-23.1
AdvanceAmerCashCenters	AEA	+0.491	2.33	2.53	31.98	18.55	4.70	74.0
Crescent Financial Bcshs	CRFM	24	4.50	1.00	28.57	4.64	2.61	117.3
FirstUnited	FUNC	37	4.95	1.10	28.57	6.06	2.76	37.5
State Auto Fincl	STFC	1.11	15.90	3.25	26.55	18.35	10.79	-8.8
CRA Intl	CRAI	65	24.72	4.58	22.68	29.80	16.42	-1.2

Percentage Losers

Company	Symbol	Volume (in000s)	Close	NetChg	%Chg	High	Low	%Chg
Hyperdynamics	HDY	13,433	1.44	-0.58	-28.71	7.15	1.01	-74.3
BuildABear	BBW	924	5.95	-2.18	-26.81	8.80	4.37	-14.1
Peerless Manufacturing Co	PMFG	2,994	16.59	-4.42	-21.04	27.40	14.22	-0.4
Digital Generation	DGIT	2,303	10.82	-2.77	-20.38	37.48	10.79	-67.8
Ancestry.com	ACOM	6,153	23.83	-4.69	-16.44	45.79	20.67	-30.7
Nobility Homes	NOBH	9	6.60	-1.17	-14.90	9.32	4.52	-17.4

©2011 Dow Jones & Company, Inc.

Explanation

This table shows which stocks have the best percent increase in their stock price for the day as well as which stocks had the largest percent decrease in price.

Formula:

$$\frac{\text{Change in price}}{\text{Yesterday's closing price (old price)}} = \text{Percent change}$$

Applying Your Business Math

Proving the percent change for Oak Ridge and Hyperdynamics

Gainer

Oak Ridge

Closing price yesterday = $3.73 − $.98 = $2.75

| Today's close | − | Change | = | Yesterday's closing price |

Calculations:

$$\frac{\$.98}{\$2.75} = .35636 = 35.64\% \text{ rounded to the nearest hundredth percent}$$

(circle diagram: P $.98 / B $2.75 × R)

Loser

Hyperdynamics

Closing price yesterday = $1.44 + $.58 = $2.02

| Today's close | + | Change | = | Yesterday's closing price |

Calculations:

$$\frac{-\$.58}{\$2.02} = .28712 = -28.71\% \text{ rounded to the nearest hundredth percent}$$

(circle diagram: P −$.58 / B $2.02 × R)

Note: To find yesterday's close we subtract change (the opposite of the actual change). If change is a minus we would add it like Hyperdynamics

10 MUTUAL FUNDS

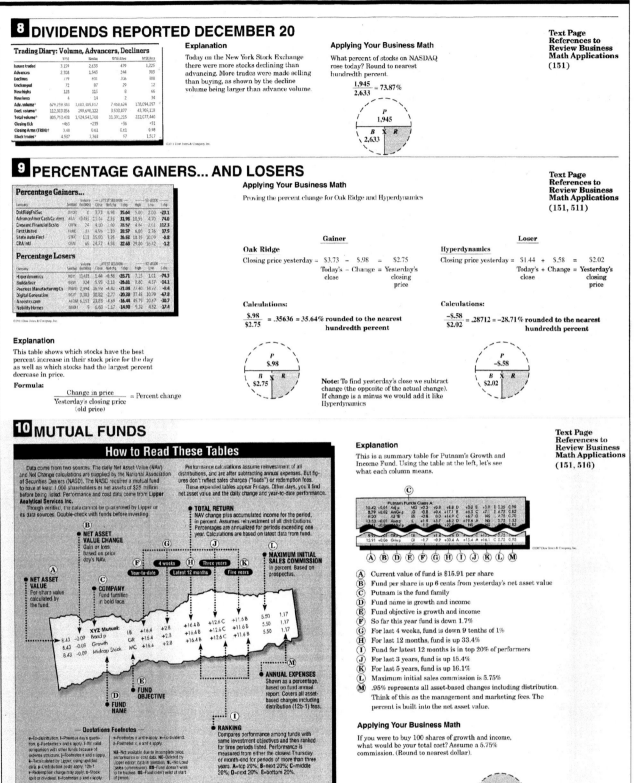

How to Read These Tables

Data come from two sources: The daily Net Asset Value (NAV) and Net Change calculations are supplied by the National Association of Securities Dealers (NASD). The NASD requires a mutual fund to have at least 1,000 shareholders or net assets of $25 million before being listed. Performance and cost data come from Lipper Analytical Services Inc.

Though verified, the data cannot be guaranteed by Lipper or its data sources. Double-check with funds before investing.

Performance calculations assume reinvestment of all distributions, and are after subtracting annual expenses. But figures don't reflect sales charges ("loads") or redemption fees. These expanded tables appear Fridays. Other days, you'll find net asset value and the daily change and year-to-date performance.

A ● NET ASSET VALUE Per share value calculated by the fund.

B ● NET ASSET VALUE CHANGE Gain or loss based on prior day's NAV.

C ● COMPANY Fund families in bold face.

D ● FUND NAME

E ● FUND OBJECTIVE

F Year-to-date

G 4 weeks

H Three years

I ● RANKING Compares performance among funds with same investment objectives and then ranked for time periods listed. Performance is measured from either the closest Thursday or month-end for periods of more than three years. A=top 20%; B=next 20%; C=middle 20%; D=next 20%; E=bottom 20%.

J Latest 12 months

K Five years

L ● MAXIMUM INITIAL SALES COMMISSION In percent. Based on prospectus.

M ● ANNUAL EXPENSES Shown as a percentage, based on fund annual report. Covers all asset-based charges including distribution (12b-1) fees.

● TOTAL RETURN NAV change plus accumulated income for the period, in percent. Assumes reinvestment of all distributions. Percentages are annualized for periods exceeding one year. Calculations are based on latest data from fund.

(table excerpt: XYZ Mutual)
8.43	-0.09	Bond	B	+16.4	+2.8	+16.4 B	+12.6 C	+11.6 B	5.50	1.17
8.43	-0.09	Growth	GR	+16.4	+2.3	+16.4 B	+12.6 C	+11.6 B	5.50	1.17
8.43	-0.09	Midcap Stock	MC	+16.4	+2.8	+16.4 B	+12.6 C	+11.6 B	5.50	1.17

— Quotations Footnotes —

e–Ex-distribution. f–Previous day's quotation. g–Footnotes x and e apply. j–No valid comparison with other funds because of expense structure. k–Recalculated by Lipper, using updated data. p–Distribution costs apply. 12b-1 r–Redemption charge may apply. s–Stock split or dividend. t–Footnotes p and e apply.

r–Footnotes x and e apply. x–Ex-dividend. z–Footnotes x, e and f apply.

NA–Not available due to incomplete price, performance or cost data. NE–Deleted by Lipper editor; data in question. NL–No Load (sales commission). NN–Fund doesn't wish to be tracked. NS–Fund didn't exist at start of period.

©2007 Dow Jones & Company, Inc.

Explanation

This is a summary table for Putnam's Growth and Income Fund. Using the table at the left, let's see what each column means.

(table excerpt: Putnam Funds Class A)
10.42	+0.01	Adj a	MG	+0.3	+0.8	+8.8 D	+3.0 E	+.9	E 5.25	0.79
8.79	+0.02	AmGv f	G	-0.8	+0.4	+17.1 B	+6.5 C	+7.1	E 4.75	0.83
9.20		A2 1E	SS	-0.8	0.0	+14.9 C	+6.7 O	NS		4.75	0.70
13.53	-0.01	Aserg	L	+1.9	+3.7	+8.2 O	+19.6 A	NS		2.73	1.53

| 9.91 | .01 | Grn p | GI | +1.2 | +3.9 | NS | +15.4 | +16.1 | C 5.75 | 0.95 |
| 15.91 | +0.06 | Grn p | GI | -1.7 | -0.9 | +33.4 A | +15.4 | +16.1 | C 5.75 | 0.95 |

©2007 Dow Jones & Company, Inc.

A B D E F G H I J K L M

Ⓐ Current value of fund is $15.91 per share
Ⓑ Fund per share is up 6 cents from yesterday's net asset value
Ⓒ Putnam is the fund family
Ⓓ Fund name is growth and income
Ⓔ Fund objective is growth and income
Ⓕ So far this year fund is down 1.7%
Ⓖ For last 4 weeks, fund is down 9 tenths of 1%
Ⓗ For last 12 months, fund is up 33.4%
Ⓘ Fund for latest 12 months is in top 20% of performers
Ⓙ For last 3 years, fund is up 15.4%
Ⓚ For last 5 years, fund is up 16.1%
Ⓛ Maximum initial sales commission is 5.75%
Ⓜ .95% represents all asset-based changes including distribution. Think of this as the management and marketing fees. The percent is built into the net asset value.

Applying Your Business Math

If you were to buy 100 shares of growth and income, what would be your total cost? Assume a 5.75% commission. (Round to nearest dollar).

```
$15.91
+   .91  (5.75%)
$16.82  x 100 shares = $1,682
```

(circle diagram: P $1,682 / B $15.91 × R 105.75%)

	Yld %	P-E Ratio	Vol. 100s	Last	Net Chg.
vc. 28	.5	39	76680	56.26	-0.02

Percent

f $.28 per share is
or a return of .5% based
k.

vidend per share
price per share

↓

= .0049768
6

ercent move the decimal
right

st tenth percent.

(511)

P-E Ratio
39

Currently the stock is selling at 39 times its
annual earnings per share.

Formula:

$$\frac{\text{Closing price per share of stock}}{\text{Annual earnings per share}}$$

P-E is rounded to a whole number solving for
unknown:

$$\frac{\$56.25}{X} = 39$$

$$\$56.25 = 39X$$

$$\frac{\$56.25}{39} = \frac{39X}{39}$$

$$\$1.44 = X$$

Annual earnings per share = $1.44. This number
is not on the stock quotation.

(511)

Vol 100s
76680

Indicates number of shares traded for day. Two
zeros are to be added on; thus Wal-Mart's traded
7,668,000 shares today. If a Z is in front of the
number, zeros would not be added.

↓

This number is multiplied by 100. Move the
decimal point two places to the right when multiplying by 100
76,680 x 100 = 7,668,000 shares

Note:
Stock with unusually high volume compared to
the stock's average trading volume is underlined.

(511)

Last
56.26

This is the price of the last
trade of the day. The stock of
Wal-Mart closed at $56.26 for
the day.

(511)

Net Change
–0.02

This is the difference between yesterday's and
today's closing prices. (This could be an increase
or a decrease.) Yesterday's closing price is not
listed here. The net change is not the difference
between today's high and low.

↓

From the previous day the last selling price of
stock is down $.02.

Yesterday's close must have been $56.28.
$56.26   today's close
+   .02 + change
$56.28   yesterday's close

Had it been up $.02, the previous day's close would
have been $56.24.
$56.26
–   .02
$56.24

(511)

Yld %	P-E Ratio	Vol. 100s	Last	Net Chg.
...	CC	57187	63.59	-2.61

Percent

idend per share
rice per share

ends, there is no yield %.
% change is 92.7%.

(511)

P-E Ratio
CC

Formula:

$$\frac{\text{Closing price per share of stock}}{\text{Annual earnings per share}}$$

CC means PE ratio is 100 or more for eBay.

(511)

Vol 100s
57187

Indicates number of shares traded for day.
Two zeros are added on; thus eBay traded
5,718,700 shares today.

↓

Move the decimal point two places to the
right when multiplying by 100.
57,187 x 100 = 5,718,700

Wal-Mart (above) traded 7,668,000 shares.
Wal-Mart traded 1,949,300 shares more than
eBay.

7,668,000
–5,718,700
1,949,300

(511)

Last
63.59

This is the price of the last trade
of the day. The stock of eBay
closed at $63.59 for the day.

(511)

Net Change
–2.61

This is the difference between yesterday's and
today's closing prices. Yesterday's closing price is
not listed here. Net change is not the difference
between the high and low for the day.

↓

Yesterday's closing price is:
$63.59 today's closing price
+ 2.61 plus change
$66.20 yesterday's close

Check: $66.20
– 2.61
$63.59

(511)

---

7 AMEX Bonds

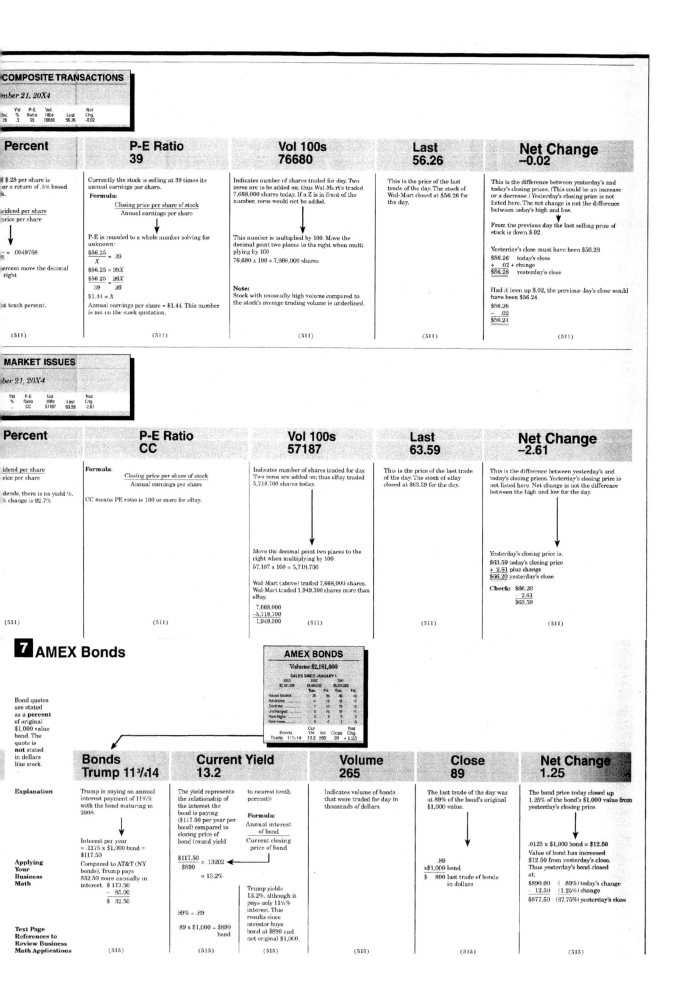

AMEX BONDS
Volume $2,181,000

SALES SINCE JANUARY 1

	20X3	20X2	20X1
	$2,181,000	$4,486,000	$6,554,000

	Tue.	Fri.	Tue.	Fri.
Issues traded	20	35	40	40
Advances	14	15	15	17
Declines	7	10	10	12
Unchanged	0	10	15	11
New highs	3	3	5	2
New lows	0	0	1	0

Bonds	Cur Yld	Vol	Close	Net Chg.
Trump 11¾ 14	13.2	265	89	+ 1.25

Bond quotes
are stated
as a **percent**
of original
$1,000 value
bond. The
quote is
not stated
in dollars
like stock.

Bonds
Trump 11³/₄14

Current Yield
13.2

Volume
265

Close
89

Net Change
1.25

Explanation

Trump is paying an annual
interest payment of 11¾%
with the bond maturing in
2008.

↓

Interest per year
= .1175 x $1,000 bond =
$117.50

**Applying
Your
Business
Math**

Compared to AT&T (NY
bonds), Trump pays
$32.50 more annually in
interest. $ 117.50
– 85.00
$ 32.50

**Text Page
References to
Review Business
Math Applications**

(515)

The yield represents
the relationship of
the interest the
bond is paying
($117.50 per year per
bond) compared to
closing price of
bond (round yield
to nearest tenth
percent))

Formula:
$$\frac{\text{Annual interest of bond}}{\text{Current closing price of bond}}$$

$$\frac{\$117.50}{\$890} = .13202$$

$$= 13.2\%$$

89% = .89

.89 x $1,000 = $890
bond

Trump yields
13.2%, although it
pays only 11¾%
interest. This
results since
investor buys
bond at $890 and
not original $1,000.

(515)

Indicates volume of bonds
that were traded for day in
thousands of dollars.

(515)

The last trade of the day was
at 89% of the bond's original
$1,000 value.

↓

.89
x$1,000 bond
$ 890 last trade of bonds
in dollars

(515)

The bond price today closed up
1.25% of the bond's $1,000 value from
yesterday's closing price.

↓

.0125 x $1,000 bond = **$12.50**
Value of bond has increased
$12.50 from yesterday's close.
Thus yesterday's bond closed
at:
$890.00   (89%) today's change
– 12.50   (1.25%) change
$877.50   (87.75%) yesterday's close

(515)

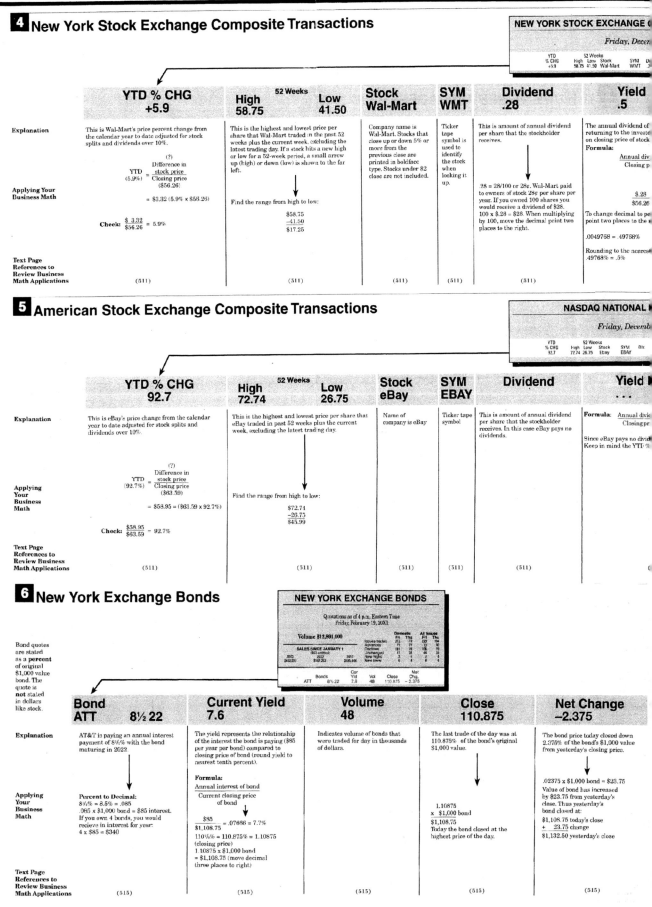

4 New York Stock Exchange Composite Transactions

NEW YORK STOCK EXCHANGE

Friday, Decer

YTD % CHG	52 Weeks		Stock	SYM	D
+5.9	High Low	Stock	Wal-Mart	WMT	
	58.75 41.50	Wal-Mart		WMT	

	YTD % CHG +5.9	**High** 58.75 **52 Weeks** **Low** 41.50	**Stock** Wal-Mart	**SYM** WMT	**Dividend** .28	**Yield** .5
Explanation	This is Wal-Mart's price percent change from the calendar year to date adjusted for stock splits and dividends over 10%.	This is the highest and lowest price per share that Wal-Mart traded in the past 52 weeks plus the current week, excluding the latest trading day. If a stock hits a new high or low for a 52-week period, a small arrow up (high) or down (low) is shown to the far left.	Company name is Wal-Mart. Stocks that close up or down 5% or more from the previous close are printed in boldface type. Stocks under $2 close are not included.	Ticker tape symbol is used to identify the stock when looking it up.	This is amount of annual dividend per share that the stockholder receives.	The annual dividend of returning to the invested on closing price of stock **Formula:** Annual div / Closing p
Applying Your Business Math	YTD (5.9%) = Difference in stock price ($56.26) / Closing price (?) = $3.32 (5.9% × $56.26) Check: $3.32 / $56.26 = 5.9%	Find the range from high to low: $58.75 −41.50 $17.25			.28 = 28/100 or 28¢. Wal-Mart paid to owners of stock 28¢ per share per year. If you owned 100 shares you would receive a dividend of $28. 100 × $.28 = $28. When multiplying by 100, move the decimal point two places to the right.	$.28 / $56.26 To change decimal to per point two places to the r .0049768 = .49768% Rounding to the nearest .49768% = .5%
Text Page References to Review Business Math Applications	(511)	(511)	(511)	(511)	(511)	

5 American Stock Exchange Composite Transactions

NASDAQ NATIONAL

Friday, Decemb

YTD % CHG	52 Weeks		Stock	SYM	Div.
92.7	High Low	Stock	eBay	EBAY	
	72.74 26.75	eBay		EBAY	

	YTD % CHG 92.7	**High** 72.74 **52 Weeks** **Low** 26.75	**Stock** eBay	**SYM** EBAY	**Dividend**	**Yield** ...
Explanation	This is eBay's price change from the calendar year to date adjusted for stock splits and dividends over 10%.	This is the highest and lowest price per share that eBay traded in past 52 weeks plus the current week, excluding the latest trading day.	Name of company is eBay	Ticker tape symbol	This is amount of annual dividend per share that the stockholder receives. In this case eBay pays no dividends.	**Formula:** Annual divi / Closing pr Since eBay pays no divid Keep in mind the YTD %
Applying Your Business Math	YTD (92.7%) = Difference in stock price ($63.59) / Closing price (?) = $58.95 = ($63.59 × 92.7%) Check: $58.95 / $63.59 = 92.7%	Find the range from high to low: $72.74 −26.75 $45.99				
Text Page References to Review Business Math Applications	(511)	(511)	(511)	(511)	(511)	

6 New York Exchange Bonds

Bond quotes are stated as a **percent** of original $1,000 value bond. The quote is **not** stated in dollars like stock.

NEW YORK EXCHANGE BONDS

Quotations as of 4 p.m. Eastern Time
Friday, February 19, 20X1

Volume $12,891,000

	Cur Yld	Vol	Close	Net Chg.
ATT 8½ 22	7.8	48	110.875	−2.375

	Bond ATT 8½ 22	**Current Yield** 7.6	**Volume** 48	**Close** 110.875	**Net Change** −2.375
Explanation	AT&T is paying an annual interest payment of 8½% with the bond maturing in 2022.	The yield represents the relationship of the interest the bond is paying ($85 per year per bond) compared to closing price of bond (round yield to nearest tenth percent).	Indicates volume of bonds that were traded for day in thousands of dollars.	The last trade of the day was at 110.875 of the bond's original $1,000 value.	The bond price today closed down 2.375% of the bond's $1,000 value from yesterday's closing price.
Applying Your Business Math	**Percent to Decimal:** 8½% = 8.5% = .085 .085 × $1,000 bond = $85 interest. If you own 4 bonds, you would receive in interest for year: 4 × $85 = $340	**Formula:** Annual interest of bond / Current closing price of bond $85 / $1,108.75 = .07666 = 7.7% 110⅞% = 110.875% = 1.10875 (closing price) 1.10875 × $1,000 bond = $1,108.75 (move decimal three places to right)		1.10875 × $1,000 bond $1,108.75 Today the bond closed at the highest price of the day.	.02375 × $1,000 bond = $23.75 Value of bond has increased by $23.75 from yesterday's close. Thus yesterday's bond closed at: $1,108.75 today's close + 23.75 change $1,132.50 yesterday's close
Text Page References to Review Business Math Applications	(515)	(515)	(515)	(515)	(515)

HOW TO LOOK AT FINANCIAL DATA IN

THE WALL STREET JOURNAL

SLATER/WITTRY—
PRACTICAL BUSINESS MATH PROCEDURES

A BUSINESS MATH APPROACH

ELEVENTH EDITION

1 THE DOW JONES AVERAGES

The Dow Jones Averages

"The stock market was strong today," a television newscaster intones. "The Dow Jones Industrial Average was up 10 points."

"Wonderful," a viewer exclaims, "but I'd like to see the day any of my stocks rose 10 points."

The confusion is justified. Stock prices are often given in points, using the term as another word for dollars. But when it comes to the Dow Jones Industrial Averages (DJIA), a different kind of yardstick is used.

The DJIA, also known as the "Dow" or "the industrials," is one of several so-called "averages" compiled and published by The Wall Street Journal and its sister publication Barron's National Business and Financial Weekly. They are designed to serve as indicators of broad movements in the securities markets.

How The Averages Began

The "Dow" in the averages comes from Charles Henry Dow, newsman, market analyst and co-founder (in 1882) of Dow Jones & Company, the publisher of The Wall Street Journal and Barron's. Like other market analysts since the earliest days of stock and bond trading, Dow attempted to discern underlying trends in the welter of each day's individual price fluctuations. Some stocks go up while others go down or stay the same, but these changes may be merely ripples atop waves and the waves in turn are subject to the underlying tide.

As a tool to help analyze these movements, Dow began computing an average of prices of stocks regarded as representative of the market as a whole. His first stock average appeared on July 3, 1884, in the Customer's Afternoon Letter, a two-page financial news bulletin which had been distributed daily by Dow Jones since November of the previous year. Only 11 stocks were included in that first index. Nine of them were railroad issues, reflecting the importance of railroads in the market in those days.

In following years, more industrial issues were added to the average and the roster expanded, first to 20 stocks and then to 30. The first publication of an average comparable to today's 30 industrial stocks was October 1, 1928.

The Dow is the oldest continuous price index of the U.S. stock market. Since those early days, public interest in the stock market has expanded greatly. A variety of indicators of price trends now is available from other sources, including such well-known ones as Standard & Poor's, Inc. and the New York Stock Exchange itself. Market technicians find each useful and no

single index, including the Dow, tells the market's whole story. But because of its history and familiarity, the Dow ranks as the most widely used indicator of stock market action.

How The Averages Are Computed

The original method of computation was elementary arithmetic. When there were 12 stocks, the prices were added together and the total divided by 12. When there were 20, the sum was divided by 20.

But the divisor is not 30 for the industrials or 20 for the transportation index or 15 for the utilities. Why not?

The answer is that the divisor is changed from time to time to maintain the historical continuity of the average. The most frequent reason for such an adjustment is a stock split. When the market price of a company's shares advances to a point where the company believes it is losing its appeal for individual investors, the stock often is split by, for example, issuing one new share for each share currently outstanding (two-for-one). Other things being equal, each share of stock is then worth half the earlier price.

Such stock splits by companies included in the average would produce distortions if the new price was simply substituted for the old one. Here is an example: Assume three stocks selling at $5, $10, and $15. Their average price is $10. Now the $15 stock is split three-for-one, which would make the new shares sell for $5. Nothing has happened to the value of an investment in these shares but the average of their prices now is $6.67—an obvious distortion in comparison with the earlier average.

An adjustment must be made to compensate so that the "average" will remain at $10. This can be done in different ways. The method used to compute the Dow Jones Averages is to change the divisor, the number divided into the total of the stock prices.

In this case the new divisor would be 2 instead of 3 and the new figure would be used in subsequent computations of the average.

The method of determining the new divisor was changed on January 1, 1992, and first used on May 12, 1992, to adjust for a two-for-one split by Coca-Cola Co., a component of the industrial average.

There were two changes. First, the divisor was increased to eight significant digits to minimize distortions due to rounding. The old calculation carried the divisor to three or four significant digits. Second, the formula used to calculate the divisor was revised as follows:

$$\text{New divisor} = \frac{\text{Current}}{\text{divisor}} \times \frac{\text{Total adjusted}}{\text{Total unadjusted}}\ \text{market value}$$

Briefly, here's how it works. At the close of regular trading, the Total Unadjusted Market Value for the Dow Jones Industrials is determined by adding the final prices of the 30 components in the average. (All stocks presently used in the averages are traded on the New York Stock Exchange except for Roadway Services, Inc., a transportation component and over-the-counter company listed on Nasdaq.)

Deduct the final price of the component involved from the total unadjusted market value and substitute the adjusted market value for the component. For example, Coca-Cola closed at 85.375 on May 11. This amount is replaced by the adjusted market value of 42.6875, reflecting the two-for-one split.

Divide the new Total Adjusted Market Value for the 30 components by the old unadjusted market value total and multiply by the current divisor. The result is the new divisor; it should be carried out nine digits, rounding to the eighth. The same formula applies to establishing a new divisor for

Dow Jones Industrial Average

12904.08 ▲ 123.13, or 0.96%

High, low, open and close for each trading day of the past three months.

	Last	Year ago
Trailing P/E ratio	14.39	15.09
P/E estimate	12.26	12.81
Dividend yield	2.51	2.35
Current divisor	0.132129493	

NYSE daily volume, in billions of shares

Company
3M
Alcoa
American Express
Bank of America
Boeing
Caterpillar
Chevron Corp.
Cisco Systems
Coca-Cola
Dupont
Exxon Mobil
General Electric
Hewlett-Packard
Home Depot
IBM
Intel
J.P. Morgan Chase
Johnson & Johnson
Kraft Foods
McDonalds
Merck
Microsoft
Pfizer
Procter & Gamble
Travelers
United Technologies
Verizon
Wal-Mart Stores
Walt Disney

the 65-stock composite average.

Over the more than 50-year history of the 30-stock average, the divisor has changed many times and now is below 2. This explains why the "average" can be reported as, for example, 1,000 while no single stock in the average is even close to that level in price. And it also explains the wide movements of the average in comparison to stock prices. With a divisor of 2, for example, an increase of $1 in the price of each of the 30 stocks produces a 15-point increase in the average.

In fact, the use of the term "average" is justified only by long usage. More accurately, it is an index or indicator.

Each day's change in each stock average is published by Dow Jones not only in points but also in percentages. The purpose of doing this is to stress the fact that the use of a divisor other than 30 doesn't in any way affect the percentage change as long as the divisor remains the same. The published percentage figure reflects more accurately than any other just how the market for the 30 stocks moved.

Currently divisors are published daily by The Journal and weekly by Barron's. They may be found with other statistics of the averages on the next-to-last page of the newspaper and in Barron's Market

Laboratory section. Other related statistics include the dividend yield and price-earnings ratio of the averages.

How The "Dow Stocks" Are Selected

With thousands of common stock issues listed on the New York Stock Exchange, not to mention thousands more traded on the American Stock Exchange, regional exchanges and in the over-the-counter market, what is the use of an index of only 30 stocks, or even 65?

In considering an answer to that frequently asked question, it should be noted that any average or index obscures a lot of diversity. (Statisticians caution against trying to walk across a lake with an average depth of three feet.) On any given day, a stock market average may zig while individual stocks are zagging. But an average like the Dow is aimed at tracking underlying trends over a period of time.

Other market indexes include more issues than the Dow, often many more. Depending on how they are computed, such indexes may react more sharply to changes in prices of low-priced stocks or to changes in a few high-priced stocks. Changes in the focus of investor interest, for example, heavy trading in certain industries, can cause market indicators to trace different courses. But experience indicates that over time the various popular indexes generally move together.

The 30 Dow Industrials are chosen as representative of the broad market and of American industry. The companies are major factors in their industries and their stocks are widely held by individuals and institutional investors.

Here are the 30 stocks that make up the Dow Jones Industrials. You can see them listed next to the Dow Jones Industrial Average. New to the 30 Dow Industrials include Bank of America, Chevron Corp., Kraft Foods, Travelers and Cisco. Companies deleted were AIG, Altria, Citicorp and Honeywell.

The editors of The Wall Street Journal decide when to make changes to the Dow Jones Industrials.

Charles Henry Dow could hardly have imagined that the occasional stock average he computed with paper and pencil would one day become part of the language of American finance. Now calculated in seconds by computer, the Dow is flashed around the world every half hour of the trading day by the Dow Jones News Service and not only published in The Wall Street Journal and Barron's but also reported by other newspapers, radio and television.

Excerpted from "The Dow Jones Averages: A Non-Professional Guide." Reprinted by permission, ©Dow Jones & Company, Inc.

2 DIARIES

Explanation

This breakdown shows the volume of stocks traded on various exchanges.

Applying Your Business Math

How many more shares were traded on the New York Exchange than in Chicago?

805,793,438
− 10,318,425
795,475,013

Text Page References to Review Business Math Applications (11, 510)

3 MOST ACTIVE ISSUES

Explanation

This is a list of the most actively traded stocks for the day. A stock that trades heavily may go up or down depending on supply and demand. This diary gives the investor a list of stocks attracting the most interest in the marketplace due to earnings reports, mergers, or other economic factors.

Applying Your Business Math

Round all the way the total volume for the most actively traded stocks. What is the actual total volume?

336,581	→	300,000
186,151	→	200,000
94,671	→	90,000
83,582	→	80,000
77,837	→	80,000
63,519	→	60,000
61,456	→	60,000
52,443	→	50,000
51,883	→	50,000
49,137	→	50,000
47,210	→	50,000
45,453	→	50,000
1,149,923		1,120,000

Text Page References to Review Business Math Applications (11, 510)